Study Abroad Opportunities for Community College Students and Strategies for Global Learning

Gregory F. Malveaux
Montgomery College, USA

Rosalind Latiner Raby
California State University Northridge, USA

A volume in the Advances in Higher Education and Professional Development (AHEPD) Book Series

Published in the United States of America by
IGI Global
Information Science Reference (an imprint of IGI Global)
701 E. Chocolate Avenue
Hershey PA, USA 17033
Tel: 717-533-8845
Fax: 717-533-8661
E-mail: cust@igi-global.com
Web site: http://www.igi-global.com

Copyright © 2019 by IGI Global. All rights reserved. No part of this publication may be reproduced, stored or distributed in any form or by any means, electronic or mechanical, including photocopying, without written permission from the publisher. Product or company names used in this set are for identification purposes only. Inclusion of the names of the products or companies does not indicate a claim of ownership by IGI Global of the trademark or registered trademark.

Library of Congress Cataloging-in-Publication Data

Names: Malveaux, Gregory F., editor. | Raby, Rosalind Latiner, editor.
Title: Study abroad opportunities for community college students and
   strategies for global learning / Gregory F. Malveaux and Rosalind Latiner
   Raby, editors.
Description: Hershey, PA : Information Science Reference, 2019. | Includes
   bibliographical references.
Identifiers: LCCN 2018005649| ISBN 9781522562528 (hardcover) | ISBN
   9781522562535 (ebook)
Subjects: LCSH: Foreign study--United States. | International
   education--United States. | Community college students--United States.
Classification: LCC LB2376 .S76 2019 | DDC 370.116/2--dc23 LC record available at https://lccn.loc.gov/2018005649

This book is published in the IGI Global book series Advances in Higher Education and Professional Development (AHEPD) (ISSN: 2327-6983; eISSN: 2327-6991)

British Cataloguing in Publication Data
A Cataloguing in Publication record for this book is available from the British Library.

All work contributed to this book is new, previously-unpublished material. The views expressed in this book are those of the authors, but not necessarily of the publisher.

For electronic access to this publication, please contact: eresources@igi-global.com.

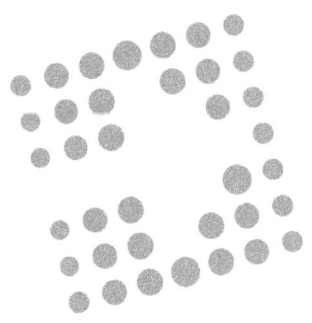

Advances in Higher Education and Professional Development (AHEPD) Book Series

Jared Keengwe
University of North Dakota, USA

ISSN:2327-6983
EISSN:2327-6991

Mission

As world economies continue to shift and change in response to global financial situations, job markets have begun to demand a more highly-skilled workforce. In many industries a college degree is the minimum requirement and further educational development is expected to advance. With these current trends in mind, the **Advances in Higher Education & Professional Development (AHEPD) Book Series** provides an outlet for researchers and academics to publish their research in these areas and to distribute these works to practitioners and other researchers.

AHEPD encompasses all research dealing with higher education pedagogy, development, and curriculum design, as well as all areas of professional development, regardless of focus.

Coverage

- Adult Education
- Assessment in Higher Education
- Career Training
- Coaching and Mentoring
- Continuing Professional Development
- Governance in Higher Education
- Higher Education Policy
- Pedagogy of Teaching Higher Education
- Vocational Education

IGI Global is currently accepting manuscripts for publication within this series. To submit a proposal for a volume in this series, please contact our Acquisition Editors at Acquisitions@igi-global.com or visit: http://www.igi-global.com/publish/.

The Advances in Higher Education and Professional Development (AHEPD) Book Series (ISSN 2327-6983) is published by IGI Global, 701 E. Chocolate Avenue, Hershey, PA 17033-1240, USA, www.igi-global.com. This series is composed of titles available for purchase individually; each title is edited to be contextually exclusive from any other title within the series. For pricing and ordering information please visit http://www.igi-global.com/book-series/advances-higher-education-professional-development/73681. Postmaster: Send all address changes to above address. Copyright © 2019 IGI Global. All rights, including translation in other languages reserved by the publisher. No part of this series may be reproduced or used in any form or by any means – graphics, electronic, or mechanical, including photocopying, recording, taping, or information and retrieval systems – without written permission from the publisher, except for non commercial, educational use, including classroom teaching purposes. The views expressed in this series are those of the authors, but not necessarily of IGI Global.

Titles in this Series

For a list of additional titles in this series, please visit: www.igi-global.com/book-series

Handbook of Research on Field-Based Teacher Education
Thomas E. Hodges (University of South Carolina, USA) and Angela C. Baum (University of South Carolina, USA)
Information Science Reference • copyright 2019 • 749pp • H/C (ISBN: 9781522562498) • US $245.00 (our price)

Student-Centered Virtual Learning Environments in Higher Education
Marius Boboc (Cleveland State University, USA) and Selma Koç (Cleveland State University, USA)
Information Science Reference • copyright 2019 • 281pp • H/C (ISBN: 9781522557692) • US $165.00 (our price)

Policies and Initiatives for the Internationalization of Higher Education
Fatoş Silman (Cyprus International University, Cyprus) Fahriye Altinay Aksal (Near East University, Cyprus) and Zehra Altinay Gazi (Near East University, Cyprus)
Information Science Reference • copyright 2019 • 229pp • H/C (ISBN: 9781522552314) • US $165.00 (our price)

Diversity, Equity, and Inclusivity in Contemporary Higher Education
Rhonda Jeffries (University of South Carolina, USA)
Information Science Reference • copyright 2019 • 334pp • H/C (ISBN: 9781522557241) • US $185.00 (our price)

Handbook of Research on Ethics, Entrepreneurship, and Governance in Higher Education
Suja R. Nair (Educe Micro Research, India) and José Manuel Saiz-Álvarez (EGADE Business School, Tecnológico de Monterrey, Mexico)
Information Science Reference • copyright 2019 • 627pp • H/C (ISBN: 9781522558378) • US $285.00 (our price)

Handbook of Research on E-Assessment in Higher Education
Ana Azevedo (Polytechnic of Porto, Portugal) and José Azevedo (Polytechnic of Porto, Portugal)
Information Science Reference • copyright 2019 • 514pp • H/C (ISBN: 9781522559368) • US $235.00 (our price)

Navigating Micro-Aggressions Toward Women in Higher Education
Ursula Thomas (Georgia Perimeter College, USA)
Information Science Reference • copyright 2019 • 304pp • H/C (ISBN: 9781522559429) • US $190.00 (our price)

Global Adaptations of Community College Infrastructure
Uttam Gaulee (Morgan State University, USA)
Information Science Reference • copyright 2019 • 305pp • H/C (ISBN: 9781522558613) • US $175.00 (our price)

701 East Chocolate Avenue, Hershey, PA 17033, USA
Tel: 717-533-8845 x100 • Fax: 717-533-8661
E-Mail: cust@igi-global.com • www.igi-global.com

Editorial Advisory Board

Monija Amani, *Georgetown University, USA*
Julie Baer, *Institute for International Education (IIE), USA*
Tanith Fowler Corsi, *Virginia International University, USA*
Rebekah de Wit, *Community College of Baltimore County, USA*
David Fell, *Carroll Community College, USA*
Mary Beth Furst, *University of Maryland, USA*
Drew Gephart, *Peralta Community College District, USA*
Ann Hubbard, *Università Cattolica del Sacro Cuore, Italy*
Mikyong Minsun Kim, *George Washington University, USA*
Jayme Kreitinger, *College Consortium for International Studies (CCIS), USA*
Anne-Marie McKee, *Volunteer State Community College, USA*
Gary Rhodes, *California State University Dominguez Hills, USA*
Jennifer Robertson, *Valencia College – Poinciana, USA*
Carola Smith, *Santa Barbara City College, USA*
David J. Smith, *George Mason University, USA*
Taryn Tangpricha, *Delaware Technical Community College, USA*
Marc Thomas, *Colorado Mountain College, USA*
Tiffany Viggiano, *Fulbright Finland, Finland*
Melissa Whatley, *University of Georgia, USA*
Dawn Wood, *Kirkwood Community College, USA*
K. Siobhan Wright, *Carroll Community College, USA*

List of Reviewers

Shabeer Amirali, *University of Louisville, USA*
Zachary T. Androulou, *Florence Ethnographic Field School, Italy*
David Comp, *Columbia College Chicago, USA*
Sylvia Findlay, *Illinois State University, USA*
Marion Froleich, *Independent Researcher, USA*
Miloni Ghandi, *Foothill/DeAnza Community College District, USA*
Emily Gorlewski, *Wesleyan University, USA*

Nick Gozik, *Boston College, USA*
Vincinio Lopez, *City College of San Francisco, USA*
Valerie Nightengale, *University of Connecticut, USA*
Tonal Simmons, *Kalamazoo College, USA*
Stacye Thompson, *Jefferson State Community College, USA*
Stephen Tippett, *State University of New York, USA*
Tasha Willis, *California State University Los Angeles, USA*
Christian Wilwohl, *State University of New York at New Paltz, USA*
Michael Woolf, *CAPA: The Global Network, USA*

Table of Contents

Foreword *by Allan Goodman* xvii

Foreword *by Brian Whalen* xviii

Preface xix

Acknowledgment xxxi

Chapter 1
Changing the Conversation: Measures That Contribute to Community College Education Abroad Success 1
    Rosalind Latiner Raby, California State University Northridge, USA

Chapter 2
Opening the Door to Study Abroad From Community Colleges 22
    Julie Baer, Institute for International Education (IIE), USA

Chapter 3
Good Practices and Program Standards: Considering the Unique Needs of Community Colleges 37
    Carola Smith, Santa Barbara City College, USA
    Ann Hubbard, American Institute for Foreign Study, USA

Chapter 4
Community College Education Abroad Health and Safety Concerns: Standards Needed to Meet the Challenges 53
    Gregory F. Malveaux, Montgomery College, USA
    Gary M. Rhodes, California State University Dominguez Hills, USA
    Rosalind L. Raby, California State University Northridge, USA

Chapter 5
Study Abroad Outcomes Assessment: A Community College Case Study 72
    Dawn R. Wood, Kirkwood Community College, USA

Chapter 6
Clearing the Hurdle: The Relationship Between Institutional Profiles and Community College Study Abroad 90
    Melissa Whatley, University of Georgia, USA

Chapter 7
The Outreach Triad for Successful Study Abroad Programs: Students, Faculty, and the Local Community 107
    Jennifer Joy Robertson, Valencia College, USA

Chapter 8
Lessons Learned: Building Inclusive Support for Study Abroad Programming at Delaware Technical Community College 120
    Taryn Gassner Tangpricha, Delaware Technical Community College, USA

Chapter 9
Enhancing Study Abroad Participation and Choices of Destination at Community Colleges 131
    Monija Amani, Georgetown University, USA
    Mikyong Minsun Kim, The George Washington University, USA

Chapter 10
The Hybrid Model: Providing Options for a Small Community College 147
    William David Fell, Carroll Community College, USA
    Siobhan Wright, Carroll Community College, USA

Chapter 11
Low-Cost Initiatives for Expanding Study Abroad Opportunities 158
    Drew Allen Gephart, Peralta Community College District, USA

Chapter 12
Institutionalizing International Education and Embedding Education Abroad Into the Campus Community 172
    Carola Smith, Santa Barbara City College, USA

Chapter 13
Thinking Globally About Social Justice 184
    Tiffany Viggiano, Fulbright Finland, Finland

Chapter 14
Peacebuilding as a Means to Global Citizenry 200
    David J. Smith, Forage Center for Peacebuilding and Humanitarian Education, USA &
    George Mason University, USA

Chapter 15
Internationalized Courses on Campus: A Complement to Study Abroad That Maximizes
International Education Participation in the Community College Context 213
    Rebekah de Wit, Community College of Baltimore County, USA
    Mary Beth Furst, Howard Community College, USA

Chapter 16
Practical Strategies for Rural-Serving Community College Global Programming 228
    Marc Thomas, Colorado Mountain College, USA

Chapter 17
A Case Study Exploring Ways to Increase Access to Education Abroad for Career and Technical
Students With Limited Availability 242
    Anne-Marie McKee, Volunteer State Community College, USA

Chapter 18
Utilizing a National Association to Increase Access to Education Abroad 255
    Jayme Kreitinger, College Consortium for International Studies, USA
    Tanith Fowler Corsi, Virginia International University, USA

Chapter 19
How to Survive and Thrive as a Community College Consortium: A Case Study of the Maryland
Community College International Education Consortium 265
    Gregory F. Malveaux, Montgomery College, USA

Compilation of References 284

About the Contributors 316

Index 322

Detailed Table of Contents

Foreword *by Allan Goodman* xvii

Foreword *by Brian Whalen* xviii

Preface xix

Acknowledgment xxxi

Chapter 1
Changing the Conversation: Measures That Contribute to Community College Education Abroad
Success 1
    Rosalind Latiner Raby, California State University Northridge, USA

Community college literature uses three distinct narratives to explain why few community colleges offer education abroad and why limited numbers of community college students study abroad. This chapter explores the viability of these narratives and counters them by showing that non-traditional community college students understand the role of education abroad to enhance their personal and professional growth, are capable of making sound decisions, and are able to balance work, school, and family. The chapter concludes with a discussion on how weak institutional choices remain the most important element that negatively impacts the choice to study abroad.

Chapter 2
Opening the Door to Study Abroad From Community Colleges 22
    Julie Baer, Institute for International Education (IIE), USA

Drawing upon data from Open Doors®, this chapter highlights the unique characteristics of study abroad from community colleges over the past decade. It explores patterns in destinations, durations, and student characteristics for study abroad at community colleges over this time period. Through lessons learned from IIE's Heiskell Award winners and Generation Study Abroad (GSA) community college commitment partners, the chapter will conclude with best practices from community colleges that have made commitments to increase and diversify their study abroad programs.

Chapter 3
Good Practices and Program Standards: Considering the Unique Needs of Community Colleges 37
Carola Smith, Santa Barbara City College, USA
Ann Hubbard, American Institute for Foreign Study, USA

With education abroad having evolved into a professional field and recognized program standards and good practices having been established, there are unique considerations that community colleges must consider regarding program development, implementation, and practices that require a particular approach to best meet the needs of both community college students and two-year institutions. By examining the nine areas of the standards of good practice developed by the Forum on Education Abroad, a narrative on each will be presented to address both their relevance and application to community colleges. Currently, with the greatest growth in U.S. education abroad occurring in short-term programming and with faculty-led programming being the most common type offered by community colleges, this review has timely relevance for the field.

Chapter 4
Community College Education Abroad Health and Safety Concerns: Standards Needed to Meet the Challenges 53
Gregory F. Malveaux, Montgomery College, USA
Gary M. Rhodes, California State University Dominguez Hills, USA
Rosalind L. Raby, California State University Northridge, USA

There has been a good deal already written about health and safety with education abroad at four-year colleges and universities. Although the authors found significant publications with a university focus, they found no published literature that specifically addresses community college overseas health, safety, and legal issues. The purpose of this chapter is to review what the literature already says about health and safety challenges and apply it to community colleges. In so doing, they bring forth US court cases and real-life examples at community college education abroad programs in order to ground recommendations and strategies for responding to today's challenges. In the same way that community colleges implement "on campus" policies and procedures to both limit and respond to student health and safety crises, community colleges should also implement policies and procedures to limit "study abroad" risks to students and be prepared to act if issues arise overseas. This chapter provides essential strategies to improve health and safety and legal standards for community college education abroad programs.

Chapter 5
Study Abroad Outcomes Assessment: A Community College Case Study 72
Dawn R. Wood, Kirkwood Community College, USA

The purpose of this chapter is to provide an overview of the literature relevant to outcomes assessment as it pertains to community college study abroad and to provide a case study of Kirkwood Community College's recent project developing institution-specific study abroad learning outcomes. The subsequent outcomes assessment conducted will be discussed along with conclusions from the process and the data gathered. This case study will illustrate how one community college developed student learning outcomes specific to its environment and a unique "home-grown" assessment model for assessing those outcomes comprehensively across all programs. The ability to engage in dialogue at all levels of the institution and speak the language of assessment has provided opportunities for unique improvements and the furthering of global learning goals.

Chapter 6
Clearing the Hurdle: The Relationship Between Institutional Profiles and Community College
Study Abroad 90
    Melissa Whatley, University of Georgia, USA

The purpose of this chapter is twofold. First, it aims to call attention to the fact that study abroad does take place in the community college sector. Second, this study aims at modeling the relationship between institutional profile characteristics and variations in study abroad participation at community colleges. In this sense, it addresses community college students' ability to access education abroad using the institution as the unit of analysis. Specifically, this study employs data from both the Institute of International Education (IIE) and the Integrated Postsecondary Education Data System (IPEDS) to examine the role institutional characteristics, such as an institution's gender and race/ethnicity composition and its location, play in community college students' participation in study abroad. The hurdle model analytic technique adopted here allows for the examination of these factors' relationship to both an institution's provision of study abroad opportunity and the percentage of students that participate. Results have implications for both policymakers and practitioners who aim to increase the prominence of education abroad in the two-year sector.

Chapter 7
The Outreach Triad for Successful Study Abroad Programs: Students, Faculty, and the Local
Community 107
    Jennifer Joy Robertson, Valencia College, USA

The old adage "build it and they will come" does not apply in the context of study abroad at the community college. Community colleges have historically struggled with study abroad enrollment due to a number of factors including inadequate funding, insufficient institutional support, and a lack of interest and awareness on behalf of their students. While there are many factors that go into successful programming for study abroad, one key element is outreach. This chapter will define outreach in terms of the marketing and communication methods to three key stakeholders in study abroad: students, faculty, and the local community. It will be argued that program administrators need to better understand the various ways in which outreach is used to increase both student enrollment, minority students in particular, and the number of faculty engaged in leading study abroad at the community college. The chapter will conclude by proposing some strategies for identifying funding opportunities from local community partners.

Chapter 8
Lessons Learned: Building Inclusive Support for Study Abroad Programming at Delaware
Technical Community College 120
    Taryn Gassner Tangpricha, Delaware Technical Community College, USA

This chapter conducts a case study of Delaware Technical Community College as it grew its programs from 2009 to present. Despite directive from the President, support and engagement was not widespread across the state: varying by campus, division, department, and instructor. Study abroad leadership was tasked with aligning the program with the college's mission, vision, and strategic directions, and building support internally and externally to boost student enrollment in the study abroad program. By targeting three key groups of stakeholders—students, faculty, and community members—and supporting shared values towards a mutual benefit, Delaware Technical Community College was able to grow its study abroad enrollment by over 400% from 2010 to 2018.

Chapter 9
Enhancing Study Abroad Participation and Choices of Destination at Community Colleges 131
    Monija Amani, Georgetown University, USA
    Mikyong Minsun Kim, The George Washington University, USA

This chapter addresses the findings of a multilayered study regarding perceptions of study abroad coordinators and students related to community college students' decisions to engage in global programs abroad and the factors that motivate their selection of a destination. In-depth interviews of study abroad program coordinators and students from three community colleges located in urban, suburban, and rural areas provided rich and diverse perspectives regarding students' access and engagement in study abroad programs and the reasons that affect their choices of destinations. Findings showed synchronicity and alignment between the study abroad coordinators' and students' perspectives. However, study abroad coordinators revealed that institutional administrators or leaders who have established connections with certain destinations influence program and destination offerings, which in turn broadens or limits students' selection of study abroad choices. Discussions and implications related to community college students, faculty, institutional leaders, and policymakers provide insight on how to make study abroad more accessible to community college students and expand their choice of destination.

Chapter 10
The Hybrid Model: Providing Options for a Small Community College 147
    William David Fell, Carroll Community College, USA
    Siobhan Wright, Carroll Community College, USA

This chapter is a case study of Carroll Community College, a small rural community college, and its plan to develop a viable travel program by using a hybrid model. This model includes three distinct cohorts: study abroad students (students who travel and take an associated credit course), lifelong learning students (travelers who take a continuing education course to prepare for the travel experience), and educational tourists (travelers who do not take an associated course). By allowing not only study abroad students but also lifelong learners (often called continuing education students) to participate in an international travel program, Carroll's mission is addressed. This chapter is a case study of how and why Carroll implemented the hybrid model as an example for other small community colleges that might wish to achieve similar results.

Chapter 11
Low-Cost Initiatives for Expanding Study Abroad Opportunities 158
    Drew Allen Gephart, Peralta Community College District, USA

Community colleges without a budget strictly allocated to study abroad programs need to be creative in how they expand opportunities for their students. This chapter will focus on the strategies developed by the Peralta Community College District's Office of International Education to develop a stronger study abroad program with limited resources and staffing. After the Peralta Colleges committed to the Institute of International Education's Generation Study Abroad initiative in 2014, it created new study abroad programs, organized annual study abroad fairs, was awarded a scholarship of $7,500, created new promotional materials and an administrative procedure, launched a new website and newsletter, organized financial aid workshops and professional development day presentations for faculty, and opened a study abroad scholarship through its foundation. The chapter will share how other colleges can learn from these efforts and institutionalize study abroad on their campuses.

Chapter 12
Institutionalizing International Education and Embedding Education Abroad Into the Campus
Community 172
    Carola Smith, Santa Barbara City College, USA

This chapter is a descriptive case study on one community college in California to show how the institution was able to successfully institutionalize study abroad through advocacy, strategic planning, and the cultivation of local, statewide, and international collaborations. Because of the longevity and vitality of the program examined in this particular case study, there is useful insight for other education abroad professionals who are at varying stages of implementing, developing, or institutionalizing study abroad programs at their respective institutions.

Chapter 13
Thinking Globally About Social Justice 184
    Tiffany Viggiano, Fulbright Finland, Finland

Scholars have identified community colleges as ideal institutions to facilitate global justice through their involvement in internationalization activities such as study abroad. This chapter explores the meaning of humanism as it relates to study abroad at the community college. Using Andreotti, Stein, Pashby, and Nicolson's Paradigms of Discourse, the chapter describes the ways in which humanism can be defined in a variety of ways based on one's own goals. The chapter also grounds a rationale for study abroad at the community college within critical humanism by applying Young's Social Connections Model. Finally, the chapter applies the critical humanist rationale to begin to question the relationship between community college study abroad initiatives: Who is included in the community mission? Whose cultures come to be understood from involvement in study abroad? How are U. S. cultures represented by study abroad?

Chapter 14
Peacebuilding as a Means to Global Citizenry 200
    David J. Smith, Forage Center for Peacebuilding and Humanitarian Education, USA &
    George Mason University, USA

The objective of this chapter is to illustrate approaches that can be used by community colleges to promote both global knowledge and global engagement—often taking the form of education abroad—using peacebuilding means. To make the case, examples and models from several U.S. community colleges will be shared. Examples from community colleges from throughout the country are given.

Chapter 15
Internationalized Courses on Campus: A Complement to Study Abroad That Maximizes
International Education Participation in the Community College Context 213
    Rebekah de Wit, Community College of Baltimore County, USA
    Mary Beth Furst, Howard Community College, USA

Internationalizing the community college curriculum offers an opportunity to reach a broad range of students completing their general education requirements. Implementing course internationalization on campus also maximizes the student body's participation in international education, particularly in community college contexts where study abroad is not a viable option for many students due to resource limitations. Efforts to internationalize the curriculum should target high-enrolled courses across campus that fit within existing programs of study. Faculty coordinating these courses are integral in extending the scope of the course objectives by integrating international perspectives. Faculty work is acknowledged through existing structures of professional development and annual review processes. An internationalized curriculum combined with study abroad and other cross-cultural experiential learning forms the framework for an academic enrichment program called Global Distinction.

Chapter 16
Practical Strategies for Rural-Serving Community College Global Programming 228
    Marc Thomas, Colorado Mountain College, USA

Nearly two-thirds of all community college districts in the United States are defined as rural serving, as reported by the Rural Community College Alliance (2017), representing 37%—or more than 3 million—of community college students nationally. These rural districts often struggle to fund and develop global education activities. This chapter will identify promising practices employed by three rural-serving colleges to improve student global competence through international-education programming.

Chapter 17
A Case Study Exploring Ways to Increase Access to Education Abroad for Career and Technical Students With Limited Availability 242
    Anne-Marie McKee, Volunteer State Community College, USA

This chapter looks into the experiences of the career and technical students who studied abroad and how their experiences affected them and transformed them in the years since studying abroad. The purpose is to examine the experiences of studying abroad for CTE students attending a rural-based community college. In this study, relevant categories and themes of meaning for CTE study abroad students were identified. One goal of this study was to see if these students' study abroad experiences affected them in the workplace and if the service-learning component of their study abroad experiences led to other altruistic practices.

Chapter 18
Utilizing a National Association to Increase Access to Education Abroad 255
    Jayme Kreitinger, College Consortium for International Studies, USA
    Tanith Fowler Corsi, Virginia International University, USA

Today, community colleges seek to internationalize amid an environment of widespread internal budget cuts and restricted resources. It has become increasingly common for community colleges to incorporate a global mission into their strategic plan despite current economic realities dictating that funding get allocated to priority projects such as student enrollment and academics before they reach international activities. A common misperception is that international education is a costly endeavor that has the potential to put a strain on the institutional budget. In reality, international education operations can be set up to be self-supporting and generate revenue for the institution through strategic study abroad pricing models. This chapter constructs a scenario to explore how community colleges can do more with less to expand their international agenda while navigating a climate of internal budget constraints and institutional downsizing.

Chapter 19
How to Survive and Thrive as a Community College Consortium: A Case Study of the Maryland
Community College International Education Consortium 265
    Gregory F. Malveaux, Montgomery College, USA

Some state and regional study abroad and international education-based consortia of community colleges have been struggling to remain operational. Key outside factors that have created trials include the United States' (US) economic downturn that ensued from 2007-2009, ongoing regulations set by government officials, and internal logistical challenges such as changes in leadership at member institutions, alterations in financial aid requirements, and emphasis placed on degree completion. There has been much analysis on "why" these consortia exist in the field; in contrast, this chapter focuses on "how" they persist. The Maryland Community College International Education Consortium (MCCIEC) is one of the nation's state consortia that continue to be active and flourish, navigating through economic trials, governmental policies that offset international student entry in to American higher education, and common logistical issues; this chapter uses MCCIEC as an illustrative model to show how community college consortia may function to prosper. MCCIEC uses four main approaches—1) gaining higher administrative buy-in, 2) encouraging full institutional support at membership colleges, 3) incorporating strong incentives for member activity, and 4) stimulating growth—to not only survive, but to thrive.

Compilation of References 284

About the Contributors 316

Index 322

Foreword

Community colleges serve a vital mission expanding access to higher education to all students, regardless of where they are in their academic journey and what stage they are at in their career. For hundreds of thousands, community colleges are a place to gain skills and new knowledge that will transform their lives.

International education is a crucial part of the college-going experience, and its role at community colleges is often misunderstood. As this book will show, study abroad plays an important role at community colleges, as community colleges were designed to meet local and regional workforce needs. What that has meant over the years is continually evolving and is increasingly important.

Globalization is changing the way the world works, making regional economies an integral part of the broader global economy. Employers want employees who have international experience and expertise, and the ability to interact with people from other countries and cultures. Study abroad cultivates those very skills, and it is crucial that community college students be afforded the same opportunities as their peers attending four-year institutions.

As the book demonstrates, many community colleges are building programs to open doors to new countries for students. In the 2015-16 academic year, 6,900 community college students studied abroad. Though still too small, this number represents great progress from decades past. In 1995-96, just 2,277 community college students studied abroad.

Community colleges, more than ever, are offering students the opportunity to take advantage of study abroad programs. This book provides important information on the college-level programs that are successfully creating new opportunities for more students to go abroad. Their stories will inspire and challenge many more colleges to follow suit.

Allan Goodman
Institute of International Education, USA

Allan Goodman, *Ph.D., is the sixth President of the Institute of International Education. He is also the CEO of the Institute of International Education. He is the author of books on international affairs published by Harvard, Princeton and Yale University presses. Previously, he was Executive Dean of the School of Foreign Service and Professor at Georgetown University. He was the first American professor to lecture at the Foreign Affairs College of Beijing, helped create the first U.S. academic exchange program with the Moscow Diplomatic Academy for the Association of Professional Schools of International Affairs, and developed the diplomatic training program of the Foreign Ministry of Vietnam. He has a Ph.D. in Government from Harvard, an M.P.A. from the John F. Kennedy School of Government and a B.S. from Northwestern University. Dr. Goodman has received awards from Georgetown, Johns Hopkins, South Florida, and Tufts universities, the Légion d'honneur from France, and the Royal Norwegian Order of Merit. He was awarded the inaugural Gilbert Medal for Internationalization by Universitas 21.*

Foreword

Higher education institutions in the United States are as diverse as the students who enroll in them. Approaches to education abroad and global learning are as vast and varied as institutions themselves. What makes sense for and works at one institution will not always be desirable or replicable at another type of institution. While the field of education abroad has well-established standards, there are a myriad of ways to meet these standards depending on institutional mission and context.

Community colleges serve more students than any other institutional type in the United States, and their students pursue educational opportunities for an incredibly diverse range of reasons and purposes. Within this fluid and dynamic context, global learning and education abroad are organized and practiced in distinctive ways.

This book describes and analyzes the distinctiveness of education abroad and global learning at community colleges. Together, the various chapters provide a framework for understanding international education at community colleges by offering perspectives on the strengths, opportunities and challenges within these institutions. The authors provide strategic analyses that will be useful for community college administrators and faculty seeking to define and develop education abroad for their institutions, and for those who are assessing current practices. This is a first of its kind and will serve as an important resource to help more community college to internationalize.

One of the most important takeaways will be a long-awaited confronting of assumptions about education abroad and global learning at community colleges. This book dispels the myth that community colleges are not as advanced in international education practices as are other types of institutions. The book documents the successes that community colleges have had in developing innovative education abroad and global learning programs that serve their local communities and diverse constituents through open access, and by implementing creative approaches and collaborations.

These are lessons well worth learning for all types of institutions.

Brian Whalen
The University at Albany (SUNY), USA & Academic Assembly, Inc., USA

Preface

About 13 million students attend 1,167 public and independent U.S. community colleges and 1,600 when including branch campuses (AACC, 2018). While the term "Community College" is preferred, these institutions are also referred to as Colleges, Junior Colleges, Technical Colleges, and Two-Year colleges (Cohen, Bawer, & Kisker, 2014). Students enroll to earn their first credential, certificate or degree, to gain multiple credentials to advance their career pathway, to enhance remedial skills, to engage in life-long education, or prepare to transfer to a four-year college/university (Cohen, Bawer, & Kisker, 2014). Instruction occurs in the liberal arts, sciences, transfer education, workforce career education, remedial education and extracurricular activities. Education abroad is included in each of these areas of instruction.

Multiple generations of community college leaders have argued that internationalization is an inherent component of community colleges that advances student knowledge, facilitates student success, and serves the needs of local communities (Gleazer, 1975; Hess, 1982; Boggs & Irwin, 2009; Raby & Valeau, 2016). For the about 24% of community college students who transfer, there is an opportunity to have international experiences at the university. The rest (about 76%), who often choose to enroll in terminal educational programs, can only gain international experiences while at the community college (Raby, 1996).

There is no national benchmark to measure the magnitude and application in which international programs are part of the community college (Raby & Valeau, 2016). The American Council on Education (ACE) surveyed 239 community colleges in 2011 and 166 in 2016 and found that less than 25% had an internationalization plan (ACE, 2012; Helms, Brajkovic, & Struthers, 2017). In an era of comprehensive internationalization (Hudzick, 2011), this means that there are few community colleges with an office that coordinates international programs across the campus and/or no comprehensive plan for growth. IIE Open Doors 2017 shows that 309 community colleges support international student programs and 141 community colleges support education abroad programs. When all databases are examined and repeat colleges are removed, about 420 community colleges, which is 36% of all community colleges, offer at least one type of an international program. Of these, 130, about 11.5% of all community colleges that offered education abroad to about 7,105 students.

A prevailing belief is that education abroad practices are the same for all institutional types. This book addresses a gap in the literature by unpacking central themes and debates that show that community colleges have unique pathways that apply to education abroad. Examples include: low to free tuition, open access that favors access over selectivity, multiple missions, guided pathway programs and stackable credentials that include highly sequences to accommodate certification requirements, career and workforce education, emphasis on performance funding linked to student learning outcomes and assessment, emphasis on accountability and transparency, minimum qualifications for faculty hiring that adhere to state and federal hiring regulations, and national enrollment and funding declines.

Community college research has focused on what is education abroad (Hess, 1982), curricular components of education abroad (Raby & Tarrow, 1996), and outreach activities (Raby, 2008). This book adds to the literature because it is the first book on community college education abroad. Chapters showcase education abroad at rural community colleges, within technical and career programs, and for racially and economically diverse students. Authors are community college education abroad directors, providers, and academics who study community colleges. Empirical and case studies reflect on the changing field and inform on important issues such as access, diversity, engagement, and assessment. Most importantly, the chapters in this book dismantle the claims that education abroad is underutilized at community colleges.

EDUCATION ABROAD, STUDY ABROAD, AND OTHER TERMS

Higher education uses many terms to define the ways in which students' study in another country. At the core, education abroad is an academically focused activity that is part of a prescribed curriculum that supports elective classes or classes that are part of a certificate or degree (NAFSA, 2018; U.S. Department of Education, 2017-2018). The title of this book uses the term "study abroad" which is most identifiable by academics and the public. The content of the book, however, celebrates the term "education abroad" which incorporates a range of outbound educational opportunities that includes for-credit courses, global service-learning, international internships, non-classroom based activities aligned with a for-credit curriculum, non-classroom based activities aligned with a non-credit curriculum, undergraduate research abroad, volunteer abroad, and student group programs such as chorus and student athletes (Forum On Education Abroad, 2018; Hamir & Gozik, 2018). A summary of these terms is included at the end of this introduction.

WHAT MAKES COMMUNITY COLLEGE EDUCATION ABROAD UNIQUE FROM UNIVERSITY STUDY ABROAD

There are unique characteristics of community college education abroad.

- **Lack of Research:** While universities have abundant literature on university efforts in education abroad, this is the first book devoted to community college education abroad.
- **Institutional Support:** Universities broadly support education abroad. The same is not true for community colleges where infusing of education abroad as an important component of the curriculum competes with decreased state and federal funding and an increasing pressure to prepare students for immediate employment (Raby & Valeau, 2016).
- **Admissions and Access:** The university junior year abroad was highly restrictive and even shorter programs still often have limitations in terms of class standing, GPA, and educational program. Community colleges are based on the open access mission in which no student is denied access to college education, including studying abroad. This results in minimal admission requirements (often with a benchmark at 2.0 or lower to accommodate for the open access mission. There is also a broad definition of who can even be a "student."

Preface

- **Institutional Structure:** Most universities have a dedicated office and working budget for education abroad. Some even have large staffing to address a range of needs and a budget allocated for professional development. Community colleges rarely have a dedicated office for education abroad, staffing is mostly faculty on release time, and a limited budget for professional development.
- **Recruitment, Placement, and Timing:** Universities work with a defined student population and have set times for program enrollment. Community colleges work with both an existing student population and with community members. Times for program enrollment are fluid as recruitment takes longer to accommodate for student needs including getting time off from work, saving money, and outreach.

Issues of Importance for Community Colleges

Student Profile and Access Changes

Community college education abroad populations are diverse since community colleges have such high non-traditional student enrollments. This includes 1st semester freshman, pre-college concurrent enrollment, adults, 1st generation students, students with disabilities, LGBTQ students, international students, undocumented students, students studying in STEAM fields, and non-degree students, ex pats, and/or community members. While many students who study abroad continue to be largely Caucasian and female, there is increasing diversification of community college students that includes under-represented populations of race, ethnicity, and economic status.

Credit Focus Changes

All education abroad is for-credit, but there are various ways in which credit is awarded. For semester and year-length programs, credit complies with credit-granting formulas on-campus. For short-term programs, a 2018 national survey (SECUSSA-April 9, 2018) respondents concurred that actual content hours per day dictates credits acquired through in-class time, site visits, and field work that directly relates to instructional time and aligns with campus credit formulas. One example is 1 hour of formal class equals 1 contact hour while 3 hours of field trips and academic excursion also equals 1 contact hour. For very short-term programs (under two weeks), credit is bundled in an affiliated class taken on-campus or as part of a hybrid program that integrates in-class, online and abroad learning.

Program Types

Community college students participate in various types of study abroad. Direct enrollment has a student enroll in an international university with fees paid directly to that university and study alongside local students. Partnership exchanges include reciprocal exchange between a community college and an international university. Tuition/fees are often paid to the home institution with credit awarded either by the host or international institution. Faculty-led programs use a designate on-campus curriculum and create a section of that class to be taught abroad by a US faculty member. US faculty also create stand-alone courses specifically for the abroad experience and credit is awarded as if the class is taught on-campus.

Embedded programs are required and/or optional add-ons to a course offered on campus during a mid-term break or at the end of the term and are one to two weeks in length. Credit is awarded for the class but can also be awarded specifically for the international component. There are also programs offered by non-accredited study abroad provider companies in which curricula is developed with US faculty and credit provided by the community college. Students can also self-enroll in formalized provider programs and receive credit from a different educational institution.

Curricular Content Changes

All academic, career, and technical courses are taught abroad including an expanded range of STEAM courses. One unique aspect of community college education abroad is that STEAM and career programs have always been a focal point (Raby, 1996) that has aligned with non-traditional locations where the STEAM courses are easily utilized. Community colleges are known for their abroad programming in career-oriented programs such as culinary arts, cosmetology, and forestry.

Location

Opportunities have expanded from programs offered mostly in Western Europe to include programs in countries all around the world. IIE (2017) shows that among the top five locations for community colleges are those in Costa Rica, Cuba, and Mexico.

Cost Changes

The cost of the education abroad program is extremely high and is a limiting factor since when compared to community college tuition that can be free or about $1,000 per year. Abroad costs include tuition/fees, room and board, medical insurance, passport and visa fees, and transportation costs. Community college education abroad costs range from a few hundred dollars to an average of $3,500 including airfare for short-term programs and $6,500 - $8,000, including airfare, for semester programs (CCIE, 2018).

Standards Changes

Some community college faculty take students abroad without coordination with a college international office and might be unaware of standards in the field. Resulting health, safety, legal, and ethical problems and resulting lawsuits are showing the importance of the adoption of standards (Malveaux, 2016). Community colleges are beginning to recognize that these standards exist and how to integrate them into their practices.

Benefits

Study abroad serves many purposes. Politically, the abroad experience supports national security and foreign policy initiatives. In a humanitarian context, the abroad experience enhances understanding of others and can build citizen ambassadors. Socially, the abroad experience builds long-lasting friendships that can also turn into business relationships. Research shows that students who study abroad often do better in their studies, graduate at a higher rate, and gain employment quicker and often at higher salaries than their peers who did not study abroad. Intercultural gains include growth in maturity, increased self-confidence, a better understanding of themselves, and an ability to evaluate their own culture in an unbiased manner. Soft skills are increasingly honored by the global economy and include being adaptable, independent, interculturally competent, curious, and being able to think critically, communicate with others, and foster understanding and collaboration in group interactions. It must be noted that while the educational context of studying abroad is at the core of all programs, what and how much is learned varies from student to student.

Business of Study Abroad

Education abroad is often a break-even enterprise and could even result in a loss of revenue. Businesses organize and sell education abroad and target students as a desirable source of revenue. A parallel business model has emerged specifically for community colleges that link program curricular design with profit margin. Yet, for community colleges, revenue generation is not in alignment with open access policy which uses the lowest cost margin to build in accessibility.

Debates in the Field

Chapters in this book discuss four debates that will affect future design of community college education abroad.

Length

Program length is linked to perceptions of quality control. Some research shows that the longer the program, the greater and the more meaningful the learning experience and that very short-term programs (under two weeks) "dumb-down" the overall learning experience. Other research shows that even the shortest programs, when effectively designed, can foster critical learning. However, when program length is linked to student demographics by assuming that some students cannot study for long periods of time, unequal patterns emerge in which very short-term programs are given to community college students while longer programs are allocated for those students with privilege.

Destination

There is on-going discussion on where students should study. Some claim that any place enables learning, even if it is to tourist locations in Western Europe. Others feel that non-European locations should be emphasized for an equity of experience. Others caution that in developing countries, there needs to recognition to avoid a colonialist view of "visiting the natives," which Lewin says is a "kind of poverty tourism that reinforces stereotypes of themselves and others" (Lewin, 2009, p. xv). A goal is to equalize location context in which both student and locals learn together and use criticism to understand context in a liberating rather than colonialization construct.

Social, Economic, and Environmental Impacts

New concerns are being raised about the consequences that students have on local economies and local environments. This awareness emphasizes the social impact on host communities in terms of transportation and safety, economic impact on investing in local infrastructure and new businesses to support education abroad community service or service learning projects, impact that students have (positive and negative) on the local community, and environmental impact on host communities that includes carbon footprint, trash, and water use. The ethical impact of creating fair wages to families and organizations that support students are creating partnerships that are ethical, collaborative, and sustainable. Potential positive impacts can be found with an increase in education abroad programs that include high impact community service or volunteer experiences.

What Is Cultural Learning?

Debates extend to the type of program learning. New frameworks question what is taught, where it is taught, and how it is taught. Tours, in which students visit places, eat new foods, and see the sights are criticized as "commercial travel masquerading as academic experience" (Lewin, 2009, p. xv) due too little to any cultural interactions. "Island" programs, in which students spend time in another location, but never break out of their isolation and mix with the locals, are criticized as minimizing cultural learning. The field suggests that the design of the programs allow students to discover themselves, to understand the interplay of globalization to local communities, and to build a link between travel experiences, social action, and academic content. In so doing, the abroad experience can help students to create a context of "empowerment," "agencies" and "self-actualization" that allow them to challenge stereotypes and oppression that exist in all societies. Finally, new discussions are building about how to be meet the needs of diverse students by acknowledging the intersectionality of racial, class, age, and gender demographics and to understand the dynamics in which peer interactions can build or weaken student comfort and thereby effect the learning process.

BOOK THEMES

The chapters in this book explore the many ways in which the field of community college education abroad is changing. Eight broad themes showcase the unique contributions made by community colleges.

Measures for Success Through Increased Access

A noted uniqueness of the community college is the open access mission that provides policy to not exclude any student from an educational experience. Raby uses open access as a focal point to change the conversation as to who gets access to education abroad, who is denied due to institutional practices and prejudices, and how to change those patterns. Advancing open access via education abroad is achieved through the consortia model (Malveaux), by embedding education abroad in general education classes (Furst and deWit), and by embedding in career and technical education curriculum (McKee). Gephart grounds the mission of the education abroad office in meeting open access while Amani and Kim provide examples of how to increase access from the perspectives of students themselves.

Preface

Embedding Into Campus Community

The first generation of community college education abroad programs were stand-alone and singular stemming from an individual faculty interest. Today, many community colleges include holistic internationalization that is achieved via curriculum integration. Examples include linking the study abroad curriculum to meet graduation requirements and to provide a Global Distinction certificate for those on campus who are unable to go abroad (Furst and deWit) and that is connected to all campus services (C. Smith). Thomas and Tangpricha show how curricular integration can be done at the departmental level while Wood shows how the entire college community is connected to designing and overseeing assessment practices. Smith and Hubbard examine campus policy that identifies and uses standards, for who teaches abroad and benefits in terms of tenure or promotion, and policy that defines student learning connections to graduation.

Stakeholders

Within the community college are a range of stakeholders, including students, faculty, administrators, and members of the community. All stakeholders are important for the overall success of the education abroad programs. Faculty lead programs, as shown by Malveaux, Gephart, Thomas, and D. Smith, and faculty can also be part of the abroad student population as shown by C. Smith and McKee. The role of faculty in development and marketing is explored by Robertson and Amani and Kim. The role of senior administrators and trustees in sanctioning the education program as well as those leaders who are in charge of education abroad are explored by Gephart, C. Smith, Tangpricha, D. Smith, Whatley, and Wood. Finally, students are the ones who enroll in the program and include mainly credit seeking students, but sometimes, as shown by Fell and Wright, can also be non-credit students. Students are expressing interest as half of all high school seniors say that they have a strong desire to study abroad in college. Student opinions intersect with enrollment, and are explored in Raby, Robertson, and Amani and Kim. Parents increasingly view education abroad as a positive experience and have personal connections to travel due to themselves having studied abroad, worked abroad, or having military experiences abroad. The important link to the local community to financially support as well as to have overall acceptance is shown by C. Smith and Robertson. Even media is routinely mentioning study abroad as a course of action for characters in television, film and in music videos. Another, and important stakeholder is the federal government also is supportive with the US Congress approved, Senator Paul Simon Study Abroad Foundation Act (2007) whose goal is to reach 1 million students studying abroad, and the newly appointed U.S. Department of State, Study Abroad office.

Institutional Factors

Recent research considers if environmental factors, such as the college being located in an urban or rural location and student demographics play a role in the offering of education abroad. Thomas, McKee and Whatley show that location may not be the key barrier as previously expected. Robertson, Amani and Kim and Baer and Calvert all show that students who attend community college education abroad are diverse in terms of socio-economic status and race/ethnicity. Raby suggests that the barriers attributed to non-traditional students are simply evidence of prejudice, while Whatley shows that the number of international students and the number of African-American students strongly correlate with the presence of education abroad.

Program Development and Offering

Case studies are provided by several authors that highlight how their community colleges develop and oversee education abroad programs. Baer shows how this plays out nationally. Malveaux and Kreitinger and Corsi explore how consortia work and provide a positive learning environment. Gephart and Thomas provide examples of running an office on a limited budget, while C. Smith shows creative means to link program development to the entire college experience. Examples of how specific curriculum are embedded in programs as well as drive the program design are shown through the example of peace education by D. Smith and through the health clinic field experiences by McKee.

Social Justice Pedagogy and Curriculum

Traditional education abroad is curricular specific, such as teaching a modern language, art history, business or culinary arts. New discussions in the field link the study abroad experience to purposeful personality and life-style changes with the intent of not only making the experience one of a lifetime, but to create the context by which global citizenship practices can be learned. Viggiano and D. Smith provide examples of how the education abroad programs are a response to the agenda of social action in which programs have a purpose that is aligned with skills needed to work in a global economy or with goals of social action. C. Smith provides examples of programs that are specifically designed to teach environmentally responsibility. Finally, C. Smith and Hubbard provide the context for an Ethical Code of Conduct that applies to the design and application of the programs themselves.

Standards and Risk Management

As the field of education abroad matures, so does recognition that there are codes of standards, code of ethics and demands for risk management. Smith and Hubbard highlight how the standards in the field need to be applied to community colleges and also showcase where community colleges are unique in the discussion. Malveaux, Rhodes, and Raby do the same in regard to risk management, health, and security.

Assessment, Outcomes, and Impact

Learning from study abroad is a relational and dynamic process shaped by structural conditions, individuals' agencies, motivations, and social and personal circumstances. Academic engagement and student success do not automatically occur and are dependent on specific factors that shape the study abroad experience. Academic engagement leads to positive college outcomes including educational attainment, change in academic profile, meeting goals, and educational or psycho-social development. Wood shows that college-impact models recognize environmental conditions that strongly impact students. Program design and learning assessment defines not only the hard skills of what the curriculum is teaching, but the soft skills that are increasingly being honored by the global economy. Soft skills include being adaptable, independent, interculturally competent, curious, and being able to think critically, communicate with others, and foster understanding and collaboration in group interactions. Assessment has changed

Preface

from student end-of-course surveys, to more elaborate measures of intercultural growth, connections to student success initiatives, and overall learning objectives. Wood reviews the various assessments that are in place and applies it to a case study of her own college. C. Smith, Tangricha, and McKee also illustrate how assessments are utilized in their own community colleges.

CONCLUSION

This book assesses prior advancements in the field of community college education abroad, current challenges, and add to the gap in the literature. The authors clearly show that a transformation is occurring in which commitment from all stakeholders is setting the pace for future educational reforms in the field of community college education abroad. A key point made by the authors in this book is that reform is not based on chance, but on intentional designs created to guide comprehensive reform efforts. As editors, we celebrate with our authors the depth of community college education abroad and the ability to change student lives for the better. We hope that the theoretical and practical commonalities found in this book will be acted upon in future publications of revised Board policies in community colleges and associations across the United States and in innovative programming dedicated to curricula and training our future international education leaders.

COMMONLY USED TERMS

The following are commonly used terms according and defined by the Forum on Education Abroad Glossary (Forum, 2018). These definitions are informed by those offered by DiversityAbroad (2018), NAFSA (2018), Hamir and Gozik (2018), and Hoffa and Pearson (2005). The distinctions between terms will be helpful for community colleges that are experimenting with format and style.

- **Education Abroad (Synonymous With and Preferred to Study Abroad):** Education that occurs outside the participants' home country, including study and study through international experiences as work, volunteering, non-credit internships, and directed travel. To be education abroad, the program must be driven to a significant degree by learning goals.
- **Study Abroad (synonymous with and preferred to Overseas Study or Foreign Study):** A subtype of Education Abroad that results in progress toward an academic degree at a student's home institution (or may also be defined as a subtype of off-campus study that takes place outside the country where the student's home institution is located). This meaning, which has become standard among international educators in the U.S., excludes the pursuit of a full academic degree at a foreign institution. The US Department of Education adds that "A study-abroad program is eligible if the home school awards academic credit for it and students in it remain concurrently enrolled at their home school" (U.S. Department of Education, 2017-2018, p. 2-38).

PROGRAM TYPES

- **Excursion (or Field Trip):** Time away from the main instructional location for educational purposes, that is part of an academic course or program-wide activity for students.
- **Field Study (or Excursion):** An education abroad program type whose pedagogy revolves around experiential study outside the classroom setting. Examples include field research programs, internship programs, service-learning programs, and field programs. A sub-type of Field Study is the *Service-Learning Program* in which the pedagogical focus is a specially designed experience combining reflection with structured participation in a community-based project to achieve specified learning outcomes as part of an education abroad program. Emphasis is on experiential education to develop an integrated approach to understanding the relationship among theory, practice, ideals, values, and community.
- **Internship Abroad (Synonymous With Practicum and Practical Training):** A work abroad placement with a primary purpose that is educational. Can be offered for the experience or combined with coursework and offered within the context of an education abroad program for academic credit. An internship may be paid or unpaid.
- **Off-Campus Study (Sub-Set of Study Abroad):** Education held off-campus that results in progress toward an academic degree at the home institution. Includes field research projects, field trips, biology or geology field courses, for-credit internships, course-embedded service-learning, as well as satisfaction of a language requirement or completion of a senior thesis.
- **Study Away (Synonym for Off-Campus Study):** Study that takes students entirely away from the home campus either within or outside the U.S. The term tends to be used most often at campuses where the same office is responsible for both education abroad and domestic off-campus study.
- **Travel Seminar (Preferable to the Synonymous Study Tour or Study Travel Program):** A program in which students travel to many different cities or countries and receive instruction in each location. Travel Seminar differs from field trips or excursions within other program types/subtypes.
- **Volunteering Abroad:** A noncredit placement in which the participant engages with the local community in a structured but unpaid capacity. While *Service-Learning* offers academic credit, Volunteering does not.
- **Work Abroad:** Immersion in an international work environment with the educational value of the experience itself being the primary purpose. May or may not be for academic credit. Work abroad is sometimes used more narrowly to mean working for pay. By design, work abroad programs are temporary, lasting from a few weeks to two or three years. Educational work abroad is to be distinguished from career-related overseas assignments, permanent jobs abroad, and migration for gainful employment.

PROGRAMMATIC VARIATIONS AFFILIATED WITH EDUCATION ABROAD

- **Co-Curricular:** Activities, programs or events that complement curricular programming or goals that are typically non-academic in nature but relate other activities and experiences to the established curriculum or pedagogy.

Preface

- **Consortium:** A group of institutions and/or organizations that share access to an abroad program(s) to provide greater access, quality control, and/or cost efficiency. Members of the consortium share fiduciary, liability, promotional, and/ or oversight responsibility for the program(s).
- **Custom Program (or Customized Program):** An education abroad program administered by a program provider organization according to specifications of the home institution.
- **Curriculum Integration:** Incorporating coursework taken abroad into the academic context of the home campus.
- **Direct Enrollment:** Study at an overseas university without the assistance of external offices such as those of a program provider.
- **Embedded Program (or Course-Embedded Study Abroad):** Adding study abroad, as a requirement and/or option, to a course given on the home campus. Often, the abroad portion is during a midterm break or after the end of the on-campus term and is just a week or two long.
- **Faculty-Led Program (or Faculty-Directed Program):** An education abroad program directed by a faculty member(s) from the home campus who accompanies students abroad.
- **Non-Credit:** Coursework or co-curricular activities that do not earn academic credit.
- **Non-Degree Student (Synonymous Non-Matriculated Student):** A student who enrolls in the education abroad class but is not admitted to the institution in a degree-seeking status, such as community members.
- **Program Provider (or Independent Program Provider, or Third-Party Provider, or Provider):** An organization that offers education abroad program services to students. A program provider may be a college or university, a nonprofit organization, a for-profit business, or a consortium.
- **Short-Term:** Lasting eight weeks or less; offered in summer, winter or spring term.

Rosalind Latiner Raby
California State University Northridge, USA

Gregory F. Malveaux
Montgomery College, USA

REFERENCES

American Association of Community Colleges (AACC). (2018). *Fast facts from our fact sheet*. Retrieved from http://www.aacc.nche.edu/AboutCC/Pages/fastfactsfactsheet.aspx

American Council on Education. (2012). *Mapping internationalization on U.S. campuses: 2012 edition*. Retrieved from http://www.acenet.edu/news-room/Documents/MappingInternationalizationUSCampuses2012-full.pdf

Boggs, G. R., & Irwin, J. (2007). What every community college leader needs to know: Building leadership for international education. In E. J. Valeau & R. L. Raby (Eds.), International reform efforts and challenges in community colleges (pp. 25-30). San Francisco, CA: Jossey-Bass. doi:10.1002/cc.278

California Colleges for International Education (CCIE). (2018). *Education Abroad*. Accessed at: www.ccieworld/studyabroad

Cohen, A. M., Brawer, F. B., & Kisker, C. B. (2014). *The American community college* (6th ed.). San Francisco, CA: Jossey-Bass.

Forum on Education Abroad. (2018). *Glossary*. Retrieved from https://forumea.org/resources/glossary

Gleazer, E. J., Jr. (1975, March 24). *Memorandum to Community College Presidents*. American Association of Community and Junior Colleges.

Hamir, H. B., & Gozik, N. (2018). *Promoting Inclusion in Education Abroad: A handbook of Research and Practice*. Stylus.

Helms, R. M., Brajkovic, L., & Struthers, B. (2017). *Mapping Internationalization on U.S. Campuses* (2017 edition). Washington, DC: American Council or Education.

Hess, G. (1982). *Freshmen and sophomores abroad: Community colleges and overseas academic programs*. New York: Teachers College Press.

Hudzik, J. K. (2011). *Comprehensive Internationalization: From Concept to Action*. Washington, DC: Association of International Educators.

Institute for International Education. (2017). *Open doors Community college education abroad data tables*. Retrieved from: https://www.iie.org/en/Research-and-Insights/Open- Doors/Data/Community-College-Data-Resource/Community-College---Study- Abroad/Leading-Institutions/2015-16

Lewin, R. (2009). The Handbook of practice and research in study abroad: higher education and the quest for global citizenship. Association of American colleges and universities.

Malveaux, G. F. (2016). *Look before leaping: Risks, liabilities, and repair of study abroad in higher education*. Lanham, MD: Rowman & Littlefield.

NAFSA. (2018). *Education Abroad Knowledge Community*. Retrieved from www.nafsa.org

Raby, R. L. (1996). International, Intercultural, and Multicultural Dimensions of Community Colleges in the United States. In Dimensions of the Community College: International and Inter/Multicultural Perspectives. Garland Pub., Inc.

Raby, R. L. (2008). *Expanding Education Abroad at U.S. Community Colleges*. New York: Institute for International Education Press.

Raby, R. L., & Tarrow, N. (Eds.). (1996). *Dimensions of the community college: International and inter/multicultural perspectives*. New York, NY: Garland.

Raby, R. L., & Valeau, E. J. (2016). *International education at community colleges: Themes, practices, research, and case studies*. New York: Palgrave Publishers. doi:10.1057/978-1-137-53336-4

SECUSSA List-Serve. (2018, April 9). *Discussion Thread on Credit Options for Study Abroad*. Author.

U.S. Department of Education. (2017-2018). *International education: Study abroad*. Retrieved from http://www2.ed.gov/students/internatl/abroad/edpicks.jhtml

Acknowledgment

We thank our community college colleagues, those who research community colleges, and all those who have and continue to support community college education abroad. Your voices are essential for the field and we are grateful you are in this book. We feel so appreciative and privileged to have worked with you on this collaboration. We especially want to thank our special reviewers who gave critical feedback and direction to all of the authors. We also want to thank the staff at IGI-Global for their support in the publication process. We write this book for the community college education abroad pioneers, Donald R. Culton, Gephard Hess, and Edmund King who never hesitated to create opportunities for their students and in so doing continue to serve as an inspiration for future generations.

On a more personal note, I, Rosalind, want to thank my husband, Ronald, for his patience and loving support in helping me peruse my academic dreams.

This book is dedicated in loving memory to my mother, Myrna Malveaux. Thank you, my loving precious wife, Lisa, for giving me the time, and making daily sacrifices to "chase my dreams." My son, Gabriel, your daily humor and sweet nature put me in the right temperament to approach this work. My encouraging siblings, Courtney, Suzette, and Suzanne; and my dear father, Floyd, I admire each of you as you fuel my desire to make a difference. Montgomery College study abroad students, your energy, intellectual curiosity, and pursuit for global competence inspire me to serve you to the best of my ability. And, I thank you, Lord, for giving me the vision and for laying down the path to make this work a reality.

Chapter 1
Changing the Conversation:
Measures That Contribute to Community College Education Abroad Success

Rosalind Latiner Raby
California State University Northridge, USA

ABSTRACT

Community college literature uses three distinct narratives to explain why few community colleges offer education abroad and why limited numbers of community college students study abroad. This chapter explores the viability of these narratives and counters them by showing that non-traditional community college students understand the role of education abroad to enhance their personal and professional growth, are capable of making sound decisions, and are able to balance work, school, and family. The chapter concludes with a discussion on how weak institutional choices remain the most important element that negatively impacts the choice to study abroad.

INTRODUCTION

I have been studying community college education abroad since 1985 and have published extensively on the changing field. I have charted the growth, identified the components required for success, analyzed the barriers, and shown how student success stems from studying abroad. In re-examining conclusions from the field, I have come to the realization that commonly held beliefs about why community college students do not study abroad are largely inaccurate as they are grounded on archaic stereotypes of student deficit characteristics. Even more problematic is that these stereotypes are used to ground community college policies and in turn, these policies negatively impact access and limit growth in the number of community colleges that offer education abroad (Raby, 2018).

Barrier literature claims that non-traditional students are less interested and/or unable to study abroad (Commission on the Abraham Lincoln Study Abroad, 2014). Non-traditional is defined by one or more of the following characteristics, low SES levels, students of color, being first-generation, working full-time, being academically under-prepared, and being an adult (Ross-Gordon, 2011). While adult status is given at the age of 18 to vote and to serve in the military, higher education defines adult as being over the age of

DOI: 10.4018/978-1-5225-6252-8.ch001

25 (Kasworm, 1990; IPEDS, 2018) with multiple classifications including "nontraditional-age students" (Jacob, 2017), "post-traditional learners" (Soares, Gagliardi, Nellum, 2017), and "career-students" (Jacob, 2017). Traditional students are those who enroll after secondary education and are full-time, while non-traditional students delay entrance, study part-time and are more racially and socioeconomically diverse (Soares, Gagliardi, Neelum, 2017). The percentage of adult and older adult students vary from college to college (Van Noy and Heidkamp, 2017).

Barrier literature at the student level focuses on cultural background, family support, and financial ability (Sanchez, Fornerino, & Zhang, 2006; Trombly, Salisbury, Tumanut & Klute, 2012). At the institutional level, barriers include lack of staff, lack of budget, and graduation requirements that limit choices (Loberg, 2012). Institutional barriers reflect a deficit narrative that guides choices to offer (or not) education abroad. There are noted dangers to adopting a deficit narrative as it provides differential educational experiences that counter the open access mission of the community college (Raby, 2018).

This chapter questions traditional barrier research because this reasoning links low expectation to lack of success. Community college counter-deficit research shows that existing stereotypes about non-traditional students are rarely correct as non-traditional students are interested in education, can balance work and school, have family and friends support, and do participate in college sponsored programs (Moschetti & Hudley, 2015; Gonzalez, Stein, & Huq, 2013, Levin, Viggiano, López Damián, Vazquez and Wolf, 2017). When examining education abroad through the lens of anti-deficit literature, those students who were stereotyped as having limitations, may in fact are able to study abroad. Community college research adds that many non-traditional students have previous international experiences from travel, working/living abroad, and military deployment and they have close family and friends who travel and some who have studied abroad. It is time to acknowledge the deficit narratives that have guided practices and eliminate them. In that community colleges serve all students, I posit that it is critical to accurately identify barriers to participation in education abroad and that it is important to understand in what ways current community college students are different from those even ten years ago.

This chapter introduces a new counter-deficit narrative that celebrates student success with the explicit intent to provide community college leaders with tools that use opportunities rather than reinforce stereotypes which create barriers. In turn, new policies can be created to positively effect substantial change in the field. This narrative includes three components, a) non-traditional students want to study abroad, b) pre-defined barriers rarely exist among the current generation of students, and c) noted growth in the field weakens key barrier arguments.

COMMUNITY COLLEGE EDUCATION ABROAD: SIX DECADES IN THE MAKING

Community college education abroad is grounded in the open access philosophy that allows admittance to educational programs for all students. Open access helped community colleges to transform the field of education abroad from a university junior year abroad with admission constraints (class standing, GPA, prerequisites) to a program that serves all students at all ability levels (Raby, 1995). Access is given to community members not enrolled as students, enrolled students, re-entry university students, and high school students who concurrently enroll in the college. In meeting the open access model to not deny any student an opportunity to learn, community colleges allow enrollment with no GPA or with one as low as 1.7 - 2.0. Often students with low GPA who study abroad gain the highest levels of success in terms of retention, completion, and even moving out of remedial studies (Raby, Rhodes, and Biscarra,

2014). Students who study at a community college represent a broad spectrum of racial, ethnic, and minoritized groups and many reside in low and middle-income communities (Raby, 2008). In that the average age of a community college student is 28, it is not surprising that adult students' study abroad. This is important because adult learners have unique educational pathways (Kasworm, 2007; Compton, Cox, & Laanan, 2006).

Flexible programming enhances access by offering different education abroad programs including year-long, semester, short-term winter, 3+ week summer, and 7- 18-day programs. While many courses are part of the general education curriculum, others give credit in technical, vocational, occupational, and career education, such as nursing, culinary arts, oenology, and cosmetology (CCIE, 2018). While all education abroad is credit-bearing, not all students, especially older adults, want that credit (Raby, 2018). Most education abroad classes are faculty-led in which faculty design, lead, and market programs, often, to their own students with whom they have developed special bonds. Even within the consortia design, faculty are still strongly involved. Group affinity is reinforced as community college students prefer being with other students from their community college (Amani, 2011; Brenner, 2016; Willis, 2016). Group affinity also provides a safe place to learn and work because adults strongly relate to one another due to their similar backgrounds and past experiences (Zhang, Lui, & Hagedorn, 2013). Finally, it is quite common for faculty to gain a following and often have repeat students on each annual program (CCIE, 2018).

UNDERSTANDING BARRIERS: THEORETICAL PERSPECTIVES

Deficit and counter-deficit narratives are used to explain why some students have lower levels of success than others. This section explores how deficit and counter-deficit narratives influence community college education abroad programming and marketing.

Deficit Narrative

The deficit narrative links low expectations about the potential success of non-traditional students to their deficiencies in social and cultural capitals (Bourdieu, 1986; Duncan-Andrade & Morrell, 2008; Gillborn, 2005). Community colleges use a deficit narrative to explain that non-traditional students lack academic preparation to succeed and lack social and cultural capitals to know how to achieve their goals (Chen & Starobin, 2017; Dennis, Phinney & Chuateco, 2005). In that some students are expected to be less successful than others, community colleges institutionalize programs to sort non-traditional students into stratified educational experiences (Brint & Karabel, 1989). In what Clark (1960) refers to as "cooling-out" these pathways are designed with an intent for limited progression and completion. Cohen and Bawer (2003) concur that an original intent of the US community college was to "divert unsuitable candidates into appropriate vocational training while making it possible for traditional universities to maintain selective admissions requirements" (p. 21). The process of sorting and "cooling-out" based on a deficit narrative has influenced community college education abroad designs and marketing.

Student Deficit Characteristics and Education Abroad

Many community college administrators and faculty use a deficit narrative to explain that non-traditional students lack the skills to make a personal choice to study abroad (Raby & Sawadogo, 2005; Raby & Rhodes, 2005). Many also label education abroad as an unnecessary luxury for poorer colleges and especially for students from lower and middle socio-economic status as it is viewed that the experience abroad is superfluous to a career pathway (Sweeney, 2013; Wick, 2011). By labeling non-traditional students as being unable to study abroad (Commission on the Abraham Lincoln Study Abroad, 2005), myths are perpetuated that do not serve these students. In actuality, the cost to the institution to build and maintain an education abroad program is minimal (Raby & Valeau, 2016) and the cost to the student can be manageable given proper time to plan (Amani & Kim, 2017). There is also an economic return for the student as there is a direct connection of career advancement as a result of studying abroad (Tillman, 2014). For many adult students, the choice to study abroad is not always aligned with a change in career pathways (Raby, 2018).

Institutional Choice to Not Offer Education Abroad

The institutional choice to exclude studying abroad from student learning pathways is a form of sorting in which some students get differential access to experiences than others. Institutional barriers result from a lack of continuity in mission (Raby, 2008), in executive leadership support (Opp & Gosetti, 2014), result in the choice to have few full-time dedicated positions to lead internationalization efforts (Kumari, 2017), and in limited professionalization of those leading programs (Raby & Valeau, 2016). Sorting is also reinforced when "community college internationalization efforts center on immediate rather than broader strategies to institutionalize such programs" (Raby, 2012, p. 14). In so doing, programs exist and expand when the budget is strong, linking accessibility to external forces.

Differential Program Design for Education Abroad

Marketing strategies are influenced by the deficit narrative about a lack of student interest coupled with a lack of family or peer support, a lack of financial capital, and a fear of the unknown, especially in relation to leaving their local community. Stereotypes suggest that few students are interested in studying abroad and hence it will be extremely difficult to get enough students to fill a class influence program design, outreach, and enrollment expectations. The very short-term education abroad program (of under 18 days) exists only because of the belief that it is the only option for non-traditional students (Gaia, 2015). Likewise, the belief that the consortia model is the only option is mostly made on the expectation that a college will be unable to attract enough students to offer education abroad on their own. In these examples, program design that may target non-traditional students ends up reinforcing inequities rather than eliminating them.

Counter-Deficit Narrative

Counter-deficit narratives challenge the deficit narrative as being stereotypical and obsolete (Ladson-Billings and Tate, 1995; Solorzano & Delgado Bernal, 2001; Yosso, 2005). Instead of attributing a deficit of capital to specific populations, the counter-deficit narrative shows that non-traditional students possess multiple forms of capitals, even those unique to different racial, ethnic, gendered and minoritized groups (Alan & Zhang, 2015; Jenkins, 2013). Non-traditional students have social and cultural capital based on life-experiences that contribute to building a strong sense of self-determination (Modood, 2004) which results in success along academic pathways (Moschetti & Hudley, 2015). Cultural capital also exists in that non-traditional students see education abroad as teaching skills that can be linked to future careers (Raby, 2018). In fact, it is this range of capitals that are important for non-traditional students to succeed in college.

It is important to note that each student comes to the community college with varying degrees of expertise and as such will have a differential learning experience. Yet, when learning opportunities are defined by institutional stratification, negative experiences result. Community colleges have existing institutional stratification that vary across race, class, gender and age (Person, Rosenbaum & Deil-Amen, 2006) and are intensified by intersectionality. Stratification in turn, contributes to under-representation in some college programs (Hodara & Jaggars, 2014; McClenney, Marti & Adkins, 2012). Even well-intended institutional policies can discriminate through exclusion of non-traditional students who are already marginalized by inequalities in curriculum (Solorzano, Cejy & Yosso, 2000) and through hostile campus environments (Harper & Quaye 2009). Thus, it is not lack of interest that is a central decision in studying abroad, but the repercussions of institutional sorting.

At the same time, when institutional programs are designed for success (CCCSE, 2017), non-traditional students will succeed. Externally, the role of parental, community, and peer support (Crozier, 2006; Dennis, Phinney & Chuateco, 2005) and internally, the role of institutional programs designed for success, (CCCSE, 2017; Hodara & Jaggars, 2014) clearly show that non-traditional community college students use their capitals to achieve success (Byun, Meece, Irvin & Hutchins, 2012; Gonzalez, Stein, & Huq, 2013; Próspero, & Vohra-Gupta, 2007). The counter-deficit narrative views institutional obstacles as thwarting student pathways more than personal histories (Bauman, Bustillos, Bensimon, Brown II, & Bartee, 2005; Rosenbaum, Deil-Amen, & Person, 2007; McClenney, Marti & Adkins, 2012). As applied to education abroad, it is the institutional choice rather than student interest (Amani & Kim, 2017; Chieffo, 2000; Stroud, 2010; Sweeney, 2013) that accounts for differential participation.

BARRIERS TO STUDYING ABROAD USING A COUNTER-DEFICIT NARRATIVE

Three examples of counter-narratives can inform new approaches to community college education abroad: a) non-traditional students want to study abroad; b) pre-defined barriers rarely exist among the current generation of non-traditional students; and c) noted growth in the field weakens key barrier arguments.

Non-Traditional Students Want to Study Abroad

Counter-deficit research shows that all non-traditional students choose to attend a community college to better themselves. These students have social and cultural capitals that build positive self-identify (Modood, 2004) and a sense of self-determination (Gipson, Mitchell & McLean, 2017) that reinforce community college success (Byun, Meece, Irvin and Hutchins, 2012; Gonzalez, Stein, & Huq, 2013; Moschetti & Hudley, 2015). This is because non-traditional students combine knowledge acquired through life-experiences (Rivera, 2015) with newly gained knowledge from college experiences to move along their academic and career pathways (Sandoval-Lucero, Maes, & Klingsmith, 2014). Adults possess a high level of self-awareness and make sound decisions regarding their education (Soares, 2013) and these choices include the ones to study abroad.

The current generation of community college students does not need to be taught to appreciate the idea of studying abroad. The desire to learn extends to studying abroad. Research consistently shows that non-traditional community college students are aware of study abroad and know it is an educational experience that they want to be part of (Amani, 2012; Quezada & Cordeior, 2016, Thomas, 2016), know the benefits gained in terms of career readiness (Zamani-Gallaher, Lang & Leon, 2016), know the benefits to broaden intercultural awareness (Arden-Ogle, 2009), have already traveled abroad (Raby & Rhodes, 2005; Robertson & Blasi, 2017), link education abroad to gaining a sense of self (Willis, 2016), and use their maturity as adults to make good choices (Raby, 2018). What they do not always know is that education abroad is even offered at their community college and how to access information about opportunities (Raby & Rhodes, 1999).

Non-traditional students have the skills to balance "multiple life roles" and have a heightened sense of purpose to take advantage of the chance to participate in college activities (Chen & Starobin, 2017; Covarrubias, 2012; Próspero, & Vohra-Gupta, 2007; Silverman, Sarvanaz & Stiles, 2009; Soria & Stebleton, 2012). In terms of studying abroad, many students know about education abroad from media, family, friends, and their faculty (Robertson & Blasi, 2017). It is true that some students have no travel experiences. Others only have indirect international experiences via social media gaming and communication and by living in multi-cultural communities where cross-cultural interactions are already occurring. Yet, others have traveled through military service and as immigrants may have traveled to visit their families abroad (Amani, 2012; Raby & Rhodes, 2005). Of critical importance is that community college students know that studying abroad is an opportunity of their lifetime (Amani & Kim, 2017; Oberstein-Deballe, 1999) and want to take advantage of it.

Changing the Narrative

In changing the narrative, community college staff, faculty, and education abroad providers, need to understand the changing dynamics of community college students in this century. This includes knowing their strengths and interests, and most importantly, how to recognize detrimental deficit stereotypes. There are two areas for focus. First, is a critical analysis of institutional practices that are based on the belief that student demographics limit choice. This critical analysis extends to review of institutional policies that seem to support non-traditional students, but in the end, discriminate against them. For example, the extreme shortening of program length, or mandate to use consortia, is based on assumed student deficits. Secondly, is the recognition of "sorting" outcomes for those who have had historical exclusion (Wick, 2011). Examples include a lack of encouragement from faculty and staff towards students of color (Murray, Brux & Fry, 2010), a lack of peer mentors (Jackson, 2005), a lack of information networks on campus (Sweeney, 2013), and a lack of a defined office and full-time administrative position that oversees international activities (Raby & Valeau, 2007). Decision makers need to be aware of current literature from community college and community college international education researchers that firmly calls into question outdated stereotypes as detrimental and fallacious. The not knowing of options to study abroad, that is institutionally bound, is not the same as not wanting to study abroad.

Pre-Defined Barriers Rarely Exist Among the Current Generation of Students

Barriers result from stereotypes that explain why white and wealthier students easily recognize the importance of studying abroad while non-traditional students need extra encouragements. These barriers include cost, fear of racism and discrimination abroad, historical exclusion, lack of encouragement from faculty and staff, lack of peer mentors, lack of intent to leave local communities, work and family obligations, lack of family support, lack of information networks on campus about study abroad issues, and lack of awareness of the benefits to studying abroad. This section explores how some of these barriers when applied to a community college student in 2018 are stereotypical.

Cost

The cost of education abroad can easily deter students from enrollment because it is simply significantly higher than annual community college tuition, which is increasingly free. Study abroad costs range from about $ 3,000 - $ 8,600 (sometimes including airfare) (CCIE, 2018). Comparably, California community college annual tuition is about $ 2,000 and nationally tuition can be as high as $ 4,892 (Community College Review, 2017). Despite the extreme cost differences, many students still interpret education abroad as a "good deal" because it is cheaper than studying abroad at a university and may be the only way some students will ever be able to travel abroad. Cost is a barrier when it is linked to inaccessibility and when programs discriminate by offering differential educational experiences to richer students. Cost is also a barrier when program design by providers inflate cost.

Travel Opportunities

Community colleges are largely located within 50 miles of where all students live to increase access. A prevailing stereotype is that students do not study abroad because they rarely travel beyond their local community, even to the next largest city, and that this insularity builds a fear of traveling. Even if students do not travel locally, that does not mean they would not travel if given the opportunity. This is supported by the fact that many students who have never traveled locally do study abroad. In our changing world, students virtually travel, may interact globally through work requirements, and travel themselves (Raby & Rhodes, 2018). Robertson and Blasi's (2017) survey of nine community colleges shows that students travel, know about other countries because of where their parents/grandparents were born, and grew up in a bicultural/multicultural community that minimizes "fear" of the unknown. The fact that students of today are far more travel savvy needs to be incorporated in all future education abroad programming.

Family and Peer Support

Another barrier is that non-traditional students lack family and peer support for studying abroad. However, community college research shows that families and friends largely support non-traditional students to study at community colleges (Gipson, Mitchell & McLean, 2017; Strayhorn & Johnson, 2014) and that this support contributes to students being able to balance study into their lives (Crozier, 2006; Dennis, Phinney & Chuateco, 2005; Strayhorn & Johnson, 2014). Motivation to study includes being a role model to younger siblings, children, or grandchildren. In fact, family support is important to high-achieving community college African-American Male (Gipson, Mitchell & McLean, 2017) and Latino male students (Sáenz, García-Louis, & Drake, 2017). Moreover, it is the familismo and familial capital that strengthens their aspirations to persist onto graduation. Community college education abroad research confirms support from family and friends also exists (Amani 2011, Amani & Kim, 2017). Numerous role models also include family, friends and faculty, who have previously studied abroad (Raby & Rhodes, 2005; Raby & Valeau, 2016; Robertson & Blasi, 2017).

Work and Family Obligations

Another barrier is that non-traditional students have competing needs due to conflicts with work and family obligations and therefore cannot give due attention to school. Research is beginning to question this as work can support student college success (Richardson, Kemp, Malinen, & Haultain, 2013). Community college research confirms that adult students are acutely aware of the need to balance competing forces and successfully navigate multiple life roles (Silverman, Sarvanaz & Stiles, 2009; Próspero, & Vohra-Gupta, 2007; Soria & Stebleton, 2012). It is important to note that non-traditional students choose to enroll in the community college because they want to improve themselves, make sound decisions regarding their education, and show this by taking advantage of college curricular and co-curricular programs (Bauman, Wang, DeLeon, Kafentzis, Lopez, & Lindsey, 2009). These students also find a way to weave studying abroad into their work (Raby, Rhodes, & Biscarra, 2014) and family obligations (Amani & Kim, 2017), even if it means leaving children, spouses, and jobs (Arden-Ogle, 2009; Willis, 2016; Zamani-Gallaher, Lang & Leon, 2016). It is the ability of community college students to navigate both educational and working worlds, that allows students to find a way to weave studying abroad into their work and family cycles.

Faculty Support

Faculty and staff build barriers by not believing in their students. Research emphasizes the positive impact faculty have to assist non-traditional students to find the balance needed to study abroad (Brenner, 2016; Murray, Brux & Fry 2010). In that most or all community college education abroad programs are faculty-led, faculty remain key in marketing and outreach (Anderson, 2007; Petzoid & Peter, 2015) because they build a safety net for linking the college experience to the real-world. Social integration obtained by involvement with on-campus programs (Gipson, Mitchell & McLean, 2017) and involvement with faculty (Wood & Harris, 2015) is a key component to student success. In a survey given to community college education abroad directors, all said that despite the advances of social media, outreach remains predominantly face-to-face, either with directed communication with their own students or with planned classroom visits campus wide (Raby & Rhodes, 2018). Thus, it remains the faculty personal connections which build trust and that trust is what builds student interest.

Program design is greatly influenced by the barrier belief that it is extremely difficult to enroll community college students in education abroad programs. A popular design used to attract non-traditional students is to shorten program length to two weeks or less to accommodate for cost and for time away from home. There are contexts in which these program choices are correct and do serve specific populations (Raby, 2008). However, when the choice is defined by a counter-deficit narrative, three concerns emerge. First, students claim that when given options, they can and do participate in longer-term programs (Raby, Rhodes, & Biscarra, 2014). Students in Robertson and Blasi's study (2017) enroll in an equal split between semester, 3-6-week summer programs, and programs less than 2 weeks. Likewise, in California 51% of education abroad students study in 3-6-week summer programs, 35% in semester programs, and 14% in less than 18 days programs (CCIE, 2018). When a college only provides very short-term programs, they are offering a differential and unequal education to selected students. Secondly, the program cost is largely determined by the third-party provider which is influenced by profit margins. Longer programs do not necessarily need to be significantly more expensive. Finally, some research suggests that while students will learn through any program that is well-constructed, some measures of student success will only occur as a result of time spent abroad. When a program is less than 18 days, it will produce the weakest results in terms of sustained student learning (Engle & Engle, 2003; Gaia, 2015; Strange & Gibson, 2017). Consequently, when community colleges offer only very short-term programs, student learning is not only not served, but is prejudicially given to those deemed as non-traditional.

Consortia Equity Building

There are two types of community college education abroad consortia (Raby, 2008). The first is based on the premise that one college cannot find enough students to meet class enrollment criteria and thus must collaborate with other colleges. In this format, each college is expected to send very few students which combined meets enrollment minimum. However, it also results in limited to no faculty involvement and administrative support to sustain the program. The minimal campus presence results in a significant lack of institutionalization that is known to be the most important barrier to advancing education abroad. A second type of consortia uses equity building in which multiple community colleges collaborate to send students, but with the expectation that each college will bring in near equal numbers and that planning, marketing, and outreach are shared among consortia participants resulting in a base for education abroad on each participating campus. This approach also uses a wider faculty base to expand course offerings and often have strategies for shared administrative duties (Raby, Culton & Valeau, 2015).

NOTED GROWTH IN THE FIELD WEAKENS KEY BARRIER ARGUMENTS

Growth in the field is charted over-time using data from the Institute for International Education Open Doors reports from 2003 - 2017 (IIE, 2003-2017). These reports rank the top 20 community colleges in terms of number of colleges that have education abroad programs, number of students that study abroad, and diversity of students who study abroad

Growth in Number of Colleges That Offer Programs

Since the first community college education abroad was offered in 1969 by Rockland community college in New York and by Cabrillo and Glendale community colleges in California, education abroad has continued to grow. In 2007/8, 85 U.S. community colleges offered education abroad programs which grew in 2016/17 to 141 community colleges. A noted concern is that this growth is not stable often due to a lack of institutionalization that results in inconsistent program offering which then eliminates multi-year planning that is essential to allow students to plan in balancing life roles (Raby and Valeau, 2016). Table 1 shows this inconsistency. Since 2003, only two community colleges (College of DuPage and Santa Barbara City) had programs in the top 20 for all 14 years. An additional two colleges (Citrus and Santa Rosa) offered programs for 13 years, two others (City College of San Francisco and Mesa) for 12 years,

Table 1. IIE Community College Study Abroad Student Enrollments: 2003-2015

YEAR	02-03	03-04	04-05	05-06	06-07	07-08	08-09	09-10	10-11	11-12	12-13	13-14	14-15	15-16
# colleges with more than 100 students	14	14	14	18	19	18	18	9	10	11	10	9	12	11
# of colleges with less than 100 students	74	74	72	92	99	99	97	64	68	56	66	70	74	69

Sources: www.iie.org/en/Research-and-Insights/Open-Doors/Data/Community-College-Data-Resource/Community-College---Study-Abroad/Leading-Institutions/2002-03 - 2015-2016

and eight others for six to twelve years. Some community college with strong student enrollment in one year are almost non-existent in another year. 16 community colleges were listed only twice in the top 20 and an additional 21 were listed only once (mostly due to new additions to the top 20 list). However, the extreme inconsistency is indicative of programs without strong institutional support.

Number of Students

In the past decade, the number of community college students who study abroad has risen exponentially, interrupted only by the 2008 economic crisis. Of great importance is that among the top 20 colleges, all send a large number of students abroad. This is important as it disproves the claim that community colleges are unable to attract large number of students to study abroad. Since 2003, 15 of the top 20 ranked community colleges sent more than 100 students abroad, with the exception of 2016-2017 when only 11 colleges sent more than 100 students abroad. In addition, since 2003, even colleges listed in the 20th ranked position sent between 56 - 99 students abroad. Since, 2014-2015, an additional 88 colleges sent 18 - 99 students abroad which suggests that enrollment criteria are being met and that disproves that a college cannot find enough students to study abroad. Table 2 illustrates student enrollment from top 20 community colleges.

When compared to universities, only a fraction of community college students study abroad. While true, a new perspective emerges when compared to different higher educational sectors. Data shows that each institutional sector has a specific cluster of the number of students who study abroad. The top 25 doctoral institutions send between 4,310 to 1,449 students as compared to the top 25 MA granting institutions which send 1,434 to 414 students and the top 25 BA granting institutions which send 653 to 278 students. Comparably, the top 25 community colleges range from 246 - 76 students (IIE, 2017b). It is apparent that education abroad favors those institutions that offer doctoral programs. Equally interesting is that a pattern emerges in which the bottom range of the higher degree granting institution is close to the higher range of the next educational sector. The lower range of doctoral granting institutions is 1,449 while the top range of MA granting institutions is 1,434. The bottom range of BA granting institutions is 278 students while the top range of the community college is 246. Thus, the low number of community colleges could simply be related to the relative offerings within each institutional sector. More research needs to be done to understand why these categorizations exist.

Table 2. IIE top 20 community colleges education abroad: 2003-2016

Listings	Colleges	TOTAL #
Colleges listed for 1 year	American River (CA); Ann Arundel (MD); Austin (TX); Cottey (NV); Delaware Technical (DE); East Los Angeles (CA); Hillsborough (FL); Howard (MD); Los Angeles Pierce (CA); Madison Tech (IL); Nassau (NY); Northhampton (PA); North Orange Co. (CA); Parkland (IL); San Diego City (CA); St. Louis (MO); Suffolk (NY); Tompkins-Cortand (NY); University of Wisconsin Colleges (WI); Wright State - Lake Campus (OH); Yosemite District (CA)	21
Colleges listed for 2 years	Baltimore (MD); Chaffey (CA); College of Canyons (CA); Consumes River (CA); Peralta (CA); Fresno City (CA); Golden West (CA); Harrisburg (PN); Mt. San Antonio (CA); Napa (CA); Ohlone (CA); Saddleback (CA); San Diego Mesa (CA); Southwest Tennessee (TN); St. Petersburg (FL); Tarrant County (TX)	16
Colleges listed for 3 years	Brookdale (NJ); Diablo Valley (CA); Hocking (OH); Lake Tahoe (CA); State Center (CA); Valencia (FL)	6
Colleges listed for 4 years	Santa Monica (CA) Sierra (CA)	2
Colleges listed for 5 years	Tulsa (OK)	1
Colleges listed for 6 years	El Camino (CA)	1
Colleges listed for 7 years	Pellissippi (TN)	1
Colleges listed for 8 years	SUNY Broome (NY)	1
Colleges listed for 9 years	Cabrillo (CA) Glendale (CA) Miami-Dade (FL)	3
Colleges listed for 10 years	Kirkwood (IA) Orange Coast (CA)	2
Colleges listed for 11 years	Mesa (AZ) San Francisco (CA)	2
Colleges listed for 12 years	Pasadena (CA) Riverside (CA)	2
Colleges listed for 13 years	Citrus College (CA) Santa Rosa (CA)	2
Colleges listed for 14 years	College of DuPage (IL) Santa Barbara (CA)	2

Sources: www.iie.org/en/Research-and-Insights/Open-Doors/Data/Community-College-Data-Resource/Community-College---Study-Abroad/Leading-Institutions/2002-03 - 2015-2016

Increased Diversity of Students

A focus in the field of education abroad is to widen participation by racial, ethnic, gender, and minoritized groups that have historically not had an opportunity to study abroad. Community colleges have a history of sending more students of color abroad than any higher education institutional sector (Raby, 2008) as shown in Table 3. The primary reason why community colleges are so successful is because the student population, and those who study abroad, reflect local multi-racial/ethnic or racial/ethnic homogenous communities (AACC, 2017). When the student population represents a homogenous profile, the study abroad population will also then represent the same profile, which then increases diversity for the education abroad field, assuming the profile includes a preponderance of or significant percentage of students of color. A key importance for a counter-narrative is that community colleges clearly show that students from various backgrounds, geographic locations, and economic profiles are interested in studying abroad when given the opportunity.

When comparing community college demographics from multiple databases, it shows that for some racial and ethnic groups, the percentage of those attending education abroad is not only meeting, but sometimes exceeding state or national averages for a racial or ethnic population. In this respect, there is a shift in the narrative of what diversity means as future discussions may not need to focus on matching demographic profiles but on increasing overall access. For example, in California, African-Americans comprise 5.78% of community college students and 8.4% of those who study abroad. Nationally, Latinos represent 22% of community college students and 17.6% of those who study abroad. New programs built on equity patterns for colleges with homogenous and heterogenous student-bodies need to be envisioned and new research on diversity patterns matching study abroad students against the college population needs to be conducted.

Table 3. Comparing student diversity across different databases

	AACC 2017	CA 2017	CCIE 2017	IIE 2000/01	IIE 2005/06	IIE 2010/11	IIE 2014/15
Caucasian	49%	26.60	25	79.1	69.0	75.5	64.8
Latino	22%	44.39	40	11.5	13.1	12.9	17.6
Asian-American, Native Hawaiian, Other Pacific Islander	6%	14.53	14	4.3	3.4	3.6	5.2
African-American	15%	5.78	10.5	4.3	5.0	5.8	8.4
Native American	1%	.42	.5	.1	.5	.5	.8
Multiracial	3%	3.67	2.7	.8	9.1	1.7	3.1
Unknown	4%	4.62	1.2				
Notes: CA separates out Asian-American (11.27%); Filipino (2.86%) and Pacific Islander (.40%) CCIE separates out Caucasian: Armenian (3%); Iranian (.25%); Russian (.25%) CCIE separates out Asian-American: Japanese (.25%); Korean (.25%); Chinese. (.5%); Indian (.25%) and Hawaiian (.05%) AACC: Based on 1300 community colleges CA: Based on 113 community colleges CCIE: Based on 36 community colleges							

Sources

American Association of Community Colleges. (2016). Fast facts from our fact sheet. Retrieved from www.aacc.nche.edu/AboutCC/Pages/fastfactsfactsheet.aspx

California Community Colleges Chancellor's Office. (2017). Management information systems data mart. Retrieved from datamart.cccco.edu

California Colleges for International Education (2018). Study abroad. Retrieved from ccieworld.org/saprograms.php

Institute of International Education. (2017). Open Doors data tables: Community college demographics. Retrieved from www.iie.org/en/Research-and-Insights/Open-Doors/Data/Community-College-Data-Resource

DISCUSSION

While in theory, community college education abroad is available to a large cross-section of the community, in practice weak institutional policies result in inconsistent programming that limits student options. To serve the widest margin of the community college student population, a counter-deficit narrative needs to be adopted that consists of five deficit-based myths that need to be reformed.

Eliminate Stereotypes

The first component for educational reform eliminates any stereotype that links a low expectation of student potential to their non-traditional profile. Enough research exists to show that these labels are obsolete and worse, that when applied, reproduce inequitable power structures which limit access and participation. All students possess a range of strengths including vision, an interest in education, and have social and cultural capitals to help them along their academic and career pathways. Colleges need to make policy only after they have listened to what students say are their needs (Harper & Quaye, 2009; Raby and Rhodes, 2005).

Institutional Deficits, Not Student Personality Limit Success

The second component for educational reform acknowledges that community college institutional deficits (Bauman, et al., 2005) that contribute to under-representation and thwarts student pathways (Hodara & Jaggars, 2014). When institutional choices label education abroad as an unnecessary luxury for a specific group of students, there is an automatic structural obstacle that denies programming. Similarly, weak institutional support for education abroad, including limited funding for full-time education abroad staff and leadership positions and limited ability for multi-year planning then limits accessibility for all students.

Provide Long-Term Program Planning

The third component for educational reform is to acknowledge that long-term planning and consistent offering helps non-traditional students to balance work, family and study. Equity models (Wick, 2011) emphasize the development of institutional factors that shape relationships between faculty and students and between staff and community. These relationships also frame the continuum of power, social hierarchy, stratification and marginalization the continually redefines access need to be developed. Another important re-design is to make education abroad part of defined educational and career pathways that seamlessly fit education abroad into academic transfer, certificate, and GenEd requirements. Thus, as students plan for their time at the community college, education abroad becomes a natural extension of that plan.

Program Length Variations

The fourth component for educational reform is to understand that while very short-term programs can serve some students, it should not be the norm. There is an unchallenged belief that the only option for community college students is in very short programming of under two-weeks. Even though both community college and university education abroad has noticeably grown shorter, concerns still exist.

First, student stereotypes are simply not true. There is nothing in research that proves that non-traditional students cannot study abroad for longer periods of time. Secondly, research suggests that the learning outcomes are different for longer vs. short vs. very short programs (Strange & Gibson, 2017). While there are ways to maximize learning opportunities for all study abroad program lengths, duration may result in unequal learning (Gaia, 2015). Thirdly, longer-term programs do not need to be more expensive. Finally, a counter-deficit narrative understands that students respond to opportunity and will participate in longer-term programs when given the chance. While the length of time may not be the most important criteria, knowing the "right time" to take off from work, the right time when the kids are grown, and the right time when a parent can leave the kids (Amani & Kim, 2017) is significant. Yet, at the same time, this "timing" is so unique that it is difficult to plan for (Amani and Kim, 2017).

Strength of Student Cohorts

The final component for educational reform is to utilize student cohorts within and between disciplines. Community college students maintain special bonds with their peers and use these bonds to build group affinity and to enhance engagement. This is due, in part, to adult learners being best able to relate to other adults because of similar backgrounds and experiences (Compton, Cox, & Laanan, 2006; Zhang, Lui, & Hagedorn, 2013). This is also true in education abroad where even the similarity of being from the same college helps to reinforce group affinity and positively influence overall learning (Willis 2016; Zamani-Gallaher, Leon, & Lang, 2016). Student cohorts remain important as peers encourage each other to study abroad and provide a familiarity important for building encouragement, comfort, and safety (Amani & Kim, 2017; Arden-Ogle 2009; Brenner, 2016; Willis 2016).

CONCLUSION

This chapter explores myths that surround the field of community college education abroad. Central is the acknowledgment that stereotypes of students' personal limits influence policy development. In re-casting this discussion, connections need to be made to highlight the fact that the low number of community college students who study abroad, is not based on a lack of student interest, but on a lack of institutional support. Non-traditional students who are lower income, racial and ethnic minorities, working, and academically struggling, are not culturally disadvantaged as they take advantage of all academic programs offered to them.

Education abroad is limited due to choices made by the institution to not offer the program, to not provide support for those leading education abroad, and to design unequal program opportunities. Instead of honoring the ability of students, deficit-based policies build a negative cycle in which disbelief in students contribute to the lack of importance given to education abroad that in turn is reflected in a lack of institutionalization. While I previously suggested that institutional programs to support education abroad are largely linked to the economy (Raby, 2012), the new narrative offered in this chapter suggests in addition, stereotypes are also driving the process.

Countering the deficit model are equity models (Wick, 2011) that emphasize the development of institutional factors to redefine access. Those involved in community college education abroad need to see where and how success exists. Change begins with counter-deficit narratives to re-shape relationships between staff, faculty, students and the community, re-focus misguided policies, and readdress areas that limit access. Evolving definitions of how to achieve student success should acknowledge the role of studying abroad as an academic and career program. Finally, new constructs need to be created to include study abroad as part of a combination of strategies that colleges adopt to counter historic achievement gaps in student success.

REFERENCES

Allen, T. O., & Zhang, Y. (2016). Dedicated to their degrees adult transfer students in engineering baccalaureate programs. *Community College Review*, *44*(1), 72–86. doi:10.1177/0091552115617018

Amani, M. (2011). *Study abroad decision and participation at community colleges: Influential factors and challenges from the voices of students and coordinators* (Dissertation). George Washington University.

Amani, M., & Kim, M. M. (2017). Study abroad participation at community colleges: Students' decision and influential factors. *Community College Journal of Research and Practice*, *41*(10), 1–15. doi: 10.1080/10668926.2017.1352544

American Association of Community Colleges (AACC). (2017). *Fast facts from our fact sheet*. Retrieved from http://www.aacc.nche.edu/AboutCC/Pages/fastfactsfactsheet.aspx

Anderson, B. D. (2007). *Students in a global village: The nexus between choice, expectation, and experience in study abroad* (Unpublished doctoral dissertation). The University of Texas, Austin, TX.

Arden-Ogle, E. (2009). *Study abroad and global competence: Exemplary community college programs which foster elements of achievement* (Dissertation). Oregon State University, Corvallis, OR.

Banks-Santilli, L. (2014). First-Generation college students and their pursuit of the American dream. *Journal of Case Studies in Education*, *5*(1), 1–32.

Bauman, G. L., Bustillos, L. T., Bensimon, E. M., Brown, M. C. II, & Bartee, R. D. (2005). *Achieving equitable educational outcomes with all students: The institution's roles and responsibilities*. Washington, DC: Association of American Colleges and Universities.

Bauman, S. S. M., Wang, N., DeLeon, C. W., Kafentzis, J., Zavala Lopez, M., & Lindsey, M. S. (2004). Nontraditional students' service needs and social support resources: A pilot study. *Journal of College Counseling*, *7*(1), 13–17. doi:10.1002/j.2161-1882.2004.tb00254.x

Bourdieu, P. (1986). The forms of capital (R. Nice, Trans.). In J. Richardson (Ed.), Handbook of theory and research for the sociology of education (pp. 241-258). New York: NY: Greenwood Press.

Brenner, A. (2016). Transformative learning through education abroad: A case study of a community college program. In R. L. Raby & E. J. Valeau (Eds.), *International education at community colleges: Themes, practices, research, and case studies (pp. 370-90)*. New York, NY: Palgrave. doi:10.1057/978-1-137-53336-4_21

Brint, S., & Karabel, J. (1989). *The diverted dream: Community colleges and the promise of educational opportunity in America, 1900-1985*. New York, NY: Oxford University Press.

Byun, S., Meece, J. L., Irvin, M. J., & Hutchins, B. (2012). The role of social capital in educational aspirations of rural youth. *Rural Sociology, 77*(3), 355–379. doi:10.1111/j.1549-0831.2012.00086.x PMID:24039302

California Colleges for International Education. (2018). *Study abroad*. Retrieved from http://ccieworld.org/saprograms.php

Center for Community College Student Engagement. (2017). *The community college student report*. Retrieved from http://www.ccsse.org/aboutsurvey/biblio/page1.cfm

Chen, Y., & Starobin, S. S. (2017). Measuring and examining general self-efficacy among community college students: A structural equation modeling approach. *Community College Journal of Research and Practice, 42*(2), 1–19. doi:10.1080/10668926.2017.1281178

Chieffo, L. (2000). *Determinants of student participation in study abroad programs at the university of Delaware: A quantitative study* (Dissertation). University of Delaware, Newark, DE.

Clark, B. (1960). The cooling-out function in higher education. *American Journal of Sociology, 65*(6), 569–576. doi:10.1086/222787

Cohen, A. M., Brawer, F. B., & Kisker, C. B. (2014). *The American community college* (6th ed.). San Francisco, CA: Jossey-Bass.

Commission on the Abraham Lincoln Study Abroad Fellowship Program. (2005). *Global competence and national needs: One million Americans studying abroad*. Washington, DC: US State Department.

Community College Review. (2017). *Tuition Statistics*. Retrieved from: https://www.communitycollegereview.com/avg-tuition-stats/national-data

Compton, J., Cox, E., & Laanan, F. (2006). Adult learners in transition. *New Directions for Student Services, 114*(114), 73–80. doi:10.1002s.208

Covarrubias, R. (2012). Unseen disadvantage: How American universities' focus on independence undermines the academic performance of first-generation college students. *Journal of Personality and Social Psychology, 102*(6), 178–197. PMID:22390227

Crozier, G. (2006). 'There's a war against our children': Black educational underachievement revisited. *British Journal of Sociology of Education, 26*(5), 585–598. doi:10.1080/01425690500293520

Dennis, J. M., Phinney, J. S., & Chuateco, L. I. (2005). The role of motivation, parental support, and peer support in the academic success of ethnic minority first-generation college students. *Journal of College Student Development, 46*(3), 223–236. doi:10.1353/csd.2005.0023

Duncan-Andrade, J. M. R., & Morrell, E. (2008). *The art of critical pedagogy: Possibilities for moving from theory to practice in urban schools.* New York, NY: Peter Lang. doi:10.3726/b12771

Engle, L., & Engle, J. (2003). Study abroad levels: Toward a classification of program types. *Frontiers: The Interdisciplinary Journal of Study Abroad, 9,* 1–20.

Gaia, A. C. (2015). Short-term faculty-led study abroad programs enhance cultural exchange and self-awareness. *International Education Journal: Comparative Perspectives, 14*(1), 21–31.

Gillborn, D. (2005). Education policy as an act of white supremacy: Whiteness, critical race theory and education reform. *Journal of Education Policy, 20*(4), 485–505. doi:10.1080/02680930500132346

Gipson, J., Mitchell, D., & McLean, C. (2017). An investigation of high-achieving African- American students attending community colleges: A mixed methods research study. *Community College Journal of Research and Practice, 41*(3), 1–13. doi:10.1080/10668926.2017.1299652

Gonzalez, L. M., Stein, G. L., & Huq, N. (2013). The influence of cultural identity and perceived barriers on college-going beliefs and aspirations of Latino youth in emerging immigrant communities. *Hispanic Journal of Behavioral Sciences, 35*(1), 103–120. doi:10.1177/0739986312463002

Hardin, C. J. (2008). Adult students in higher education: A portrait of transitions. *New Directions for Higher Education, 144*(1), 49–57. doi:10.1002/he.325

Harper, S. R., & Quaye, S. J. (2009). Beyond sameness, with engagement and outcomes for all: An introduction. In S. R. Harper & S. J. Quaye (Eds.), *Student engagement in higher education: Theoretical perspectives and practical approaches for diverse populations* (pp. 1–15). New York, NY: Routledge.

Hodara, M., & Jaggars, S. S. (2014). An examination of the impact of accelerating community college students' progression through developmental education. *The Journal of Higher Education, 85*(2), 246–276. doi:10.1353/jhe.2014.0006

Institute for International Education (IIE). (2017a). *Community college education abroad data tables (2002-2017).* Retrieved from www.iie.org/en/Research-and-Insights/ Open-Doors/Data/Community-College-Data-Resource/Community-College---Study- Abroad/Leading-Institutions/

Institute for International Education (IIE). (2017b). *Education abroad data tables.* Retrieved from www.iie.org/en/Research-and- Insights/Open-Doors/Data/Study-Abroad/Leading-Institutions/2016-17

Jackson, M. J. (2005, Fall). Breaking the barriers to overseas study for students of color and minorities. *IIE Networker,* 16-18.

Jacob, J. (2017). Adults and community college degrees. *Chronicle of Higher Education.* Retrieved from https://www.insidehighered.com/views/2017/10/09/community-colleges-should-focus-more-educating-adults-essay

Jenkins, S. K. (2013, January 1). *Faculty perceptions of, and experiences with, African American male students at a community college* (Dissertation). The University of North Carolina at Charlotte. ERIC NU. (ED558944)

Kasworm, C. (1990). Adult undergraduates in higher education: A review of past research perspectives. *Review of Educational Research*, *60*(3), 345–372. doi:10.3102/00346543060003345

Kasworm, C. (2007). *Adult Undergraduate Student Identity: A Proposed Model*. Paper presented at the American Educational Research Association, Chicago, IL.

Kumari, S. (2017). *Leadership in higher education: Role of persons-in-charge of internationalization efforts in community colleges* (Dissertation). University of South Florida.

Ladson-Billings, G., & Tate, W. F. (1995). Toward a critical race theory of education. *Teachers College Record*, *97*(1), 47.

Levin, J. S., Viggiano, T., López Damián, A. I., Morales Vazquez, E., & Wolf, J. P. (2017). Polymorphic students: New descriptions and conceptions of community college students from the perspectives of administrators and faculty. *Community College Review*, *45*(2), 119–143. doi:10.1177/0091552116679731

Loberg, L. (2012). *Exploring factors that lead to participation in study abroad* (Dissertation). University of California at Los Angeles.

McClenney, K., Marti, C. N., & Adkins, C. (2012). *Student engagement and student outcomes: Key findings from CCSSE validation research*. Austin, TX: Community College Survey of Student Engagement. Retrieved from www.ccsse.org/aboutsurvey/docs/CCSSE%20Validation%20Summary.pdf

Modood, T. (2004). Capitals, ethnic identity and educational qualifications. *Cultural Trends*, *13*(50), 87–105. doi:10.1080/0954896042000267170

Moschetti, R. V., & Hudley, C. (2015). Social capital and academic motivation among first- generation community college students. *Community College Journal of Research and Practice*, *39*(2), 235–251. doi:10.1080/10668926.2013.819304

Murray Brux, J., & Fry, B. (2010). Multicultural students in study abroad: Their interests, their issues, and their constraints. *Journal of Studies in International Education*, *14*(5), 508–527. doi:10.1177/1028315309342486

National Center on Education Statistics. (2009). *Integrated Postsecondary Education Data System (IPEDS)*. Retrieved from: http://nces.ed.gov/ipeds/

Oberstein-Delvalle, E. (1999). *Study abroad programs in three California community colleges* (Dissertation). Pepperdine University, Malibu, CA.

Opp, D., & Gosetti, P. P. (2014). The role of key administrators in internationalizing the c ommunity college. In Strengthening Community Colleges Through Institutional Collaborations (pp. 67-75). San Francisco, CA: Jossey-Bass.

Person, A., Rosenbaum, J. E., & Deil-Amen, R. (2006). Student planning and information problems in different college structures. *Teachers College Record*, *108*(3), 374–396. doi:10.1111/j.1467-9620.2006.00655.x

Petzoid, K., & Peter, T. (2015). The social norm to study abroad: Determinants and effects. *Higher Education*, *69*(8), 885–900. doi:10.100710734-014-9811-4

Próspero, M., & Vohra-Gupta, S. (2007). First generation college students: Motivation, integration, and academic achievement. *Community College Journal of Research and Practice, 31*(12), 963–975. doi:10.1080/10668920600902051

Quezada, R. L., & Cordeiro, P. A. (2016). Creating and enhancing a global consciousness among students of color in our community colleges. In International education at community colleges: Themes, practices, research, and case studies (pp. 335-355). New York, NY: Palgrave.

Raby, R. L. (1997). *Community college models: Myths and realities of access and equality.* ERIC ED402973.

Raby, R. L. (2008). *Meeting America's global education challenge: Expanding education abroad at U.S. community colleges.* New York: Institute for International Education.

Raby, R. L. (2012). Re-Imagining international education at community colleges. *Audem: International Journal of Higher Education and Democracy, 3,* 81–99.

Raby, R. L. (2018). Adult students studying abroad through community colleges. In E. Brewer & A. C. Ogden (Eds.), *Critical Perspectives on Education Abroad: Leveraging the Educational Continuum.* New York, NY: Stylus.

Raby, R. L., Culton, D. R., & Valeau, E. J. (2014). Collaboration: Use of consortium to promote international education. In Strengthening Community Colleges Through Institutional Collaborations (pp. 77-87). San Francisco, CA: Jossey-Bass.

Raby, R. L., & Rhodes, G. M. (2005). *Barriers for Under-Represented Students Participation in California Community College Study Abroad Programs.* Sacramento, CA: Chancellor's Office of California Community Colleges, Fund for Instructional Improvement Publications.

Raby, R. L., & Rhodes, G. M. (2018). Promoting education abroad among community college students: Overcoming obstacles and developing inclusive practices. In *Promoting Inclusion in Education Abroad.* London: Stylus.

Raby, R. L., Rhodes, G. M., & Biscarra, A. (2014). Community college study abroad: Implications for student success. *Community College Journal of Research and Practice, 38*(2-3), 174–183. doi:10.1080/10668926.2014.851961

Raby, R. L., & Sawadogo, G. (2005). Community colleges and study abroad. In NAFSA's Guide to Education Abroad for Advisers and Administrators (3rd ed.). New York: NAFSA Publications.

Raby, R. L., & Valeau, E. J. (2007). International reform efforts and challenges in community colleges. In *New Directions.* San Francisco, CA: Jossey-Bass.

Raby, R. L., & Valeau, E. J. (2016). *International education at community colleges: Themes, practices, research, and case studies.* New York, NY: Palgrave Macmillian Publishers. doi:10.1057/978-1-137-53336-4

Richardson, J., Kemp, S., Malinen, S., & Haultain, S. A. (2013). The academic achievement of students in a New Zealand university: Does it pay to work? *Journal of Further and Higher Education, 37*(6), 864–882. doi:10.1080/0309877X.2012.699517

Rivera, L. A. (2015). *Pedigree: How elite students get elite jobs*. Oxford, UK: Princeton University Press. doi:10.1515/9781400865895

Robertson, J. J., & Blasi, L. (2017). Community college student perceptions of their experiences related to global learning: Understanding the impact of family, faculty, and the curriculum. *Community College Journal of Research and Practice*, *41*(11), 697–718. doi:10.1080/10668926.2016.1222974

Rosenbaum, J. E., Deil-Amen, R., & Person, A. E. (2007). *After admission: From college access to college success*. New York, NY: Russell Sage Foundation.

Sáenz, V. B., García-Louis, C., & Drake, A. P. (2017). Leveraging their family capital: How Latino males successfully navigate the community college. *Community College Review*, *45*(5), 1–17.

Sanchez, C. M., Fornerino, M., & Zhang, M. (2006). Motivations and the intent to study abroad among U.S., French, and Chinese Students. *Journal of Teaching in International Business*, *18*(1), 27–52. doi:10.1300/J066v18n01_03

Sandoval-Lucero, E., Maes, J. B., & Klingsmith, L. (2014). African American and Latina(o) community college students' social capital and student success. *College Student Journal*, *48*(3), 522–533.

Silverman, S. C., Sarvenaz, A., & Stiles, M. R. (2009). Meeting the needs of commuter, part-time, transfer, and returning students. In Student engagement in higher education: Theoretical perspectives and practical approaches for diverse populations (pp. 223-242). New York, NY: Routledge.

Soares, L. (2013). *Post-traditional learners and the transformation of postsecondary education: A manifesto for college leaders*. Washington, DC: American Council on Education.

Soares, L., Gagliardi, J. S., & Nellum, C. J. (2017). *The post-traditional learners manifesto revisited: Aligning postsecondary education with real life for adult student success*. Retrieved from: http://www.acenet.edu/news-room/Pages/The-Post-Traditional-Learners-Manifesto-Revisited.aspx

Solorzano, D., & Delgado Bernal, D. (2001). Critical race theory, transformational resistance, and social justice: Chicana and Chicano students in an urban context. *Urban Education*, *36*, 308–342. doi:10.1177/0042085901363002

Solorzano, D. G., & Yosso, T. J. (2001). Critical race and LatCrit theory and method: Counter-storytelling. *International Journal of Qualitative Studies in Education: QSE*, *14*(4), 471–495. doi:10.1080/09518390110063365

Soria, K. M., & Stebleton, M. J. (2012). First-Generation students' academic engagement and retention. *Teaching in Higher Education*, *17*(6), 673–685. doi:10.1080/13562517.2012.666735

Strange, H., & Gibson, H. J. (2017). An investigation of experiential and transformative learning in study abroad programs. *Frontiers: The Interdisciplinary Journal of Study Abroad*, *29*, 85–100.

Strayhorn, T. L., & Johnson, R. M. (2014). Black female community college students' satisfaction: A national regression analysis. *Community College Journal of Research and Practice*, *38*(6), 534–550. doi:10.1080/10668926.2013.866060

Stroud, A. H. (2010). Who plans (not) to study abroad? An examination of U. S. student intent. *Journal of Studies in International Education, 14*(5), 491–507. doi:10.1177/1028315309357942

Sweeney, K. (2013). Inclusive excellence and underrepresentation of students of color in study abroad. *Frontiers: The Interdisciplinary Journal of Study Abroad, 23*. Retrieved from https://frontiersjournal.org/wp-content/uploads/2015/09/SWEENEY-FrontiersXXIII- InclusiveExcellenceandUnderrepresentationofStudentsofColorinStudyAbroad.pdf

Thomas, T. (2016). Community college education abroad and business internship programs cultivation of competency in communicating, collaborating, and critical thinking. In R. L. Raby & E. J. Valeau (Eds.), *International education at community colleges: Themes, practices, research, and case studies*. New York, NY: Palgrave Macmillian Publishers. doi:10.1057/978-1-137-53336-4_23

Tillman, M. (2010). *Diversity in international education hands-on workshop: Summary Report*. Washington, DC: American Institute for Foreign Study.

Twombly, S. B., Salisbury, M. H., Tumanut, S. D., & Klute, P. (2012). Special Issue: Study Abroad in a New Global Century--Renewing the Promise, Refining the Purpose. *ASHE Higher Education Report, 38*(4), 1–152.

Van Noy, M., & Heidkamp, M. (2017). *Working for adults: State policies and community college practices to better serve adult learners at community colleges during the great recession and beyond*. Retrieved from: https://www.dol.gov/odep/pdf/WorkingForAdults.pdf

Wick, D. J. (2011). *Study abroad for students of color: A third space for negotiating agency and identity* (Unpublished doctoral dissertation). San Francisco State University.

Willis, T. Y. (2016). Microaggressions and intersectionality in the experiences of Black women studying abroad through community colleges: Implications for practice. In International education at community colleges: Themes, practices, research, and case studies (pp. 167-186). New York: Palgrave Macmillian Publishers.

Wood, J. L., & Harris, F., III. (2015). The effect of academic engagement on sense of belonging: A hierarchical, multilevel analysis of Black men in the community colleges. *Spectrum: A Journal on Black Men, 4*(1), 21–47. doi:10.2979pectrum.4.1.0

Yosso, T. J. (2005). Whose culture has capital? A critical race theory discussion of community cultural wealth. *Race, Ethnicity and Education, 8*(1), 69–91. doi:10.1080/1361332052000341006

Zamani-Gallaher, E. M., Leon, R. A., & Lang, J. (2016). Self-authorship beyond borders: Reconceptualizing college and career readiness. In R. L. Raby & E. J. Valeau (Eds.), *International education at community colleges: Themes, practices, research, and case studies (pp. 146-66)*. New York, NY: Palgrave. doi:10.1057/978-1-137-53336-4_8

Zhang, Y. (2011). Education abroad in the U.S. Community Colleges. *Community College Review, 39*(2), 181–200. doi:10.1177/0091552111404552

Zhang, Y. L., Lui, J., & Hagedorn, L. S. (2013). Post transfer experiences: Adult undergraduate students at a research university. *Journal of Applied Research in the Community College, 21*, 31–40.

Chapter 2
Opening the Door to Study Abroad From Community Colleges

Julie Baer
Institute for International Education, USA

ABSTRACT

Drawing upon data from Open Doors®, this chapter highlights the unique characteristics of study abroad from community colleges over the past decade. It explores patterns in destinations, durations, and student characteristics for study abroad at community colleges over this time period. Through lessons learned from IIE's Heiskell Award winners and Generation Study Abroad (GSA) community college commitment partners, the chapter will conclude with best practices from community colleges that have made commitments to increase and diversify their study abroad programs.

WHY STUDY ABROAD?

While many four-year institutions in the United States offer education abroad opportunities for their students, a much smaller proportion of community colleges send U.S. students abroad. If community colleges are primarily focused on serving the local community and providing millions of students with workforce education, how do students studying abroad in another country support that mission? To illuminate the answer, it is important to understand the breadth and depth of benefits that study abroad yields for all students, including those at community colleges.

Research has suggested that study abroad impacts students' academic and professional careers. The National Survey of Student Engagement (NSSE) classifies study abroad among the six "high impact practices" due to positive associations with student learning and retention (National Survey of Student Engagement, 2018). Research has linked study abroad to improved grade point averages, completion rates, retention rates, and transfer rates, particularly for minority and at-risk students (Sutton & Rubin, 2010; Willett, Pellegrin, & Cooper, 2013). It is particularly notable that these effects were evident at the community college level in the California Community College Student Outcomes Abroad Research

DOI: 10.4018/978-1-5225-6252-8.ch002

Opening the Door to Study Abroad From Community Colleges

(Raby, Rhodes, & Biscarra, 2014). Furthermore, studies have indicated that students who study abroad develop intrapersonal competencies, cognitive abilities, interpersonal skills, cultural understanding, global awareness, and positive associations with their overall educational experience (Dwyer, 2004; Gaia, 2015; Farrugia & Sanger, 2017; Coker, Heiser, and Taylor, 2018; Hubbard, Rexeisen, & Watson, 2018). For example, Farrugia and Sanger's (2017) national study of 4,500 U.S. college and university alumni found that over half of respondents self-reported that their study abroad experiences significantly developed or improved their flexibility/adaptability, self-awareness, curiosity, confidence, problem-solving, intercultural, interpersonal, and communication skills (Figure 1), and that the majority of survey respondents believed that their time abroad directly contributed to a job offer. Once students have secured a job, Partlo and Ampaw's (2018) research found that students who participated in study abroad had higher earnings in the workforce one year after graduation.

HOW MANY U.S. STUDENTS STUDY ABROAD FROM COMMUNITY COLLEGES?

Despite research indicating positive impacts academically and professionally, few community college students study abroad. Only 6,905 U.S. community college students studied abroad in 2015/16 accord-

Figure 1. Reported skill development or improvement through study abroad
Source: Farrugia, C. & J. Sanger. (2017). Gaining an Employment Edge: The impact of Study Abroad on 21st Century Skills and Career Prospects in the United States. New York: Institute of International Education.

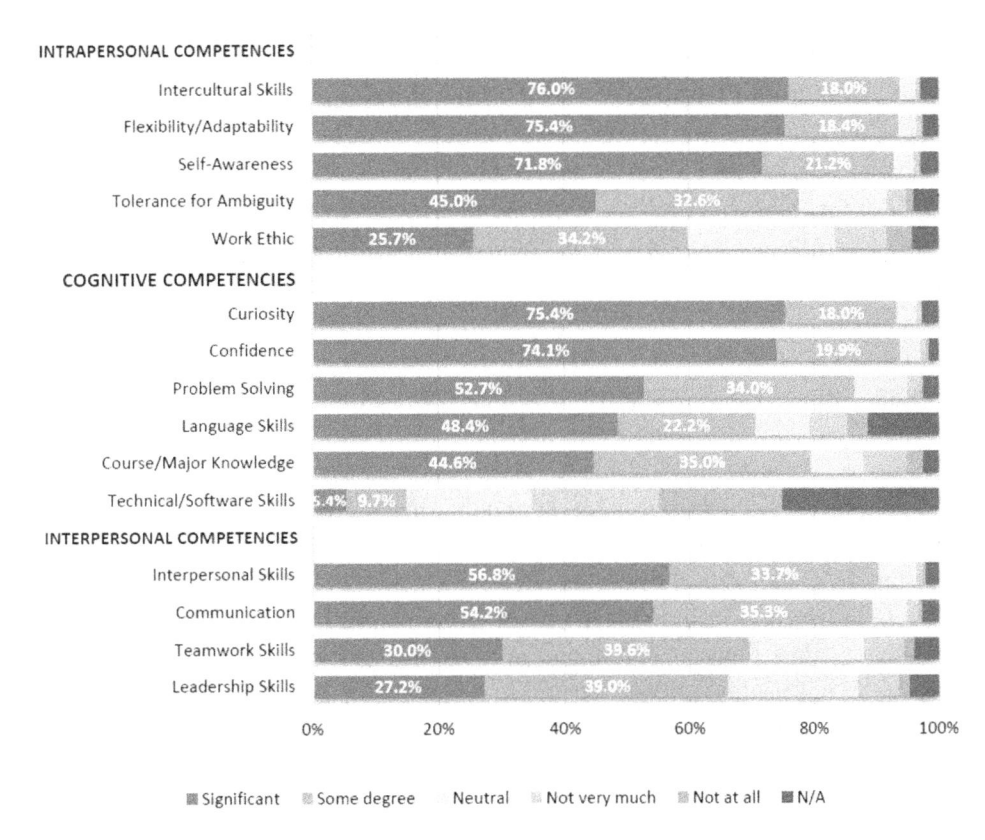

Competency	Significant	Some degree
INTRAPERSONAL COMPETENCIES		
Intercultural Skills	76.0%	18.0%
Flexibility/Adaptability	75.4%	18.4%
Self-Awareness	71.8%	21.2%
Tolerance for Ambiguity	45.0%	32.6%
Work Ethic	25.7%	34.2%
COGNITIVE COMPETENCIES		
Curiosity	75.4%	18.0%
Confidence	74.1%	19.9%
Problem Solving	52.7%	34.0%
Language Skills	48.4%	22.2%
Course/Major Knowledge	44.6%	35.0%
Technical/Software Skills	5.4%	9.7%
INTERPERSONAL COMPETENCIES		
Interpersonal Skills	56.8%	33.7%
Communication	54.2%	35.3%
Teamwork Skills	30.0%	39.6%
Leadership Skills	27.2%	39.0%

Legend: Significant | Some degree | Neutral | Not very much | Not at all | N/A

ing to the *Open Doors Report on International Educational Exchange,* a yearly study carried out by IIE in partnership with the U.S. Department of State's Bureau of Educational and Cultural Affairs that collects information from U.S. higher education institutions on international students and scholars as well as U.S. study abroad. This number represents a small proportion (2%) of the over 325,000 U.S. students that went abroad in 2015/16, a trend that has been consistent for the past twenty years. With community colleges enrolling 41% of undergraduate students in the United States (American Association of Community Colleges, 2018), a large segment of the undergraduate population is not afforded the opportunity to study abroad.

At community colleges there are both institutional challenges and student barriers that may impede significant growth in study abroad opportunities. Institutionally, community colleges may face challenges around internationalization not being a strategic priority, limited resources or administrative support, and a lack of integration with other departments. For institutions without robust support, this may contribute to difficulties offering diverse programs, marketing study abroad opportunities, working with faculty to understand the benefits and advocate for study abroad, assessing study abroad outcomes, and reporting to national data collection efforts. To address some of these challenges, the Consortium for Analysis of Student Success through International Education (2018) was launched with funding from the US Department of Education to build institutional capacity and promote research for tracking study abroad outcomes.

There are also a number of personal student barriers that may prevent students from studying abroad, including a lack of student awareness of programs, anxiety about traveling to new places or leaving friends, and health or safety concerns. One of the greatest factors influencing a student's decision to go abroad is the cost of the experience, which includes both the direct price as well as potential opportunity costs of absences from family or work obligations. This ongoing challenge was documented through a snapshot survey conducted by IIE and the California Colleges for International Education, which found that the vast majority of institutions (83%) indicated that the cost of study abroad was the most significant challenge to expanding education abroad at community colleges (Raby, 2008). Subsequent research by Raby and Rhodes (2018) found that the average cost of going abroad among California community colleges in 2015/16 was $3,500 for a short-term summer program and $7,500 for a semester program, which is a considerably higher cost than the average annual California tuition of $1,200. Research has shown that providing students with scholarships may incentivize students to overcome cost concerns (Amani & Kim, 2018).

The impact of education abroad price sensitivity is particularly acute at the community college level and becomes apparent when examining historical data over the past decade. As seen in Figure 2, the number of community college students going abroad decreased in 2007/08 when the global financial crisis and U.S. recession occurred. While national study abroad trends fell for one year in 2008/09 following the recession, those numbers quickly rebounded the following year and have steadily grown since. Comparatively, from 2007/08 until 2010/11, the number of study abroad students from community colleges fell to approximately 4,500 students. This is particularly surprising given that over this same period, enrollment in two-year institutions increased from 6.6 million in fall 2007 to 7.7 million in fall 2010, which is the all-time high for enrollment at two-year institutions (Snyder, de Brey, & Dillow, 2018). The reason for this decline is likely due to a combination of students' inability to afford the study abroad costs and institutions scaling back study abroad offerings in the fiscally constrained recession environment (Raby, 2012).

Figure 2. U.S. study abroad at community colleges, 2005/06 – 2015/16
Source: Institute of International Education. (2017). "U.S. Study Abroad at Associate's Institutions, 2005/06 - 2015/16." Open Doors Report on International Educational Exchange.

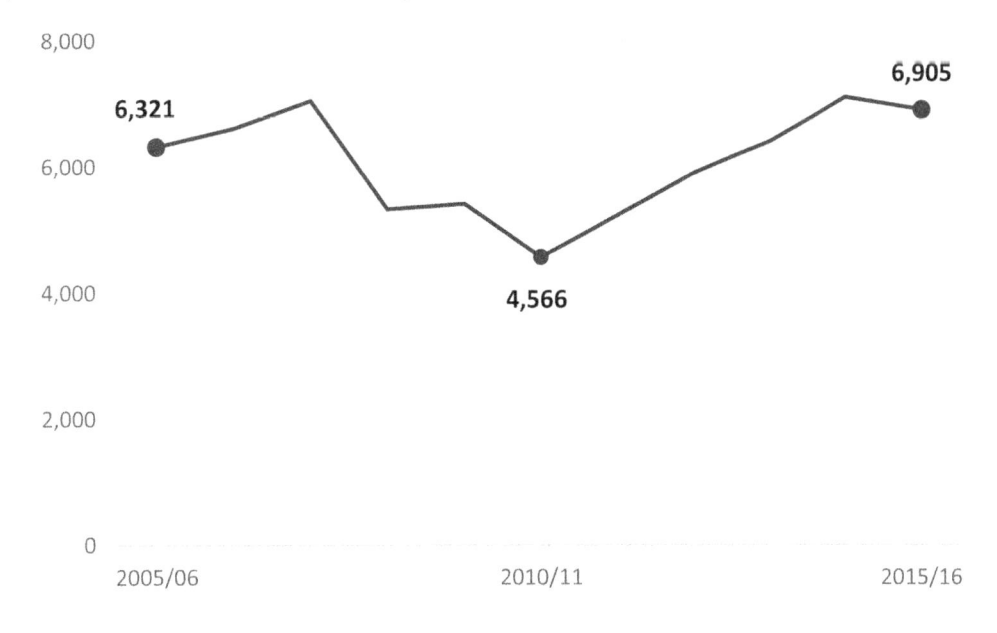

[Line graph showing values: 6,321 at 2005/06; 4,566 at 2010/11; 6,905 at 2015/16]

While study abroad at community colleges has slowly grown since the recession, there are indicators that these institutions are continuously working to overcome challenges to study abroad and provide opportunities for global experiences. According to the American Council on Education's *Mapping Internationalization on U.S. Campuses 2017 Edition*, over the past five years, community colleges have increasingly developed strategic plans or tasks forces focused on internationalizing the campus and implemented global learning outcomes (Helms & Brajkovic, 2017). Additionally, community colleges have engaged with initiatives that strategically promote and support best practices across the field, such as IIE's Generation Study Abroad initiative.

WHERE HAVE WE BEEN AND WHERE ARE WE NOW?

With community colleges recognizing the value of study abroad programs, it is important to understand the profile and interests of U.S. students going abroad to build programs that serve their needs, particularly as community colleges have distinct missions and student populations compared with other institutional types. This section draws upon *Open Doors* data to analyze the evolving patterns of U.S. study abroad from community colleges over time in comparison with national trends.

Where Do U.S. Community College Students Go Abroad?

Overseas experiences from community colleges are often concentrated in certain key destinations. Students from community colleges studied abroad in just 67 destinations, compared to over 200 destinations for U.S. students across all institutional types. Of students from all U.S. institutions, 56% of students travelled to the top ten destinations of the United Kingdom, Italy, Spain, France, Germany, China, Ireland, Australia,

Costa Rica, and Japan. Comparatively, nearly three-quarters (72%) of community college students were concentrated in the top ten destinations of Italy, Spain, United Kingdom, Costa Rica, France, Ireland, Cuba, Mexico, China, and Japan. With additional opportunities to study abroad, more community college students may be able to gain increased international exposure to diverse destinations around the globe.

Similar to national trends of overall study abroad, the majority of community college students studied in Europe in 2015/16 (Figure 3). Within Europe, however, notable distinctions emerge when analyzing the leading host destinations. Over the past decade, Italy and Spain have ranked as the top destination for community college students. This differs from the top destination nationally – the United Kingdom – which has ranked as the number one destination since *Open Doors* began collecting data on study abroad in 1985/86. Outside of the traditional top three European destinations (Italy, Spain, and the United Kingdom), France and Ireland also fall within the top ten destinations for community college students. In 2017, the "Community College Abroad in France" initiative was announced by the Cultural and Scientific Services of the French Embassy in partnership with Community Colleges for International Development (CCID) and the n+i network (network of 50 top engineering schools in France) to provide opportunities for traditionally underserved students to pursue studies within France as part of the U.S. Department of State and French Ministry of Foreign Affairs' "Transatlantic Friendship and Mobility Initiative" (Cultural Services French Embassy in the United States, 2017). The number of community college students pursuing study abroad in Ireland has also rapidly increased over the past decade. In 2005/06 Ireland was not listed within the top ten destinations, but as of 2015/16 Ireland ranked as the sixth leading destination, likely due to its popularity as an English-speaking country and initiatives by Education in Ireland.

Outside of Europe, an increasing number of community college students are studying abroad to Latin America and the Caribbean (Figure 3). In 2001/02, 17% of community college students went abroad to this region, which had increased to 28% by 2015/16. In comparison, only 16% of all students nationally studied abroad in Latin America and the Caribbean in 2015/16, indicating a stronger interest among community college students.

This interest is likely driven by several factors that encourage study abroad to the region including historical, language, and cultural connections, particularly as nearly a quarter of community college students studying abroad identify as Hispanic, as well as affordable costs and large governmental initiatives. For example, the 100,000 Strong in the Americas initiative launched in 2014 with the goal of creating innovative and sustainable student exchange and training programs. This initiative is a public-private partnership between the U.S. Department of State, Partners of the Americas, and NAFSA that promotes academic exchange through awarding Innovation Fund grants to teams of higher education institutions. Over a dozen U.S. community colleges have received awards to create partnerships in countries throughout the Western Hemisphere (100,000 Strong in the Americas, 2018). The strong growth in the region is also supported by student interest in several increasingly popular destinations, such as Costa Rica, Cuba, and Mexico.

How Long Do U.S. Community College Students Go Abroad?

Nationally, the majority of study abroad students go overseas for short-term durations of eight weeks or less during the academic year or for summer programs. This trend across all institution types has increased by approximately 15% points over the past fifteen years from 48% of all students in 2000/01 to 63% in 2015/16. The pattern towards short-term study abroad has been even more pronounced at

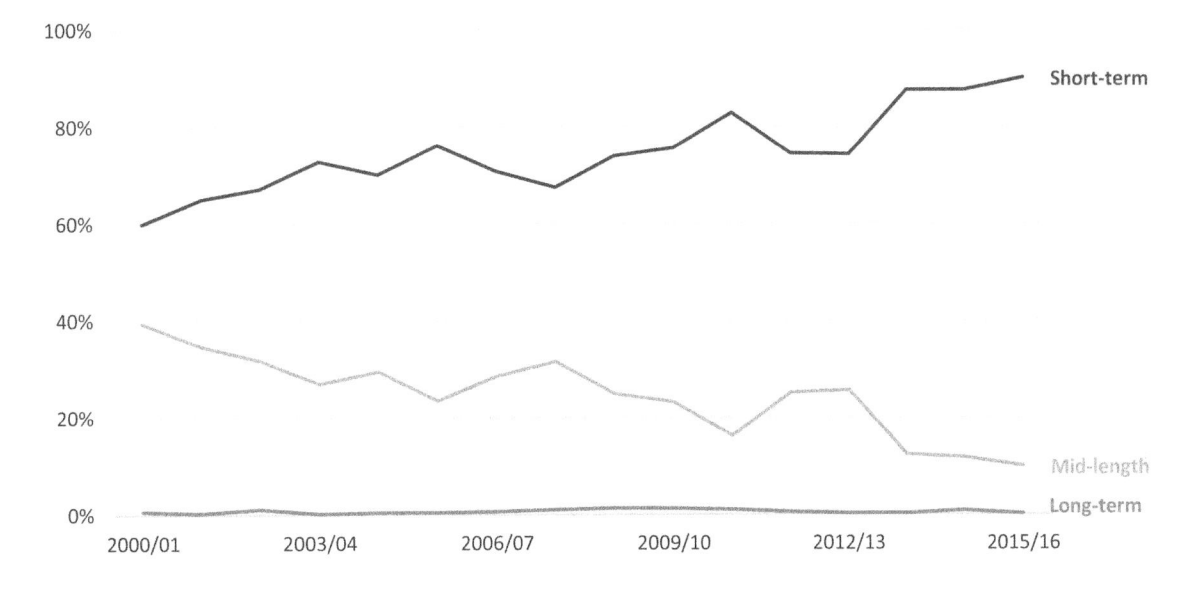

Figure 3. Study abroad at community colleges by world regions, selected years 2003/04 – 2015/16
Source: Institute of International Education. (2017). "Host Regions of U.S. Study Abroad at Associate's Institutions, 2001/02 - 2015/16." Open Doors Report on International Educational Exchange.

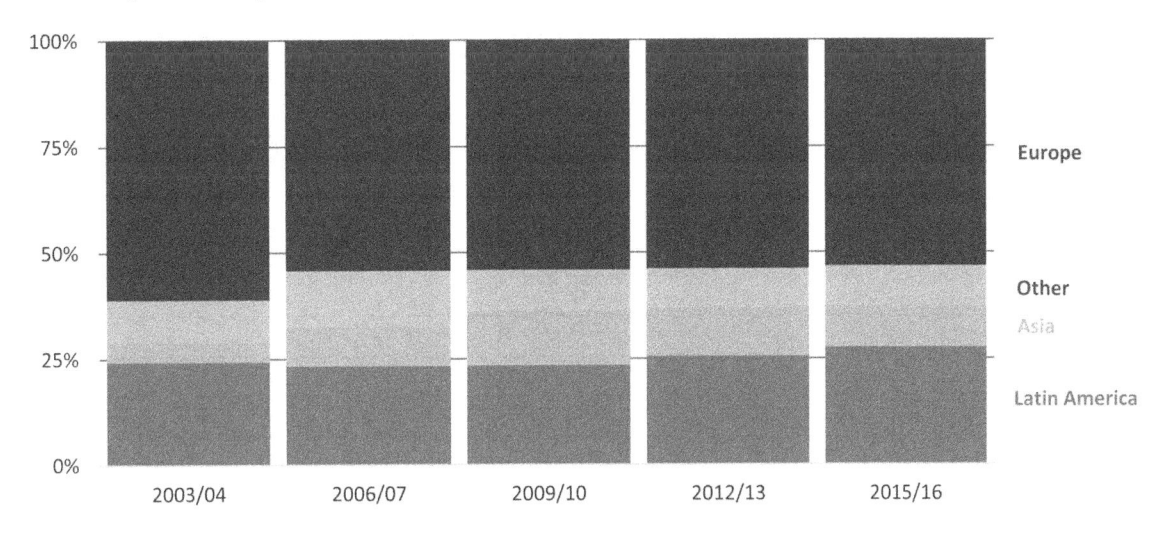

community colleges. In 2000/01, approximately 60% of community college students went abroad on short-term experiences, while 39% studied abroad for mid-term durations of a semester or one to two quarters (Figure 4). Since then, an increasing number and proportion of students have pursued short-term study abroad experiences. In 2015/16, approximately 90% of all community college study abroad was short-term, while only 10% of students pursued mid-term durations abroad (Table 1).

While research in the field has indicated that longer term study abroad is often associated with a wider variety of benefits (Dwyer, 2004; Kehl and Morris, 2008; Trooboff, Vande Berg, & Rayman, 2008;

Figure 4. Duration of study abroad at community colleges, 2000/01 – 2015/16
Institute of International Education. (2017). "Duration of U.S. Study Abroad at Associate's Institutions, 2000/01 - 2015/16." Open Doors Report on International Educational Exchange.

Table 1. Detailed duration of U.S. study abroad at community colleges and all institutional types, 2015/16

Detailed Duration of U.S. Study Abroad, 2015/16	Associate's Institutions Study Abroad (%)	All Institutions Study Abroad (%)
Summer Term	66.6	30.0
Summer: More than eight weeks	0.5	2.6
Summer: Two to eight weeks	42.5	30.4
Summer: Fewer than two weeks	23.6	5.0
One Semester	8.3	31.9
8 Weeks or Less During Academic Year	16.8	17.4
Two to eight weeks	6.0	6.6
Fewer than two weeks	10.8	10.8
January Term	6.1	7.4
Academic Year	0.1	2.3
One Quarter	1.5	2.3
Two Quarters	0.1	0.3
Calendar Year	0.0	0.1
Other	0.5	0.4

Source: Institute of International Education. (2017). "Detailed Duration of U.S. Study Abroad at Community Colleges and All Institutional Types, 2015/16." *Open Doors Report on International Educational Exchange*.

Coker, Heiser, and Taylor, 2018), evidence also suggests that short-term durations abroad can also have a positive impact on students (Chieffo & Griffiths, 2004; Dwyer, 2004; Anderson, Lawton, Rexeisen, & Hubbard, 2006; Gaia, 2015, Farrugia & Sanger, 2017; Coker, Heiser, & Taylor, 2018). For example, Gaia (2015) reported that two- to three-week faculty-led programs can improve cultural awareness and global perspectives, and Farrugia and Sanger (2017) noted that shorter-term study abroad experiences were more effective at fostering teamwork, likely due to short-term experiences being more structured and team oriented. Additionally, short-term durations can often be an excellent opportunity for community college students who may not be able to go abroad for longer durations due to financial, work, athletic, or family obligations

Which Community College Students Go Abroad?

Due to their academic profile, community colleges contribute to the increasingly diverse group of students who study abroad. As institutions seek to provide opportunities to all students, it is helpful to understand the characteristics of students who go abroad, such as their race/ethnicity, gender, and chosen majors.

Overall, the number of racial and ethnic minority students going abroad modestly increased over the past decade. Among community colleges in the United States, students identifying as a racial or ethnic minority who studied abroad grew from 30% of the total population in 2001/02 to 39% in 2015/16. Of note, a greater proportion of study abroad students at community colleges identify as racial and ethnic minorities, 39% versus the 28% of students studying abroad nationally (Figure 5). This higher percentage may be primarily due to the demographics of students attending community colleges. Data from the *Digest of Education Statistics 2016* indicates that among all two-year institutions, approximately

50% of community college students identify as racial or ethnic minority students (Snyder, de Brey, & Dillow, 2018).

While community colleges work to increase the proportion of underrepresented students going abroad, one area of success has been the proportion of Hispanic or Latino(a) students that study abroad compared to the overall population enrolled at these institutions. Hispanic or Latino(a) students comprise 24% of all enrolled students at community colleges according to the *Digest of Education Statistics 2016* (Snyder, de Brey, & Dillow, 2018) and account for 23% of students studying abroad from community colleges. As institutions seek to benchmark the profile of students, it may also be useful to work with state systems or local networks to understand these trends at a regional level. For example, Raby and Rhodes (2018) note that while there is national success among the representation of Hispanic and Latino(a) students going abroad, there are still opportunities for growth among this population in California where 46% of enrolled students in Fall 2017 identify as Hispanic and Latino(a) (California Community Colleges Chancellor's Office, 2018).

While there have been improvements in the number of students identifying as racial and ethnic minorities going abroad each year, the gender gap in study abroad persists, with a higher proportion of women pursuing education abroad. While it is expected that more women may study abroad due to the fact that 57% of all enrolled students at two-year institutions were women in Fall 2016 (Snyder, de Brey, & Dil-

Figure 5. Race and ethnicity of enrollment and study abroad students at all U.S. institutions and community colleges
*Snyder, T.D., de Brey, C., and Dillow, S.A. (2018). Digest of Education Statistics 2016 (NCES 2017-094). National Center for Education Statistics, Institute of Education Sciences, U.S. Department of Education. Washington, DC.
**Institute of International Education. (2017). "Race and Ethnicity Student Characteristics for U.S. Study Abroad, 2015/16." Open Doors Report on International Educational Exchange.

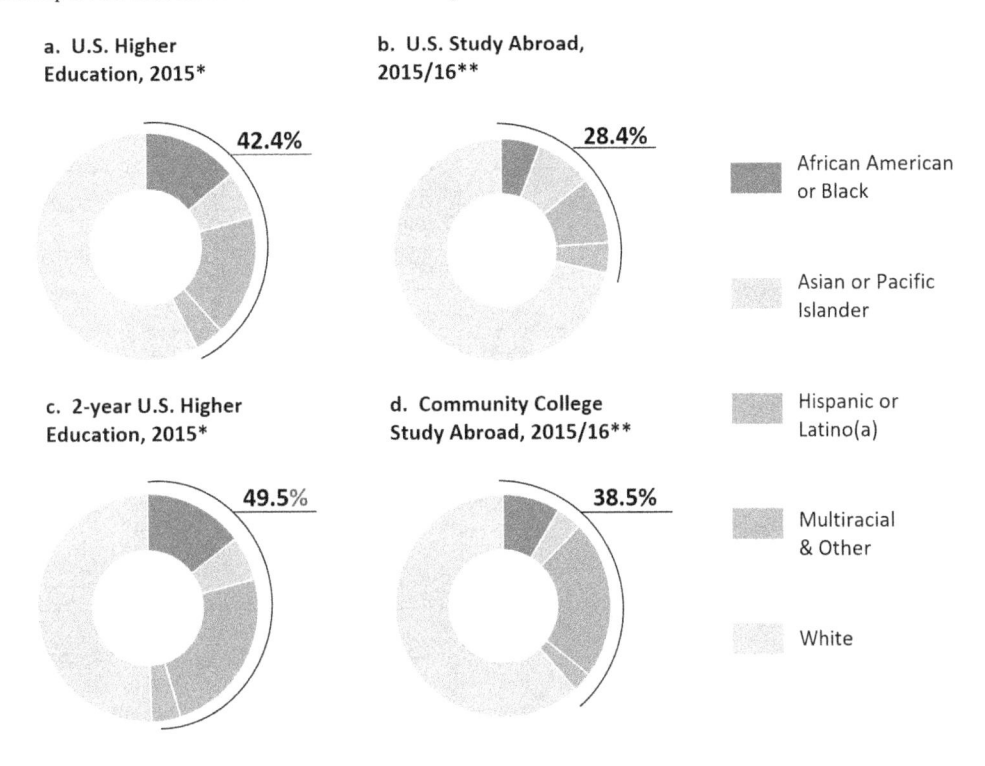

a. U.S. Higher Education, 2015* — 42.4%

b. U.S. Study Abroad, 2015/16** — 28.4%

c. 2-year U.S. Higher Education, 2015* — 49.5%

d. Community College Study Abroad, 2015/16** — 38.5%

Legend:
- African American or Black
- Asian or Pacific Islander
- Hispanic or Latino(a)
- Multiracial & Other
- White

low, 2018), the gender gap is much wider among students studying abroad. In 2015/16, 65% of study abroad students from community college were women. This trend has remained remarkably consistent as women accounted for 66% of community college students abroad a decade ago in 2005/06. Some researchers have noted that steps can be taken to promote education abroad to men through marketing that appeals to their academic interests and the ability to challenge themselves, as well as highlighting how study abroad can have lasting benefits for academic achievement and career development (Lucas, 2009; Fischer, 2012; Yankey, 2014).

Another factor impacting the ability to go abroad may be a student's field of study, as certain majors remain underrepresented in study abroad, particularly in the science, technology, engineering, and mathematics (STEM) fields. A decade ago in 2005/06, only 16% of community college students studied abroad in the STEM fields, with less than 1% of students pursuing abroad opportunities in engineering (0.9%), agriculture (0.5%), and math or computer science (0.3%). By 2015/16, the percent of students studying abroad in the STEM fields had increased to 24% (Table 2). However, according to the most recent data on student majors at Associate's institutions from the 2016 National Postsecondary Student Aid Study, 41% of community college students majored in the STEM areas, particularly within the health professions (U.S. Department of Education, 2018). As such, while there has been strong growth in STEM majors accessing study abroad opportunities, these STEM students continue to be underrepresented in comparison with overall STEM enrollment at community colleges.

Table 2. Major fields of study at community colleges for study abroad 2015/16 and overall enrollment 2016

Major Field of Study	Associate's Institutions Study Abroad* (%)	Associate's Institutions Enrollment** (%)
Science, Technology, Engineering, and Math Fields (STEM)	23.7	41.3
Health Professions	9.4	22.8
Engineering	3.0	10.1
Physical and Life Sciences	6.4	2.6
Math and Computer Science	1.9	4.8
Agriculture	3.0	1.0
Business and Management	9.2	12.1
Social Sciences	4.9	5.0
Fine and Applied Arts	3.1	3.5
Foreign Language and International Studies	5.3	0.3
Education	5.2	4.0
Humanities	1.5	0.6
Communications and Journalism	4.2	1.3
Legal Studies and Law Enforcement	0.9	5.7
Other Fields of Study	34.0	22.5
Undeclared	8.0	3.7

Sources
*Institute of International Education. (2017). "Field of Study Student Characteristics for U.S. Study Abroad, 2015/16." *Open Doors Report on International Educational Exchange.*
**U.S. Department of Education. Institute of Education Sciences, National Center for Education Statistics. (2018). "Detailed Fields of Study by U.S. Citizenship at Associate's Institutions." National Postsecondary Student Aid Study (*NPSAS*): 2016.

OPENING THE DOOR WIDER FOR STUDY ABROAD FROM COMMUNITY COLLEGES: WHERE DO WE GO FROM HERE?

Over the past twenty years, IIE has worked to provide best practices and to encourage institutions to develop a strategic vision to broaden study abroad at the community college level. In order to better understand how institutions creatively build unique programs and share best practices, IIE created the Heiskell Awards. These awards recognize outstanding initiatives to internationalize higher education by IIENetwork member universities and colleges, which includes an award for Internationalizing the Community College. In order to disseminate these successes, the best practices from each of the Heiskell Award winners are highlighted on IIE's website, which include further details about the conceptual framework of successful programs and how they were implemented (IIE, 2018b). (https://www.iie.org/Research-and-Insights/Best-Practices-Resource). Community colleges also actively participate in IIE's Generation Study Abroad initiative, a network of institutions dedicated to mobilizing resources and making commitments with the goal of doubling and diversifying the number of U.S. students studying abroad by the end of the decade (IIE, 2018a). Through these networks, IIE identified the following examples of best practices to expand study abroad at community colleges:

Cultivate Institutional Commitments

Building institutional commitments can aid in engaging stakeholders to recognize the importance of developing international opportunities, often leading to increased access to education abroad experiences. Examples of this include developing an internationalization vision, strategic plan or task force, working with senior administrators, and building support from offices across campus.

Institutional Examples

- *Spokane Falls Community College (Washington)* created a 2020 Global Vision Program that takes a multi-tiered approach. This program integrated international instructional content into the curriculum, brought global activities to campus through their International Guest Speaker Series, and established a commitment through IIE's Generation Study Abroad initiative to increase the number of study abroad students.
- *Santa Monica College (California)* initiated a Global Citizenship Initiative that grew out of a 2008 faculty task force. The Global Citizenship Initiative focused on internationalizing the college's mission, culture, and values through specific programming. This included a yearly Global Citizenship theme, a Research Symposium focusing on international issues, faculty mini-grants to bring international programs to campus, short-term study abroad for students, and professional development programs abroad for faculty and staff.

Develop Creative Funding Streams

As costs can be a major impediment to study abroad, community colleges have taken many approaches to building funding streams that support study abroad, which includes institutional commitments to scholarships, US Department of Education Title VI grants, local and national foundational support, and fundraising programs.

Institutional Examples

- *The College of Lake County (Illinois)* began their semester-long program in China in 2008 with support from a Title VI grant. In understanding the importance of financial aid to go abroad, the institution also pledged $275,000 in matching funds for study abroad.
- *Ohio State University Agricultural Technical Institute (Ohio),* upon their founding 15 years ago began the Ghana Research and Education Abroad (GREA) program to send associate degree-seeking students on a month-long experiential learning program. To support this program, Ohio State ATI has received donations from the Noble and Romich Foundations.
- *Alamo Colleges (Texas),* Board of Trustees, in December 2016, approved a $1 International Education Fee per student, per semester. The funds from this fee are designed to support a Study Abroad Scholarship for students to access education abroad opportunities. The institution has also worked with the Alamo Colleges Scholarship Foundation to establish sustainable student scholarship funding.

Engage Faculty

Working closely with faculty and staff to highlight the value of study abroad or enable them to travel abroad themselves can be useful in encouraging faculty to globalize their curriculum and to advocate for students to pursue study abroad opportunities.

Institutional Examples

- *Pitt Community College (North Carolina)* provided grants to both students and faculty through an International Education Travel Scholarship (IETS). Faculty are then expected to share their experiences with students and become recruiters for future abroad programs.
- *Valencia College (Florida)* developed a Study Abroad Program Leader Certificate to help faculty develop programs and understand safety considerations in leading students abroad. They also created a Program Leader-in-Training mentorship initiative, partnering veteran faculty with new faculty leaders. These initiatives resulted in increased number of faculty leading short-term programs and an uptick in study abroad enrollment.

Establish Partnerships

As community colleges seek to expand study abroad opportunities, taking advantage of internal and external collaborative partnerships is an additional way to fund programs and implement best practices.

Institutional Examples

- *Northwestern Michigan College (Michigan)* identified several ways to build partnerships for meaningful academic programs abroad. They identified their unique freshwater studies program as an opportunity and partnered with Earth University in Costa Rica, so their students could conduct lab work in the field and help local farmers with technical skills in Costa Rica. They also built an internal partnership between the study abroad office, the culinary school, and the business school

to enhance opportunities for students. These three departments connected with a local partner to carry out experiential learning in Ecuador where students assisted locals in setting up a restaurant and established methods to promote new business with tourists.
- *Pellissippi State College (Tennessee)* is a member of and serves as the headquarters for the Tennessee Consortium for International Studies (TnCIS), bringing together 19 Tennessee community colleges and universities to drive international education and study abroad efforts through collaboration and partnership. This includes expanded program offerings for students and faculty at all member schools and providing training, support, and program development.

Initiate Outreach to Students

Students, especially in underrepresented communities, may not know about study abroad opportunities and the benefits of going abroad. As such, some institutions have created outreach through initiatives designed to target specific populations or have invested in cultivating on-campus ambassadors to encourage student participation in study abroad.

Institutional Examples

- *Pitt Community College (North Carolina)* students are required to become campus ambassadors for study abroad in order to receive one of the Pitt Community College International Education Travel Scholarships. Additionally, students must complete a community and college sharing plan, requiring them to disseminate their experience with those who did not have the opportunity to travel abroad as well as writing a letter to the Global Education committee and college administration about how their experience impacted their academic, professional, and personal growth.
- *Miami Dade College (Florida)* graduates the most Hispanic and African American students in the United States, the Medical Campus created a Diasporic Knowledge Remittance Study Abroad Program designed to allow students to study abroad and reconnect with their countries of heritage in the Caribbean and Latin America.

NEXT STEPS

Over the past decade, the door to study abroad at community colleges has continued to open with approximately 6,900 students going abroad in 2015/16. From the *Open Doors* data, successes are evident, such as the growth in study abroad over the past fifteen years and an increasing diversification of underrepresented students pursuing education abroad opportunities. As institutions commit to ensuring that students develop skills aligned with the global competencies required for today's interconnected workforce, study abroad is an avenue that community colleges are increasingly pursuing despite institutional challenges. However, with community colleges comprising only 2% of all U.S. study abroad, work remains to be done in encouraging study abroad at community college. Through developing commitments, sharing best practices, and increasing the focus on the benefits of these experiences, community colleges can make a significant impact in increasing study abroad at their institutions.

REFERENCES

100,000 Strong in the Americas. (2018). *Meet the winners*. Retrieved from http://www.100kstrongamericas.org/category/meet-the-winners/

Amani, M., & Kim, M. M. (2018). Study abroad participation at community colleges: Students' decision and influential factors. *Community College Journal of Research and Practice*, *42*(10), 678–692. doi:10.1080/10668926.2017.1352544

American Association of Community Colleges. (2018). *Fast facts 2018*. Retrieved from https://www.aacc.nche.edu/research-trends/fast-facts/

Anderson, P. H., Lawton, L., Rexeisen, R. J., & Hubbard, A. C. (2006). Short-term study abroad and intercultural sensitivity: A pilot study. *International Journal of Intercultural Relations*, *30*(4), 457–469. doi:10.1016/j.ijintrel.2005.10.004

California Community Colleges Chancellor's Office. (2018). *Management information systems data mart – Statewide enrollment status summary report of Fall 2017 students by ethnicity*. Retrieved from https://datamart.cccco.edu/Students/Enrollment_Status.aspx

Chieffo, L., & Griffiths, L. (2004). Large-scale assessment of student attitudes after a short-term study abroad program. *Frontiers: The Interdisciplinary Journal of Study Abroad*, *10*, 165–177. Retrieved from https://frontiersjournal.org/wp-content/uploads/2015/09/CHIEFFO-GRIFFITHS-FrontiersX-LargeScaleAssessmentofStudentAttitudeafteraShortTermStudyAbroadProgram.pdf

Coker, J. S., Heiser, E., & Taylor, L. (2018). Student outcomes associated with short-term and semester study abroad programs. *Frontiers: The Interdisciplinary Journal of Study Abroad*, *30*(2), 92–105. Retrieved from https://frontiersjournal.org/wp-content/uploads/2018/04/Coker-Heiser-Taylor-XXX-2-Student-Learning-Outcomes.pdf

Consortium for Analysis of Student Success through International Education. (2018). Retrieved from https://www.usg.edu/cassie

Cultural Services French Embassy in the United States. (2017). *Community college abroad in France - A new and affordable opportunities to study in France*. Retrieved from http://frenchculture.org/about-us/press-room/4887-community-college-abroad-france-new-and-affordable-opportunities-study

Dwyer, M. M. (2004). More is better: The impact of study abroad program duration. *Frontiers: The Interdisciplinary Journal of Study Abroad*, *10*, 151–164. Retrieved from https://frontiersjournal.org/wp-content/uploads/2015/09/DWYER-FrontiersX-MoreIsBetter.pdf

Farrugia, C., Bhandari, R., Baer, J., Robles, C., & Andrejko, N. (2017). *Open Doors 2017 Report on International Educational Exchange*. New York: Institute of International Education.

Farrugia, C., & Sanger, J. (2017). *Gaining an employment edge: The impact of study abroad on 21st century skills and career prospects in the United States*. New York, NY: Institute of International Education. Retrieved from https://www.iie.org/Research-and-Insights/Publications/Gaining-an-Employment-Edge---The-Impact-of-Study-Abroad

Fischer, K. (2012). In study abroad, men are hard to find. *The Chronicle of Higher Education.* Retrieved from http://chronicle.com/article/In-Study-Abroad-Men-Are-Hard/130853

Gaia, A. C. (2015). Short-term faculty-led study abroad programs enhance cultural exchange and self-awareness. *International Education Journal: Comparative Perspectives, 14*(1), 21-31. Retrieved from https://openjournals.library.sydney.edu.au/index.php/IEJ/article/viewFile/7627/8839

Helms, R. M., & Brajkovic, L. (2017). *Mapping internationalization on U.S campuses* (2017 edition). Washington, DC: American Council on Education. Retrieved from http://www.acenet.edu/news-room/Documents/Mapping-Internationalization-2017.pdf

Hubbard, A., Rexeisen, R., & Watson, P. (2018). *AIFS study abroad alumni outcomes: A longitudinal study of personal, intercultural and career development based on a survey of our alumni from 1990 to 2017.* American Institute of Foreign Study (AIFS). Retrieved from https://www.aifsabroad.com/outcomes2018.pdf

Institute of International Education. (2017a). *U.S. Study Abroad at Associate's Institutions, 2005/06 - 2015/16.* Open Doors Report on International Educational Exchange.

Institute of International Education. (2017b). *Host Regions of U.S. Study Abroad at Associate's Institutions, 2001/02 - 2015/16.* Open Doors Report on International Educational Exchange.

Institute of International Education. (2017c). *Duration of U.S. Study Abroad at Associate's Institutions, 2000/01 - 2015/16.* Open Doors Report on International Educational Exchange.

Institute of International Education. (2017d). *Race and Ethnicity Student Characteristics for U.S. Study Abroad, 2015/16.* Open Doors Report on International Educational Exchange.

Institute of International Education. (2017e). *Field of Study Student Characteristics for U.S. Study Abroad, 2015/16.* Open Doors Report on International Educational Exchange.

Institute of International Education. (2018a). *IIE generation study abroad initiative.* Retrieved from https://www.iie.org/en/Programs/Generation-Study-Abroad

Institute of International Education. (2018b). *Heiskell award.* Retrieved from https://www.iie.org/Research-and-Insights/Best-Practices-Resource

Kehl, K., & Morris, J. (2008). Differences in global-mindedness between short-term and semester-long study abroad participants at selected private universities. *Frontiers: The Interdisciplinary Journal of Study Abroad, 15,* 67–79. Retrieved from https://frontiersjournal.org/wp-content/uploads/2015/09/KEHL-MORRIS-FrontiersXV- DifferencesinGlobalMindednessbetweenShortTermandSemesterLong-StudyAbroadPartici pants.pdf

Lucas, J. M. (2009). *Where are all the males?: A mixed methods inquiry into male study abroad participation* (Doctoral dissertation). Retrieved from Dissertations and Theses database. (UMI No. 3381358)

National Survey of Student Engagement. (2018). *High-Impact practices.* Retrieved from http://nsse.indiana.edu/html/high_impact_practices.cfm

OECD. (2016). *Getting skills right: Assessing and anticipating changing skill needs*. Paris: OECD Publishing; doi:10.1787/9789264252073-

Partlo, M., & Ampaw, F. (2018). Using income effects to market undergraduate education abroad participation in higher education. *Journal of Marketing for Higher Education, 28*(1), 66–89. doi:10.1080/08841241.2018.1425230

Raby, R. L. (2008). *Expanding education abroad at U.S. community colleges (IIE Study Abroad White Paper Series, Issue No. 3)*. New York, NY: Institute of International Education. Retrieved from https://www.iie.org/Research-and-Insights/Publications/Expanding-Education-Abroad-at-US-Community-Colleges

Raby, R. L. (2012). Re-Imagining international education at community colleges. *Audem: International Journal of Higher Education and Democracy, 3,* 81-99. Retrieved from https://muse.jhu.edu/issue/27073

Raby, R. L., & Rhodes, G. M. (2018). Promoting education abroad among community college students: Overcoming obstacles and developing inclusive practices. In H. Barclay Hamir & N. Gozik (Eds.), Promoting Inclusion in Education Abroad: A Handbook of Research and Practice (pp. 114-133). Sterling, VA: Stylus.

Raby, R. L., Rhodes, G. M., & Biscarra, A. (2014). Community college study abroad: Implications for student success. *Community College Journal of Research and Practice, 38*(2-3), 174–183. doi:10.1080/10668926.2014.851961

Snyder, T. D., de Brey, C., & Dillow, S. A. (2018). *Digest of Education Statistics 2016 (NCES 2017-094)*. Washington, DC: National Center for Education Statistics, Institute of Education Sciences, U.S. Department of Education. Retrieved from https://nces.ed.gov/pubs2017/2017094.pdf

Sutton, R. C., & Rubin, D. L. (2010). *Documenting the academic impact of study abroad: Final report of the GlOSSARI project* [PowerPoint slides]. Retrieved from http://glossari.uga.edu/datasets/pdfs/FINAL.pdf

U.S. Department of Education, Institute of Education Sciences, National Center for Education Statistics. (2018). *Detailed fields of study by U.S citizenship at associate's institutions*. Washington, DC: National Postsecondary Student Aid Study (NPSAS).

Willett, T., Pellegrin, N., & Cooper, D. (2013). *Study abroad impact technical report*. Retrieved from http://globaled.us/cccsoar/docs/CCC-SOAR-StudyAbroadTechReportFinal.pdf

Yankey, J. B. (2014). *Dude, where's my passport?: An exploration of masculine identity of college men who study abroad*. Graduate Theses and Dissertations. 13666. Iowa State University. Retrieved from https://lib.dr.iastate.edu/cgi/viewcontent.cgi?article=4673&context=etd

Chapter 3
Good Practices and Program Standards:
Considering the Unique Needs of Community Colleges

Carola Smith
Santa Barbara City College, USA

Ann Hubbard
American Institute for Foreign Study, USA

ABSTRACT

With education abroad having evolved into a professional field and recognized program standards and good practices having been established, there are unique considerations that community colleges must consider regarding program development, implementation, and practices that require a particular approach to best meet the needs of both community college students and two-year institutions. By examining the nine areas of the standards of good practice developed by the Forum on Education Abroad, a narrative on each will be presented to address both their relevance and application to community colleges. Currently, with the greatest growth in U.S. education abroad occurring in short-term programming and with faculty-led programming being the most common type offered by community colleges, this review has timely relevance for the field.

INTRODUCTION

As community colleges develop or expand their study abroad options, careful time, attention, and resources are needed to align the academic objectives with the practical aspects of planning and programming. Education abroad is a complex and labor-intensive undertaking. It requires not only staff with specific responsibilities for the programming itself, but collaboration and cooperation from many offices on campus such as financial aid, admissions, student support services, and the institution's risk management staff. While institutions manage the requirements in both innovative and practical ways, knowledge of

DOI: 10.4018/978-1-5225-6252-8.ch003

best practices is essential for successful programs – especially for the customized, faculty-led model utilized by many community colleges, which will be the primary focus of this chapter.

There are a number of professional organizations, which have developed standards of good practice for the field of education abroad. The Community Colleges for International Development's (CCID) *Framework for Comprehensive Internationalization* (cited in Bissonnette & Woodin, 2013) provides a useful tool for institutions to assess the critical areas that promote and support all international activity. The Council for the Advancement of Standards in Higher Education promotes general standards and ethical principles, which have relevance for all higher education service areas, as well as functional area standards for specialized programs including education abroad. Additionally, CAS developed a set of learning outcomes and self-assessment tools to be used in "the development, assessment, and improvement of quality student learning, programs, and services" (Council for the Advancement of Standards in Higher Education, 2014). NAFSA: Association of International Educators developed a *Statement of Ethical Principles*, which is intended to promote ethical conduct and help guide professionals in the field of international education in decision-making in the development, coordination, and administration of programs and services (NAFSA, 2009). Additionally, NAFSA has developed extensive resources on best practices and regulations affecting education abroad, which are continuously reviewed and updated; they also offer information on comprehensive internationalization (see Hudzik, 2011; Hudzik, 2012). The Forum on Education Abroad, which serves as the collective voice of post-secondary education abroad, was established in 2001 by a group of professionals who felt the need for an organization that would focus on standards and support research in the field.

In 2005, The Forum was recognized by the U.S. Department of Justice and the Federal Trade Commission to serve as the Standards Development Organization (SDO) for the field of education abroad. The role of a SDO is to encourage self-regulation and compliance with standards in a specified field. As a SDO, The Forum is obligated to exhibit the following elements in developing and disseminating standards: *Openness, Balance, Transparency, Consensus, and Due Process* (The Forum on Education Abroad, 2015). In addition, The Forum has developed *Guidelines* (The Forum on Education Abroad, 2017b) for each standard area, which are under continual review and which provide another level of detail in guiding policies and practices.

The *Standards*[1] are intended to serve as a quality assurance measure and are meant to equally apply to all types of institutions engaged in the field of education abroad (including U.S. colleges and universities, third party providers, and overseas host institutions as well study abroad consortia or professional organizations in the field). Because the authors could find no documented application of the Standards specifically to community colleges and because of The Forum's recognized status as the Standards Development Organization in the U.S., the following chapter applies The Forum's *Standards* to the unique needs and goals of community college education abroad, specifically to faculty-led programming. By using The Forum's *Standards of Good Practice* (2015) as a framework, a narrative as well as some considerations for each of its nine *Standards* will be presented in this chapter to address both their relevance and application to community college faculty-led education abroad programming. The text of the standards' statements and accompanying bullet points as published in the fifth edition of the *Standards of Good Practice for Education Abroad* are reproduced in their entirety at the beginning of each section with permission from The Forum on Education Abroad. "Queries" for each can also be found in the *Standards* publication, which may be used for self-assessment and evaluation processes.

MISSION AND GOALS: THE ORGANIZATION HAS A MISSION STATEMENT AND ARTICULATES CLEAR GOALS FOR ITS EDUCATION ABROAD PROGRAMMING

- *The mission statement defines the scope of the organization's work, its objectives, and its aspirations, and it is made available to the organization's internal and external constituents.*
- *Specific learning goals are articulated for each of the organization's individual programs.*
- *The organization regularly assesses the degree to which it is achieving its mission and program goals and uses these findings to pursue continuous improvement of the quality of its programming* (The Forum on Education Abroad, 2015, p. 3).

To provide a brief historic perspective, in the early 20th century U.S. community colleges were founded with the intent to provide higher education and workforce training to the surrounding communities. For many years, community colleges were heavily reliant on local funding sources, which led to the frequently held belief that the services offered by community colleges should not extend beyond the parameters of the local community and that "serving the local community is the opposite of a global connection" (Raby & Valeau, 2016, p 10). Throughout the past four decades, the U.S. job market has undergone fundamental changes, requiring adaptability, highly specialized and rapidly evolving technical skills, as well as strong interpersonal and intercultural skills to meet the rapidly changing needs of our increasingly interdependent and globalized economy. Simultaneously, community colleges have experienced "increasing financial pressure as state appropriations for higher education have declined" (Bailey, Smith Jaggars, & Jenkins, 2015, p. 174). These funding restrictions have resulted in community colleges looking for alternate revenue sources and actively recruiting out-of-state and non-resident students. As a result of these changes, many community colleges have broadened their reach and perspective beyond the physical boundaries of their local communities to prepare a progressively more diverse student body for an increasingly interdependent and globalized 21st century job market.

A recent review of the mission statements of all California community colleges conducted by the authors revealed that while many colleges engage in internationalization efforts, only few community colleges explicitly reference internationalization in their institutional mission statements. Of the 114 California community colleges, which represent the largest system of higher education in the U.S. (California Community Colleges Chancellor's Office, 2018), 71 colleges explicitly recognize the diversity of their student population and/or reference the importance of embracing diversity. Thirty colleges reference the importance of promoting global awareness and of preparing students to become engaged members of the global community. Eighteen colleges state the importance of promoting cultural awareness, vitality, or growth. Twenty-three community colleges do not include any reference to diversity, cultural awareness, or global perspectives within their mission statements. Only three community colleges specifically mention serving international students as core to their institutional missions, and none specifically include reference to education abroad or other types of international engagement. Likewise, while the majority of California community colleges promote diversity and inclusion, only a few institutions specifically reference international education or education abroad in their mission statements.

Student Learning and Development

The organization's mission, goals and operations prioritize student learning and development.

- *Educational objectives remain central to program design and management.*
- *Regular evaluations are conducted to assess student learning and development.*
- *Organizations seek to create and maintain continuity with student learning and development on the home campus* (The Forum on Education Abroad, 2015, p. 4).

Applying best practices in this standard area results in programs that align not only with the academic objectives of a specific course, but also with the mission of the institution while addressing the international or intercultural learning component. It is important to determine what the intended outcomes are in taking a course abroad. What added elements will benefit students and align with the institutional mission and institutional student learning outcomes? What is the educational "value-added" of going abroad? While learning about another culture is an obvious goal (and an important element of intercultural learning), intercultural competence includes cognitive, affective, and behavioral elements (Bennett, 2012). Current research indicates that intentional facilitation of the students' intercultural experience is the best predictor of positive impact (Bennett, 2012; Engle & Engle, 2004; Hemming Lou & Weber Bosley, 2012; Paige & Vande Berg, 2012). Thus, a balance must be achieved between the course being "a kind of tourism" and students being "over-programmed" (Swart & Spaeth, 2017, p. 103).

Establishing measurable learning outcomes is equally important. While it is too vast of a topic to address here, a process to assess academic objectives in education abroad should be a feature of every institution's plan for success. While existing courses that are offered abroad have established learning outcomes (since they are part of the state-approved curriculum), determining how intercultural learning will be incorporated into the coursework is a primary consideration. Faculty who familiarize themselves with the intercultural theories and developmental models will know that allowing time for reflection and promoting discussion help incorporate the affective learning domain (Peifer & Meyer-Lee, 2017). Learning appropriate behaviors abroad is one element of intercultural sensitivity; research also points to the impact study abroad can have on students' behavior upon returning home and throughout their lifetime. Recent research points to study abroad alumni who report that the study abroad experience impacted their friendships, career paths, civic involvement and philanthropy (Engberg & Fox, 2011; Paige, Fry, Stallman, Josić, & Jon, 2009).

Faculty and staff development with regard to intercultural learning is another important aspect of education abroad. Resources on intercultural development may exist within the institution's own faculty. Additionally, numerous resources are available in the form of student workbooks and curricula, faculty conferences, and trainers (White, 2007). See resources such as "Maximizing Study Abroad" (Center for Advanced Language Acquisition, 2017), the Workshop on Intercultural Skills Enhancement (Wake Forest University, 2017), the Summer Institute for Intercultural Communication (ICI, 2018), and the websites "What's Up with Culture" (University of the Pacific, 2017) and "Global Scholars" (Center for Global Education, 2017).

While not necessarily unique to two-year institutions, many faculty-led programs are specific to majors that are highly sequenced and must accommodate certification requirements (e.g., Nursing). Without a large set of common or core requirements across majors, some programs may be best for or only suited for a particular target group of students. Rather than focusing on traditional areas of study abroad, such as languages or art history, programs may focus on the practices of specific sectors (e.g., social service agencies or financial markets) or specialized topics (e.g., topics pertaining to health, sciences, immigration, social justice, or the environment). This means that customized, faculty-led courses must facilitate connections with leaders, organizations, and businesses to add relevant in-country 'content'.

Good Practices and Program Standards

Another best practice is to provide for a continuation of the international learning experience once students have returned to campus. Having students share their learning in campus forums, publications, or events helps disseminate knowledge and build awareness of other cultures and global issues while also generating interest in study abroad. Since community college students tend to be more transient and frequently study abroad in their final year or semester of studies, programming for returned students should be offered in different modalities and be accessible to all program participants. Helping returned students undergo a self-reflection about the experience (to give meaning to what they saw and did) also contributes to holistic learning. Given that there should be prime opportunity for students to demonstrate a number of transferable skills while abroad (e.g., flexibility, adaptability, open-mindedness, problem-solving), helping students learn to identify and articulate these skills helps students in recognizing their own employability. One common characteristic of community colleges is the diversity of the student population – including a range of ages or developmental life stages. Education abroad programming should encompass this spectrum and consider special needs of non-traditional students.

Looking to faculty who have taught abroad as a resource or mentor for those less experienced is another best practice. Faculty who have international experience are a rich resource for the institution. They are typically around much longer than students who return from abroad and who typically graduate shortly after their return. Successful practices include faculty director mentorship or buddy systems, pairing first-time directors with experienced directors, or having experienced directors participate in prospective director training workshops. Engaging experienced faculty in advisory roles on committees to steer the vision and implementation of continued education abroad programming is also key to the sustainability and viability of the program.

Academic Framework

The organization delivers academic content appropriate to its stated mission and goals, ensures adequate academic supervision and evaluation, and maintains clear and transparent academic policies.

- *Curriculum supports the program's stated goals and leverages the unique learning opportunities offered by the host context.*
- *Students' academic work is adequately supervised and fairly evaluated by faculty with appropriate training and credentials.*
- *The organization's policies and procedures related to evaluation, awarding of credit, grade appeals, research ethics, and academic integrity are clear and accessible* (The Forum on Education Abroad, 2015, p. 5).

There are several academic planning considerations, which must be weighed when planning, developing and coordinating community college education abroad programs. These considerations pertain to curriculum design, faculty selection and evaluation, program development and assessment, compliance with state regulations and reporting requirements, accommodations for students with special needs, and adherence to established academic standards. Questions to consider include how to identify academic disciplines and specific courses that lend themselves to be offered in the particular host environment; how to identify qualified faculty to teach the courses; and how to adapt the curriculum to take advantage of the unique learning opportunities offered by the host country while adhering to the state-approved course of study outlines? While some of these issues are not unique to community college programs, there are others that deserve special consideration within the framework of community college education abroad programming.

Community colleges are based on the premise of providing open access. Therefore, any courses offered abroad must also be available on campus to ensure access to all students, regardless of whether students study at their home campus or whether they participate in an education abroad program. This requires faculty who teach abroad to adapt existing courses to take advantage of the host environment and to accommodate a frequently condensed class schedule while ensuring that the approved course content is covered and that academic standards are met. To attract a broad pool of applicants, highly transferable courses should be identified, which appeal to a large audience of students from different fields of study and which do not carry enrollment limitations. At the same time, alternate course credit may need to be offered to students who have already completed the course(s) to be offered abroad. Another primary concern is to maintain the academic rigor of the courses taught abroad while adapting the course curriculum to the particular host environment and program setting. Since the majority of community college education abroad programs are short-term programs, courses offered abroad are likely to be taught in a shortened or condensed format. This can be accommodated either by holding pre-departure or post-return classes on the home campus to account for part of the required instruction hours, by frontloading assignments, or by offering courses in a hybrid format, enabling students to complete the courses online either prior to their departure or upon their return.

If local adjunct faculty are hired to teach some or all of the courses to be offered abroad, additional questions arise pertaining to minimum qualifications and hiring requirements. The hiring practices for hiring local adjunct faculty must be aligned with hiring policies and processes at the home campus and must adhere to state and federal hiring regulations. Clear policies and processes on how to screen overseas adjunct faculty, if and how to evaluate international degrees to determine minimum qualifications, how to handle required faculty health and background checks, and how to pay and hire local adjunct faculty must be developed in collaboration with human resources, legal counsel, faculty and administrators, and the program service provider. Additionally, local adjunct faculty should be thoroughly trained on course requirements, grading and attendance policies, student learning outcomes reporting requirements, accommodations for students with disabilities, and course assessment to ensure that the institutional academic standards are met abroad.

Student Selection, Preparation, and Advising

The organization maintains fair and ethical recruitment and selection processes, adequate student preparation and advising, and ongoing student support.

- *Recruitment and selection processes are fair, ethical, and transparent.*
- *Students are adequately prepared for the challenges of the education abroad context, with pre-departure training and on-site orientation that equips them to achieve academic success and broader program goals; anticipates personal, health or safety issues that might arise; and where appropriate, re-entry measures that prepare them for their return.*
- *The organization offers students pre-departure and on-site academic advising, ensures placement in appropriate course and language levels, encourages academic planning and integration of coursework abroad and at the home campus, and integrates career and professional planning where possible and appropriate* (The Forum on Education Abroad, 2015, p. 6).

Good Practices and Program Standards

The process of sufficiently enrolling a study abroad program can be a challenge for many community colleges. Obviously, students most likely to participate in the course are targeted, but many community colleges find it builds interest and momentum to promote all of the upcoming study abroad programs in a unified fashion (i.e. on a single website with the same/similar promotional periods for the same term and the same enrollment deadlines). Best practices entail offering an academic description, stating the academic requirements, the program cost (what is included and an estimate for what is not), application processes and deadlines, and any information regarding unique physical demands of the program. Community colleges often have multiple campus sites and students who are learning online. To accommodate all students, a plan must be in place to coordinate a thorough and equitable application and approval process. If selection interviews will take place, the access and format must be established and consistently implemented. Additionally, accommodations should be made for students who are not physically on campus, such as conducting online interviews.

While community colleges are generally open-access institutions providing access to all students who can benefit from instruction, special requirements may apply for study abroad program participants. In addition to setting academic requirements (such as minimum GPA or specific course/program prerequisites), other criteria may also be considered in the screening process. For instance, many campuses routinely review student conduct records to confirm eligibility. Another decision that community colleges frequently face is whether to allow non-enrolled "guests" to participate in study abroad programs, such as family members of enrolled students or community members who do not enroll in the academic courses offered abroad. Potential implications of this decision should be very carefully considered, including the institution's exposure to added liability risks. Another potential risk of allowing non-students to participate is for the program to be regarded as a "trip" rather than as a rigorous academic program. If non-enrolled students are allowed to participate, written policies and waivers should be provided outlining expectations for non-enrolled students and emphasizing that all behavioral rules apply to all participants.

Thorough pre-departure advising, including a required orientation, is critically important to prepare students for their experience abroad. If there are staff members dedicated to international programming, they may be able to take the lead; yet staff from student affairs and health services should also be willing to present relevant information at a pre-departure orientation (e.g., behavioral expectations or cross-cultural awareness; preventative health measures, including any recommended or required immunizations; student conduct; and health and safety advisories). Different offices on campus must work in unison with the study abroad staff and/or faculty directors to ensure that students are properly prepared (See resources on the websites of NAFSA: Association of International Educators and The Forum on Education Abroad). Some institutions offer the orientation either face-to-face, in an online live webinar format, or in an asynchronous format, allowing students to watch the recording on their own schedule.

Student Code of Conduct and Disciplinary Measures: The Organization Articulates Clear and Accessible Guidelines for Student Behavior and Consequences Resulting From Violations

- *Expectations for student conduct are provided to students both prior to departure and on-site, with clearly articulated policies regarding drug and alcohol use, culturally-appropriate behavior, sexual harassment or assault, rules related to travel and housing, and any other policies that would carry disciplinary sanctions if violated.*

- *Sanctions for the violation of policies governing student conduct are clearly defined and shared with students prior to departure and on-site.*
- *An appeal process for disciplinary measures exists and is accessible to students* (The Forum on Education Abroad, 2015, p. 7)

Community colleges tend to rely heavily on faculty to develop, plan and coordinate education abroad programs, frequently without the support of a centralized study abroad office. Whether a designated education abroad office is in place or whether education abroad programs are planned, coordinated, and led by reassigned faculty, clearly defined student conduct policies and procedures must be developed in close collaboration with the institution's student conduct and discipline officials, administrators, and legal counsel prior to offering education abroad programs.

To minimize disciplinary issues abroad, a transparent screening process for determining students' eligibility to study abroad should be established, which includes the review of students' disciplinary records. As part of this process, colleges should determine which types of violations may be allowable (such as minor conduct violations, including noise or curfew violations), which may require further action (such as accepting students on a probationary contract), and which may result in the denial of the applicant. By identifying students with prior conduct violations early on at the time of application, colleges can take a proactive approach to supporting at-risk students and to limiting potential liability risks for the institution (Hulstrand, 2013).

While most of the institution's student conduct policies, which govern student conduct on campus, are likely to apply to education abroad programs, supplemental study abroad student conduct policies may need to be developed to address unique issues pertaining to education abroad programs. Special consideration should be given to developing clear and consistent policies and sanctions pertaining to usage of alcohol and controlled substances, academic expectations including attendance and participation requirements, as well as a study abroad code of conduct, outlining how students are expected to conduct themselves abroad and emphasizing their ambassadorial role abroad. In addition to the institutional policies and procedures governing student conduct abroad, third party program providers, overseas housing providers, and study centers are likely to have their own conduct rules, sanctions, and procedures. These rules and procedures have to be thoroughly researched and clearly communicated to students and accompanying faculty.

Once the conduct policies have been developed, a protocol should be established on how to handle student discipline abroad. Working closely with the college's student discipline officials and the appropriate faculty and administrators, it should be determined which types of disciplinary issues should be handled by the accompanying faculty or the overseas study center and at which point the institution's discipline official should be involved. The availability of video conferencing software greatly facilitates close collaboration between the overseas staff and the home institution. Video conferencing enables home campus discipline officials to remotely conduct hearings and adjudicate disciplinary cases, thereby relieving the accompanying faculty or overseas center staff of this responsibility and ensuring adherence to established processes.

Faculty program directors must have a clear understanding of their role in monitoring student conduct and enforcing college regulations while abroad and be properly trained on student conduct expectations, student disciplinary procedures, local laws, as well as Title IX and Clery Act reporting requirements. Additionally, clear channels of communication between the respective offices at the home campus, the service provider, the overseas study center, and the faculty director should be established as part of the program development process to facilitate effective communication. If problems arise, the appropriate offices on campus should maintain close communication with overseas faculty to ensure a seamless collaboration with the home institution.

Student conduct expectations, policies, appeal processes, and potential sanctions must be clearly communicated to students, both in writing as well as during the pre-departure and arrival orientations. At the time of application, students should be advised that their student conduct record will be reviewed to determine their eligibility to study abroad. Upon acceptance into the program, students should be provided with written copies of the institution's general student conduct policies as well as policies and disciplinary procedures that are specific to study abroad. The pre-departure orientation provides another opportunity to review these policies in more depth within a broader discussion about health, safety, and cultural development.

Policies and Procedures

The organization has well defined and clearly articulated policies and procedures that govern its programs and practices, ensures that they are fairly and consistently implemented, and conducts regular reviews to assess their effectiveness.

- *The organization has transparent and accessible policies that govern student affairs and student finances.*
- *The organization has transparent and accessible employment policies regarding staff and faculty.*
- *The organization has guidelines governing its marketing practices, partnerships, and institutional relations* (The Forum on Education Abroad, 2015, p. 8).

Considering the fact that very few two-year institutions have a centralized office that is responsible for international programming, the goal for community colleges may best be stated as having standardized policies and procedures. Woody Pelton points to "distinct advantages of a model that is at least semi-centralized" (Pelton, 2017, p. 49), ensuring consistency across programs and addressing risk and liability factors. Either way, institutional policies and procedures should be established and vetted in consultation with the appropriate stakeholders and disseminated in writing, especially if individual faculty take on the program planning on their own.

When developing policies and processes for education abroad programming, some items to consider include how to establish a formalized process for program provider selection and evaluation; how to determine appropriate program length, housing options and necessary onsite support services; which program components to customarily include; which costs to absorb as an institution and which to pass on to students; how to protect the institution financially and to minimize potential liability risks; and how to identify and avoid potential conflicts of interest.

As part of the academic program approval and development process, an established formula should be utilized to determine required contact hours, baseline academic requirements for the institution, and how teaching abroad is counted towards the faculty course load. Similarly, policies should be developed on and how faculty are compensated for travel expenses (most commonly, faculty travel expenses are built into the student program fees). Frequently, district or state requirements will dictate whether a per diem is to be awarded or a cost reimbursement for meals is to be awarded. District or state policies may need to be considered in the development of institutional policies and processes pertaining to the financial program management. If colleges decide to work directly with overseas host institutions (without the assistance of a U.S. program provider), fiscal program management can be complicated due to the need to pay a multitude of different vendors in a foreign currency and to monitor the fulfillment of multiple contractual agreements.

In facilitating program payments, student application deposits and program payments should be managed either by the institution's fiscal services or the program provider rather than shifting this responsibility to the accompanying faculty. Similarly, faculty should be discouraged from using their own personal credit card to secure flights or to pay for other program services.

International programming is unique in that it often requires adjustments to established campus processes. For instance, term start and end dates may be different for the overseas course, the fee structure may be different for courses taught abroad, registration/enrollment processes may differ from regular enrollment processes, and thorough student preparation is necessary before stepping on the plane. Coordinating successful education abroad programs "takes a campus" requiring proactive and dedicated support and active engagement from many different departments on campus (Paige et al., 2009). A directive from high-level administration with fair and adequate assignment of responsibilities across all of the offices involved will help ensure the success of the program by maintaining academic integrity, proper fiscal management, and risk reduction.

Organizational and Program Resources: The Organization Ensures That Its Programs Are Adequately Funded and Staffed

- *Faculty and staff are qualified for their roles, fairly compensated, and appropriately trained, with workloads that enable them to support the educational goals of the program and devote sufficient time to their students.*
- *Programs are funded at levels that ensure safe, clean, and hospitable student housing; co- or extra-curricular activities that support the program's educational aims, and responsible health, safety, and security measures.*
- *Facilities and infrastructure are suited to realizing the goals of the program, providing a safe environment that is conducive to learning, and accommodating students of varying needs and abilities* (The Forum on Education Abroad, 2015, p. 9).

Due to significant enrollment and funding declines experienced by most community colleges throughout the recent past, community college education abroad programs are frequently operated on a shoestring budget and human and financial resources tend to be scarce. These financial and human resource limitations present unique challenges for community colleges having to operate with minimal resources while trying to provide the necessary resources, infrastructure, and training to ensure the safety and wellbeing of program participants.

Program affordability is of primary concern for community colleges, which typically serve large populations of economically disadvantaged and traditionally underrepresented students. Many private and 4-year institutions include programmatic and operational expenses in the student program fees, thereby shifting much of the financial responsibility to students. Community colleges, on the other hand, must make every possible effort to offer low-cost education abroad programs to facilitate and encourage participation of economically disadvantaged students. This ethical and social mandate frequently requires community college education abroad programs to explore alternative funding sources.

Good Practices and Program Standards

For those community colleges, which do not have a designated education abroad budget, important steps towards developing a sustainable education abroad budget include working with stakeholders across campus to closely align the program's goals with the strategic goals of the institution, establishing an education abroad cost center, and aligning education abroad resource requests with institutional funding resource request cycles and processes, such as the annual program review. Additionally, close collaboration with financial aid, cashiers, extended opportunities programs and services, student equity, and the institution's development office helps bolster institutional support and ensures that current processes are reviewed and streamlined to remove potential barriers to access to study abroad. Similarly, partnerships with local community organizations are often instrumental to securing external funding and providing financial assistance to students who would otherwise not be able to participate. The program budget should include funding for faculty support, professional development and training, student advising and orientation programming, operational and ancillary expenses, as well as a provision to build up reserve funds to be used for scholarships and unexpected emergencies and contingencies.

To ensure the long-term viability of the program, faculty and staff must be fairly compensated for their involvement in education abroad. Faculty director responsibilities prior, during, and after the program's return should be clearly defined and communicated. These responsibilities may include recruiting students, screening potential program participants, providing oversight for the academic component of the program, assisting students in case of emergencies, administering the program budget, and overseeing the onsite implementation of the contractual agreement with the program provider or host institution. The faculty directors' teaching load and compensation should take into account all the additional responsibilities overseas faculty directors have to assume in addition to their regular teaching load.

Providing faculty directors and education abroad staff with training and professional development opportunities is particularly important at community colleges where education abroad faculty and staff may be required to "wear many different hats" and to assume responsibilities, which are outside their primary area of expertise. International education conferences, regional education abroad consortium workshops, and online webinars all provide opportunities to stay current on developments in the field, to learn about best practices, and to exchange information and ideas with colleagues in the field.

Whether community colleges choose to work with a U.S. program provider or to partner directly with an overseas school or university, clear criteria and standards ought to be established for the selection of program providers and/or overseas host institutions. Factors to be considered include the availability of onsite support services, housing options, transportation and logistical support services, safety protocols, emergency preparedness, and insurance coverage. Program providers and overseas host institutions must be thoroughly vetted and regularly evaluated. For new program providers, reference checks from colleagues at other institutions may provide valuable insight. Site visits provide an opportunity to inspect housing and teaching facilities, to meet onsite staff, and to ensure that the services provided by the program provider meet the quality standards of the institution. A site visit checklist and a written site visit report are helpful in ensuring that all programmatic aspects are systematically reviewed.

Health, Safety, Security, and Risk Management

The organization prioritizes the health, safety and security of its students through policies, procedures, advising, orientation and training.

- *The organization prioritizes health, safety, and security in program development, implementation, and management, conducting appropriate risk assessments for program sites and activities, maintaining written emergency plans and protocols, and identifying and leveraging relevant authorities, networks and resources.*
- *Staff are trained to anticipate and respond responsibly to student health, safety, or security issues; students are trained to responsibly manage their own health, safety, and security while abroad; and measures are in place for ongoing monitoring of and advising on health, safety, and security issues through a range of U.S. Department of State and other appropriate resources.*
- *The organization maintains appropriate kinds of insurance at recommended levels, operates in compliance with local laws, and follows best practices in reporting on critical incidents* (The Forum on Education Abroad, 2015, p. 10).

This standard is heavy with responsibility and cannot be managed by a single faculty member, or by even a large number of faculty, without involvement from other entities on campus. Best practices (and likely legal counsel) require institutions to have carefully reviewed policies and practices for all stages of education abroad programming in order to ensure students' health and safety. Some important steps include:

- Identifying and securing an insurance policy required for all programs abroad (with specific coverage approved by legal counsel). Many program providers include emergency health and travel insurance in the program package while others may require students to show proof of insurance. A number of student travel insurance companies can make enrollment relatively swift and provide coverage at a reasonable cost to include medical, repatriation and evacuation, as well as trip cancellation coverage.
- Establishing an institutional policy on whether programs scheduled to a country with a U.S. State Department Travel Warning may proceed. The U.S. State Department issued a revised system of alerts and warnings in December 2017. Best practices call for the establishment of clear and consistent policies on how to respond to each of the four levels of travel advisories. Specifically, these policies should address under which circumstances travel may be allowed to countries of concern, which additional safety precautions to take if a higher-level advisory is in place, and at which level to suspend travel. https://travel.state.gov/content/travel/en/traveladvisories/traveladvisories.html
- Encouraging or requiring program participants to register their information with the *Safe Travelers Enrollment Program* in order to be notified of any events or situations of concern. https://step.state.gov/step/
- Consulting with the office(s) responsible for risk management to review all policies and practices related to international travel to minimize financial and liability risks. Colleges should have defined policies on alcohol use and the use of illegal substances as well as on behavior expectations during non-instruction times. Clearly defined processes must be established on how to communicate these policies to faculty and students as well as on reporting requirements for different types of emergencies.
- Developing a crisis management plan, which requires the involvement of the appropriate offices on campus. It is important to put together a crisis management team, to identify an emergency preparedness plan (to be vetted by legal counsel), to develop emergency protocols, and to identify potential emergencies or events that may raise safety concerns. College officials who manage the

institution's Title IX, Violence Against Women Act (VAWA), and Clery Act compliance must be involved in the establishment of study abroad emergency management and reporting protocols.
- Managing health risks and advising students about potential health and safety risks and precautionary health measures, including managing mental health issues abroad. Institutions must establish consistent policies on whether to require medical clearance or proof of immunization. Additionally, institutions must determine how to advise students on potential health risks and specific program requirements (e.g., immunization requirements, physical requirements, availability of accommodations for students with disabilities).

Ethics

The organization operates its programs in accordance with ethical principles, and trains its staff and students in ethical decision-making and practices:

- *The organization has adopted its own code of ethics or that of The Forum on Education Abroad.*
- *The organization conducts its activities and advises students in an ethically responsible manner; faculty adhere to ethical practices in teaching and student research; and students are sensitized to the ethical implications of their academic work and activities abroad.*
- *The organization promotes respect for the cultures and values of the communities in which it operates* (The Forum on Education Abroad, 2015, p. 11).

The *Code of Ethics for Education Abroad* developed by The Forum on Education Abroad (2011) provides institutions and professionals engaged in education abroad with guidance and direction on ethical principles, which ought to be considered when developing, marketing, and coordinating education abroad programs and engaging with students, faculty, program providers, and overseas host institutions. Another valuable resource is the *Statement of Ethical Principles* developed by NAFSA: Association of International Educators, which can be accessed on the NAFSA website and which is referenced below.

Program administrators and faculty engaged in education abroad have to carefully weigh competing interests, priorities, and responsibilities to ensure that education abroad programs are developed and coordinated with the highest level of transparency, integrity, and responsibility. While the *Code of Ethics* (The Forum on Education Abroad, 2011) is meant to apply universally to all institutions engaged in education abroad, there are some special considerations for community colleges, which primarily center around issues pertaining to access; fiscal, program, and risk management; and the practices previously discussed in this chapter.

Since access, equity, and inclusion are cornerstones of the community college system, community colleges must provide access to education abroad by developing affordable, high-quality education abroad programs and by encouraging and financially assisting traditionally underrepresented students to participate in education abroad. To ensure program affordability, fair, transparent, and competitive processes must be established for selecting program destinations, faculty program directors, and program providers. In selecting program destinations, the availability of low-cost program options ought to be considered as one of the selection criteria. In selecting faculty directors, an impartial selection committee should be appointed, which recommends faculty directors based on a set of established selection criteria. To avoid potential conflicts of interest and to ensure that quality standards are consistently met, policies must be developed pertaining to sustainable and ethical program development and administration;

program provider selection; program pricing; budget development and monitoring; as well as ongoing program assessment and improvement.

This responsibility cannot be shouldered by a few individuals on campus who work in isolation or without the support of the broader campus community. Instead, responsible, ethical, and sustainable education abroad programming requires the explicit support from the institutional leadership and the allocation of financial and human resources to develop the necessary program resources and infrastructure to maintain the quality of the program, to ensure the safety and wellbeing of students, and to maximize the educational benefits of the program.

CONCLUSION

Due to the open-access nature of the community college system and its primary mission of providing low-cost education to a highly diverse student population, there are unique aspects of community colleges to be considered in implementing good practices in faculty-led education abroad. Within the community college system, each institution has unique qualities, requiring community colleges to navigate their own path with good practices guiding their approach to designing and implementing education abroad. The following list serves as a summary of the practices discussed in this chapter, which help ensure the accessibility, integrity, and quality of community college education abroad programs:

- Closely align internationalization strategies and education abroad programming with the institution's mission and broader strategic goals.
- Develop clearly defined and measurable learning outcomes for education abroad programs and incorporate learning opportunities intentionally designed to enhance interpersonal and intercultural competencies to maximize educational benefits.
- Collaborate with faculty to establish guidelines and on how to adapt existing courses to be taught abroad to ensure that established learning outcomes are met while taking advantage of learning opportunities within the host environment.
- Develop transparent and consistent policies for student screening, student conduct, and student discipline and clearly communicate behavioral expectations and potential disciplinary sanctions and appeals processes to students, faculty, and program providers.
- Provide comprehensive, accurate, and proactive education abroad advising and orientation services both before, during, and upon termination of the program.
- Establish selection criteria for program, faculty, and program provider selection and develop consistent processes for continuous program assessment and improvement.
- Clearly outline faculty director responsibilities prior, during, and after the program's return and provide education abroad faculty and staff with the necessary training and resources to safely and responsibly conduct education abroad programs.
- Establish carefully reviewed policies and practices for all stages of education abroad programming in order to ensure students' health and safety.
- Adhere to the ethical principles and standards developed by The Forum on Education Abroad, NAFSA, and other professional organizations, ensuring that education abroad programs are developed and coordinated with the highest level of integrity, transparency, and responsibility.

REFERENCES

Bailey, T. R., Jaggars, S. S., & Jenkins, D. (2015). *Redesigning America's community colleges: A clearer path to student success*. Cambridge, MA: Harvard University Press. doi:10.4159/9780674425934

Bennett, M. J. (2012). Paradigmatic assumptions and a developmental approach to intercultural learning. In *Student Learning Abroad: What our students are learning, what they're not and what we can do about it* (pp. 90–114). Sterling, VA: Stylus.

Bissonnette, B., & Woodin, S. (2013). Building support for internationalization through institutional assessment and leadership engagement. In Resituating the community college in a global context (p. 11-26). San Francisco: Jossey-Bass Publications. Doi:10.1002/cc20045

California Community Colleges Chancellor's Office. (2018). Datamart. *California Community Colleges*. Retrieved from: https://www.cccco.edu/

Center for Advanced Language Acquisition. (2017). *Maximizing Study Abroad*. Retrieved from http://carla.umn.edu/maxsa/

Center for Global Education. (2017). *Global Scholars*. Retrieved from http://www.globalscholar.us/

Council for the Advancement of Standards in Higher Education. (2015). *CAS professional standards for higher education* (9th ed.). Washington, DC: Wells.

Engberg, M. E., & Fox, K. (2011). Exploring the relationship between undergraduate service- learning experiences and global perspective-taking. *Journal of Student Affairs Research and Practice, 48*(1), 85–105. doi:10.2202/1949-6605.6192

Engle, L., & Engle, J. (2003). Study Abroad Levels: Toward a Classification of Program Types 1. *Frontiers: The Interdisciplinary Journal of Study Abroad, 9*(1), 1–20.

Hemming, L. K., & Bosley, W. G. (2012). Facilitating intercultural learning abroad. In M. Vande Berg, R. M. Paige, & K. Hemming Lou (Eds.), *Student Learning Abroad: what our students are learning, what they're not and what we can do about it* (pp. 335–359). Sterling, VA: Stylus.

Hudzik, J. K. (2011). Comprehensive internationalization: From concept to action. Washington, DC: NAFSA: Association of International Educators.

Hudzik, J. K., & McCarthy, J. S. (2012). Leading comprehensive internationalization: Strategies and tactics for action. Washington, DC: NAFSA: Association of International Educators.

Hulstrand, J. (2013). Should they go? Academic and disciplinary considerations for education abroad. *International Educator, 22*(4).

Institute for Intercultural Communication. (2018). *Summer Institute for Intercultural Education*. Retrieved from http://intercultural.org/siic.html

NAFSA. (2018). *Statement of ethical principles*. Retrieved from: http://www.nafsa.org/About_Us/About_NAFSA/Leadership_and_ Governance/NAFSA_s_Statement_of_Ethical_Principles/

Paige, R. M., Fry, G. W., Stallman, E. M., Josić, J., & Jon, J. (2009). Study abroad for global engagement: The long-term impact of mobility experiences. *Intercultural Education, 20*(Supplement 1), S29–S44. doi:10.1080/14675980903370847

Paige, R. M., & Vande Berg, M. (2012). Why students are and are not learning abroad. In M. Vande Berg, R. M. Paige, & K. H. Lou (Eds.), *Student learning abroad: what our students are learning, what they're not* (pp. 29–58). Sterling, VA: Stylus.

Peifer, J., & Meyer-Lee, E. (2017). Program Design for Intercultural Development. In The Guide to Successful Short-Term Programs Abroad (3rd ed.; pp. 157–170). Washington, DC: NAFSA.

Pelton, W. (2017). Administrative Processes. In The Guide to Successful Short-Term Programs Abroad (3rd ed.; pp. 45-63). Washington, DC: NAFSA.

Raby, R. L., & Valeau, E. J. (Eds.). (2016). *International education at community colleges: Themes, practices, and case studies.* New York, NY: Palgrave Macmillan. doi:10.1057/978-1-137-53336-4

Swart, W. J., & Spaeth, C. (2017). Designing the Academic Course: Principles and Practicalities. In The Guide to Successful Short-Term Programs Abroad (3rd ed.; pp. 103-155). Washington, DC: NAFSA.

The Forum on Education Abroad. (2011). *Code of Ethics for Education Abroad* (2nd ed.). Carlisle, PA: The Forum on Education Abroad. Retrieved from: https://forumea.org/resources/standards-of-good-practice/code-of-ethics

The Forum on Education Abroad. (2015). *Standards of Good Practice for Education Abroad* (5th ed.). Carlisle, PA: The Forum on Education Abroad.

The Forum on Education Abroad. (2017a). *Forum History.* Retrieved from https://forumea.org/about-us/mission/history/

The Forum on Education Abroad. (2017b). *Guidelines.* Retrieved from https://forumea.org/resources/standards-of-good-practice/standards-guidelines

University of the Pacific. (2017). *What's Up with Culture?* Retrieved from: http://www2.pacific.edu/sis/culture/

Wake Forest University. (2017). *WISE Conference.* Retrieved December 30, 2017, from http://global.wfu.edu/global-campus/wise-conference/

White, D. (2007). It takes a campus to run a study abroad program. In The Guide to Successful Short-Term Programs Abroad (pp. 29–37). Washington, DC: NAFSA.

ENDNOTE

[1] The authors would like to express their gratitude to Amelia Dietrich, Ph.D., Associate Director for Programs and Resources at The Forum on Education Abroad, for granting permission of the full text of each Standard of Best Practice in this chapter. Document is available from https://forumea.org/resources/standards-of-good-practice

Chapter 4
Community College Education Abroad Health and Safety Concerns:
Standards Needed to Meet the Challenges

Gregory F. Malveaux
Montgomery College, USA

Gary M. Rhodes
California State University Dominguez Hills, USA

Rosalind L. Raby
California State University Northridge, USA

ABSTRACT

There has been a good deal already written about health and safety with education abroad at four-year colleges and universities. Although the authors found significant publications with a university focus, they found no published literature that specifically addresses community college overseas health, safety, and legal issues. The purpose of this chapter is to review what the literature already says about health and safety challenges and apply it to community colleges. In so doing, they bring forth US court cases and real-life examples at community college education abroad programs in order to ground recommendations and strategies for responding to today's challenges. In the same way that community colleges implement "on campus" policies and procedures to both limit and respond to student health and safety crises, community colleges should also implement policies and procedures to limit "study abroad" risks to students and be prepared to act if issues arise overseas. This chapter provides essential strategies to improve health and safety and legal standards for community college education abroad programs.

DOI: 10.4018/978-1-5225-6252-8.ch004

INTRODUCTION

Research confirms broad-ranging positive impacts of education abroad on students (Institute of International Education, 2014). Positive impacts include international learning, personal development, support for retention and success, and enhancing professional and career development (Donohue & Altaf, 2012). We can conclude that this applies to community colleges who also offer study abroad opportunities. Additional benefits include bringing international learning back to the campus upon re-entry, allowing community college students to have institutional residential experiences as a full-time student while abroad, and being fully engaged in education without needing to focus on external responsibilities (Raby & Rhodes, 2018).

Despite the benefits of studying abroad, there are potential negative health, safety, and legal problems. Problems extend to issues with program design, academic learning, housing, and other aspects of program implementation. In our experiences of working with community colleges for more than 30 years, we have seen three ways in which community college administrators respond to health and safety challenges. First, is to fear the potential problems and close down the education abroad program. Second, is to either not know that there are risks or know that there are risks but to choose to not take any actions to protect and support students. Third, is to understand that ignorance of policies and standards is dangerous and that well-planned administrative practices are important to effectively support student health and safety, and to limit potential liability to the institution.

While it is typical for US community colleges to have risk management policies that govern student actions on campus, including issues related to land and property, campus vehicles, student programming, science laboratories, and competitive athletics, the same is not always applied to students who study abroad. While there is vast literature on health and safety and education abroad at four-year institutions, we only found one unpublished manuscript specific to community colleges that outlines a legal framework for California community college education abroad (Henry, 1985; 2006).

The purpose of this chapter is to review what the education abroad literature states about health, safety, and legal challenges and apply it to community colleges. We use United States (US) court cases and real-life examples to ground recommendations, strategies, and standards.

BACKGROUND ON STUDY ABROAD POLICIES AND HOW THEY APPLY TO COMMUNITY COLLEGES

A prevailing belief is that education abroad practices are the same for all institutional types. However, the uniqueness of community colleges mandates some specific modifications. For example, community colleges have low to free tuition which impacts the cost of studying abroad. Open access favors access over selectivity, which impacts who studies abroad and questions program and administrative hidden fee costs. Multiple missions, guided pathway programs, and stackable credentials result in highly sequenced classes that accommodate career and workforce certification, but that can negatively impact who is able to study abroad. Emphasis on performance funding that is linked to student learning outcomes and assessment often ignore contributions made by studying abroad. Minimum qualifications for faculty hiring that adhere to state and federal hiring regulations impact faculty who teach on campus and abroad. Finally, national enrollment and funding declines are challenging community colleges to remain open. In sum, community college study abroad policies must support the safety of program participants, limit liability to the college, and support an administrative office to implement study abroad (Henry, 1985; 2006).

This section reviews policy responses to study abroad health and safety by major professional organizations and merges findings to application in community colleges.

The Interassociational Advisory Committee on Safety and Responsibility in Education Abroad

The Interassociational Advisory Committee on Safety and Responsibility in Education Abroad (formerly the Interorganizational Task Force on Safety and Responsibility in Education Abroad) began as a joint venture of professional organizations and education abroad providers. One outcome was the "Responsible Education Abroad: Good Practices for Health & Safety" (2001).

Because the health and safety of education abroad participants are primary concerns, these statements of good practice have been developed to provide guidance to institutions, participants (including faculty and staff), and parents/ guardians/families. These statements are intended to be aspirational in nature. They address issues that merit attention and thoughtful consideration by everyone involved with education abroad. They are intentionally general; they are not intended to account for all the many variations in education abroad programs and actual health, safety, and security cases that will inevitably occur. In dealing with any specific situation, those responsible must also rely upon their collective experience and judgment while considering their specific circumstances (2001, p. 1).

This policy is applicable to community colleges as it is a checklist to gauge if institutional policies and procedures are at an appropriate level, provides a good overview of what community colleges should take into account, and can serve as a potential tool for plaintiffs' attorneys if something goes wrong.

CAS Standards for Health and Safety With Education Abroad

The Council for the Advancement of Standards (CAS) (2018) promotes intra-campus collaboration and reflects good practices agreed upon by the profession-at-large. Members represent 41 CAS member organizations with over 115,000 professionals in higher education. CAS includes 44 sets of functional area standards to support programs and services, including a set of standards for education abroad that highlights the responsibilities of education abroad program staff to be knowledgeable and competent in the following areas (August 2015, p. 11):

- Cultural competence
- Experiential education
- Legal affairs and risk management
- Intercultural communication
- Culture shock, reverse culture shock, and cultural adjustment
- Student advising and counseling
- Emergency and crisis management
- Budgetary and financial management
- Collaboration with academic stakeholders at home and at host institutions

- Organizational policies (e.g. Admissions, credit transfer, financial aid, travel regulations, immigration policies, and insurance)
- Pre-departure and re-entry issues
- Travel and living abroad
- Higher education administration
- Technology (e.g. Application and data management systems, and virtual communication)
- Country specific health, safety, and security concerns.

This policy is applicable to community colleges as it details generally accepted topics that community college professional staff should also be knowledgeable.

The Forum on Education Abroad Standards of Good Practice

The Forum on Education Abroad, a higher education association, is recognized as a standards development organization (SDO) for education abroad by the US government (Standard 8, Health, Safety, Security, and Risk Management) (Standards of Practice, 2018). There are a number of community colleges that are members of the Forum (Forum on Education Abroad, 2018). The Forum provides recommendations for program development, conducting appropriate risk assessments for program sites and activities, maintaining written emergency plans and protocols, and for identifying and leveraging relevant authorities, networks and resources. In addition, staff are to be trained to anticipate and respond responsibly to student health, safety, or security issues; students are trained to responsibly manage their own health, safety, and security while abroad; and measures are in place for ongoing monitoring of and advising on health, safety, and security issues through a range of US Department of State and other appropriate resources. Finally, the organization maintains appropriate kinds of insurance at recommended levels, operates in compliance with local laws, and follows best practices in reporting on critical incidents.

The chapter in this book by Carola Smith and Ann Hubbard detail the application of the Standards for community colleges. While some community colleges have gone through the professional training based on these standards, most community colleges are still not aware that these standards exist.

SAFETI CLEARINGHOUSE

In the 1990s, there were several highly publicized incidents of death and injury during education abroad, involving both community colleges and universities (Malveaux, 2016). In 1998, the Center for Global Education (currently housed at California State University, Dominquez Hills) built the Safety Abroad First – Educational Travel Information (SAFETI) Clearinghouse (Center for Global Education, 2018c). Professionals from throughout the country helped to build components of the SAFETI Clearinghouse that provides a range of resources, including sample forms and policies, to support the development and implementation of education abroad programs with health and safety issues at the forefront. Community college study abroad professionals also contributed to the development of these resources. Annually, these resources are updated to reflect changing times. Table 1 shows the Globaled on-line tutorials (Center for Global Education, 2018a). These resources are applicable to community colleges as they can be a preventative audit checklist to gauge if current policies are at the appropriate standard of care.

CURRENT ISSUES IMPACTING HEALTH AND SAFETY AT COMMUNITY COLLEGES

There is a recognized need for leaders of education abroad to be well-informed about an ever-changing overseas landscape due to political and economic shifts that create new and ongoing health and safety concerns. Unique applications of these standards for community colleges result from an open access mission, diverse student body, and limited designated and trained staff leading education abroad programs.

Statutory Authority

There is precedent for community colleges to offer education abroad. In California, authority to offer education abroad includes a balance of the Education Code section 66025.7 (state encouragement of community college international programs) with "open access" found in Section 55450 of Title 5 of the California Code of Regulations. Henry (1985; 2006) concludes that this balance takes two forms. First is the need to accommodate the "no exclusion of students to enroll" with transparent links for where students can find financial support. Second is to make all abroad courses are also available on campus as a way to ensure access to all students.

Duty of Care and Age

Aligned with open access mission, education abroad must be in compliance with Title VI and Title IX regulations (Henry, 2006) by accommodating all students, including those with special physical or mental health challenges and seniors who may need special support. Duty of Care is unique for community colleges who have a wide range of student participants.

Minors and Guardian Consent

Community colleges have dual enrollment that allows high school students to concurrently take community college classes (Fink, Davis, & Takeshi, 2017), including study abroad. For minors, there is a responsibility for the college to give in-loco parentis (serving in the place of the parent) care to those students since they are legally minors and their parents are not available. For those under age 18, a separate consent form for guardians to sign or a section in the existing program release/waiver of liability that allows for the guardian to accept the conditions of the program on behalf of their daughter or son is needed. Malveaux (2016, p. 185) shares a sample statement, used in release forms at Montgomery College and other community colleges:

I: (a) am the parent or legal guardian of the above participant/student; (b) have read the foregoing Release (including such parts as may subject me to personal financial responsibility); (c) am and will be legally responsible for the obligations and acts of the student/participant as described in this Release, and (d) agree for myself and for the student/participant to be bound by its terms.

Adult Students

The average age of a community college student is 28 and as such, application of health and safety standards is aligned with adult understanding. There is thus a balance of responsibility that the college acknowledges and the ability of students to act as adult consumers of education abroad where they can comprehend the information provided about potential risks during education abroad and how to manage those risks and respond to them. In addition, adult students should be provided the opportunity to thrive when working through rudimentary language skills, awareness of appropriate behavior, and limited student services that are different than what they would find on the home college campus.

Older Adults

Community colleges accept older adult (50+) students to participate in study abroad programs. Duty of care then includes informing students about the level of the programs' physicality and provisions of optional alternate activity. For example, a Montgomery College Iceland ecological program offered an activity in an underground lava cave that had a multi-mile tunnel requiring a lot of bending and maneuvering along slippery rocks. An alternative activity included an aboveground hike. Alternative activities can reduce the likelihood of participant injury or death and allow students to not miss out on an important itinerary item when an alternate, suitable activity is offered.

Immigrant, Refugee, and DACA Students

Community college open enrollment allows for a diverse array of students to attend the community college and who are eligible to study abroad. This population includes recent immigrants, refugees, and Deferred Action for Children Arrivals (DACA) students. There is a need to counsel these students specific to their individual needs.

International Students

Community colleges enroll a sizable international student population who may also enroll in education abroad programs. Community college program leaders must consider potential issues for international students who study abroad if they are from countries where the US government may make it difficult for them to return after overseas program completion. Even if an international student is not from a travel restricted country, and holds a legal visa, they could still be detained at an airport, or even be blocked from re-entering the US. Program advisors need to be clear about the potential challenges for re-entry into the US for international students who want to study abroad.

Terrorism

Community colleges need to monitor the ongoing issue of terrorism throughout the world. This is especially true for geographic areas that were once considered relatively safe in Western Europe as terrorism was responsible for shootings in Paris at the *Charlie Hebdoe* office in France (2015); bombings at a Jewish museum, the airport, and metro stations in Brussels (2016); and for the use of large vehicles used to run down pedestrians in Nice (2016) and in London (2017) at the Houses of Parliament (United

Kingdom, August 2018). The US State Department issues travel advice that provides guidance about the level of risks found in each country. Like universities, some community colleges will not offer education abroad programs in countries where the US State Department has highlighted specific concerns, while others, examine the travel advice on a case-by-case basis. It is important to give increased caution to students about safety concerns abroad as well as highlight concerns for international students of study abroad—their re-entry to the US may be more challenging due to these issues. Of critical importance for community colleges is that any choice regarding location needs to be approved by the community college Board of Trustees. As such, education of site, of safety, and of levels of risk, needs to be part of a long-range strategy.

Lacking Institutional Support and Professionalization of Study Abroad Leaders

While some community colleges have broad based support, central administrative office, and professional staff, many do not. A lack of professional staff along with coordinated campus-wide efforts increases vulnerability for lawsuits with study abroad offices. It would be oversimplified to just blame administrators for this culture as study abroad faculty and staff also fail to advocate for funding and visibility of education abroad. Moreover, a prevailing belief is that those leading study abroad only need to be passionate and as such support to attend professional conferences where they can develop needed expertise is rarely given (Valeau and Raby, 2016). A contributing factor is the lack of community college professional and associational literature on minimum standards for education abroad that is available to senior community college leadership and Trustees. Without access to literature that supports community college education abroad, senior leadership may make decisions about study abroad without sufficient expertise. The result is limited professional skills related to health, safety, and legal issues of study abroad. To the detriment of community colleges, legal counsel for the plaintiff in lawsuits may compare the level of program and student support to that of a highly-resourced university which often has larger, more permanent education abroad staffing. For example, some universities and non-university provider companies have 10 to 100 full-time employees for implementing study abroad programs with designated staff to oversee health and safety.

Faculty Selection

Community college collective bargaining agreements mandate clear and transparent policies on how faculty are selected to lead a study abroad program and how they are compensated (Henry, 1985; 2006). This extends to local adjunct faculty who may be hired to teach abroad and who must adhere to the minimum qualifications and hiring requirements found on-campus and that adhere to state and federal hiring regulations.

Choosing an Education Abroad Provider

An education abroad provider is not required at community colleges. At the same time, there are issues of conflict of interest in which public employees cannot be financially interested in contracts that they participate in making (Henry, 1985; 2006). Thus, unless leadership know health, safety and legal issues, it is highly recommended that an education abroad provider assist with program offerings. In turn, each provider needs to be carefully vetted as some have staff dedicated to health and safety matters, while others do not. Likewise, not all providers know about community college policies, institutional liability policies, and regulations.

All community colleges need to be aware of contract liability, including contractual relationships with third party vendors for billing disputes and breach of contract (Henry, 1985; 2006). In the mid-1990s, multiple California community colleges experienced the challenge of having a well-respected study abroad provider, who specialized in community colleges, go out of business in the middle of a community college's education abroad program. The impacted college needed to create emergency funds and processes to support the program at the last minute and all other community colleges in the state that used this provider also ended up adding contingency plans for their future programs. In the case of health or safety problems resulting in litigation, both the community college and the provider will probably be defendants in legal action.

POLICIES GROUNDED IN COURT CASES

The following are examples of policies that are grounded in court cases and which community colleges need to be aware of to implement in their program design.

Staffing

Due to limited support, community colleges may attempt to have faculty-led study abroad programs in which only one faculty member accompanies and teaches students. Best practice suggest that at least two faculty and/or a combination of one faculty and one or more staff members (depending on the number of students) accompany to be better able to implement programs and to respond to any health and safety concerns, in particular if one faculty member becomes ill or injured and cannot provide support or a student becomes ill or injured and one faculty or staff member can support the needs of that student while the other can support the rest of the program students.

Case in Point With Fay v. Thiel College

The case of *Fay v. Thiel College* (2001) describes an incident resulting in the injury of an education abroad student when the home campus had no one on site. In this case, the program leaders left a student alone for extended periods, resulting in the contention that if the program leaders were with the student at those times, the health or safety problem would not have taken place. The program was supervised by three faculty members (Fay v. Thiel Coll., 55 Pa. D. & C.4th 353, 354-55 (Com. Pl. 2001)). During the program, the student, Fay, became ill and was admitted at a medical clinic in Cuzco, Peru (Fay v. Thiel Coll., 55 Pa. D. & C.4th 355 (Com. Pl. 2001)). After she was admitted, all staff and the other students left on a prescheduled multi-day trip and left the student alone at the clinic with only a Lutheran missionary to act as Fay's translator (Fay v. Thiel Coll., 55 Pa. D. & C.4th 355 (Com. Pl. 2001)). While at the medical clinic, Fay was subjected to unnecessary surgical removal of her appendix; after the appendectomy was completed, she was sexually assaulted by her surgeon and anesthesiologist (Fay v. Thiel Coll., 55 Pa. D. & C.4th 356 (Com. Pl. 2001)).

The recommendation of having more than one staff member accompany students is a result of this case. Since the student and their parents view programs as "sponsored by the home college or university," the legal action will usually name all possible institutions and individuals in the lawsuit.

Pre-Departure Advising and Orientation Programs

Pre-departure orientation programs provide a background about the realities of study abroad programs, including specific health and safety information and enable students to better avoid and manage study abroad risks and liabilities. These programs must provide adequate details so that the student's experience abroad matches the information provided prior to departure (Henry, 2006) including academic credit and transfer policies, visa and passport requirements, housing and travel arrangements, and academic program information (Malveaux, 2016). The Jeanne Clery Disclosure of Campus Security Policy and Campus Crime Statistics Act (The Clery Act) requires that study abroad program collect and disseminate specific health and safety data connected to crime and safety statistics, including off-campus programs like study abroad when community colleges own or control aspects of program implementation. Some US States also have specific laws requiring special processes for implementing study abroad programs.

It is critical to note that neither a release of liability/hold harmless form nor a claim that community colleges have fewer resources will hold up in court if there were litigation after a problematic health and safety event. It is therefore important to have written materials which clarify the relationship or lack of relationship between the college and their education abroad options as well as potential risks to students associated with programs abroad, limitations in resources abroad, and ways for students to respond to those risks.

Case in Point With Bloss v. The University of Minnesota Board of Regents

Bloss v. The University of Minnesota Board of Regents illustrates why the courts recognize pre-departure orientation as a best practice for education abroad. A student in the University of Minnesota's cultural immersion program in Cuernavaca, Mexico, alleges that while traveling to meet friends for a social evening she was raped at knifepoint by a taxi driver (Bloss v. Univ. of Minn. Bd. of Regents, 590 N.W.2d 661, 662 (Minn. Ct. App. 1999)). The student, Bloss, sued the University of Minnesota for negligence due to failure to secure housing closer to the Cemanahuac campus, imprudence in not providing transportation to and from the campus, and inattention to impart warnings about various serious risks including the use of taxicabs in Cuernavaca (Bloss v. Univ. of Minn. Bd. of Regents, 590 N.W.2d 663 (Minn. Ct. App. 1999)). A favorable court decision was awarded to the university due in large part to having provided orientation materials about proper standards of conduct expected of participants who partake in the program (Bloss v. Univ. of Minn. Bd. of Regents, 590 N.W.2d 666 (Minn. Ct. App. 1999)). The materials gave warning about dangerous conduct for the region (Bloss v. Univ. of Minn. Bd. of Regents, 590 N.W.2d 666 (Minn. Ct. App. 1999)). The warnings included specific admonitions that it was dangerous for women to go out alone at night, [they] should call for a taxi at night rather than hail a taxi on the street, and that women should never sit in the front seat of taxis (Bloss v. Univ. of Minn. Bd. of Regents, 590 N.W.2d 666 (Minn. Ct. App. 1999)). These warnings specifically addressed the circumstances under which the student sustained her injuries (Bloss v. Univ. of Minn. Bd. of Regents, 590 N.W.2d 666 (Minn. Ct. App. 1999)).

This case confirms the importance of providing pre-departure orientation information to aid student conduct to remain healthy and safe during study abroad, and providing guidance that students need to be active in supporting their safety, while also limiting institutional liability.

Disclosure of Student Health Information

Pre-study abroad orientation should include requests for students to share information about any on-going physical and mental health support needs before their departure. This is often an area that is neglected because many community colleges have limited staffing and limited knowledge of study abroad best practices.

Case in Point With Furrh v. Arizona Board of Regents

Furrh v. Arizona Board of Regents is an example of a case which reveals that unexpected dangers can arise when an overseas program participant fails to disclose essential medical background details. A Court of Appeals of Arizona related that a University of Arizona student, who had chronic mental disorders, needed to be physically restrained while on a study abroad program in the Baja peninsula, Mexico (676 P.2 1142-43 (Ariz. Ct. App. 1983)). After finishing the program, Furrh sued the university, claiming that program leaders unlawfully restrained him, assaulted him, and caused him to become lost and unprotected to [dangerous] elements in Mexico (676 P.2 1142 (Ariz. Ct. App. 1983)). The trial court judged in favor of the defendants, or the university (676 P.2 1142 (Ariz. Ct. App. 1983)), and then the higher Court of Appeals affirmed the trial court ruling (676 P.2 1146 (Ariz. Ct. App. 1983)). Two of the program leaders were unaware of Furrh's chronic mental and emotional disorder, or the fact that he had been under the care of a psychiatrist for several years (676 P.2 1141 (Ariz. Ct. App. 1983)). This mental illness was exacerbated by the experience of the program to the point where Furrh was a threat to the safety of himself and other members of the group (676 P.2 1142 (Ariz. Ct. App. 1983)). Malveaux (2016) discusses that without full disclosure of a student's health risks, major issues can arise while overseas. The challenge of addressing an undisclosed medical issue overseas makes it more difficult to effectively respond to support the program and its participants. It is critical that any information that is disclosed is evaluated and responded to effectively by the college and any partners abroad.

Prescription Medication

An increasing number of students in US higher education are taking medications for physical issues, mental health issues, and to enhance their ability to succeed as college students. Rhodes, DeRomana, & Pedone (2018) highlight the importance of planning to have necessary medications and ensure that the medications that are legal in the United States may not be legal or available abroad. This includes leadership to inform students to check with their health care provider, their insurance or emergency assistance provider, a US embassy or consulate in the host country, and/or the International Narcotics Control Board (https://www.incb.org) regarding the legality of their prescription medications. In addition, students need to be advised to discuss with their health care providers whether some medications should be changed and to allow sufficient time to make adjustments before departure as students should avoid switching medications immediately before departure. Students must travel with a signed prescription for all medications. The prescription must indicate the name of the student, the name of the medication (both brand name and generic), the dosage and quantity prescribed, and be translated into the language of the country where the student will study. The student should also have a letter from the US treating physician explaining the recommended dosage, the student's diagnosis, and the treatment. This is especially important for controlled substances and injectable medications. Translations of these documents to the host country language may be helpful. It is a good idea to leave copies of prescriptions with a family member or friend at home. In most countries, arriving with quantities exceeding those prescribed for personal use is prohibited. Students should pack all medications in the original, labeled containers in their carry-on baggage.

Students With Special Needs and Disabilities

When a student discloses special physical or mental health information, leadership need to effectively determine the limitations that the program presents for these students. For community colleges, this needs to be conducted within the open access framework and in compliance with ADA/Section 504 (Henry, 2006). Requesting and obtaining that information provides the concept to students and their parents that the college will be taking the next step of finding out in advance what approaches will be necessary to support those special needs. It is important to work with appropriate staff on campus to determine whether reasonable accommodations can be made to support healthy, safe, and productive participation in the program by a student. At the same time, collaborations with the community college legal office needs to result in policies in which appropriate care is not available abroad and students should be advised to not study abroad. For instance, if a student needed dialysis and a program in a rural location did not have dialysis support, serious health problems will result. It may be better to defend a legal action for not allowing the student to participate in that study abroad program than to defend a legal action resulting from the illness or death of the student. An effective institutional response could include providing the student with other study abroad options where adequate support was available. There are privacy protections that raise concerns about obtaining and sharing information including Family Educational Rights and Privacy Act of 1974 (FERPA), Health Insurance Portability and Accountability Act of 1996 (HIPAA), and some countries have their own privacy regulations.

Case in Point With Bird v. Lewis & Clark College

The lawsuit *Bird v. Lewis & Clark College* claimed that Lewis & Clark College officials were in violation of ADA and Title III of the Rehabilitation Act for an undergraduate student who used a wheelchair to participate in Lewis & Clark College's study abroad program in Australia (303 F.3d 1017 (9th Cir. 2002)). The student felt that college officials were not as transparent as they could be with disclosing limited accommodations which included a need for her to be carried from the bathroom to her bedroom, as well as up a flight of stairs to get to the cafeteria (303 F.3d 1017-18 (9th Cir. 2002)). The college was sued for being in violation of Section 504 and ADA, negligent misrepresentation, and other issues (303 F.3d 1019 (9th Cir. 2002)). All of the claims share a similar premise that the College discriminated against her on the basis of disability by failing to provide wheelchair access (303 F.3d 1019 (9th Cir. 2002)).

There are some resources to serve students with disabilities who desire overseas study found at www.abilityinfo.com, www.disabledtravelers.com/airlines.htm, *emerginghorizons.com*, www.miusa.org *(Mobility International)*. If the college makes a claim that they are taking those steps but fail to do so, a plaintiff's attorney could contend that was an act of negligence by the college (if it could be connected to an accident or injury impacting the student).

Code of Conduct

Home college and host institution codes of conduct that apply to students while abroad must be clearly articulated and consequences of not following conduct codes must be clearly defined and communicated. This includes including guidance to students about appropriate behavior during study abroad and defining prior to leaving, who has authority to impose discipline and hear appeals (Henry, 1985; 2006).

Case in Point: Court Cases

One example is *King v. Board of Control of Eastern Michigan University* in which a program leader disregarded his college's policy for proper codes of conduct and allowed male students to also disregard the school's set policies, creating a hostile environment in South Africa. The faculty supervisor allowed male students to sexually harass female students without censure (King v. Bd. of Control of E. Mich. Univ., 221 F.Supp.2d 783, 786 (E.D. Mich. 2002)). In consequence, the court directly pointed out where the university's policies and code of conduct were not followed (King v. Bd. of Control of E. Mich. Univ., 221 F.Supp.2d 790-91 (E.D. Mich. 2002)). The university has a set campus policy that allows students a secure instructional environment; when this code is violated, faculty instructors are supposed to diffuse the disruption (King v. Bd. of Control of E. Mich. Univ., 221 F.Supp.2d 791 (E.D. Mich. 2002)). The court supported that the faculty supervisor was in violation of the university's set policy, and as an agent working on behalf of the university, the university was also in violation of its own set policies (King v. Bd. of Control of E. Mich. Univ., 221 F.Supp.2d 791 (E.D. Mich. 2002)). The coordinator put future programs and their institution at risk by not following the institutional policy and codes of conduct while abroad. The policies and code of conduct that were outlined in institutional handbooks, mission statements, and other educational materials should have been followed.

Courts concur home and host institution codes of conduct should be clearly stated. Some colleges have students sign a Code of Conduct or Conditions of Participation Form as a part of the application process. Study Abroad Coordinators should confer with student affairs professionals, risk managers and campus legal counsel to see if the document is a compatible fit with their own institutional policies. Institutions should consider that removing students from a study abroad program based on health and safety concerns may need to be immediate and should inform students that this would require less due process than removing them from a degree program on the home college campus.

Risk Assessment for Program Site Accommodations and Activities

Risk assessment of program accommodations and activities need to be regularly conduced. Pasadena Community College and Duke University learned this lesson in the form of lawsuits.

Case in Point With Paneno v. Centres

Paneno v. Centres reveals the sad fact that overseas injuries are a major concern due to potential challenges with accommodations provided to students, leading to merited lawsuits. Challenges with the housing provided by the program led to the critical injury of student Rocky Paneno (Paneno v. Centres for Acad. Programmes Abroad, Ltd., 13 Cal. Rptr. 3d 759, 762-63 ((Cal. Ct. App. 2004)). Paneno was on the balcony of housing provided by Centres for Academic Programmes Abroad (CAPA), leaned against the railing where a portion of it gave way, and fell six stories resulting in his paralysis; Paneno filed a lawsuit against Pasadena Community College (PCC) and CAPA as a result (Paneno v. Centres for Acad. Programmes Abroad, Ltd., 13 Cal. Rptr. 3d 759, 762-63 ((Cal. Ct. App. 2004)).

Case in Point With Thackurdeen v. Duke University

Thackurdeen v. Duke University underscores the need for institutions to carefully assess risks involved with overseas sites and activities. The case involved the death of a Duke University student on a program through an Organization for Tropical Studies Program (OTS), which was offered in coordination with Duke University, to Costa Rica in 2012 (Complaint at 3, 6, Thackurdeen v. Duke Univ., No. 14-cv-6311 (Aug. 8, 2014 S.D.N.Y.)). The program included a trip to a beach that has been part of its OTS program for three consecutive years (Complaint at 5, Thackurdeen v. Duke Univ., No. 14-cv-6311 (Aug. 8, 2014 S.D.N.Y.)). The students were told that it was safe to swim in the waters and they were given only the following instruction: to swim parallel to the shore if they were caught in a rip current (Complaint at 5, Thackurdeen v. Duke Univ., No. 14-cv-6311 (Aug. 8, 2014 S.D.N.Y.)). One student got caught in a rip current and drowned (Complaint at 6, Thackurdeen v. Duke Univ., No. 14-cv-6311 (Aug. 8, 2014 S.D.N.Y.)). The complaint notes that almost every website or brochure that discussed visiting Playa Tortuga mentioned the dangerously strong rip currents and that swimming at the beach was not advisable (Complaint at 12-13, Thackurdeen v. Duke Univ., No. 14-cv-6311 (Aug. 8, 2014 S.D.N.Y.)). What made Playa Tortuga even more dangerous is that there are no lifeguards on duty at the beach (Complaint at 13, Thackurdeen v. Duke Univ., No. 14-cv-6311 (Aug. 8, 2014 S.D.N.Y.)). This complaint directly highlights concerns for proper risk assessment of a program activity by the institution as well as identifying special health and safety risks associated with each study abroad program.

These cases underscore that coordinators must closely evaluate housing, venues, and activities provided by their foreign partnering agencies prior to including them in the program. This is part of providing a proper duty of care for students and protects all parties from accidents. It may also be helpful to provide students with a checklist of housing and other building safety issues as the same building standards they expect in the US may not be in place abroad. For example, after the 2011 fire in an apartment building in Paris in which four international students died (Four Girls, 2011), the Jasmine Jahanshahi Fire Safety Foundation (http://www.firesafetyfoundation.org) was created to provide information and support for study abroad students to share training and fire safety practices. Finally, community colleges need to question if an abroad activity is being implemented effectively, identify potential health hazards to participants, reduce the potential of those hazards, and prepare to respond to health and safety incidents that take place.

TRAINING COMMUNITY COLLEGE EDUCATION ABROAD PROFESSIONAL STAFF

Having a professional staff who is trained in up to date policies, standards, and legal requirements and that centralizes education abroad efforts is critical. As noted, this does not always occur as funding for professional development is limited, expectations for professionalization are limited, and there is a revolving door of faculty who lead programs without college coordination (Valeau and Raby, 2016). The following details needed skills for community college education abroad staff.

Professionalization

The Council for the Advancement of Standards (CAS) suggests that education abroad professional staff must hold an earned graduate or professional degree in a field relevant to the position they hold or must possess an appropriate combination of educational credentials and related work experience (CAS, 2018, p. 10). This is problematic for community colleges as Valeau and Raby (2016) survey of 91 community college international leaders found that 78% had, as their highest degree, a master's degree, and that only three had taken graduate courses in international education or education abroad. The depth of knowledge needed to support study abroad program development and implementation underscores the importance of professional development (Valeau and Raby, 2016) that is difficult to obtain for only a part-time staff.

Training for Health and Safety Risk Management

Program faculty and staff should be trained to include transparent emergency and crisis management procedures to avoid and respond to potential health and safety challenges so that they can orient students to avoid and respond to health and safety incidents abroad, including Alcohol and Drug Use and Abuse; Crime and Violence; Crisis Management; Kidnapping and Terrorism; Medical/Physical Health Response; Responding to Discrimination Abroad; Responding to Guidance of the US Centers for Disease Control and Prevention Abroad; Responding to Guidance by US Department of State Abroad; Sexual Harassment and Assault; and Supporting Students with Special Needs and Disabilities (Center for Global Education, 2018c). It is also important to provide information related to health and safety challenges in other cities and countries in a balanced context, confirming that these challenges also exist in the US. In some areas (gun violence, alcohol and drug abuse, sexual assault, terrorism, etc.) conditions in the US may be more challenging than those found in international locations.

Training for Pre-Departure Orientation and Re-Entry

Pre-departure orientation programs vary substantially for community colleges that range from a semester-long pre-departure course, a week of sessions, a one-day or half-day session, a required on-line program, or reliance on providers to conduct the orientation on the first day of instruction abroad. Support for training can be found from the University of California Education Abroad Programs (2018) and Center for Global Education (2018b).

Training on Maintaining Regular Updates

The US Department of State's "Smart Traveler Enrollment Program," or STEP (US Department of State, 2018) provides timely updates on health, safety, and security issues. Once registered with STEP, country-specific information, travel alerts and warnings, fact sheets, and emergency messages are current and notifications may come through a smart phone APP, Facebook, or Twitter. In addition, the free service helps with recovering lost or stolen passports, and aids with evacuation of US citizens in emergency situations (US Department of State, 2018).

Training on Legal Issues

CAS Standards Part 6 notes that EAPS must be in compliance with laws, regulations, and policies that relate to their respective responsibilities and that pose legal obligations, limitations, risks, and liabilities for the institution as a whole. Examples include constitutional, statutory, regulatory, case and Tort liability which include personal injury, defamation, invasion of privacy, applying civil rights of student and employee while participating in study abroad, contract of enrollment and promotional materials that takes into consideration consumer rights, and dispute resolutions (Henry, 1985; 2006). The community colleges should obtain the host institution's crisis management plan and to refer students to information on host country laws and host institution policies and procedures. All community college education abroad leadership should have insurance for emergency medical, medical evacuation, repatriation of remains, and security evacuation coverage (General Standards revised in 2011; EAPS content developed in 2005 & 2014, CAS). Finally, the community college should have a policy detailing the consequences of breaking in-country laws and program policies. In California, this includes knowledge of the fundamentals of risk management, defense and California indemnification, and immunity in which "all persons making the abroad program waive all claims against the district or the State for injury, accident, illness, or death occurring during or by reason of the abroad program" (Henry, 2006, p. 5).

Garnering Broad-Based Institutional Support

Each campus should have a centralized office/person in charge of education abroad with broad-based institutional support resulting in permanent study abroad office, professional development, and needed institutional support against a lawsuit. We recommend the NAFSA: Association of International Educators comprehensive internationalization strategies (Hudzik & Mcarthy, 2012).

1. Engage in a campus dialog about comprehensive internationalization.
2. Build an institutional climate of support for comprehensive internationalization.
3. Connect comprehensive internationalization to core institutional missions and values.
4. Expand and extend the leadership team for comprehensive internationalization.
5. Articulate a bold vision and goals.
6. Measure for accountability and reward for success.
7. Recruit for internationalization.
8. Integrate comprehensive internationalization into institutional missions and existing programs as broad based support allows study abroad to become a more indispensable part of the community college's operations.

Registrar

The registrar aids with applying finished overseas course credits to the student's official transcript. The registrar also proves to be a valuable ally with determining alternative designations "special topic," "umbrella," and/or "global perspective"—to issue course credit when there is not an exact match between the home college and overseas institution.

Bursar

Members of the bursar's office should understand how the set-up of the college's data system might play a role in which payment structure works best – whether the travel is considered a "course fee" with the bursar's office, a "program fee," or is paid via another office or mechanism. Also, they will work in conjunction with financial aid on preferences for how and where the funds are applied to student bills and paid, in case a certain structure will ease students' use of aid at their school.

Financial Aid

This office facilitates student payments and provides financial aid recommendations on payment structure and timing for study abroad students. Collaboration with education abroad leadership should be done to establish study abroad payment due dates, integrating special funding for study abroad, and to coincide study abroad with key financial aid events, such as when refund checks become available to students.

Legal Counsel and Risk Managers

The college's attorneys and risk managers should be consulted about potential liability concerns with study abroad program activities and to review all waivers of liability and risk management documents. Attorneys and risk managers should inform policy development that details study abroad students of potential program risks and safeguards the education abroad office from lawsuits.

Student Affairs

Student affairs professionals should be consulted about a variety of concerns related to student support issues for study abroad. They can assist with developing and supporting student conduct policies, issues related to sexual harassment and assault, support for students with special needs, and provide support for students from diverse backgrounds who study abroad.

Academic Advising

Counselors and advisors are essential for assisting students with linking education abroad with directed pathway and stackable credential programs. The academic advisor works in unison with the study abroad advisor and registrar to place study abroad students in proper classes.

CONCLUSION

All community colleges that have or will develop education abroad need effective support services for students with health and safety as a priority and to share these policies to students before, during and after study abroad. It is also important to provide students with realistic cultural norms abroad and challenge false stereotypes for students prior to departure, while abroad, and after the return home. While much of the information in this chapter focuses on faculty-led short-term programs (the most common at community colleges), since community college students also enroll directly at universities abroad, it is important for community colleges to develop policies about local laws, host institutional policies, and transcript credit reviews.

There are unique issues in CC that influence EA

Open access policies mandate that all students be allowed access to education abroad and that equal opportunities need to be made for student on - and off campus. Low to free tuition need to be aligned with the overall cost of studying abroad.

While education abroad programs must be approved by the Board of Trustees, the Trustee association publications do not adequately inform them on community college education abroad. Community colleges have multiple missions that provide unique pathways that may have untraditional connections to studying abroad. Career and workforce education is aligned with labor market skill demands and workforce guided pathway programs include sequenced courses to accommodate certification requirements that may limit choices to study abroad. Community colleges that offer baccalaureate degrees add new issues for consideration. Performance funding formulas link accountability to student learning outcomes and assessment which may not take into consideration study abroad. Inconsistent leadership professional training along with a lack of centralization hinders leaders ability to oversee faculty compliance. Finally, enrollment declines and funding declines greatly influence course offerings and even the viability of the community college itself.

Likewise, there are unique issues that intersect with health, safety, and legal issues that have yet to be researched. We found limited literature on the application of health, safety, and legal issues to community colleges. As such, there is a need to develop information and resources that speak to the needs of community colleges for them to effectively develop and implement study abroad programs with health and safety issues as a primary concern towards effective training and support for program leaders and student participants. Effective program implementation includes orientation and training of students before, during, and after study abroad to maximize the impact and minimize the potential for negative health and safety outcomes. In the same way that community colleges implement policies and procedures on campus to limit risks to student health and safety and prepare to respond to potential risks, so too can community colleges implement policies and procedures to limit health and safety hazards for education abroad and prepare to respond to them in the adoption of important and necessary standards. Community college commitment to study abroad should provide resources to maximize the benefits to students and minimize health and safety challenges and limit institutional liability.

REFERENCES

Bird v. Lewis & Clark College, 104 F. Supp. 2d 1271 (D. Or. 2000) aff'd, 303 F.3d 1015 (9th Cir. 2002).

Bird v. Lewis & Clark College, 303 F.3d 1015 (9th Cir. 2002).

Center for Global Education. (2018a). *Globaled.us*. Retrieved from http://globaled.us/index.asp

Center for Global Education. (2018b). GlobalScholar.us. Retrieved from http://globaled.us/index.asp

Center for Global Education. (2018c). SAFETI. Retrieved from http://globaled.us./index.asp

Council for the Advancement of Standards in Higher Education. (2018). CAS Standards. In *CAS Professional Standards for Higher Education* (9th ed.). Cabot, AZ: Author. Retrieved from: http://www.nafsa.org/_/File/_/eaps_ statement.pdf

Dawn.Com. (2011, April 19). *Four girls killed in Paris inferno*. Retrieved from: https://www.dawn.com/news/622237

Donohue, D., & Altaf, S. (2012, May). *Learn by doing: expanding international internships/work abroad opportunities for U.S. STEM students—A briefing paper from IIE's Center for Academic Mobility Research*. Retrieved from www.file://C:/ Users/Montgomery%20College/Downloads/Learn%20by%20 Doing%20Final.pdf

Fay v. Thiel College, 55 Pa. D. & C.4th 353 (Com. Pl. 2001).

Fink, J., Davis, J., & Takeshi, Y. (2017). *What happens to students who take community college "Dual Enrollment" courses in high school?* Community College Research Center (CCRC). Retrieved from: https://ccrc.tc.columbia.edu/publications/what-happens-community-college-dual- enrollment-students.html

Forum on Education Abroad. (2018). *Forum's standards focus on health and safety Standards of Practice*. Retrieved from: https://forumea.org/resources/standards-of-good- practice/standard-8/

Forum on Education Abroad. (2018). *Membership Listing*. Retrieved from: https://forumea.org/about-us/who-we-are/member-listing/

Furrh v. Arizona Board of Regents, 676 P.2d 1141 (Ariz. Ct. App. 1983).

Henry, R. (1985). California's Community Colleges and International Education: Legal Issues. Santa Rosa, CA: School and College Legal Services of California. (Unpublished Document)

Hudzik & McCarthy. (2012). *Leading Comprehensive Internationalization: Strategies and Tactics for Action*. Washington, DC: NAFSA.

Institute of International Education. (2014). *Press release Open Doors 2014: International students in the United States and study abroad by American students are at all-time high*. Retrieved from http://www.iie.org/Who-We-Are/News-and-Events/Press-Center/Press-Releases/2014/2014-11-17-Open-Doors-Data

Interassociational Advisory Committee on Safety and Responsibility in Education Abroad. (2001). *Responsible education abroad: Good practices for health & safety*. Retrieved from https://www.nafsa.org/Professional_Resources/Browse_by _Interest/ Education_Abroad/Network_Resources/Education_Abroad/Responsible_ Study_Abroad__Good_Practices_for_Health___Safety/

Jasmine Jahanshahi Fire Safety Foundation. (2018). *Homepage*. Retrieved From: http://www.firesafetyfoundation.org

King v. Board of Control of Eastern Michigan University, 221 F. Supp. 2d 783 (E.D. Mich. 2002).

Malveaux, G. F. (2016). *Look Before Leaping: Risks, Liabilities and Repair of Study Abroad in Higher Education*. Lanham, MD: Rowman & Littlefield.

NAFSA. (2018). *Responsible education abroad: Good practices for health and safety*. Retrieved from: https://www.nafsa.org/uploadedFiles/responsible_ education_abroad.pdf

Paneno v. Centres for Academic Programmes Abroad Ltd., 13 Cal. Rptr. 3d 759 (Cal. Ct. App. 2004).

Raby, R. L., & Rhodes, G. M. (2018). Promoting education abroad among community college students: Overcoming obstacles and developing inclusive practices. In H. B. Hamir & N. Gozik (Eds.), *Promoting Inclusion in Education Abroad* (pp. 114–133). London: Stylus.

Rhodes, G., DeRomana, I., & Pedone, X. (2018). *Education Abroad & Other International Travel. Center for Disease Control (CDC) Yellow Book*. Retrieved from: https://wwwnc.cdc.gov/travel/yellowbook/2018/advising-travelers-with-specific- needs/education-abroad-other-international-student-travel

Thackurdeen v. Duke University, 2014 WL 3886037 (S.D.N.Y. Aug. 8, 2014).

University of California Education Abroad Programs. (2018). *Health and Safety*. Retrieved at: http://eap.ucop.edu/ForParents/Pages/health_safety.aspx

US Department of State. (2018). *US passports & international travel*. US Department of State - Bureau of Consular Affairs. Retrieved from http://travel.state.gov/content/passports/english/country/guatemala.html

Valeau, E. J., & Raby, R. L. (2016). Building the pipeline for community college international education leadership. In R. L. Raby & E. J. Valeau (Eds.), *International Education at Community Colleges: Themes, Practices, Research, and Case Studies* (pp. 163–173). New York, NY: Palgrave Macmillian. doi:10.1057/978-1-137-53336-4_11

Chapter 5
Study Abroad Outcomes Assessment:
A Community College Case Study

Dawn R. Wood
Kirkwood Community College, USA

ABSTRACT

The purpose of this chapter is to provide an overview of the literature relevant to outcomes assessment as it pertains to community college study abroad and to provide a case study of Kirkwood Community College's recent project developing institution-specific study abroad learning outcomes. The subsequent outcomes assessment conducted will be discussed along with conclusions from the process and the data gathered. This case study will illustrate how one community college developed student learning outcomes specific to its environment and a unique "home-grown" assessment model for assessing those outcomes comprehensively across all programs. The ability to engage in dialogue at all levels of the institution and speak the language of assessment has provided opportunities for unique improvements and the furthering of global learning goals.

INTRODUCTION

In today's higher education environment, the development and assessment of study abroad learning outcomes is undoubtedly crucial to improving study abroad program success and integrating global learning into the overall learning outcomes of higher education institutions. Given the focus on outcomes assessment at community colleges (Nunley, Beers & Manning, 2011; Jenkins, Lahr, Fink, & Ganga, 2018), the development and implementation of a quality outcomes assessment method specifically for study abroad is especially necessary. There is no doubt that anecdotal evidence of life-changing experiences through study abroad will continue to be imperative to sharing the story of study abroad impact. The importance of collecting these stories through an empirical method and integrating the process into the community college structure is critical. Outcomes assessment provides complementary tools

DOI: 10.4018/978-1-5225-6252-8.ch005

and additional qualitative as well as quantitative information relevant to institutions and institutional stakeholders' communities.

According to NAFSA International Education Professionals Core Competencies (2017), intercultural communication is a cross-cutting core competency in the profession of international education. This intercultural communication competency allows international education professionals to "adapt to other cultural norms when appropriate." Many international education professionals have successfully traveled and/or lived in other cultures around the world to further their competency in intercultural adaptation. These same international education professionals leading internationalization efforts at community colleges operate within the larger context of a higher education institution. As with any institution, a certain organizational culture exists. The culture of the community college includes an "assessment culture" in which international educators must learn to adapt and operate.

It is time for international education professionals to step up, adapt and apply their intercultural skills and core competencies to ensure global learning occupies a prioritized spot in the assessment culture of higher education. Start by recognizing the organizational culture of one's own institution, learning the language of outcomes assessment, dialoguing with college faculty and leaders about assessment methodology, and ensuring global learning is at the table when the assessment dialogue occurs. By learning the language and culture of outcomes assessment, international educators have the opportunity to weave global learning into the fabric of the community college and create more opportunity for the institutionalization of global learning.

The first part of this chapter will provide an overview of the literature and research that has been conducted relevant to outcomes assessment in general with a focus specifically on community colleges and study abroad. The review of the literature will show that very little empirical research is available in this area specific to study abroad outcomes assessment at community colleges and that more case studies and data are needed to directly address the unique environment and culture of the community college.

The second part of this chapter will present a case study of Kirkwood Community College's development of study abroad learning outcomes. The subsequent outcomes assessment conducted will be discussed along with conclusions from the process and the data gathered. This case study will illustrate how one community college developed student learning outcomes specific to its environment and a unique "home-grown" assessment model for assessing those outcomes comprehensively across all programs. The ability to engage in dialogue at all levels of the institution and speak the language of assessment has provided opportunities for unique improvements and the furthering of global learning goals.

LITERATURE REVIEW: STUDY ABROAD OUTCOMES ASSESSMENT AT COMMUNITY COLLEGE

Study Abroad at Community Colleges

According to the Institute of International Education's (IIE) Open Doors Report (2017), in the 2016–2017 academic year, 90,802 students from community colleges participated in study abroad programs. More and more community college students are choosing to study abroad with the majority selecting short-term faculty led programs for their study abroad experience (Open Doors, 2017). This uptick in global experiences at community colleges is creating a growing awareness by administration that study abroad and global learning are essential. With this awareness comes an increasing number of community colleges seeking to expand and improve study abroad programming on their campuses.

Community colleges have an affinity for hands-on teaching methods, experiential learning, and high impact programming; thus a natural home for study abroad. Study abroad has been described as a "high impact" learning experience (Kuh, 2008). Kuh (2008) describes examples of high impact experiences including service learning, global learning, study abroad, learning communities, etc. Characteristics of high impact experiences include experiences where students work collaboratively in a community of peers, experience real-world applications of knowledge and reflect on their own learning experience. Students often describe these high impact learning experiences as having "changed their lives." Community colleges use strategies that promote increased faculty and peer contact (Endo & Harpel, 1982; Stovall, 2001) to increase levels of retention and persistence. Increased faculty and peer contact is a characteristic of high impact programming (Kuh, 2008) and a characteristic of a typical short-term faculty-led study abroad program.

Community colleges focus on workforce readiness, specifically on the workforce needs of their local communities. Recent publications related to the link between study abroad and workforce readiness have found that study abroad contributes to the development of work-related skills such as problem-solving, teamwork, self-awareness, interpersonal skills, leadership skills, etc. (Harder, Andenoro, Roberts, Stedman, Newberry, Parker, & Rodriguez, 2015; Farrugia & Sanger, J., 2017). In 2017, Farrugia and Sanger showed that study abroad has a direct impact on the skills needed for career success. With community colleges tied so closely to workforce needs in their community, this finding is very significant. Farrugia and Sanger (2017) state that study abroad has an overall positive impact on job skills needed in the job market today. Teamwork was one of those job skills/outcomes that resulted from structured short-term study abroad programs specifically. Other such skill development outcomes included communication, interpersonal skills, flexibility, adaptability, and intercultural skills.

A recent white paper published jointly by Institute of International Education and American Institute for Foreign Study (2018), about linking higher education to the workplace through international experience made conclusions directly relevant to community colleges. The first was that study abroad should start earlier in students' college education. Community colleges are the first two years of over half of US undergraduates, thus are the first two years of the college education. This finding, then, about how study abroad should start earlier, is relevant directly to the population of community college students and a call to action to community college leaders preparing students for transfer and/or workforce. Another finding from this study is that higher education institutions should encourage students of all backgrounds to study abroad. This finding is relevant in its direct relationship to the diverse nature of the community college population. Community colleges serve a diverse range of students in terms of age, race/ethnicity, and socioeconomic background, providing an important pathway to many (Ma & Baum, 2016). The global economy demands that students of all backgrounds and academic disciplines including technical areas, will need global skills that experiences abroad provide.

The community college focuses on preparing students for the workforce, for transfer and for being a valued member of the communities they serve. Global learning is a critical component to this preparation and each subset may have a different set of expectations. There is a recognition on community college campuses that campus leaders need to be more intentional about aligning the goals of education with the realities of an interconnected world (Hovland, 2010).

Outcomes Assessment Methods at Community Colleges

The community college organizational culture is unique and ascribes to a unique set of values and priorities. With a dedication to access and open admissions, community colleges operate within a culture that often, although there are exceptions, favors access over selectivity. The environment at community colleges is one that demands accountability and transparency on many levels. From the forward of the National Institute for Learning Outcomes Assessment paper dated July 2011

The open access mission of community colleges demands working with individuals with widely varying academic skill levels and diverse educational backgrounds. As a result, learning outcomes assessment in community colleges presents an array of opportunities and challenges distinctive to these institutions and the students that they serve (Nunley, Beers & Manning, 2011, p. 3).

Literature about outcomes assessment at community colleges is primarily focused on institution-wide assessment and very little is found about study abroad assessment specifically. According the AAC&U paper

Assessment is probably the aspect of global learning that has crystallized the least. As the complex notion of global learning is still in a state of flux, assessment plans at various institutions are at different stages of development (Nair & Henning, 2017, p. 13).

It is beneficial to recognize the importance of community college assessment at an institutional level and recognize that certain movements such as the guided pathway reforms (Jenkins, Lahr, Fink, & Ganga, 2014) have magnified the focus on student learning outcomes and assessment. This has created an environment on community college campuses that includes an assessment-driven faculty and administration laden in direct hands-on assessment. There are a wide variety of stages of development of outcomes assessment, institution-wide, across all 1200+ community colleges in the U.S. Community colleges, as all institutions of higher learning, are becoming accustomed to the process of developing and accessing student learning outcomes (Nunley, Bers, & Manning, 2011); however, not all institutions are at the same stage of development. Not all institutions have a consistent scheme of assessment across the institution nor are necessarily effectively utilizing the assessment process for quality improvements. Most community colleges have established some form of learning outcomes and most do collect some type of data; however, many have not established a consistent and effective campus-wide process.

Study Abroad Outcomes Assessment

The literature about study abroad outcomes assessment is developed to a point where there are several excellent publications about the importance of outcomes assessment in study abroad that provide good guidance for institutions beginning the process (Deardorf & Banta, 2015; Savicki & Brewer, 2015). Organizations such as the Forum for Education Abroad (Bolen, 2014), NAFSA, and Organization for Economic Co-operation and Development (OECD) (2018) have all put forward guidelines, toolboxes and publications related to outcomes assessment in study abroad, global competence, etc.

A study that looked at hundreds of college surveys sent out to students after studying abroad found that over 95% of colleges utilize assessment tools or questionnaires that assess student satisfaction in study abroad programs, but very few measure gains in academic information or intercultural skills gained from study abroad (Sideli, 2001; Engle, 2012). This seems to suggest that international educators are often focused on asking questions that pertain to the customer service experience achieved through study abroad instead of asking more substantive assessment-based questions that get to the actual learning outcomes desired. Engle (2012) explains this focus on "satisfaction" as an ethnocentric way to evaluate a program. There is a clear imperative to document the impact of study abroad beyond mere "satisfaction" and to instead evaluate the actual global learning, the actual intercultural competencies, and/or the level of intercultural sensitivity acquired through the experience. According to many resources this area of research in learning outcomes has been quite undeveloped (Rubin & Sutton, 2001; Sideli, 2001; Vande Ber, 2001; Conley & Tudor, 2006) but recently advancements have taken place and resources related to learning outcomes have increased.

There are many tools available by which to measure intercultural and global competence and/or intercultural sensitivity. One framework available is the AAC&U VALUE rubrics which include rubrics on Global Learning as well as Intercultural Knowledge and Competence (Rhodes, 2009). Many study abroad assessment strategies involve utilizing a common tool for assessment that involves students self-reporting knowledge, attitudes, skills, etc. For a list of these type of tools, see West (2015) or Fantini (2006). Some examples are the Global Perspectives Inventory (GPI), Intercultural Development Inventory (IDI), and Global Competence Aptitude Assessment (GCAA) to assess outcomes and attempt to measure intercultural sensitivity or increased knowledge about world events/cultures.

Another area of research has focused on determining if and how study abroad impacts student success. The CCC SOAR study is one of very few published research studies directly addressing community college outcomes assessment. The SOAR study focused on how study abroad can contribute to community college students completing their program and improved academic achievement (Raby, Rhodes, & Biscarra, 2014). The findings of the SOAR study are very convincing that students who participate in study abroad have a greater tendency toward academic success than students who did not participate in study abroad.

Another notable large-scale research project was conducted by the University of Georgia system and is known as the GLOSSARI project (Sutton & Rubin, 2004). The GLOSSARI project compared study abroad participants to non-participants at a specific set of institutions and measured the difference in their learning outcomes on certain contact areas such as intercultural interaction, world geography, etc. The study found that students who studied abroad exceeded the comparison group on several factors, but not all. One of the conclusions of the data was that it was reasonable to argue that any differences between those who studied abroad and those who did not could have been attributed to the elite academic status of those who typically choose to study abroad, and not at all attributable to the study abroad experience.

Merging Community College Assessment With Study Abroad Assessment

There is a very clear benefit to integrating study abroad assessment into the broader assessment of the institutional learning outcomes (NAFSA Teaching, Learning, & Scholarship Knowledge Community 2009 Task Force on Assessment and Evaluation). Each institution will need to develop their own process and practice based on their own parameters. One of the tenants of a solid assessment model is that the institution not apply a "one-size-fits-all" approach but rather customize the assessment to meet the unique learning environment (Deardorff, 2014). In the literature, several guidelines are suggested for designing an outcomes assessment plan at an institution or within programs (Nunley, Bers, & Manning,

2011; West, 2015). In the case study that follows, a college will be presented that has developed its own assessment process and rating process that is consistent with the wider institution assessment process.

CASE STUDY: STUDY ABROAD OUTCOMES ASSESSMENT AT KIRKWOOD COMMUNITY COLLEGE

In light of the literature review above lacking specific practical examples of community colleges engaging in study abroad outcomes assessment, the remaining segment of this chapter will examine a case study of one community college's unique experience developing and implementing study abroad outcomes assessment. The purpose in presenting this case study here is not to exhibit perfection in methodology but rather to demonstrate how taking concrete steps in alignment with institutional assessment strategies and best practices can accomplish a conversation and institutional dialogue with purpose and strategies for global learning. The case study presented here is a "work in progress" whereby continuous improvement and changes are still taking place to enhance the process. In addition, presenting this case study will illustrate some of the challenges and successes experienced by one college who intentionally embarked upon the journey of study abroad learning outcomes assessment.

Kirkwood Community College Background Information

Kirkwood is a large community college with approximately 14,745 unduplicated head count in 2016 (http://www.kirkwood.edu/pdf/uploaded/394/fall_mis_data_sheet_-_enrollment.pdf). Global learning is one of Kirkwood's priorities and college resources have been dedicated to furthering access for Kirkwood students to study abroad. At Kirkwood there are typically 15-18 annual short-term faculty-lead study abroad programs to over 10 different countries. Kirkwood sends approximately 32 faculty leaders and over 160 students per year on study abroad. According to IIE Open Doors Community College Data Tables, Kirkwood ranks 6th in the nation for number of students studying abroad among all associate's institutions (IIE Open Doors, 2016). Kirkwood study abroad programs are all delivered for academic credit and are diverse in course content as well as location. Each program is led by faculty teaching at least one academic credit course connected to the study abroad program offering.

Kirkwood's International Programs has a stated vision that every Kirkwood faculty, staff and student will engage in an intercultural experience as part of their Kirkwood experience. This "intercultural experience" is defined broadly as any experience that includes a person-to-person interaction between students, faculty and/or staff from other cultures. These in-classroom or out-of-classroom experiences could include, but are not limited to, an experience working with an international student and/or immigrant student, a virtual exchange experience connecting a classroom to students overseas, a curriculum module that allows students to meet and interact with people from other cultures, a student organization focused on multiculturalism, etc. Some of these experiences will of course be more impactful than others. Study abroad is, without a doubt, a high impact intercultural experience that works as a high impact method to achieve the vision.

Kirkwood Community College has recently implemented its own self-developed version of study abroad outcomes assessment. Like many institutions, Kirkwood Study Abroad had for many years assessed its study abroad programs by means of a self-reported student satisfaction survey, asking students to assess their satisfaction with programs and rate themselves on their own learning about themselves and the world. The satisfaction surveys asked students many questions about how they liked the experience, if they would recommend the program to other students, how much they thought the program related to the academic class, if they improved their worldview, etc. In the majority of the programs, the satisfaction surveys were overwhelmingly positive but did not allow a deeper level of analysis about what global learning was occurring on study abroad, what growth could be measured, and what could be improved in the student learning component of study abroad. The satisfaction survey provided indirect measures of learning and Kirkwood desired to add a more direct measure assessing student learning outcomes.

In addition to the satisfaction survey, other methods of assessment were utilized by individual faculty leaders, at their own initiative, to assess learning on study abroad. Some of these faculty-led assessment methods were aimed at their own course learning outcomes and some were targeted more toward generalized global competency or intercultural sensitivity goals.

Recognizing the need for a direct measure of student learning outcomes, Kirkwood took the following five steps toward implementing a study abroad outcomes assessment strategy. These five steps are outlined below and then discussed in more detail in the subsequent sections of this chapter. The steps are generic and are outlined here in order to provide some direction for other institutions interested in developing their own assessment plan:

1. Define Study Abroad Learning Outcomes and Align with College Assessment Plan
2. Determine the Method for Assessing the Learning Outcomes
3. Establish Rater Reliability while Balancing Flexibility
4. Collect and Analyze the Data
5. Disseminate the Data and Engage in Conversation

First Step: Define Study Abroad Learning Outcomes and Align With College Assessment Plan

As Kirkwood endeavored upon the idea of a more comprehensive method for assessing study abroad learning outcomes, the very first step involved initiating discussions about exactly what Kirkwood's objectives are for global learning. What was it exactly that Kirkwood wanted study abroad students to learn? What was the purpose of study abroad? What did Kirkwood want to measure in terms of learning?

In 2013, Kirkwood Community College initiated their study abroad learning outcomes assessment journey by assembling a team. The team consisted primarily of faculty study abroad leaders, a Kirkwood assessment specialist, and international programs staff. Several meetings were held to brainstorm study abroad learning outcomes and faculty involvement was critical to the discussion.

Initially, there was a general perception or assumption made by the faculty and administrators at Kirkwood that the Career and Technical Education (CTE) faculty and the Liberal Arts faculty would have different perspectives on the desired learning outcomes. Because of this initial assumption that these two faculty groups would view study abroad learning outcomes in different ways, two separate teams were formed and two separate meetings were held. One team included faculty from the Career and Technical Education (CTE) area and the second team included faculty from the Liberal Arts areas of study. The International Programs Director and the Kirkwood Assessment Specialist participated in both meetings. In these initial meetings, each team began the process of developing a set of common Kirkwood study abroad learning outcomes. After only a few initial meetings, the two separate teams realized they were both headed in the same direction and the decision was made to merge the two groups into one team.

Study Abroad Outcomes Assessment

Although the subject matter varied dramatically in study abroad programming from Agriculture, Environmental Science, Culinary Arts, Architecture, Humanities, and so forth, the core learning desired because of study abroad was consistent: growth in intercultural sensitivity and competence.

After several additional team meetings and email correspondence, the multi-disciplinary faculty team eventually arrived at the following three common study abroad learning outcomes to apply across all Kirkwood study abroad programs:

Outcome 1: Compare/contrast components of home culture and host culture experienced through the study abroad program.
Outcome 2: Develop intercultural competencies and tools to enable the ability to move across boundaries and see the world from multiple perspectives.
Outcome 3: Reflect and apply cultural learning obtained from the study abroad experience to one's own academic discipline and/or career direction.

These three outcomes were chosen because of the recurring themes in the faculty discussion: self-awareness, skill building, and future impact. Detailed notes were taken at each team meeting and three common themes emerged from the notes that eventually became the three outcomes.

Outcome #1 was borne out of the discussion related to the student growth faculty leaders had directly witnessed in their study abroad students' self-awareness. Faculty cited examples of students who came to the realization because of study abroad that they themselves had a "culture" that was valuable and comparable to other cultures. This acknowledgement of self-culture and the ability to compare recurred in the faculty leader discussion. Several action words were discussed but, in the end, "compare and contrast" seemed the most applicable for outcome one.

Outcome #2 encapsulated a discussion about skill-building. Kirkwood faculty wanted to ensure students walked away with skills and tools to use in the future. The theme here included references that the study abroad experience was not designed to be a tourist adventure, but rather a skill-building experience that would allow students to cross borders and see the world from alternative perspectives.

Outcome #3 focused on impact and how study abroad would carry through to the students' futures. The general theme in the discussion about Outcome #3 was about the need to ensure the experiences were future-focused and could be directly applied to students' futures. Faculty wanted to find a way to assess whether the experience would "change lives" and that the learning gained could be directly applied to the student's future and career.

Throughout this discussion about the outcomes themselves, there were also several discussion points about the implementation strategy including the following: how to apply the learning outcomes to each unique academic course, how to integrate the assessment process within the overall Kirkwood assessment scheme, and how to allow for faculty freedom in the method of assessment.

There was considerable discussion among the team members about the difficulty of adding the three common learning outcomes to the faculty leader's existing course learning outcomes. At, Kirkwood, faculty leaders teach a variety of different academic courses as part of the study abroad program. For example, the Kirkwood program to Costa Rica involves a faculty member teaching a course on Environmental Ethics. The Spanish study abroad program involves a language faculty teaching a foreign language course. The study abroad program to Australia for technical students involves the faculty member teaching Education Experience Abroad, a course designed to guide the study abroad experience itself.

The team discussed the importance of separating the academic course outcomes from the three study abroad learning outcomes, although there would undoubtedly be overlap. The team agreed that all faculty leaders would overlay these three outcomes in the syllabus for their study abroad course so that the goal would be to focus activities for the program on both the academic course outcomes and the study abroad outcomes. Kirkwood faculty were somewhat accustomed to this "overlay" concept due to the institutional wide assessment strategy that allows for course outcomes, program outcomes and institutional general education outcomes to overlay each other in the larger scheme of assessment. This particular discussion benefited from the presence of the assessment specialist on the team and the overall understanding both the faculty team and the International Programs Dean had of the institutional language of assessment.

There were other ways that the language and culture of the overall assessment process at the institution was woven into the new study abroad outcomes assessment discussion. In discussions with Academic Affairs and Kirkwood's Assessment Specialist, Study Abroad was categorized as its own academic program so that the annual review and assessment process aligned with other academic programs and the annual review process mirrored other academic areas of the college. This paralleling of the assessment process allowed faculty and administrators to see study abroad assessment data in the same way they viewed academic program assessment data.

The learning outcomes themselves were also integrated into several other aspects of study abroad programming. The Faculty Proposal form was revised to include concrete proposal elements about how activities in the program would be structured around the learning outcomes. The study abroad pre-departure student orientation was redesigned so that the agenda for the orientation was clearly tied to the three learning outcomes thus creating a higher level of student, faculty and parent awareness of the outcomes and the methods be using to achieve those outcomes. Some programs have also implemented re-entry strategies and activities upon return of the students in their post-travel meetings to reflect on the three learning outcomes and discuss their relevance.

Second Step: Determine the Method for Assessing the Learning Outcomes

Once the three study abroad learning outcomes were established and the faculty agreed on how to apply them to their course syllabi and program activities, the next step was to discuss the method for rating the growth of students along the DMIS scale.

As we have seen in the literature, the initial discussion found the Kirkwood team searching for the "right tool" to measure intercultural sensitivity. Many ideas for tools such as the Intercultural Development Inventory (IDI), Global Competence Aptitude Assessment (GCAA), Global Perspectives Inventory (GPI), and so forth came up in the discussion. The IDI seemed like a good fit due to its tie to the DMIS scale for example. For a more comprehensive listing of such assessment tools, see West (2015) or Fantini (2006). As these specific tools were evaluated by the team, it seemed difficult to apply the tools directly to the three Kirkwood learning outcomes. The tools did not directly match the learning outcomes developed and also seemed too broad to be applied to Kirkwood's intent. For example, the IDI assesses intercultural competence as a whole and the progression of intercultural competence along the continuum; however, the IDI does not address Kirkwood's three learning outcomes specifically. The five stages themselves were relevant to each of the three outcomes but the results of the overall IDI assessment would not drill down to this level. Because of this incongruence, the team, through its research on intercultural sensitivity, then endeavored upon a more homegrown approach.

Study Abroad Outcomes Assessment

The team found that intercultural sensitivity and intercultural competence were desired outcomes that ran through all three learning outcomes. The team settled on the idea that growth was the critical measurement that needed to be measured and that they wanted to measure growth in intercultural sensitivity and intercultural competence. As the team explored several articles about intercultural sensitivity, the team found that it could relate best to Bennett's Developmental Model of Intercultural Sensitivity (DMIS) scale as a tool for adapting and using as a type of rating tool. Figure 1 illustrates the DMIS scale's five stages. The team proposed utilizing the five stages to measure growth in intercultural sensitivity along all three study abroad student learning outcomes.

The team proposed that assessment of student learning outcomes be conducted through faculty rating of artifacts from their academic course. Kirkwood faculty rating of artifacts was already an established practice at the institution and the team seemed comfortable with developing a rubric for rating and utilizing it in the assessment. Table 1 shows the learning outcomes rating sheet and Table 2 shows the rating rubric.

The team suggested that the faculty collect pre- and post- written assignments and/or use a different type of artifact assignment such as a standard pre- and post- survey, interview, presentation, video, etc. The pre- and post- artifact measures would be rated on each learning outcome according to the five stages from Bennett's Developmental Model of Intercultural Sensitivity (DMIS) (Bennett, 1993).

This faculty discussion of Bennett's model was the first time cross-disciplinary faculty at Kirkwood had discussed the topic of growth in intercultural sensitivity as a defined outcome for study abroad. It was the first time it was discussed utilizing a theoretical approach such as the DMIS that acknowledged

Figure 1. Developmental model of intercultural sensitivity
Source: Bennett, Milton J. (1993)

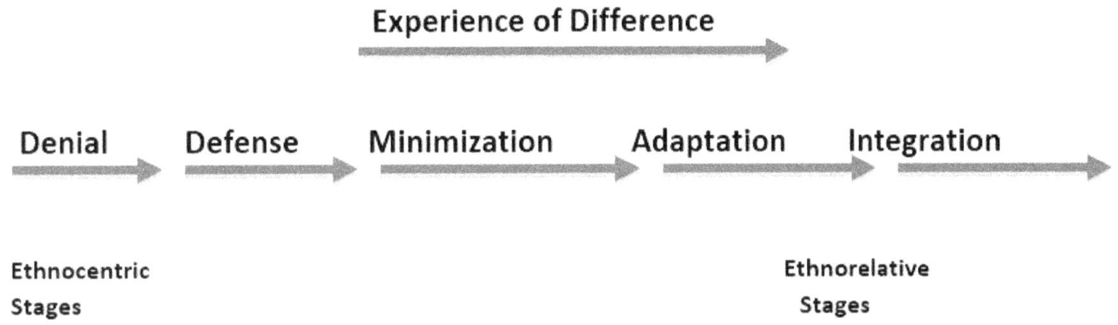

Experience of Difference

Denial → Defense → Minimization → Adaptation → Integration

Ethnocentric Stages   Ethnorelative Stages

Table 1. Kirkwood Community College international programs study abroad learning outcomes and rubric

Study Abroad Learning Outcomes	Pre-Rating (1-5)	Post-Rating (1-5)	Growth (Post-Pre)
Compare/contrast components of home culture and host culture experienced though the study abroad program			
Develop intercultural competencies and tools to enable the ability to move across boundaries and see the world from multiple perspectives			
Reflect and apply cultural learning obtained from the study abroad experience to one's own academic discipline and/or career direction.			

Table 2. Kirkwood Community College study abroad rating rubric

Rating Stage	Definition of Stage	Writing Samples that would fit in this stage
1: Denial	Learner is unable to recognize cultural difference	"All I need to know when I'm in another culture is how to get around" "I have traveled before and found no real differences in people"
2: Defense	Learner negatively evaluates cultural difference; polarizes "us" and "them"; stereotypes; manifests attitude of superiority of home culture over other cultures	"When you go to other countries, it makes you realize how much better the US is" "People from other cultures are not open-minded like mine" "I signed up for this program because people there need to much help"
3: Minimization	Learners recognize and accept superficial cultural differences while holding that all human beings are essentially the same; emphasize the similarities of people and commonality of basic values and define universal standards as related to self	"I am tired of hearing what makes people different; we need to recognize that we are all human beings" "The best way to get along is to just be yourself" "Deep down we are all the same - people just trying to lead our lives"
4: Acceptance	Learners recognize and appreciate cultural differences in behavior and values, and accept cultural differences as viable alternative solutions; consciously elaborates on categories of differences	"It would be boring to be around the same type of people all the time" "I generally enjoy differences between myself and others" "I am just starting to learn more about culture and it is amazing to find all of the similarities and differences"
5: Adaptation or Integration	Learners develop skills that enable intercultural communication, empathy, and the ability to shift cultural frame of reference to understand and be understood across cultural boundaries; Learners internalize multicultural frames of reference and see themselves as "in process."	"I can maintain my values and behave in culturally appropriate ways" "The more I understand this culture, the better I get at the language" "I really enjoy some of what I learned. Some behaviors though, are ones I can never imagine feeling comfortable" "I can look at any situation now from multiple points of view" "I may not like everything here, but I am willing to accept things I cannot understand"

Adapted from: Bennett, Milton (1993).

concrete stages of growth through which Kirkwood students grew from the study abroad experience. The discussion was rich and faculty shared concrete examples of students they had led on programs that exhibited criteria from each of the stages.

As the team meetings continued, the team was committed to allowing flexibility for faculty in the assessment process. Faculty flexibility and freedom was identified as important to Kirkwood faculty. To allow for this freedom in the process, the rating process may be conducted by the lead faculty alone, the lead faculty and the faculty shadow, or a committee made up of selected members. The lead faculty and International Programs Dean are accountable to ensure the assessment is carried out.

Each student studying abroad was rated pre- and post- study abroad on each of the three learning outcomes. Faculty entered the two ratings on a spreadsheet that calculates the growth for each student. Table 3 shows how the two measures were rated on each outcome and used to gauge individual student and group growth as follows:

Table 3. Measures to gauge student and group growth

Measure 1	Pre-Study Abroad	Rate each of the three outcomes 1-5
Measure 2	Post-Study Abroad	Rate each of the three outcomes 1-5
Growth = Measure 2 - Measure 1 on each of the 3 learning outcomes		

Third Step: Establish Rater Reliability While Balancing Flexibility

The team recognized that there could be some inconsistencies in the rating by the faculty members due to the level of freedom allowed in choosing the artifact and the natural tendency of individual faculty to understand the five stages differently. The following rating notes were developed and are distributed to faculty leaders to provide guidance on the rating process with the goal of establishing rater reliability:

- Levels 1-5 were representative of each stage of the DMIS (Bennett, 1993). For example, level 1 = "Denial" and level 5 = "Adaptation or Integration." It was recognized that these integer numbers were not meant to signify their numeric value but instead illustrated a certain discrete stage.
- It is important to note that the ratings from the DMIS represent ordinal data. That is, the five stages are logically ordered; however, the distance between two levels is not necessarily the same mathematically. There is not a consistent amount of time, experience, or learning necessary to move from one level to the next and one must be careful in calculating and comparing growth. There is also not a clear interpretation of a rating of 2.3, for example, so all ratings must be an integer – no decimals or fractions.
- A rating rubric was developed providing examples of statements that would be evident at each level of the DMIS. For example, writing examples illustrate a level 1 rating are:
  - *All I need to know when I'm in another culture is how to get around.*
  - *I have traveled before and found no real differences in people.*
- A writing example used to illustrate a level 4 Acceptance is:
I generally enjoy differences between myself and others.
- There is not a value judgment placed on the 5 stages in the Model of Intercultural Sensitivity rubric. Students will be at a variety of stages at entry to the program, during and after the experience. There is no "good" or "bad" stage.
- Results from this rating will not be used as an evaluation of the effectiveness of the academic course or faculty leader.
- Rating measures should not be gauged by the quality of grammar, punctuation, writing competency but rather on the content of the replies.
- Honesty will be encouraged in students for the purpose of the rating.
- Faculty leaders are encouraged to build in guiding questions in pre-/post- assignments to more directly capture some of the learning outcome topics.
- Rating results will remain anonymous. Individual growth and group growth will be measured; however, names of students will not be shared in the final results.
- Students may be made aware of their own results if requested and deemed appropriate by the faculty leader.

Fourth Step: Collect and Analyze the Data

The team determined that the process for collecting the data was best centralized in International Programs. This centralized collection strategy aligned International Programs with other Kirkwood academic departments that also collect assessment data for Annual Review purposes. A spreadsheet was distributed to all faculty leaders whereby they entered their individual ratings on the spreadsheet for both the pre- and post- assessment. The growth column populates based on a formula that subtracted the pre- from the post- rating. The completed spreadsheets are submitted to International Programs for compiling and analyzing. Charts and graphs are then created by the assessment specialist and international programs staff to differentiate between type of program, length of program, program focus, etc.

An example of a chart developed from the data over a two-year period is shown below in the charting of the growth calculation over all 3 outcomes. Figure 2 illustrates one example of a chart developed showing growth in 2016 seemed to be higher on Learning Outcomes 1 and 2 as well as overall growth, but slightly down on Learning Outcome 3.

For example, Kirkwood has a number of service learning/volunteer abroad type programs in its list of programs. These were grouped together and then compared against programs that may have had a more liberal arts focus, or a more technical/career focus. The results were then distributed to the entire group of faculty leaders and a meeting was held to discuss the data and its meaning. The first year of the meeting data was compiled comparing each program and the growth measured by averages. The third year of the meeting, data was analyzed based upon categories of study abroad experiences. The categories reflected the primary intent of the study abroad experience; career-oriented, humanities-focused, language learning, service-focused. Figure 3 illustrates the differences in growth rates among these different program types.

Figure 2. Overall growth results on Kirkwood 2015-2016 study abroad learning outcomes

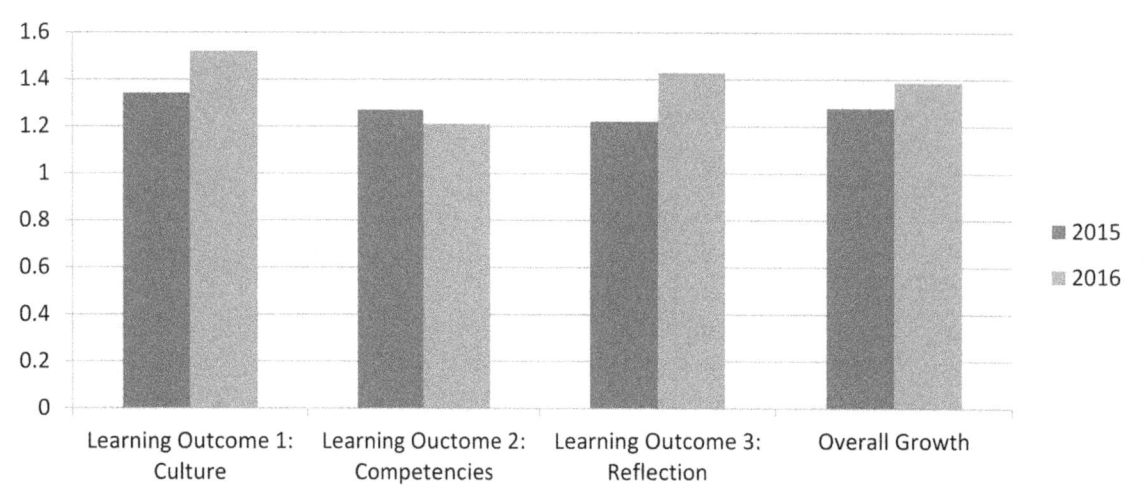

Figure 3. Average initial and final ratings and growth by study abroad category

Graph 1
Outcome 1: Average Initial and Final Ratings and Growth by Study Abroad Category

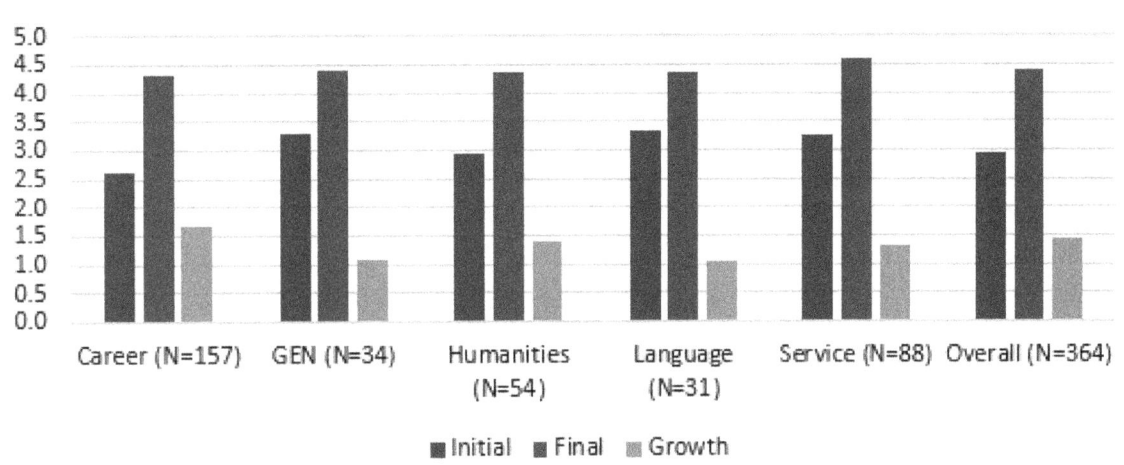

One interesting discussion that came out of the data was that nearly half of the students participating in career focused study abroad had an initial rating of 1 or 2 on the DMIS scale. The other categories had a lower proportion of students with initial ratings of 1 or 2. This particular rating data point led to some very interesting discussions and conversations with faculty about what pre-departure materials may be more appropriate for career-focused study abroad students than for those in the service-focused programs.

Fifth Step: Disseminate the Data and Engage in Conversation

A total of 464 students participated in 46 study abroad experiences at Kirkwood between 2015 and 2017. The Kirkwood Study Abroad Program assessed three student learning outcomes for all experiences offered. The data collected by Kirkwood's outcomes assessment showed that growth did occur as a result of study abroad in Kirkwood students. Growth was achieved overall in all three learning outcomes.

Data analysis was conducted to compare the different types of programs and the growth results in each. Faculty gathered to discuss the data and came up with ideas related to why the data displayed certain trends or illustrated differences. For example, some programs had multiple "repeat" students, students who had participated in study abroad before, and may have exhibited less growth than those students who were novices to the study abroad experience. The discussion was held about how the curriculum could be adapted to personalize the learning for those students at a deeper level and/or ask those students to take on a more leadership role in the experience to facilitate leadership skill development. These types of faculty-driven discussions facilitated concrete improvements in the study abroad process.

Kirkwood's process of involving faculty throughout the assessment process from delivery to analyzing to suggesting improvements provided a rich level of discussion. Several real benefits were realized.

By inviting all faculty leaders to the table, the dialogue and conversation was deepened. It was exceptional to observe cross-disciplinary faculty discussing the impact of global learning as it related not only to their specific program, but to the institution as a whole. Kirkwood was able to allow for flexibility and faculty freedom in the rating process, the selection of artifacts for rating, and other details that created a trusting community where everyone's ideas were valued.

Another benefit realized was the real connection made between study abroad and growth. Kirkwood had always asserted that study abroad is responsible for personal, professional and intellectual growth in students. The stories and student testimonials repeated this time and time again. This process of assessment validated that Study Abroad is a means toward individual growth of Kirkwood students and established a common language to use to discuss that growth and measure it.

The real benefit that outweighs all of the benefits discussed here is the enhanced communication and opportunities for open dialogue about the reasons for what Kirkwood is doing – The conversation itself had immense value in improving Kirkwood study abroad programs, structure and processes/procedures. There were concrete improvements made to support faculty, to orient students, to adapt program activities, to create a faculty shared resource area/toolkit for study abroad, to clarify study abroad processes and procedures, etc.

CONCLUSION

The literature review at the beginning of this chapter illustrates the need for additional study of learning outcomes for study abroad at community colleges and more examples of community colleges conducting outcomes assessment. Overall, community colleges are growing in the number of students studying abroad and in order to keep up with the pace of growth and to support programs, international educators at community colleges need to "brave the world" of assessment, speak the language of learning outcomes, and integrate the study abroad learning outcomes and assessment process with the overall assessment process at their institutions.

The study abroad outcomes assessment process is important for the conversation it creates. In the words of Nelson Mandela, "If you talk to a man in a language he understands, that goes to his head. If you talk to him in his language, that goes to his heart" (Peace Corps, 1996, p. vi.)

The majority of study abroad professionals and higher education leaders agree on the proposition that study abroad experiences changes lives. When study abroad professionals can engage decision makers at institutions and converse in the language of higher education - the language of learning outcomes and assessment, real understanding can be found. When the change and growth study abroad creates is demonstrated clearly and profoundly in the language of assessment native to your institution, whether at a community college or other institutional type, heartfelt conversation and improvements will be made to create even more transformational global learning experiences for students.

REFERENCES

Bennett, M. J. (1986). A developmental approach to training intercultural sensitivity. International Journal of Intercultural Relations, 10(2), 179-186.

Bennett, M. J. (1993). Towards ethnorelativism: A developmental model of intercultural sensitivity (revised). In R. M. Paige (Ed.), *Education for the Intercultural Experience*. Yarmouth, ME: Intercultural Press.

Bolen, M. C. (2014). *A guide to outcomes assessment in education abroad*. Carlisle, PA: Publication of the Forum on Education Abroad.

Carley, S., & Tudor, R. K. (2010) Assessing the impact of short-term study abroad. *Journal of Global Initiatives: Policy, Pedagogy, Perspective, 1*(2), Article 5. Available at: https://digitalcommons.kennesaw.edu/jgi/vol1/iss2/5

Corps, P. (1996). *At home in the world: The Peace Corps story*. Washington, DC: Peace Corps.

Deardorff, D. K. (2014). Outcomes assessment in international education. *Industry and Higher Education, 75*, 8–10.

Deardorff, D. K. (2015). *Demystifying outcomes assessment for international educators: A practical approach*. Sterling, VA: Stylus Publishing.

Engle, L. (2012). The rewards of qualitative assessment appropriate to study abroad. *Frontiers: The Interdisciplinary Journal of Study Abroad, 22*, 111–126.

Farrugia, C., & Sanger, J. (2017). *Gaining an employment edge: The impact of study abroad on 21st century skills and career prospects in the United States, 2013-2016*. New York, NY: Institute for International Education.

Green, M. F. (2007). Internationalizing community colleges: Barriers and strategies. New Directions for Community Colleges, 138, 15-24. Doi:10.1002/cc.277

Hammer, M. R., Bennett, M. J., & Wiseman, R. (2003). Measuring intercultural sensitivitiy: The intercultural development inventory. *International Journal of Intercultural Relations, 27*(4), 421–443. doi:10.1016/S0147-1767(03)00032-4

Harder, A., Andenoro, A., Roberts, T., Stedman, N., Newberry, M. I., Parker, S., & Rodriguez, M. (2015). Does study abroad increase employability? *NACTA Journal, 59*(1).

Hovland, K. (2010). *Global learning: aligning student learning outcomes with study abroad. The Center for Capacity Building in Study Abroad. NAFSA and APLU*. Washington, DC: NAFSA Publications.

Hovland, K. (2014). *Global learning: defining, designing and demonstrating*. Joint publication of NAFSA and AAC&U. Washington, DC: NAFSA Publications. Institute of International Education (IIE).

Hovland, K. (2017). *Open Doors Report*. New York, NY: Academic Press.

Hovland, K. (2018). *Study Abroad Matters: Linking Higher Education to the Contemporary Workplace through International Experience.* Washington, DC: IIE Publications.

Jenkins, D., Lahr, H., Fink, J. & Ganga, E. (2018). *What we are learning about guided pathways.* Community College Research Center.

Kuh, G. D. (2008). *High-Impact educational practices: A brief overview.* Washington, DC: American Association of Colleges and Universities. Retrieved from http://www.aacu.org/leap/hip.cfm

Kuh, G. D. (2008). *High-Impact educational practices: What they are, who has access to them, and why they matter.* Washington, DC: Association of American Colleges and Universities. Retrieved from www.aacu.org/publications/

Ma, J., & Baum, S. (2016). *Trends in community colleges: Enrollment, prices, student debt and completion.* College Board Research Brief: April 2016. Retrieved from: https://trends.collegeboard.org/sites/default/files/trends-in-community-colleges-research- brief.pdf

Musil, C. M. (2006). *Assessing Global Learning: Matching Good Intentions with Good Practice.* Washington, DC: American Association of Colleges and Universities Publications.

NAFSA. (2017). *NAFSA International Education Professional Competencies.* Accessed from www.nafsa.org/competencies

NAFSA Task Force. (2010). *Assessment and evaluation for international educators.* Accessed from http://www.nafsa.org/uploadedFiles/NAFSA_Home/Resource_Library_Assets/Networks/RS/Assess%20and%20Eval%20in%20IE.pdf

Nair, I., & Henning, M. (2017). *Models of global learning.* Washington, DC: Association of American Colleges and Universities.

Nunley, C., Bers, T., & Manning, T. (2011). *Learning outcomes assessment in community colleges.* National Institute for Learning Outcome's Assessment. Retrieved from www.learningoutcomesassessment.org

OECD/Asia Society. (2018). *Teaching for global competence in a rapidly changing world.* Retrieved from: https://asiasociety.org/sites/default/files/inline-files/teaching-for-global- competence-in-a-rapidly-changing-world-edu.pdf

Raby, R. L., Rhodes, G. M., & Biscarra, A. (2014). Community college study abroad: Implications for student success. *Community College Journal of Research and Practice, 38*(2-3), 174–183. doi:10.1080/10668926.2014.851961

Rhodes, T. (2009). *Assessing outcomes and improving achievement: Tips and tools for using the rubrics.* Washington, DC: Association of American Colleges and Universities.

Savicki, V., & Brewer, E. (2015). *Assessing Study Abroad: Theory, Tools and Practice.* Sterling, VA: Stylus Publishing.

Sideli, K. (2001, Spring). Outcomes assessment and study abroad programs: Commentary on the results of a SECUSSA/IIE electronic sampling. *International Educator*, 30.

Stovall, M. (2001). Using success courses for promoting persistence and completion. In Beyond access: Methods and models for increasing retention and learning among minority students (pp. 45–54). San Francisco, CA: Jossey Bass.

Sutton, R. C., & Rubin, D. L. (2004). The GLOSSARI project: Initial findings from a system-wide research initiative on study abroad learning outcomes. *Frontiers: The Interdisciplinary Journal of Study Abroad*, *10*(Fall), 65–82.

Sutton, R. C., & Rubin, D. L. (2010). *Documenting the academic impact of study abroad: Final report of the GLOSSARI project*. Paper presented at NAFSA National Conference, Kansas City, MO.

West, C. (2015, October). Assessing learning outcomes for study abroad. *International Educator*, 36-41.

Chapter 6
Clearing the Hurdle:
The Relationship Between Institutional Profiles and Community College Study Abroad

Melissa Whatley
University of Georgia, USA

ABSTRACT

The purpose of this chapter is twofold. First, it aims to call attention to the fact that study abroad does take place in the community college sector. Second, this study aims at modeling the relationship between institutional profile characteristics and variations in study abroad participation at community colleges. In this sense, it addresses community college students' ability to access education abroad using the institution as the unit of analysis. Specifically, this study employs data from both the Institute of International Education (IIE) and the Integrated Postsecondary Education Data System (IPEDS) to examine the role institutional characteristics, such as an institution's gender and race/ethnicity composition and its location, play in community college students' participation in study abroad. The hurdle model analytic technique adopted here allows for the examination of these factors' relationship to both an institution's provision of study abroad opportunity and the percentage of students that participate. Results have implications for both policymakers and practitioners who aim to increase the prominence of education abroad in the two-year sector.

INTRODUCTION

Community college students comprise an underrepresented student population in U.S. study abroad. Even though study abroad has been offered at community colleges since 1967 (Zhang, 2011), students enrolled at public two-year institutions represented only 1.7% of students studying abroad in the 2015-16 academic year, while they comprised approximately 32% of total enrollments in U.S. higher education (Institute of International Education, 2017; National Center for Education Statistics, 2016). Although Blair, Phinney, and Phillipe (2001) note a considerable increase in international practices at community

DOI: 10.4018/978-1-5225-6252-8.ch006

Clearing the Hurdle

colleges between 1995 and 2000, and Zhang (2011) reports a fourfold increase in the number of community college students studying abroad between the 1999-00 and 2007-08 academic years, this sector continues to face considerable obstacles to sending students abroad. Indeed, the average number of students studying abroad annually from public associates-granting institutions has remained between 45 and 50 each year since the 2008-09 academic year (author's calculations, Institute of International Education, 2017).

Despite low levels of participation, study abroad represents the most common strategy for internationalization among community colleges (Green & Siaya, 2005). These comprehensive internationalization efforts seek to incorporate cross-cultural elements into community college coursework and academic programs (Raby, 2007). The specific provision of study abroad opportunities to students enrolled at community colleges is particularly relevant for students who never intend or are not able to transfer to the four-year post-secondary sector (Raby & Valeau, 2007; Frost & Raby, 2009; Zhang, 2011; Raby, 2012). Indeed, Raby and Valeau (2007) view the inclusion of international components in the two-year sector as central to the community college mission to provide access to quality educational opportunities to populations that are often denied such opportunities at more traditional, four-year institutions. These authors conclude that the open access philosophy of the community college is placed at risk if students attending four-year institutions have access educational experiences, such as international programs, that enhance their degree quality and competitiveness, but students attending community colleges do not. That is, the provision of certain educational activities such as study abroad only at institutions with a competitive admissions process (e.g., four-year institutions) effectively excludes certain segments of the student population from these opportunities. Concerning study abroad in particular, Raby (2008) posits that "community colleges that do not offer education abroad are not meeting their mandate of preparing students for their future roles in a global economy, where international literacy is a basic skill needed in the workplace" (9). Nevertheless, despite a growing interest in international activities such as study abroad among community college students, international education remains very much at the periphery of practice and policy in the two-year sector (Oberstein-Delvalle, 1999; Raby, 2008; Robertson & Blasi, 2017).

Currently, very little is known about the contexts wherein community college students are most likely to access study abroad, meaning that they are not only presented with, but also take advantage of the opportunity. While researchers such as Emert and Pearson (2007), Raby, Rhodes, and Biscarra (2014), and Thomas (2016) provide evidence of the positive relationship between study abroad participation and community college students' success, focusing on outcomes such as transfer to the four-year sector and the development of global competence, evidence of institutional and individual-level factors that encourage community college students to study abroad in the first place remains thin. The research around this topic that does exist concentrates its focus at the student level rather than the institutional level, finding that students perceive that factors related to academic demands and aspirations, the influence of family and friends, perceptions of affordability, group membership affinity, and faculty encouragement of study abroad promote participation (Amani, 2011; Amani & Kim, 2017). Although conceptual models such as the one framing this chapter, Perna's (2006) integrated model of student access and choice, predict that institutional profiles also hold considerable influence on the decisions students make about post-secondary education, researchers have yet to examine this relationship concerning study abroad participation among community college students.

The purpose of this study is twofold. First, it aims to call attention to the fact that study abroad does take place in the community college sector. In this sense, it follows a recent study (González Canché,

2018) that found that the two-year sector attracts almost 10% of all non-resident students across the nine sectors configuring the U.S. higher education system, a figure that had previously been assumed to be nonexistent. Second, this study aims at modeling the relationship between institutional profile characteristics and variations in study abroad participation at community colleges. In this sense, it addresses community college students' ability to access to education abroad using the institution as the unit of analysis. Specifically, this study employs data from both the Institute of International Education (IIE) and the Integrated Postsecondary Education Data System (IPEDS) to examine the role institutional characteristics, such as an institution's gender and race/ethnicity composition and its location, play in community college students' participation in study abroad. The hurdle model analytic technique adopted here allows for the examination of these factors' relationship to both an institution's provision of study abroad opportunity and the percentage of students that participate. Results have implications for both policy-makers and practitioners who aim to increase the prominence of education abroad in the two-year sector.

CONCEPTUAL MODEL

This study is framed by Perna's (2006) conceptual model of student college access and choice, which was initially intended to explain students' decisions about whether and where to attend college. This model conceptualizes student decision-making as happening within four contextual layers. The inner-most layer consists of students' habitus, that is, an individual's internalized system of outlooks and beliefs about the world, determined by past experiences, that shape students' educational expectations and aspirations (Bourdieu, 1977; McDonough, 1994). This level includes factors related to students' academic preparation, financial resources, sources for information about college, and demographic characteristics. A student's high school and community context constitutes the second level of Perna's model and includes characteristics such as structural supports and barriers to post-secondary attendance, the availability of resources, and types of resources available. The higher education context comprises the third layer of this model and consists of factors related to institutional profiles such as location and demographics of the student population. In applying this model to student decision-making beyond initial college choice, these second and third layers may be collapsed into one, corresponding to McDonough's (1997) concept of *organizational habitus*, which recognizes the importance of institutional resources and social structures as they relate to students' choices. Finally, the fourth layer of Perna's model includes the social, economic, and policy context, which correspond to characteristics of students' external environments beyond their immediate institutional context.

Recent work has extended Perna's model to the study of access and choice beyond initial college attendance. Figure 1 depicts how this conceptual model may be applied to study abroad. Concerning study abroad in particular, Salisbury, Paulsen, and Pascarella (2010, 2011) and Salisbury, Umbach, Paulsen, and Pascarella (2009) found that factors related to the inner-most layer of Perna's model, such as the educational attainment of students' parents and the type of financial aid students received, significantly related to students' intent to study abroad. Generally speaking, these studies found that students attending community colleges were less likely to intend to study abroad compared to students at four-year institutions. However, in terms of institution-level characteristics, their analyses did not go beyond the inclusion of institution type in predictive models. To expand on this prior research, the current investigation approaches the study of community college students' participation in education abroad from the

Clearing the Hurdle

perspective of Perna's second and third contextual layers (collapsed into one here) by examining factors related to institutional profile and context. This framework predicts that factors within students' higher education contexts, such as the amount they pay in tuition and fee charges and characteristics of their peers, relate to whether students participate in education abroad activities.

LITERATURE REVIEW

Community College Students' Study Abroad Participation

As mentioned briefly in the introduction to this chapter, only two studies, Amani (2011) and Amani and Kim (2017), have examined community college students' initial decision-making about study abroad participation. Both these studies focused attention at the individual student level. Amani (2011) explored why students at a single community college decided to study abroad and the challenges they faced when making this decision. In examining semi-structured interviews with community college students who had either already studied abroad or had committed to doing so, Amani found that individual-level factors, such as academic demands and aspirations (e.g., intensity of coursework, desire to transfer to the four-year sector), social factors (e.g., the influence of family and friends), and institutional factors (e.g., faculty encouragement) contributed to students' decisions to participate in study abroad. Students especially viewed study abroad as an opportunity of a lifetime, one that they wanted to experience specifically while enrolled at a community college due to a desire to strengthen their applications to transfer to four-year institutions and to fears that academic demands on their time would increase once they transferred. Students in this study identified three primary obstacles to participation in study abroad, namely funding, fear of traveling, and academic and family responsibilities. Similar to Amani (2011), Amani and Kim (2017) employed interview data from community college students enrolled at three different institutions to examine the reasons why they chose to participate in study abroad and the

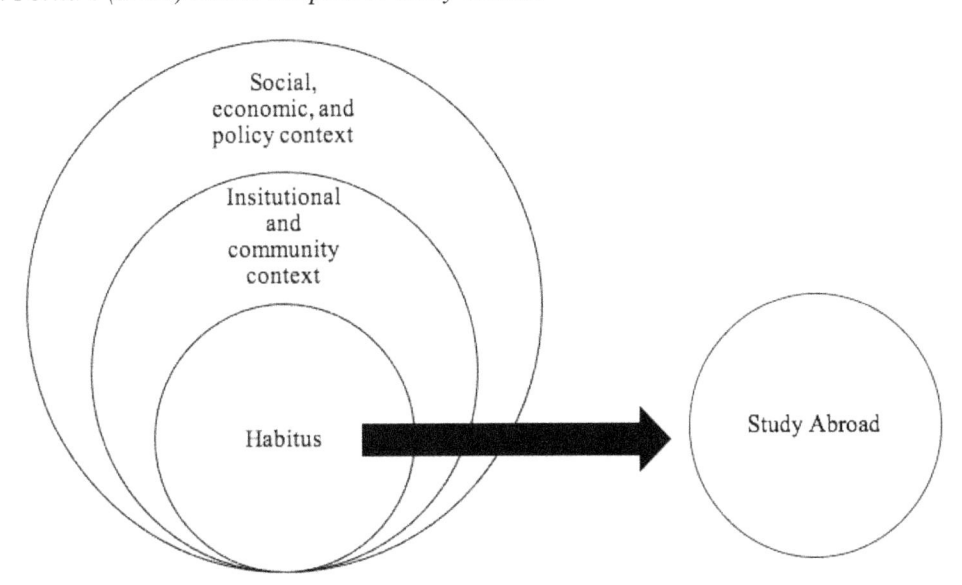

Figure 1. Perna's (2006) model adapted to study abroad

challenges they faced as they made this decision. These researchers identified eight institutional, social, and personal reasons for which students at community colleges chose to study abroad: opportunity of a lifetime, academic transfer, personal timing, cost affordability, faculty encouragement, family support, honors program offerings abroad, and affinity to a group of peers also studying abroad. Challenges faced by these students when considering study abroad included funding concerns, anxiety/fear of travel, and academic-life balance. Taken together, these two studies highlight the fact that many community college students consider study abroad through their institution to be a once-in-a-lifetime opportunity. This finding underscores the importance of providing education abroad at two-year institutions in spite of low overall participation rates.

The Role of the Institution in Study Abroad Access and Choice

Similar to the community college study abroad literature, the general study abroad literature primarily explores students' decisions to participate in study abroad from the individual student perspective. Exceptions to this rule include BaileyShea (2009), Williams (2007), and Simon and Ainsworth (2012), all of whom examine study abroad participation at four-year institutions. In an exploration of the relationships between institution-level characteristics and individual-student participation in study abroad, BaileyShea (2009) found that positive predictors of study abroad included an institution's graduation rate and the proportion of an institution's student body that identified as Latino or American Indian, while negative predictors included the size of an institution's African American and Hawaiian/Pacific Islander population. Williams (2007) found that the number of administrators and staff working in an institution's study abroad office positively related to the number of students able to access study abroad at that institution, while the percentage of the student population receiving financial aid and the institution's average SAT score were negatively associated. Finally, Simon and Ainsworth (2012) highlight the barrier that institutional-level bureaucratic structures may pose for minority students who would like to participate in study abroad, particularly those who lack the background knowledge needed to successfully navigate such bureaucracy. The results of these three studies emphasize the importance of examining institution-level characteristics when studying student participation in study abroad.

METHOD

To reach an understanding of the correspondence between institutional profiles and community college study abroad, this study employs data from two U.S. national datasets, the Institute of International Education's (IIE) annual Open Doors survey and the Integrated Postsecondary Education Data System (IPEDS). Analyses explore the relationship between the percentage of students participating in study abroad and institutional profile characteristics falling into four categories: student body characteristics, institutional charges to students, location of the institution, and instructional characteristics.

Data

Both data sources employed in this study, IIE and IPEDS, consist of annual surveys administered to institutions of higher education across the United States. While institutions are required to report data to IPEDS to receive federal funding, IIE reporting is voluntary, and therefore somewhat sparser in comparison. These two datasets were merged to create a larger dataset wherein IIE data represents the source of information about students' study abroad participation and IPEDS is the source of all institutional characteristics.

In this study, data represent the most recent academic year for which study abroad data are available (2015-16). These data come from the 2017 release of IIE data and from either the 2015 or 2016 release of IPEDS, depending on the survey component (Jaquette & Parra, 2014). The institution-specific UNITID number present in both datasets enabled the merging of the two data sources. In total, the merged dataset contained 1,027 public two-year institutions, 893 of which reported data for all variables of interest (listed in Table 1 below and discussed in the following paragraph). Of these 893 institutions, 101 institutions reported sending students abroad during the 2015-16 academic year to IIE (approximately 11%) while 792 did not (approximately 89%). The institutions representing those that did report sending students abroad are displayed graphically in Figure 2, where they are organized by the percentage of their student populations that participated in education abroad. On average, these 101 institutions reported that 0.4% of their student population studied abroad during the 2015-16 academic year, with a minimum of 0.04% and a maximum of 4.61%. When including all institutions, those who did and those who did not report students studying abroad, an average of 0.05% of students enrolled at institutions in this dataset studied abroad during the 2015-16 academic year. This percentage of students participating in study abroad was calculated by dividing the total number of students studying abroad reported to IIE by the total number of students enrolled at each institution during the Fall 2015 semester as reported in IPEDS.

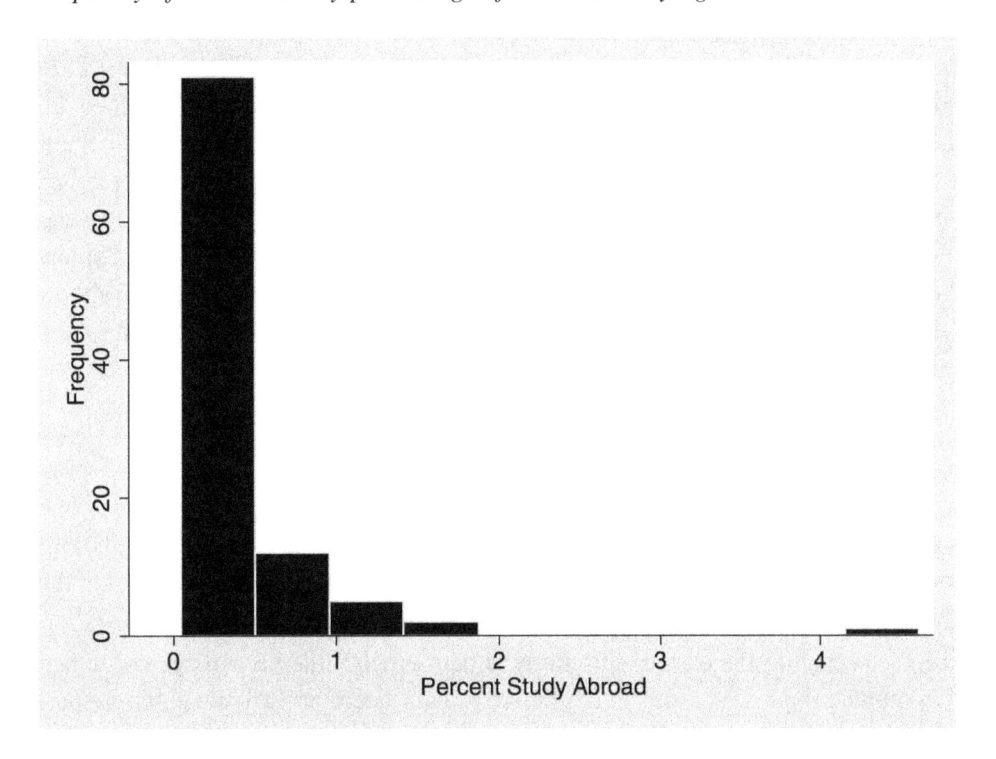

Figure 2. Frequency of institutions by percentage of students studying abroad

Additional institution-level indicators either taken directly from or calculated using IPEDS data fell into four categories: student body characteristics, institutional charges to students, location of the institution, and instructional characteristics. Table 1 lists these variables and provides summary statistics (discussed in the Results section) for each one. It is important to note that these variables correspond to an institution's entire student population, not the subset of students that participated in study abroad. Among the characteristics of institutions' student bodies taken into consideration were several demographic characteristics, including percentage female, percentage non-U.S. residents, percentage Black, percentage Asian, percentage Hispanic, percentage White, and percentage aged 25 or older. Additionally, student enrollment patterns were considered through the inclusion of a variable representing the percentage of an institution's student population that was enrolled part time. To account for students' general socioeconomic status, at least to an extent, the percentage of an institution's student population receiving Pell grant funding was also included. Data on institutions' charges to students, namely the average tuition and fees charged to in-state and out-of-state students during the 2015-16 academic year, comprised the next group of variables. An institution's location (city, suburb, town, or rural) was considered to account for some of the differences in the communities these institutions served. Finally, two factors corresponding to characteristics of the instruction students received were included - the institution's reported student-to-faculty ratio and the percent of its instructional staff that was employed part time.

Analysis

The variables belonging to the four categories of institution-level characteristics just described were employed to predict the percentage of students studying abroad from each institution during the 2015-16 academic year. Given the numerous instances of community colleges that did not report sending any students abroad to IIE, usual means of testing for the relationship between multiple variables and a single continuous outcome (i.e., the percentage of students studying abroad from each institution), such as Ordinary Least Squares regression, were not appropriate in the case of this study. Such analyses may render biased or unrealistic estimates given the skewness of the data. To account for the considerable number of institutions associated with zero students studying abroad, instead a Cragg hurdle regression was fitted to the data. Cragg (1971) proposed this type of regression model to explore outcomes wherein individuals (in this case, institutions) report either zero or a positive value for the outcome of interest (in this case, percentage of students studying abroad). Specifically, hurdle analyses model the relationship depicted in (1)

$$y_i = s_i h_i^* \tag{1}$$

where y_i represents the outcome of interest, in this case, the percentage of students studying abroad in the 2015-16 academic year. The two components on the right-hand side of equation (1) represent two stages of a hurdle model, a probit model (s_i) and a truncated regression model (h_i^*). s_i represents the selection variable, which in the case of this study is equal to 1 if the percentage of students studying abroad is not bounded (that is, not 0), and 0 otherwise. This selection variable is represented in (2)

Table 1. Variables included in models and summary statistics

Variable	N	Mean	Std. Dev.
Percent study abroad	893	0.05	-
Student Body Characteristics			
Percent female	893	57.53	-
Percent nonresident	893	1.05	-
Percent Black	893	13.34	-
Percent Asian	893	3.59	-
Percent Hispanic	893	16.11	-
Percent White	893	56.29	-
Percent part-time students	893	59.77	-
Percent age 25+	893	34.08	-
Percent awarded Pell	893	37.75	-
Student Charges			
In-state tuition and fees[a]	893	3.94	2.00
Out-of-state tuition and fees[a]	893	7.77	3.02
Location[b]			
Percent City	893	31.36	-
Percent Suburb	893	20.38	-
Percent Town	893	23.18	-
Percent Rural	893	25.75	-
Instructional Characteristics			
Student-to-faculty ratio	893	18.87	5.52
Percent part-time instructional staff	893	63.42	-

[a] In thousands; [b] Based on a school's physical address, assigned through a methodology developed by the U.S. Census Bureau's Population Division in 2005

$$s_i = \begin{cases} 1 & if\ z_i \gamma + \varepsilon_i > 0 \\ 0 & otherwise \end{cases} \quad (2)$$

where z_i corresponds to a vector of explanatory variables representing those just outlined in Table 1, γ is a vector of associated coefficients, and ε_i is a standard error term. In other words, the first stage of this model simply predicts whether an institution's students participated in study abroad or not without accounting for the actual percentage of students studying abroad. The second component of the right-hand side of equation (1), h_i^*, represents a continuous latent variable (percentage of students studying abroad), which is only observed if s_i is equal to 1 (that is, only if institutions sent students abroad during the 2015-16 academic year). In this case of this study, this variable was modeled linearly, as in (3)

$$h_i^* = x_i\beta + v_i \tag{3}$$

In (3), x_i represents the same explanatory variables listed in Table 1 while β represents their corresponding coefficients and v_i is an error term. In other words, this second stage of the model predicts the continuous outcome of interest, that is the percentage of students studying abroad from a given institution during the 2015-16 academic year. Taken together, the two stages of a Cragg hurdle model account for the lower-boundedness of the outcome of interest in this study (an institution cannot send fewer than 0% of its students abroad) to produce more reliable and less biased estimates of the outcome of interest.

LIMITATIONS

Lack of institutional reporting to the two data sources employed in this study, IPEDS and IIE, represents a primary limitation of this study. Of note is that overlap in non-reporting patterns existed in that institutions that did not report information to one data source also often did not report information to the other. Concerning IPEDS, while institutions are required to complete data surveys to receive federal funding, still a total of 134 community colleges did not report data for at least some of the variables included in this study. This limitation becomes twofold when considering IIE data. That is, institutional reporting of study abroad data is voluntary, while institutions are only listed in IIE's data reports if they sent ten or more students abroad during a given academic year. As such, the non-inclusion of an institution in IIE's data may be indicative of one of three potential scenarios: an institution did not send students abroad, an institution elected not to report their study abroad numbers, or fewer than ten students from an institution studied abroad in a given academic year. In the case of this study, all three of these scenarios were inevitably collapsed into the same category of zero students participating in education abroad. A second limitation is that IIE data currently only count credit-bearing study abroad. As a consequence, students who study abroad but who do not earn academic credit for their participation (e.g., students who study abroad for personal rather than academic reasons) are not included in this dataset.

RESULTS

Data Overview

Table 1 in the previous section displays summary statistics for each of the variables included in this study. On average, the community colleges in this dataset reported approximately 0.05% of their student populations studying abroad during the 2015-16 academic year. Around 1% of institutions' student populations were comprised of non-U.S. residents, over half of students (60%) were enrolled part time, and approximately 34% were aged 25 or older, on average. Concerning race/ethnicity, approximately 13% of student populations were Black, 4% were Asian, 16% were Hispanic, and 56% were White. Finally, an average of around 38% of student populations received Pell funding to pay for their studies.

Clearing the Hurdle

Concerning tuition and fee charges (represented in $1,000 increments in Table 1), institutions on average charged slightly less than $4,000 to in-state students and almost $8,000 to out-of-state students for the academic year. Around 31% of institutions in this dataset were in urban locations, while 20%, 23%, and 25% were located in suburban, town, and rural locations, respectively. The average student-to-faculty ratio at these institutions was 19:1, and almost 64% of institutions' instructional staff was employed part time, on average.

Hurdle Model

Results of both hurdle model stages are displayed in Table 2. For ease of interpretation, all coefficients represent marginal effects, thus rendering estimates that are interpreted as percent changes in the likelihood of the outcome variable of each respective stage. In the first stage of the model, significant predictors of institutions providing access to study abroad included the percentage of the student body that was comprised of non-U.S. residents, the percentages of both Black and Asian students in the student body, and location in a town or rural area (compared to an urban area). More specifically, the average effect of a percent increase in the non-resident student population at a community college was related with an approximate 2% increase in the likelihood that an institution's students would study abroad. A percent increase in the proportion of Black students comprising the student body was associated with an approximate 0.3% decrease in the likelihood of study abroad opportunity, while the same increase in the proportion of Asian students enrolled at an institution was associated with a 0.4% increase in the likelihood. Compared to community colleges located in urban areas (the reference group), those in both towns and rural areas are approximately 18% and 8%, respectively, less likely to have students studying abroad.

In the second stage of the hurdle model, which controls for the fact that many institutions in this dataset did not report students studying abroad at all, two variables returned significant results: the percentage of the student body comprised of part-time students and the student-to-faculty ratio. A one percent increase in the percent of students enrolled part time was associated with a decrease of approximately 0.2 of a percentage point in the proportion of students studying abroad, while a one unit increase in the student-to-faculty ratio was associated with a similarly-sized negative effect.

DISCUSSION AND IMPLICATIONS

The theoretical framework guiding this study suggests that institutional profile relates to students' access to study abroad opportunities and as such their participation patterns. This study has focused on the institutional profiles of community colleges. Table 3 summarizes this study's significant results and implications for policy and practice that derive from each one. Specifically, it was found that the percentage of a community college's student body that was comprised of non-U.S. residents positively related to study abroad opportunities, while location in a town or rural area was negatively related to this outcome (compared to urban locations). The former result likely reflects an institution's commitment to internationalization more broadly. That is, institutions that bring in international students to study may also direct more resources towards sending their own domestic students abroad. Concerning geographic location, it may be that community colleges located in less urban environments struggle to connect study abroad with their community-focused missions, resulting in fewer institutions in rural locations and towns providing students with study abroad opportunities. Institutions located in these

Table 2. Hurdle model results

	Stage 1: Probit (outcome: study abroad participation)		Stage 2: Truncated Regression (outcome: percentage of students studying abroad)	
	Marginal Effect	Standard Error	Marginal Effect	Standard Error
Percent female	0.000	0.002	0.000	0.005
Percent nonresident	0.017***	0.004	0.008	0.004
Percent Black	-0.003*	0.001	-0.001	0.001
Percent Asian	0.004*	0.002	0.002	0.003
Percent Hispanic	0.000	0.001	0.001+	0.015
Percent White	0.000	0.001	0.000	0.005
Percent part-time students	-0.002	0.001	-0.002*	0.023
Percent age 25+	0.000	0.001	-0.001	0.014
Percent awarded Pell	-0.002+	0.001	-0.001	0.003
In-state tuition and fees[a]	-0.008	0.005	-0.004	0.007
Out-of-state tuition/fees[a]	0.006	0.004	0.004	0.030
Suburb[b]	0.022	0.022	0.009	0.025
Town[b]	-0.178***	0.046	-0.055	0.530
Rural[b]	-0.078**	0.029	-0.032	0.094
Student-to-faculty ratio	0.001	0.002	-0.002*	0.049
Pct part-time instr. staff	0.002+	0.001	0.000	0.009
Constant	-0.961	1.145	4.126	3.091
Sample Size	893		893	
Pseudo R2	0.270		0.317	
Log likelihood	-230.176		-218.229	

+ p<.10, * p<.05, ** p<.01, *** p<.001
Reference group for location is Urban
[a] In thousands, [b] Based on a school's physical address, assigned through a methodology developed by the U.S. Census Bureau's Population Division in 2005

environments may benefit from direct communication with local employers and other entities in the community concerning their international skill needs. An additional potential explanation for this finding is that it reflects differences in the amount of funding available to community colleges located in different environments, and consequently differences in the amount of funding institutions are able to dedicate to study abroad. Generally speaking, this result points to a need for future research focusing on differences in the implementation of internationalization efforts among community colleges located in different local environments. An interesting connection that future research might make is between an institution's location and its attraction of international students on the one hand as they relate to study abroad participation on the other.

Concerning demographics of the student population at a given community college, the percentage of this population identified as Black predicted a decrease in the likelihood of students studying abroad, a result in line with that of BaileyShea (2009), who studied institution-level predictors of study abroad

Clearing the Hurdle

in the four-year higher education sector. However, in contrast to BaileyShea (2009), the proportion of the student body that identified as Asian positively predicted study abroad participation. This finding is somewhat surprising, as this student group tends to be underrepresented in four-year institution study abroad (Institute of International Education, 2017; Van Der Meid, 2003). Future research is needed to focus specifically on the study abroad participation patterns of both Black and Asian students enrolled at community colleges. It may be that while community colleges represent a place of access to international education among Asian students, Black community college students are not able to access these opportunities as easily. The findings of this study suggest that this non-participation is not due to Black students' lack of interest in or ability to study abroad, but rather is because they tend to attend institutions that do not offer such experiences. This finding has potential important implications for needed change in the organizational structures of community colleges that serve large proportions of Black students.

While not a significant predictor of the provision of study abroad opportunity (Stage 1), the percentage of an institution's student population attending part-time was negatively associated with the percentage of students studying abroad (Stage 2). This finding is not surprising, as part-time student populations are more likely to have other responsibilities, such as full-time employment, that discourage study abroad. While community colleges already work to design flexible study abroad programs aimed particularly at this student population (Bartzis, Kirkwood, & Mulvihill, 2016), this finding suggests a need for renewed and enhanced efforts in this area. Institutional decision-makers cannot assume that part-time attendance implies a lack of desire or ability to participate in education-enhancing activities such as study abroad. Also significant in this second stage was the student-to-faculty ratio, which was negatively related to the percentage of student studying abroad from a given institution. This finding coupled with that of Amani (2011) and Amani and Kim (2017) that community college students identified faculty encouragement as an important influence in their decision to participate in education abroad highlights the importance of the unique, and personal, role that faculty and instructors play in encouraging students to participate in academic and career-enhancing activities such as study abroad. This finding has important implications for faculty training and professional development, which may be modified to include attention to students' international engagement while enrolled at a community college. Such training is particularly important given research findings that indicate that underrepresented racial minorities at community colleges interact with faculty and derive benefits from this interaction in a variety of ways (Chang, 2005).

Clearly, the significant findings of the hurdle model employed in this study present interesting food for thought for any administrator or decision-maker at a community college interested in increasing participation in study abroad. However, the non-significant findings of this study are equally as interesting and important. For example, findings related to the gender compositions of the student bodies of community colleges indicated that this factor was not a significant predictor of study abroad provision or participation. Future research is needed to explore why institutional gender composition does not appear to significantly relate to study abroad at community colleges. Similarly, the percentage of the student body receiving Pell funding, a variable often taken as a proxy for students' socioeconomic status, was not significant in either phase of the hurdle model. This finding may be indicative of a certain level of affordability of study abroad programs that are sponsored by community colleges. In other words, students who are not able to access study abroad through other institutions due to financial concerns may be able to access these opportunities in the two-year sector. Indeed, these findings are in sharp contrast with prior research on study abroad participation among students enrolled primarily in four-year institutions, which finds that male students and students with higher levels of financial need are less likely to study abroad (e.g., Brux & Fry, 2010; Salisbury et al., 2010, 2011; Shirley, 2006; Simon & Ainsworth, 2012).

These discrepancies between the current study and studies involving students enrolled in the four-year sector indicate that community colleges may be a place where opportunities to participate in study abroad are more readily available to students belonging to traditionally underrepresented groups, such as male students and students from lower socioeconomic status groups. Although future research around this topic is needed, these results are promising in that they point to the community college as a potential site for the democratization of study abroad opportunity. Additional inquiry might especially explore policies and practices at community colleges that open up opportunities for and encourage underrepresented students' participation in study abroad. For example, institutions might consider articulation agreements with four-year institutions that encourage study abroad participation at the point when students transfer from a two- to a four-year institution. Another line of future research that may prove to be fruitful is a comparative study wherein the study abroad participation patterns of community college students is compared to that of students enrolled at other institution types.

IMPLICATIONS FOR FUTURE RESEARCH ON COMMUNITY COLLEGE STUDY ABROAD

The previous section has pointed to several directions for future research on study abroad participation among community college students, ranging from a deeper exploration of the role of institutional geographic location in students' study abroad participation patterns to the role that community colleges may play in providing study abroad opportunities to students who otherwise are underrepresented in

Table 3. Summary of significant findings and implications for policy and practice

Finding	Implication(s)
Stage 1: Study Abroad Participation	
The percentage of the student body comprised of non-U.S. residents positively related to study abroad.	Study abroad may be a function of general institutional commitment to internationalization goals. Institutions that focus on bringing in international students may also direct more resources towards sending their own domestic students abroad
Location in a town or rural area was negatively related to study abroad (compared to urban locations).	Institutions located in less urban environments may benefit from direct communication with local employers and other entities in the community concerning their international skill needs.
The percentage of students identified as Black negatively related to study abroad.	Change in the organizational structures of community colleges that serve large proportions of Black students may be necessary to provide access to study abroad to a diverse student population.
The percentage of students identified as Asian positively related to study abroad.	Community colleges may represent a place of access to international education among Asian students.
Stage 2: Percentage of Students Studying Abroad	
The percentage of an institution's student population attending part-time negatively related to study abroad.	Institutional decision-makers need to renew and enhance focus on designing flexible study abroad programs aimed especially at part-time students.
An institution's student-to-faculty ratio negatively related to study abroad.	Faculty training and professional development may need to be modified to include attention to students' international engagement while enrolled at a community college, particularly when considering underrepresented student populations.

Clearing the Hurdle

U.S. study abroad. It is clear that the community college sector holds much promise for future endeavors that seek to increase and enhance the international experiences of students that attend U.S. institutions of higher education. In closing, however, a limitation of this study must be highlighted once more. This study is inherently limited by the data that are available to conduct research on study abroad participation at community colleges. For example, in the dataset used for this study, a community college associated with sending zero students abroad may not have sent any students abroad but may also have sent students abroad and not reported this information to the Institute of International Education or may have sent fewer than ten students abroad. The inclusion of more accurate data on this front could alter the estimates of the statistical model presented here. It is important that institutions prioritize the reporting of their study abroad information.

An additional concern involving data availability relates to the identification of community colleges as potential sites for the democratization of study abroad. Future research is needed to explore other elements of Perna's (2006) model of student access and choice, such as individual student-level factors (e.g., markers of socioeconomic status and students' pre-college resources), that significantly relate to study abroad participation among community college students themselves. This study was limited to the examination of institutional profiles and institution-level study abroad participation numbers as these data represent what is currently available to researchers. Investigations that are able to account for both individual student-level characteristics along with institutional profile characteristics would be able to further examine the potential for democratization in study abroad at community colleges. These studies should address student background characteristics and, importantly, incorporate considerations of prestige and privilege into their research designs. Investigations along these lines would contribute to an important conversation surrounding study abroad at community colleges. More detailed information about the nature of community college students' study abroad experiences (e.g., destination and length of study abroad) is also needed to explore potential issues surrounding not only the quantity but also the quality of community college study abroad. Indeed, investigations concerned with access to study abroad are incomplete if they do not also address questions concerning what types of experiences students are able to access. Future efforts that involve partnerships between researchers and practitioners at community colleges have the potential to make available more precise information about community college students' study abroad participation patterns. These data, in turn, will enable better-informed and more nuanced research to inform community college study abroad policy and practice.

ACKNOWLEDGMENT

The author is grateful to both Manuel González Canché and Rob Toutkoushian for their advice and feedback on prior versions of this chapter and to Rosalind Raby, Gregory Malveaux, and two anonymous reviewers for their comments during this chapter's revisions. All remaining errors are my own.

REFERENCES

Amani, M. (2011). *Study abroad decision and participation at community colleges: Influential factors and challenges from the voices of students and coordinators* (Unpublished doctoral dissertation). George Washington University, Washington, DC.

Amani, M., & Kim, M.M. (2017). Study abroad participation at community colleges: Students' decision and influential factors. *Community College Journal of Research and Practice.*

BaileyShea. C. (2009). *Factors that affect American college students' participation in study abroad* (Unpublished doctoral dissertation). University of Rochester, Rochester, NY.

Bartzis, O. L., Kirkwood, K. J., & Mulvihill, T. M. (2016). Innovative approaches to study abroad at Harper College and Fox Valley Technical College. In R. L. Raby & E. J. Valeau (Eds.), *International education at community colleges: Themes, practices, and case studies* (pp. 237–246). Palgrave Macmillan. doi:10.1057/978-1-137-53336-4_17

Blair, D. P., Phinney, L., & Phillippe, K. A. (2001). *International programs at community colleges.* Washington, DC: American Association of Community Colleges.

Bourdieu, P. (1977). *Outline of theory and practice* (R. Nice, Trans.). Cambridge, UK: Cambridge University Press. doi:10.1017/CBO9780511812507

Brux, J., & Fry, B. (2010). Multicultural students in study abroad: Their interests, their issues, and their constraints. *Journal of Studies in International Education, 14*(5), 508–527. doi:10.1177/1028315309342486

Chang, J. C. (2005). Faculty-student interaction at the community college: A focus on students of color. *Research in Higher Education, 46*(7), 769–802. doi:10.100711162-004-6225-7

Cragg, J. G. (1971). Some statistical models for limited dependent variables with application to the demand for durable goods. *Econometrica, 39*(5), 829–844. doi:10.2307/1909582

Emert, H. A., & Pearson, D. L. (2007). Expanding the vision of international education: Collaboration, assessment, and intercultural development. *New Directions for Community Colleges, 2007*(138), 67–75. doi:10.1002/cc.283

Frost, R. A., & Raby, R. L. (2009). Democratizing study abroad: Challenges of open access, local commitments, and global competence in community colleges. In R. Lewin (Ed.), *Handbook of practice and research in study abroad* (pp. 170–190). New York: Routledge.

González Canché, M. S. (2018). Geographical network analysis and spatial econometrics as tools to enhance our understanding of student migration patterns and benefits in the U.S. higher education network. *The Review of Higher Education, 41*(2), 169–216. doi:10.1353/rhe.2018.0001

Green, M. F., & Siaya, L. (2005). *Measuring internationalization at community colleges.* Report from the American Council on Education Center for Institutional and International Initiatives. Retrieved from http://www.acenet.edu/news-room/Documents/Measuring-CommunityCollege.pdf

Institute of International Education. (2017). *Open Doors 2017: Report on international educational exchange.* Retrieved from http://www.iie.org/Research-and-Publications/Open-Doors

Jaquette, O., & Parra, E. E. (2014). Using IPEDS for panel analyses: Core concepts, data challenges, and empirical applications. In M.B. Paulsen (Ed.), Higher education: Handbook of theory and research (vol. 29, pp. 467-533). New York: Springer Science+Business Media.

McDonough, P. (1994). Buying and selling higher education: The social construction of the college applicant. *The Journal of Higher Education, 65*, 427–446.

McDonough, P. (1997). *Choosing colleges: How social class and schools structure opportunity*. Albany, NY: SUNY University Press.

National Center for Education Statistics. (2016). *Digest of Education Statistics*. Retrieved from https://nces.ed.gov/programs/digest/

Oberstein-Delvalle, E. (1999). *Study abroad programs in three California community colleges* (Unpublished doctoral dissertation). Pepperdine University, Malibu, CA.

Perna, L. W. (2006). Studying college access and choice: A proposed conceptual model. In J. C. Smart (Ed.), *Higher education: Handbook of theory and research* (Vol. 21, pp. 99–157). New York: Springer Press.

Raby, R. L. (2007). Internationalizing the curriculum: On- and off-campus strategies. *New Directions for Community Colleges, 138*(138), 57–66. doi:10.1002/cc.282

Raby, R. L. (2008, September). *Meeting America's global education challenge: Expanding education abroad at U.S. Community colleges* (Institute of International Education Study Abroad White Paper Series 3). New York: Institute for International Education Press.

Raby, R. L. (2012). Re-imagining international education at community colleges. *Audem: International Journal of Higher Education and Democracy, 3*, 81–98.

Raby, R. L., Rhodes, G. M., & Biscarra, A. (2014). Community college study abroad: Implications for student success. *Community College Journal of Research and Practice, 38*(2-3), 174–183. doi:10.1080/10668926.2014.851961

Raby, R. L., & Valeau, E. J. (2007). Community college international education: Looking back to forecast the future. *New Directions for Community Colleges, 2007*(138), 5–14. doi:10.1002/cc.276

Robertson, J. F., & Blasi, L. (2017). Community college student perceptions of their experiences related to global learning: Understanding the impact of family, faculty, and the curriculum. *Community College Journal of Research and Practice, 41*(11), 697–718. doi:10.1080/10668926.2016.1222974

Salisbury, M. H., Paulsen, M. B., & Pascarella, E. T. (2010). To see the world or stay at home: Applying an integrated student choice model to explore the gender gap in the intent to study abroad. *Research in Higher Education, 51*(7), 615–640. doi:10.100711162-010-9171-6

Salisbury, M. H., Paulsen, M. B., & Pascarella, E. T. (2011). Why do all the study abroad students look alike? Applying an integrated student choice model to explore differences in the factors that influence white and minority students' intent to study abroad. *Research in Higher Education, 52*(2), 123–150. doi:10.100711162-010-9191-2

Salisbury, M. H., Umbach, P. D., Paulsen, M. B., & Pascarella, E. T. (2009). Going global: Understanding the choice process of the intent to study abroad. *Research in Higher Education, 50*(2), 119–143. doi:10.100711162-008-9111-x

Shirley, S. (2006). *The gender gap in post-secondary study abroad: Understanding and marketing to males* (Unpublished doctoral dissertation). University of North Dakota, Grand Forks, ND.

Simon, J., & Ainsworth, J.W. (2012). Race and socioeconomic status differences in study abroad participation: The role of habitus, social networks, and cultural capital. *ISRN Education*.

Thomas, M. (2016). Community college education abroad and business internship programs' cultivation of competency in communicating, collaborating, and critical thinking? In R. L. Raby & E. J. Valeau (Eds.), *International education at community colleges: Themes, practices, and case studies* (pp. 323–336). Palgrave Macmillan. doi:10.1057/978-1-137-53336-4_23

Van Der Meid, J. S. (2003). Asian Americans: Factors influencing the decision to study abroad. *Frontiers: The Interdisciplinary Journal of Study Abroad*, *9*(4), 71–110.

Williams, F. (2007). *Study abroad and Carnegie doctoral/research extensive universities: Preparing students from underrepresented racial groups to live in a global environment* (Unpublished doctoral dissertation). Virginia Commonwealth University, Richmond, VA.

Zhang, Y. (2011). CSCC review series essay: Education abroad in the U.S. community colleges. *Community College Review*, *39*(2), 181–200. doi:10.1177/0091552111404552

Chapter 7
The Outreach Triad for Successful Study Abroad Programs:
Students, Faculty, and the Local Community

Jennifer Joy Robertson
Valencia College, USA

ABSTRACT

The old adage "build it and they will come" does not apply in the context of study abroad at the community college. Community colleges have historically struggled with study abroad enrollment due to a number of factors including inadequate funding, insufficient institutional support, and a lack of interest and awareness on behalf of their students. While there are many factors that go into successful programming for study abroad, one key element is outreach. This chapter will define outreach in terms of the marketing and communication methods to three key stakeholders in study abroad: students, faculty, and the local community. It will be argued that program administrators need to better understand the various ways in which outreach is used to increase both student enrollment, minority students in particular, and the number of faculty engaged in leading study abroad at the community college. The chapter will conclude by proposing some strategies for identifying funding opportunities from local community partners.

INTRODUCTION

The benefits of study abroad in higher education are well documented in the academic literature, particularly when it comes to sufficiently preparing our future leaders how to effectively navigate the global marketplace. However, community colleges have historically faced a myriad of challenges when it comes to study abroad program enrollment. A common theme among many program administrators has been the lack funding and staffing to sufficiently develop and promote study abroad programs on campus. With tight state budgets for higher education, international education has become a peripheral activity

DOI: 10.4018/978-1-5225-6252-8.ch007

to the core mission of workforce education in many the community colleges. Moreover, community college faculty may not have the experience or knowledge to effectively develop and promote study abroad programs on campus. Compounding these challenges is a student body, especially minority students, who do not pursue international experiences as part of their academic goals.

The purpose of this chapter is to identify the influences on a community college student's interest in global learning opportunities, outline the obstacles they face when it comes to study abroad participation, and offer suggestions to campus administrators and faculty on how to increase outreach efforts to market and promote study abroad experiences particularly to racial and ethnic minority students. Recommendations are also provided on how to engage the local community in study abroad.

It is important to note that several of the studies presented in this chapter come from research done at community colleges in the state of Florida, which is one of a growing number of states that allow community colleges to offer bachelor's degrees to increase students' access to higher education at a lower cost (Povich, 2018). While these institutions may be changing their names and degree offerings, the mission continues to be to serve the local community; and therefore these community colleges can serve as models for other institutions of higher education when it comes to internationalizing the campus and curriculum.

BACKGROUND

Student Interest in Global Learning

Many post-secondary educational institutions rank "improving student preparedness for a global era" among one of their most pressing goals (American Council on Education, 2017). In 2006, the Secretary of Education, Margaret Spellings, commissioned a year-long study of the United States higher education system and found that much work was still needed to develop "a world-class higher-education system that creates new knowledge, contributes to economic prosperity and global competitiveness, and empowers citizens… a higher-education system that gives Americans the workplace skills they need to adapt to a rapidly changing economy" (Spellings, 2006, pg. viii).

Over a decade later, the question is still asked as to why so few college students in the United States study abroad. According to the Institute of International Education's Open Doors Report (2016), only 1.6% of all U.S. undergraduates studied abroad in 2014-2015. The question begs to answer if college students are just not interested in the world at large, and if they are not then is college too late to spark that interest? In a study of one large community college in Florida, the author found that only 24% of students (n=68) had a strong interest in global topics or events. One student in the study responded: "I have too much to worry about within my own country and mind, I will begin to worry about international events when they begin to adversely affect me" (Robertson, 2014, p. 10).

In a follow up study at nine community colleges in Florida by Robertson and Blasi (2017) using similar research protocols, the authors found similar results with 36% of students (n=175) very interested in global learning. Only one-third (33%) of the students strongly preferred courses with global content and 40% strongly preferred courses with cultural content. However, the authors did find that the majority of students had traveled internationally or planned to travel in the near future (86%), but only 4% reported participating in a study abroad program. According to a separate qualitative study with seven students enrolled in four community colleges in Florida, there were five primary factors found to influence a student's interest in global learning: family, friends, academic experiences, workplace experiences, and the external environment (Figure 1).

The study found that the students' interest in global learning occurred well before the college experience however, they "had no clear understanding of global learning from an academic perspective, and what they did know came from a series of disconnected life experiences that students may or may not be able to one day piece together" (Robertson, 2016, p. 178). The takeaway from some of this prior research is that many students arrive to the community college with a variety of life experiences that expose them to the world, but they still lack an understanding of or interest in global topics such as current events, geography, culture, or the benefits of study abroad. There is a distinct difference between knowledge and experience, so a student might have friends from Latin American but never truly understand the differences between American and Hispanic culture. Therefore, the community college can be a place to help students bridge the experience to knowledge gap (Robertson 2016). This poses a challenge for study abroad administrators and faculty who want to increase program enrollment at their institutions because many of these students do not see the value of study abroad, particularly in terms of cost and time away from home.

Study Abroad at the Community College

There has already been much research done on the benefits of study abroad, although mostly at the four-year universities. One study conducted in the California Community College System by Raby, Rhodes, and Biscarra (2014) used a mixed-method research design to explore if participation in study abroad had an impact on academic success. The study showed those students had higher levels of retention and completion rates than students who did not. The study also found that academic gains were even higher for Hispanic students, which is a noteworthy outcome since Hispanic achievement has historically lagged behind Whites and Asians (Raby, Rhodes, & Biscarra, 2014).

Figure 1. The global learning circle of influence

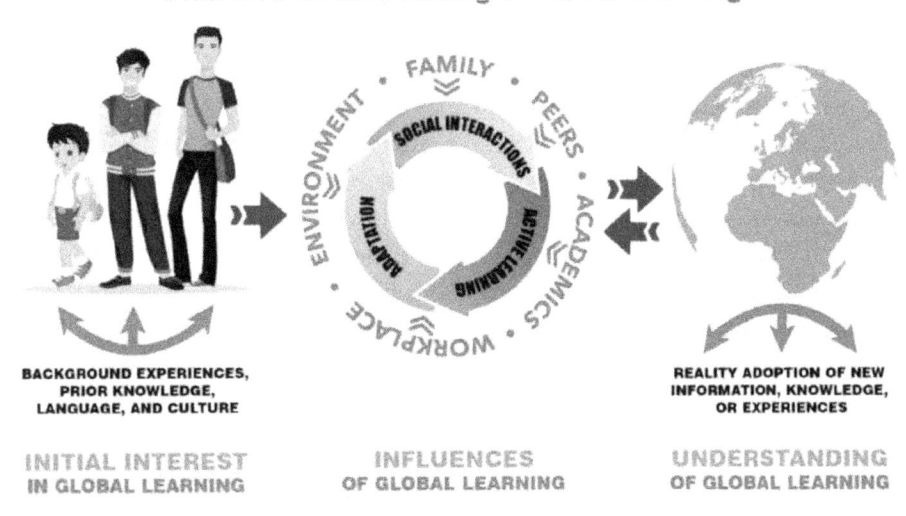

In the fall of 2015, there were 7.2 million students enrolled in community colleges across the United States (American Association of Community Colleges, 2017) yet only 1.7% of them participated in study abroad compared to 9.1% of students enrolled at four-year institutions (Institute for International Education, 2017). While internationalizing efforts in the community college have historically lagged behind four-year universities, efforts to increase study abroad enrollment ranked as the number one priority across all institution types in the American Council on Education's (2017) Mapping Internationalizing 2017 study. Study abroad is one type of education abroad, which also includes international internships and international service learning, and is a term used to describe "activities that take students to other countries and contribute to their learning and development" (American Council on Education, 2017).

There are many challenges that can impact study abroad enrollment in higher education. From the institutional perspective, it can be an expensive and labor-intensive endeavor for an institution; only about one-fifth of the 1,164 institutions in the American Council on Education's Mapping Internationalization 2017 study had a formal strategy to financially support internationalization efforts, and less than half had an organized office led by an administrator. These numbers were much smaller for community colleges, however, there were only 118 community college respondents in the survey. The Forum on Education Abroad (2017) State of the Field report found that the top five concerns in education abroad included crisis and risk management, the need for better student funding, adequate preparation for students supporting underrepresented students, and concerns over the academic quality of the programs. Raby, Rhodes, and Biscarra (2014) noted that one of the greatest challenges for community colleges specifically is their locally-focused workforce development mission which conflicts with a broader focus on internationalization.

In addition to the challenge of increasing study abroad enrollment in the community college, there exists the even more complex dilemma of increasing the number of students from diverse racial and ethnic backgrounds. According to the Institute of International Education (2017), of all college students who studied abroad in 2015-2016, 71.6% were White, 9.7% Hispanic or Latino, and 5.9% were Black or African American; in contrast, community college students represented 61.4% White, 23.2% Hispanic, and 8.6% Black or African American.

There are several studies which examine the complex set of reasons why community college students do not enroll in study abroad programs such as lack of knowledge about the programs, personal finances, work and family responsibilities, fear of racism and discrimination abroad, anxiety over traveling abroad, lack of academically relevant study abroad programs, lack of institutional financial support, safety concerns, and a feeling that these programs offer no value (Institute for International Education, 2008; Brux & Fry, 2010; Robertson,2014; Forum on Education Abroad, 2017; Barclay Hamir & Gozik, 2018). In one community college research study that included 38% minorities, students were asked why they did not want to study abroad and they listed financial reasons (66%), work responsibilities (37%), family responsibilities (35%), and academic reasons (25%) as the primary factors (Robertson & Blasi, 2017). Study abroad program administrators and faculty should review the literature that is already available on financing study abroad programs in the community college (Sutin, Derrico, Raby, & Valeau, 2011; Hernandez, Wiedenhoeft, & Wick, 2014; Chieffo & Spaeth, 2017).

THE OUTREACH TRIAD FOR STUDY ABROAD: STUDENTS, FACULTY, AND THE LOCAL COMMUNITY

The mission of the community college system in the United States focuses on the local community, which can make some administrators uneasy at the idea of investing funds into efforts that focus on international education. This reality can then lead to insufficient funding and resource allocation to the programming of study abroad opportunities for community college students. In order to increase study abroad participation on campus, it must be promoted to students, faculty, and the local community as a high impact learning activity that connects to the institution's mission statement, values, and strategic goals.

Marketing to Students

One of the challenges in growing an institution's study abroad enrollment is the lack of knowledge that some administrators and faculty have when it comes to effectively marketing programs to students. Many times there is a "build it and they will come" approach without fully realizing the importance of developing a marketing strategy behind each program, which includes a mix of tactics to communicate out to all intended audiences and stakeholders. Moreover, sometimes faculty believe that administrators get in the way of their efforts to promote study abroad opportunities on campus when ideally this must be a shared responsibility between both faculty and administration to be most effective (Keese & O'Brien, 2011).

The first step to increasing student participation in study abroad at the community college is understanding the student demographics on campus, particularly when it comes to knowing what the obstacles will be and the student's decision-making process. The goal is to be inclusive across all racial, ethnic, and socioeconomic backgrounds when it comes to study abroad participation. According to previous research studies, we know that the family is an important factor in a student's global learning interest level (Robertson & Blasi, 2017), so overcoming negative family perceptions about the dangers, high costs, and misconceptions of study abroad is paramount to student outreach and recruitment. Preparation for the development of all study abroad programs should include a student survey, either electronically or through in-person focus groups, on their programs of interest in terms of destination, duration, course offering, time of year, price point, and student concerns. This information will be useful when determining the right mix of study abroad program offerings to best meet students' academic goals.

The next step in the process of student outreach is to develop a communication strategy using a variety of tactics that include information on program benefits, academic requirements, registration and payment processes, scholarship opportunities, and how financial aid can be used to cover the costs of study abroad. The marketing tactics used should include a combination of print media, in-person promotion, and electronic media. The following is a list of suggestions based on the successful experiences of community college administrators and faculty who are members of the Florida Consortium of International Education, an organization where individuals come together annually in a small conference-style event to share ideas and cross-promote study abroad opportunities:

- **Print Media:** A key marketing tactic must include the development of visually appealing posters, flyers, brochures, and/or rack cards to place around campus in high-traffic locations. Ensure faculty program leaders have input on the final printed materials and also consider validating the messaging with current students to see if they find it appealing. If lack of sufficient wall space for brochure racks is an issue, use the T-style sandwich board displays to make your own mobile brochure holder. More cost-effective print media solutions include the creation of program bookmarks or business cards with contact information that can be printed in high quantity numbers for distribution. The information that is provided to students should include contact phone numbers, websites, and course information and be made available in different languages for parents which can be done electronically rather than hard copy if there are budgetary restraints.
- **In-Person Promotion:** Hosting an open house on campus and inviting family members is an excellent way to begin to dispel the myths and dangers of study abroad and convince students that these international experiences are beneficial to their long-term academic and career goals (Bandyopadhyay & Bandyopadhyay, 2015). It is important to invite parents and family members to informational events since these individuals have a strong influence on a student's decision to participate in study abroad (Robertson, 2016). In addition to the open house concept, some other highly effective methods of promotion include tabling at high-traffic sites around campus, facilitating classroom presentations with the professor's permission to target students who might want to take the course as an elective or toward their major, and making presentations to student clubs and organizations.
- **Electronic Media:** A well-designed and easy-to-navigate website for study abroad is paramount to a successful recruitment strategy. The website must include a general landing page with links to informational pages to showcase overall study abroad program benefits, timeline, payment deadlines, program processes, application requirements, and upcoming informational events. There should be additional pages that go into detail for each study abroad program with information on the course, destination, costs, and faculty contacts. A clearly organized website is particularly important since market research points to the fact that "school websites remain pivotal during students' post-secondary decision-making journey" (Higher Education Marketing, 2016, p. 1). A second component of electronic media promotion is to have a comprehensive social media strategy across multiple platforms to keep students engaged and "following" you. According to Hanover Research (2014, p. 9), "Institutions are making greater use of social media and digital platforms like Twitter, Facebook, YouTube, and podcasts to market their programs, while website design and interface is proving a crucial component in how colleges and universities present themselves to prospective students." While this statement was originally intended for overall institutional marketing, it still applies at the programmatic level as well. It can be overwhelming to post to multiple social media sites several times a week so tools such as Hootsuite and Zoho will help manage your social media efforts since they give you the ability to schedule posts in advance and post to multiple sites at once with one click. A final recommendation includes developing an open informational "course" on the college's learning management system (LMS) such as Canvas or Blackboard, which will be easily accessible to students at all times. There is a way in which messages can be shared out in all online classes in the network college-wide. This can be accomplished by working with colleagues on campus responsible for academic support technology, instructional technology, or digital learning.

As previously mentioned, marketing must be done as a partnership between study abroad administrators and faculty to achieve the greatest return on investment. It is recommended that a document is drafted that specifically outlines who handles which marketing and outreach activities so that it is clear for all stakeholders, particularly when there is a centralized office and/or support staff. In the case when there is no centralized study abroad office, faculty can try to recruit the help of staff in the various campus units and make use of the mobile brochure racks. All campus units including admissions, student services, advising, the business office, and financial aid staff should be fully informed and/or trained on the process of study abroad, and the registration and payment processes for these programs should not be overly cumbersome or complex for students or this may hamper overall recruitment efforts. The payment deadlines should align with financial aid disbursement if at all possible to relieve the debt burden on students. It is recommended to build a study abroad program timeline backwards starting with the deadlines when payments are due to program providers and forward through when professors submit their paperwork to lead a study abroad program. This will ensure that stakeholders have sufficient lead time from the application deadline to implement the marketing plan. It is suggested that students have at least one to two full semesters in advance of the application deadline to plan their course load and save money. See Valencia College's website for a sample timeline for faculty proposals, program promotion, and student application deadlines: http://valenciacollege.edu/international/studyabroad/faculty-staff/leadstudyabroad/

Promoting to Faculty

According to the American Council on Education's Mapping Internationalizing 2017 study, less than 40% of the 118 community colleges reported that they have faculty who lead study abroad programs. There are many contributing factors for low participation of faculty leading study abroad in the community college system. Program administrators and faculty in community colleges in the Florida Consortium for International Education have reported that faculty lack sufficient funding for programs, a centralized office, marketing expertise, and program development expertise. The challenge is that many community college faculty do not understand what is involved in developing, marketing, and leading a study abroad program (Keese & O'Brien, 2011). However, it is possible for faculty to design programs that are credit bearing and affordable to students who can use their financial aid (Hernandez, Wiedenhoeft, & Wick, 2014). The first step is to assist faculty with the process of developing safe, affordable, and academically rigorous study abroad programs for students, and this requires a formal program approval process. First, identify a committee composed of faculty, administrators, and student affairs personnel to work in collaboration on a program approval process that includes a proposal form, evaluation rubric, and timeline. Ensure that the rubric evaluates criteria on the faculty member's international experience, program safety, affordability, program provider selection, academic rigor, program minimum and maximum enrollment guidelines, and student selection. The evaluation rubric should also be designed to address the challenge of having the same people leading study abroad over and over again since many times it is the same few faculty members. One way to get new faculty into the mix is to create a scoring system that allows faculty to get more points only for the first several years and then they have to step down and allow other faculty to lead. Once a system is put into place, these opportunities should be communicated out to all faculty. The following are recommendations from the author, which outline some best practices to engage more faculty in study abroad:

- Encourage a culture of embracing new faculty who want to lead study abroad. Create an advisory council and/or mentoring program made up of experienced faculty who have led study abroad in the past to share their knowledge and expertise with new faculty getting started in developing programs.
- Create a "Program Leader in Training" opportunity where new faculty are funded and become co-program leaders with veteran faculty the first year and then they apply to lead their own program the following year.
- Develop a workshop (or a series of workshops) that prepares faculty for the process of creating a study abroad program that includes everything from how to evaluate a program provider to developing day-by-day itinerary, infusing social and cultural activities into the curriculum, ensuring safety for study abroad, and creating a program budget. This will allow faculty members to work together and brainstorm ideas, and it will allow the facilitator the opportunity to identify any weaknesses in the proposals that can be adjusted before final submission. Work with the Faculty Development Office so participants can earn professional development credit if this is available at the institution.
- Communicate the study abroad proposal process, timeline, and workshop well in advance by offering a series of information sessions for faculty members that provide a summary of what they need to do to offer a successful study abroad program. Attending division meetings and meeting with deans are also other effective ways to communicate out how to engage in this work. The timeline is a very important component of this work because it must allow faculty members sufficient time to develop their proposals, get them approved, market their programs to students, enroll students and accept payments, and prepare for the overseas travel through a series of orientation sessions with the program leaders.
- Communicate the process for faculty to apply to lead study abroad by posting the information on the college's website. It is a best practice to have webpages dedicated to student navigation of the study abroad programs and faculty webpages dedicated to the proposal process and forms needed to apply to lead a study abroad program. Visit the Valencia College Study Abroad website for ideas: http://valenciacollege.edu/international/studyabroad/

Although this chapter does not specifically address program design, the author would be remiss not to make specific mention of its importance. One of the fatal flaws in study abroad is to design program offerings based on what administrators and faculty think students want and need or offer programs based on faculty interest in a subject matter than does not articulate to any type of degree, which could actually put students in danger of going over the maximum credits allowed for financial aid in the long run. The following is a list of suggestions to keep in mind when designing a study abroad program at the community college:

- **Program Duration:** Short-term study abroad programs are gaining in popularity due to the limited time required away from work and family and the lower price point for students. While a full semester abroad would give students a more immersive experience, the short-term programs are better suited for many community college students who otherwise would not have the opportunity to participate in study abroad due to the cost and time away from work and study.

- **Academic Engagement:** It is important to note that short-term study abroad programs taking place less than two weeks overseas may require additional class time and/or online course activities Federal financial aid regulations concerning credit hours constitute "not less than one hour of classroom or direct faculty instruction and a minimum of two hours of out-of-class work each week for approximately 15 weeks for one semester... or at least the equivalent amount of work over a different amount of time" (U.S. Department of Education, 2017-2018, pg. 2-38). This equates to at least 45 academic engagement hours for every one credit hour so time spent traveling, sleeping, or socializing with no learning outcome should not be counted towards the total academic engagement hours.
- **Course Offering:** In terms of choosing a credit-course offering, some faculty offer "boutique-type" courses that do not count toward general education or a specific major. While there may be value in the course content, these programs are harder to market to students who may not have any elective credits left to take in their program of study. A much safer bet for faculty who need to boost program enrollment is to choose courses that are part of the college's general education or degree major requirements.
- **Cultural and Country-Specific Content:** It is very important that faculty infuse the curriculum with learning outcomes that address the culture and country-specific nuances that students may encounter when traveling overseas. This should be done both prior to travel, during the overseas component, and in a reflection at the end of the course upon return to the United States.

There are a variety of resources to assist faculty with the development of study abroad programs, which include *NAFSA's Guide to Education Abroad for Advisors and Administrators* (4th Ed.) and *The Guide to Successful Short-Term Programs Abroad* (3rd Ed.), Raby's (2008) *Institute of International Education Study Abroad White Paper Series Issue Number 3*, and the Forum on Education Abroad also has a wealth of information at their annual conference and on their website at: https://forumea.org.

Engaging the Local Community

Student participation in study abroad directly benefits our communities by preparing students to be global citizens and support our nation's goal of competing in the global marketplace (Spellings, 2006). Today's global marketplace also includes local U.S. employers who hire people from diverse backgrounds, do business with clients from all over the world, or have offices located overseas. Since the cost factor is a barrier to participation in study abroad for many community college students (Brux & Fry, 2010), there are several actions that program administrators can take to help offset program costs for students. One way is to identify local employers who may want to support study abroad through scholarship opportunities. For example, a local hospital could create a scholarship in their name for students who want to participate in a nursing study abroad program. The local chamber of commerce groups, Rotary Club, and minority-specific organizations are excellent places to start. Remember to connect with your institution's foundation prior to reaching out to any local business or organization to determine if a relationship already exists. The foundation may also be able to assist in pursing new opportunities for funding or contributing existing funds to support study abroad scholarships.

A second approach to securing additional funding for study abroad is through fundraising opportunities in the local community. Fundraising can be done at the study abroad department level where an opportunity is created for students across all programs to engage in, or it can be done at the program level where only students in a specific program participate. Some ideas for fundraising include hosting a golf tournament or some other type of sporting event, putting on an international meal with restaurants donating or heavily discounting the food, or simply having students set up a GoFundMe account and sharing the link through social media. While these activities take time to set up initially, they will pay off over time as more individuals look forward to these fun events and want to help support college students.

While lowering program costs is one reason to engage the community, another reason is to conduct outreach to future college students. As mentioned previously, many students experience global learning early in life and those pre-college academic experiences have a big impact on future interest in the world at large (Robertson, 2016). Therefore, one way to create a pipeline of incoming college students primed for study abroad is to do outreach to the local secondary schools through classroom presentations and tabling at school events. Partnering with local secondary schools during International Education Week and possibly bringing groups on campus is another way to promote global learning opportunities to students and also provide information on the benefits of study abroad.

SOLUTIONS AND RECOMMENDATIONS

Community colleges across the country vary greatly when it comes to location, government funding, student demographics, and community needs, therefore, there is no "one size fits all" when it comes to solutions and recommendations. Some institutions are far along in this work while others have not even yet begun, plus everything in between. The advice to those institutions that are still struggling to get study abroad off the ground or gain some traction is to start small and try to build the study abroad efforts over time. There are institutions that have small programs in place with no centralized office or funding, and while not optimal, at least it is a start. To take your study abroad efforts to the next level includes short-term and long-term strategic planning with a comprehensive funding and outreach strategy to students, faculty, and the community. Within that strategy, there must be a healthy relationship between study abroad program administrators and faculty leading study abroad when it comes to building the department. Finally, it is important to target minority students with intentionality by focusing outreach efforts on student clubs and organizations on campus to ensure that students from many different backgrounds have the opportunity to participate in study abroad at the community college.

FUTURE RESEARCH DIRECTIONS

A recommendation for future research in the community college setting is a longitudinal study to determine students' level of interest in study abroad upon starting college and then again three to five years later. This type of study would more accurately pinpoint the success rate of global learning interventions on students' interest and participation in study abroad in college. At the same time, a study is recommended for students in the community college who have studied abroad to identify where their initial interest in global learning began to determine if it aligns with prior research finding. These types of studies would help answer the proverbial question if students who study abroad are already those most likely to participate or if they participate because of their experiences in the community college setting.

CONCLUSION

If the goal of community colleges is to prepare students to meet the demands of today's global workforce, then internationalization must be an equal partner to the other goals of the mission and vision of the institution. However, the reality is that state budgets are constantly being stretched and funding to colleges may not be as robust as hoped. In this context, internationalization efforts on campus can be easily stymied without the support of institutional leadership as they compete with more pressing initiatives in academia. For those institutions that are trying to increase study abroad enrollment as part of their global learning initiatives, the outreach function is paramount in building its base and that outreach must extend equally to three key groups – students, faculty, and the local community. Marketing to students must be a partnership between administrators and faculty and include a variety of tactics that involve print, electronic, and in-person methods to many different student groups on campus. The key to growing study abroad opportunities on campus lies with the faculty and providing them with the training that they need to develop safe and academically rigorous programs for students. Finally, engaging the local community is key to help students offset the costs of study abroad and promote these opportunities to future generations.

REFERENCES

American Association of Community Colleges. (2017). *Fast facts 2017*. Retrieved from https://www.aacc.nche.edu/research-tends/fast-facts/

American Council on Education. (2017). *Mapping internationalization on U.S. campuses* (2017 edition). Washington, DC: American Council on Education.

Bandyopadhyay, S., & Bandyopadhyay, K. (2015). Factors influencing student participation in college study abroad programs. *Journal of International Education Research*, *11*(2), 87–94.

Barclay Hamir, H., & Gozik, N. (2018). *Promoting inclusion in education aboard: A handbook of research and practice*. Herndon, VA: Stylus Publishing, LLC.

Brux, J. M., & Fry, B. (2010). Multicultural students in study abroad: Their interests, their issues, and their constraints. *Journal of Studies in International Education*, *14*(5), 508–527. doi:10.1177/1028315309342486

Chieffo, L., & Spaeth, C. (2017). *The guide to successful short-term programs abroad* (3rd ed.). Annapolis, MD: NAFSA.

Community College Review. (2015). *What is a community college?* Retrieved from http://www.communitycollegereview.com/blog/what-is-a-community-college

Forum on Education Abroad. (2017). *State of the field 2017*. Retrieved from https://forumea.org/wp-content/uploads/2018/03/ForumEA-State-of-the-Field-18-web-version.pdf

Green, M., & Olsen, C. (2003). *Internationalizing the campus: A user's guide*. Washington, DC: American Council on Education.

Hanover Research. (2014). *Trends in higher education marketing, recruitment, and technology*. Washington, DC: Hanover Research.

Hernandez, M., Wiedenhoeft, M., & Wick, D. (Eds.). (2014). *NAFSA's guide to education abroad for advisors and administrators* (4th ed.). Annapolis, MD: NAFSA.

Higher Education Marketing. (2016). *7 signs your website is sabotaging student recruitment*. Retrieved from http://www.higher-education-marketing.com/blog/website-student-recruitment

Institute of International Education. (2008). *Expanding education abroad at U.S. community colleges*. Retrieved from https://www.iie.org/Research-and-Insights/Publications/Expanding-Education-Abroad-at-US-Community-Colleges

Institute of International Education. (2017). *Open doors 2017*. Retrieved from https://www.iie.org/Research-and-Insights/Open-Doors

Keese, J., & O'Brien, J. (2011). Learn by going: Critical issues for faculty-led study-abroad programs. *The California Geographer, 51*, 2–24.

Knight, J. (2003). Updating the definition of internationalization. *Industry and Higher Education, 33*, 2–3.

NAFSA. (2016). *Trends in US study abroad*. Retrieved from http://www.nafsa.org/Policy_and_Advocacy/Policy_Resources/Policy_Trends_and_Data/ Trends_in_U_S__Study_Abroad/

Povich, E. (2018). *More community colleges are offering bachelor's degrees — and four-year universities aren't happy about it*. Retrieved from http://www.pewtrusts.org/en/research- and-analysis/blogs/stateline/2018/04/26/more-community-colleges-are-offering-bachelors-degrees

Raby, R. L. (2008). *IIE study abroad white paper series number 3: Expanding education abroad at U.S. community colleges*. New York: Institute for International Education.

Raby, R. L., Rhodes, G., & Biscarra, A. (2014). Community college study abroad: Implications for student success. *Community College Journal of Research and Practice, 38*(2-3), 174–183. doi:10.1080/10668926.2014.851961

Robertson, J. (2014). Student interest in international education at the community college. *Community College Journal of Research and Practice, 39*(5), 473–484. doi:10.1080/10668926.2013.879377

Robertson, J. (2016). *The community college student's social construction of global learning in the Florida college system* (Doctoral dissertation). Orlando, FL: University of Central Florida.

Robertson, J., & Blasi, L. (2017). Community college student perceptions of their experiences related to global learning: Understanding the impact of family, faculty, and the curriculum. *Community College Journal of Research and Practice, 41*(11), 697–718. doi:10.1080/10668926.2016.1222974

Spellings, M. (2006). *A test of leadership: Charting the future of U.S. higher education*. Washington, DC: United States Department of Education.

Sutin, S., Derrico, D., Raby, R. L., & Valeau, E. (2011). *Increasing effectiveness of the community college financial model: A global perspective for the global economy.* New York: Palgrave MacMillan. doi:10.1057/9780230120006

U.S. Department of Education. (2017-2018). *2017-2018 federal student aid handbook.* Retrieved from https://ifap.ed.gov/fsahandbook/attachments/1415FSAHdbkAppendices FSAGlossaryAppendixA.pdf

Chapter 8
Lessons Learned:
Building Inclusive Support for Study Abroad Programming at Delaware Technical Community College

Taryn Gassner Tangpricha
Delaware Technical Community College, USA

ABSTRACT

This chapter conducts a case study of Delaware Technical Community College as it grew its programs from 2009 to present. Despite directive from the President, support and engagement was not widespread across the state: varying by campus, division, department, and instructor. Study abroad leadership was tasked with aligning the program with the college's mission, vision, and strategic directions, and building support internally and externally to boost student enrollment in the study abroad program. By targeting three key groups of stakeholders—students, faculty, and community members—and supporting shared values towards a mutual benefit, Delaware Technical Community College was able to grow its study abroad enrollment by over 400% from 2010 to 2018.

INTRODUCTION

Educators likely agree "it takes a village" to build and sustain study abroad programs at higher education institutions. At community colleges, study abroad is often times initiated by a handful of passionate stakeholders. However, a program driven by a few individuals alone will struggle to maintain sustainable, long-term growth (West, 2012). Identifying the individuals or groups that have a fundamental impact on the study abroad program and building inclusive support can further ensure the longevity of the program and build financial resources for future initiatives (Kenny, 2014).

Nearly a decade ago, Delaware Technical Community College found itself at a crossroads in terms of growing its study abroad program. Locally referred to as "Delaware Tech," the college is a statewide institution with four campus locations serving over 14,000 full-time and part-time students. The college's campus locations range from two urban campuses in Delaware's northern New Castle County,

DOI: 10.4018/978-1-5225-6252-8.ch008

a suburban campus in the state capital of Dover in Kent County, and a rural campus in the southern county of Sussex. In the 2009-2010 academic year, the study abroad program enrolled fourteen students in two faculty-led courses, consisting of two groups of seven students and two faculty; one traveling to Quito, Ecuador, and one to London, England. Despite the financial strains of the global recession, the college president and administration remained unwavering in their support of the program and its role at the college as a high-impact educational experience for students. However, support and engagement was not widespread across the state - varying by campus, division, department, and instructor. Study abroad leadership was tasked with aligning the program with the college's mission, vision, and strategic directions, and building support internally and externally to boost student enrollment in the study abroad program. By targeting three key groups of stakeholders- students, faculty, and community members- and supporting shared values towards a mutual benefit, Delaware Technical Community College was able to grow its study abroad enrollment by over 400% from 2010 to 2018.

Utilizing Student Input to Guide Study Abroad Programming and Support Services

While not traditionally included in the development process, student input and engagement remain critical factors in building support for the study abroad program. Community college student bodies are historically comprised of non-traditional students, minorities, first generation, low-socioeconomic groups- and are vastly underrepresented in study abroad (Raby, 2008). Allan E. Goodman, President and CEO of the Institute of International Education writes, "if this trend is allowed to continue, these underrepresented groups will remain on the sidelines and will not have equal access to the life-changing opportunities that will prepare them for today's global society" (Raby, 2008, p. 4-5). However, the perception that the community college student demographic is not suitable for the study abroad experience can be debunked (Raby, 2008). Study abroad leadership at Delaware Tech found that by providing appropriate opportunities for input and feedback, students, both traditional and non-traditional, served as an invaluable resources in driving the direction study abroad programming and helping the college to provide experiences to students that were both appealing and accessible.

At Delaware Tech, the international education leadership team consists of an international education director, who is supervised by the vice president for academic affairs and is tasked with the strategic oversight of the study abroad program, F-1 student visa compliance, and on-campus internationalization. At each campus location, one faculty or staff member serves in a paid supplemental coordinator position to oversee and implement study abroad recruitment, advising and on-campus programming. Since 2010, the international education leadership team has met monthly to collaborate and coordinate initiatives college-wide.

International education leadership first analyzed the college's study abroad offerings and the data driving its programming. They found that there was little quantitative data or student input collected as part of the development process. As a result, leadership worked to connect with students on and off campus to gather information to identify students' key interests in and motivation for studying abroad. Analyzing current practices, they concluded that there was little value in holding stand-alone information sessions on campus, finding it more effective to seek students out during their regular activities and classes, especially in 100-level and introductory student success courses where first-semester students were enrolled. The leadership team began to track interest in study abroad by soliciting student contact information at on-campus events. In addition, they tracked attendance and collected contact information at the on-campus global understanding series. The team also worked with student affairs to include questions related to study abroad in college-wide student surveys. The data collected addressed:

- The destinations and types of experiences students desired;
- Information on how students make decisions regarding course enrollment;
- Who/what were their major influencers (both positive and negative); and
- Whether they had access to the financial resources needed to study abroad.

Student feedback indicated that interests of and influencers on a student's decision to study abroad ranged, but the strongest factors were indicated to be: the destination, faculty teaching the course, and relation of content to their program and future career field. Feedback collected annually also demonstrated trends in students utilizing the study abroad experience as a first-time out of the country and even the state of Delaware.

The team also utilized surveys to identify major factors that served as barriers to participation such as family or work obligations (not being able to take the time away from work), and financial constraints. Financial constraints are a major consideration for community college students, and often pose as one of the greatest barriers to studying abroad (Hulstrand, 2016). In an effort to address these constraints, the college began to offer a monthly payment plan with a flexible payment schedule that allowed students to fund the experience. "It goes without saying that the lower the program cost, the more students will participate, and this will ensure compliance with community college open access policies." (Raby, 2008, p. 19). To address this, leadership set maximum limits on program costs, and worked with administration to establish study abroad scholarship funds and an international education endowment. "The enrollment process itself can be daunting for students," says Amy Russell, International Education Coordinator and Academic Support Assistant, "We meet with students during and walk them to the registrar to ensure they enroll and submit their first payment without issues. We always follow the program cost by saying that we have scholarships and we will help them to apply" (A. Russell, personal communication, March 5, 2018).

International education coordinators also noted that interested students vocalized that time constraints related to their everyday responsibilities such as work, childcare, and schoolwork were viewed as barriers to enrolling in study abroad courses. Russell noted, "In addition to the cost of the program, we must also consider the amount wages lost for students, as many of them work hourly positions with no paid time off" (A. Russell, personal communication, March 5, 2018). To address these time constraints, the college also committed to offering study abroad programs that were shorter in length, and classes offered in an online or hybrid format at flexible times. For courses that require more face-to-face meeting time, driving time between the college's campuses was also an issue. Taking into account, that there is over two hours of driving distance between the college's northernmost and southernmost campuses, faculty utilized the college's distance learning centers to live-broadcast classes across all four campuses.

The leadership team also discovered gaps in how the college supported students through the study abroad advising and enrollment process. They found that it was critical to ensure that employees who directly support students in non-academic areas were educated about the programs, well-informed, and accessible to students. Counselors and student affairs advisors served as the first point of contact for incoming students. Leadership found that though there was a direct question in the initial advising session related to study abroad, the question was rarely completed by the counselor in the Student Education Plan or (SEP). The leadership team interviewed student affairs staff on each campus to document:

Lessons Learned

- When or what time of year academic advising occurred;
- What staff in an advising role needed to know;
- The customer service touch-points related to admissions, enrollment, and payments that students must navigate; and
- The changes and/or additional resources that might assist in the process.

As a result of these interviews, leadership discovered that counselors often felt they lacked the knowledge to adequately advise students on study abroad opportunities. Therefore, international education leadership created an annual advising sheet, listing frequently asked questions and information on each study abroad course for counselors to have on hand to review with students. To expand the partnership with student affairs, international education leadership worked together with counselors and staff to ensure that the study abroad opportunities are represented at student-focused events such as new student orientations, open house events, student resource fairs, and dual-enrollment information sessions and local high and middle schools.

International education leadership found it critical to take a proactive approach to communicate with employees to ensure those serving in all support roles had access to and were knowledgeable knowledge about study abroad in order to assist students. For example, after establishing a regular meeting with financial aid and business services, study abroad leadership was dismayed to find that they had been sending students to the financial aid offices to discuss the timing of their loan disbursements, when in actuality, the business services offices were where this information was housed and provided to students. Clarifying this information pathway was the first step to ending a high level of frustration amongst students. A similar analysis was conducted to address communication with other groups that provide support services to students such as career services, disability support services, and public safety. Feedback from students indicated that when they were turned away, or staff were unable to assist them, it many times was the deciding factor between enrolling in versus walking away from the study abroad experience during their time at the institution.

In addition, the team identified additional support divisions at the institution that were critical to the implementation of study abroad but did not have direct contact with students. For example, the timely transfer of needed information and regular assessment of internal processes was critical to the functionality of the study abroad program. Likewise, legal affairs or general counsel approved contracts with third-party providers, applications and forms, and provide advising for risk management. Articulation ensured that study abroad courses meet transfer requirements to four-year institutions (Raby, 2008). The marketing department produced promotional materials, website announcements, and other media on and off campus. Human resources was integral in approving travel stipends, instructional contracts, and permission for faculty time leave from campus. The fiscal department processed vendor payments, travel reimbursements, and distributed scholarship funds. All of these relationships were multi-dimensional nature, and the team noted the need for mutual benefit to add value to common goals and initiatives. After identifying these functions, the international education team strategized ways to provide cross-training related to study abroad and support for the respective division's initiatives at the college.

It is also critical to support students throughout the study abroad process. Many times, community college students are first-time travelers and may not have the support mechanisms at home to assist them through the lengthy enrollment, preparation, travel, and return process (Raby & Rhodes, 2018). To address this, the college implemented mandatory study abroad orientations on each campus, covering travel tips, health and safety, and a career workshop related to how students can use the study abroad experience to further their careers. It is equally important for study abroad leadership to support students during the re-entry phase and re-assimilation to their home culture after studying abroad (Brubaker, 2017). Scholarship recipients are required to participate in and assist with the execution of on-campus fundraisers, study abroad fairs, and other events, while students in general are encouraged to help out On-campus programming developed and offered to students should complement and aim to engage students in the study abroad program. Connect on-campus events to feature study abroad opportunities, past programs, study abroad alumni, or other relevant initiatives. Future and past scholarship recipients, study abroad alumni, faculty, staff, and community members can participate together for the common cause of promoting global awareness and cross-cultural understanding.

Working With Faculty and Academic Departments to Develop Sustainable Programming

Collaborating with faculty and academic departments to bring content to life for students is equally important to the process of building a sustainable study abroad program. Particularly, communicating effectively with faculty and departmental leadership to engage in collaborative development is key to success (Hulstrand, 2016). Ogden and Barnes claim that "At many U.S. universities or colleges today, the faculty own and control the curriculum" (Ogden & Barnes, 2016). They add that "and any real success in advancing education abroad as a high-impact educational practice will be found by working with, and through, the faculty" (Ogden & Barnes, 2016). The same is true for community colleges in which faculty remain a central component of study abroad (Raby, 2016).

In many cases, the responsibility for making the connection between the individual program, study abroad, and the larger college vision, mission, and goals will rest with international education leadership. At Delaware Tech, international education leadership likewise found that faculty lacked or was unaware of the college-wide vision for study abroad and international education. This proved especially true for adjunct instructors. International education leadership began a public relations campaign of sorts, addressing faculty both informally and formally through employee updates, department meetings, and other professional development opportunities to enhance knowledge and buy-in related to study abroad's role in the college-wide agenda. It was also critical before faculty engaged in program development, to frontload efforts with an emphasis on how internationalization helps meet objectives related to student learning (West, 2012).

Upon examining the college's overall mission, goals, vision statement, and strategic directions, study abroad leadership identified two strong linkages to its programming: (*Mission, Vision, Strategic Directions, and Values Statement*, 2015):

1. Advance the delivery of innovative instructional offerings, such as pathways and stackable credentials, to meet competitive workforce needs and increase educational and career opportunities for students.; and
2. Foster a culture of inclusion that values, respects, recruits, and retains a diverse college community.

Similarly, the study abroad leadership team identified that targeted "soft skills" developed during the study abroad experience such as communication, critical thinking, and cross-cultural competency aligned with the college's "Core Curriculum Competencies" listed in the curriculum guidelines that sets

Lessons Learned

standards for all courses offered at the institution (*Delaware Technical Community College Curriculum Guidelines,* 2017):

1. Apply clear and effective communication skills.
2. Use critical thinking to solve problems.
3. Collaborate to achieve a common goal.
4. Demonstrate professional and ethical conduct.
5. Use information literacy for effective vocational and/or academic research.
6. Apply quantitative reasoning and/or scientific inquiry to solve practical problems.

As a result of this planning in the initial stages of program development, study abroad leadership established a 3-year set of strategic goals and objectives closely linked to the college-wide strategic plan. For example, the division's College Plan Goals for the FY2019-FY2021 year period are:

1. Strengthen and maximize international education offerings.
2. Collaborate with partners to develop and promote innovative international educational programming.
3. Provide strategic college wide leadership to foster a climate of diversity and inclusion.

These goals possess corresponding annual objectives that the division addresses and reports out to the administration and local community through an annual publication.

International education leadership continued to work with the Deans of Instruction on the college's campuses to educate departments on how to approach and develop study abroad programming that was relevant to their program content and to share leadership and approval of said programing college-wide. They found that ensuring that certain issues were addressed at the outset of program development created a balance between "great ideas" and the reality of whether the program proposal is sustainable and a wise expenditure of college resources. This shared leadership and commitment to long-term programming ensures the stability of the study abroad program, where students can plan academic coursework through assured offerings (Ogden & Barnes, 2018). Table 1 shares a worksheet that features a series of questions for instructors and department leadership to be addressed in the initial phases of study abroad development.

In addition to program development, faculty serve in an equally important role in engaging students to participate in study abroad courses. Over the years, international education leadership found that the student's relationship with the faculty leading the study abroad course was often ranked between the numbers one and two factors influencing a student's decision to participate in study abroad (Delaware Technical Community College, 2010-2018). Noting the significance of faculty influence and involvement in the program, study abroad leadership established an annual training schedule for instructors in study abroad leadership roles to support instructors in setting up and delivering course content to students and provide them with the tools they need to implement the program abroad and function effectively during crisis situations. This training regularly employed the expertise of faculty and staff who have previously led courses to ensure relevancy of training content. They also found it to be critical to communicate and collaborate with faculty during program marketing, recruitment, enrollment and implementation of each departmental study abroad course, and established a regular communication structure to communicate important dates, scholarships opportunities, and provide updates to instructors.

Table 1. Worksheet for instruction: Study abroad expansion in program departments

Program- Specific Competencies	Which program (major) competencies will students develop through the study abroad experience?
Cultural Competencies	Which cultural competencies will students to develop through the study abroad experience (examples listed below)? • Interacting with diverse groups of people • Understanding cultural differences in the workplace • Adapting to change • Independent exploration of country site
Courses/Curriculum Appropriate for the Study Abroad Experience	Which courses within the program demonstrate a strong linkage to the study abroad experience and why?
Course Enrollment Considerations	• Is this a required course in the program? • How many students enroll in the course annually? • Is projected enrollment sufficient to offer the course annually, or should another time rotation be considered? • Which semester do students typically take the course in the program course sequence?
Linkage between Destination and Program Content	What is the connection between the venues/sites available in this destination and academic content in the program?
Potential or Existing Partnerships	Can an institutional/academic partner/third-party provider in the destination be identified?
Sustainability	• Is this a sustainable destination for the program? • Will the in-country partners support a multi-year program? • Does the department have qualified and able faculty willing to lead or support the course? • How do groups plan to collaborate college-wide to offer the program over a period of time? • What are the safety and security conditions in-country? Do they meet the college's guidelines on safety standards?
Student Interest	Which destinations clearly connect to the program's content will most likely be interesting to students?

Mobilizing Administrators, Employers, and Community Members for Program Support

Nationwide, community colleges' missions and strategic goals consistently relate to preparing students for the workforce through the educational experience and training. According to Castro-Salazar, Merriam-Castro, & Lopez, "the importance of preparing an internationally competent workforce has increased due to rapid developments in transportation, communication, and economic globalization" (2016, p. 176). However, a disconnect remains between the local mission of the community college and value of the study abroad experience. According to Raby, "there are still many who question how education abroad serves the local mandate of the community college mission which prepares students to transfer to four-year institutions or for employment at local businesses." (2008, p.20). Raby's statement accentuates the need for international education leadership to ensure that the strategic goals for the study abroad program align with those of the college president and to communicate the mutual benefits of such to the top levels of administration.

At Delaware Tech, international education leadership was fortunate to have access to upper-level administration meetings. However, the team found it useful to examine the communication structure of the college on the whole to determine the effectiveness of its messaging an upper-level meetings. They found that differences existed in messaging needs related to administrators versus instructional departments. For example, during upper-level meetings, international education leadership provided sweeping

Lessons Learned

updates and college-wide initiatives. However, when campus administrators passes these updates along to deans and department chairs, they lacked the details necessary for faculty and staff to effectively engage with the program. The most effective way to convey its message was to communicate with faculty directly through existing campus and departmental updates.

By attending open board of trustee meetings, leadership found that members of the board of trustees possessed great potential to serve as champions of study abroad. Board members typically possess extensive professional backgrounds and are serving in their capacity because of their connection to your institution. A little bit of research can reveal whether individual board members have international backgrounds or experience that they could contribute to the program. It may be possible to establish programming such as donor travel or on-campus content that would appeal to them and their constituents. The college initiated regular updates regarding international education, and invited board members to participate in the college's annual international professional development program. After attending the college's international professional development program to Turkey in 2011, a board member invited all faculty and staff participants to his home for a celebration the following year. Another board member who held professional expertise in the international field attended the program to China in 2012, and then led the program to Germany in 2013.

Local employers and members of the community members are often untapped resources for support. The international education leadership team communicated with employers and community members during program advisory board meetings to promote awareness about the study abroad program, and inquired about what the international education program could do to meet their business needs. It was also important that collaborations between the college and external partners were a good fit and demonstrated mutual benefit (West, 2012). The college also utilized input and feedback from local employers gathered during program advisory meetings to guide programming. International education leadership was able to access these meetings to ask employers directly about their connection to the study abroad experience. Furthermore, during a listening session in the college's administrative retreat in 2018, employers clearly expressed that Delaware Tech graduates excelled in the area of technical skills, but there was opportunity for growth in their level of "soft skills." These were the same target skills identified in the international education leadership team's planning process.

This support for the college's international education program within the administration, board of trustees, employers, and local community led to the establishment and implementation of an annual fundraiser on each campus to fund study abroad scholarships. The college engaged faculty, staff, students, and local businesses to participate in the planning and execution of these events. Over the years, the fundraisers have ranged from gala events, 5k races, and online raffles. To date, the international education fundraisers at the college have raised over $100,000 to support study abroad scholarships for students and on-campus programming that addresses global understanding. Annually, the college is able to fund approximately $30,000 in scholarships due to these campus fundraisers. Using these funds, the college was also able to strategize ways to further engage community members on campus. This included holding free events and workshops related to international themes and inviting local K-12 schools, establishing partnerships with community organizations to host events, and offering family friendly events on campus.

CONCLUSION

In conclusion, effective communication and collaboration between the individuals and groups that are critical to the success of the study abroad program. Study abroad leadership must serve as the link to ensure this collaboration works for all involved stakeholders. It is useful to complete an analysis of how different stakeholders interact and provide information back and forth to each other, and the nature of assistance needed to bridge the gap. While each institution's map will differ, there is likely an interconnected relationship between all stakeholders to support international education initiatives. Figure 1 demonstrates the relationship between Delaware Tech's internal and external stakeholders and international education initiatives and priorities at the college.

In the end there is no one solution to building inclusive support for study abroad at community colleges. It is an often-times painstakingly slow process that involves a large volume of communication and time investment - all set to the backdrop of a high speed day-to-day academic calendar and changing student body. However, aligning mission and goals with those of the institution and taking the time to identify and understand the individuals and groups critical to the program, can ensure future success and result in institutionalization of holistic support for international education and study abroad initiatives for years to come.

Figure 1. Mapping stakeholder relationships on and off-campus

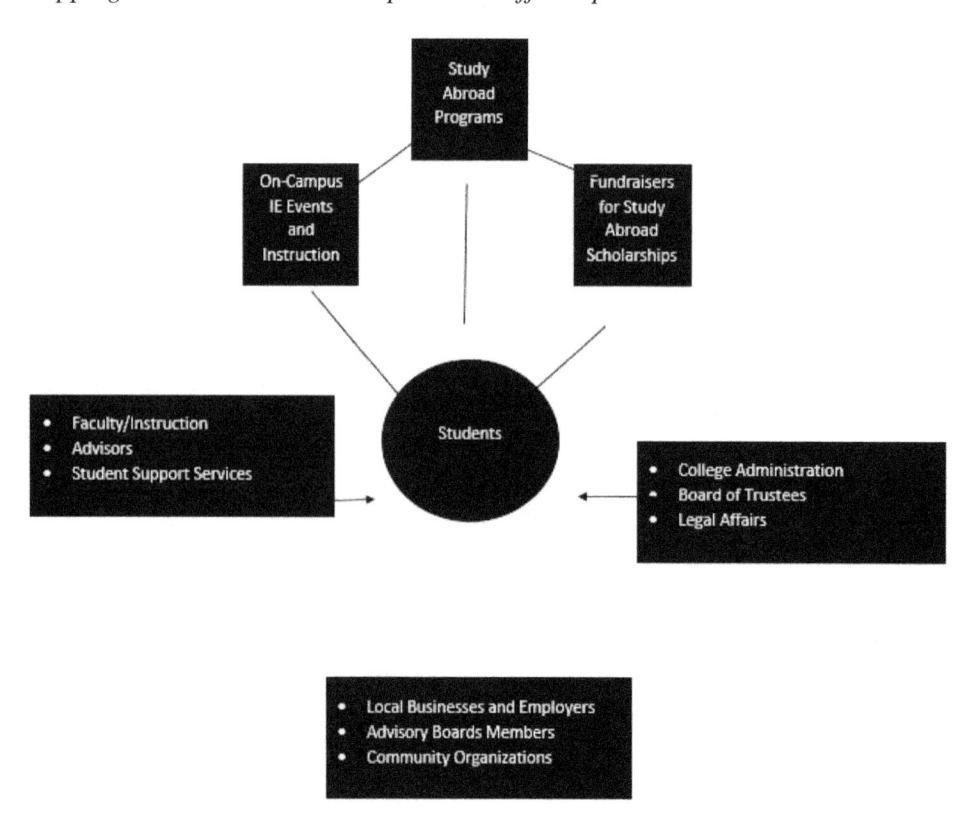

Checklist

- Define study abroad mission, vision, and goals and ensure alignment with institution's strategic goals.
- Identify key groups or individuals that are fundamental to study abroad program support.
- Connect by gathering information on key points of interest to address mutual needs.
- Communicate to articulate common goals and operational needs.
- Collaborate to implement program day-to-day and improvements.
- Map out college-wide relationships and points of interaction.
- Assess effectiveness and best practices annually.

REFERENCES

Brubaker, C. (2017). Re-thinking re-entry: New approaches to supporting students after study zbroad. *Die Unterrichtspraxis/Teaching German, 50*(2), 109.

Castro-Salazar, R., Merriam-Castro, K., & Perez Lopez, Y. A. (2016). Building a world class college: Creating a global community at Pima community college. In R. L. Raby & E. J. Valeau (Eds.), *International Education at Community Colleges: Themes, Practices, Research, and Case Studies*. New York, NY: Palgrave Macmillian Publishers. doi:10.1057/978-1-137-53336-4_12

Delaware Technical Community College. (2015). *Mission, Vision, Strategic Directions and Values Statement*. Retrieved from https://www.dtcc.edu/about/mission-vision-and-strategic-directions

Delaware Technical Community College. (2017). *Curriculum Guidelines*. Retrieved from https://efiles.dtcc.edu/CURR_GUIDE/Archive/Curriculum%20 Guidelines%20201851.pdf

Delaware Technical Community College. (2018). *Exit surveys: 2010-2018*. Dover, DE: Delaware Technical Community College Study Abroad Program.

Delaware Technical Community College. (2018). *FY2019-2021 College Plan Goals and Objectives: International Education*. Dover, DE: Delaware Technical Community College.

Hulstrand, J. (2016). Advancing faculty-led programs at community colleges. *International Educator*. Retrieved from: www.nafsa.org/_File/_/ie_ novdec16_education_abroad.pdf

Kenny, G. (2014). Five questions to identify key stakeholders. *Harvard Business Review*. Retrieved from: https://hbr.org/2014/03/five-questions-to-identify-key-stakeholders

Ogden, A., & Barnes, B. E. (2018, July 5). Expanding education abroad through faculty engagement [blog post]. Retrieved from: https://isatoday.wordpress.com/2018/07 /05/expanding-education-abroad-through-faculty-engagement/

Raby, R. L. (2008). *Expanding education abroad at U.S. community colleges.* IIE Study Abroad White Paper Series 3. New York: NY: Institute for International Education Press.

Raby, R. L., & Rhodes, G. M. (2018). Promoting education abroad among community college students: Overcoming obstacles and developing inclusive practices. In N. Gozik & H. B. Hamir (Eds.), *Promoting Inclusion in Education Abroad*. London: Stylus Publishing, LLC.

West, C. (2012). *Engaging stakeholders in internationalization: Strategies for collaboration*. NAFSA. Retrieved from: https://www.nafsa.org/uploadedFiles/Chez_NAFSA/Find_Resources/Internationalizing_Higher_Education/engaging_stakeholders.pdf

Chapter 9
Enhancing Study Abroad Participation and Choices of Destination at Community Colleges

Monija Amani
Georgetown University, USA

Mikyong Minsun Kim
The George Washington University, USA

ABSTRACT

This chapter addresses the findings of a multilayered study regarding perceptions of study abroad coordinators and students related to community college students' decisions to engage in global programs abroad and the factors that motivate their selection of a destination. In-depth interviews of study abroad program coordinators and students from three community colleges located in urban, suburban, and rural areas provided rich and diverse perspectives regarding students' access and engagement in study abroad programs and the reasons that affect their choices of destinations. Findings showed synchronicity and alignment between the study abroad coordinators' and students' perspectives. However, study abroad coordinators revealed that institutional administrators or leaders who have established connections with certain destinations influence program and destination offerings, which in turn broadens or limits students' selection of study abroad choices. Discussions and implications related to community college students, faculty, institutional leaders, and policymakers provide insight on how to make study abroad more accessible to community college students and expand their choice of destination.

DOI: 10.4018/978-1-5225-6252-8.ch009

INTRODUCTION

At the onset of the 21st century, the geopolitical, economic, and technological forces across the globe have driven colleges and universities to internationalize their curriculum and implement policies that are considered valuable in better preparing students for success in a rising global economy. To address this demand, higher education institutions have focused on internationalizing student experiences on many levels (Carlson et al., 1990; Knight, 2004; Opp & Gesetti, 2014). Participation in education abroad programs is one way in which U.S. colleges and universities have endeavored to provide global opportunities that will help students lay the foundation of an international education by expanding their intercultural exposure, awareness, and understanding during and beyond college (Commission on the Abraham Lincoln Study Abroad Fellowship Program, 2005). Internationalization efforts through study abroad are, however, minimal at community colleges compared with efforts at four-year institutions. Based on the Institute of International Education's (IIE) *Open Doors Report* (2017), in the 2016–2017 academic year, 279,792 bachelor's-seeking students studied abroad, while only 90,802 students from community colleges participated in education abroad programs. Salisbury, Umbach, Paulsen, and Pascarella (2009) further maintain that the number of community college students intending to study abroad is 30% less than the number of students at liberal arts colleges intending to study abroad. If community colleges are expected to provide their students with access and opportunities to global programs, with the purposes of training them to have an international mindset, gaining intercultural awareness, and developing their proficiency in foreign languages, the low participation rate of students engaging in study abroad programs at these institutions must be examined.

Students' decisions regarding their choice of study abroad destination have also raised concerns among educators (Abraham Lincoln Commission, 2005). To equalize choice of destination, The Lincoln Commission's (2005) Recommendation II suggested that efforts must be made to increase study abroad participation among students enrolled in community colleges and to expand their travel to nontraditional destinations. If the purpose of enhancing study abroad engagement at community colleges is to expand students' knowledge and understanding of other cultures, then students' choices of destination and influential decision factors need to be further explored and understood.

Community colleges have been an integral component of the American higher education system since 1901. With the mission of providing various educational paths to students who come from diverse racial, ethnic, and socioeconomic backgrounds (Brint & Karabel, 1989; Kasper, 2002-2003; Cohen & Brawer, 2003; Bragg & Townsend, 2006), today, these institutions have grown tremendously, serving over 12 million students across the nation (American Association of Community Colleges, 2018). Students who begin their academic pursuits at the community college level can have different academic and professional objectives. While some choose to transfer credits to a four-year institution, others may select a different educational or vocational path that leads to a terminal degree at the community college. Despite students' academic and professional goals, today's globalized world is making it necessary for community college students to develop and enhance their understanding of intercultural issues that could affect their personal, social, and professional spheres.

Although the necessity of experiencing a global education has been widely established, there is a dearth of research on the impact of global education or study abroad programs on students attending community colleges. According to Raby's analysis (2012), the community colleges' lack of internationalization efforts was affected by their "historical context, mission, and application" (p.82), and that there seemed to be unique patterns or trajectories at the community colleges. This qualitative research at three community colleges might add to the knowledge gap regarding students' study abroad decisions and their choice of destinations.

LITERATURE REVIEW

Study Abroad Participation and Outcomes

Participation in education programs abroad has been a topic of inquiry and scholarship among social and educational researchers. Studies have shown that studying abroad leads to students' intellectual and psychosocial gains (Dwyer, 2004), cross-cultural awareness (Keith, 2004), cross-cultural knowledge and sensitivity (Carpenter & Garcia, 2012), intercultural competence (Dwyer, 2004; Bandyopadhyay & Bandyopadhyay, 2015), and foreign language development (Shiri, 2013). Craig (1999) noted that being immersed in the culture of the host country compels individuals to re-examine their views and develop a global perspective that is vital to the interdependent nature of today's environment.

Dwyer (2004) studied the differing outcomes of 1,700 student alumni from the Institute for the International Education of Students (IES) who studied abroad between 1950 and 1999. With a 25% response rate, Dwyer's findings (2004) demonstrated that (a) respondents' participation in a study abroad program was due to being enrolled in a foreign language course, (b) internship abroad influenced respondents' career decisions after graduation, leading them to work for multinational organizations or work abroad, (c) respondents worked as teachers abroad or worked in private industries, as a result of their studying abroad, (d) studying abroad influenced respondent's worldview of art and culture and encouraged them to seek diverse friendships, and (e) studying abroad affected respondents' personal and social development.

Miller, Perrin & Thompson (2014) reported that outcomes of study abroad participation are understood from two perspectives—one relating to external influences (e.g., cultural and foreign language development) and the other associating with "internal redirection, resulting in a deepening sense of one's identity and self-awareness" (p. 78). Harrell, Sterner, Alter, and Lonie (2017) attributed the benefits of studying abroad to students' becoming environmentally conscious, gaining new perspective on personal matters, becoming more independent, and developing overall flexibility and adaptability.

Blake-Campbell (2014) examined the transformative elements of study abroad experiences among 15 students from an urban community college, using the pre and post survey methods. Findings demonstrated major themes such as students increased academic, cultural, and global knowledge as the outcomes of study abroad participation. About 66% of the study participants also stated that their awareness of "intercultural skills" was significantly improved after a short-term study abroad. While findings of this study are based on one urban community college, our study is grounded on three community colleges from different geographic locations.

Findings of these study abroad studies demonstrate the values of studying abroad and portray the shifts that can be achieved in attitudes and skills of students that parallel the current social trends regarding personal, societal, and intercultural matters. Acquiring intercultural competencies (Deardorff, 2011), traveling with friends and being a part of a group or social network (Amani & Kim, 2017), fulfilling academic/degree requirements (Carlson, et al., 1990; Claughly,1991), and developing foreign language proficiency (Anderson, 2007; Shiri, 2013), are some of the reasons that inspire study abroad participation among college students.

Bandyopadhyay and Bandyopadhyay (2015) proposed a study abroad framework asserting that students' study abroad intention and participation is influenced by intercultural awareness and expectations regarding the personal, professional, and intellectual outcome of studying abroad. Program duration and demographic characteristics such as gender and race also play a role in influencing study abroad intention and participation. In better understanding the study abroad participation decision of African

American students, Lu, Reddick, Dean, and Pecero (2015) found that in addition to the role that family, friends, and ethnic communities play in influencing study abroad participation, faculty encouragement and support is the dominant element affecting study abroad engagement among students.

Salisbury, Umbach, Paulsen, & Pascarella (2009) discussed students' socio-economic status and social capital (family background and encouragement from peer groups) in influencing study abroad participation. Harrell, Sterner, Alter, & Lonie (2017) discussed the intrinsic and extrinsic factors that influence participants' decisions among college students. Regarding intrinsic factors, the opportunity to experience and appreciate another culture, desire for travel, and longings for a change of scenery motivated students to study abroad. With respect to extrinsic factors, academic objectives and the opportunity for improving language skills and fulfilling degree requirements led them to engage in a global abroad program.

Amani and Kim (2017) noted that community college study abroad engagement was influenced by individual, social, and institutional factors. Engagement in study abroad was perceived as an opportunity of a lifetime and as a platform for supporting academic transfer application to a four-year institution; timing of the study abroad opportunity, work responsibilities, and academic goals also contributed to study abroad engagement. In addition, encouragement from faculty and family, and curricular offerings of the institution and students' network of peers and friends were instrumental in deciding to study abroad. Although participants discussed concerns such as cost, fear of travel, and family obligations as hindrances to studying abroad, the participants were able to transform those concerns into opportunities through a personal cost-benefit analysis and by recognizing the utility of studying abroad in gaining personal development.

Factors Influencing Destination Choice

Regarding students' choice of destination, American students are often eager to select Western European countries for their study abroad experiences, and study abroad participation in developing countries and Arab countries remains low. *The Open Doors Report* (2017) indicated that the majority of students continue to study abroad in Europe, followed by Latin, Central, and South America, Asia, Africa, and the Middle East. Other literature has generally focused on the experiences of international students or non-US students as they choose their study abroad site. Mazzarol & Soutar (2002) described a push-pull model explaining international students' decisions regarding study abroad and institutional choice of destination. Nyaupane, Paris, & Teye (2010) also studied the choice of destination and pre-departure attitude of international students. These researchers reported that factors such as students' budget, socioeconomic status, institutional logistics, as well as historical and social networks affect geographic inclinations and destination preferences. Shiri (2013) examined language-learning American students' destination choices regarding different Arabic-speaking nations, their attitude about learning certain Arabic dialects, and the factors influencing those attitudes. With respect to the desirability of destination, the dialect of the host country (language preference), area of focus, and perceptions related to the safety of the destination influenced participants' preferences.

Hulstrand (2011) suggests that one way to expand study abroad programs is to survey students about where they wish to go and what they hope to study. Doing so will also provide information about students' preferred choice of destination that could lead to enhanced participation in education abroad programs.

While the majority of the current literature discusses students' study abroad participation decisions from the students' perspectives, a limited number of studies have sought to understand perceptions of study abroad faculty coordinators as they relate to the reasons that prompt students to study abroad and the factors that affect their choice of destination. To address this gap, this research was undertaken to understand the perspectives of study abroad coordinators and students related to their choice of destination and factors that tend to influence community college students' engagement in global study abroad programs.

PARTICIPANTS AND METHODS

Through this study, we intended to understand and discuss students and study abroad faculty coordinators' perceptions regarding the factors that influence community college students' engagement in study abroad programs and the reasons that affect destination choices. This study relied on a qualitative design grounded in a social construction paradigm of inquiry. Qualitative research involves an in-depth understanding of an event, phenomenon, and human behavior in its unique natural setting (Denzin & Lincoln, 2002; Merriam, 2002; Maxwell, 2013; Creswell & Poth, 2018).

The participants of this study included six study abroad faculty coordinators and 24 students from three community colleges that were located in urban, rural, and suburban areas in a mid-Atlantic state. Community colleges from three different regions of the same state were chosen to integrate multiple and rich perspectives from different geographical contexts. Two study abroad coordinators and eight students from each of these three community colleges were purposively selected through criterion-based and snowball sampling. Of the 24 students across all institutions, 17 (71%) were female and 7 (29%) were male participants. In terms of ethnicity, 19 participants self-identified as White/Non-Hispanic, 1 as Black/Non-Hispanic, 1 as Hispanic, 1 as Hispanic- Biracial, 1 as Biracial, and 1 as Asian. Regarding the six coordinators, 3 were male (50%) and 3 were female (50%).

Interviews lasting between 60 and 70 minutes were conducted with each participant. Pseudonyms were used to ensure the confidentiality of the institutions and participants. For example, Professors Hall and Brown were from Institution A, Professors Johnson and Smith from Institution B, and Professors Woods and Watkins from Institution C. The in-depth interviews generated rich information regarding participants' perceptions related to why students choose to study abroad and what factors affect their choice of destination. Interviews were transcribed to obtain an overall sense of the participants' ideas, tones, and perspectives and then coded using participants' words or phrases that demonstrated their views about the phenomena. Codes were further reduced to themes that either converged with the existing literature or differed from it.

FINDINGS

Factors Influencing Study Abroad Participation

Studying abroad for the purpose of personal development and cultural enrichment was commonly perceived as motivating students' participation. Professor Woods stated, "I think that a lot of [students] may see it as their only chance to travel or one of their few possibilities for [going] abroad." Similarly, Professor Brown believed that the opportunity to experience new places motivates students to study abroad. She explained, "As a young college student, you hear about these exotic places that you can go to. And, I think, there is that genuine instinct of 'oh I want to see new places.'" Professor Woods added that often "[students] think of traveling as going to new places and having excitement and enjoyable experiences." Professor Johnson agreed by adding that "[students'] reasons really run all over the place. But a lot of it has to do with [their] personal experience and growth."

Echoing these faculty coordinators' sentiments, Kyle, one of the students who had studied abroad, explained that his decision was based on his desire to explore other cultures and gain new insight. He stated, "It just sounded like it would be an interesting trip and that I would learn some interesting things . . . that [I] would not be able to do inside the United States." Similarly, Jamie, a student who was preparing for her upcoming study abroad experience, believed that studying abroad would help her become more independent. She wanted to study abroad because the opportunity would allow her "to see the world, to meet new people, to learn through the new perspectives." She added, "I guess you could say [I would] sort of be more independent." Experiencing new adventures, traveling to new places, gaining cultural insights, and becoming more independent were all factors mirrored by both faculty participants and students concerning the reasons why students decide to participate in study abroad programs.

Engagement in study abroad programs was also perceived to be influenced by social determinants. Several faculty coordinators referenced the critical role that family and friends play in motiving students to study abroad. Professor Woods believed that encouragement from parents and their assumptions about study abroad often influence students' participation decision. Professor Woods also emphasized that when students meet their peers who have traveled abroad or are planning an academic trip, "it becomes a reality for them, saying that this person has done it, and maybe I can do it too. If this person can afford it, maybe I can too." Professor Hall also believed that both friends and family can influence students' study abroad participation decisions. He remarked:

Some students learn from other students that there's a [study abroad] course available that is interesting and fun. And some, I would imagine, [find that] their parents had a concept of study abroad and encouraged them to look for these programs and take advantage of it.

Professor Hall further commented that merely knowing that other students would travel as part of a unified group contributes to the study abroad decision among students at community colleges. He added, "It is possible that the . . . [students] would like the protection of the group, sort of the security that it affords them." Several student participants agreed with the study abroad directors. Professor Johnson also agreed that students are influenced by their peers to study abroad. He stated that students don't often know that studying abroad is a possibility until they hear about it from their friends who have gone abroad. So, that role model helps to motivate students to study abroad. John, a student who had just returned from his study abroad experience during the previous semester, agreed with Hall's analysis about traveling as part of a pack. Similarly, for Jamie, studying abroad with a group of friends and peers made her study abroad decision and experience more enjoyable. Daniela also agreed with Professor Hall's analysis that students' families play a part in motivating study abroad engagement. She stated, "My mom always motivated me . . . probably because she is from another country. And she always encourages a lot of traveling, discovering new things."

As viewed through these faculty coordinators, support by both family and peers is an important factor in promoting students' study abroad engagement. While peers' prior study abroad experiences are helpful in motivating students to study abroad, families' enthusiasm for global programs and desire to support their son or daughter to take advantage of global programs are important considerations for study abroad decisions among participants.

In addition to individual and social determinants influencing study abroad participation among community college students, institutional determinants can also play a role. Faculty coordinators agreed that studying abroad decisions can be influenced by curricular and degree requirements of the institution. Professor Smith, for example, explained that one of the courses embedded in the Honors Program requires students to study abroad. Although the course is a requirement of the Honors Program, its global experience component attracts students' attention the most. She added that students who are part of the Honors Program often say, "One of the greatest attractions of the program is to study abroad." Similarly, Professor Hall commented that for many students the credits earned through a study abroad course can help fulfill students' academic requirements.

Consistent with the faculty coordinators' perceptions regarding institutional factors that can affect study abroad participation, Calvin, one of the students who was expecting to study abroad, confessed that his participation decision was based on the premise that the credits earned as part of the study abroad course would be applied to his anticipated Associate of Arts (AA) degree.

Although curricular or degree requirements may affect community college students' engagement in global programs abroad, many faculty agreed that student–teacher relationships and faculty's enthusiasm and promotion of international programs can be motivating factors for students' decisions. Professor Brown acknowledged that the professor plays a role in whether students enroll in a faculty-led program. He added, "The professor has a huge influence. If you have had a professor and don't like them, you are not going to spend [time abroad] with them. I think most of the students who go with me know me." Professor Watkins agreed, asserting, "Faculty have a huge influence. . . . If we demonstrate a lot of enthusiasm for [study abroad programs] and do it the right way, you know, a little bit at a time, [students] get the idea." Professor Smith also agreed that students are often influenced by their teachers to study abroad or not to. She stated, "Sometimes it is their own teachers, a particular teacher," that encourages students to study abroad. Similarly, Professor Woods added, "I would like to think that maybe my class prompted them to study abroad and see great works of art and architecture." In addition, Professor Woods added that a professor's background in terms of previous travel abroad and leading study abroad courses can affect students' decisions to study abroad. Adding to these faculty coordinators' observations, Matt, a student who had studied abroad, also talked about how his faculty influenced his study abroad decision and participation.

Table 1. Factors influencing study abroad participation decision and destination choices

Coordinators	College Location	Decision factors		Destination choice	
		Personal Factors (Personal & Cultural Enrichment)	**Social Factors** (Family & Peers)	**Institutional Factors** (Curricular & Degree Requirements)	**Linguistic & Geographical Familiarity**
Woods	Rural	✓	✓	✓	✓
Hall	Rural		✓	✓	✓
Brown	Suburban	✓		✓	✓
Watkins	Suburban		✓	✓	
Smith	Urban			✓	
Johnson	Urban	✓	✓		

These testimonials provide a good understanding of how study abroad faculty coordinators perceive the institution's curricular and degree requirements and their own role in motivating students' study abroad participation. Faculty directors' perceptions about students' determinants for studying abroad mirrored student participants' experiences. These findings, along with the knowledge that faculty directors' perceptions aligned with those of students, can be utilized by institutional leaders and policy makers in developing and implementing programs that will increase study abroad access and participation among students attending community colleges. Table 1 illustrates the faculty coordinators' perceptions about factors related to students' participation decision in study abroad programs. Faculty coordinators believe that study abroad participation is motivated by personal, social, and institutional determinant. This finding is consistent with the current literature.

Choice of Study Abroad Destination

The availability and type of study abroad courses offered to students tend to affect choice of destination. Several faculty coordinators agreed that institutional elements such as the availability of study abroad courses or program factors affect students' selection of study abroad destination. Professor Watkins, for example, elaborated on this point:

How hard a college will push certain programs influences students' choices. There are just certain efforts by the college for certain countries. And sometimes it's a personal interest of the administration. . . . . Why? Because one of their people was from that area and he really wanted that kind of thing going on. .... Our vice president is very interested in Scandinavia. So Denmark took off.

Professor Watkins portrays how institutional administrators can influence the availability of programs and students' choice of destination mainly because of current or prior personal and/or professional networks. Professor Smith who directs an Honors Program with an embedded global component, explained that studying in a well-known institution in England has been a part of that particular program since its inception. While she questioned her predecessors' rationale for the selection of this destination, she did believe that studying in England is more efficient and economical for her students than going to another country. She remarked, "... there are many fine universities. But for practical reasons, cost is important. England is, believe it or not, one of the reasonable ones out there."

Professor Johnson also asserted that students rely particularly on programs that are offered through their respective institutions, explaining, "We don't have, necessarily, set locations every year except for the more traditional locations like Cambridge with the Honors Program or the Art Scholars Program." Professor Johnson further commented that, to some extent, he and the institution do influence where students study abroad, but he also considers students' aspirations:

I influence the students [and] where they're going to go by advertising, making certain locations available, particularly with the short-term study abroad. The school does influence that, for sure. But the other side of it is that students who come to my office may want to [study abroad for] long semesters . . . we can consider that. . . . I also consider what they want. So it happens both ways.

"Turkey and China were [offered] in my time-frame. So, I decided on Turkey."

Beth noted that her choice of destination was due to the availability of one study abroad course offered during the semester she wanted to go abroad. She explained, "I never actually imagined myself going to Scotland or Ireland. And those particular countries were offered through the [Honors Program]." While administrators played a vital role in the availability of study abroad destinations, they also considered program cost and logistics that are critical to the overall design and access of global programs abroad.

The second frequently discussed dimension regarding choice of destination was related to students' linguistic familiarity with the host country (see the last column of Table 1). Several faculty coordinators agreed that the language of the host country seemed an important gauge for measuring students' decisions with certain education abroad destinations. Professor Brown, for example, believed that students often select English-speaking countries because of their level of linguistic comfort. She explained, "Some of my students are going to Ireland because English is spoken there and they feel that if they are going to be in a foreign country, [they] don't want to have to wrestle with that part of the [experience]." Professor Brown also agreed that students feel a sense of connection and familiarity with English-speaking countries that motivates their choices.

While Professor Brown's intention is to ensure students' ease when abroad, her comment could be perceived as influencing the direction of students' choice of destination. From the perspective of students, Corrine admitted that studying abroad in an English-speaking country was important for her because "there wouldn't be a language barrier and it would be easier to learn from them." Casey, another student, who had studied abroad in the United Kingdom, agreed that the English language served as a bridge for her daily activities.

A third aspect of destination selection was related to some students' familiarity and prior knowledge of the host country. Professor Brown, for example, asserted that students' choice of study abroad destination largely depends on how they view the world. She remarked, "Either students are familiar with a couple of places that they go to, like Scotland and Ireland, [or] they have grown up knowing those places more so than they would know about Egypt." Similarly, Professor Woods maintained that despite having options, students would still select certain destinations based on their background and familiarity:

I would love to say that they would take the opportunity to go to other places. But, I think a lot of them would choose to go to Western Europe, even if they have other options. And I think part of the problem or the reasoning behind that would be seemingly familiarity for them as well . . . a lot of times they have more familiarity of the history of France and history of England and history of Italy over the history of India, the history of Iraq or Iran or even Egypt.

Following faculty coordinators' perspectives, several students also agreed that their study abroad choice of destinations was based on their existing knowledge of and familiarity with certain regions compared with others. Shelly, for example, explained her attraction to Europe compared with other nations by stating, "I'm very attached to Europe. I guess . . . I think, it's like a lot more familiar than a place like Egypt or China or something like that." Similarly, Laura admitted that her lack of knowledge and familiarity with non-European countries affected her choice of study abroad in France:

Some places I know more about like specific regions than others. But probably I would stay within Western Europe because I know the most about that . . . like I don't know enough about other countries to be able to talk about it. [For example], I know a lot about Scotland and the days before the Romans came. I don't know that much about Eastern European history.

For Kelly, who studied abroad in Prague, it was more important to take "one step at a time" than to immerse herself in situations that she did not feel comfortable in and ready to embrace. She acknowledged that studying abroad in a European country would be less of a culture shock for her than China, for example. Moreover, she revealed her perception about the safety net that European destinations provide compared with others.

Students' choice of destinations as perceived by study abroad faculty coordinators, and as corroborated by students, portrays the variety of factors that can influence selection of destinations. The availability of courses and programs and the critical role of the language of the host country—in addition to the students' knowledge and familiarity with some regions of the world and not others—are vital in explaining students' motives behind their choice of study abroad destination.

Community colleges with limited resources for international education programs may not have the luxury of offering myriad global programs to their students. As a result, student choices are limited to the destinations that are pre-determined by faculty who lead study abroad programs or by the institutional administrators who lend support to some programs and not others. Institutional decisions to promote study abroad programs offered through other community colleges or programs offered through the for-profit organizations may depend on each community college's organizational and leadership philosophy. Moreover, students' familiarity of the region and language seems to be a major decision factor when selecting a destination.

DISCUSSIONS

Factors Influencing Study Abroad Participation

Community college students' motivations for studying abroad and the factors that affect their choice of destination were examined from the perceptions of study abroad academic coordinators and students. Findings reveal vital information that will be addressed in the context of current literature and future research while providing practical strategies for institutional stakeholders and policy makers.

Consistent with the current literature, overall, study abroad faculty coordinators perceived personal, social, and institutional determinants (Amani & Kim, 2017; Anderson, 2005) as influencing students' attendance in study abroad programs. With respect to personal influences, study abroad participation was perceived as being influenced by attitudes regarding the students' personal growth and cultural enrichment. Half of the coordinators believed that community college students were engaging in academic global experiences for the purpose of fun and travel opportunities. Students were also mindful of the current state of world affairs and wished to gain international experiences similar to those available to their four-year counterparts. Moreover, in the midst of a global economy, community college students, as perceived by the coordinators and students in this study, were believed to understand the implications of education abroad experiences and how to utilize those opportunities as a stepping-stone to becoming independent adults.

More than 60% of the coordinators believed that peer groups and family's support were critical in promoting study abroad participation. Coordinators believed that students with prior travel abroad engagement could share stories and experiences that motivate their peers. Moreover, students, particularly women, were thought to prefer studying abroad with friends and traveling as part of a structured program rather than studying abroad on their own (Amani & Kim, 2017). For this reason friends are critical, as they continue to serve as socialization agents by encouraging and supporting study abroad participation among their peers. Faculty coordinators interviewed agreed that influences from the students' family and peers, in addition to students' preference to study abroad as part of a group or a cohort of peers (e.g. personal network), are important considerations that inspire students to study abroad. They also commented that parental attitude and mindset about the world and the extent to which they view it as a vital part of their son's or daughter's future success influences study abroad engagement.

Regarding institutional determinants, the current literature discusses the type and availability of institutionally sponsored study abroad programs and the role of faculty as a critical factor in influencing students' choice of participation in global programs abroad (Trevor, 1995; Koh, 2004). Similarly, 80% of faculty coordinators in this study perceived the nature and availability of study abroad courses and programs, curricular policies of the institution, and faculty's enthusiasm and encouragement as significant decision factors in students' studying abroad decision and participation.

According to coordinators, programs or courses (e.g., the Honors Programs) with a mandatory study abroad dimension and similar curricula that include study abroad as a required element of the program encourage increased student participation in global programs. Additionally, degree requirements of the institution were perceived as affecting study abroad engagement, particularly among students who wish to complete degree requirements sooner than expected and transfer credits earned through studying abroad to a four-year institution.

Faculty coordinators also reported that among the institutional elements, faculty encouragement and support are critical to study abroad participation among students at their respective community colleges. This was somewhat consistent with the Lu, Reddic, Dean, and Pecero's (2015) study in which African American students shared how their relationship with their faculty affected their study abroad engagement. In Amani and Kim's (2017) study, nearly 60% of the participants from community colleges rated faculty as being influential to their study abroad decisions. Similarly, other scholars have confirmed the vital role that faculty members play in informing students about study abroad opportunities (Chieffo, 2000; Peterson, 2003; Green, 2005) and supporting their study abroad decisions (Sideli & Kreutzer, 2005).

Choices of Destination

Based on the coordinators' perceptions regarding selection of study abroad destination, the availability and types of program offerings, at the institutional level, were factors that seemed to influence participants' choice of certain locations compared with others. Having course options was particularly important to students who were interested in current world affairs and wished to study abroad in destinations such as the Middle East. However, studying abroad in such locations was limited due to the unavailability of courses offered at the students' home institutions. Considering that study abroad coordinators or institutional administrators select the direction of study abroad programs through professional networks and personal connections, as discussed in the findings' section, it can be deduced that students are perhaps being channeled to programs and locations depending on the institution's resources, priorities, and objectives as well as the administrators' networks. This finding mirrors discussions regarding institutional politics and the differing agendas posed by the community college administrators, boards of governors, and international education directors that can affect the institution's internationalization efforts (Knight, 2004; Ng, 2007), including study abroad programs.

Studying abroad in English-speaking destinations was also perceived as prevalent among participants in this study. Coordinators believed that studying abroad in an English-speaking nation leads to a lesser degree of culture shock and helps students to feel at ease and avoid miscommunications while navigating the academic and social surroundings of their host country.

This finding can be contradictory to the intent of the Abraham Lincoln Commission (2005) that called for preparing graduates who are well equipped with foreign language skills to help them compete in the global economy. If students continue to shy away from learning new languages and instead travel to destinations where English is the predominant or second language, foreign language illiteracy among American graduates will perpetuate, leading them to be less competitive in todays' global environment. While this argument is important, others are as critical. It can also be argued that recommending students to study abroad in non-English speaking destinations that cause them discomfort and alarm will not be beneficial in any way. Therefore, international educators must assess not only the intellectual ability of students who are studying abroad but also the emotional readiness and well-being of their students and advise them accordingly. Clarifying myths or bolstering cultural competence by providing avenues through which students are exposed to on-campus opportunities that build their awareness of foreign nations and languages may also minimize this issue and lead to greater participation of students in non-English speaking countries.

Faculty coordinators also noted that prior knowledge of and familiarity with the host country or region influences students' choice of destination. Coordinators believed that such knowledge is an important indicator of students' destination preferences.

Educators who design study abroad programs should consider the familial (e.g., parental global value) and educational settings (e.g., positive discussion of non-European societies at US schools) that are instrumental in conditioning and perpetuating students' knowledge of less familiar regions. For example, it was found that students' motivations for studying abroad were encouraged by family members' global-mindedness; those who were perceived as valuing the exposure and experiences of an international education also supported their son's or daughter's decision to study abroad. It was also shown that some family members encouraged participation in European regions rather than in Asian countries, such as China. It can be inferred that students' lack of broader knowledge of non-European countries and their zest for studying abroad in European nations may have been the result of their upbringing as well as their family's perceptions of various nations. One is also led to suspect that the K–12 curriculum may have failed to adequately prepare students with sufficient knowledge of the world map and non-European cultures that affects students' choices of destinations during college. Examining the K–12 educational policies and curriculum, therefore, is critical to better understanding the low number of community college students' participation in non-European programs.

Overall, findings regarding students' choice of destination demonstrated that availability of courses and programs and familiarity with the language of the host country—in addition to the students' knowledge and awareness of some regions of the world—are vital in explaining students' motives behind their choice of study abroad destination. However, unique to this finding is the knowledge that community college students do not have sufficient program choices available to them. Program offerings are decided by either the faculty coordinator or the institution's administrator, which ultimately affects students' selection of destination at the time of their participation.

RECOMMENDATAIONS FOR PRACTICE AND STUDY ABROAD ACCESS

Studying abroad for the purpose of gaining intellectual insight and personal development is not a new phenomenon but nature of today's interdependent world deems it even more important for students to travel beyond their nation's borders, not only for obtaining intellectual advances and personal growth, but also for interacting with people, ideas, and cultures that are different from their own. Findings of this study, however, provide insights that can help enhance study abroad access and engagement among students attending community colleges.

First, encouraging community colleges to expand the availability of various study abroad programs and destinations might be the first step to fulfilling the Lincoln Commission's goals. Understanding the challenges can provide a platform for dialogue and an opportunity for re-examining institutional structures and policies for boosting participation in study abroad programs. Developing programs that have an embedded global or study abroad component such as the Honors Program can also attract students' attention and help their participation decisions.

Second, community colleges should consider updating their curricular requirements, so that all entering degree-seeking students could enroll in a cross-cultural or a cross-national course, thereby increasing students' knowledge of geographic regions and countries beyond the boundaries of their nation state. This would help students interested in studying abroad, particularly those students who have limited knowledge of or familiarity with different regions and countries, to become more aware and make informed decisions.

Third, considering the vital role of faculty coordinators in influencing study abroad decisions and participation, community college administrators could confer with coordinators in selecting destinations and developing systemic strategies for informing and exposing students to study abroad programs that could lead to increased participation in global programs abroad.

Fourth, as revealed by the faculty coordinators' perceptions, students' engagement in study abroad programs for the purpose of personal and cultural enrichment provides the context for discussion and promotion of study abroad programs at community colleges. Information fairs and presentations can focus on the fun and adventurous nature of studying abroad in addition to the transformative elements of these programs that lead to personal and cultural enrichment.

Fifth, student concerns regarding safety matters abroad as related to their choice of destination should be considered seriously. The coordinators should address the safety issues clearly and communicate approaches to emergencies and the resources available to all student participants to ensure their safety while abroad. However, when necessary, myths and misconceptions should also be corrected so that students can make informed decisions regarding their study abroad choices.

Sixth, students' academic background and psychological readiness must be considered. Since faculty coordinators are in continual contact with students who study abroad, students could be made aware of the positive aspects of studying abroad in non-Western or non-traditional destinations. For example, outlining for enhancing students' foreign language skills as well as reducing students' misconceptions related to non-European nations could reduce students' anxieties, possibly, leading to greater participation in education abroad in non-traditional destinations. Since faculty coordinators are in continual contact with students who study abroad, students could be made aware of the positive aspects of studying abroad in non-Western or non-traditional destinations.

Considering these recommendations, our hope is to witness a greater number of program offerings and choices of destinations at community colleges that will allow students to engage in global programs abroad. This can be achieved through institutional decisions of making global programs a priority and by encouraging constructive dialogues among the educators, students, and study abroad coordinators.

CONCLUSION

International education has been a prevalent aspect of curricular and co-curricular programming at four-year academic institutions across the US. Its necessity at community colleges did not attract much attention until the onset of globalization in the late 1980s. Continued advances in technology and the diminishing geographic boundaries across many nation states has emphasized the importance of participation in global opportunities such as education abroad. Studying abroad allows students to discover what is possible, recognizing similarities across nations and transforming differences into opportunities for economic, social, and political collaborations.

Moreover, engagement in study abroad programs can contribute to students' personal, cultural, and intellectual growth. While the concept of studying abroad is promising, not all community college students take advantage of the opportunities before graduating. The development and implementation of global programs in community colleges are also limited because of funding or budgetary restrictions. Therefore, federal and state investments should be made for study abroad activities at the community college level to enrich the educational quality and outcomes needed to produce global citizens, develop an effective workforce, and prepare future leaders so that they can contribute to the myriad aspects of their local and global communities.

REFERENCES

Amani, M. & Kim, M. M. (in press) Study Abroad Participation at Community Colleges: Students' Decision and Influential Factors. *Community College Journal of Research and Practice, 42*, 678-92.

American Association of Community Colleges. (2018). *Fast Facts*. Retrieved from: http://www.aacc.nche.edu

Anderson, B. D. (2007). *Students in a global village: The nexus between choice, expectation, and experience in study abroad* (Unpublished doctoral dissertation). The University of Texas, Austin, TX.

Bandyopadhyay, S., & Bandyopadhyay, K. (2015). Factors influencing student participation in college study abroad program. *Journal of International Education Research, 11*(2), 87–94.

Blake-Campbell, B. (2014). More Than Just a Sampling of Study Abroad: Transformative Possibilities at Best. *The Community College Enterprise, 20*(2), 60–71.

Boggs, G. R., & Irwin, J. (2007). What every community college leader needs to know: Building leadership for international education. In International reform efforts and challenges in community colleges (pp. 25-30). San Francisco: Jossey-Bass.

Brint, S., & Karabal, J. (1989). *The diverted dream: Community colleges and the promise of educational opportunity in America, 1900-1985*. New York: Oxford University Press, Inc.

Carlson, J. S., Burn, B., Useem, J., & Yachimowicz. (1990). *Study abroad: The experience of American undergraduates*. New York: Greenwood Press.

Chieffo, L. (2000). *Determinants of student participation in study abroad programs at the university of Delaware: A quantitative study* (Unpublished doctoral dissertation). University of Delaware, Newark, DE.

Cloughly, C. (1991). Integrating study abroad into the undergraduate liberal arts curriculum: Eight institutional case studies. In *Factors influencing students' decisions to study abroad* (pp. 65–86). Westport, CT: Greenwood Publishing Group, Inc.

Coffey, A., & Atkinson, P. (1996). *Making sense of qualitative data: Complimentary research strategies*. Thousand Oaks, CA: Sage Publications, Inc.

Cohen, A. M., & Brawer, F. B. (2013). *The American community college* (6th ed.). San Francisco, CA: Jossey-Bass.

Commission on the Abraham Lincoln Study Abroad Fellowship Program. (2005). *Global competence & national needs: 640 One million Americans studying aboard*. Retrieved from https://www.aifs.com/pdf/lincoln_final_report.pdf

Council on International Intercultural Exchange. (1988). *Educating for global competence: Report of the Advisory Council for International Educational Exchange*. New York, NY: Council on International Intercultural Exchange.

Craig, S. (1999). Study abroad 101: The basic facts. *The Black Collegian*, 138-143.

Creswell, J. W., & Poth, C. N. (2018). *Qualitative inquiry & research design: Choosing among five approaches*. Los Angeles, CA: Sage.

Crotty, M. (1998). *The foundations of social research: Meaning and perspective in the research process*. London, UK: Sage.

Deardorff, D. K. (2011). Assessing intercultural competence. *New Directions for Institutional Research*, *149*(149), 65–79. doi:10.1002/ir.381

Dwyer, M. M. (2004). Charting the impact of studying abroad. *International Educator*, *13*(1), 14–20.

Green, M. F. (2007). Internationalizing community colleges: Barriers and strategies. In International reform efforts and challenges in community colleges (pp. 15-24). San Francisco: Jossey-Bass.

Harrell, A., Sterner, G., Alter, T., & Lonie, J. (2017). Student perceptions of the impact of their diverse study abroad experiences. *NACTA Journal*, *61*(1).

Hett, J. (1993). *Development of an instrument to measure global-mindedness* (Unpublished doctoral dissertation). University of San Diego, San Diego, CA.

Hossler, D., & Gallagher, K. S. (1987). Studying student college choice: A three-phase model and the implications for policymakers. *College and University*, *62*(3), 207–221.

Hulstrand, J. (2011, September). Developing Education Abroad at Community Colleges. *International Educator*, 46-49.

Institute on International Education (IIE). (2017). *Open Doors Report*. New York, NY: IIE.

Kasper, H. T. (2002). The changing role of community college. *Occupational Outlook Quarterly*, *46*(4), 14–21.

Knight, J. (2004). Internationalization remodeled: Definition, approaches, and rationales. *Journal of Studies in International Education*, *8*(1), 5–31. doi:10.1177/1028315303260832

Lu, C., Reddick, R., Dean, D., & Pecero, V. (2015). Coloring up study abroad: Exploring black students' decision to study in China. *Journal of Student Affairs Research and Practice*, *52*(4), 440–451. doi:10.1080/19496591.2015.1050032

Mazzarol, T., & Soutar, G. N. (2002). "Push-Pull" factors influencing international student destination choice. *International Journal of Educational Management*, *16*(82).

Merriam, S. B. (2002). *Qualitative research in practice: Examples for discussion and analysis*. San Francisco, CA: Jossey-Bass.

Miller-Perrin, C., & Thompson, D. (2014). Outcomes of global education: External and internal change associated with study abroad. *New Directions for Student Services*, *146*(146), 77–89. doi:10.1002s.20093

Nyaupane, G., Paris, C. M., & Teye, V. (2010). Study abroad motivations, destination selection and pre-trip attitude formation. *International Journal of Tourism Research*, *13*(3), 205–217. doi:10.1002/jtr.811

Opp, R. D., & Gosetti, P. P. (2014). The role of key administrators in internationalizing the community college student experience. *New Directions for Community Colleges*, *165*(165), 67–75. doi:10.1002/cc.20092

Raby, R. L. (2006, Fall). *Community college study abroad: Making study abroad accessible to all students*. Retrieved from: http://www.iienetwork.org

Raby, R. L. (2012). Re-Imagining International Community Colleges *Audem*. *International Journal of Higher Education and Democracy*, *3*, 81–99.

Salisbury, M. H., Umbach, P., Paulsen, M. B., & Pascarella, E. T. (2009). Going global: Understand the choice process of the intent to study abroad. *Research in Higher Education*, *50*(2), 119–143. doi:10.100711162-008-9111-x

Shiri, S. (2013). Learners' Attitudes toward regional dialects and destinations preferences in study abroad. *Foreign Language Annals*, *46*(4), 565–587. doi:10.1111/flan.12058

Chapter 10
The Hybrid Model:
Providing Options for a Small Community College

William David Fell
Carroll Community College, USA

Siobhan Wright
Carroll Community College, USA

ABSTRACT

This chapter is a case study of Carroll Community College, a small rural community college, and its plan to develop a viable travel program by using a hybrid model. This model includes three distinct cohorts: study abroad students (students who travel and take an associated credit course), lifelong learning students (travelers who take a continuing education course to prepare for the travel experience), and educational tourists (travelers who do not take an associated course). By allowing not only study abroad students but also lifelong learners (often called continuing education students) to participate in an international travel program, Carroll's mission is addressed. This chapter is a case study of how and why Carroll implemented the hybrid model as an example for other small community colleges that might wish to achieve similar results.

INTRODUCTION

Nestled in the rolling hills of northern Maryland, Carroll Community College seems an unlikely locale for a vibrant educational travel program. One of the smallest community colleges in the state, Carroll's full-time students (FTE) number fewer than 3,000 (Carroll Community College, 2017, p. 2), and most are drawn from family farms, small towns, and distant suburbs.

Yet in the spring of 2017, the college took 39 participants on a 10-day travel program to Ireland. The program filled up six weeks prior to the registration deadline and there was a waiting list that was never exhausted. Indeed, this scenario has played out not just for the most recent programs to Ireland and Italy, but for the past several years as the college has taken between 26 and 39 participants in the past

DOI: 10.4018/978-1-5225-6252-8.ch010

four years to England, France, Italy, and Ireland—and before that, to many other European countries, dating back to 1992.

So how does a small rural community college manage to develop a viable travel program? One answer is by using a hybrid model, one that includes three distinct cohorts.

- Study abroad students (students who travel and take an associated credit course)
- Lifelong learning students (travelers who take a continuing education course to prepare for the travel experience)
- Educational tourists (travelers who do not take an associated for-credit course).

This model is in keeping with Carroll's mission, which is to provide "active learn[ing]" experiences for all students, both traditional and lifelong learners; to prepare them "for an increasingly diverse and changing world"; and to provide them with opportunities for "personal and cultural enrichment" (CCC, 2016, p. 4). By allowing not only study abroad students, but also lifelong learners (often called continuing education students) to participate in an international travel program, this mission is more than addressed. For all travelers, the college offers both academic (or credit) and continuing education (non-credit) courses to deepen its travelers' educational experiences abroad, although taking a course is not a requirement for any traveler. To be clear, only the first type of participant—the study abroad student—receives academic credit for an associated travel course, which transpires over an entire semester and which includes but is not limited to a ten-day educational travel experience. This component of the hybrid program allows students "to get a toe wet" (Woolf, 2007, p. 497) in education abroad. For Carroll community college, this study abroad opportunity is made possible by the participants in the other two cohorts, whose inclusion makes the program affordable and, thus, viable.

This chapter is a case study of how and why Carroll implemented the hybrid model as an example for other small community colleges that might wish to achieve similar results. As Malveaux (2016) notes, the motivation to study abroad among today's students is "a desire to travel" and "a desire to experience a new culture" (p. 2), which are the same motivations that underlie successful educational tourism programs.

BACKGROUND: DEFINITION OF TERMS

The following terms are used in this chapter to describe the different types of travel program participants included in the hybrid model:

- *Study abroad student* describes a participant in "formal educational programs that occur outside the participant's home country" and for "which students receive degree credits" from an associated travel course (Zhang, 2011, p. 182-183).
- *Lifelong learner* describes a participant in an international travel program who takes a non-credit continuing education course to prepare for the travel experience—because he or she is "inspired by personal development activities that stimulate creativity, broaden knowledge, expand perspectives, and support healthy living" (CCC, 2016, p. 159).
- *Educational tourist* describes a participant in an international travel program who may or may not be a credit-earning student, one who takes neither an academic course nor a continuing education

The Hybrid Model

course to enhance their travel experience, but one whose participation constitutes "an intentional, structured, *in situ* learning experience" (Pitman, Broomhall, McEwan, & Majocha, 2010, p. 226)

THE PROBLEM: FISHING IN A SMALL POND

The reason for using a hybrid model is simple: small community colleges serve a finite population. They are fishing in a small pond for study abroad students. As Twombly, Salisbury, Tumanut, and Klute (2012) note, "Community college students participate in study abroad at considerably lower rates than students from other kinds of institutions" (p. 43). The most recent numbers from the Institute of International Education (IIE) (2017b) indicate that only 1.7% of all study abroad students are Associate's students. For small community colleges, this lower rate of participation can make it difficult to develop a viable program, if the program is limited just to study abroad students. For example, at Carroll, the number of study abroad students is typically three or fewer per year. It is hard to justify a travel program for just a handful of students.

THE SOLUTION: EXPANDING THE POOL

In order to overcome the problem of program viability, Carroll Community College expanded the pool of possible participants to include lifelong learners and educational tourists. Every participant in the program registers through continuing education, which serves some practical functions, particularly in regard to risk management concerns and streamlining paperwork. However, study abroad students take a companion course during the semester of travel. In the companion course, students design a capstone project that is partially completed while abroad. Lifelong learning students register for continuing education classes that promise to enhance their travel experience: non-credit courses in cuisine, photography, languages, and culture. The courses vary according to the location of a given travel program.

The goal is to create a mix of participants who supplement their travel experience with coursework. The mix of participants creates diverse group of travelers, especially in terms of age. For the educational tourist who does not take an associated course, the program is short-term: a nine-to-ten-day educational travel experience during the college's spring break. Lifelong learners prepare for the travel experience for personal reasons, but—in effect—they become more expert about the destination and often add to the program in educationally supportive ways, especially in their interactions with educational tourists. For study abroad students, the experience encompasses a semester, as they register for a three-credit study abroad course offered through Humanities, History, or Art. The class tends to be small and highly individualized. For instance, students have latitude to identify topics connected to international travel that they wish to study, focusing on landmarks, artwork, or endeavors connected to the country to which they will travel over spring break. A common course number exists in three different academic areas for students: Humanities-160, History-160, and Art-160. These are, in academic terms, special topics courses that are developed to suit the academic interests of the enrolled students. In addition, some study abroad students use the travel program to answer the objectives of different courses in which they are enrolled, which falls outside the scope of the faculty coordinators who organize the programs.

The three cohorts in the hybrid model (study abroad students, lifelong learners, and educational tourists), as shown in Table 1, create a bigger pool of travelers and a viable number of participants.

Table 1. Carroll Community College travel program: Demographic breakdown of participants

Year	Program	Number of Study Abroad Students	Number of Lifelong Learners	Number of Educational Tourists	Total Number of Participants
2013	Italy	3	2	15	20
2014	England	3	1	22	26
2015	France	2	2	26	30
2016	Italy	1	2	33	36
2017	Ireland	2	1	36	39
2018	Italy	0	4	32	36

As these numbers show, the addition of lifelong learners and educational tourists helps to create a robust program of 39 participants, as in the case of the college's 2017 program to Ireland. At Carroll Community College, a viable travel program is one with at least 20 participants. 20 students is the college's threshold number because its travel vendor requires at least 10 paying travelers for each complimentary faculty leader, and the college's policy is to have at least two faculty leaders so that at least one can be with the group in case the other has to handle an emergency. Having two faculty leaders also addresses a risk management concern: guaranteeing ongoing coordination if one leader is incapacitated or required to solve a major problem, such as dealing with a lost passport. The good news is that even a small community college such as Carroll can mount a travel program of 20+ participants if it is willing to broaden its view of who can participate and embrace a non-traditional program that, in turn, meets the mission of that college.

At the same time, the hybrid model can still be an educational one for all who participate, not just the study abroad students. At Carroll, this goal is accomplished by designing itineraries that focus on historical sites and cultural experiences rather than on recreational ones. For example, the college's upcoming 2019 Greece program will include no time at the beach, no cruise around the islands. Rather, it will focus on sites such as the Acropolis, the National Archaeological Museum, Delphi, and Olympia. Second, Carroll's travel programs include local guides, provided by the travel vendor, that offer expert lectures about key sites and a chance for participants to ask questions. During the 2018 Italy program, the local guide at Pompeii had formerly worked as an archaeologist at the site, prompting an intense discussion between him and an expert archeologist who was an educational tourist. This discussion engaged other participants as well. Finally, the vendor-provided tour manager and the college's faculty leaders are content experts in several academic areas relevant to the program itinerary, particularly literature, history, and art. The tour manager that the college uses for its British programs has a degree from Oxford University and is a specialist in Charles Dickens. Two of the study abroad students had designed projects about literary figures, so the tour manager proved to be a great source of information, alerting students to a theatrical production that was taking place and facilitating the purchase of tickets. In addition to the study abroad students, others purchased tickets to the recommended theatrical production. So, even for those participants who are not taking a credit course associated with the program—educational tourists—the program still offers an educational experience.

Completion Rates

For Carroll students who participate in the travel program, completion rates are significantly higher than the college average, including for students traveling as educational tourists, suggesting that students who participate are much more likely to graduate. In the chart below, two types of completion rates are presented: the persistence-completion rate and the graduation-transfer rate. The persistence-completion rate is defined as students who are still enrolled in the college, have graduated, or have transferred. The graduation-transfer rate is defined as students who have graduated from the college or who have transferred to a four-year institution. Both rates are shown in Table 2.

As these numbers illustrate, not only are the completion rates of study abroad students higher than the college average, but so too are those of students participating as educational tourists. In fact, the persistence-completion rate of the latter group is slightly higher than that of study abroad students, although the graduation-transfer rate of study abroad students is higher. In any case, the completion rates of both types of students are higher than the college average by more than 20 percentage points. While the completion rate likely reflects the grit of a self-selecting student cohort, it also suggests that the hybrid model attracts serious students. In fact, several study abroad students in the program also went on to study abroad at their transfer colleges and to travel independently over international borders.

Other Benefits

Broadening Opportunities for Learning

Just as importantly, a hybrid model makes possible learning opportunities that otherwise would not exist. It allows a handful of students at a small community college to have a study abroad experience: to travel abroad while taking a three-credit course associated with the travel experience that is taught by a college faculty member who is a travel program leader. As a non-traditional student who works full-time said, "Traveling to the place I had been studying provided me with a deeper meaning and a context for my final project on Ireland . . . and [the hybrid program] made it possible for me to study abroad, as I can take off 10 days from work but not several weeks or a full semester" (K. Schroyer, personal communication, July 23, 2018). Without the hybrid model, *no one* would have the opportunity to travel with Carroll Community College.

Table 2. Carroll Community College completion rates for students participating in the travel program: 2013-2017

Completion Rates	Study Abroad Students	Students Participating As Educational Tourists	All Full-time Carroll Students
Persistence-completion rate (fall-to-fall)	90.9%	92.8%	70%
Graduation-transfer rate (fall-to-fall)	90.9%	76.1%	50%

Second, it allows students who do not have room in their schedules for a study abroad course to participate in an educational travel experience. Even though these students may not receive academic credit for their travel experience, their experience can still contribute to their learning in credit courses not connected directly to the travel program. During the college's 2015 Paris program, a journalism student, Deborah, captured the entire travel experience for the student newspaper, *The Quill*. In a blog that she updated every evening from Paris, she exercised her photography and writing skills, creating a body of work on which she was evaluated by her journalism professor. For Deborah, this was a unique strategy for making use of the travel experience in an academic endeavor.

Karin, a study abroad student for the 2016 Italy program and an artist, designed a final project on Michelangelo. Both a photographer and a painter, Karin spent the entire time with a camera around her neck. After visiting the Statue of David at Galleria dell'Accademia di Firenze, she strolled the Piazza della Signoria taking photographs. One of the photographs captured an elderly man feeding the pigeons. He became her muse. She developed the photograph in black and white, entered into photography competitions, and won some awards. Karin also painted "Pigeon Man." Her painting earned her local recognition. Soon she wanted to connect with her muse again. During the 2018 program to Italy, Karin traveled as an educational tourist—one with a mission. While the group visited landmarks in Rome, Karin took an independent day trip to Florence to find her muse—and she did. His name is Mario, and she spent an hour with him feeding pigeons and showing him the artwork that he had inspired. While Karin did not spend a semester at Accademia d'Arte, she nonetheless had a meaningful artistic, educational, and human experience, one that spanned two years. When asked about the study abroad course, Art-160, and study abroad program, Karin responded simply, "I would recommend it to any [art] student at Carroll Community College" (K. Johnsson, personal communication, July 25, 2018).

One of the greatest benefits of the hybrid model is that it is flexible. A student can initially register for the program as an educational tourist and then later decide to take the associated course as well and become a study abroad student. This flexibility is possible because the vendor's registration deadline is in November and the course's registration deadline is in the following January. More importantly, this flexibility is possible because both options—study abroad and educational tourism—are available to students, making educational tourism an entry point into study abroad for some students. In fact, approximately half of the study abroad students listed in the preceding chart had initially registered as educational tourists and then later decided to register for the associated study abroad course.

With fewer study abroad students, it is possible to tailor each student's travel course to his or her interests rather than forcing all students to follow the same set curriculum. In the college's study abroad course, which is a three-credit elective humanities course, students study a topic of their choosing from the beginning to the end of the spring semester, culminating in a capstone presentation. At the beginning of the spring semester, faculty leaders meet with each student to discuss his or her interests as they relate to the program destination. Faculty leaders then assign pre-travel readings, develop journal prompts, and collaborate with students on ideas for capstone projects that reflect this interest. At the end of the program, students present these capstone projects not only to faculty leaders and other students in the travel program, but also to the wider college audience, including other faculty members, students, and administrators. Of course, the topics chosen by students must be academic (for example, in the areas of literature, history, and art), and they must be related to the program itinerary, but beyond that, students are free to choose their topic as long as it is approved by the faculty leaders who teach the course. The benefit of study abroad programs, as noted by Malveaux (2016), also applies to the study abroad student at Carroll Community College (p. 2). The student who studies both on campus and at a travel destina-

The Hybrid Model

tion—and then chooses a topic to examine and experience in another country to support their learning—is "not a passive participant, but a proactive contributor to activities while studying abroad" (p. 3). Simply, the study takes place before, during, and after the physical experience of traveling abroad.

This individual tailoring of project topics, along with the small number of study abroad students, also allows faculty leaders to be flexible during the travel experience when mishaps occur or student interests change. For example, in advance of the college's 2017 program to Ireland, Katie set out to study *The Book of Kells*. The itinerary had been designed to include a tour of Trinity College, in part to accommodate her project, only for her to discover upon arriving that because of a college formal, which was not publicized, Trinity was closed. On site, faculty leaders worked with her to redesign her project to include the monastery Glendalough. Her presentation was outstanding. Two years before, in advance of the college's 2015 Paris program, one student, Jordan, had set out to study Napoleon. However, while in Paris, she realized that the person she was really interested in was Napoleon III, Napoleon's nephew and the man responsible for many of the sites she visited, such as Napoleon's Tomb, the Arc de Triomphe, and the street plan of Paris. On site, faculty leaders revised her journal prompts so that they would correlate to this new area of interest.

Last, the hybrid model facilitates lifelong learning. For example, in advance of the college's 2015 Paris program, a senior continuing education student, Joe, researched several of the sites on the itinerary and prepared a packet with pictures and historical information about each site. With Joe's permission, faculty leaders copied and distributed this packet to other travelers just before departure. In fact, many who sign up for the travel program decide to take supporting courses through continuing education, becoming part of the cohort of lifelong learners. For instance, a middle-aged couple, Tamara and Dante, took continuing education classes in conversational Italian and Italian culture to prepare for the travel program to Italy in 2018. They wrote that "taking the Italian language and Italian culture classes reawakened their art of learning" and inspired them to "connect with a distant relative" in Italy while abroad, a relative who spoke very little English (T. Almonte and D. Almonte, personal communication, July 24, 2018). It is hard not to see that Tamara and Dante's experience in Italy was deepened because of the coursework they took at the college in preparation for their travel experience. In fact, over the last five years, ten lifelong learners have been drawn to the college to take credit and non-credit language courses. As a result, the hybrid model also promotes awareness of the college and both its credit and non-credit offerings, making the hybrid program an accidental marketing and enrollment tool for the college.

Research on the benefits of educational tourism for older and middle-age participants confirms its cognitive as well as health benefits. In a study of Elderhostel, an educational tourism program for seniors, Ahn and Janke (2011) found that "participation in Elderhostel, and other educational travel experiences, promotes the three components of successful aging: avoiding disease, maintaining high levels of physical and cognitive function, and engagement with life" (p. 667). They conclude that "involvement in educational travel experiences may be one avenue for promoting optimal aging in middle aged and older adults" (Ahn, & Janke, 2011, p. 667). Carroll's hybrid approach involves interested lifelong learners in planning travel program itineraries, deepening educational tourism for at least those who participate in the travel advisory planning sessions. This creates a satisfying and educational experience, as noted by an active senior traveler:

Now that I'm retired, Carroll Community College's travel study trips have given me the opportunity to visit some of the historical and cultural places I studied in high school and college. Each year I research the battles, art, architecture and other features that makes a place worth visiting. The travel study advisory group allows me to use my research to help develop an itinerary that is both educational and enjoyable. (J. Markovic, personal communication, July 24, 2018)

Given that the majority of lifelong learners in Carroll's travel programs are middle aged and older adults, the hybrid model includes avid participants in the planning process of each itinerary for the next year.

Reducing Costs for Students

The addition of non-student participants also reduces the cost of the program for students. As research has shown, "Socioeconomic status and parental income are among the primary factors influencing the decision to study abroad" (Twombly et al., 2012, p. 44), with "cost" being "an especially salient consideration for community college students" (p. 63). Indeed, the most common response that Carroll faculty leaders hear from students when the program is presented to them is some version of "I'd love to go, but I don't have the money."

Fortunately, vendors often price travel programs more cheaply for greater numbers of participants, which means that a hybrid program can take advantage of economies of scale in order to lower costs. For example, when the college asks for a quote from its vendor, it usually asks that the program be priced for 30 participants, which means that the price-per-participant is substantially less (sometimes by hundreds of dollars) than if the program had been priced for only 20 or 25 participants. This difference becomes significant when looking at the results of the student focus groups that Carroll convenes prior to each program. One of the advisory group questions asks for the students' price point. In the past several years, that price point has ranged between $3,300 and $3,600. Therefore, when a quote is $3,400 per participant for a group of 30—rather than $3,800 for a group of 20—the impact on student participation becomes obvious.

When the number of participants exceeds the college's expectation of 30, as it has in recent years, the vendor can offer even more benefits—at no additional cost—such as additional guides and tour managers, better accommodations, additional included meals, and even additional days and destinations. For example, in 2017, the large group size (39) allowed the program to include a full-time tour manager for the first time. In 2016, the group size (36) allowed an extra day to be added to the itinerary as well as an additional destination (Venice).

Creating a Diverse Community of Travelers

The hybrid model also creates a demographically diverse community of travelers. The irony of a community college is that it can be, in its worst moments, a hub of commuters who share few experiences with each other. Carroll's travel program creates a bonding experience among travelers. New relationships emerge. It's moving. During the 2014 London program, it soon became apparent that one young traveler, Kevin, was leaving for boot camp in the weeks following his return. Faculty leaders celebrated him. Just prior to the 2015 Paris program, a student named Tyler had buried his grandfather and began the program in a state of grief. While in Paris, he bonded with Lou, a retiree and senior citizen, and they spent much of their time together. Tyler said that Lou helped him process his grandfather's death. During the 2017 Ireland program, one of the retired travelers, Lynn, developed friendships with traditional aged college students, and she enjoyed herself so much that she spent a year developing her photography

The Hybrid Model

skills for the subsequent Italy program. Community travelers enrich the lives of students and contribute to their education.

In the same way, the hybrid model builds a genuine sense of community within the college. A consistent number of college employees sign-up for the program, and many take at least one continuing education class to prepare for the travel experience. They are, therefore, lifelong learning students. While abroad, students and faculty alike become acquainted with staff members. Often staff members emerge as informal group leaders, lending their expertise in the college at critical times. For instance, an administrative associate in the Student Life Office helped arrange a coach bus from the college to the airport, and a couple months after the program ended, she organized a reunion party at her home. The Director of Lifelong Learning assisted with designing sensible forms and offered classes to support those continuing education students who had signed up for a travel program. Travelers become aware of each other—whether student, faculty, or staff—which strengthens the sense of community across the campus. Students and faculty learn the names of staff members, the offices they work in, the critical work that they perform at the college, and their interests in life. The walls between the Testing Center, the Cashier's Office, the Student Life Office, and the Career Development Center disappear, and the college community develops a special rapport. This phenomenon is noted as a strength by Malveaux (2016) in study abroad programs that cater to the needs of only degree-seeking students (p. 2). He says that they develop "a far greater bond between study and coordinator than most courses. With this close bond often a special relationship forms between university officials and students" (p. 2). The bonding experience is one of the guaranteed benefits of a hybrid program.

Planning

Planning travel programs involves previous travelers, who represent each of the three cohorts. Participants gather for at least two meetings to identify and begin the process of designing the program that will commence about 18 months later. They prepare materials and discuss educational opportunities in different locations. The conversations at these meetings are rich, ranging from relevant world events to educational opportunities in different locations. While some of the participants in the past have signed up for the program they helped plan, such is not necessarily the case. About half of the participants in the planning sessions have no intention of signing up and are motivated by a commitment to the program, to world travel, and to the college's students. This advisory group meets at least twice, typically in October. At the first meeting, faculty leaders introduce a problem (there is always a problem). The current problem is that the college is changing its spring break week to the end of March, so climate will be a challenge if the college continues to travel to colder destinations at that time of year.

The second—and more delightful—order of business is choosing a destination. Faculty leaders have noticed that travelers are interested in locations for iconic sites, ancestral connections, religious pilgrimage, intellectual curiosity, and weather. When creating the advisory group, faculty leaders try to keep in mind people who have traveled with the college for each of these reasons. Beyond the work that is accomplished during these sessions, they often serve as mini-reunions for former travelers.

Faculty leaders must also consider academic factors when choosing a destination. For example, the college has chosen Greece for its 2019 travel program. The timing of the program is partly to align with a credit Greek mythology course that is offered during the spring semester every other year. The advisory group suggested that a Greek mythology course offered through continuing education would bolster the experience for lifelong learners participating in the program. The Continuing Education Office, therefore, is working closely with the faculty leaders to answer the charge.

Naturally, this approach to program planning requires that the travel vendor be flexible enough to design a program proposed by the college and not just offer a list of pre-packaged hop-on, hop-off itineraries. That is why the college uses a vendor that can provide a tailor-made itinerary that best satisfies the unique interests of prospective participants as well while addressing the college's mission. This flexibility is essential to meeting the needs of the three cohorts of travelers. In truth, and as Michael Woolf (2007) suggests, the hybrid model "blurs the distinction between education and educational tourism" (p. 503)—but without lessoning the credibility of any approach to education abroad, as he fears.

Advertising

Once planning is completed, faculty leaders then turn to advertising, which targets both students and community members. To reach students, the college advertises the travel program on its website and on digital and print signs throughout the college. Faculty leaders also develop oral and visual presentations for their own classes as well as for other classes that might be interested, such as the college's honors cohort.

To target community members, faculty leaders work closely with the marketing department at the college to create professional-looking tri-fold brochures and to place an advertisement in the local *Carroll Magazine*, which appeals to a 55+ age group. After so many years, the travel program has momentum of its own, one created by the travelers themselves, many of whom recommend the program to others and take advantage of it two or more times.

CONCLUSION

Carroll's experience demonstrates that even a small community college can develop a viable travel program—*if* it is willing to expand its audience of participants. As Twombly et al. (2012) have concluded, "limiting the institutional definition of study abroad to credit-bearing experiences may limit study abroad participation" (p. 107-198). The hybrid model offers one way of moving beyond those limits. Indeed, educational tourism, paired with study abroad, is perhaps the most viable model for the small community college. The notion that such programs "weaken the credibility of international education" (Woolf, 2007, p. 503), as stated by the former president of the Foundation for International Education, is elitist and represents a criticism that community colleges have long withstood. Carroll's statistics for completion mirror those of traditional programs. Additionally, community colleges serve a community cohort. Obviously, those privileged students who are able study abroad for a semester or more develop greater "linguistic ability" and "lifelong" international connections (Coker, Heiser, Taylor, & Book, 2017, p. 6) than those who can afford only an educational tour, but the unthinkable option for the latter would be for all our travelers to just stay home.

CHECKLIST

The following are some recommendations for developing a hybrid travel program:

- Expand the pool of travelers to reflect all cohorts defined by the college's mission: credit students, lifelong learners, and community members (educational tourists).
- Collaborate with the Continuing Education Office to offer meaningful lifelong learning courses to potential travelers who are not degree-seeking students.
- Convene an advisory board that reflects the cohort of travel program participants: credit students, lifelong learners, and community members (educational tourists).
- Select a vendor that will allow for a customized travel program and that will provide expert-level educational support in-country.
- Advertise to all members of the community, using professionally designed materials.

REFERENCES

Ahn, Y., & Janke, M. C. (2011). Motivations and benefits of the travel experience of older adults. *Educational Gerontology*, *37*(8), 653–673. doi:10.1080/03601271003716010

Carroll Community College. (2016). *Carroll community college catalogue: 2016-2017*. Westminster, MD: Carroll Community College.

Carroll Community College. (2017). *Institutional assessment effectiveness report*. Westminster, MD: Carroll Community College.

Coker, J. S., Heiser, E., Taylor, L., & Book, C. (2017). Impacts of experiential learning depth and breadth on student outcomes. *Journal of Experiential Education*, *40*(1), 5–23. doi:10.1177/1053825916678265

Institute of International Education. (2017a). *Open doors 2017 executive summary*. Retrieved from https://www.iie.org/Why-IIE/Announcements/2017-11-13-Open-Doors-2017-ExecutiveSummary

Institute of International Education. (2017b). *Profile of U.S. study abroad students, 2004/05-2015/16*. Retrieved from https://www.iie.org/Research-and-Insights/Open-Doors/Data/US-Study-Abroad/Student-Profile

Malveaux, G. (2016). *Look before leaping: Risks, liability, and repair of study abroad in higher education*. Lanham, MD: Rowman & Littlefield.

Pitman, T., Broomhall, S., McEwan, J., & Majocha, E. (2010). Adult learning in educational tourism. *Australian Journal of Adult Learning*, *50*(2), 219–238.

Twombly, S. B., Salisbury, M. H., Tumanut, S. D., & Klute, P. (2012). Study abroad in a new global century—Renewing the promise, refining the purpose. *ASHE Higher Education Report*, *38*(4), 1–152. Retrieved from http://eds.a.ebscohost.com/

Woolf, M. (2007). Impossible things before breakfast: Myths in education abroad. *Journal of Studies in International Education*, *11*(3-4), 496–509. doi:10.1177/1028315307304186

Zhang, Y. (2011). CSCC Review series essay: Education abroad in the U.S.: Community colleges. *Community College Review*, *39*(2), 181–200. doi:10.1177/0091552111404552

Chapter 11
Low-Cost Initiatives for Expanding Study Abroad Opportunities

Drew Allen Gephart
Peralta Community College District, USA

ABSTRACT

Community colleges without a budget strictly allocated to study abroad programs need to be creative in how they expand opportunities for their students. This chapter will focus on the strategies developed by the Peralta Community College District's Office of International Education to develop a stronger study abroad program with limited resources and staffing. After the Peralta Colleges committed to the Institute of International Education's Generation Study Abroad initiative in 2014, it created new study abroad programs, organized annual study abroad fairs, was awarded a scholarship of $7,500, created new promotional materials and an administrative procedure, launched a new website and newsletter, organized financial aid workshops and professional development day presentations for faculty, and opened a study abroad scholarship through its foundation. The chapter will share how other colleges can learn from these efforts and institutionalize study abroad on their campuses.

PERALTA COMMUNITY COLLEGE DISTRICT BACKGROUND

Located in the East Bay Area of Northern California, the Peralta Community College District, which is referred to as Peralta Colleges, consists of four community colleges (Berkeley City College, College of Alameda, Laney College and Merritt College) that are accredited by the Accrediting Commission for Community and Junior Colleges (ACCJC, 2018). The colleges have a diverse student population which adds to the richness of its learning community and study abroad programs. In spring 2017, approximately 25,000 students enrolled at the Peralta Colleges, which includes 1,000 international students studying from over 80 different countries. On average Peralta Colleges sends approximately 50-70 students to other countries each year on its faculty led study abroad programs. The Peralta Colleges students mirror the Bay Area's ethnic, cultural and socioeconomic diversity. They include single parents, international

DOI: 10.4018/978-1-5225-6252-8.ch011

students, full-time workers, re-entry students, career changers and high school students. Ethnicities for all students includes 27% Asian, 23% African American, 22% Hispanic, 17% White Non-Hispanic, 3% Filipino, and 8% Unknown/Other. More than half of Peralta Colleges' students are between 19 and 24 years of age. 55% are female, 42% are male and 3% are unknown or declined to state (California Community College's Chancellors Office, 2017).

Prior to 2018, very limited data was collected regarding specific student demographics participating in study abroad programs. Beginning in 2018, Peralta Colleges required all students participating in a faculty-led program to fill out a Pre-Travel Study Abroad Information Form which includes demographic data, travel history, educational goals, medical history and other information which will be used for future studies in understanding the types of students who are enrolling. For Peralta Colleges' study abroad programs to Cuba, Japan and China (35 students total) offered during the summer 2018 term, 37% were male and 63% were female. The average age of students was 29 (ranging from 17 to 70). Ethnicities include 8% Asian or Pacific Islander, 44% African American, 20% Hispanic, 8% Multiracial, 8% White Non-Hispanic and 12% Unknown/Decline to State. Students who enrolled in these study abroad programs indicated their current educational goals as 51% obtain an associate degree and transfer to a 4-year institution, 20% transfer to a 4-year institution without an associate degree, 6% obtain a 2-year associate degree without transfer, 6% earn a career technical certificate without transfer, 3% prepare for a new career (acquire job skills), 6% advance in current job/career (update job skills), 6% educational development and 2% undecided on goal. 28% of the students were first generation college students, and 80% of the students indicated that they were the first person in their family to study abroad. 37% of the students said they had never traveled abroad before.

Peralta Colleges Educational Programs

Peralta Colleges offer many two-year Associate of Arts/Associate of Science (A.A./A.S.) Degrees and Certificate programs in fields such as Business, Performing Arts, Computer Information Systems, English for Speakers of Other Languages (ESOL), as well as many Science, Technology, Engineering, Art and Math (STEAM) fields of study. Peralta Colleges also offer Career and Technical Education programs such as Aviation Maintenance Technology, Culinary Arts, Cosmetology, Cyber-security, Automotive Technology, Apparel and Fashion Design, Dental Assisting, and Nursing (PCCD Career and Technical Education, 2018). All college level units taken at Peralta Colleges are transferable to the University of California (UC) and California State University (CSU) systems, as well as most other 4-Year public and private Universities. Faculty from any department may choose to propose a study abroad program in their discipline. Peralta Colleges offers study abroad courses which are transferrable and help fulfill the General Education transfer requirements to a 4-Year University. Additionally, Peralta Colleges has also created career education study abroad programs in fields such as Cosmetology.

Peralta Colleges Education Abroad Programs

In line with current trends across higher education, Peralta Colleges has steadily increased the number of faculty-led programs since the early 2000's. Each program has approximately 10-15 students participating. Each program is linked to an individual class, which is determined by the faculty leader working alongside with the Chair of their department and Division Dean to decide on minimum course enrollment needed.

Since 2007, Peralta Colleges have created different programs in over 13 countries including Dance programs in Vietnam, Haiti, Cuba and Ghana; African American Studies programs in Belize, Jamaica, Brazil, Ghana, and Cuba; Business in Cuba and Japan; Social Justice in Jamaica; Intercultural Communications in Ghana; History in El Salvador; Cosmetology in England; Spanish in Mexico; Language and Culture in China; and Natural History in Iceland, Costa Rica and Switzerland. All of Peralta Colleges study abroad programs are 1-3 week short term programs offered during the summer or spring/winter intersessions at the end of the fall and spring semesters. Each program is also affiliated with one of Peralta Colleges' four colleges but are open to any student at any of the colleges. Peralta Colleges has also offered a unique medical Spanish language course in Cuba, which included a joint venture with Kaiser Permanente medical group, where medical Spanish was taught for the Kaiser personnel who concurrently enrolled in Berkeley City College's Spanish Study Abroad in Cuba program. New programs are consistently being discussed and developed with faculty interested in teaching their courses abroad. Other courses which have been proposed are Anthropology courses in New Zealand and Iceland; Arabic in Egypt; Automotive Technology in Cuba; Art History courses in Germany, England and France; Physical Geography in Costa Rica; and student athlete abroad experiences in Costa Rica.

Each faculty who proposes a course decides on the location and which class they are most interested in teaching which also has curriculum related to their destination and activities. Faculty are recommended to select a course that is already approved to be offered on campus, so they do not have to go through a longer curriculum review process in creating a new course. However, there have been a few faculty members who have developed their own classes specifically designed for study abroad. For example, the Dance department created Dance 7 - Dance Study Abroad which is also a California State University transferrable course offering 3-5 units over the summer term. The Cosmetology department at Laney College is working on new curriculum designed specifically for their study abroad programs for current Cosmetology students and alumni. Another study abroad course was created by the Department of Spanish at Berkeley City College which focused on the traditions, culture and language of Cubans. Creating new curriculum for courses is time consuming but can be done without a budget, as long as there are faculty who are willing to put in the time and effort to work on the course information needed to be approved. Study abroad offices can support faculty through the curriculum review process by understanding the timelines and requirements for creating new courses for study abroad programs. They can also work closely with faculty to be creative in course offerings that link curriculum to the country and promote programs that help meet the minimum enrollment needed to run a course.

Peralta Colleges Mission

The Mission of the Peralta Colleges is to provide educational leadership for the East Bay, delivering programs and services that sustainably enhance the region's human, economic, environmental, and social development. Peralta Colleges empower students to achieve their highest aspirations and develops leaders who create opportunities and transform lives. Together with its partners, Peralta Colleges provide diverse students and communities with equitable access to the educational resources, experiences, and life-long opportunities to meet and exceed their goals (PCCD Mission Statement, 2015).

Currently, the words "study abroad" do not appear in the actual mission statement for Peralta Colleges, although "international" is mentioned as part of Peralta Colleges' strategic goals where it reads to "expand and document *international* partnerships" (PCCD Strategic Goals & Institutional Objectives, 2015-2016). The work to institutionalize study abroad has been established by working with committed faculty members to believe in the importance of offering courses abroad. Many of the benefits of study abroad come through in the mission statement, such as developing leaders and transforming the lives of students. Study abroad should be a part of every college's mission statement which enhances the awareness and importance of programs being offered. As a college without a study abroad budget, having it mentioned in the strategic goals and working with faculty closely allows study abroad to not be forgotten.

Peralta Colleges Study Abroad Administrative Procedures

In my position as International Services Manager, I work with the College Deans and faculty to consistently improve the work of Peralta Colleges' study abroad programs. In 2015, I developed Peralta Colleges' first official Administrative Procedure (AP) entitled "Philosophy and Criteria for Study Abroad Education" (PCCD Board Policies & Administrative Procedures, 2015). The procedure can be found on Peralta Colleges' Board of Trustees website under Board Policies and Administrative Procedures. I found it important to develop this procedure as Peralta Colleges' process for faculty were somewhat unclear and constantly changing. A Dean at Laney College, one of the four colleges of Peralta Colleges, came to me with a template he used to create procedure when he worked at another California community college. Topics in the current AP include criteria for program development/implementation, proposal for establishing a study abroad program, student participation program requirements, and working with third-party providers. Having the support of a Dean on campus is very important for colleges who do not have a budget for developing programs. Below are some steps study abroad offices can take to develop clear and transparent procedures on their own:

1. Develop a one-page overview for faculty to understand the step by step process needed to create a study abroad program. This should include a complete overview of the proposal approval process, steps on how to finalize program details, how to market programs for free and which pre-departure information is needed to provide to students.
2. Have a clear proposal process and form for faculty to have their study abroad programs approved by their department.
3. Work with faculty to develop program and decide on budget and how logistics are to be handled.
4. Assist with recruitment and marketing along with faculty member.
5. Conduct pre-departure orientations and ensure students understand risks and student code of conduct.
6. Meet with faculty after the program is completed to discuss future planning.

PERALTA COLLEGES STUDY ABROAD HISTORY AND OUTREACH ACTIVITIES

Historical Context

When I started at Peralta Colleges in 2007 as an International Student Support Specialist there was a limited number of offerings for study abroad. As far as I know, only a few departments, including, African American Studies and Natural History were offering programs.

The first program I had the opportunity to work on was a Chinese Language studies program to Beijing in 2008 during the time of the Summer Olympics. Since we wanted to keep the costs low for our students, a connection was made with a university in China to house the students at a very low cost. In addition to creating a marketing flyer for the program and collecting payments from students, I worked directly with the travel agent to arrange student flights, as well as some connecting flights to other locations once the program concluded. We did not utilize a third-party program provider which removed some additional fees students would have needed to pay if we did go that route. While this was time consuming, the students and faculty were appreciative of the effort we spent creating and marketing the program. These types of efforts go a long way in helping a program to be successful, such as having a team that is dedicated to get the program off of the ground and finding creative ways to keep the costs down to ensure the program has enough students for the program to be offered. For this program, the team included myself and a dedicated faculty member who was willing to put in extra time to work with a travel agent to book flights, and utilizing existing partnerships with universities where available. If there is no budget for travel to meet with overseas universities to view their facilities and discuss accommodations, there may be other ways to accomplish this such as through online communication, or utilizing other staff or faculty traveling abroad on their own who might be able to make a connection for you.

Over the years, I have learned that supporting faculty to establish new study abroad programs does always not mean financially. Faculty need the support to market their programs by connecting with outside organizations, marketing in the classroom, using free campus resources (email and website), hosting information sessions, or using social media. Other ways to support faculty without a budget are helping them through the campus approval process and establishing a program that ties in well with the curriculum. Some faculty may need to create a new course which needs assistance, and others may need several meetings with their Chairs or Deans to get the program approved. Promoting the benefits of study abroad on campus through professional development presentations or seeking outside funding opportunities through grants and scholarships are other great ways to build study abroad without a budget. When referring to budget, I am speaking about discretionary funding which can be used for marketing, travel, or other expenses. A percentage of my salary is spent on study abroad, however there is no additional funding which is readily available to support the programs.

Professional Development and Partnerships

In 2014, I was given the responsibility to spend more time in my position to expand the study abroad program. With this new role, I began researching what other colleges were doing with study abroad and expanded outreach in search of dedicated faculty interested in developing a study abroad course of their own. To learn more, I enrolled in NAFSA's e-Learning Course, "Education Abroad Advising," to learn more about the types of study abroad programs a college can offer and how to direct conversations with students (NAFSA.org, 2015). Funding for this program came directly from the Peralta District international student budget. I also worked to expand connections with universities abroad who were interested in having our students study at their university. Articulation agreements are a way to create a clear pathway for students to be guaranteed acceptance and transfer of credits to the foreign universities upon completion of studies at their home campus. This is a new undertaking at Peralta Colleges and hopefully these new partnerships will be successful. Providing clear pathways for students is another way to support study abroad without a budget as it designs a plan which makes it easier for students to see studying abroad as a reality.

Generation Study Abroad

In 2014, Peralta Colleges joined the Institute of International Education's (IIE) Generation Study Abroad (GSA) initiative. Through IIE, I learned that fewer than 10% of American college students participate in international study programs, and less than 25% of those students are from underrepresented minority groups (IIE Generation Study Abroad, 2014). Many of Peralta Colleges' students come from those underrepresented minority groups and have not had the opportunity to travel outside of where they are from, let alone another country. Funds from the Peralta District international students program were used to allow me to attend IIE annual conferences in Washington D.C. to join study abroad professionals who are aiming to strive towards the goal of expanding study abroad opportunities for students. For the first seven years of my career in international education, I had no idea how many professionals were working directly in the study abroad field. Joining IIE's GSA inspired me to focus on increasing study abroad participation each year since 2014 through initiatives such as organizing a study abroad fair and creating new marketing materials. The goals in the original initiative were to have 400 students study abroad by 2019. I may have been a little overly ambitious, however, the number of students have increased each year, with 53 studying abroad in 2015/16 and 55 in 2016/17. If programs reach their enrollment targets for 2017/18, the number of students could be as high as 70-90, which would reach the top 10 for Associates Institutions in IIE's Open Doors report released each year (IIE Open Doors, 2017). I was fortunate to have funds allocated from the international students' budget to allow me to attend the conference. Colleges without a study abroad budget may want to seek other departments for assistance, beginning with other areas of international education.

Institutional Survey

In 2017, I created a survey which was sent to all Peralta Colleges employees. This is a great way to build buy-in without having a budget. The goal was to gain a better understanding of the awareness of study abroad across the district, what countries should programs be offered in, how important they believe study abroad is to the institution, and if they were interested in developing a study abroad program of their own. The overall response was positive as faculty, staff and administrators shared how the offerings need to be expanded:

It continues to show current as well as prospective students that Peralta Colleges is committed to the highest standards of excellence in regards to their education and that we can compete with the offerings of local four-year institutions (Fashion Design Instructor, College of Alameda).

It is important because Peralta Colleges, especially Merritt, mission has a global perspective in its mandate to "care-of" for humanity. Its moral value speaks to Social Justice. And our ambassadors should be the youth leaders of tomorrow (English Instructor, Merritt College).

Study Abroad and travel in general allows students to grow and see the community from a more holistic perspective. Students will start to understand (if they already don't) that the world is huge and their place in it matters. Also, the viewpoint of people everywhere is not the same so it would help to understand that and to get to know their neighbors in the world as we are now in a global society, politically, socially, and economically (Project Manager, College of Alameda).

Global awareness and cross-cultural flexibility are traits desired by many employers and universities. Studying abroad can also be a way to build empathy among students for the experiences of others (Political Science Instructor, Berkeley City College).

While the value of study abroad is clear, such as creating global awareness and building cultural competency which will help students be successful in this global economy, expanding study abroad opportunities with little to no budget is a tough challenge. Study abroad professionals need to discover who their advocates are on campus that will help them fight to sustain study abroad as an essential aspect of offerings for the college. As the word spreads among colleagues at Peralta Colleges, the interest in creating new programs for students is growing as well. I believe the awareness is building the momentum our programs need to eventually have a full-time office staff dedicated to serving faculty and advising students.

Study Abroad Fair

Since 2014, Peralta Colleges have organized its own study abroad fair each year for students to understand the benefits and opportunities available. This can be accomplished without a budget, as long as time can be allocated for staff to prepare. I visited the UC Berkeley's study abroad fair to get an idea of what to aim for prior to organizing our own fair. UCB's fair did give some inspiration, especially seeing all of the students and vendors which were present. UCB also has study abroad ambassadors who work at the fair, something for other colleges to consider as well. The first Peralta Colleges Study Abroad Fair was held at Laney College and the vendors included study abroad program providers, 4-Year University study abroad programs, as well as Peralta Colleges' faculty promoting their own programs. The Laney College Department of Dance provided some entertainment for the students and vendors with an elaborate African dance performance for free. Peralta Colleges have continued to organize fairs in the fall of each year. During the fall 2015 fair, Peralta Colleges Director of Energy and Environmental Sustainability saw the event going on and wanted to include it as part of the annual EcoFest in the spring which attracts 2,000 to 3,000 visitors each year. So now, there are two study abroad fairs offered each year, one at EcoFest in the spring and another one at the college during the fall. Although EcoFest is focused on sustainability, the study abroad vendors are able to share information about any of their programs to the community members who come to the fair. Vendors are asked to make a donation to the Peralta Colleges study abroad scholarship where one $500 scholarship is awarded each semester to a student going abroad. Each semester, the fair is listed as part of the NAFSA Region XII resource calendar which provides necessary advertising and planning to ensure the greatest vendor and student participation (NAFSA Region XII, 2017). The study abroad fair is a great way to support programs with a very limited or zero budget. The only cost typically incurred is for lunch provided to the vendors for attending.

Study Abroad Pamphlet

Peralta Colleges were also awarded a small grant from California Colleges for International Education (CCIE) which was used to create new study abroad materials, including a pamphlet for students of Peralta Colleges (PCCD Study Abroad Booklet, 2015). The pamphlet has information on the top 10 reasons why students should study abroad, where they can search for study abroad programs, how to fund the programs, quotes from former students and new study abroad initiatives. It also contains a section for faculty who are interested in leading their own program and where to find the information to submit a proposal. This pamphlet is available on each campus and has increased the awareness for Peralta Colleges' students and allows them to know about the opportunities which are offered. It serves as a reminder that Peralta Colleges does offer study abroad programs and helps with promotion and marketing of programs to students and community members. It was a great way to build awareness on campus without having our own budget to develop promotional materials.

IIE Scholarship

Because of the initiatives taken, Peralta Colleges applied to and was awarded a Generation Study Abroad scholarship through IIE. IIE awarded $7,500 to Peralta Colleges which was required to be matched. With no study abroad budget available, the Department of Dance at Laney College pitched in to match the grant from funds raised on their own via dance recitals and other activities. The IIE grant funds were then used to support students specifically to study abroad through the Dance program. The Department of Dance decided that students who were to receive the grant must also attend a leadership conference prior to their study abroad experience to show their commitment to the program. Grant funds were disbursed through student scholarships with the help of the Peralta Colleges Foundation. Six students from Peralta Colleges were awarded $2,500 each and presented at Peralta Colleges' Board of Trustees meeting. One Board member was inspired enough to donate some additional funds for study abroad scholarships as well.

DEVELOPING A STUDY ABROAD PROGRAM AT PERALTA COLLEGES

This section describes how peralta colleges develop study abroad programs.

Program Criteria

Courses to be offered on a study abroad program must be listed in the Peralta Colleges schedule of classes during the academic term for which the program is being offered. If there is not a course connected to the program, the educational components must be clearly outlined to justify the program. When courses are selected, faculty members must consult with their department Chair and Division Dean to ensure contact hours are met for the number of units being offered. For example, if the instructor is offering a 3 unit course, but the study abroad portion is only 1 week, the faculty must require additional contact hours before or after the trip for students to earn complete credits for the course. All courses must comply with all Peralta Colleges' policies and regulations as if the course were being offered on campus. This is why all students must read and verify that they understand the Standards of Student Conduct (Peralta Colleges Student Conduct, 2013). The faculty leader must provide mandatory pre-departure orientation sessions. These sessions are handled in conjunction with the Office of International Education to cover academic and cultural information, safety precautions, student code of conduct, and medical insurance information, so that students are well-informed and fully prepared to participate in the program. Information and resources for these sessions are provided on the Peralta Colleges' study abroad website.

Offices without a budget can still ensure safety procedures are met and students follow protocols. While on the study abroad program, the faculty leader must include relevant cultural activities to significantly enhance the educational experience where the program is offered. They are also encouraged to provide lectures and group conversations related to the course. The faculty leader must adhere to established planning timelines which are set for course approval. Any full-time or part-time faculty employed by Peralta Colleges may propose a study abroad program, as long as they meet the suggested criteria as follows: subject matter expertise as required by the program of study; demonstrated ability to work in unfamiliar conditions and under often severe time constraints; adaptability, flexibility, and self-sufficiency; previous experience leading or participating in study abroad programs; level of familiarity with host country, including language and culture; and other criteria as deemed appropriate by their department Chair, division Dean or Vice President of Instruction. The decision on faculty leading programs will ultimately be determined by the Dean, in consultation with the department Chair, who oversees the division for which the faculty is a part of. All of these criteria can be met without a budget by building strong relationships with the faculty and their departments to develop a culture of trust and teamwork to create and sustain these programs.

Program Proposals

The first step for instructors interested in proposing a study abroad course is to meet with the Office of International Education to discuss proposal components and country of destination, course offering, travel dates, and possible logistics. Proposals should be discussed and recommended for approval by the Department Chair prior to sending to the Division Dean and Vice President for approval. Once the proposal form is approved, the instructor will work together with me to finalize the program details, logistics and budget. Once the program details are finalized, I draft an "Agreement for Short-Term Study Abroad Program" contract between Peralta Colleges and the Program Provider, which will be reviewed by District Legal Counsel and the Program Provider. The faculty leader works together with our office to decide on which program provider, if necessary, will work to organize the program. This step takes some time to decide, determined by how much work the faculty is willing to do on their own, as well as the prices offered by the provider. Once the agreement for the study abroad program is approved by Legal Counsel, an official contract is signed by the program provider, College President, International Services Manager and the Chancellor. The District does retain an outside legal counsel and as such, a separate budget is not required for a specific study abroad legal advice. In addition, most of the colleges already have a legal department and risk managers that can be leveraged for supporting study abroad opportunities.

Peralta Colleges Study Abroad Programs

Programs offered by Peralta Colleges reflect diversity in location and in courses. Students are required to enroll in the course related to the program and are encouraged to apply for financial aid and scholarship opportunities. All of the programs offered are short-term (1-2 weeks) and are mainly offered during the summer term. From time to time, a faculty member will create a program for either the spring or winter intersession periods which take place directly after the fall or spring semesters. Since all faculty teach other classes during the semester terms of fall and spring, it has been difficult to design a full semester long study abroad program. For these programs, students mainly stay in university style dorms or hotels arranged by a travel provider of the faculty themselves.

Low-Cost Initiatives for Expanding Study Abroad Opportunities

Merritt College has two departments with the longest running study abroad programs for the Peralta Colleges. The African American Studies department has been offering programs for over a decade and has taken students to countries such as Belize, Brazil, Jamaica, Cuba and Ghana. The program is known as the "Black Consciousness Raising Study and Tour" which focuses on Afro Caribbean history, politics and culture.

The Merritt College Environmental Studies department has offered programs to countries including Japan, Switzerland, Costa Rica, and Iceland. These "Natural History" field courses take visits to the rainforest and focus on the ecosystems of different countries.

The Laney College Department of Dance has the next longest running programs which have been offered in Cuba, Ghana and Haiti. They have developed a new "Ceremony, Tradition & Urban Dynamics" program in Ghana, which is a 14-day program that allows student to take two classes, Dance 7 – Dance Study Abroad (5 units) and Communications 6 - Intercultural Communications (3 units). Most of the actual instruction takes place during the summer session prior to the actual trip to Ghana, in order to ensure contact hours are met for the number of units being offered. The Department of Dance created its own Dance Study Abroad class which is approved for transfer credits to the California State Universities, which they have used for past programs. Summer 2018 was the first time Peralta Colleges integrated classes as a team teaching model which allowed faculty from different departments to work together to recruit enough students for the program. Instead of one faculty member needing to recruit 15-20 students, each faculty only needed to recruit 7-10 students to meet enrollment targets since students will be enrolling in multiple courses.

Cuba has been a popular country over the years for study abroad programs offered through Peralta Colleges. In addition to African American Studies, Dance and Spanish, a "Business program in Havana, Cuba" was created in 2018 which is a 7-day program offering a Business 10 – Introduction to Business (3 units). Students spend one week in Cuba followed by two weeks online upon return to the U.S to complete the course requirements. Students in the program develop a business plan based on the sites visited in Cuba, which include community development organizations and local businesses. The students work in groups and decide on a business plan which will help support the Cuban businesses they visited on the trip. Site visits include community development organizations that focus on providing workshops for children in dance, theater, art and movie making; bike tour/rental companies, barber shops, restaurants and a local publishing company which creates books made from recyclable materials. Students in Cuba spend most of their time journaling and meeting in groups to discuss their projects, and receive instruction on selected business topics. Upon return to the U.S. the students work online to complete the plans and present a final project.

The "Art History program in Berlin, Germany" is a 16-day program offering Art 3 – History of Western Art (3 units). In total, students will be enrolled in the class for 6 weeks, however, only 2 of those weeks are actually in Germany. This model allows students who are not able to go to Germany to still possibly take this course. In this model, some students study abroad while the rest stay on-campus and take online assignment. The benefit to this model is that it helps to meet enrollment targets, and allows students who cannot afford the trip or are not interested in the study abroad portion to still take the class. In addition, these students interact with those abroad which helps to build future interest. Site visits include the Berlin Wall and customized Berlin Art walk tours.

The "Geography program in Costa Rica" is a 13-day program offering Geography 1 – Physical Geography (3 units). The first four weeks of the program are taught in person prior to the trip to Costa Rica, with the final two weeks of instruction taking place in Costa Rica. Students unable to travel to Costa

Rica are given similar assignments to those who are able to travel. Field trip emphasis is on the physical geography of Costa Rica covering rainforest trails, volcanic craters and observing the abundant wildlife.

The "Business program in Japan" is a 7-day program in Business 72 – Principles of Retailing (3 units) with one week in Japan followed by two Saturday session classes which will be required for students to attend to earn the units for the course. Students have the opportunity to explore and analyze retail of every type in Japan from large department stores to outside vendors. Students also have an in depth experience with the culture of Japan by visiting museums, restaurants and interacting with locals in the community by conducting brief interviews with Japanese people on the street.

The "Cosmetology program in London" is a 10-day educational experience created specifically for those in the Cosmetology field to learn new techniques and styles. The department has a new course approved which is specifically designed for a Cosmetology experience abroad. This program includes visits to salons and hair shows, and students receive specialized training and classes in hair styling. As far as I know, it is the only community college study abroad program designed specifically for Cosmetology students.

Since 2016, Peralta Colleges has been selected each year to represent Congresswoman Barbara Lee's California – 13th District which is an African America initiative started in 2010 to study in China through the United States Exchange Foundation. The delegate of students spend 12 days in China and visit three cities: Beijing, Hangzhou and Shanghai. During the trip, students get an overview of Chinese language, culture, politics and history, as well as visit historical sites including the Great Wall, Forbidden City and the Yu Garden.

Peralta Colleges are constantly looking for ways to support new faculty to design programs. Interest for new study abroad programs includes "Economy in China", "Spanish in Mexico and Argentina," "Art and Science of War in England and France", "Anthropology in New Zealand and Iceland", "Chinese Culture in China, Arabic in Egypt", "Social Sciences in Germany and English/Critical Thinking in Belize."

ELEMENTS THAT HELP EXPAND STUDY ABROAD WITHOUT A BUDGET

Communication and Outreach to Students

I did not study abroad as a college student and was not aware of the opportunities or sure if the opportunities even existed. It actually never crossed my mind to consider it as an option, especially during my time at a community college. I did not understand how study abroad could benefit me as an individual and that opportunities existed where I would not lose valuable time in my studies. Prior to 2014, many Peralta Colleges students were also not familiar with the process for studying abroad, even though some programs were being offered. In addition, students did not know how to finance a program and where to begin looking. Communication needs to focus on eliminating a common misperception that only students at 4-year universities can study abroad. To change this attitude, and to make students more aware, I worked with three Graduate students from the Monterey Institute for International Studies (MIIS) to design handbooks for faculty and students with the purpose of helping to expand study abroad opportunities for students. The projects included a faculty handbook for developing and leading study abroad programs, as well as student handbooks focused on the benefits of study abroad for Peralta Colleges students to decide if study abroad is the right choice, program selection, finances & application, pre-departure and re-entry. The faculty handbook is a living document which was most recently updated with new procedures at the beginning of 2018. Being a mentor for these graduate students was a great experience to help them, as well as receive some assistance for free while they were working on their project for us.

CONCLUSION/RECOMMENDATIONS

Study abroad education should encourage programs that support learning about other cultures and global issues, as well as provide opportunities for students in all majors to enrich their academic training, perspectives, and personal development. Community colleges possess a significant opportunity to create a positive impact in the lives of students by adding to the cultural diversity of the colleges and generating an exchange of worldviews in the classroom setting. This type of campus internationalization leads to an overall improvement in the quality of instruction and especially on student learning.

The expansion of study abroad programs plays a key role in this process. Due to the necessity for international exposure in the global economy, studying abroad will help students become better situated to be successful in their careers and lives. Professionals in the field may choose to address this opportunity by making it possible for more students to study abroad by working with colleges and partners overseas to create affordable programs and providing information on financial aid resources and scholarship opportunities for students who want to study abroad. This requires a commitment to finding new and creative solutions to enable students to participate in the study abroad experience which includes organizing study abroad fairs, strategically planning for study abroad financing of classes, continuing to learn best practices for safety and security in education abroad, and networking with other colleges and organizations to promote study abroad. Study abroad improves student learning by integrating knowledge with real life experiences, creates a lasting learning experience for students, promotes colleges and their programs on a global level, as well as helps students and faculty to develop a greater appreciation for other cultures and become more globally aware.

Peralta Colleges were able to create a thriving study abroad program without a budget by finding dedicated faculty who are willing to put their time and effort into building a program with little support. By utilizing free online tools, hosting study abroad fairs, and applying for small grants, the Office of International Education has been creative in how it continues to expand opportunities for students. Having a six figure budget is not necessary for a college looking to grow its study abroad program. However, having a full-time, or even part time staff person dedicated to building the study abroad program is necessary. The program will not grow on its own. Someone at the college needs to take ownership or have it as part of their job description to make the growth happen. Employees willing to take on the extra work and initiative to make study abroad a priority on campus could open up future career opportunities for themselves, not to mention that it is a very unique field with many rewards. Staff who are creative and willing to find affordable ways to support faculty will eventually lead to more offerings and students going abroad. As the saying goes, the grass is greener where you water it.

For colleges that want to start a study abroad program without a budget, the first step I recommend is to find a dedicated instructor who is interested in teaching their course abroad. Some staff members may be willing to donate some of their own free time to support the programs as well. Colleges should decide on a marketing strategy and come up with a proposal to the department on why study abroad is essential to student learning. As noted above, there are many creative ways to build a study abroad program without a budget by utilizing outside program providers which can help build the program without having to travel to the destination. The college should build the faculty's expenses into the program budget which is distributed evenly among student fees paid so the college does not incur any costs. By joining professional networks, such as IIE's Generation Study abroad and NAFSA, free resources and tips on how to expand study abroad options are shared and can then be adapted at other colleges. Growing study abroad will take dedication and time, but much can be done to get things started if you truly want to create these memorable and life changing experiences for students.

REFERENCES

Accrediting Commission for Community and Junior Colleges. (2018). Western Association of Schools and Colleges. Retrieved from: https://accjc.org/

California Community Colleges Chancellor's Office. (2017). *Management information systems data mart*. Retrieved from: http://datamart.cccco.edu/

Institute of International Education. (2014). *Generation study abroad*. Retrieved from: https://www.iie.org/Programs/Generation-Study-Abroad

Institute of International Education. (2017). *Open doors*. Retrieved from: https://www.iie.org/opendoors

NAFSA. (2015). *Education abroad advising e-learning courses*. Retrieved from: http://www.nafsa.org/Professional_Resources/Learning_and_Training/e-Learning_Courses/Courses/Education_Abroad_Advising/

NAFSA. (2017). *Region XII Calendar*. Retrieved from: http://www.nafsa.org/Connect_and_Network/NAFSA_Regions/Region_XII/Resources/

Peralta Community College District. (2015). *Board policies & district administrative procedures home*. Retrieved from: http://web.peralta.edu/trustees/files/2013/12/AP-4026-Philosphy-and-Criteria-for-Study-Abroad-Education-DRAFT-revised-8-6-15.pdf

Peralta Community College District. (2015). *Strategic plan home, our mission*. Retrieved from: http://web.peralta.edu/strategicplan/

Peralta Community College District. (2015). *Study abroad booklet*. Retrieved from: http://web.peralta.edu/international/wp-content/uploads/2008/09/PCCD-Study-Abroad-Booklet.pdf

Peralta Community College District. (2016). *Board policies & district administrative procedures home*. Retrieved from: http://web.peralta.edu/trustees/files/2013/12/AP-5500-Standards-of-Student-Conduct-Discipline-Procedures-and-Due-Process5.pdf

Peralta Community College District. (2018). *Career and technical education home*. Retrieved from: http://web.peralta.edu/cte/

Peralta Community College District. (2018). *Pre-Travel study abroad information form.* Retrieved from: https://www.surveymonkey.com/r/peraltapretravel

Peralta Community College District. (2015-2016). *2015-2016 Strategic goals and institutional objectives.* Retrieved from: http://web.peralta.edu/strategicplan/files/2009/02/PCCD-2015-2016-Strategic-Goals-and-Institutional-Objectives1.docx

Chapter 12
Institutionalizing International Education and Embedding Education Abroad Into the Campus Community

Carola Smith
Santa Barbara City College, USA

ABSTRACT

This chapter is a descriptive case study on one community college in California to show how the institution was able to successfully institutionalize study abroad through advocacy, strategic planning, and the cultivation of local, statewide, and international collaborations. Because of the longevity and vitality of the program examined in this particular case study, there is useful insight for other education abroad professionals who are at varying stages of implementing, developing, or institutionalizing study abroad programs at their respective institutions.

INTRODUCTION

Many community colleges have been offering study abroad programs for several decades, and most educators and administrators recognize the need to prepare students for an increasingly globalized world and work environment. At the same time, community colleges continue to be faced with a number of challenges and obstacles, which frequently stand in the way of the systemic integration of education abroad within the institution.

This chapter employs a qualitative research approach, utilizing a singular descriptive case study to provide an in-depth analysis of how one community college in California was able to successfully institutionalize study abroad through advocacy, strategic planning, and the cultivation of local, statewide, and international collaborations. The initiatives and strategies discussed in this chapter are not only intended to provide insight into this particular institution's approach to institutionalizing education abroad, but also to provide a "detailed consideration of the contextual factors" (Starman, 2013, p. 36) and a holistic

DOI: 10.4018/978-1-5225-6252-8.ch012

Institutionalizing International Education and Embedding Education Abroad

overview of the conditions, which need to be in place to successfully garner broad-based institutional support for community college education abroad. While the author is cognizant of the inherent limitations and common misperceptions of qualitative case studies, including the author's potential tendency towards subjectivity, a case study approach was chosen to provide detailed insight into the historic development of the program and to examine the causes and factors that led to the program's long-term viability and success (Flyvbjerg, 2006, 2011; Starman, 2013). Because of the longevity and vitality of the program examined in this particular case study, the author hopes to be able to provide useful insight for other education abroad professionals who are at varying stages of implementing, developing, or institutionalizing study abroad programs at their respective institutions.

The study focuses on Santa Barbara City College (SBCC), which is located in central California and which has had a long-standing commitment to international education. SBCC is a Hispanic-serving institution in an urban location, which serves approximately 17,500 students. Approximately 42% of the students are white, 40% of the students are Hispanic, 8% are Asian/Filipino/Pacific Islander, and 3% are African American. Approximately 67% of the students are part-time students, and 64% of the students are 24 years of age or younger. Approximately, 15% of the students are fully online students. Almost 37% of the students are California College Promise Grant recipients and almost 40% of the students receive either state, federal, and/or private financial assistance. The above cited institutional data are intended to provide a snapshot of SBCC's student demographics; however, it should be acknowledged that these demographic characteristics do not adequately capture the diversity and "polymorphic identities" of community college students and that community college students may have multiple identities and may change identities over time (Levin, Viggiano, López Damián, Morales, & Wolf, 2017, p.120).

The author first became familiar with SBCC's Study Abroad program in 1989, when she attended SBCC as an international student and participated in a semester study abroad program in Cambridge, England. In 1995, she returned to the college – initially in the role of faculty and subsequently as an administrator. For the past 21 years, she has provided oversight for the institution's Study Abroad Program. Information on the origin and early development of the program was derived from interviews with the previous program director and former study abroad faculty directors.

FROM ADVOCACY TO PROGRAM IMPLEMENTATION

SBCC's first study abroad program was developed in 1973. Credit is owed to two visionaries within the field of international education. Dr. Donald Culton, former Director of International Education for the Los Angeles Community College District served as the first full-time international education community college administrator in the State and was instrumental in forming the non-profit consortium *California Colleges for International Education*, which continues to serve as the primary international education resource to the California Community Colleges Chancellor's Office (California Colleges for International Education, 2018). Mr. Pablo Buckelew, Vice President Emeritus at SBCC, pioneered SBCC's first internationalization efforts and implemented SBCC's Study Abroad program.[1] These two former faculty members, turned administrators, closely collaborated for three decades to lay much of the groundwork for study abroad at California community colleges by developing comprehensive education abroad principles and policies, by sharing resources with other institutions across the State, and by promoting international education on an institutional, regional, and statewide level. Both of them had personally benefitted from a study abroad experience, worked closely with underrepresented students, and ended up devoting much of their careers to advocating for international education and making study abroad accessible to all students, regardless of their socio-economic and educational backgrounds.

When the idea of offering SBCC students the opportunity to study abroad was first proposed, it was initially met with reservation. Some members of the campus community and the Board of Trustees questioned the appropriateness and rationale for offering study abroad at the community college level, based on the prevailing perception that community colleges were intended to serve students within the local community. At the time, California community colleges were primarily funded by local property tax revenues, which led to the widely held belief that community colleges should serve students within "specific local boundaries" and the misperception that "there is a diametrical connection between local and global" (Raby & Valeau 2016, p. 16). Thanks to the advocacy efforts of a few outspoken faculty and administrators who had personally benefitted from an international experience, the SBCC campus community came to a broader understanding that the college should serve the educational needs and interests of its students regardless of their physical location. The institution gradually came to recognize that students' needs extended well beyond the city's geographic limits and that community college students were equally deserving of the opportunity to study abroad as their peers at four-year institutions. One of the factors, which helped to tip the discussion in favor of adopting a more global perspective, was the top-level support from the executive leadership. As Raby suggests, "when reform comes from senior-level administrators, it is sometimes easier to modify college missions and policy documents" (Raby, 2007, p. 58). This was the case at SBCC, which benefitted from the steady and visionary leadership of one of the longest-serving college presidents in the State who led the institution for more than two decades and who encouraged faculty to develop innovative study abroad programs and to actively engage in international exchanges.

The college's first summer study abroad program to Guadalajara, Mexico, in 1973 was offered in conjunction with the University of San Diego and La Universidad Jesuita de Guadalajara and attracted a group of 55 SBCC students and members of the local community. The program would become the first of a series of more than twenty annual summer Spanish language programs in Mexico. In 1983, the college expanded its program offerings to include semester-length programs. In 1985, SBCC was the first community college nationally to offer a semester-length program in China. The program was initiated and developed by one of SBCC's emeritus faculty and current member of the SBCC Board of Trustees who had participated in a Fulbright faculty exchange in China. In 1989, this program provided subsequent program participants with the opportunity to witness first-hand the pro-democracy demonstrations in Tiananmen Square. In 1990, Santa Barbara City College was the first community college nationally to offer a full-length credit semester program in the Ukraine when it was still part of the former Soviet Union (led by the same bold and forward-thinking faculty) where students were able to observe the nationalist and political independence movements, which preceded the breakup of the Soviet Union. In 2002, SBCC was one of the first community colleges to offer a summer program in Cuba. More recently, SBCC has developed programs in India, Rwanda, South Africa, and other non-traditional locations. Since the inception of the program, more than 6,000 SBCC students from a large variety of disciplines have participated in study abroad programs in more than 20 different countries. The participating students reflect the diversity of SBCC's general student population.

INSTITUTIONALIZING STUDY ABROAD

While SBCC's first internationalization efforts were initially led by a few outspoken faculty and the long-term viability of the program would not have been sustainable without broad-based organizational support and without broad stakeholder buy-in from faculty, staff, administrators, community members, and the Board. The following section describes how Santa Barbara City College evolved from developing isolated international education initiatives to building a campus community, which is infused by international perspectives and which embraces international education as an important component of its mission.

Developing a Global Campus Community

Santa Barbara City College has been accepting international students into its academic programs since the 1950s when the college experienced an influx of international students from the Middle East and particularly Iran (Interview with Pablo Buckelew, 2018). In 1959, the college first assigned an academic counselor to provide oversight and support for SBCC's International Student Program. In the 1970s, the college began to accept international students into its ESL program in an effort to diversify and internationalize its ESL student body and to increase non-resident tuition revenues. An intensive English Language Support Program (ELSP) was established, which provided dedicated support to international ESL students. At the time, the faculty who would subsequently establish SBCC's Study Abroad Program coordinated the ELSP program. When the original funding proposal for the establishment of a dedicated Study Abroad office was first developed in the late 1970s, the proposed Study Abroad budget was intentionally tied to the institution's ELSP budget, which had started to generate additional revenues for the institution (Interview with Pablo Buckelew, 2018). The argument was made that education abroad programming constituted yet another important component in the institution's internationalization efforts and that the additional expenses associated with establishing and staffing a dedicated Study Abroad office could be offset by the revenues generated from non-resident tuition fees. Combining the proposed Study Abroad budget, which required the allocation of ongoing general district funds, with the revenue-generating ELSP budget initially made the proposal for a permanently funded Study Abroad office more appealing to the institutional leadership and proved to be a successful strategy to shield the program from future budget cuts. Once the Study Abroad Program was implemented, the institution allocated general district funding to permanently staff a dedicated office. Within the past three decades, many California community colleges repeatedly suspended or drastically reduced its study abroad program offerings as a result of budget reductions and the ongoing defunding of higher education in the State of California. Santa Barbara City College is one of the few community colleges in the State, which has maintained consistent funding for Study Abroad and continued providing students with robust study abroad program offerings.

The institution has long recognized that campus internationalization should not be limited to sending U.S. students abroad and/or to welcoming international students on campus. Instead, internationalization efforts must include all programs and stakeholders of the institution and impact "the entirety of campus life and learning and fundamentally shape the institution's external frames of reference, partnerships, and relations" (Hudzik, 2011, p. 10). As Hudzik and McCarthy posit, comprehensive internationalization requires a "significant and ongoing commitment to action" and must have "both strategic and operational dimensions" (Hudzik & McCarthy, 2012, p. 2). On a strategic level, SBCC has created a campus climate that is supportive of all components of international education and encouraged the emphasis of global perspectives in the institution's vision and mission statements, its institutional student learning outcomes, and its instructional programs. On an operational level, the college designated a permanent full-time administrator to coordinate the institution's international programs and developed a number of academic programs and initiatives, which have contributed to the institution's overall internationalization efforts. These include associate and certificate degree programs in Global Studies, Modern Languages, Middle East Studies, International Business, Global Entrepreneurship, and, most recently, Global Leadership; international partnerships and articulation agreements with overseas universities; comprehensive international student support services as well as robust study abroad program offerings. All of these initiatives have helped to internationalize the curriculum and generate increased student interest in study abroad.

Fostering Faculty Engagement

Faculty members and academic departments are frequently the drivers and catalysts for initiating study abroad and faculty exchanges and internationalizing the institution (Sutton & Obst, 2011; Gorlewski, 2014). This has been the case at SBCC where numerous faculty have engaged in Fulbright Faculty Exchanges, initiated longstanding partnerships with overseas universities, and successfully established partnerships with local and international non-profit organizations. In turn, this broad-based faculty engagement in different global initiatives has helped to generate strong faculty support and interest in study abroad and has served to bolster the study abroad program.

From the inception of the program, the institution has recognized and promoted education abroad as a valuable professional development opportunity, which is made available to interested faculty based on a rotation principle. Early on, the college succeeded in gaining the buy-in and support from its faculty by actively reaching out to faculty and by successfully conveying the educational benefits of internationalizing the curriculum. Faculty buy-in was sustained by providing faculty with financial incentives to develop and direct study abroad programs. Incentives included release time for faculty to market and coordinate study abroad programs, travel stipends for faculty with young children, and sabbatical leave projects to develop study abroad programs in new destinations. To date, more than 60 SBCC faculty have served as faculty study abroad program directors, which represents almost a quarter of the total number of tenured faculty. These faculty have brought their experiences back to SBCC classrooms through research conducted abroad, case studies, and their own broadened perspective. For instance, one of SBCC's art history professors and veteran study abroad directors recently traveled to Mexico City and researched Hispanic and Mexican art as part of a sabbatical project. This international experience as well as her prior study abroad experiences enabled the faculty to redesign her curriculum, shifting away from a primarily euro-centric perspective and introducing new course content that is more reflective and inclusive of SBCC's student population. Similarly, many other returning faculty directors have infused their classes with international perspectives and continue to use examples from their study abroad experience, thereby broadening students' global awareness and greatly enhancing the visibility of the program. In addition to participating in study abroad as program directors, a number of faculty have participated in short-term programs as students to enhance their language proficiency or intercultural competency, reversing roles and experiencing the programs from a student perspective. This experience has provided invaluable insight for faculty members who have subsequently led programs.

The administrator who oversees the institution's international programs closely collaborates with faculty across disciplines on curriculum design and the development, coordination, and assessment of study abroad programs to create synergies between individual programs. This collaboration across departments and programs ensures that global perspectives and international learning opportunities are firmly embedded in the institution's academic programs. As a result of this close partnership, the college has been able to rely on faculty playing a key role in promoting education abroad and integrating it into its academic programs. Thanks to the strong support from faculty, the institution's executive leadership, the Board of Trustees, as well as from members of the local community, the Study Abroad Program has come to be considered a signature program for the institution, largely protecting it from budget cuts and program reductions.

Faculty Representation on the International Education Advisory Committee

The college's International Education Advisory Committee has been active since 1986 and is comprised of faculty from a variety of disciplines and support programs, including Disability Services Program for Students (DSPS), Extended Opportunity Programs and Services (EOPS), and Academic Counseling. The committee is instrumental in ensuring broad-based faculty representation and serves as the primary advisory body on all issues pertaining to international education and specifically education abroad. The committee gives faculty the primary voice in recommending programs and faculty directors to the administration and planning and conducting outreach and training workshops for prospective faculty directors. SBCC's International Education Advisory Committee has developed a set of criteria to formalize the selection process for study abroad program proposals and faculty directors, ensuring a transparent and consistent selection process. Faculty selection criteria include teaching expertise, experience in directing a program and traveling/living abroad and demonstrated interest in working with students outside the classroom. In an effort to encourage broad-based faculty participation and program variety, priority is given to first-time faculty directors from different disciplines. First-time directors are encouraged to pair up with seasoned program directors that provide training and mentoring. Returning faculty directors report to the committee on their experience abroad, and the committee serves an advisory role in continuous program evaluation and program improvement.

INTERNATIONAL AND EXTERNAL COLLABORATIONS

The program's long-term viability has largely depended on successful collaborations both within the campus and the broader community. Through collaboration and cooperation, the institution has been able to minimize administrative costs, to secure scholarship funding for students with financial needs, and to offer a variety of affordable, high-impact study abroad and service learning programs. The following section highlights some of the institution's collaborations.

Collaboration With the SBCC Foundation to Secure External Funding

From the onset, the SBCC Study Abroad Program was designed with the premise that every effort must be made to encourage and financially assist traditionally underserved students. In order to facilitate participation of economically disadvantaged students, the institution undertakes ongoing fundraising efforts.

Working closely with the SBCC Foundation, one of the most active community college foundations in the country, ten different study abroad scholarships have been established and donations of almost half a million dollars have been secured to provide ongoing financial assistance to study abroad students who would otherwise not be able to participate. In addition to the study abroad specific scholarships, most of the general SBCC Foundation scholarships have been set up to allow students to apply general scholarship funds towards studying abroad. The Foundation's Chief Development Officer participated in several summer study abroad programs as a student and has been a strong advocate for the program. The Study Abroad Program works closely with Financial Aid, Student Equity, Student Outreach, the Veterans Support Program, and Extended Opportunity Programs and Services (EOPS) to raise awareness of existing scholarship funding, to assist students with the scholarship application process, and to ensure that payment accommodations are made for students with financial needs. Additionally, the Study Abroad Program conducts regular workshops and a variety of outreach activities to promote the Benjamin A. Gilman Scholarship Program, a national scholarship for traditionally underrepresented students. Trained staff in the Study Abroad Office, the Writing Center, and EOPS assist students with the scholarship application process. As a result, in 2018 SBCC was recognized by the U.S. Department of State as a Gilman Scholarship Program Top Producing Institution for the 2016-2017 academic year.

Faculty and administrators have played an important role in the institution's fundraising efforts by leveraging their personal connections within the local community and by actively reaching out to members of the community and local businesses to seek financial support. Similarly, faculty have been instrumental in the planning and coordination of program-specific fundraiser events, which have yielded significant one-time funding for individual programs while helping to increase the program visibility within the local community. One recent example is a gourmet dinner and wine tasting event, which was co-sponsored by the Wine Cask (one of Santa Barbara's most highly rated restaurants), the SBCC School of Culinary Arts, and the SBCC Foundation. The event raised sufficient funds to provide all culinary arts study abroad program participants who helped at the event with a $1,000 stipend in addition to their other study abroad scholarship awards. The study abroad-specific scholarships, departmental awards, and stipends from program-specific fundraisers may amount to 50 – 75% of the total program cost. The availability of financial support makes study abroad accessible to students with significant financial needs.

Statewide Collaborations

Throughout the years, the college has collaborated with institutions across the State and the country, and the program's policies and procedures have been replicated by numerous other colleges both regionally and nationally.

SBCC was one of the original colleges to join California Colleges for International Education (CCIE), a non-profit educational consortium, which has been in existence since 1985 and which has become the primary international education advocacy and research body for California community colleges. For more than two decades, SBCC been an active member of the consortium and collaborated on a variety of state and federal initiatives, including research grants, professional development conferences, and the development of good practices in the field.

Since 1996, SBCC has served as host institution to the Central Coast Study Abroad Consortium, which currently includes five community colleges in central California (Allan Hancock College, Cuesta College, Ventura College, Moorpark College, and Santa Barbara City College). Under the provisions of this regional consortium, SBCC serves as the lead college administering short-term and semester-length study abroad programs on an ongoing basis and providing administrative support for all consortium programs. The member colleges actively advertise the consortium programs, and students from member colleges have the same priority and access to scholarships as SBCC students. Member colleges can determine which programs, if any, are to be offered by their institution in a given year and are not required to advertise consortium programs if they compete with their own faculty-led programs. Through the consortium, SBCC has been able to extend the program to enable consortium members that are currently unable to offer study abroad programs on a regular basis and to make study abroad opportunities readily available to their students. A review of the program's recent application statistics indicates that approximately 15-20% of SBCC's study abroad program participants come from other consortium member institutions. Throughout the years, the consortium has made study abroad accessible to hundreds of students who would otherwise not have had the opportunity to go abroad and provided students with access to scholarship funding, which is not currently available at their respective home institutions. In turn, the consortium agreement has benefitted SBCC in that it has enabled the institution to fill programs, which might otherwise have been canceled due to low enrollments.

SBCC is currently exploring other types of formal and informal collaboration models with additional community colleges in the State. One model, which is currently being developed in collaboration with Glendale Community College, is a joint faculty-led program in Bali, Indonesia, to be co-directed by faculty from both institutions. This joint program model enables institutions to benefit from each other's connections and expertise, to lower student program fees, and to increase program offerings for students.

Collaborations With Local and International Non-Profits

In an effort to provide students with meaningful experiential learning opportunities and to be responsive to the particular needs of the people in the host community, SBCC has been partnering with local and international non-profits to integrate structured credit-bearing experiential learning components into a number of its programs. The following section highlights some of the institution's successful collaborations.

For the last two *Global Studies Semester Programs* offered in China, the faculty director was able to secure financial assistance through a grant from the Freeman Asia Foundation to offer students the opportunity to work as paid interns, teaching English to small groups of Chinese high school and university students. Student program evaluation surveys indicated that the internship was widely perceived by the students as one of the most valuable components of the program. Students reported that the internship component contributed to their personal and academic learning experience by providing them with a deepened understanding and appreciation for Chinese culture and life.

In 2009, SBCC offered a *Service Learning Program in Rwanda*, partnering with two international non-profit organizations (Network4Africa and Fair Children/Youth Foundation). The program provided students with the opportunity to volunteer at a Rwandan community center, a nursery school, and a school for hearing impaired students where students provided English language training and conducted basic training workshops in documentary film making. Prior to the commencement of the program, students from a variety of disciplines organized a series of fundraisers. Sufficient funds were raised to build a house for genocide survivors who live in child-headed households in the Survivors Fund (SURF) Peace Village in Kigali, Rwanda, and program participants had the opportunity to visit the village and to meet the youth who live in the SBCC-funded house. Since the SBCC group's return from Rwanda, SBCC students and faculty have continued to collaborate with various Rwandan non-profits, to host Rwandan guest lecturers on campus, and to provide continued support for its Rwandan partner organizations. As a result of these ongoing efforts, lasting partnerships between SBCC, the local community, and various Rwandan non-profits have been developed and cultivated. Several SBCC students have returned to Rwanda on their own to volunteer at different Rwandan non-profits. The SBCC Student Ambassadors, a student leadership group consisting of both international and local students, have partnered with a local non-profit, World Dance for Humanity, for the past three years to sponsor a Rwandan student throughout his last year of high school and university studies. Another group of SBCC students partnered with a local non-profit to introduce reusable cloth menstrual pad kits to Rwandan women and to teach Rwandan women how to produce and market these reusable cloth pads and how to educate Rwandans about reproductive health and hygiene.

Another successful collaboration with external partners both within the local community and abroad resulted in the development of a *History and Philosophy Study Abroad Program in Vietnam and Cambodia*, for which SBCC partnered with a local travel provider and *A Year Without War*, a global network of 40,000 members, which was established by an emeritus SBCC faculty member and a group of SBCC student volunteers. The organization's mission is to work towards the goal of making 2020 a year of global ceasefire. The *Vietnam and Cambodia* study abroad program provided students with the opportunity to learn about the history and ethics of the Vietnam War by meeting with survivors, engaging with Vietnamese and Cambodian youth, historians, and peace activists, and volunteering together with Vietnamese students at a rehabilitation facility for children with Agent Orange related health complications. Since the group's return, several program participants have continued to volunteer for *A Year Without War* and to be engaged in various peace-building efforts. Most recently, the SBCC *A Year Without War* Club hosted a panel discussion with a Cambodian peace activist who had served as a guide on the SBCC Vietnam and Cambodia program.

The above-mentioned study abroad programs have served as catalysts for lasting collaborations with the local and global community, provided students and faculty with opportunities to become engaged both locally and globally, and deepened the institution's connection with the broader community. SBCC continues to broaden the scope of its international internship, service learning and volunteer opportunities and to establish partnerships with local and international non-profits. The integration of service learning components supports the institution's vision to "build a socially conscious community where knowledge and respect empower individuals to transform our world" and fulfills an integral part of the institution's mission to provide a "diverse learning environment," to promote "global responsibility," and to "foster opportunity for all."

CONCLUSION

In the absence of state or federal guidelines and directives on the role and relevance of international education within the community college system, community college study abroad programs have evolved organically over time, largely relying on the vision and leadership of individual faculty or administrators committed to promoting education abroad. To date, no significant efforts have been made to systemically internationalize community college curricula and to institutionalize education abroad system-wide. As a result, at many institutions study abroad programs largely remain to exist on the periphery, and individual community colleges have adopted different approaches to developing, funding, and staffing education abroad programs. Due to the lack of a consistent system-wide approach, programs are more susceptible to changes in institutional leadership, budget cuts, and the reprioritization of funds.

Institutionalizing International Education and Embedding Education Abroad

Similar to many other community colleges, SBCC's Study Abroad Program was initially developed by a few committed faculty members and administrators. What makes Santa Barbara City College unique is the confluence of a number of factors and the implementation of different strategies and initiatives, which resulted in the institutionalization of education abroad. With the support from the executive leadership, faculty and administrators succeeded early on in generating momentum and gaining institutional support for the program. Subsequent implementation strategies included ongoing outreach activities to garner broad-based faculty support, financial incentives and professional development opportunities for faculty study abroad directors, the establishment of a designated Study Abroad Office and an International Education Advisory Committee, the implementation of formal education abroad policies, processes, and procedures, the infusion of international perspectives into the curriculum, and the establishment of study abroad scholarships.

The continued success of the institution's international education programs has largely depended on broad-based stakeholder support, the institution's ongoing financial commitment, and successful collaborations with state, national, and international consortia and partner organizations. The Study Abroad Program continues to expand and cultivate a network of partners, advocates, and allies across campus and within the broader community to ensure the ongoing financial and administrative support from the institution's executive leadership, to foster active and sustained faculty engagement, and to enhance the overall visibility of the program.

While significant progress towards internationalizing the campus has been made, more work remains to be done. The institution must continue to be responsive to the constantly evolving local and global environment, particularly in light of the recent changes in the political climate, which have ushered in a new era of nationalism inspired and emboldened by President Trump's "America First" rhetoric. These changes are likely to have a significant impact on the field of international education and on student mobility. More so than ever before the institution must remain committed to creating an inclusive, globally minded learning environment to provide students with the necessary skills and knowledge to compete in this increasingly interconnected and globalized world.

Within the community college system, different institutions have taken their own unique approach towards implementing education abroad and towards providing students with international learning opportunities. These efforts widely range from single programs initiated by individual faculty to fully established programs. Recognizing existing differences in institutional priorities, funding formulas, and organizational structures, this case study is intended to highlight some of the implementation strategies, which have broader application. The following checklist serves as a summary of the aforementioned strategies.

Checklist

- Build alliances with different stakeholders across the institution to create a campus climate that is supportive of international education and to gain broad-based buy-in from faculty, staff, administrators, and students.
- Allocate staff and financial resources to provide ongoing support for Study Abroad and provide faculty with international professional development opportunities.
- Closely collaborate with faculty across departments on curriculum design and the development, coordination, and assessment of study abroad programs.

- Foster faculty engagement by promoting education abroad as a professional development opportunity, by continuously reaching out to new faculty, and by providing financial incentives to faculty to develop, market, and coordinate programs.
- Develop transparent and consistent criteria for selecting study abroad programs and faculty directors and involve faculty in the selection process through the establishment of a formal international education advisory committee.
- Partner with the institution's development office to seek external funding for scholarships and to promote education abroad within the local community.
- Leverage faculty and staff connections to develop partnerships with local and international organizations to promote service learning and to facilitate ongoing student engagement with local and international non-profit organizations.
- Collaborate with other community colleges to pool financial resources and to leverage specialized expertise and human resource capacity.

REFERENCES

California Colleges for International Education. (2018). *Mission*. Retrieved from http://www.ccieworld.org/missionstatement.htm

Flyvbjerg, B. (2006). Five misunderstandings about case-study research. *Qualitative Inquiry, 12*(2), 219–245. doi:10.1177/1077800405284363

Flyvbjerg, B. (2011). Case Study. In N. K. Denzin & Y. S. Lincoln (Eds.), *The Sage Handbook of Qualitative Research* (4th ed.; pp. 301–316). Thousand Oaks, CA: Sage.

Gorlewski, Ey. (2014). Partnerships and advocacy. In Education Abroad for Advisers and Administrators. Washington, DC: NAFSA.

Hudzik, J. K. (2011). Comprehensive internationalization: From concept to action. Washington, DC: NAFSA.

Hudzik, J. K., & McCarthy, A. (2012). Leading comprehensive internationalization: Strategies and tactics for action. Washington, DC: NAFSA.

Levin, J. S., Viggiano, T., López Damián, A. I., Morales Vazquez, E., & Wolf, J. P. (2017). Polymorphic students: New descriptions and conceptions of community college students from the perspectives of administrators and faculty. *Community College Review, 45*(2), 119–143. doi:10.1177/0091552116679731

Raby, R. L. (2007). Internationalizing the Curriculum: On- and Off-Campus Strategies. In International Reform Efforts and Challenges in Community Colleges. Jossey-Bass.

Raby, R. L. (2008). *Expanding Education Abroad at U.S. Community Colleges*. IIE Study Abroad White Paper Series 3 (September 2008). New York: NY: Institute for International Education Press.

Raby, R. L., & Valeau, E. J. (Eds.). (2016). *International education at community colleges: Themes, practices, and case studies*. New York, NY: Palgrave Macmillan. doi:10.1057/978-1-137-53336-4

Starman, A. B. (2013). The case study as a type of qualitative research. *Journal of Contemporary European Studies, 1,* 28–43.

Stutton, S. B., & Obst, D. (Eds.). (2011). *Developing strategic international partnerships: Models for initiating and sustaining innovative institutional linkages. Global Education Research Reports.* New York: Institute of International Education and the AIFS Foundation.

ENDNOTE

[1] The author would like to express her gratitude to Mr. Buckelew who provided detailed information on the inception and historic evolution of the SBCC Study Abroad Program, which is summarized in this chapter.

Chapter 13
Thinking Globally About Social Justice

Tiffany Viggiano
Fulbright Finland, Finland

ABSTRACT

Scholars have identified community colleges as ideal institutions to facilitate global justice through their involvement in internationalization activities such as study abroad. This chapter explores the meaning of humanism as it relates to study abroad at the community college. Using Andreotti, Stein, Pashby, and Nicolson's Paradigms of Discourse, the chapter describes the ways in which humanism can be defined in a variety of ways based on one's own goals. The chapter also grounds a rationale for study abroad at the community college within critical humanism by applying Young's Social Connections Model. Finally, the chapter applies the critical humanist rationale to begin to question the relationship between community college study abroad initiatives: Who is included in the community mission? Whose cultures come to be understood from involvement in study abroad? How are U. S. cultures represented by study abroad?

INTRODUCTION

Prior to this century, most understandings of justice were bound within the nation state: discussed in terms of citizens' rights within a nation, but not applied globally (Young, 2006). However, in the current millennium, noted philosopher Martha Nussbaum asserted that, "extending justice to all world citizens, showing theoretically how we might realize a world that is just as a whole, in which accidents of birth and national origin do not warp people's life chances pervasively and from the start" is one of the most urgent unsolved problems of social justice (2006, p. 1). To address this problem, Iris Marion Young (2006) moved away from the confines of the nation state to argue that "all agents who contribute by their actions to the structural processes that produce injustice have responsibilities to work to remedy these injustices" (pp. 102-103). Thus, any institution engaged in internationalization is socially responsible to work to mitigate global social injustice.

DOI: 10.4018/978-1-5225-6252-8.ch013

Community colleges are a type of institution that transcend national borders, and therefore, through the lens of modern justice theory, community college actors have a responsibility to people outside of their local communities. Although data that tracks community college participation in internationalization activities is sparse (Copeland, McCrink, & Starratt, 2017), there is significant evidence that the community college has not operated solely within national boundaries for decades and continues to actively pursue an international agenda (American Council on Education [ACE], 2016; Levin, 2001; 2002; 2017). Community colleges transcend national borders through study abroad programs, branch campuses, and by providing services to non-domestic stake holders (ACE, 2016). Raby (2012) points to changing student demographics in which many of the students are themselves international or have strong social and familial ties to international communities. In the 2014/15 academic year, over 7,000 community college students studied abroad, and U. S. community colleges hosted over 91,000 international students (IIE, 2016). Of the associates granting institutions that participated in the ACE (2016) survey, 41% indicated that increasing the number of students that study abroad was their primary internationalization goal and roughly 72% indicated that internationalization had accelerated at, at least a moderate rate between the years of 2011 to 2015. Importantly, the very presence of study abroad programs at the community college demonstrate that community colleges no longer operate solely within the perimeter of the nation state. Therefore, community colleges are in fact active international institutions. In alignment with Young's (2006) social connections model, community college stakeholders have an ethical responsibility to serve the interest of those outside of their immediate community and to think about the long term and global implications of their actions.

Scholars have identified community colleges as ideal institutions to facilitate global justice through their involvement in internationalization activities such as study abroad. Treat and Hagedorn (2013) find that characteristics associated with the community college such as open access, adaptability, and their student-centered mission make these institutions well placed to serve the expanding middle class of low and middle GDP countries. In addition, Copeland et al. (2017) suggest that community college rationales for internationalization may differ from the motivations of their four-year counterparts, suggesting that community college administrators may value internationalization because of their open-door mission rather than an explicit mission to internationalize for the purposes of revenue generation or prestige (Copeland et al., 2017). While narrow conceptions of community have caused practitioners and scholars to question the role of internationalization at the community college (Raby, 2012), Ayers and Palmadessa (2015) find evidence that community college actors may still support a global justice agenda.

While community college practitioners have a responsibility and inclination to pursue socially just study abroad initiatives, it can be difficult to articulate issues of global social justice and to justify the pursuit of such initiatives to those in power. As such, the purpose of this chapter is to build a sturdy foundation for rationalizing socially just study abroad at the community college—called for by Raby (2012)—by grounding a humanist rationale firmly in justice theory. From the discussion of humanism comes a new term, the critical humanist rationale: an argument that applies principles of global justice to the community college so as to highlight the global responsibility of community college study abroad programs have beyond the parameters of the community and the nation state. The theoretical frame will help scholars and practitioners begin to identify and question the ways in which their actions influence those outside of their community, and the responsibilities that accompany their international relationships. Practitioners can use this frame to articulate, justify, and shape their approach to globally just study abroad initiatives at the community college.

The critical humanist rationale is a theoretically grounded foundation from which to discuss and advocate for globally just study abroad programs at the community college. While the neoliberal and liberal rationales for study abroad at the community college are often cited, the critical humanist rationale aligns best with the pursuit of social justice. The critical humanist rationale is that institutional actors at community colleges have a responsibility to facilitate study abroad initiatives that mediate global injustice by recognizing global power differentials and the interconnected globalized world. This rationale includes all humans and holds social justice, rather than economics or history, as the most important policy guidepost.

The remainder of this chapter is divided into three sections. The first section explores the meaning of humanism as it relates to study abroad at the community college. Using Andreotti, Stein, Pashby, and Nicolson's (2016) Paradigms of Discourse, the chapter describes the ways in which humanism can be defined in a variety of ways based on one's own goals. The section breaks down the humanist roots of conflicting rationales for study abroad, thus demonstrating that humanism alone is not a firm enough foundation for a globally just rationale. The second section grounds a rationale for study abroad at the community college within critical humanism by applying Young's (2006) Social Connections Model. The third section applies the critical humanist rationale to begin to question the relationship between community college study abroad initiatives: Who is included in the community mission? Whose cultures come to be understood from involvement in study abroad? How are U. S. cultures represented by study abroad? This chapter concludes by discussing the ways in which community college practitioners can use this framework to determine if they are successful at meeting their responsibilities to global justice.

HUMANISM AND STUDY ABROAD AT THE COMMUNITY COLLEGE

Scholars use different concepts to describe the underlining motivations for the pursuit of internationalization at the community college for the purpose of promoting outcomes associated with global social justice such as cultural tolerance, empathy, and privilege (e.g. Raby & Valeau, 2007; Raby, 2012). Ayers and Palmadessa (2015) identify the presence of a global citizenship discourse tied to the concept of justice globalism first identified by Steger (2008). These concepts align with what other scholarship (e.g. Raby & Valeau, 2007; Raby, 2012) has labelled the humanist rationale.

In the broadest sense, humanism can be defined as a rationale that attaches prime importance to the human. But Foucault has commented on the vague nature of this word humanism, "...the humanistic thematic is in itself too supple, too diverse, too inconsistent to serve as an axis for reflection" (Foucault, 1984, p. 44). Raby and Valeau (2007) attempted to clarify this word as it applies to internationalization at the community college. They suggest that the humanist rationale is grounded within a discourse that promotes student understanding of a multicultural society whilst facilitating peaceful relationships between nations (Raby & Valeau, 2007). The authors separate the humanist rationale completely from economic, political, and academic rationales (Raby & Valeau, 2007).

Within the humanist rationale there is sometimes a rationale of humanitarianism tied to ideals of global justice (Raby, 2012; Ayers & Palmadessa, 2015). Ayers & Palmadessa's (2015) analysis of 254 issues of the Community College Journal "...reveals a humanitarian discourse of responsibility to fellow human beings irrespective of national boundaries..." present amongst community college stakeholders (p. 886). Ayers and Palmadessa (2015) express hope for this discourse to serve as a counterhegemonic ideology to combat the well documented side effects of the prevalent neoliberal discourse at the community college

Thinking Globally About Social Justice

that has challenged the pursuit of social justice (see Ayers, 2005; Levin, 2007; Pashby & Andreotti, 2016). International development projects and the international development humanist perspective described by Cook (1996) may fall into the humanitarianism category, but seemingly humanitarian initiatives do not necessarily facilitate globally just behavior (Pashby & Andreotti, 2016). For example, Viggiano, López Damián, Morales Vázquez, and Levin (2018) found that community college practitioners in their study actively promoted student outcomes associated with humanism and social justice for domestic students but not necessarily international students.

One reason for inconsistent humanist rationales may be that the humanist rationale is not yet firmly grounded within justice theory. While institutional actors have employed the humanitarian rationale in relation to natural disasters and political events—such as tsunami relief aid in Indonesia in 2004 (Ayers & Palmadessa, 2015) and the Los Angeles Riots of the early 1990's (Raby, 2012)—Raby (2012) warns against internationalization rationales that are linked to temporarily relevant world events. She argues that founding rationales for internationalization within a socio-political framework weakens practitioners' abilities to advocate for internationalization activities. As such, she calls for a rationale for internationalization at the community college with a sturdier foundation than socio-political climate (Raby, 2012).

The following theoretical exploration of humanism as it applies to study abroad at the community college reveals that the humanist rationale alone is too nimble. Humanism is a vulnerable term that has historically been manipulated to suit the agenda of the time and come to mean nothing specific or coherent in many contexts (Foucault, 1984). Raby (2012) suggests that "…hidden and often conflicting messages that mask intent…" are contributing factors to the marginalization of internationalization at the community college (p. 89). In this section I argue that the humanist rationale is a part of those conflicting messages that mask intent and contribute to this marginalization. This is shown in Figure 1.

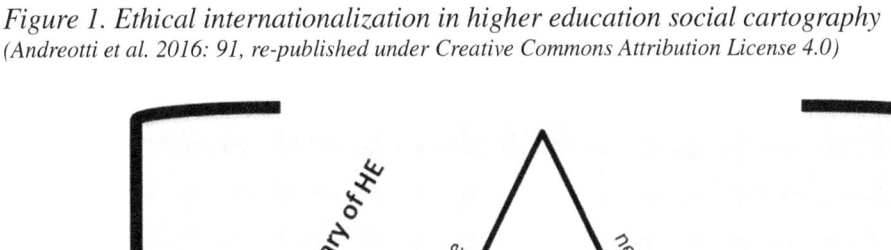

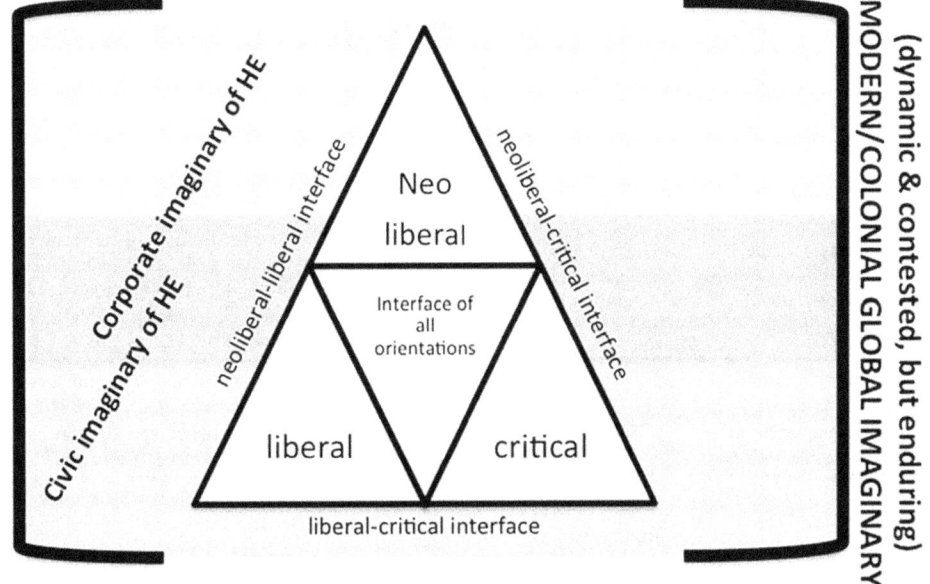

Figure 1. Ethical internationalization in higher education social cartography
(Andreotti et al. 2016: 91, re-published under Creative Commons Attribution License 4.0)

As a way of bringing to light taken for granted assumptions of internationalization, Andreotti et al. (2016) explore internationalization from three distinct and interconnected paradigms of discourse: the neoliberal, the liberal, and the critical. The neoliberal category is associated with discourses relating to economics, the liberal category with traditional values, and the critical with social reform. These terms are defined and applied in more detail in the sections below. Formatted as triangles within a triangle, there are points at which these ideologies intersect, but at times they are also fundamentally distinct. Figure 1 demonstrates this relationship. Pashby and Andreotti (2016) have utilized this triangle to explore the ethics of international education broadly.

The following section utilizes Andreotti et al.'s (2016) cartograph as a tool to discuss specifically the various forms of the humanist rationale as it relates to study abroad at the community college. In trying to plot humanism on the cardiograph, the relationship between humanism and each of these domains stimulates conversation about the purpose of study abroad at the community college whilst illuminating the multiple conceptions of the humanist rationale. Table 1 summarizes these differing humanist rationales.

The Neoliberal Domain

The neoliberal domain is associated with the privatization of education, the free market, a disinvestment in welfare programs (Ayers, 2005; Levin, 2007; 2017; Pashby & Andreotti, 2016) and the global colonial imaginary (Pashby & Andreotti, 2016). In many ways the neoliberal discourse is thought to represent the opposite of core community college values (Ayers, 2005). It is a belief that education is a private good, which individuals can leverage to personal advantage that will eventually lead to geographically bounded economic societal benefit; though in practice neoliberal policies do not benefit society, but instead the already economically and socially advantaged (Harvey, 2005; Viggiano, et al., 2018). Therefore, the broadly neoliberal perspective is associated with the argument that internationalization at the community college is useful for the purpose of revenue generation.

Within the neoliberal domain, the neoliberal humanist rationale is that study abroad at the community college is useful because it helps domestic students from less privileged backgrounds to become more marketable by providing skills necessary to compete in a global economy. From this perspective, it is the obligation of the community college to offer a global education to ensure that economically disad-

Table 1. Rationales for study abroad at the community college

Domain	Foundation	Objective	Humanist Rationale
Neoliberal	Money: revenue, competition, prestige, individual responsibility	Revenue generation for individual students that will contribute to U. S. GDP	Study abroad is a means of facilitating the development of skills associated with global competency for underserved domestic students so as to provide them the opportunity to generate greater economic return from their degrees in the globalized job market (e.g. Brennan & Dellow, 2013; Manns, 2014).
Liberal	History: mission of open access, civic engagement, community	Citizens prepared to participate in democratic society	Study abroad is a means for developing cultural competence amongst students in the local community, which is useful for democratic participation in the diverse U. S. society (e.g. Raby & Valeau, 2007; Green, 2007; Treat & Hagedorn, 2013).
Critical	Social Justice: service to the less powerful	Mitigate injustice	Study abroad is a means to mitigate global social injustice by promoting initiatives and positive outcomes, for all people involved. It is associated with the interconnected nature of the world and global power differentials (defined in this chapter).

vantaged students are not economically disadvantaged further (Brennan & Dellow, 2013; Manns, 2014). Skills associated with global competency learned from study abroad will give underserved students the potential of generating greater economic return from their degrees in the globalized job market (Brennan & Dellow, 2013; Manns, 2014). This is what Lilley, Barker, and Harris (2017) call a "neoliberal global citizen." Rather than seeing study abroad initiatives at the community college as a means of revenue generation for the campus, those who employ a humanist rationale and operate from the neoliberal domain argue for study abroad as a means of future revenue generation for the students. The humanist rationale brings the focus from the institution toward the students, but still operates under the guiding principles of the neoliberal domain: revenue generation and competition. From this perspective, study abroad is only useful so long as it serves to economically advantage the student in the future.

The Liberal Domain

The liberal domain is associated with the traditional community college ideals of open access, civic engagement, social mobility, and community. The liberal domain highlights the role of education as a public good for society but bounds this good clearly within social precedent and geographic boundaries (Andreotti et al., 2016). Those in the liberal domain fear altering an institutional foundation that they perceive to be sturdy, but instead choose to focus on improving the already existing foundation (Andreotti et al., 2016). The problem with the liberal domain is that it reproduces historical injustice by rooting the solutions to social injustice within the same framework that created the social injustice (Stein, 2017).

Practitioners that operate from the foundation of the liberal humanist rationale try to fit study abroad within the existing mission of the community college. From this perspective discrimination and unjust policies are justified based on a historical responsibility to only a preselected privileged group of people, such as the local community or tax payer. Those that employ the liberal humanist rationale would argue that community colleges should pursue study abroad because it helps 'their students'—U.S. nationals and community members—to develop cultural competence that is useful for participation in the U. S.'s or local community's diverse society (e.g. Raby & Valeau, 2007; Green, 2007; Treat & Hagedorn, 2013). Many proponents of study abroad at the community college fall within this domain. Conflict and confusion arise when "their students" are no longer only U. S. nationals (Viggiano, et. al, 2018).

Although motivated by student centered goals, the liberal humanist rationale for study abroad at the community college is exclusionary. Because those within the liberal domain want only to work within the parameters of the current mission, expanding the structure to include new stakeholders becomes a conceptual challenge. Those in the liberal domain may find themselves stuck in a hegemonic and nationalist frame (Shahjahan & Kezar, 2015) that privileges traditional stakeholders—U. S. students and citizens—at the expense of new stakeholders—students and citizens of other countries. Thus, the liberal humanist rationale does not pay regard to the global impact of community colleges and neglects to question the reciprocity of a study abroad relationship across borders: How do students influence the world outside of the U. S.? What is it that the host country will receive in return?

The Critical Domain

The critical domain is associated with equity, diversity, and social justice (Andreotti et al., 2016), and therefore very aligned with the core values of the community college (Ayers, 2005), but it is not constrained by tradition. While the critical discourse is similar to the liberal discourse, the crucial difference is that the critical discourse prioritizes actions that are to the advantage of those that are the most disadvantaged by society (Andreotti et al., 2016). From the critical perspective, liberal arguments about historical missions of the community college and national boundaries are invalid, if they are utilized to perpetuate injustice. Where the liberal domain privileges a cohesive society founded in tradition, the critical domain privileges a socially just society, and recognizes that at times the two may be in conflict (Andreotti et al., 2016). The critical domain promotes alterations to the foundational assumptions of institutions so as to correct for historical social injustice and to accommodate for a more socially just future (Pashby & Andreotti, 2016). As such, the critical humanist rationale is that community colleges actors at institutions that are engaged in internationalization initiatives, such as study abroad, have an equal responsibility to facilitate socially just outcomes for all humans influenced by the activity regardless of national boundaries. From this perspective, social-justice is synonymous with global-justice at internationalized community colleges.

Scholars and practitioners who consider their work to be within the critical domain may still fail themselves to employ a globally critical rationale to study abroad at the community college. Even those who identify with the critical domain may struggle to see beyond national boundaries (Pashby & Andreotti, 2016). Shahjahan and Kezar's (2015) work on methodological nationalism demonstrates that many critical scholars often fail to apply critical principles beyond the nation state. Study abroad practitioners and scholars that fall within the critical humanist domain would be interested in promoting policies that consider the impact of study abroad on the host country, and students within the host country; they consider global power differentials and privilege; and they aim to recognize diversity between and within nations. While the critical voice is often employed to highlight the ways in which institutions are complicit in structural inequality (Martínez-Alemán, Pusser, & Bensimon, 2015; Stein, 2017), scholars have yet to highlight the way in which community college study abroad programs facilitate structural inequality. A globally critical humanist rationale for study abroad at the community college is absent from the scholarly literature.

This chapter introduces the critical humanist rationale for internationalization at the community college by grounding the humanist rationale within Young's (2006) justice theory. Because the definition and application of humanism changes based on one's domain of reference, as it currently stands, humanism alone can be seen as another inconsistent agenda that Raby (2012) finds pushes internationalization at the community college towards the periphery. Moreover, this section demonstrated that some applications of humanism, as it applies to study abroad at the community college, push some humans towards the periphery. Consistent with recent literature (Levin, Viggiano, López Damián, Morales Vázquez, & Wolf, 2017), as the foundation of rationales change, so too does the degree to which different humans are included in the mission. While rationales for study abroad at the community college fit snugly in the neoliberal and liberal domains, a critical rationale that includes non-domestic humans is absent from the scholarly literature. To address these issues, the following section clearly defines the parameters of a critical humanist rationale. To do so, these sections utilize Young's (2006) Social Connections Model to explain ways in which community colleges and their actors can begin to reexamine their roles in structural injustice.

GROUNDING THE CRITICAL HUMANIST RATIONALE

Global competence and citizenship are relatively agreed upon and expected outcomes of study abroad initiatives (Green, 2007; Lilley et al., 2017), so practitioners that facilitate such programs should also hold and utilize the skills associated with these outcomes. Green suggests that successful study abroad initiatives teach that "…the fates of individuals, nations, and the planet are inextricably linked" (Green, 2007, p. 15). Lilley et al.'s (2017) interview-based study of strategically selected higher education experts yielded a definition for global citizenship which included "shows openness, tolerance, respect, and responsibility for self, others, and the planet… has a global mind-set and makes interconnections about the impacts of globalization…" (p. 15). Thus, community college scholars and practitioners expect globally competent individuals to be able to easily identify global connections and responsibilities. These are anti-nationalist concepts aligned with the critical humanist domain. Young's (2006) Social Connections Model may help practitioners apply their own global competence to facilitate the globally just study abroad programs. This chapter suggests that institutional members of community colleges can utilize the principles of Young's (2006) model to help them to rationalize and facilitate globally just study abroad programs at the community college.

Young's (2006) Social Connections Model

Justice theory is often related to Rawls (1971) interpretation of a social contract. Given that people do not have a choice in which place in society that they will be born, then societies built on the foundation of a social contract should ensure that all people have a fair and equal opportunity to ascend the social hierarchy. Inequality is tolerable in society so long as it is to the greatest benefit of the most disadvantaged peoples.

While originally applied only to those that reside within the nation state (Rawls, 1971), scholars (e.g. Beitz, 1979; Pogge, 1989; Viggiano et al., 2018; Young, 2006) extend the notion of a social contract to a global system: a global contract. Proponents of a global contract assert that given strict immigration laws and the vastly unequal global wealth distribution, people do not have a choice in which society they will join (Young, 2006). The political borders of today were formed and continue to be maintained only by historically unequitable power relationships tied to colonialism (Pashby & Andreotti, 2016; Shahjahan & Kezar, 2015; Mignolo & Tlostanova, 2006; Stein, 2017; Young, 2006). Thus, arguments of discrimination and exclusion based on geographical borders are based on birth right and therefore unjust (Bietz, 1979; Nussbaum, 2006; Pashby & Andreotti, 2016; Pogge, 1989; Young, 2006). Young (2006) argues that global structural injustice continues to exist because international institutions and their actors facilitate this injustice: "[s]tructural injustice occurs as a consequence of many individuals and institutions acting in pursuit of their particular goals and interests, within given institutional rules and accepted norms" (p. 114). In alignment with this assertion, Viggiano et al. (2018) found that community college practitioners within their study of three highly internationalized community colleges were indeed in violation of Rawlsian (1971) justice theory from the perspective of a global social contract.

From Young's (2006) perspective, the rules of a global social contract apply as soon as an international relationship is formed. All institutions and institutional actors that facilitate international relationships have a responsibility to ensure fair and equitable treatment of all humans influenced—be it directly or indirectly—by the relationship. This responsibility is not dependent on geographic boundary. Individuals are responsible for the ways in which their actions, in the pursuit of these institutional goals, influence people regardless of their national origin. As such, the central tenant of this model is that, "all agents who contribute by their actions to the structural processes that produce injustice have responsibilities to work to remedy these injustices" (p. 102-103).

Young's (2006) Social Connection Model holds five basic tenants. 1) the responsibility of one party does not absolve the responsibility of other parties; 2) rather than taking a purely liberal approach that attempts to work within preestablished rules of the system, actors should call into question the foundation of the system; 3) rather than paying reparation for past misconducts, actors are encouraged to prevent future wrongdoings; 4) individuals are responsible for outcomes rather than ambiguous entities in which the institutional actors are left unaccountable; 5) individuals can discharge their responsibility only by acting within their own power, privilege, interest, and collective ability whilst encouraging others to do the same.

It is from the foundation of the global contract and Young's (2006) Social Connections Model that the critical humanist rationale defines the responsibility of community colleges and their actors to the pursuit of justice. To facilitate just outcomes institutional actors must pursue equity-based policies that acknowledge the interconnected nature of the world as well as global power differentials. The following section applies the logic of the critical humanist rationale to begin to discuss globally just study abroad at the community college.

Incorporating the Critical Humanist Rationale Into Mission and Action

Asking the Right Questions

The critical humanist rationale sets a solid foundation from which to formulate questions about the nature and implementation of globally just study abroad programs at the community college. Given that space constraints prevent a comprehensive exploration of all possible questions, the following sections focus on questions relating to the ways in which community college practitioners and students come to conceptualize the social justice related problems of the world. The final subsection suggests additional questions that could be explored from the foundation of the critical humanist rationale.

Who Is Included in Community?

Practitioners and scholars have defined the boundary of community colleges by utilizing what Raby (2012, p. 84) calls a "narrow definition of community." International comes into direct competition with a geographically bounded conception of community, breeding competition between the local and international and therefore promoting bounded citizenship (Raby, 2012).

In the context of higher education scholarship, methodological nationalists assume that institutions of higher education operate within national boundaries and should therefore serve a national agenda (Shahjahan & Kezar, 2015). Shahjahan and Kezar (2013) argue that viewing stakeholders from a nationalist frame contributes to "…unequal power relationships and reduced responsibility for human suffering tied to national boundaries" (p. 27). Decolonial scholarship such as Mignolo and Tlostanova (2006) argue that societies, institutions, and their actors utilize borders to promote a historical power structure of colonization by granting some groups of people greater privileges based solely on the location of their birth:

Thinking Globally About Social Justice

Borders in this precise sense, are not a natural outcome of a natural or divine historical processes in human history, but were created in the very constitution of the modern/colonial world (i.e. in the imaginary of Western and Atlantic capitalist empires formed in the past five hundred years). (p. 208)

Education can be perceived as one such resource and the narrow conception of community can be seen as one such border.

Practitioners that employ a narrow definition of community are not recognizing international social connections and not honoring their responsibility to stakeholders outside of their immediate community. Those that apply the narrow definition of community neglect to consider the critical humanist rationale and therefore do not demonstrate mastery of global citizenship. Specifically, this narrow conception ignores, "…responsibility for… others, and the planet" (Lilley et al., 2017, p. 15).

How Do Students Come to Understand Problems of Global Social Justice?

Open Doors Data from the Institute for International Education ([IIE], 2017) demonstrates that students from associate granting institutions in the U. S. are not studying abroad in a diverse assortment of countries: most choose to study in one of a handful of high-GDP countries in the Global North. In the 2015/16 academic year 42% of U.S. associate granting students that studied abroad did so in just four countries—Italy, Spain, France, and the UK. Over half of all U.S. students, including community college students, are choosing to study abroad in European countries. Given that Europe is home to just over 11% of the world population and less than 10% of the world land mass, this distribution is disproportional.

From the critical humanist foundation, these data illuminate a potential problem. If students are disproportionately exposed to the communities of high-GDP countries in the Global North, then we offer students a warped view of the state of global problems. This is to say that students that study abroad in only privileged countries are not exposed to global problems such as extreme poverty, disease, differential effects of climate change in the same way as if they were to study abroad in a less privileged country. As such, it may be that students that study in these privileged countries will struggle to perceive the severity and scope of global problems. It may be more difficult for students that study in these privileged countries to conceptualize global social justice. Practitioners that suggest that students that study abroad will gain global competence, should consider that outcomes associated with global competence will likely differ based on the country of study. Future research should investigate this potential outcome disparity.

Increasing study abroad participation at the community college may marginally increase rates of study abroad to Latin America. Interestingly, community college students study abroad in Latin American more than their university counterparts. For example, in the 2014/15 academic year 24.5% of students from associate granting institutions studied abroad in Latin America versus 16%, of students across all institutional types (IIE, 2016). Costa Rica was the third most popular study abroad destination of associate students studying abroad: 8.5% in the 2015/16 year. This shows that community colleges have made some strides in the diversification of study abroad destinations that is not yet observed at four-year institutions.

How Does the U. S. Come to Be Understood?

When socio-economically and ethnically diverse students do not participate in study abroad, then students in other countries that U. S. students visit may develop a warped view of the state of society within the U. S. This is to say that students in countries where U. S. students go to study abroad may come to understand U. S. culture from the perspective of white affluence, without conceptualizing the multi-faceted and polymorphic identities of the larger U. S. population. This would misrepresent the multicultural perspectives and views of the U. S., potentially presenting a distorted view of the state of society within the U. S. For this reason, practitioners that apply the critical humanist rationale should recognize their responsibility to participate and promote the involvement of students from diverse backgrounds in study abroad initiatives. Future research should be conducted to assess this theoretical relationship.

Across all institutional types students that study abroad from the U.S. are disproportionately white and affluent (Luo & Jamieson-Drake, 2015; Salisbury, Paulsen, & Pascarella, 2011; Salisbury et al., 2009). In Salisbury et al.'s (2009) quantitative study on student motivations to engage in study abroad, the scholars analyzed survey responses from 2,772 students across various institutional types. They found that, despite the documented difference in actual participation rates, there was no difference between students of color and white students in their desire to study abroad (Salisbury et al., 2009). However, students receiving financial aid were 11 percentage points less likely to report that they planned to study abroad than their more affluent counterparts (Salisbury et al., 2009). In addition, the greatest predictor of a student's likelihood to express a desire to study abroad was parent's education level. Thus, community college practitioners looking to send students that represent the diversity of perspectives within the U. S. should actively attempt to engage low-SES and first-generation students in study abroad.

Given that the community college enrolls more low-SES, non-traditional, first generation, and minority students than its four-year counterparts (Cohen, Brawer, & Kisker, 2013), study abroad initiatives at the community college may engage more diverse students in study abroad activities (Salisbury et al., 2009). This is the case for students of color. In the 2015-16 academic year, more students of color studied abroad from the community college than from other institutional types: approximately 39% of the students that studied abroad at associates granting institutions were students that identified as a racial identity other than white, as opposed to 28% across all institutional types (IIE, 2017). Although students identifying as Black/African American participated in study abroad at the community college at a marginally higher rate than other institutional types, the major difference stemmed from students identifying as Hispanic/Latino: 23.2% of the study abroad participants at associates granting institutions identified as Hispanic/Latino contrasted with 9.7% across all institutional types (IIE, 2017). However, community college students in Salisbury et al.'s (2009) sample were 30 percentage points less likely to report that they plan to engage in study abroad activities than their liberal arts counterparts (Salisbury et al., 2009). Therefore, practitioners should work to actively promote the participation of community college students in study abroad initiatives.

Remaining Questions

These questions serve as examples of the application of the critical humanist perspective but are by no means exhaustive. Though again not a comprehensive list, additional questions might include: Whose cultures are marginalized by education abroad? Whose cultures come to be understood? How do students come to understand the multiple cultures within a culture? How does involvement in study abroad disadvantage the host country, institution, and peoples? Does the Social Connections Model apply to community colleges outside of the U. S.? In what ways? How can community college study abroad programs balance their responsibility without pursuing a development discourse tied to colonialism (Stein, Andreotti, & Suša, 2016)? In the future, practitioners and scholars can begin to explore these questions and more from within the framework of the critical humanist rationale.

CONCLUSION AND DISCUSSION

The critical humanist rationale incorporates all humans and holds social justice, rather than monetary benefit or historical president, as the superior policy guidepost. This rationale argues that, given that community colleges have become globalized institutions (Levin, 2001; 2002; Levin, 2017), community colleges are equally responsible to stakeholders outside and inside of their geographical community. Through the lens of this rationale, the purpose of study abroad programs at the community college are to mitigate structural social injustice, which will require practitioners to recognize the interconnected nature of the world as well as global power differentials.

This foundation can serve as a compass for practitioners looking to facilitate globally - just study abroad programs. To pursue global social justice, community college practitioners must consider the ways in which study abroad initiatives influence both domestic and international stakeholders and must take personal responsibility for the effects that their institution's international involvement has on all humans. In accordance with Young's (2006) social justice theory, practitioners should reflect on their own positionality to determine the ways in which they can work to minimize their contribution to this structural injustice and guide their institution's actions accordingly. While not comprehensive, the questions discussed in this chapter were examples of the ways in which community college study abroad practitioners could begin to reimagine the ways in which their institutions conceptualize their influence outside of their local communities.

Guiding Conversations Towards Humanism and Critical Humanism

Practitioners can utilize Andreotti et al.'s (2016) cartograph to explore their rationales for study abroad at the community college. This exercise can help to construct concrete goals and reveal motivations and assumptions that were previously inaudible or unexplored (Andreotti et al., 2016). Departments might use this as a group exercise to stimulate conversation that clarifies, explains, and explores goals as they relate to study abroad. Ask questions like "which goals of our department fall into each domain?", "which domain does the department and institution actively pursue?", "which domain do you personally identify with most?", "how might you shift your focus from one domain to another?". Supporters of the critical humanist rationale can use the argument constructed in this chapter to discuss the importance of globally just initiatives—those that are non-nationalist, consider global power differentials, and acknowledge the interconnected nature of the world.

Consider that the neoliberal discourse is often associated with injustice and is much louder than that of the critical or liberal discourses (Andreotti et al., 2016; Pashby & Andreotti, 2016). Members of the community college are quick to use neoliberal logic of resource strain or competition to justify their position and silence other perspectives (Ayers & Palmadessa, 2015). Although the critical voice is often closely aligned with justice (Pashby & Andreotti, 2016), Andreotti et al. (2016) have found that the critical voice was the most silent of all. As such, those that pursue a broadly humanist study abroad program will need to take great care to purposefully and mindfully incorporate critical and liberal perspectives. Purposefully incorporating the critical humanist rationale into the departmental or institutional mission could help to accomplish this goal.

Steps to incorporate the critical humanist rationale:

1. Be aware of the global implications of your actions
   a. Has your team considered the global implications of their global program? In what ways might your actions be facilitating injustice? How are you and your team actively working to advance the goals of global social justice?
   b. Are students completing with realistic expectations of their "global competence"?
   c. Do staff and students recognize their own privilege and involvement in global social injustice?
2. Purposefully rethink your mission with global justice in mind
   a. Are you engaging and considering all dimensions of the triangle?
   b. Is one piece of the triangle more dominant than another? How can you ensure that the neoliberal discourse does not drown out the critical or liberal discourse?
3. Incorporate into practice
   a. Are there differences in how you treat your partner institutions? If there are differences, are these differences to the greatest advantage of the least advantaged peoples involved? How might you begin or nurture partnerships with institutions that are less advantaged than your own institution?
   b. Are students studying in a wide range of countries?
   c. Are domestic students (from a variety of backgrounds) engaging with international students (from a variety of backgrounds)?
   d. How are students conceptualizing and representing their understanding of global problems, the multiplicity of cultures, and their own roles in global social injustice?

REFERENCES

Altbach, P. G., & De Wit, H. (2016). Internationalization and global tensions: Lessons from history. In P. G. Altbach (Ed.), *Global perspectives on higher education*. Baltimore, MD: John Hopkins University Press.

American Council on Education (ACE). (2016). *Survey Responses by Institution Type*. Washington, DC: Center for International and Global Engagement. Retrieved from http://www.acenet.edu/news-room/Documents/Mapping-Internationalization-Tables-2017.pdf

Andreotti, V., Stein, S., Pashby, K., & Nicolson, M. (2016). Social cartographies as performative devices in research on higher education. *Higher Education Research & Development*, *35*(1), 84–99. doi:10.1080/07294360.2015.1125857

Ayers, D. F. (2005). Neoliberal ideology in community college mission statements: A critical discourse analysis. *The Review of Higher Education*, *28*(4), 527–549. doi:10.1353/rhe.2005.0033

Ayers, D. F., & Palmadessa, A. L. (2015). The community college and a rising global imaginary: An analysis of practical reasoning, 1950-2013. *The Journal of Higher Education*, *86*(6), 864–892.

Beitz, C. R. (1979). *Political theory and international relations*. Princeton, NJ: Princeton University Press.

Brennan, M., & Dellow, D. A. (2013). International students as a resource for achieving comprehensive internationalization. *New Directions for Community Colleges*, *2013*(161), 27–37. doi:10.1002/cc.20046

Cohen, A. M., Brawer, F. B., & Kisker, C. B. (2013). *The American community college*. San Francisco, CA: Jossey-Bass.

Cook, J. (1996). Community self-help international development projects. In N. Tarrow & R. L. Raby (Eds.), *Dimensions of the community college: International, intercultural, and multicultural perspectives*. New York, NY: Routledge.

Copeland, J. M., McCrink, C. L., & Starratt, G. K. (2017). Development of the community college internationalization index. *Journal of Studies in International Education*, *21*(4), 349–374. doi:10.1177/1028315317697541

Foucault, M. (1984). What is Enlightenment? In P. Rabinow (Ed.), *The Foucault Reader* (pp. 31–50). New York, NY: Pantheon.

Green, M. F. (2007). Internationalizing community colleges: Barriers and strategies. *New Directions for Community Colleges*, *2007*(138), 15–24. doi:10.1002/cc.277

Harvey, D. (2007). *A brief history of neoliberalism*. Oxford, UK: Oxford University Press.

Hunter, B., White, G. P., & Godbey, G. C. (2006). What does it mean to be globally competent? *Journal of Studies in International Education*, *10*(3), 267–285. doi:10.1177/1028315306286930

Institute of International Education. (2017). *Open doors report on international educational exchange*. New York, NY: Institute for International Education.

Levin, J. S. (2001). *Globalizing the community college: Strategies for change in the twenty-first century*. New York, NY: Palgrave MacMillan. doi:10.1057/9780312292836

Levin, J. S. (2002). Global culture and the community college. *Community College Journal of Research and Practice*, *26*(2), 121–145. doi:10.1080/106689202753385474

Levin, J. S. (2007). *Nontraditional students and community colleges: The conflict of justice and neoliberalism*. New York, NY: Palgrave MacMillan. doi:10.1057/9780230607286

Levin, J. S. (2017). *Community colleges and new universities under neoliberal pressures: Institutional change, institutional stability*. New York, NY: Palgrave MacMillan. doi:10.1057/978-1-137-48020-0

Levin, J. S., Viggiano, T., López Damián, A. I., Morales Vázquez, E., & Wolf, J. P. (2017). Polymorphic students: New descriptions and conceptions of community college students from the perspectives of administrators and faculty. *Community College Review*, *45*(2), 119–143. doi:10.1177/0091552116679731

Lilley, K., Barker, M., & Harris, N. (2017). The global citizen conceptualized: Accommodating ambiguity. *Journal of Studies in International Education*, *21*(1), 6–21. doi:10.1177/1028315316637354

Luo, J., & Jamieson-Drake, D. (2015). Predictors of study abroad intent, participation, and college outcomes. *Research in Higher Education*, *56*(1), 29–56. doi:10.100711162-014-9338-7

Manns, D. (2014). Redefining the role, scope, and mission of community colleges in an international context. *Community College Journal of Research and Practice*, *38*(8), 705–709. doi:10.1080/10668926.2014.897079

Martínez-Alemán, A. M., Pusser, B., & Bensimon, E. M. (Eds.). (2015). *Critical approaches to the study of higher education: A practical introduction*. Baltimore, MD: John Hopkins University Press.

Mignolo, W. D., & Tlostanova, M. V. (2006). Theorizing from the borders: Shifting to geo-and body-politics of knowledge. *European Journal of Social Theory*, 9(2), 205–221. doi:10.1177/1368431006063333

Nussbaum, M. (2006). *Frontiers of justice: Disability, nationality, species membership*. Cambridge, MA: Harvard University Press.

Olssen, M., & Peters, M. A. (2005). Neoliberalism, higher education and the knowledge economy: From the free market to knowledge capitalism. *Journal of Education Policy*, 20(3), 313–345. doi:10.1080/02680930500108718

Opp, R. D., & Gosetti, P. P. (2014). The role of key administrators in internationalizing the community college student experience. *New Directions for Community Colleges*, 2014(165), 67–75. doi:10.1002/cc.20092

Pashby, K., & Andreotti, V. D. O. (2016). Ethical internationalisation in higher education: Interfaces with international development and sustainability. *Environmental Education Research*, 22(6), 771–787. doi:10.1080/13504622.2016.1201789

Pogge, T. W. M. (1989). *Realizing Rawls*. Ithaca, NY: Cornell University Press.

Quijano, A. (2007). Coloniality and modernity/rationaleity. *Cultural Studies*, 21(2-3), 168–178. doi:10.1080/09502380601164353

Raby, R. L. (2012). Reimagining international education at community colleges. *AUDEM: The International Journal of Higher Education and Democracy*, 3(1), 81–98.

Raby, R. L., & Valeau, E. J. (2007). Community college international education: Looking back to forecast the future. *New Directions for Community Colleges*, 2007(138), 5–14. doi:10.1002/cc.276

Rawls, J. (1971). *A theory of justice*. Cambridge, MA: Harvard University.

Salisbury, M. H., Paulsen, M. B., & Pascarella, E. T. (2011). Why do all the study abroad students look alike? Applying an integrated student choice model to explore differences in the factors that influence white and minority students' intent to study abroad. *Research in Higher Education*, 52(2), 123–150. doi:10.100711162-010-9191-2

Salisbury, M. H., Umbach, P. D., Paulsen, M. B., & Pascarella, E. T. (2009). Going global: Understanding the choice process of the intent to study abroad. *Research in Higher Education*, 50(2), 119–143. doi:10.100711162-008-9111-x

Shahjahan, R. A. (2013). Coloniality and a global testing regime in higher education: Unpacking the OECD's AHELO initiative. *Journal of Education Policy*, 28(5), 676–694. doi:10.1080/02680939.2012.758831

Shahjahan, R. A., & Kezar, A. J. (2013). Beyond the "national container" addressing methodological nationalism in higher education research. *Educational Researcher*, 42(1), 20–29. doi:10.3102/0013189X12463050

Steger, M. B. (2008). *Globalisms: The great ideological struggle of the twenty-first century*. Lanham, MD: Rowman & Littlefield Publishers.

Stein, S. (2017). Internationalization for an uncertain future: Tensions, paradoxes, and possibilities. *The Review of Higher Education*, *41*(1), 3–32. doi:10.1353/rhe.2017.0031

Stein, S., Andreotti, V. D. O., & Suša, R. (2016). 'Beyond 2015', within the modern/colonial global imaginary? Global development and higher education. *Critical Studies in Education*, 1–21. doi:10.1080/17508487.2016.1247737

Treat, T., & Hagedorn, L. S. (2013). Resituating the community college in a global context. *New Directions for Community Colleges*, *2013*(161), 5–9. doi:10.1002/cc.20044

Viggiano, T., López Damián, A. I., Morales Vázquez, E., & Levin, J. S. (2018). The others: Equitable access, international students, and the community college. *Journal of Studies in International Education*, *22*(1), 71–85. doi:10.1177/1028315317725883

Chapter 14
Peacebuilding as a Means to Global Citizenry

David J. Smith
Forage Center for Peacebuilding and Humanitarian Education, USA & George Mason University, USA

ABSTRACT

The objective of this chapter is to illustrate approaches that can be used by community colleges to promote both global knowledge and global engagement—often taking the form of education abroad—using peacebuilding means. To make the case, examples and models from several U.S. community colleges will be shared. Examples from community colleges from throughout the country are given.

INTRODUCTION

Remarkably in the United States, a country fraught with conflict and violence, promoting peace is often viewed as controversial and misunderstood. The reasons for this dichotomy are many and beyond the scope of this chapter. But it can be said that those who advocate for peace-oriented approaches and strategies to curbing violence and conflict are at times viewed either as impractical idealists or political (and possibly unpatriotic) subversives. A constructive counterview is that they are realistic professionals looking to solve serious challenges to peace using research-based and tested methods (Fitzduff & Jean, 2011).

Our notions of peace are often taken from depictions and symbols of political and social activism. The ubiquitous peace symbol designed by graphic artist Gerald Holtom in 1958 for an anti-nuclear march in the United Kingdom frames the sensibilities of many about peace: We are either drawn to the symbol and what it represents (e.g., nonviolence, social justice, environmentalism, and human rights) or are put off by it and might use the American flag as a juxtapositional symbol (Smith, 2002). Symbolic standoffs typify political and social debates and can lead to (hopefully) civic (and civil) discussions on how to deal with the challenges shared by Americans and internationals alike.

DOI: 10.4018/978-1-5225-6252-8.ch014

The presence of violence in our society is undisputable. It often takes the form of overt violence but includes "exploitative social relations that cause unnecessary suffering" (Maill, Ramsbotham, & Woodhouse, 2011, p. 31). This later form is referred to as structural violence and focuses "on the systemic disadvantages conferred on marginalized groups in society" (Liu & Opotow, 2014, p. 692). Examples include "hunger, political repression, and psychological alienation" (Barash & Webel, 2002, p. 7). Violence is equally present in elite colleges and state universities, as in community colleges. But because community colleges enroll Americans of all social backgrounds, cultures, and income groups, and are often viewed as democracy's colleges because of their open doors and affordability, the consequences of failing to address overt and structural violence on community college campuses has dire consequences for societal stability, human rights protection, economic prosperity, social mobility, and social justice.

Global citizenry has taken on a range of interpretations including being linked to global peacefulness (Farnsworth, 2013). They are considered entwined with each other, with peace a "precondition for global citizenship" (Noddings, 2005, p. 17). Global citizenship education looks to empower all "to assume active roles, both locally and globally, in building more peaceful, tolerant, inclusive and secure societies" (UNESCO, 2018). To be "global" is considered an essential characteristic of a liberally educated learner (Sterns, 2010). Programs, initiatives, and strategies are present in institutions to help students achieve global knowledge as well as foster active global engagement. While global knowledge might include foreign language proficiency, geographic savviness, or an understanding of cross-cultural behaviors and expectations, to be globally engaged can be viewed as the active pursuit of opportunities to further one's global personal and professional interests. While this can be done in a range of ways, typically in 4- year institutions, and less often in community colleges, study abroad provides that opportunity.

In community colleges, the availability of opportunities to advance global education has not been as available as in 4- year institutions (American Council on Education, 2012). One reason for this may be the low level of support and lack of prioritization in many community colleges (Raby, 2016). However, as community college populations transform due to the arrival of foreign multicultural and multiethnic students – some having legal status and others not – there will be increasing pressures on these institutions to support meaningful and measurable ways to advance global education. Since community colleges reflect the demographics of local communities, this seems an expected evolution.

The objective of this chapter is to illustrate approaches that can be used by community colleges to promote both global knowledge and global engagement – often taking the form of education abroad – using peacebuilding means. To make the case, examples and models from several U.S. community colleges will be shared.

PEACEBUILDING

Peace can be viewed as a means to an end, as Mahatma Gandhi famously remarked, "as the means, so the end." Though his reflection was offered in viewing how Indians might achieve independence from the British with the use of nonviolence, his means/end construct can be applied in considering peace to achieve global awareness goals and fostering engagement in learners. In today's community colleges, where students of all backgrounds, ethnicities, experiences, and aspirations are found, this is more important than ever. Society's present challenges are immense, and graduates of America's community colleges will take on the important work of shaping local, state, national, and international policy, and implement strategies that will seek to build bridges with others across political, geographic, and virtual boundaries and borders. A hopeful sign is that American political leaders are increasingly being educated in community colleges (Sheehy, 2014).

Peacebuilding describes the active pursuit of peace. At times appearing as peace-building, it encompasses a wide range of strategies, approaches, and policies that support and sustain local and global communities to be healthy, safe, and nonviolent. Peacebuilding seeks to assist all, especially the marginalized, in achieving their personal and professional hopes. According to the Alliance for Peacebuilding (n.d.), "Peacebuilding ultimately supports human security—where people have freedom from fear, freedom from want, and freedom from humiliation." Specific approaches to peacebuilding include:

Providing humanitarian relief, protecting human rights, ensuring security, establishing nonviolent modes of resolving conflicts, fostering reconciliation, providing trauma healing services, repatriating refugees and resettling internally displaced persons, supporting broad-based education, and aiding in economic reconstruction (Snodderly, 2011, p. 40-41).

Traditionally, peacebuilding strategies were applied after conflict and war to prevent a relapse into violence by focusing on improving long-term relationships and rebuilding civil society institutions and infrastructure (Boutros-Ghali, 1992). The efficacy of peacebuilding is recognized as a programmatic strategy by Catholic Relief Services (Catholic Relief Services, n.d.) and an educational strategy by the U.S. Institute of Peace (Milofsky & Berdan, 2011). Peacebuilding today takes an expansive view and includes the "full array of processes, approaches, and stages needed to transform conflict toward more sustainable, peaceful relationships" regardless of whether the application is post-conflict or not (Lederach, 1997, p. 20). And it is no longer limited to looking only at global contexts but is also considered in domestic and local circumstances and applications (Peace Alliance, n.d.). In situations where violence and conflict are present, peacebuilding engagement is seen as a viable means to building long-term stability and security in communities.

ROLE OF EDUCATION

Education has played a significant role in advancing peacebuilding. Peace education describes peacebuilding efforts in secondary education, while peace studies is more often the emphasis in higher education. An important goal of peace education is to create in youth a desire to understand and learn "how nonviolence and positive visions of peace can provide the basis for a just and sustainable future" (Harris & Morrison, 2013, p. 18). It has been urged that teaching peace is crucial to advancing the objectives of international education including many of the objectives and aspirations of the United Nations (Navarro-Castro & Nario-Galace, 2008).

Peace studies is defined as:

An interdisciplinary field of study with varying themes and foci, including but not limited to analysis of conflict, management of conflict, and resolution of conflict; non-violent sanctions; peace paradigms, peace building, peacekeeping, and peace enforcement; social and economic justice; war's causes and conduct; and a variety of conceptions of international and domestic security (Miller & King, 2005, p. 60).

Peace studies theory is based on the idea that "conflict is a result of social, economic, or political inequities" and that focusing on the sources of these injustices is critical to remedial action (Aall, Helsing & Tidwell, 2007, p. 335). A closely aligned field to peace studies is conflict resolution (sometimes referred to as conflict management). Where peace studies examines various forms of injustice arising from conflict, conflict resolution is more applied and focuses on reaching compromise and settlement in order to avoid further conflict (Aall, Helsing & Tidwell, 2007.

Peacebuilding related degree programs are well-established with major graduate and undergraduate efforts in the U.S. at the University of Notre Dame, Kennesaw State University, George Mason University, and Portland State University. Though a precise number of programs does not exist, the Peace and Justice Studies Association estimates that there are approximately 40 graduate and close to 160 undergraduate credit programs (Directory, n.d.). It is estimated that there are programs or initiatives on peace and conflict at nearly 40 community colleges in the U.S. and Canada (Davidjsmithconsulting.com, 2017).

The presence of international students can play an important role in ensuring currency and relevancy in teaching peace. For international students who might arrive from conflict-affected areas, many of the issues and topics covered in peacebuilding curricula and related student activities can reverberate personally. Students who arrive as refugees or as asylum seekers may have experienced the types of violence and injustice that are at the roots of human rights protection. In addition, social justice issues in the U.S. and abroad including social and economic inequities, violence against minority groups, and addressing violent extremism, can also be incorporated into peacebuilding education and generate student interest. An example is the law enforcement and criminal justice/social justice degree option at Anne Arundel Community College (MD) (Anne Arundel Community College, n.d.).

COMMUNITY EVENTS AND CURRICULUM

Peacebuilding education can be the access point for promoting international education topics and issues. Some strategies are led by those who focus on student services and activities and might take the form of international and thematic fairs and celebrations. An example is Florida's Pasco-Hernando State College's (formerly Pasco-Hernando Community College) Peace Week held annually on the college's five campuses. A number of community colleges have offered similar community-based fairs where global peacebuilding and intercultural awareness are featured including at Arizona Western College, Bluegrass Community and Technical College (KY) (BCTC), Grand Rapids Community College (MI), Lane Community College (OR), and San Diego City College (CA) (SDCC). BCTC's 2012 peace fair included representatives of the Peace Corps, presentations by non-governmental organizations, and programs by Iraqi, Burundian, and Guatemalan cultural groups. In order to raise awareness of global challenges, SDCC's 2008 event featured programs and presentations by international humanitarian groups (Davis, 2013).

Curricular efforts can include offering courses that advance global issues such as a course in cultural awareness or by infusing peacebuilding themes in already established courses. Human rights education is increasingly seen as a viable curricular path in teaching about global peacebuilding issues. Daoust and Epperson (2013) write about the course, Universal Human Rights, that Epperson teaches at St. Louis Community College (MO) that emphasizes the relevancy of humanitarianism as a means to advancing global peacebuilding. The course includes topics such as the plight of child soldiers and the protections that are found in the Geneva Conventions. They argue that this has become more important than ever before in light of the events of September 11, 2001.

Human interaction is central to peace. Peacebuilding is about working, engaging, and, at times, struggling with and advocating for others who may be different from ourselves. Study aboard permits students to experience an unfamiliar environment, learning about the lives of others and their struggles in the face of challenges and obstacles. In the end, peacebuilding permits the opening of a window to understanding challenges and opportunities faced by the global community. Through study abroad and experiential learning students not only develop aptitudes that better permit them to engage, but these experiences provide them with a chance to practice what they have learned.

FOUR COMMUNITY COLLEGE APPROACHES

Four community colleges, Johnson County Community College (KS), Golden West College (CA), Cuyahoga Community College (OH), and Valencia College (FL), geographically in different parts of the U.S. – Kansas, California, Ohio, and Florida – have taken diverse approaches to using peacebuilding as a vehicle to promote global education, citizenry, and overseas experiences. The efforts of these colleges illustrate what can be done by faculty and college leadership, often collaborating with local community and educational partners, to foster global learning with their students.

For the past six years, the author has directed the National Community College Peacebuilding Seminar, an annual program for community college faculty and staff interested in promoting peacebuilding based in Washington, DC. The seminar focuses broadly on curricular efforts and content relative to global peacebuilding. Some 120 faculty and administrators have participated in the program. The four colleges featured below have participated in or contributed to the seminar.

Johnson County Community College's Annual Peacebuilding Conference

Johnson County Community College (JCCC), established in 1969, serves the Overland Park and Johnson County areas of eastern Kansas. In 2012, the college received financial support from the U.S. Institute of Peace as part of the Public Education for Peacebuilding Support Awards, offered from 2011-2013. The program was jointly administered with the Institute of International Education. The goal of the program was to support local groups including public libraries and higher education institutions with small funding to promote global peacebuilding efforts (Institute of International Education, About USIP Support, n.d.). For the two years that the program was in operation, 250 awards of $2,000 were made to advance global peacebuilding education, with almost 20% awarded to community colleges (Institute of International Education, Support Recipients, n.d.). Community colleges were funded for a range of peacebuilding projects including teaching about humanitarian assistance in a program titled "Global Health and Peacebuilding" at Anne Arundel Community College (MD) (AACC) and awarded to the college's nursing program (Davidjsmithconsulting.com, 2013b). Madison College (WI) was given an award for the college's Center for International Education (Davidjsmithconsulting.com, 2013a). At AACC, the application was submitted by nursing faculty member Lena Choudhary (currently an associate professor of nursing at Montgomery College in Maryland). In an interview for a blog at the time AACC received the award she commented that "it is important that healthcare workers today – especially those coming from community colleges, which are seeing growing international populations – are aware of the critical needs in war zones and support the efforts of health care professionals doing battlefield work" (Davidjsmithconsulting.com, 2013b).

Peacebuilding as a Means to Global Citizenry

The goal of the JCCC grant was to provide initial funding for a sustainable and recurring peacebuilding conference. The focus of the first conference was conflict in Uganda and titled "Local Peacebuilding Lessons from Uganda." Because the college's nursing program at the time was taking students on study abroad to Uganda, this theme seemed an ideal one (T. Patterson, personal communication, February 16, 2018). The annual conference has provided an opportunity to establish relationships with other academic institutions in the area. Over the course of five conferences, JCCC has partnered with the University of Kansas, Rockhurst University, Avila University, and most regularly with the Center for Global Peace Journalism at Park University, all based in the Kansas City area. The 2013 conference was a one-day event; by 2017 it had grown to three-days. The theme of the 2017 conference focused on nonviolence and peacebuilding with sessions strongly focused on international topics including the use of nonviolence in Central America and Africa. The keynote talk was on "Women as Essential Nonviolent Peacebuilding Leaders: Lessons from Africa" (Johnson County Community College, 2017). Overall, some 150 students have attended the conferences, many going on to study abroad programs at JCCC.

The college sends around 100 students a year overseas to the Netherlands, Italy, the United Kingdom, and Russia. The college also sponsors service learning projects including one in Mexico that focuses on health care and community development. JCCC's director of international education feels the Mexico program has benefited considerably from the content and programming of the annual conference themes particularly in sensitizing students to the needs of local marginalized communities (T. Patterson, personal communication, February 23, 2018). An important outcome of the annual conference has been to foster an area wide effort on peacebuilding, centered at JCCC. The first meeting of the Greater Kansas City Peacebuilding Consortium met in early 2018 with invitations extended to 130 organizations that focus on peacebuilding and international issues (T. Patterson, personal communication, February 16, 2018).

Peace Studies at Golden West College

Golden West College, located in Huntington Beach, CA, established its peace studies program in 2007. An associate of arts degree program, the college has articulation agreements for peace studies graduates with area 4-year institutions including the University of California and California State University. In 2017, the first full-time faculty member was hired in peace studies (F. Farazdaghi, personal communication, February 27, 2018). The program is premised on the belief that:

As the world is becoming increasingly interconnected, interdependent, diverse and complex, there is a greater need for peace, equity and sustainability. New skills of leadership are required in creating peaceful communities that are just, compassionate and sustainable (Golden West College, Peace Studies Program, n.d.)

To connect with the greater community and advance the objectives of the program, the college since 2007 has sponsored a spring peacebuilding conference. The 2018 conference theme was "Peace and the Global Economy: Emerging Issues & Practical Solutions" and focused on the role of economics in helping to shape societies defined by "social justice, environmental sustainability, and cultural equity" (Golden West College, Peace Conference, n.d.). Generally, the one-day conference attracts about 300 students and community members. The conference includes lectures, interactive workshops, and entertainment with multicultural and global peacebuilding themes (F. Farazdaghi, personal communication, February 23, 2018). Past conference themes have included:

- Peace & Equity Conference (2017)
- Peace, Justice & Sustainability Conference (2016)
- Peace & Leadership Conference – Leadership and Peace Building (2015)
- Peace Conference – Our Challenge, Our Opportunity, Our Legacy (2014)
- Peace Conference – Sustainable Peace (2013)
- Peace Conference – Creating Peace Through Sustainability, Education, Nonviolence, Conscious Democracy, Health, and Artistic Creativity (2012)
- Peace Conference – A Better Tomorrow: Making Peace a Global Reality in the 21st Century (2011)
- Peace Conference – Strategies for a Nonviolent Future – How to Create a Peaceful World (2010)
- Peace Conference – Creating Peace through Conscious Action (2009)
- Peace Conference – Peace is Possible Now (2008)
- Peace Conference – Celebrating Our Diversities, Trusting Our Unity (2007) (Golden West College, Previous Peace Conferences, n.d.).

Golden West College dedicated a peace pole in 2013 as a way of emphasizing its commitment to global peacebuilding. Typically, a peace poll is inscribed with "may peace prevail on earth" on its sides – as many as six: one being in English, and the others in the languages that are often the most predominate on campus. The college's pole is inscribed in Vietnamese, Spanish, Farsi, Chinese (Mandarin), Chumash (representing the language of native peoples who inhabited the area of the college before European settlement), and English (F. Farazdaghi, personal communication, March 1, 2018). Richland College (TX), which offers a peace studies program, has 25 peace poles on its campus with inscriptions in 76 different languages. One is planted each spring as part of the college's intercultural festival (Richland College, n.d.). As far as study abroad, the Golden West peace studies program coordinator is working with the University for Peace in Costa Rica to establish a short-term program (F. Farazdaghi, personal communication, June 26, 2018).

Peace and Justice Institute at Valencia College

Established in 1967, Valencia College serves the greater Orlando area with five campuses and 60,000 students. Its Peace and Justice Institute was informally founded in 2007 (R. Allen, personal communication, February 24, 2018). Today, the institute is a comprehensive initiative offering programming year-round on all campuses. Its 40-person advisory board represents both campus and community constituencies including representatives from the Muslim and Jewish religious communities (Valencia College, Peace and Justice Institute Advisory Council, n.d.). Valencia College has strived to position itself as a trusted community support entity for the Orlando area. A major focus of the institute has been helping students see their futures as peacebuilders. Students participating in the program have gone on to the Peace Corps, AmeriCorps, and become leaders in social activism (Valencia College, Peace and Justice Institute About, n.d.). Past speakers at the institute have included former diplomats and global peace activists (Valencia College, Peace and Justice Institute Past Speakers, n.d.). The institute has worked closely with other centers at the college to developed service learning and study abroad programs in Haiti. In the past, in partnership with a local church, the institute held a 3-day peace conference in Jacmel, Haiti. The conference brought together Haitians with Valencia College faculty and students to consider nonviolence and develop conflict resolution skills. Called "Konferans Lape Jakmel" – Haitian Creole for Peace Conference Jacmel – a major goal of the effort was supporting a sustainable peace program for Haitian youth. The program was last held in 2016 and the institute is looking to start it up again (R. Allen, personal communication, February 24, 2018). In addition, the institute has developed an ongoing relationship with Rift Valley Technical Training Institute (RVTTI) in Kenya. Faculty affiliated with the institute have provided technical support to RVTTI in the school's effort to develop a peacebuilding program ("Peace and Justice Initiative Newsletter," 2015). Finally, Global Peace Week is held every September to coincide with the International Day of Peace annually held on September 21 and established by the United Nations in 1981. The institute's 2017 program included a film festival that included films on overfishing in Palau and on the dropping of the atomic bomb on Hiroshima at the end of World War II (Valencia College, Peace and Justice Institute Programs, n.d.).

Cuyahoga Community College's Study Abroad to Costa Rica

Cleveland, Ohio's Cuyahoga Community College offers a 21-27 credit hour certificate in conflict resolution and peace studies. The program was established in 2010 and is articulated with Kent State University. Because the program developers wanted to provide students with an applied opportunity abroad, a program elective is the course Study Abroad in Peace and Conflict Resolution, offered every spring. The experience takes students to Costa Rica for 10 days. Among the objectives of the course is "to understand issues from multiple cultural perspectives, enhance their intercultural communication and adjustment skills, and analyze conflict resolution efforts and their impact at multiple levels" (Cuyahoga Community College, Study Abroad, 2018).

The course, listed as POL 2050 (in political science), requires preparatory work by students before embarking as a group to Costa Rica. This includes learning about Oscar Arias Sanchez, a former president and Nobel Peace Prize recipient. Students learn about why Costa Rica is demilitarized as a country. Upon returning to the U.S., students continue readings in contemporary peace studies including learning about multitrack diplomacy and conflict transformation (Olsen & Lipinski, 2017). In 2017, students while in-country visited with the country's Office of Justice and Peace to understand and compare Costa Rican justice approaches to American ones, and spent a day at the University for Peace, a UN mandated institution, to learn about higher education and career opportunities in the field. In that environmental sustainability is a component of peacebuilding approaches, students every year visit an organic farm to learn about local practices, and again, make comparisons to what takes place in the U.S. (I. Castillo, personal communication, June 22, 2018). In evaluating the experience and the overall program of study, one student commented:

My time in Costa Rica is very dear to me and I will treasure it always, both because of the wealth of knowledge I gained from the many speakers and my instructors and because of the wonderful friendships I made and experiences I had. It is my wish that all people should have an understanding of peace and conflict resolution as I believe it fosters a mind that is more empathetic, understanding, and more likely to meet obstacles and conflict with an open and creative mind (Course Survey, 2018).

OTHER APPROACHES

Besides Cuyahoga's approach, Pennsylvania's Northampton Community College's Anatasakos (2013) has developed study abroad opportunities for her students to visit Turkey to build peace and improve intercultural understanding. She writes:

Increasingly, community colleges are adopting study-abroad programs as part of their larger efforts to enhance students' global literacy. When community colleges successfully combine a curriculum infused with a global perspective, study-abroad programs, and other types of experiential learning, they can become powerful agents of world peace (p.105).

Delta College (MI) established a global peace studies certificate program in 2012. The peacebuilding awareness that students have attained has advanced the college's service learning programs in Costa Rica, where students have built bookshelves in elementary schools, and Kenya, where they have worked in medical clinics (C. Dykhuizen, personal communication, February 23, 2018).

These approaches suggest the intentionality that is important to creating meaningful peacebuilding experiences. Peacebuilding as a means to global awareness can be effective in advancing concrete objectives that can be measured and recognized. In that peacebuilding seeks to bring about change, incorporating peacebuilding strategies can work towards not only instilling students with awareness, but also fostering in them specific personal and professional aptitudes and skills that can be used to promote their global aspirations. Forage (2013) in offering a humanitarian training exercise at Indian River State College (FL) found that students used their experience to obtain careers in "municipal emergency management agencies, and others have gone on to serve in humanitarian agencies overseas" (p. 198). He writes about one student from Northern Oklahoma College who attended his exercise and then went to work with refugees in Nigeria for the UN High Commissioner for Refugees in displacement camps in Kenya. She attributed her success overseas directly to the exercise that Forage offered (Forage, 2013).

The U.S. Institute of Peace (USIP) has worked to help promote overseas experiences maintaining that "educators, policymakers and students have long recognized the importance of international study in developing new skills and perspectives, which can, in turn, advance peacebuilding skills and goals" using study abroad (U.S. Institute of Peace, Study Abroad, 2017). USIP is an important resource – particularly its public education efforts – for educators contemplating how a travel experience can be aligned with peacebuilding objectives.

CONCLUSION

The potential for advancing global awareness and engagement using peacebuilding as the linchpin is vast. Today, the myriad issues that we face as a global society provide fodder for educators to grab students' attention and engage them in considering and facing global challenges. Community college classrooms will continue to transform, not just with international students, but with U.S. based learners who have been touched by global experiences. Many of these experiences will be based on interaction with conflict and violence, or in dealing with marginalization, which are at the core of peacebuilding. Consider that community colleges are the destination of many men and women who have served in the U.S. military, recently in combat situations in Iraq and Afghanistan. Their experiences strategically and compassionately shared in a classroom can be valuable to helping students develop geographic, political, social, and historic global understanding.

Using peacebuilding as the "means" to the "end" provides context and relevancy for educators striving to get their students to attain global citizenship. As such, students can develop the confidence in the classroom to take steps beyond that which may result in their engaging in a study abroad or travel experience as part of their learning journey. Peacebuilding education can lay the essential ground work for this to happen and result in meaningful experiences for learners.

REFERENCES

Aall, P. R., Helsing, J. W., & Tidwell, A. C. (2007). Addressing conflict through education. In I. W. Zartman (Ed.), *Peacemaking in international conflict: methods & techniques* (pp. 327–353). Washington, DC: United States Institute of Peace.

Alliance for Peacebuilding. (n.d.). *What is Peacebuilding?* Retrieved from http://www.allianceforpeacebuilding.org/what-is-peacebuilding/

American Council on Education. (2012). *Mapping Internationalization on U.S. Campuses: 2012 Edition* (Rep.). Washington, DC: American Council on Education. Retrieved from http://www.acenet.edu/news-room/Documents/Mapping-Internationalizationon-US-Campuses-2012-full.pdf

Anastasakos, V. (2013). Teaching peace through short-term study abroad. In D. J. Smith (Ed.), *Peacebuilding in community colleges: a teaching resource* (pp. 105–117). Washington, DC: United States Institute of Peace.

Anne Arundel Community College. (n.d.). *Law enforcement and criminal justice, social justice option.* Retrieved from https://catalog.aacc.edu/preview_program.php?catoid=16&poid=5853&returnto=2431

Barash, D., & Webel, C. (2002). *Peace and conflict studies*. Thousand Oaks, CA: Sage Publications.

Boutros-Ghali, B. (1992). *An agenda for peace: Preventive diplomacy, peacemaking, and peace-keeping: report of the Secretary-General pursuant to the statement adopted by the summit meeting of the Security Council on 31 January 1992*. New York, NY: United Nations.

Catholic Relief Services. (n.d.). *Peacebuilding*. Retrieved from https://www.crs.org/our-work- overseas/program-areas/peacebuilding

Cuyahoga Community College. (2018). *Course survey*. Cleveland, OH: Cuyahoga Community College.

Cuyahoga Community College. (2018). *Study Abroad*. Retrieved from http://www.tri-c.edu/ programs/studyabroad/index.html

Daoust, I., & Epperson, C. (2013). Teaching human rights and international humanitarian law. In D. J. Smith (Ed.), *Peacebuilding in community colleges: a teaching resource* (pp. 149–163). Washington, DC: United States Institute of Peace Press.

Davidjsmithconsulting.com. (2013a). *Madison College Receives Peacebuilding Support Award*. Retrieved from https://davidjsmithconsulting.com/2013/07/10/madison-college-receives-peacebuilding-support-award/

Davidjsmithconsulting.com. (2013b). *ICRC Expert Speaks at Anne Arundel Community College as part of USIP/IIE Public Education for Peacebuilding Support Program*. Retrieved from https://davidjsmithconsulting.com/2013/03/10/icrc-expert-speaks-at- anne-arundel-community-college-as-part-of-usipiie-public-education-for-peacebuilding- support-program/

Davidjsmithconsulting.com. (2017). *U.S. and Canadian Community College Peacebuilding Programs and Initiatives (including peace studies, conflict resolution, social justice, justice studies, human rights, and mediation)*. Retrieved from https://davidjsmithconsulting.com/north-american-community-college-peacebuilding-programs-and-initiatives-including-peace-studies-conflict-resolution- social-justice-justice-studies-human-rights-and-mediation/

Davis, K. (2013). Community building through a peace and social justice institute. In D. J. Smith (Ed.), *Peacebuilding in community colleges: a teaching resource* (pp. 93–104). Washington, DC: United States Institute of Peace Press.

Farnsworth, K. A. (2013). Peace, conflict resolution, and the essential need for international education. In D. J. Smith (Ed.), *Peacebuilding in community colleges: a teaching resource* (pp. 29–39). Washington, DC: United States Institute of Peace Press.

Fitzduff, M., & Jean, I. (2011). *Peace education: State of the field and lessons learned from USIP grantmaking (Publication No. 74)*. Washington, DC: United States Institute of Peace.

Forage, P. C. (2013). Field training for humanitarians and peacebuilders. In D. J. Smith (Ed.), *Peacebuilding in community colleges: a teaching resource* (pp. 189–198). Washington, DC: United States Institute of Peace Press.

Golden West College. (n.d.). *Peace conference 2018 – Golden West College*. Retrieved from http://www.goldenwestcollege.edu/peace-conference/

Golden West College. (n.d.). *Peace studies program - Golden West College*. Retrieved from http://www.goldenwestcollege.edu/peace/

Golden West College. (n.d.). *Previous peace conferences*. Retrieved from http://www.goldenwestcollege.edu/peace/past-events/

Harris, I. M., & Morrison, M. L. (2013). *Peace education*. Jefferson, NC: McFarland & Company.

Institute of International Education. (n.d.). *About USIP support*. Retrieved from https://www.iie.org/Programs/USIP-Support/About

Institute of International Education. (n.d.). *Support recipients*. Retrieved from https://www.iie.org/Programs/USIP-Support/Support-Recipients

Johnson County Community College. (n.d.). *Peacebuilding and nonviolence: Beyond the Cliches November 2-4, 2017.* Retrieved from http://www.jccc.edu/conferences/peacebuilding/

Lederach, J. P. (1997). *Building peace: sustainable reconciliation in divided societies.* Washington, DC: U.S. Institute of Peace Press

Liu, W., & Opotow, S. (2014). Aggression and violence. In P. T. Coleman, M. Deutsch, & E. C. Marcus (Eds.), *The handbook of conflict resolution theory and practice* (pp. 681–707). San Francisco, CA: Jossey-Bass.

Maill, H., Ramsbotham, O., & Woodhouse, T. (2011). *Contemporary conflict resolution.* Cambridge, UK: Polity.

Miller, C. A., & King, M. E. (2005). *A glossary of terms and concepts in peace and conflict studies.* Geneva: University for Peace.

Milofsky, A., & Berdan, K. (Eds.). (2011). *Peacebuilding toolkit for educators: high school lessons.* Washington, DC: United States Institute of Peace.

Navarro-Castro, L., & Nario-Galace, J. (2008). *Peace education: a pathway to a culture of peace.* Quezon City, Philippines: Center for Peace Education.

Noddings, N. (2005). Global citizenship: promises and problems. In N. Noddings (Ed.), *Educating citizens for global awareness* (pp. 1–21). New York, NY: Teachers College Press.

Olsen, T., & Lipinsky, B. (2017). *Peace studies and conflict resolution – Study abroad syllabus.* Cleveland, OH: Cuyahoga Community College.

Peace Alliance. (n.d.). *Domestic peacekeeping.* Retrieved from https://peacealliance.org/issues-advocacy/domestic-peacekeeping/

Peace and Justice Initiative Newsletter. (2015). Going global, sister school with Kenya institute. *Peace and Justice Initiative Newsletter, 6,* 13.

Peace and Justice Studies Association. (n.d.). *Directory of peace studies and conflict resolution programs.* Retrieved from https://pjsa.lib.miamioh.edu/

Raby, R. L. (2016, July 18). *Community college education abroad foundation and future concerns.* Retrieved from: https://www.diversitynetwork.org/news/298875/Community-College-Education-Abroad-Foundation-and-Future-Concerns.htm

Richland College. (n.d.). *Richland college path for peace.* Retrieved from https://alt.richlandcollege.edu/peace-poles/

Sheehy, K. (2014, November 4). *5 politicians who started at community colleges.* Retrieved from https://www.usnews.com/education/community-colleges/articles/2014/11/04/5-politicians-who-started-at-community-colleges

Smith, D. J. (2002, March 21). Let's give peace sign a chance. *Baltimore Sun.* Retrieved from http://articles.baltimoresun.com/2002-03-21/news/0203210153_1_peace-sign-nuclear-disarmament-popular-culture

Snodderly, D. R. (2011). *Peace terms glossary of terms for conflict management and peacebuilding.* Washington, DC: United States Institute of Peace Press.

Sterns, P. (2010). Global Education & Liberal Education. *Liberal Education, 96*(3). Retrieved from https://www.aacu.org/publications-research/periodicals/global-education-liberal-education

UNESCO. (2018). *What is global citizenship education?* Retrieved from https://en.unesco.org/themese/gced/definition

U.S. Institute of Peace. (2017). *Study abroad.* Retrieved from https://www.usip.org/public-education/students/study-abroad

Valencia College. (n.d.a). *Peace and justice institute, Advisory Council.* Retrieved March 1, 2018, from https://valenciacollege.edu/PJI/advisory-council.cfm

Valencia College. (n.d.b). *Peace and justice institute, about.* Retrieved from http://valenciacollege.edu/pji/about.cfm

Valencia College. (n.d.c). *Peace and justice institute, past speakers.* Retrieved from http://valenciacollege.edu/PJI/programs/past-speakers.cfm

Valencia College. (n.d.d). *Peace and justice institute, programs.* Retrieved from http://valenciacollege.edu/PJI/programs/global-peace-week.cfm

ADDITIONAL READING

Cortright, D. (2013). *Peace a history of movements and ideas.* Cambridge: Cambridge University Press.

McElwee, T. (Ed.). (2009). *Peace, justice, and security studies: a curriculum guide.* Boulder, CO: L. Rienner.

Tongeren, P. V. (Ed.). (2005). *People building peace II: successful stories of civil society.* London: L. Rienner.

Wood, H. (2016). *Invitation to peace studies.* Oxford: Oxford University Press.

KEY TERMS AND DEFINITIONS

Global Engagement: The active pursuit of global experiences.
Global Knowledge: Understanding of global concepts and issues.
Peace Education: The examination of positive visions of peace and correlated actions.
Peace Studies: The interdisciplinary study of conflict, violence, and global solutions.
Peacebuilding: The active pursuit of peace.

Chapter 15
Internationalized Courses on Campus:
A Complement to Study Abroad That Maximizes International Education Participation in the Community College Context

Rebekah de Wit
Community College of Baltimore County, USA

Mary Beth Furst
Howard Community College, USA

ABSTRACT

Internationalizing the community college curriculum offers an opportunity to reach a broad range of students completing their general education requirements. Implementing course internationalization on campus also maximizes the student body's participation in international education, particularly in community college contexts where study abroad is not a viable option for many students due to resource limitations. Efforts to internationalize the curriculum should target high-enrolled courses across campus that fit within existing programs of study. Faculty coordinating these courses are integral in extending the scope of the course objectives by integrating international perspectives. Faculty work is acknowledged through existing structures of professional development and annual review processes. An internationalized curriculum combined with study abroad and other cross-cultural experiential learning forms the framework for an academic enrichment program called Global Distinction.

DOI: 10.4018/978-1-5225-6252-8.ch015

INTRODUCTION

Because few community college students study abroad, and many have work and family commitments that preclude extensive extra- and co-curricular involvement on campus, curriculum internationalization provides a significant opportunity for community colleges to pursue an internationalization agenda. The literature in the field debates whether the appropriate term for this process is "internationalization" or "globalization," and De Wit (2011) offers a particularly concise discussion and definition. We will not extend this discussion here but will note that although our colleges opted for "globalization," in this chapter we use "internationalization" because it is the most common term in the published literature.

This chapter discusses internationalization of the curriculum in the community college context. Specifically, it describes how two Maryland community colleges, the Community College of Baltimore County (CCBC) and Howard Community College (HCC), together developed a curriculum internationalization program and a comprehensive academic enrichment program, Global Distinction, to incorporate internationalized curriculum, study abroad or local cross-cultural experiential learning, and engagement with intercultural activities. This model can serve as a guide for other community colleges that seek to develop or systematize their curriculum internationalization efforts.

CONTEXT

Starting in the 1980s and 1990s, curriculum internationalization became an increasingly prominent topic of discussion and a solid foundation of theory has been cited to support its benefits to students. Groennings' and Wiley's (1990) edited volume *Group Portrait: Internationalizing the Disciplines* is one prominent example that assembled diverse essays on this topic. Numerous large-scale studies and reports have subsequently documented the growth of curriculum internationalization initiatives across the United States (Lambert, 1989; ACE, 2017). These reports indicate that curriculum internationalization is a primary method for U.S. colleges and universities to internationalize their campuses. The following overview provides a rationale.

Study Abroad

Even the most cursory review of published literature on campus internationalization – and curriculum internationalization specifically – over the past several decades reveals that the widest body of studies and essays concern the study abroad context (Dutschke (2009) provided a particularly in-depth discussion of this issue). While study abroad has become more common in the community college context, community college students still participate at rates far below those of students at four-year institutions. Indeed, the most recent *Open Doors* report indicated that in 2015-2016, only 1.7% of study abroad participants from the United States were students pursuing an associate degree (IIE, 2017). Community colleges consequently must turn much of their focus to campus-based initiatives to achieve internationalization goals.

Study abroad has also been by far the internationalization initiative subject to the most research, including research on outcomes. However, a shortcoming of much study abroad research – as well as curriculum internationalization research – has been a multitude of small scale, qualitative approaches and studies without a comparison group. Parsons (2010) is a rare researcher who examined internationalization initiatives in a quantitative, triangulated, and comparative way, exploring how study abroad outcomes compared to outcomes from on-campus internationalization efforts that included curriculum internationalization. Notably, her findings indicate that on-campus initiatives can be as effective as study abroad in supporting students' acquisition of intercultural competence, which further supports the importance of curriculum internationalization for community colleges.

General Education

General education courses (i.e., English, mathematics, science, social sciences, and arts and humanities) are often a focus for curriculum internationalization efforts. Because associate degree programs consist largely of general education courses, a focus on general education is a particularly efficient and fruitful way to internationalize the curriculum in a community college context. Several studies have focused specifically on internationalization of general education courses in the community college, describing generally positive attitudes toward and recommending strategies to support such efforts (Clark, 2013; O'Connor, Farnsworth, & Utley, 2013; Oredein, 2016).

Other Major Published Topics on Curriculum and Campus Internationalization

Curriculum internationalization has also been examined from other angles. One of the most prominent topics is internationalizing courses in specific disciplines (Shooshtari & Manuel, 2009; NAFSA's colloquia from 2015-2018;). Studies focusing on community colleges also highlight the importance of faculty involvement and institutional support (Harder, 2011; Clark, 2013) and surveying students, faculty, and others about their perspectives on curriculum internationalization (Burdzinski, 2014; Robertson, 2015; McRaven & Somers, 2017).

Finally, several case studies of campus internationalization provide an overview of varied approaches that individual community colleges have taken to internationalize their campuses and courses, which include useful models (e.g., Ivey, 2009). Comparatively few publications, however, have provided highly detailed strategies for implementing curricular internationalization across a community college. Among the stronger examples are Butler (2016), who used three case studies to delineate broad strategies to support leadership, faculty buy-in, sustainability, and other key areas; Raby (1995, 2007), who provided lists of strategies for community colleges to pursue; and Patriquin (2016), who reviewed a significant body of related literature in the field to determine the broad approaches to internationalization that might work best for community colleges' career and technical programs. The present chapter further develops the body of resources on specific strategies for implementing a general education-focused curriculum internationalization initiative in the community college context based on the experience at two colleges.

THE PATH TO CURRICULUM INTERNATIONALIZATION AT TWO MARYLAND COMMUNITY COLLEGES

CCBC and HCC, located in central Maryland, sought to expand their international activities and initially focused heavily on campus-wide events with an emphasis on "food, flags, and festivals" (Korbelak, 2014) showcased during International Education Week, Diversity Week, or peppered throughout the academic year. These events centered on international foods and traditions from highlighted countries and generated campus interest by promising an entertaining look at culture. While special events like these were high profile, the faculty organizers ultimately recognized that they often supported only superficial learning, were resource intensive, and sometimes lacked a unifying theme. They then began to explore how a more systematic, transformative, and cost-effective approach to developing global competency would incorporate curriculum.

In 2010, a small team of internationally minded faculty members from both colleges came together in response to concerns over the "food, flags, and festivals" focus and to the modest number of students participating in study abroad programs. The group met monthly to develop strategies for increasing students' intercultural competence on a more significant scale and to build on the contributions made at each college by prior study abroad and other smaller-scale campus internationalization efforts. The group decided to call its internationalization initiative Global Distinction (Furst & Ebersole, 2012). It was designed as an academic enrichment program combining curricular and co-curricular activities and was open to students across all majors and GPAs. Global Distinction was instituted the same year at both community colleges.

The Global Distinction initiative's mission was to provide a framework to support students' becoming "global citizens" through preparation for "academic and professional endeavors in the interconnected and interdependent world of the 21st century." Specifically, the initiative aimed to improve students' global competency through three means: curriculum, cultural immersion, and active campus engagement, as indicated in Table 1.

To facilitate Global Distinction program completion, both colleges soon recognized the need for additional internationalized courses across more disciplines. The program's faculty administrators realized that while the Global Distinction initiative had merit, the curriculum internationalization initiative that supported it (i.e., the process of designating certain courses as internationalized) was potentially even more valuable because of the breadth of the student population affected and the depth of internationalized content that could be achieved.

In their initial approach to defining certain courses as internationalized, the faculty team closely examined their college course catalogs, which included outstanding examples of sociology, anthropology, history, and world language courses already thoroughly infused with internationalized objectives and content. Because of the heavy concentration of these courses in the humanities and social sciences, the faculty team decided that its next goals should be twofold:

1. Ensure that more internationalized course offerings were available across the colleges to reach students in all degree programs.

Table 1. Global Distinction goals and program components

Goal	Program Component
Pursuit of an internationalized curriculum	15 credits of general education courses classified as internationalized, including two semesters of a world language
Cultural immersion/experiential learning	Study abroad or an approved 40-hour domestic cross-cultural work or volunteer experience
Active and reflective intercultural engagement	Internationally-themed activities and events on campus each semester and a reflective essay from students about their co- and extra-curricular learning experiences including activities on campus, abroad, and in the community

2. Define the framework for course internationalized for faculty and establish a formal process for reviewing new internationalized course proposals. The new process would ensure quality and institutionalize the initiative.

The following sections describe in detail the strategies that HCC and CCBC used to develop internationalized course offerings and processes across the colleges.

INTERNATIONALIZING COURSES ACROSS CAMPUS

In 2012, HCC and CCBC received the Institute of International Education's Andrew Heiskell Award for Internationalizing the Community College. Separately, CCBC also subsequently received a positive assessment from an external evaluator with the National Endowment for the Humanities who assessed CCBC's internationalization efforts and described the curriculum internationalization initiative as "the heart of the [college's entire] Global Education program" (Zaki, 2016). The process that the colleges followed to reach this point is offered below as a model for a systematic course internationalization process.

Identifying Courses

The primary internationalization strategy that the colleges were moving toward, reaching students through routine course selection in general education courses, required building a broad repertoire of courses with an international focus. To be both systematic and cross-disciplinary, the faculty teams worked with their colleges' institutional research office staff and identified highly enrolled courses across a range of disciplines to reach the most students and fit within the requirements of existing degrees. The courses that emerged from this analysis were primarily introductory-level general education courses in English, mathematics, psychology, sociology, and biology.

The next step was to explore opportunities to engage the faculty members coordinating those courses. A challenge in garnering faculty support for the effort required demonstrating to faculty that the curriculum internationalization initiative need not involve adding course objectives but rather reframing them. For example, an introductory psychology course objective at HCC was to "compare and contrast the various influences on issues of mental health" (HCC, 2017a). Revised with an international focus, the course objective became "to compare and contrast the various influences on issues of mental health *around the world*" [emphasis added]. This change encourages the study of mental health issues cross-culturally, including increasing awareness; analyzing multiple perspectives; and evaluating approaches, values, and worldviews. Malkan and Pisani (2011) offer a good table with further examples of framing internationally themed learning activities and objectives from a range of disciplines (p. 832).

Some faculty found that changing the verbiage of course objectives opened the door to changing pedagogy. For example, at HCC the revised course objective "Discriminate among various types of economic systems *present in the world*" [emphasis added] (HCC, 2017b) led to exploration in an introductory business course of economic systems as they exist in various countries. Students studied articles from business periodicals and academic sources that illuminated the impact of various economic systems on people in several countries (see, e.g., *What Will Become of China's Ghost Cities?* by Rapoza [2015] for a sample reading added from a popular magazine). Lively discussions, assessments, and student course evaluations indicated students' depth of understanding and connection with the concepts. Reframing course objectives thus spurred instructors to reframe and refresh course content.

Many faculty members considered science, mathematics, and technology courses to be more challenging to internationalize. However, creative approaches to these courses ultimately resulted in successful internationalization of several courses or course sections in these disciplines at both colleges. Among other changes, science and mathematics problems and projects were brought to life using real-world data from organizations like the United Nations and the Organisation for Economic Co-operation and Development (OECD), which collect statistics on subjects ranging from population to economic prosperity. The literature includes numerous examples of internationalized courses and course work in the sciences and mathematics (e.g., NAFSA, 2015-2018).

Early in the process of curriculum internationalization at HCC, faculty leaders in the effort found it useful to classify courses engaged in various stages of the process. Courses with a single internationalized course objective or unit were categorized as Method 1, and courses with infusion of international content through half the objectives or units as Method 2. Table 2 provides a detailed taxonomy. The language of "method" rather than "level" was chosen to minimize the implication of a value judgment and to illustrate that the faculty developers were progressing toward full internationalization of their courses.

Connecting Faculty to Resources

CCBC and HCC found that some faculty needed direction in identifying good sources for information on internationalizing the curriculum. Resources particularly helpful in supporting development of internationalized curriculum were open resources published by the American Association of Colleges and Universities (AAC&U). The AAC&U created 16 *Valid Assessment of Learning in Undergraduate Education* (VALUE) learning rubrics, among them a rubric called *Global Learning*, to assist in sharpening institutional focus and promoting a shared language for student competency (AAC&U, 2015). The rubrics are available for institutional use free of charge and provide a valuable starting point for crafting general education goals. Another strong and free resource for internationalizing courses that is available online is the American Council on Education's *Internationalization in Action* series called *Internationalizing the Curriculum* (2013-2014). This series expands on the course internationalization initiative by also providing guidance on internationalization efforts at the program, degree, and discipline levels. The State University of New York's COIL program (http://coil.suny.edu) also makes some useful resources available free of charge.

Table 2. Methods for internationalizing course content

Method 1	The course has a single internationalized course objective or unit of study.
Method 2	The course has multiple objectives or units (between two and half of them) that are internationalized.
Method 3	More than half the course's elements are internationalized.
Method 4	The course is internationalized throughout.

Providing Faculty Incentives

Some faculty needed little incentive to internationalize their courses. To them, teaching from this point of view came naturally. It was productive to identify these allies early on, as they became ambassadors for broadening the effort. These faculty leaders harnessed their influence and knowledge strategically to maximize their impact on other colleagues and to minimize their feeling of being tasked with yet another campus initiative. Specific incentives that the colleges built over time are addressed under "Step 3" in the next section.

Recognizing Paths via Existing Systems

Identifying opportunities offered within existing structures on the campuses helped HCC and CCBC to align and then expand efforts to internationalize curriculum. For example, both colleges already offered a semester-long learning community program that paired courses with potentially complementary content for the pursuit of joint topics and learning activities. Increasing the numbers of pairings of credit courses with ESL courses helped to support the internationalization of additional credit courses at CCBC. Mentorship programs that paired new faculty members with experienced faculty guides provided another means to support and recruit new faculty to the curriculum internationalization effort. For example, at HCC, internationalizing the curriculum, participating in learning communities, and piloting single units or course objectives with international elements infused were all recognized on annual performance assessments as teaching improvement projects.

Increasing Student Engagement

Bonet and Walters (2016) found that a sociology curriculum with an experiential component and an international perspective increased student engagement and reduced absenteeism. They quipped, "Pity the sociologist who avoids reaching out for the experiential learning afforded by working with refugee and immigrant student populations" (p. 231). The experiential learning that Bonet and Walters (2016) advocate for and that Kuh (2008) and others cite as transformative were achieved at our colleges through such efforts as partnering with the colleges' service learning programs and career offices to expand volunteer and internship options for students to include guided internationalized opportunities. Examples include volunteering to support local immigrants in various capacities or working with local companies (e.g., airlines, importers, tour and travel agencies, etc.) and non-profit organizations (e.g., environmental groups, museums, etc.) in a wide range of positions – from tutor to tour guide to bookkeeper. Such placements paired with mentoring from an experienced faculty member on campus can help students to gain intercultural skills and to better understand the ubiquitous connections between local matters and their international sources, co-developments, and consequences.

Professional development events and information sessions helped to increase faculty members' self-efficacy in incorporating internationalized content via diverse types of learning activities into their courses. Here again, experienced and confident faculty served as program ambassadors in modeling internationalized experiential learning opportunities in the domestic setting and providing hands-on professional development opportunities for their peers.

A number of paths can lead to successful curriculum internationalization. Beginning with some or all the steps above that HCC and CCBC found helpful may to propel a new initiative forward. The next sections offer specific guidance from HCC's and CCBC's experience that may be useful to colleges ready for the next steps: formalizing and systematically growing their internationalized curriculum initiative.

THE INTERNATIONALIZED COURSE PROPOSAL AND ADJUDICATION PROCESS

Once key administrators and a corps of faculty members were invested in planning a course internationalization initiative and grassroots efforts to internationalize new courses were bearing fruit, HCC's and CCBC's next steps were to establish and publish a formal proposal and adjudication process. The process that follows was implemented at both colleges.

Step 1: Both HCC and CCBC formed a faculty committee to develop and oversee the process. Faculty members on the committee represented a range of disciplines so that the proposal criteria and the review process were inclusive, pertinent, and appropriately rigorous. Most committee members had significant experience teaching content with an international angle and meaningful experience with both U.S. and non-U.S. cultures.

Step 2: The colleges developed criteria for assessing proposals for new internationalized courses and used the criteria as the basis for the proposal form. Because the process needed to accommodate a wide range of disciplines and course types, a holistic review process that included quantitative and qualitative measures of internationalization was appropriate. As explained on CCBC's proposal form,

A course need not be strong in all areas since how course content is globalized will, by necessity, vary by discipline. Strengths in one area or areas of a course may offset shortcomings in others. However, all globalized courses must include significant objectives and content with a scope extending beyond U.S. borders.

Examples of quantitative measures of internationalization included such items as the quantity of key course materials involving internationalized content and the percentage of assessments that included critical thinking about international issues. Examples of qualitative measures included descriptions of and rationales for sample learning activities, and samples of assignments involving international themes. The following is a breakdown of the internationalized course proposal components that CCBC opted to assess.

- **Internationalization Across the Course:** Descriptions and percentages internationalized:
    - Objectives
    - Materials (textbook and other resources)
    - Learning activities (including special initiatives such as guest speakers, field trips and other forms of experiential learning, and campus events)
    - Assessments (tests, papers, projects, presentations, research, etc.)
- **Narratives and materials:**
    - Faculty member's reflections on the percentages assigned to the categories above
    - Syllabus

- Sample learning activities and assessments involving internationalized content, each accompanied by description, rationale, and instructional context

Step 3: The colleges formalized and articulated ways to reward and recognize participating faculty. The following initiatives were among those used at CCBC and HCC to foster interest in and support from faculty and administrators for course internationalization.
- Count approved internationalized course proposal(s) as an achievement on faculty members' annual evaluations and grant greater credit to faculty who collaborate with colleagues to internationalize all sections of a given course – not just their own sections.
- Deem development and instruction of internationalized courses institutional service on the annual performance evaluation, or if a faculty member instructing an internationalized course for the first time did not develop the course him-/herself, deem it a one-time professional development achievement.
- Provide high-visibility opportunities for faculty who internationalize their courses to present their strategies and outcomes to colleagues at campus-wide showcases and discipline-specific meetings.
- Award a limited amount of institutional funding to faculty to internationalize curriculum, prioritizing proposals that internationalize all sections of a given course and/or result in enhanced outcomes – for example, the establishment of partnerships with institutions abroad for collaborative distance learning projects.

Step 4: Each college publicized the process. Faculty whose proposals were approved, faculty who taught long-standing internationalized courses, and internationalized course review committee members serving as discipline or school liaisons were deemed effective ambassadors for the program.

Step 5: The colleges developed a process for adjudicating course proposals. Faculty decided that after committee review applicants would receive either immediate approval or suggestions for revision and a subsequent review. Approved courses were designated in the course catalog and semester schedules as internationalized.

Ensuring continued course compliance with program goals was another key part of developing the adjudication process. For example, at HCC, the course review committee was charged with reviewing internationalized courses during institutional course, general education, and program outcomes assessments to ensure continued compliance with the goals of the initiative. At CCBC, instructors who internationalized their own section(s) of a course were reauthorized each semester for inclusion of their internationalized course in the class schedule. The faculty committee also determined a rotating multi-year cycle for the review of courses for which all sections were internationalized.

PROMOTING ENROLLMENT IN INTERNATIONALIZED COURSES

With a critical mass of internationalized courses in the general education curriculum, many students found themselves in courses with an international perspective by happy accident – which is a welcome outcome, as it has enabled the initiative to reach many students who otherwise would not self-select as participants in international education. A more intentional approach to some students' course selection was achieved through the following strategies.

- **Advertisements:** Just as a faculty member offering a new course for the first time might advertise to attract students, the colleges marketed internationalized courses in places such as bulletin boards, online student portals, and campus welcome events.
- **Syllabi and Explicit Discussion:** Ongoing assessment of the course internationalization initiative revealed that students' understanding of the benefits of internationalized course work helped them to see and appreciate connections between their present learning and their future engagement with the world as they progressed in their studies and careers. Students who received explicit information throughout the semester about their course's internationalized design and goals had a more positive response to the course and were more likely to express a desire to pursue further international education activities. This process began with a note on the course syllabus to clarify the overarching aim of the course internationalization process: for example, "This course has been designed to involve content and perspectives from both inside and outside U.S. borders to enhance your intercultural skills and knowledge about today's interconnected world" and was reiterated by faculty throughout the semester. The following is sample end-of-term feedback from CCBC students in a 2014 internationalized course in IT that made its internationalization goals explicit.

The global assignments were my very favorite part of the class. They made me more aware about what is going on around the world instead of just what is going on in my little world. They definitely increased my global and global technology awareness. I got the chance to learn about things that I had not heard talked about and things I had no concern with until now and I am appreciative of that.

The multi-phased project and other global assignments really helped me to open my eyes more. There are many things around the world that are happening right under our noses and we don't even know about them. These issues are big, affecting people worldwide.

The assignments encouraged me to see things from a different perspective. One of the topics that had a huge effect on me is the issue of the "digital dump" and how we dispose of old technology.

- **Earning Global Distinction:** To motivate students to pursue more internationalized courses, both colleges created opportunities for successful completion of the courses to contribute to a credential or an honor. To that end, faculty teaching internationalized courses at HCC and CCBC were asked to include a notation on their syllabi that "successful completion of this course counts as one of five globalized courses needed to earn the certificate of Global Distinction. Learn more at [program website]."
- **Internationalized Course Contract:** At CCBC, a multi-campus institution, the faculty committee developed a "contract" process so that students could arrange with a faculty member to pursue extra assignments to convert a traditional course into an internationalized course. This process had the goal of expanding participation in internationalized courses to students on campuses where fewer course options were available and to students who were advanced enough in their program that few or no internationalized course options existed among the courses still needed for their degree. The contract process also eased the path to credential completion for participants in the Global Distinction program.

- **Recruiting Announcements:** Publicity on the benefits of internationalized courses and the Global Distinction program was a natural fit for first-year students and students enrolled in academic programs with particularly large numbers of fully internationalized courses (notably world languages, anthropology, history, and the like). Faculty administering the internationalized curriculum initiative also created announcements and links to be pasted into syllabi, posted in online course platforms, and added to letters sent to students in the programs with heavily internationalized curricula. These notes alerted students to internationalized offerings in the course catalog and the upcoming semester's schedule and directed them to the Global Distinction website.
- **Internationalized Courses as "Enhanced" General Education Options:** Both colleges were careful to explain in publicity efforts to students that pursuing internationalized courses need not add extra credits to their studies. If they chose to pursue an internationalized course that also fulfills a general education requirement, they would receive the benefits of both types of courses at once.
- **Articulation Agreements With Four-Year Institutions:** HCC and CCBC also collaborated to develop transferrable credits and articulation agreements. Students who complete their associate's degree and earn Global Distinction and then transfer to universities with the agreements can apply several of their Global Distinction credits toward various minor and certificate programs with an international focus.

CONCLUSION

HCC's and CCBC's experience show that a successful and far-reaching curriculum internationalization program can arise from the grassroots efforts of a small group of dedicated faculty. The first step is to appreciate the range of internationally oriented courses already on campus and then to identify opportunities to reach more students via the most highly enrolled courses. The next steps are to identify faculty colleagues who recognize the importance and appeal of engaging students through internationalization and to help the faculty to re-focus their courses with an eye toward international objectives and content. Deliberate efforts that harness faculty energy within the existing college structures of general education and faculty development create more opportunities for students to reap the benefits of an internationalized curriculum. The rewards are internationalization that engages more disciplines, reaches more students, and results in more meaningful student learning.

BUILDING AN INTERNATIONALIZED CURRICULUM AND GLOBALLY DISTINCT CAMPUS CHECKLIST

1. Identify faculty leaders for the effort.
2. Analyze current courses and assess the degree to which they already offer an internationalized curriculum (see Table 2).
3. Identify faculty who naturally explore international topics in their curriculum and offer opportunities for them to engage in efforts to increase the level at which their courses are internationalized – with full internationalization as the ultimate goal.

4. Assess opportunities for existing college structures—curriculum, professional development, learning communities, and faculty evaluation—to support internationalization efforts and expand faculty involvement in the course initiative.
5. Develop institutional processes to adjudicate new internationalized course proposals and to review continuing offerings on a regular schedule. These steps formalize the program to render it strong and sustainable.
6. Help students to understand the goals of the internationalized curriculum and the opportunities it affords them.
7. Sustain and grow the internationalized campus by weaving together internationalized course work, study abroad and domestic cultural immersion experiences, and campus events and activities to create a broad culture of internationalization on campus.
8. Offer credentials and honors that recognize student participation in international programs (i.e., Global Distinction) and develop relationships with transfer universities that acknowledge the students' achievements.

REFERENCES

American Association of Colleges and Universities. (2015). *Global learning VALUE rubric.* American Association of Colleges and Universities Value Rubric Development Project. Retrieved from https://www.aacu.org/value/rubrics/global-learning

American Council on Education. (2017). *ACE releases signature mapping internationalization on U.S. campuses report.* Retrieved from http://www.acenet.edu/news-room/Pages/ACE-Releases-Signature-Mapping-Internationalization-on-U-S-Campuses-Report.aspx

American Council on Education. (2013-2014). *Internationalization in action: Internationalizing the curriculum.* Retrieved from http://www.acenet.edu/news-room/Pages/Internationalization-in-Action.aspx

Bonet, G., & Walters, B. (2016). High impact practices: Student engagement and retention. *College Student Journal, 50*(2), 224–235.

Burdzinski, D. R. (2014). *Attitudes about globalization, internationalization, and the role of student affairs administrators in internationalizing Florida's community and state colleges* (Doctoral dissertation). Retrieved from ProQuest Dissertations and Theses. (UMI No. 3615607)

Butler, D. C. (2016). *Comprehensive internationalization: Examining the what, why, and how at community colleges.* Retrieved from ProQuest Dissertations and Theses. (UMI No. 10111570)

Clark, B. M. (2013). *Faculty perceptions of the importance of internationalizing the general education curriculum in the Florida college system* (Doctoral dissertation). Retrieved from ProQuest Dissertations and Theses. (UMI No. 3558998)

de Wit, H. (2011). Globalisation and internationalisation of higher education (Introduction to online monograph). *Revista de Universidad y Sociedad del Conocimiento (RUSC), 8*(2), 241-248. Retrieved from http://rusc.uoc.edu/ojs/index.php/rusc/article/view/v8n2-dewit/v8n2-dewit-eng

Dutschke, D. (2009). Campus internationalization initiatives and study abroad. *College and University, 84*(3), 67–73.

Furst, M., & Ebersole, T. (2012). *Global Distinction: A Student Pathway to Global Competence, Presentation to The League for Innovation.* Retrieved from https://www.league.org/innovation-showcase/going-global-students-distinction

Groennings, S., & Wiley, D. S. (Eds.). (1990). *Group portrait: Internationalizing the disciplines.* New York, NY: The American Forum.

Harder, N. J. (2011). Internationalization efforts in United States community colleges: A comparative analysis of urban, suburban, and rural institutions. *Community College Journal of Research and Practice, 35*(1-2), 152–164. doi:10.1080/10668926.2011.525186

Howard Community College (HCC). (2017a). College catalog: PSYC 101 General Psychology. *Howard Community College SmartCatalog, 2017-2018.* Retrieved from http://howardcc.smartcatalogiq.com/en/2017-2018/Catalog/Courses/PSYC-Psychology/100/PSYC-101

Howard Community College (HCC). (2017b). College catalog: BMGT 100 Introduction to Business. *Howard Community College SmartCatalog, 2017-2018.* Retrieved from http://howardcc.smartcatalogiq.com/2017-2018/Catalog/Courses/BMGT-Business/100/BMGT-100

Institute of International Education. (2017). *Profile of U.S. study abroad students, 2004/05-2015/16.* Open Doors Report on International Educational Exchange. Retrieved from https://www.iie.org/Research-and-Insights/Open-Doors/Data/US-Study-Abroad/Student-Profile

Ivey, T. (2009). *Curriculum internationalization and the community college* (Doctoral dissertation). Retrieved from http://thescholarship.ecu.edu/handle/10342/2212

Korbelak, S. (2014, April). *The internationalization of community college education: Moving beyond food, flags, and festivals.* Panel presentation at a meeting entitled Internationalization of U.S. Education in the 21st Century: The Future of International and Foreign Language Studies at the College of William & Mary, Williamsburg, VA. Retrieved from www.wm.edu/offices/revescenter/globalengagement/internationalization/ papers%20and%20presentations/StacyKorbelakpresentation2014.pptx

Kuh, G. D. (2008). *High impact educational practices: What they are, who has access to them, and why they matter.* Washington, DC: Association of American Colleges and Universities.

Lambert, R. A. (1989). *International studies and the undergraduate.* Washington, DC: American Council on Education.

Malkay, R., & Pisani, M. J. (2011). Internationalizing the community college experience. *Community College Journal of Research and Practice, 35*(11), 825–841. doi:10.1080/10668920802201377

McRaven, N., & Somers, P. (2017). Internationalizing a community college: A view from the top. *Community College Journal of Research and Practice, 41*(7), 436–446. doi:10.1080/10668926.2016.1195306

NAFSA. (2015). *2015 Global learning colloquia presentations and handouts*. Retrieved from https://www.nafsa.org/Programs_and_Events/Global_Learning_Colloquia/2015_Global_Learning_Colloquia_Presentations_and_Handouts

NAFSA. (2016). *2016 Global learning colloquia presentations and handouts*. Retrieved from https://www.nafsa.org/Programs_and_Events/Global_Learning_Colloquia/2016_Global_Learning_Colloquia_Presentations_and_Handouts

NAFSA. (2017). *2017 Global learning colloquia presentations and handouts*. Retrieved from https://www.nafsa.org/Programs_and_Events/Global_Learning_Colloquia/2017_Global_Learning_Colloquia_Presentations_and_Handouts

NAFSA. (2018). *2018 global learning signature programs: Presentations and handouts*. Retrieved from http://www.nafsa.org/Programs_and_Events/Global_Learning_Colloquia/2018_Global_Learning_Signature_Programs__Presentations_and_Handouts

O'Connor, G., Farnsworth, K. A., & Utley, M. E. (2013). Internationalization of general education curricula in community colleges: A faculty perspective. *Community College Journal of Research and Practice, 37*(12), 966–978. doi:10.1080/10668926.2010.515512

Oredein, A. E. (2016). *Faculty perceptions of factors affecting the internationalization of general education curriculum in Mississippi community colleges* (Doctoral dissertation). Retrieved from ProQuest Dissertations and Theses. (UMI No. 10100418)

Parsons, R. L. (2010). The effects of an internationalized university experience on domestic students in the United States and Australia. *Journal of Studies in International Education, 14*(4), 313–334. doi:10.1177/1028315309331390

Patriquin, W. M. (2016). *Developing intercultural competence in community college career and technical programs* (Doctoral dissertation). Retrieved from ProQuest Dissertations and Theses. (UMI No. 10193559)

Raby, R. L. (1995). *Internationalizing the curriculum: Ideals vs. reality*. Paper presented at the Annual Conference of the Association of California Community College Administrators, San Jose, CA.

Raby, R. L., & Valeau, E. J. (2007). Community college international education: Looking back to forecast the future. In International Reform Efforts and Challenges in Community Colleges (pp. 5-14). San Francisco, CA: Jossey-Bass.

Rapoza, K. (2015). What will become of China's ghost cities? *Forbes*. Retrieved from https://www.forbes.com/sites/kenrapoza/2015/07/20/what-will-become-of-chinas-ghost-cities/4/#683ed15927b2

Robertson, J. J. (2015). Student interest in international education at the community college. *Community College Journal of Research and Practice*, *39*(5), 473–484. doi:10.1080/10668926.2013.879377

Shooshtari, N. H., & Manuel, T. A. (2009). Curriculum internationalization at AACSB schools: Immersive experiences, student placement, and assessment. *Journal of Teaching in International Business*, *25*(2), 134–156. doi:10.1080/08975930.2014.888965

Zaki, H. (2016). *CCBC's center for global education: External review report, August 2016* (Unpublished manuscript). National Endowment for the Humanities, Washington, DC.

Chapter 16
Practical Strategies for Rural-Serving Community College Global Programming

Marc Thomas
Colorado Mountain College, USA

ABSTRACT

Nearly two-thirds of all community college districts in the United States are defined as rural serving, as reported by the Rural Community College Alliance (2017), representing 37%—or more than 3 million—of community college students nationally. These rural districts often struggle to fund and develop global education activities. This chapter will identify promising practices employed by three rural-serving colleges to improve student global competence through international-education programming.

INTRODUCTION

Nearly two-thirds of all community college districts in the United States are defined as rural serving, as reported by the Rural Community College Alliance (2017), representing 37% -- or more than 3 million -- of community college students nationally. These rural districts often struggle to fund and develop global education activities. This chapter will identify promising practices employed by three rural-serving colleges to improve student global competence through international-education programming.

THE RURAL ECONOMIC LANDSCAPE

Challenges faced by rural communities influence the ability of their local community colleges to thrive. Pennington, Williams and Karvonen (2006) reported continued economic barriers for rural communities, including educational attainment and declining tax revenues to support higher education. Gains in student completion in rural areas are happening but are not keeping pace with other geographic areas. The U.S. Department of Agriculture (2017) reported that rural areas are "converging with urban areas

DOI: 10.4018/978-1-5225-6252-8.ch016

in the share of adults without a high school diploma or equivalent, but the share of adults with at least a bachelor's degree is growing faster in urban areas" (p. 2).

The economic barriers rural colleges face often are compounded by heightened community expectations. Miller and Kissinger (2007) described the activities of these community colleges as being "felt more intensely in rural communities than in urban centers," including playing a key role in leisure education from summer sports camps to international study programs (p. 28-29). Rural community colleges are expected to provide comprehensive programming to a relatively small number of students; the inefficiencies that accompany this demand prevent institutions from taking advantage of the economies of scale that benefit larger institutions (Williams et. al., 2007, p. 25).

The Rural Community College: Challenges

Financial stress is an often-cited reality of the rural community college. Pennington, Williams and Karvonen (2006) outlined the core challenge: "Rural community colleges are charged with providing comprehensive programs to a relatively small student population" (p. 642) spread over a large geographic area. Other research has emphasized the weakened agricultural economy as adversely affecting rural colleges. Howley, Chavis and Kester (2013) described "farm closures or consolidation, the movement of industry overseas, contracting labor markets, growing unemployment, declining tax bases and weakening infrastructure" as detriments to the rural community college bottom line.

The funding hurdles faced by the rural community college also contribute to other organizational challenges. Hicks and Jones (2011), in a comprehensive study of three rural community colleges, reported that recruiting and keeping qualified faculty and staff is a challenge for most institutions, "but it is acute for those located in rural areas" (p. 37).

Other challenges regularly cited as challenges for rural institutions include technology and the ability to compete with larger institutions' success at providing online course delivery, an evolving mission from offering primarily transfer courses to increasing demand for workforce training, and a struggle to make the case of their remote academic programs to decision makers in the population center (Pennington et. al., 2006).

Rural Community Colleges: Opportunities

While funding support and economies of scale may offer an advantage to urban and suburban institutions, some researchers have suggested that the nature of rural institutions also can benefit students. Howley, Chavis and Kester (2013) pointed to simpler bureaucratic systems of the small- and medium-sized rural institutions. Their research identified nimbleness in establishing new initiatives. Students interviewed for the study often reported benefits of "responsiveness of faculty and staff, and the relationships facilitated by a small community, made staying in school easier for them and had a positive impact on their retention" (p. 8).

Sparks and Nuñez (2014) reported no disparity in college persistence rates between students attending rural and urban institutions. However, the background and experiences of these two sets of students are distinct, perhaps to the benefit of rural students. "The research indicates that college students in rural settings, through their increased engagement in social activities and community service, could have unique advantages over their urban counterparts in developing social capital that supports their postsecondary persistence" (p. 13).

Rural Community College Internationalization

Data about the quantity and quality of community-college international education at rural institutions is sparse. Farrugia and Bhandari (2016) reported that fewer than one percent of International students studied at rural institutions (p. 8). Harder (2010) surveyed more than 400 U.S. community colleges about their level of overall internationalization, including institutional support for global initiatives, academic programs and activities, faculty opportunities, and number of international students. The formula calculation revealed that 81% of rural institutions had a low internationalization rate, compared to 57% of urban and 54% of suburban colleges (p.157).

Methodology

The case-study colleges for this chapter were selected based on their representativeness as rural-serving institutions and their efforts to meet the challenges of offering global programming. For example, Carl Sandburg College has experienced recent financial disinvestment from Illinois political leaders and has responded with the development of more focused efforts to allow for continued global programming. The Colorado Mountain College was established in 1967 to meet the education needs of remote Rocky Mountain communities and has begun a recent renewed visioning of its global strategy. Snow College in rural Utah has experienced ebbs and flows in its ability to provide students with international education opportunities, but its efforts to intersect campus internationalization and study-abroad operations appear to have inspired new energy for global education.

Fact-finding at each institution included interviews with administrators and faculty leaders who oversee global programming. Students were interviewed whenever possible, but the cycle of two-year institutions meant that students who took part in previous programs sometimes were not available. The research also included review of documents, including syllabi, strategic plans, and budgets. In the case of Snow College, student reflection papers from the College's study-abroad program in Guatemala were reviewed for evidence of cultural competence gains. More detailed explanation of that review process appears in the Snow College case study.

This chapter will review examples of best practices in international education programming from three rural community colleges, focusing on how they strived to provide affordable opportunities abroad amid economic and programmatic challenges. The chapter's emphasis is on sharing practical knowledge that has the potential to be implemented elsewhere.

CARL SANDBURG COLLEGE

The nation watched as Illinois struggled to meet its obligations to college students. Lobosco (2017) for CNN Money, reported on the Illinois budget calamity: "The state's 12 public universities and 48 community colleges have been tightening their belts since before the drastic cuts. State funding, which typically makes up one-third of a school's budget, had already decreased 41% from 2002 to 2015" (para. 4). Selzer (2017) for Inside Higher Ed, reporting on the end of two years without approved higher education budgets, described an uncertain future even after a legislative override of the Governor's budget veto that put education funds in place: "The full ramifications of the new budget -- and the end of the impasse -- can't be fully measured so soon. Still, it is unclear that the impasse seriously hurt both institutions and students by forcing painful cuts, eroding enrollments and driving down confidence in public education. It is also clear that it has changed the outlook of many leaders for the future" (para. 8).

Study abroad at Carl Sandburg College, a community college in western Illinois, is completed within the context of these state funding rollbacks and the College's annual budget performance measures. Its budget strategy for study abroad is included in the "commitment to diversity" category but is connected to the broader enrollment strategy of increasing student participation in study abroad program to help the College "compete with Four Year and Colleges in terms of recruiting students who desire that experience" (Carl Sandburg, 2015, p. 108). This budget document made its case for budget support for study abroad through a key performance indicator for the overall college goal to double the student participation.

Sandburg's Associate Dean, James Hutchings, described the reality: "We live in a debt-ridden, tax-heavy state ... and our students are often working multiple jobs to make ends meet. Finding creative ways to stretch the money is an ongoing creative process" (J. Hutchings, personal communication, October 30, 2017).

Carl Sandburg's Strategy

In response to uncertainty over public funding in Illinois, Sandburg adopted the following strategy to help reduce expenses for their education abroad programs: cutting program costs abroad on individual programs, shifting from third-party travel providers to internal logistics management, and refocusing from longer programs to shorter faculty-led experiences. This strategy has offered challenges and opportunities: "While this has presented an extra workload for those involved, cutting out the tour companies has been key in reducing cost, increasing personalization, and recruiting students" (J. Hutchings, personal communication, Oct. 30, 2017).

Strategy: Shift From External to Internal Capacity

The College is making a shift from a third-party provider model to one centered on building internal capacity to offer global programming at lower costs to students.

In 2017-18, Sandburg's quote for an Italy program from a third-party provider was $3,260 per student, while its cost for running the program internally was $2,500 per student, including a lower student-teacher ratio under the internal model. Cost savings for the virtually identical itineraries included air transportation, use of city public transportation, a hostel rather than hotel and as-needed instead of a full-time guide. In-country logistics have moved from transportation via motor coaches to public transit. Formal dinners were transformed into casual meetings at local hangouts. More free time for exploration and cultural engagement supplanted some planned excursions. The College reported that no liability insurance cost increases resulted from these changes.

Strategy: Reduce Student Costs Through Shorter, More Focused Programs

The Sandburg strategy is anchored by a focus on shorter programs, often 8 to 10 days, instead of summer or semester experiences. Programs are developed solely by faculty, with the goal of providing meaningful and directed programming abroad. The College has a handful of faculty who have developed expertise in travel logistics and group organization and have the capacity to take on this work.

Strategy: Build More Partnerships

Sandburg has reported success in establishing bilateral scholarships. A recent example is a collaboration with Lincoln Land Community College for a six-day biology program in Belize. Under this model, both colleges earned the benefit of meeting enrollment numbers and drawing upon faculty expertise from both institutions but having the flexibility to maintain individual pricing structures.

Students have the option of taking part in study abroad sponsored by the Illinois Consortium for International Study Programs (ICISP) for semester offerings. Sandburg regards this as a good option for students who want longer experiences abroad than is now the institution's focus. Participation in these consortium programs for Sandburg has been an average of one student per year over from 2013-14 to 2017-18.

Strategy: Transform the Student Funding Model

The traditional model at Sandburg has been to fund programs abroad solely through fees billed to students, with the option of a payment plan. As the college transitions its funding model, the following strategies are in the works at this writing:

- Working with the College Foundation to secure grants to help defray student costs, including for items like travel visas and museum entrance fees.
- Establishing a long-term fund from overages and processing fees to allow shifting faculty travel expenses away from the student participant.

Carl Sandburg's enrollment for internal study-abroad programs has grown steadily from three students in 2013-14 to 19 students in 2017-18. The College attributes the increase in participation to the College's efforts to shorten program length and simplify in-country logistics.

Strategy: Maintain Academic Quality and Personalization

In a video recounting their experiences abroad, Carl Sandburg students discussed the essential nature of blending classroom and field learning abroad. Holocaust program participant Abbie Miller described this synergy: "You can sit in a classroom and learn about things for years and years and years and then you might forget it. But once you are doing hands-on experience and learning these things and being a part of the history, it's a little bit different and it sticks with you a lot more" (Carl Sandburg College, 2016). Another student, Angel Peterson, described the vivid emotions attached to experiential learning: "And then we saw the ovens where they burned them, sometimes dead, sometimes alive. And those kinds of experiences are hard to comprehend when you are reading them. Seeing them in person just makes it that much harder" (Carl Sandburg College, 2016).

Practical Strategies for Rural-Serving Community College Global Programming

COLORADO MOUNTAIN COLLEGE

The Colorado Mountain College (CMC), established in the 1960s to bring higher education to rural communities, is spread across eleven locations in the Rocky Mountains. Much of its academic focus is on experiential learning including outdoor education and ski area operations.

CMC Global Strategy: Connect to the College Mission

CMC Vice President Kathryn Regjo described her College's shift in global education philosophy: "Rural community colleges have niches that respond to the needs of their communities. In Wyoming it might be connected to ranching. In Colorado it might be wilderness rescue." (K. Regjo, personal communication, October 2, 2017). The College's Himalayan study-abroad program is one example of developing global programming that transplants local priorities to an international experience.

Abroad Program Strategy and Implementation

Under Hindu tradition, India's Ganges River is "an extension of a celestial river that corresponds to the Milky Way" (Long & Sullivan, 2011, p. 122). The 1,500-mile waterway offers opportunities for rafting, seeing the Hindu pilgrimage for purification in the river, and nearby mountain trekking in the Himalayas. CMC outdoor education faculty member Jeremy Deem wanted to design a learning opportunity that captured outdoor studies along with the history and philosophy associated with India. His thoughts drifted to Rishikesh, India, which he described as the "birthplace and Hindu and prime terrain for outdoor education" (J. Deem, personal communication, November 16, 2017).

The CMC Himalayan program began with the development of a course on the history of India. The first learning outcome describes the overriding course theme: "Demonstrate knowledge of the history of Indian subcontinent as it has developed over time, and specific understanding of the cultural, environmental, religious, and gender-based nuances of the nation's past" (Colorado Community College System, n.d.).

After arrival in India, the learning shifted to the Himalayas, including field courses in River Orientation and Trekking, along with cultural visits and reflection on those collective experiences. The river navigation and mountain trekking experiences centered around the Ganges River. The waterway's origin is in the Himalayas, flowing from several glacial-fed streams, becoming the Ganges where the Bhagirathi and Alaknanda rivers join. Students first entered the Ganges for days trips in-between Devprayag and Rishikesh. Then, they hiked the Tungnath region. Their field work concluded with three days of rafting on the Alaknanda between Rudraprayag and Rishikesh.

Learning outcomes for the technical rafting course included steering, safety, and rescue skills, challenging students in ways different from generally smaller rivers in America.

While the river provides a challenging learning environment for technical skills, faculty described the primary benefit is described as what happens before and after. Students often shifted from acute focus on technical rafting skills to intense reflection. In describing encountering a sacred bathing ceremony at Devprayag, Professor Deem recounted: "We just floated in there on our rafts, at a place where people had spent entire lives planning this sacred trek. Students were jaw-dropped" (Deem, personal communication, November 16, 2017).

In an email to his family, one student described his thoughts about fusing the Indian history he'd read with a mountain trek to a hallowed Hindu destination:

233

The next day we did a morning hike after our 15 miles starting at 330am... This hike was to the highest Hindu temple in India. Very sacred and important to Hindu. Many Indians spend a life time trying to afford to get here or die on the way getting here so this was very special. At around 12000 feet in elevation it was a crazy hike. Very quiet and euphoric moment in my life. (A. Lanata, personal communication, May 24, 2016)

During the 18-day field experience, faculty planted seeds of more humanist learning outcomes including better understanding of inequality and global competition and cooperation. Faculty and students pieced together perspectives on India through what they saw: babies in cardboard boxes, open sewage flowing from rooftops, and large families huddled on a single moped. Student reaction to the stark economic and cultural differences was revealing. "I saw children begging for food under the bridge, and kids scratching at the window of our tuc tuc asking for food. I have never seen that struggle in my life. It was super intense" (A. Lanata, personal communication, December 6, 2017).

End-of-program student reflection on the learning experience began with an icebreaker: write a Haiku poem to inspire conversation among the group. The final course project had each student submit one photograph and description for each course learning outcome.

Strategy: Build Internal and External Alliances

For many years, CMC focused primarily on faculty-led programs, often connected to only one of its Colorado campuses. Sometimes these programs enrolled enough students for a program abroad, sometimes they did not. Starting in 2017, CMC re-evaluated its approach to global programming, beginning to tie programming abroad to more than one campus, explore intersession programs between semesters, secure international partnerships for reciprocal student exchange, and shift its $15,000 international programs budget from a faculty professional development focus to one with more emphasis on supporting global partnerships and costs associated with study abroad (K. Regjo, personal communication, October 2, 2017).

Strategy: Negotiate With a Global Mindset

Respect and humility were at the core of Professor Deem's negotiation strategy to secure the best possible student experience -- and cost -- for students on the India study-abroad program. "Westerners sometimes have an attitude of being the foremost experts" (Deem, personal communication, November 16, 2017). His initial approach with potential guides -- a necessary feature in the sometimes treacherous Himalayan waterways -- included questions like, "Here's the experience we want for our students. What do you recommend?" The early discussions emphasized the potential involvement of the guide service, but not the cost.

The only negotiation topic that required the need for the American faculty to assert their position was on their desire for students to have an extreme learning experience, including faster rapids and enduring more heat than a typical tourist excursion might offer.

Faculty leaders got three bids for guide services in the Himalayas: $4,200, $4,800, $2,500. The low bid was comprehensive, including all:

- In-country transportation, from airport to expeditions to off-day cultural visits;
- Lodging, including two- and four-star hotels;

- Equipment (including tents, rafts, and river and mountain safety equipment);
- Guides from beginning to end.

Deem had an online discussion about the bid with the low bidder, hoping to confirm what he viewed as an extremely favorable bid and assured that all goods and services proposed were included. The American faculty were told: "If American college students are coming to India, we want them to travel with our team. We are the best." The Colorado faculty attribute their negotiation success to their sensitivity to cross-cultural differences.

SNOW COLLEGE

Snow College was founded in 1888 and serves a six-county Utah region including a diverse geography of mountain peaks, deserts, national forests, and waterways. Its economy is anchored by a large turkey ranching and processing industry. The Snow College (n.d.) strategic mission charts an institutional path for "learning and service opportunities, locally and globally, to engage students, faculty, staff and surrounding communities." The College's Center for Global Engagement has carried out that mission through interweaving international student and study-abroad activities. This section will outline how those priorities have been carried out in tandem.

The Snow Strategy: Make Global Education Part of the Institution's Fabric

The strategy includes keeping the importance of international education in front of the faculty, administration, students, and community by actively working to include international education in the college's strategic planning, from the mission statement to annual budget. "Large schools will always have money set aside for global. At a small community college, this could be seen as fringe to the mission" (A. Peterson, personal communication, December 4, 2017). Keeping global competence at the forefront of college and community leaders' mindset is important, including the workplace skills in communication, teamwork, and problem solving that can result from international education. Peterson described a "value placed on global awareness by the administration in the school" that lead to increased support for international education (A. Peterson, personal communication, May 21, 2018). While Peterson cited some initial interest from Snow in international student recruitment as a part of the College's overall enrollment targets, he pointed to growing support from College leaders, stemming from faculty and staff who support global engagement, leading to incorporation of international education into the "cultural fabric" of the institution. The College's location in Utah, where the Church of Jesus Christ of Latter-day Saints' commitment to international mission work is common, also appears to have helped weave this institutional fabric through increased community support for international education.

Strategy: Bring International Activities to Students From Day One

Recognizing that the traditional time for student study-abroad is in the junior year, Snow has opted for a balanced enhancement of international opportunities for its two-year students in campus internationalization and study abroad, with growth in both areas as resources allowed.

Students are likely encounter the College's international focus from the onset of their two-year mission at Snow, from "Culture Night" presentations by international students to increased opportunities for language study and area study through liberal-arts courses. Snow's focus has been on partnerships that facilitate exchange in both directions, two or three faculty led programs, and a recent affiliation with a college consortium in support of increased student study-abroad opportunities. This chapter section includes a review of Snow's partnership with a Guatemalan school that offers a study-abroad opportunity for Snow students and for Latin American students to attend Snow.

Strategy: Intentional International Partnerships

To help build a diverse campus, Snow looks for students who are a good fit with Snow's academic program focus. For example, Snow has put emphasis on recruitment at private bilingual high schools in Ecuador, where student current language abilities and tuition cost lend themselves to study at a U.S. community college.

Strategy: Communicate the Rural Brand

"Places like rural Alaska or Utah are not usually places international students think of going" (A. Peterson, personal communication, December 4, 2017). Selling points often include a:

- Good education at an economical price
- Safe learning and living environment
- Strong feeling and practice of continuous service and support
- Holistic educational experience, including experiencing the American dream, along with meeting young people from other countries.

Abroad Program Strategy and Implementation

Realizing that many teachers were not well-prepared to work with the diverse populations that make up many American classrooms, Snow College Education Chair Richard Squire took steps to integrate multicultural lessons in the classroom with field experience abroad. The result was EDUC 2851, "Global Perspectives on Education, Latin America," a two-credit classroom course with the option of an additional credit for students who took part in a Guatemalan classroom experience.

Julio Salazar, the founder and principal of the K-12 Colegio Mesoamericano school in Guatemala, was familiar with the traditional model of English instruction in Latin America, which allowed for an hour or so of English a week, separate from other subjects. Salazar believed that his master's degree in productivity engineering could help him approach instructional design in a different way – from the perspective of process and product. In systems engineering, the inputs used in the process often include taking into account the customer needs, the project mission, and strategy for measuring effectiveness of the resulting product or output. As an engineer, Salazar said he "didn't know that certain things couldn't be done. If I encountered a problem I simply sat down and analyzed it, looked at the desired output, and figured out what I needed" (J. Salazar, personal communication, January 15, 2018).

Practical Strategies for Rural-Serving Community College Global Programming

What was the result of this engineering-inspired process? Dual-immersion instruction, with English embedded in almost every instructional activity at the school. In the spring of 2017, this model was aided by Snow College education majors, who team taught with Guatemalan teachers for 12 days, jointly planning English learning activities and working with elementary students in small classroom groups and over recess.

English activities and practice starts in preschool program at Colegio Mesoamericano. By upper elementary, social studies, science, and language arts are taught in English. Lessons typically start with vocabulary, such as *la erupción* in a science lesson on volcanoes, and continue with illustrations, videos, hands-on practice, and student explanations of key concepts. To ensure that students capture learning outcomes, teachers watch for common threads of misunderstanding and revisit those concepts.

With this dual immersion project, the emphasis is on both Americans and Guatemalans learning. "Their mindset changes. Their intensity and attention changes. Both students learned that the world is smaller than they thought it was" (J. Salazar, personal communication, December 4, 2017).

One activity with reported cultural and competency benefit was when Guatemalan students served as tour guides for Snow students at nearby Iximché, a Mayan archeological site. As example, the Guatemalan students learned how to play an ancient Mayan ballgame, and practiced pronunciation and gestures to teach the college students how to play. Salazar reported enhanced employment and higher education opportunities for his students who used activities like this to become proficient in English.

What do Snow students hope to achieve from the course? The course syllabus sets out the following overarching learning goal: "They will gain an awareness that by understanding the culture students and their families come from, they can then make educationally sound decisions for their students and increase the students' educational success" (Snow College, 2017).

Student learning abroad was assessed by Snow primarily through student reflection papers. Students responded to the prompt, "How has this experience changed you and your perspective on helping students? How has this experience opened your eyes to the needs of students coming from not only other countries but diverse backgrounds?"

To offer an independent assessment, this author reviewed the 14 papers for evidence of cultural competence gains during the study-abroad experience through the lens of the Association of American Colleges and Universities (n.d.) Intercultural Knowledge rubric. The AAC&U rubric category that most closely corresponds to the question students answered is "empathy," which outlines the following criteria for each step along the competence continuum:

1. **Benchmark:** Views the experience of others but does so through own cultural worldview.
2. **Milestone:** Identifies components of other cultural perspectives but responds in all situations with own worldview.
3. **Milestone:** Recognizes intellectual and emotional dimensions of more than one worldview and sometimes uses more than one worldview in interactions.
4. **Capstone:** Interprets intercultural experience from the perspective of own and more than one worldview and demonstrates ability to act in a supportive manner that recognizes the feelings of another cultural group.

Table 1. Assessment of rubric level of student paper

Student Paper	Evidence of Cultural Competence	Assigned Intercultural Competence Rubric Level
Paper 1	"This trip helped me broaden my cultural horizon which led me to new understandings … there are different people no matter where we are and they all need to be treated as such: differently"	2 – Milestone
Paper 2	"Seeing the tears of joy of a principal collecting books for the children of her school, or the damp eyes of grateful parents who have sent their child to attend Snow College from Guatemala is a sight the heart won't forget."	2 – Milestone
Paper 3	"I had never realized how difficult school can be for some people. By the end of the week, we were communicating quite effectively in a mixture of Spanish, English, and non-verbal messages."	3 – Milestone
Paper 4	"I was surprised at how well some of the students spoke English."	1 - Benchmark
Paper 5	"I saw how environmental concepts are implemented in a different culture, and socioeconomic background. Nature and civilization seem to be more intertwined here."	3 – Milestone
Paper 6	"We were able to talk with them in English."	1 - Benchmark
Paper 7	"I got to see first-hand how typical children in third-world countries live. This was such a tender experience."	2 - Milestone
Paper 8	"The sixth-graders were also more willing to find other ways to communicate. Such as pointing, writing on the board, and asking friends for help … If we are not willing to learn their language we cannot expect them to learn our language"	3 – Milestone
Paper 9	"Even for the students who knew more English, my accent is vastly different than someone who is from Guatemala teaching English so it was hard for them to understand me sometimes."	3 – Milestone
Paper 10	"In one of the classrooms that I was working I noticed it had no crayons, no paper, no toys for recess, no computers … After going on the trip I am having a hard time complaining about the little things."	2 – Milestone
Paper 11	"Students in the states moan and complain about most of the tasks they were asked to complete, but these kids jumped right into what they were asked."	2 - Milestone
Paper 12	"I felt so lost and confused when they would speak Spanish. This is how it feels when someone isn't used to English."	3 – Milestone
Paper 13	"Even though we could not verbally communicate we found many different ways such as acting out what we wanted each other to do. Even though I know I looked goofy to the kids, this really helped me because I got out of my comfort zone."	2 - Milestone
Paper 14	"Understanding your culture … will help you succeed. While it is important to understand this about themselves, it is also important … to learn about different cultures."	3 – Milestone

The ability to gauge cultural competence gains depended on the students' willingness to provide concrete examples of and reflect on their experiences. For example, a paper that described a "life-changing experience" or "expanded world view" but was absent examples of the interactions that led to competence gains was not assigned a rubric level beyond "1 Benchmark" because evidence of development beyond that level was not shared. Table 1 below includes evidence from each student paper that is representative of the cultural gains presented by the student, along with this author's assessment of the rubric level.

When applying the AAC&U rubric, Snow study-abroad students demonstrated gains in intercultural competency. While a pre- and post-test assessing gains during the abroad period did not happen, the students' written reflections are noteworthy because each example included represents a specific intercultural experience occurring in Guatemala that would not have otherwise occurred. Under this author's review, five of the 14 papers demonstrated reflection reaching the rubric level 3 of "intellectual and emotional dimensions of more than one worldview."

CONCLUSION AND RECOMMENDATIONS

While global education practitioners at rural-serving institutions encounter common challenges, their solutions are varied, as revealed in the case studies in this chapter. Common themes found across the case studies, but resulting in different outcomes, included:

- **Connecting Study Abroad to Other Institutional Strategies:** The Colorado Mountain College has worked to link its global programming to the needs of its rural community, while Carl Sandburg has correlated its study abroad participation to its College's overall student recruitment strategy.
- **Devising Strategies for More Efficient Study-Abroad Operations:** The blueprints ranged from a shift away from third-party providers to shorter faculty-led programs at Carl Sandburg to some shift from traditional faculty-led opportunities to third-party-provided mutual exchange opportunities at the Colorado Mountain College.
- **Cultivating More Partnerships:** Carl Sandburg's strategy included fostering domestic partnerships to share study-abroad resources, while Snow College looked for global partnerships to leverage the potential synergies between study abroad and campus internationalization.

The most compelling lessons from the experiences of these small institutions lie in their focus on making strategic connections. These links range from connections between study-abroad programs and the institutional strategic mission to integrating local economic priorities with international programming. The continued ability of small and rural-serving community colleges to make a commitment to international education likely depends on their ability to amalgamate these often disparate priorities.

REFERENCES

Association of American Colleges and Universities. (n.d.). *Intercultural knowledge and competence VALUE rubric*. Retrieved from https://www.aacu.org/value/rubrics/intercultural-knowledge

Carl Sandburg College. (2015). *July 1, 2015 to June 30, 2016 budget*. Retrieved from http://www.sandburg.edu/About/Budgets-And-Financial-Information/2016-budget- final.pdf

Carl Sandburg College. (2016). *Experiencing the Holocaust*. Retrieved from https://livesandburg-my.sharepoint.com/personal/jhutchings_sandburg_edu/Documents/Sandburg/Abroad/Experiencing%20the%20Holocaust.mp4?slrid=fc73409e-8031-5000-d3fa-b27af9cb4128

Colorado Community College System. (n.d.). *Common course numbering system*. Retrieved from https://www.cccs.edu/educator-resources/common-course-numbering-system/

Farrugia, C., & Bhandari, R. (2016). *Open Doors*. New York, NY: Institute of International Education.

Harder, N. (2010). Internationalization efforts in United States community colleges: A comparative analysis of urban, suburban, and rural institutions. *Community College Journal of Research and Practice*, *35*(1-2), 152–164. doi:10.1080/10668926.2011.525186

Hicks, C., & Jones, S.J. (2011, Fall). At issue: survival tactics for small, rural-serving community colleges. *The Community College Enterprise*, 28-45.

Howley, C., Chavis, B., & Kester, J. (2013). 'Like human beings': Responsive relationships and institutional flexibility at a rural community college. *Journal of Research in Rural Education*, *28*(8), 1–14.

Lobosco, K. (2017, June 29). *Illinois is starving state colleges and universities*. Retrieved from http://money.cnn.com/2017/06/29/pf/college/illinois-budget-higher-education/index.html

Long, J., & Sullivan, B. (2011). *Historical dictionary of Hinduism*. Lanham, MD: Scarecrow Press.

Miller, M., & Kissinger, D. (2007). Connecting rural community colleges to their communities. In P. Eddy and J. Murray. eds. Rural community colleges: Teaching, learning, and leading in the heartland. *New Directions for Community Colleges*, *137*(Spring), 27–34. doi:10.1002/cc.267

Pennington, K., Williams, M., & Karvonen, M. (2006). Challenges facing rural community colleges: Issues and problems today and over the past 30 years. *Community College Journal of Research and Practice*, *30*(8), 641–655. doi:10.1080/10668920600746086

Rural Community College Alliance. (2017). *Opening doors they alone open*. Retrieved from http://ruralccalliance.org/opening-doors

Seltzer, R. (2017, July 10). Picking up the pieces in Illinois. *Inside Higher Education*. Retrieved from https://www.insidehighered.com/news/2017/07/10/illinois-leaders-re-evaluate-higher-education-after-first-state-budget-two-years

Snow College. (2017). *EDUC 2851. Global perspectives on education, Latin America syllabus. Instructor: Richard Squire*. Ephraim, UT: Snow College.

Snow College. (n.d.). *Core themes, goals, and objectives*. Retrieved from https://www.snow.edu/academics/office/themes.html

Sparks, P. J., & Nuñez, A. (2014). The role of postsecondary institutional urbanicity in college persistence. *Journal of Research in Rural Education*, *29*(6), 1–19.

U. S. Department of Agriculture, Economic Research Service. (2017). *Rural education at a glance: 2017 edition*. Retrieved from https://www.ers.usda.gov/webdocs/publications/83078/eib-171.pdf?v=42830

Williams, M. R., Pennington, K. L., Couch, G., & Dougherty, M. A. (2007). Preparing rural community college professionals. *Community College Enterprise*, *13*(1), 23–35.

Chapter 17
A Case Study Exploring Ways to Increase Access to Education Abroad for Career and Technical Students With Limited Availability

Anne-Marie McKee
Volunteer State Community College, USA

ABSTRACT

This chapter looks into the experiences of the career and technical students who studied abroad and how their experiences affected them and transformed them in the years since studying abroad. The purpose is to examine the experiences of studying abroad for CTE students attending a rural-based community college. In this study, relevant categories and themes of meaning for CTE study abroad students were identified. One goal of this study was to see if these students' study abroad experiences affected them in the workplace and if the service-learning component of their study abroad experiences led to other altruistic practices.

INTRODUCTION

Community colleges serve nearly close to half of the undergraduate students in the United States. While some community college students choose to transfer to four-year institutions, other students attend community colleges for career and technical education (CTE). CTE students pursue associate degrees in applied science (AAS). An AAS degree is for students who want to gain technical expertise in a specific career field (TNeCampus, 2018).

The majority of U.S. community college students enroll in educational programs to gain knowledge to advance in a chosen career path. Community colleges prepare the majority of health field workers, and more than 80% of first responders with postsecondary credentials, paramedics, emergency medical

DOI: 10.4018/978-1-5225-6252-8.ch017

A Case Study Exploring Ways to Increase Access to Education Abroad

technicians, firefighters, and police officers (Boggs, 2010). The only opportunity a CTE student has to study abroad to gain global knowledge is during the short time he or she is a student at a community college (Raby, 2008). At VSCC, CTE programs include Ophthalmic Technician Program, Diagnostic Medical Sonography, Sleep Diagnostic Technology, Physical Therapist Assistant, Dental Assistant Program, Respiratory Care Program, Health Information Management, Fire Science, Paramedic, Emergency Medical Technician, and Radiologic Technology.

Within the community college landscape, CTE students are less likely than other community college students to study abroad for numerous reasons. One hurdle for CTE students to study abroad is that their coursework is consecutive are include the summer semester. The summer academic term still remains the most popular time for students to study abroad, with 38% of students who study abroad doing so during the summer term (USA Study Abroad, 2018). Students who are pursuing ophthalmic technology certification at Volunteer State Community College (VSCC), complete their college and clinical studies in 18 consecutive months without taking traditional academic breaks. Alternative study abroad options for CTE students must be developed to meet the needs of this student niche. As such, VSCC, a study abroad opportunity was built into students' preexisting course of study, enabling these students to have an international education experience.

To determine whether study abroad affected CTE students, I conducted this case study in which I examined seven years of ophthalmology career program students who participated in a study abroad program that was created to meet their academic scheduling needs. These ophthalmic students had the opportunity to study abroad because their program director was able to develop, in concert with a national service club, and VSCC, a study abroad program that fits within their 18-month program. Had this study abroad opportunity not been built into these students' academic program, these students would not have been able to participate in study abroad.

In addition to the study abroad component in Guatemala, students also engaged in a service-learning component. Ophthalmology students worked with more than 200 Guatemalans each day to fit them with donated eyeglasses. Therefore, while students were studying and learning, they were also providing services to individuals in need. Without the services the students provided the Guatemalans served would not have obtained much needed ophthalmic care. While Guatemalans benefited from the students' work, the students were also able to gain more than 40 hours of personal hand-on training.

This study provided a look into the experiences of the students who studied abroad and how their experiences affected them and transformed them in the years since studying abroad. The purpose of this study was to examine the experiences of studying abroad for CTE students attending a rural-based community college. In this study, relevant categories and themes of meaning for CTE study abroad students were identified. One goal of this study was to see if these students' study abroad experiences affected them in the workplace and if the service-learning component of their study abroad experiences led to other altruistic practices.

METHODS

This study collected both primary data and secondary data. I examined nine years of documents, interviewed, and observed 14 students and two faculty members using a variety of qualitative method strategies. A nonprobabilistic, purposive sampling approach was used to identify subjects.

The interviews were one-on-one and were thematic, topic centered, and biographical. I reviewed several documents from students who participated in the education abroad program from 2009 - 2018 to understand the learning process. These documents included pretravel essays, study abroad applications, and post-study abroad reflection paper. Themes were developed and analyzed, and patterns identified.

Initial data analysis was conducted as data were collected and memos were written in conjunction with each interview to preserve perspectives and potential linkages as they became apparent during data collection (Merriam, 2007; Glesne, 2010). Since interviews can build on each other, it was critical to review each transcript for missed opportunities, which could become part of the next interview. The analysis in this manner also allowed for the development of potential themes and emerging answers to research questions.

CASE STUDY PROFILE

From 2009 to 2017, 44 students enrolled in the VSCC ophthalmic career program participated in a study abroad program that was aligned to meet the program's requirements. Out of the 44 students who participated in the study abroad program, fourteen students and two faculty members agreed to participate in this case study. The ophthalmic career program consisted of general education courses plus ophthalmic-specific technical courses.

Study participants were asked questions regarding the impact of traveling and learning with a cohort, cultural adaptation attitudes, and descriptions of what it was like working and learning in another country with faculty members who had previously taught students in a traditional classroom environment. Students ranged from traditional-aged students to individuals who were returning to college to cross train into other careers. Table 1 describes the case study participants. As found in the literature, Caucasian women are the majority of study abroad participants. While this case study's population was primarily Caucasian women, the age of the women was not typical for study abroad participants.

Building Career Pathways Through Study Abroad

When participating in this program, students receive many benefits such as technical skills, language skills, and an understanding of their place in the global environment while working alongside instructors. George S. Barrett, Chairman, and CEO of Cardinal Health in Dublin, Ohio said, "Successfully working across borders—both geographical and cultural—is critical to our long-term success. Global fluency is a critical business skill. And the greater our global fluency, the better we are at breaking down barriers and building bridges" (Draper, 2015, para. 9).

Field Training

Over the past 15 years, community colleges have experienced three major changes that resulted in a new institutional paradigm. The concepts that led to this paradigm shift are the community colleges as the Learning College; New Vocationalism; and the Entrepreneurial College. Today, community college administrators and faculty look at issues and ask how a problem can be addressed so the result positively affects student learning. Instruction is designed to meet the needs of economic development as well as the needs of students. With increasing pressure to find new funding sources, this new paradigm provides

A Case Study Exploring Ways to Increase Access to Education Abroad

Table 1. Participant demographics

Pseudonym	Cohort	Race	Age	Gender	Occupation	Prior Global Travel
Ann	2011	w	28	f	stay-at-home mom	Yes
Dr. Smith		w	43	f	instructor	Yes
Barbara	2016	w	20	f	ophthalmic tech	No
Hannah	2016	w	24	f	student	No
Kathy	2015	w	24	f	student	No
Helen	2016	w	21	f	ophthalmic tech	No
Katherine	2014	w	33	f	ophthalmic tech	Yes
Paula	2015	w	26	f	ophthalmic tech	No
Tom	2009	b	29	m	Navy	No
Alex	2014	w	30	f	ophthalmic tech	No
Kenesha	2013	w		f	receptionist	No
Wilma	2014	w	32	f	ophthalmic tech	No
Nancy	2013	w	48	f	admin assistant	Yes

a rationale for career-focused study abroad programs (Brennan, 2005, pg. 8). "The vocational community college student is not shopping for a vacation, an experience, a course she needs, or perhaps even a vague learning opportunity. She is shopping primarily for an affordable way to gain qualifying, or new skills to increase her job prospects in an increasingly competitive economy" (Brennan, 2005, pg. 9). CTE educators must work to prepare students to meet the challenges and demands of the career pathway they have chosen. Workforce development is essential for CTE students. How an international study experience affects students' "qualifications for future employment and their successful participation in community life" (Brennan, 2005, p. 16) must be considered with designing programs for CTE students. One way to accomplish this goal is to have students participate in actual job experiences. For CTE students, this means while they are studying abroad, they need to be able to participate in work similar to what they will do once they graduate. For the ophthalmic study abroad program, the hands-on learning happens in the overseas health clinic and this learning is coupled with what has been taught in the classroom. The combination of the traditional classroom with hands-on learning is what CTE students are seeking in study abroad programming. Gaining international work experience helps students build skills toward their competency-based education, and directly prepares them for their careers.

Mastering specific skills necessary to be a successful technician in an ophthalmologist office is a primary goal for students in the VSCC ophthalmic program. The study abroad trip to Guatemala gives participating students the opportunity to hone ophthalmic skills by learning via field training. While in Guatemala, the students worked in a local makeshift health clinic helping hundreds of patients each day. Barbara, 20 years old (cohort 2016), described the students' workday. "We would set up our clinic and start admitting patients. We worked consistently until lunch screening patients. If the patients see at least 20/30 or better, we did not refract them or give them glasses. We took a short lunch break and then headed back to the clinic until 4:30. Then we loaded back on the bus and drove back to Antiqua."

Katherine, 33 (cohort 2014), who held a B.S. degree in business, returned to the community college in 2014 to pursue her interest in health care. She said, "Dr. Smith set us up for success. We knew exactly what we were going to encounter." Nancy (cohort 2013), the oldest student in the study, expressed she felt she performed better in the field than she did in the classroom. "Classroom settings are very different as opposed to hands-on situations. I get nervous with question, answer/testing atmosphere, and forget a lot of things that I do know. But when in a working atmosphere I am hands on."

Ann (cohort 2011) said, "The days were exceedingly long and somewhat grueling, but I have never felt as though I have made more of an impact in any other activity. I loved having to think on my feet and adapt my skills to meet the needs of the patient sitting in front of me. My absolute favorite memory is when we were able to give a patient with 20/400 vision (barely able to see the big 'E') a pair of glasses that instantly correcting her vision to 20/20. She honestly had no idea what she had been missing until her vision was corrected." After graduating from the ophthalmic program, Ann worked in a Texas medical practice. The field training helped her gain technical skills. At the time of the study, she was a stay-at-home mom.

The time students spent assisting patients in Guatemala gave them practical experience that carried over to the workplace once they returned home. Paula (cohort 2015) who worked as a certified ophthalmology technician in a small, rural, southern ophthalmology office, said, "Refracting we had to use trial frames. When you are having to switch lenses in and out, number one it gets a little confusing. Then when you come to something that is so much easier to use like when we use our phoropter it just makes it so much easier. I think about that time, and how hard it was and you kind of had to get a rough estimate. You had to do the best that you could. Then you come home to work, and you think this is so easy. It gave you a better skill set. I feel more confident when I do patients' glasses now from doing that because that was rough. We had to use such basic equipment in Guatemala. When I go back here, I was like kissing my phoropter. I was like, I have missed you."

"I love being able to see and learn different cultures outside of my own," said Helen (cohort 2016 and graduate volunteer 2017). "Refracting was a piece of cake when I came back home. I fly through it now. I seriously could do it with my eyes closed in a dark room. I refract like a boss!"

Learning skills in an environment absent of first-world luxuries changed the VSCC students' perspectives. "Lack of equipment is one of the biggest challenges encountered while working in the clinic," said Dr. Smith. "Tests performed on expensive pieces of equipment in the U.S. are performed by hand using very basic equipment in Guatemala. Students come back from Guatemala as better clinicians with a different perspective of what constitutes a difficult clinical case. Patients that one might have thought were difficult before Guatemala are much easier upon your return, knowing you have all of the state-of-the-art equipment at your disposal."

Program director, Dr. Smith said goals were set for ophthalmic students to determine their ability to utilize the knowledge they gained in class, lab, and clinical field experience. Students not only demonstrated a high level of critical thinking but also grew in their skill and confidence levels while working abroad.

Prior to students embarking on Guatemala study abroad, the ophthalmic director established learning objectives. These learning objectives were:

1. Students will be able to use and apply the principles of refractometry and ophthalmic optics to obtain the needed glasses prescription using manual trial frame refraction methods.
2. Students will be able to use and apply the knowledge learned in the Ophthalmic Program to obtain the glasses prescription on patients speaking a language other than English.

A Case Study Exploring Ways to Increase Access to Education Abroad

"A lot of the patients we saw had problems with their eyes that were far more than what we had ever encountered before back in the states at our rotations. My medical values were always questioned I feel like. There were many situations in which it seemed that even though I had been in the classroom learning for almost a year about the eyes, I was still so unsure of what was going on at times" said Kathy (cohort 2015).

When students work in an environment that is less than ideal, they learn to think on their feet and not always depend on technology. These career-training opportunities enable students to hone occupational skills that can be transferred back into the workplace.

Language Skills

Acquiring additional language skills is important in the healthcare field. Several of the students prior to traveling to Guatemala had previously taken Spanish courses either in college or during their K-12 education; however, none of the students was at a conversational level with their Spanish skills. Although there were translators at the Guatemala clinic available to help, the students commented that the language barrier affected their study abroad experience and made them more aware of not being proficient in a second language.

"The language would probably be the most difficult to adapt to. Although Spanish is the official language, they have about 20 other languages there, and they speak extremely fast," said Kenesha, (cohort 2013). Wilma, 23 (cohort 2014), who at the time of the study, was an ophthalmic technician and an ophthalmic photographer, she explained the Hispanic culture had interested her for some time. "I had taken Spanish classes, so I have always been interested in the Hispanic culture. I found it very interesting and getting to see how the language and people play into their culture is amazing. Being in Guatemala helped me understand the language more."

"I had to communicate with people who did not speak English. We were given translators to help us in our work; however, we still had to do a great deal of communication on our own. My Spanish improved as I worked alongside people who only spoke Spanish," related Ann (cohort 2011).

Although some of the VSCC students spoke a little Spanish, most only had a basic understanding of the language. "I understand letters in Spanish. Being in Guatemala made me more patient with those who do not speak English or people who are deaf," said Alex (cohort 2014). Kathy said the language barrier was difficult. She said that at times it was challenging to communicate with patients. Wilma (cohort 2014) said that the trip helps her now in her job when treating Spanish-speaking clients.

"When I was at Lodens, there was a patient who just spoke Spanish. Having gone to Guatemala and being able to refract people there helped me get through a very basic exam with a patient who didn't speak English," said Hannah (cohort 2016 and graduate volunteer 2017). "Facial expressions helped a lot. It did encourage me to learn a second language," said Tom (cohort 2009).

"The most challenging aspect of dealing with people from other cultures is learning how to communicate in a respectful manner. So much of our communication is nonverbal and nonverbal communication varies greatly between cultures. Being able to communicate not only effectively, but respectfully requires skill and finesse. When I served with an ophthalmic team in Guatemala, some of these scenarios included properly identifying the ophthalmic complaint, communicating with those who are incapable of reading a standard eye chart, providing adequate care to a greater volume of patients and communicating respect while also providing care," said Ann (cohort 2011).

"I have no problem treating people who don't speak English," said Helen (cohort 2016). Helen also said she would still like to study Spanish and planned to go back to Guatemala. Working with patients in the United States who do not speak English as their first language is different from working in a country where English is a second language. Immersing students in a country, whose first language is not English, put students in a position where they had to adapt. Once the students returned to the United States, they had more empathy and patience for people who spoke English as a second language.

Working and Learning With Instructors Outside the Classroom vs. Inside a Traditional Classroom

Graduates revealed that their experiences in study abroad enabled them to increase their ophthalmic skills beyond what was possible in a traditional classroom or a clinical setting because they learned side-by-side with their faculty. Students expressed when they studied in a conventional classroom, problems could be anticipated and predicted. Working side-by-side in a rural, international health clinic produced unanticipated interactions with patients. Alex, a certified ophthalmic technician, 30, reflected on being able to connect with her instructors. "I got to see them both wear different hats than just in the classroom. Dr. Smith challenged us to use our skills in a different way." Being able to work with their instructors mimicked a working environment versus a classroom environment. This type of mentoring enabled the students to grow in their ophthalmic skills. Ann (cohort 2011) responded:

One has a one-sided perception of educators when only seeing them in a traditional classroom environment. When we are learning from and working alongside these educators in a different country, I was able to see more of their humanity. The distinction between 'us and them' became somewhat blurred as we all worked together toward a common goal. The teacher/student roles were still there as we relied on direction and knowledge from our educators, but we each had our place as adults. I think this was possibly one of the greatest lessons that I learned while on the trip. We are each responsible for our abilities, education, knowledge, initiative, etc. It is easy to rely on educators to bear the brunt of the load in a traditional classroom setting. When one is working side by side with these same educators in a country with a different language and limited supplies, you realize how much you need to lean on each other to make things happen. Respect grows in both directions: Students for educator and educator for student.

Time students spend with instructors in the classroom is limited. However, when students work in the field alongside instructors, the learning opportunities stretch. Students are able to see instructors actually performing procedures that are merely demonstrated in traditional classrooms.

Other study participants expressed similar benefits to working and learning with an instructor outside the classroom versus inside a traditional classroom.

"A classroom environment teaches you skills and knowledge, but working in the field really teaches you problem-solving techniques and hands-on skills that you can only learn by doing. Working with Dr. Smith was even better because I got to see her work and get advice from her and she could use every opportunity as a teaching moment. I learned so much working side by side with her. I also got to know her as a person, which I consider to be very valuable," said Barbara, 20 (cohort 2016).

When students learn from instructors in a traditional classroom, they compartmentalize the instructor as a teacher. Out in the field, the role of the faculty member expands from merely lecturing to real-life, real-time demonstration. Not only do students learn as they observe the faculty in the field, the students also participate with the faculty member assisting an actual client. This type of learning cannot be duplicated in a traditional classroom.

Empathy and Compassion

Many of the students mentioned they were drawn to study in the healthcare field because of a genuine desire to help and care for others. Students developed a new awareness of the benefits United States citizens have compared with individuals in developing countries, specifically as they relate to healthcare. Because of being exposed to patients living in poverty, students developed empathy and compassion for the people they were treating.

Katherine (cohort 2014) explained that providing a person in Guatemala with over-the-counter reading glasses made significant changes in a person's life. "A lot of patients we saw could not read anything, not even their bible. You would give them something as simple as readers, and it changes their life. It really put into perspective that a lot of people don't have what I have, and that put me in check."

Barbara, 20 (cohort 2016), related, "When you are shown extreme poverty firsthand, it is really hard to cope with that. When you are looking out of your bus window, and there is a girl, no more than three years old wandering half-dressed through a barren, deserted camp, it is hard not to yell at the bus driver to pull over so that you can do something. I had never been out of the country before, and I certainly had never seen these kinds of living conditions."

The participants noted conveniences taken for granted in America, were not readily assessable in in Guatemala. "In America, we have access to all kinds of healthcare, and we are used to being able to receive it quickly. But there are those who live in less developed societies and need the help of others. Each and every one of us has different skills and trades. Sometimes giving just means taking your time to do what you do best for other people. It is easy to get caught up in life and forget that we are fortunate to have healthcare," said Barbara, 20 (cohort 2016). Ann (cohort 2011) said, "I better understand the extreme poverty and wealth disparity. I understand the culture and people better as well as the lack of proper medical care for the destitute."

Paula, 26 (cohort 2015) expressed "the hardest part was the poverty. It makes you look at people in a totally different light. When I came home, I can't even describe the feeling. I just felt so empty. I just felt like there was nothing. I was sad and almost depressed."

Living and working in the United States without exposure to global issues limits students to see only situations from one perspective. Having the opportunity to travel and work internationally with patients who do not have the opportunity for basic eye care, demonstrated to the students the advanced level of technology and healthcare available in the United States.

Soft Skills

Learning and honing career skills are top priorities to CTE students. Due to the shorter period of time CTE students are in college, it is important to these students to utilize all available time in and out of class. While in Guatemala, students say they learned soft skills, and their actual ophthalmology skills improved because of the work they did.

Katherine (cohort 2014) said being in Guatemala helped her see things differently. "It really put into perspective that a lot of people don't have what I have. That really put me in check."

Participants expressed that due to their international experience, they were more confident, more understanding with patients, and were more open minded toward people who were different from themselves. Several students mentioned they were more altruistic since studying abroad and now participated in more volunteer activities than before they studied abroad.

Soft skills are learned when students study abroad. Students develop new mindsets that cannot be taught in classrooms. "Being there with my classmates made us a good team. We learned to work together. I think we would all say that we came back a strong team," added Barbara (cohort 2016).

"A lot of the patients we saw had problems with their eyes that were far more than what we had ever encountered before back in the states at our rotations. My medical values were always questioned I feel like. There were many situations in which it seemed that even though I had been in the classroom learning for almost a year about the eyes, I was still so unsure of what was going on at times. We did experience some overwhelming times, but I always would ask the girls for help, or Dr. Smith," said Kathy (cohort 2015).

According to a report in the publication Fast Company, there is a skills gap between what managers are looking for and what college graduates have to offer. The top soft skills hiring managers found lacking in recent graduates were communication, leadership and teamwork (Dishman, 2016). Studying abroad directly addresses this gap by enabling students to be in an environment where they must learn to communicate, lead and work as a team in order to meet the goals of the study abroad experience.

Understanding Cultural Differences

Cultural differences can affect employees in any career field. For healthcare workers, understanding cultural differences can affect the quality of care individuals receive. "It is the goal of faculty involved in our international project to educate the students with which we work on cultural differences. We want our students to have respect for different foods, variations in the meaning of words, differences in the celebrations of various events including religious events, and different political views when traveling. We teach that you don't have to agree or like something, but you do have to respect the differences someone may have," said Dr. Smith.

Now on active duty for the U.S. Navy as an E-5 Petty Officer 2nd Class (cohort 2009), Tom said he would never forget "Helping all those children who could not see get glasses and leave there happy. I one time had this little girl who cried because she could finally see better. I am currently in the military, and we have to adjust to different cultures all the time. I learned a lot while I was there and it taught me to appreciate what I have here." Tom is a father of three young sons, ages three, four and five. He says that although he does not work in ophthalmology anymore, the experience in Guatemala was one of the first times he worked with people from other cultures and that helped him in the military, as he had to adjust to different cultures all the time.

Employment Edge Competencies Necessary for the 21st Century

Studying abroad gives students an employment edge and equips them with skills and competencies that employers say are necessary for the 21st century (Farrugia, 2017). There are specific critical skills that employers in the 21st century are seeking and study abroad opportunities can be created to meet these workplace needs. "Guatemala was my first trip overseas, or even in a plane for that matter. I came back a changed person. I have since flown 15 times in three years. I utilize my experience in Guatemala in my current workplace 3-5 times a week. I now have a better understanding of the Hispanic culture and language barriers between me and a patient," said Wilma. Participants commented that participating in study abroad helped them become more adaptable and improved their international skills. Most of the students had never traveled outside the United States, and several had never flown on an airplane. "I feel I have more of a global mindset since participating in the trip to Guatemala," said Ann (cohort 2009). "I was definitely more small-minded before the trip, and I have worked consistently to push my boundaries and step outside of my comfort zone since returning home."

RECOMMENDATIONS

More study abroad research specific to CTE students attending community colleges would help build successful study abroad programs that could be replicated at other community colleges.

- Protect what students learn during study abroad through reflection. Reflection should be made during the trip via notebooks or informal discussions. Students should also write a reflection piece upon return from their trip (Strange, 2017).
- Alternative study abroad options for CTE students must be developed to meet the needs of this student niche.
- Study abroad administrators at community colleges can use this study to plan, implement, and evaluate study abroad programs for CTE students.
- Study abroad opportunities can be built into CTE students' preexisting program of study, enabling these students to have an international education experience.
- Students stated in interviews that learning while working side-by-side with faculty was a powerful learning paradigm. Opportunities for student to learn with faculty outside the classroom should be encouraged.

DISCUSSION

Study abroad for CTE students at community colleges requires planning differently from study abroad at 4-year institutions. Unless a study abroad component had been embedded into their coursework, these students would not have been able to participate in study abroad because they do not have traditional breaks such as spring break and summer break. In addition to creating a specifically timed study abroad program, the director also deliberately created actual career experience for students while they were abroad. The work skills gained during the study abroad enhanced these students' career skillsets and improved their confidence.

CTE students do not view study abroad as just an opportunity for cultural immersion, but instead a chance to gain on the job experience. CTE students at community colleges who take part in study abroad programs gain enhanced work skills. For example, if ophthalmic students can successfully refract a patient who does not speak English using manual equipment in a hot, basic facility, which may or may not have electricity, they can certainly work with individuals in the United States who do not speak English well.

As demonstrated in this study, study abroad does help develop CTE students' cognitive, intrapersonal, and interpersonal skills. Students participating in this study articulated how because of participating in study abroad, they were now more flexible, confident, and self-aware. The students remarked how while abroad, their worldviews were challenged and as a result, their ability to demonstrate leadership and tolerance for ambiguity developed.

In general, what works for most CTE students are highly structured experiences that include in-depth interactions, versus just moving from place-to-place without any authentic connection to the local environment. Study abroad for CTE students is a viable way for community college students to gain exposure to the world and develop more of a global perspective. It is imperative that accurate planning and implementation is considered when creating a study abroad experience for CTE students at community colleges. CTE students at community colleges want an international experience where they can gain job skills that make them more marketable for jobs and better careers.

CONCLUSION

The purpose of this study was to explore a study abroad program that was developed at a community college to accommodate CTE students. Nine cohorts spanning from 2009-2017 were examined, and it was found that short-term study abroad for CTE students attending a community college did have positive effects on the students both personally and professionally. The students in this research project said that because they had participated in a study abroad experience, they had a better idea of how they fit into the world. Prior their study abroad these students understood some international issues, but after experiencing poverty, language barriers, and other situations firsthand, these students had a better appreciation for the importance of understanding and empathizing with cultural differences.

During this study, it became apparent that the students who participated in study abroad program had impactful experiences that lasted many years after the conclusion of the program. Participants commented that participating in study abroad helped them become more adaptable and improved their international skills. Most of the students in this study had never traveled outside the United States, and several had never flown on an airplane. The students elaborated on their study abroad experiences and how taking part in the activity changed their perceptions of the world. Moreover, students remarked how participation in study abroad would not have been possible without the development of a study abroad program designed explicitly for their career and technical program at a community college.

CTE students want a study abroad experience with actual job experience integrated into the trip (Tillman, n.d.). This study shows a CTE program at a community college can be included in study abroad opportunities if steps are taken to develop a program that fits the specific needs of the students.

International engagement following this study abroad experience was evident. While students may not have been able to travel extensively abroad due to job and financial responsibilities, participants expressed because of their international experience, they were more confident, more understanding with patients, and were more open-minded toward people who were different from themselves. Several students mentioned they were more altruistic since studying abroad and now participate in more volunteer activities than before they studied abroad.

REFERENCES

Amani, M. (2011). *Study abroad decision and participation at community colleges: Influential factors and challenges from the voices of students and coordinators* (Doctoral dissertation). Available from Proquest Dissertations and Theses database. (UMI No. 3438831)

Arps, K. (2013). *Study abroad for community college students.* Retrieved from Monterey Institute of International Studies website: http://sites.miis.edu/kristenarps/files/2013/12/Study-Abroad-at-Community-Colleges-Presentation.pdf

Boggs, G. R. (2010). The evolution of the community college in America: Democracy colleges. *Community College Journal, 82*(4), 36–39.

Brennan, M., Frost, R., Hagadorn, E., Martin, M., & Natali, J. (2005) Education abroad and the career development of community college students: Four case studies. In M. Tillman (Ed.), Impact of Education Abroad on Career Development: Four Community College Case Studies II (pp. 7-16). Stamford, CT: American Institute for Foreign Study Publications.

Chieffo, L., & Griffiths, L. (2004). Large-scale assessment of student attitudes after a short-term study abroad program. *Frontiers: The Interdisciplinary Journal of Study Abroad*, (10): 165–177.

CollegeBoard. (2008, January). *Winning the skills race and strengthening America's middle class: An action agenda for community colleges*. Retrieved from http://professionals.collegeboard.com/profdownload/winning_the_skills_race.pdf

Curran, S. J. (2007, November-December). The career value of education abroad. *International Educator*, 48-52.

Dishman, L. (2016). These are the biggest skills that new graduates lack. *Fast Company*. Retrieved from https://www.fastcompany.com/3059940/these-are-the-biggest-skills-that-new-graduates-lack

Draper, K. (2015). CTE and global education: The perfect marriage. *Education Week*.

Education Advisory Board. (2017). *Survey: 70% of community college students work—and for many, it's too much.* Retrieved from EAB website: https://www.eab.com/daily-briefing/2015/10/29/seventy-percent-of-community-college-students-work

Farrugia, C., & Sanger, J. (2017). *Gaining an employment edge: The impact of study abroad on the 21st-century skills and career prospects in the United States, 2013-2016.* New York, NY: Institute of International Education.

Glesne, C. (2010). *Becoming qualitative researchers: An introduction.* Pearson.

Hulstrand, J. (2016, November-December). Advancing faculty-led programs at community colleges. *International Educator*, 44-47.

Jenkins, D., & Weiss, M. (2011). *Charting pathways to completion for low-income community college students.* New York, NY: Teachers College, Columbia University.

Jones, S. R.-K., Rowan-Kenyon, H. T., Ireland, S. M.-Y., Niehaus, E., & Skendall, K. C. (2012). The meaning students make as participants in short-term immersion programs. *Journal of College Student Development, 53*(2), 201–220. doi:10.1353/csd.2012.0026

Kolodner, M. (2016). *Fewer than one in seven community college students transfer and gets a bachelor's degree---but there is new hope.* The Hechinger Report.

Kowarski, L. (2010). Colleges help students to translate the benefits of study abroad. *Chronicle of Higher Education*. Retrieved from the Chronicle of Higher Education website: https://www.chronicle.com/article/Colleges-Help-Students-to/123653

Merriam, S. B. (2007). *Qualitative research and case study applications in education.* San Francisco, CA: Jossey-Bass.

Mezirow, J. (2000). *Learning as transformation: Critical perspectives on a theory in progress.* San Francisco, CA: Jossey-Bass.

Pussar, B., & Levin, J. (2009). *Re-imagining community colleges in the 21st century.* Retrieved From https://cdn.americanprogress.org/wp-content/uploads/issues/2009/12/pdf/community_colleges_reimagined.pdf

Raby, R. L. (2008, September). *Expanding education abroad at U.S. community colleges.* New York, NY: Institute of International Education Study Abroad.

Simon, P. (1980). *The tongue-tied American: Confronting the foreign language crisis.* New York, NY: Crossroad.

Spencer, S. E., & Tuma, K. (2002). The guide to successful short-term programs abroad. Washington, DC: NAFSA.

Strange, H., & Gibson, H. J. (2017). An investigation of experiential and transformative learning in study abroad programs. *Frontiers: The Interdisciplinary Journal of Study Abroad*, 85–100.

Tillman, M. (Ed.). (2005). *Impact of education abroad on career development: Four community college case studies.* Stamford, CT: American Institute for Foreign Study.

Tillman, M. (2014). *On the linkage of international experience and student employability, in career integration: Reviewing impact of experience abroad on employment.* CAPA & Learning Abroad Center, University of Minnesota. Retrieved from https://www.capa.org/sites/default/files/Career_Integration_Booklet_lowres.pdf

TNeCampus. (n.d.). *Earn an associate degree online in Tennessee.* Retrieved from https://tnecampus.org/associates

USA Study Abroad. (2017). *Study abroad data.* Retrieved from: https://studyabroad.state.gov/

Yin, R. (1989). *Case study research: Design and method.* Newbury Park, CA: Sage.

Chapter 18
Utilizing a National Association to Increase Access to Education Abroad

Jayme Kreitinger
College Consortium for International Studies, USA

Tanith Fowler Corsi
Virginia International University, USA

ABSTRACT

Today, community colleges seek to internationalize amid an environment of widespread internal budget cuts and restricted resources. It has become increasingly common for community colleges to incorporate a global mission into their strategic plan despite current economic realities dictating that funding get allocated to priority projects such as student enrollment and academics before they reach international activities. A common misperception is that international education is a costly endeavor that has the potential to put a strain on the institutional budget. In reality, international education operations can be set up to be self-supporting and generate revenue for the institution through strategic study abroad pricing models. This chapter constructs a scenario to explore how community colleges can do more with less to expand their international agenda while navigating a climate of internal budget constraints and institutional downsizing.

THE CURRENT U.S. COMMUNITY COLLEGE LANDSCAPE

There is no denying that the world we live in is driven by accelerating economic and social change fueled by technological advances and all-encompassing globalization. It has now become a practical imperative, and no longer a choice, for institutions of higher education to incorporate a global dimension into their mission and curriculum to prepare students to successfully navigate and contribute to a global workforce.

In the past decade, many community colleges have embraced this internationalization strategy and incorporated it into their learning communities. In 2015, 7,105 community college students studied abroad, and 95,376 international students were enrolled at two-year institutions (Institute of Interna-

DOI: 10.4018/978-1-5225-6252-8.ch018

tional Education, 2016). According to the American Association of Community Colleges, over 60% of community college students were employed either full-time or part-time and 50% were low-income and received financial aid in 2015. Work responsibilities and insufficient personal funds represent major challenges to studying abroad (American Association of Community Colleges, 2017).

In recent years, many community colleges have also seen a sharp increase in the requests for international partnerships and initiatives on the part of overseas institutions and businesses seeking to capitalize on the growth and economic potential of U.S community colleges (Dembicki, 2015). International partnership requests include but are not limited to student and faculty exchanges, dual-degree programs, and general partnerships that leave room for a variety of creative collaborative options. This increase in interest in international partnership can be attributed to the fact that overseas institutions recognize that there is a market for sending students to U.S community colleges which offer lower tuition and an alternative way to access the U.S higher education system which has historically been a powerful magnet. Overseas institutions are also looking for ways to leverage new relationships to exchange faculty and students and share best practices around curriculum development and community college/local business partnership models that can be applied in their home countries.

Houston Community College (HCC) has expanded the term of "community" to "global community" as it recognizes that globalization has made the world smaller. HCC's global identity stems from a large international student program, with over 5,000 international students from 200 countries, more foreign students than any other two-year college. HCC attracts international students looking for affordable tuition and a welcoming campus environment. The college has also been pro-active in raising its international profile by recruiting students from Asia, offering global seminars and study abroad opportunities, and signing agreements with overseas institutions (Fernandez, 2015).

Many community colleges that have strong internationalization programs also have a President or Provost who is committed to developing strategic plans for global awareness and competence connecting the institution, local businesses and governmental entities (Boggs & Irwin, 2007). The joint global community mission is to think globally and act locally to create a climate of global connectedness and understanding (Raby & Valeau, 2016). In this cooperative relationship, community colleges develop policies that support international education whereas local businesses are depended upon to provide funding for internationally-related activities (American Association of Community Colleges and Association of Community College Trustees, 2006). Both the American Association of Community Colleges and the Association of Community College Trustees maintain respective global missions and memberships in recognition of the interconnectedness of our society.

A major paradox with this trend towards global stewardship is that community colleges seek to internationalize amid an environment of widespread internal budget cuts and restricted resources. It has become increasingly common for community colleges to incorporate a global mission into their strategic plan despite current economic realities dictating that funding get allocated to priority projects such as student enrollment and academics before they reach international activities. A common misperception is that international education is a costly endeavor that has the potential to put a strain on the institutional budget. In reality, international education operations can be set up to be self-supporting and generate revenue for the institution through strategic study abroad pricing models (Raby & Valeau, 2016). Northern Virginia Community College (NOVA) is a good illustration of this paradox as it developed a global mission statement in 2005 considering its large number of international students and global programs, but even as this institution's global mission developed the organizational framework remained largely lacking (Stearns, 2009). At many community colleges, such as NOVA, current global initiatives including study abroad have been paused to focus on other priorities such as enrollment and internal budget. Consequently, there is a growing disconnect between the community college mission and the reality which puts a strain on growth of global initiatives on many campuses. How can community colleges do more with less?

INTRODUCING A HYPOTHETICAL EXAMPLE

To illustrate this point, let's construct the following scenario which the authors, in working with community colleges, have seen to be common as colleges seek to expand their international agenda while navigating a climate of internal budget constraints and institutional downsizing.

In our hypothetical example, Community College X has experienced growing momentum over the last decade led by the higher administration's desire to globalize and broaden its mission to the rest of the world to capitalize on enrollment growth and global economic collaborations. This drive stalled in recent years with enrollment decreases and internal budget struggles, yet the college's mission remains focused on opening the college and surrounding community to the world.

In the past year, a new Vice President was put in place to guide College X out of its financial difficulties. This Vice President has asked staff and faculty to take on global education responsibilities in addition to regular duties, while limited additional financial resources or professional training have been made available. As a result, administrators are left to struggle with how to grow international education opportunities and help foster the college's global mission without having the necessary infrastructure in place. This results in a financial and professional strain on staff and faculty and study abroad is often put on hold preventing students from benefiting from global learning opportunities.

A common myth is that study abroad is that it is an expensive extracurricular endeavor limited to certain disciplines (Nevadomski Berdan, 2014). Based on the authors' experience working with a broad variety of community colleges, this misperception is often evident at institutions where faculty and administrators are tasked with advising students on study abroad opportunities while operating with limited resources and access to professional training. Consequently, students are not always made aware of all available study abroad and financing options and choose to overlook these important experiential learning opportunities (Noel, 2016).

Key elements needed for community colleges to successfully fulfill their institutional global mission are established internal procedures, a dedicated infrastructure and available staff training. If these elements are missing or not accessible due to lack of resources and structure, there are study abroad models that can help alleviate the pressure on staff and administrators while allowing students to take advantage of global learning opportunities.

THE CONSORTIUM MODEL ADVANTAGE

One potential solution to the challenges many community colleges face in developing and expanding education abroad is the consortium model. A consortium can be defined as a "formal association of institutions in a state or region choosing to pool their human and financial resources to offer collaborative programs for all member institutions" (Korbel, 2007, p. 48). When discussing a consortium model within international education, this means a group of institutions and even possibly organizations that are coming together to collectively provide avenues of support, services, and resources. Consortia are formed to provide an avenue to produce solutions to institutional needs, projects, and programs that they would not or could not attempt on their own (Korbel, 2007). The consortium model can also unite a group of peers towards a common mission and to sustain the passion, energy, and creativity that is needed to move forward international objectives when staff, time, and financial resources are limited. A consortium is only as strong as its members as each member brings knowledge, skills, and resources that contribute to the objective of creating something larger than the sum of its parts.

There are several avenues in which community colleges can create access and opportunity for both the institution and their students in education abroad through the association or consortium model. By leveraging an established circuit of international education opportunities and resources, technical or community colleges can significantly expand their institutional capacities with limited startup and ongoing administrative costs. A consortium can provide its members immediately with access to a portfolio of quality and affordable education abroad programs (McLean, 1990, p. 50), capacity building and professional development resources, and a network of international education peers to share knowledge and expertise. This model provides an avenue towards efficiency, lows costs, and stability while maintaining quality and low barriers to access (McLean, 1990, pp. 48-50). Each institution can have ownership over the product and result without being solely responsible for the input, which provides the institution with the ability to scale and maintain low administrative costs (Heisel & Kissler, 2010, pp. 11-12).

Associations and consortia exist at varying levels with different focuses encompassing the breadth and depth of international education, including large national groups as well as more targeted state and institution driven initiatives. As an example of a national association, the Community Colleges for International Development (CCID) includes both U.S. and international institutions and supports U.S. two-year institutions in furthering their internationalization initiatives and supporting their efforts in developing a global workforce (CCID, 2018). The Florida Consortium for International Education (FCIE) is an institution-driven consortium that was created by state community colleges and universities to promote internationalization and foster collaboration on comprehensive internationalization (FCIE, 2018a). As a state consortium, FCIE is positioned to advocate on unique international education initiatives faced by Florida institutions and acts as a liaison with state and federal agencies to advocate for international education within Florida (FCIE, 2018b). Another example of a state consortium is the California Colleges for International Education (CCIE). CCIE is comprised of over 80 California community colleges and together they support a variety of programs to increase international understanding through education, including faculty exchanges, international business, international development, international students, internationalizing the curriculum, and study abroad (CCIE, 2018). There are different costs and benefits associated with participating in these varying types of consortia and associations, including membership fees, travel, participation in conferences, level of support, and stability (Korbel, 2007).

Leveraging Opportunities and Resources

To explore avenues allowing institutions to leverage an established circuit of international education opportunities and resources while reducing costs, barriers, and maintaining stability, we will use the example of the College Consortium for International Studies (CCIS). CCIS was founded in 1973 when three two-year institutions in New York, New Jersey, and Pennsylvania had concerns of access in education abroad and wanted to provide more opportunities for their students. The model initially started with these institutions forming a confederation to allow each other's students on their institution's education

Utilizing a National Association to Increase Access to Education Abroad

abroad programs with CCIS coordinating and overseeing the education abroad programs (Hess, 1982, p. 29). The model's aim was exponentially increasing the students' access to quality education abroad programs without straining existing institutional resources. CCIS has maintained its mission to create access and opportunity in education abroad with three major pillars to support this mission: education abroad programs, institution and individual capacity building and professional development, and advocacy in the field.

Since its founding, CCIS has grown from a loose federation of three two-year colleges to an incorporated non-profit with over 100 U.S and international members. Membership includes higher education institutions with varying backgrounds, sizes, U.S. and international, public and private, to intentionally create a community of international educators working toward a common goal while bringing a variety of perspectives (McLean, 1990; CCIS, 2018a). The unique ability to bring together varying perspectives allows the consortium model to be constantly innovative and support the ever-changing needs of students and institutions.

As a formal association of members, CCIS has a set of bylaws to ensure proper governance and rights of the members while maintaining stability within the organization. A board of directors provides guidance on the strategic direction of CCIS to best support its members and sustain the consortium through the years as higher education and international education change. An additional set of governing councils and committees that develop policies, procedures, best practices, and the monitoring and evaluating of all CCIS services provide an additional level of management. All members have voting rights and CCIS is essentially owned and managed by the members for the members. A small central office provides a needed degree of support in creating and maintaining the avenues for member collaboration as well as non-profit management and leadership.

Members are ultimately the providers of the programs and services offered through the consortium, but members can be and are involved to varying degrees based on their needs and their institution's objectives. Membership is institutional and higher education administrators, senior international offices, faculty, and education abroad coordinators and advisors are all welcomed and included in the institutional membership representation. Membership types and roles include sponsors, hosts, and sending institutions. CCIS sponsors are U.S. member institutions that sponsor and administer the study abroad programs and capacity building programs. The international institution members, CCIS hosts, provide the academic and programmatic logistics on the ground. The majority of U.S. members participate in CCIS as sending institutions and utilize the programs and services provided by the sponsors, hosts, and CCIS central office. Member institutions both provide and utilize the sharing of best practices, resources, materials, and trainings to collaboratively support their work in education abroad. CCIS also produces an annual conference that creates the time and space to learn from each other and plan for future collaborations. CCIS's foundation is built on this idea of programs and services created and produced by member collaborations.

The primary collaboration and benefit to members is the portfolio of education abroad opportunities. An accredited U.S. institution and CCIS member can become a program sponsor and this sponsor institution develops the education abroad program in collaboration with the international institution, also known as CCIS host institution. Currently, CCIS host institutions are spread across the globe in 28 countries (CCIS, 2018b). Some examples include Edge Hill University in England, Al-Akhawayn University in Morocco, and Shanghai University in China. Because programs are initiated and administered by U.S. institutions, the program opportunities go beyond the most popular destinations to focus on providing the right opportunities for all students. The sponsor institution manages the program administration, student advising, application processing, billing, transcripts, and health and safety. The host institution provides the academic and programmatic services on the ground with oversight from the sponsor institution. CCIS governance committees, made up of members, manage the program assessment and quality control processes.

Through this model of sponsor and host institutions, members can benefit from programs that are academically vetted by an accredited U.S. institution as well as the CCIS governance committees and board of directors. One agreement with CCIS acts as an agreement with all consortium programs, greatly simplifying the program agreement process and allowing for the transfer of financial aid and credits. The model of programs being based and run by the U.S. member institution also keeps program costs low by reducing the overhead needed to run programs centrally through a large organization. Additionally, the sponsor institutions can benefit from program stability by increasing access to students and filling programs as well as reducing program costs as student enrollments increase.

Each new program is proposed by the sponsor institution to the CCIS Academic Programs Committee for review and acceptance into the CCIS program portfolio. The Academic Programs Committee conducts a thorough review for academic and program quality as well as the capabilities of the sponsor institutions to administer the program. Once this committee approves a program, it is proposed to the board of directors for adoption. Once a program is accepted into the consortium, it must abide by the CCIS program monitoring and evaluation policies, which includes periodic surveys, assessments, and comprehensive program reviews including site visits. Programs must be re-approved by CCIS on an ongoing basis to ensure academic and programmatic quality.

Beyond the education abroad programs, capacity building is another key tenant of the CCIS consortium model. The annual conference is the largest endeavor, which focuses on identifying members' needs and pooling member knowledge and expertise in the field. The annual conferences go beyond knowledge-sharing by creating a space for members to begin collaborations on other education abroad initiatives to essentially do more with less resources. Another way members collaborate to be greater than the sum of their parts is through the sharing of best practices and resources through trainings such as webinars but also through the direct sharing of materials such as faculty manuals, protocols for risk management, and student advising toolkits. The CCIS central organization also facilitates peer mentoring, particularly for new members that are establishing their education abroad operations.

The benefits of a community of international educators with established trust and respect has the potential for collaborations that extend beyond the essential services. U.S. members can leverage a base of vetted international institutions to develop faculty-led programs with expertise and facilities on the ground to improve program quality while reducing the program cost significantly. U.S. and international member institutions can collaborate on research initiatives, as well as faculty and student exchange. Institutions are able to leverage the vetted network of peers for joint grant proposals. Additionally, U.S. institutions looking to increase their international student populations or even expand into dual or accelerated degree programs have a group of international institutions with a sound history of international collaborations from which to draw partners.

BENEFITS OF THE CCIS CONSORTIUM MODEL: CASE EXAMPLES

As clearly shown, CCIS and its model of an organization is a beneficial model of organization and support for community colleges which often identify with the common Community College X hypothetical scenario described earlier. The challenges associated with a campus mission to internationalize without added resources can be alleviated through the external peer support network provided by an institutional consortium model. This model can help diminish the additional burden of responsibilities on campus administrators who benefit from outside professional expertise and guidance with the added peace of mind that global learning opportunities are vetted by U.S sponsoring institutions. Community colleges also have the added benefit of leveraging an expanded professional network in the U.S and abroad which often leads to further professional development and engagement with the field. The tools, structures and networks provided through a consortium model help to decrease the perception that study abroad is a high-maintenance and expensive endeavor and provides students access to high-impact global learning opportunities.

The following three long-standing CCIS member community colleges concretely illustrate common themes such as student access, campus internationalization and collaboration that reflect the institutional positive impact created by affiliation with a consortium model.

Bergen Community College, NJ

Bergen Community College, an accredited, co-educational, two-year, public community college located in Bergen County, New Jersey with a current enrollment of over 17,000 students joined the CCIS Consortium in 2000. Affiliation with a national consortium has provided concrete support for Bergen to consider itself a global institution through access to education abroad programs, increased infrastructure and staff expertise, as well as a global network for academic collaborations. Bergen identifies three areas which have directly benefited from affiliation with the CCIS Consortium model (phone interview with Amparo Codding, International Student Counselor & Study Abroad Advisor at Bergen Community College, August 2017).

- **Student Access:** The consortium affiliation expanded Bergen's peer institutional networking opportunities and introduced the College to CCIS study abroad scholarship opportunities for their students which has helped to reduce costs associated with study abroad.
- **Campus Internationalization:** Despite a lack of institutional resources, consortium affiliation allows Bergen students to participate on global education programs that connect the local campus to the rest of the world through the broad CCIS program portfolio.
- **Collaboration**: Bergen's participation on CCIS academic program reviews has provided opportunities for institutional collaboration and professional development as well as a better understanding of CCIS programs. This professional development provided by CCIS has allowed Bergen faculty to develop knowledge and experience to increase the institution's capacity to expand international education at their institution and to better mentor and advise their students on available affordable study abroad options.

Brookdale Community College, NJ

Brookdale Community College, an accredited coeducational public community college in Lincroft, Monmouth County, New Jersey with a current enrollment of over 14,000 students joined the CCIS Consortium in 2007. The support of a national association made it possible for Brookdale to both expand access to education abroad programs and develop campus specific internationalization initiatives through access to a global network and professional development opportunities. Brookdale identifies three main areas which have benefited from affiliation with a consortium model (phone interview with Janice Thomas, Director at Brookdale Community College, August 2017).

- **Student Access:** CCIS scholarships have allowed Brookdale students to have access to study abroad programs they would otherwise not have access to. Access to CCIS programs and scholarships has in turn helped to increased Brookdale study abroad participation rates.
- **Campus Internationalization:** Through its affiliation with CCIS, Brookdale students participating on CCIS study abroad programs can graduate from Brookdale with a Global Citizenship Distinction certificate issued by the institution.
- **Collaboration:** Through its affiliation with the consortium model, Brookdale co-authored a book chapter and presented at professional conferences on the topic of Study Abroad Implications for Student Success at Community Colleges with peer network community colleges.

Broward College, Fl

Broward College, a state college in Fort Lauderdale, Florida with a current enrollment of over 40,000 students joined the CCIS Consortium in 2001. Through affiliation with the CCIS model, Broward was able to expand its education abroad offerings to its students and other peer institutions' students, while increasing funding internally for its own internationalization initiatives. Broward identifies three main areas which have benefited from affiliation with a consortium mode (phone interview with David Moore, Dean of International Education at Broward College, August 2017).

- **Student Access:** Through its affiliation with CCIS as a program sponsor, Broward was able to create program need-based scholarships through study abroad revenue which increased access to study abroad for Broward College students. Broward's students have access to over 100 education abroad programs run by accredited U.S. institutions that otherwise Broward would not have the resources to develop independently.
- **Campus Internationalization:** Through its CCIS program sponsorship status, Broward can fund a full-time study abroad coordinator position on campus through its study abroad pricing model. This additional source of revenue allows Broward to expand its international footprint without an increase in internally allocated funding.
- **Collaborations:** Sponsorship of CCIS programs has helped Broward develop collaborations with other U.S and international institutions and boost study abroad participation numbers. The consortium model has provided support in education abroad, which has freed up time and resources for Broward to expand its scope and expertise in international education and become a leader in the field.

CONCLUSION

In an environment where community colleges are frequently charged with internationalizing their campuses and producing global citizens without an internal influx of staff and resources to achieve this mission, technical and community colleges can look towards study abroad models where resources are pooled and shared to support their efforts, as briefly illustrated in the three-case studies above. The CCIS study abroad consortium model, when developed by the members and for the members, can effectively create the necessary community, infrastructure, and financial resources to achieve these global imperatives without a large institutional investment of dedicated money and staff.

Affiliation with a national study abroad consortium, such as CCIS, provides the means for institutions to increase access to education abroad programs, fund internal staffing positions, and develop a professional network for academic collaboration. The support of a national association also makes it possible for institutions to develop campus-specific internationalization initiatives through access to a global network and professional development opportunities.

In sum, the CCIS study abroad consortium model as articulated in this chapter is one of the easiest and most accessible ways to increase access and opportunity in education abroad at two-year institutions interested in growing their global footprint.

Checklist for Growing Education Abroad Through the Consortium Model

- Review institutional global mission and goals to fully understand the mandate.
- Determine assigned roles and responsibilities pertaining to internationalization.
- Assess available internal structure and resources related to the global mission.
- Break down the global mission into concrete measurable outcomes to determine success.
- Review study abroad models that can help advance the institution's global mission.
- Utilize a consortium model to lower the administrative burden on staff and faculty.
- Focus on promoting student access to education abroad through affordable programing.
- Advance internationalization through external support such as scholarships/grants.
- Leverage global collaborations through an extensive consortium network.
- Utilize internationalization measurable outcomes to advocate for additional resources.

REFERENCES

American Association of Community Colleges (AACC). (2017). *ACC international programs and services*. Retrieved from http://www.aacc.nche.edu/About/PInternational.aspx

American Association of Community Colleges and Association of Community College Trustees. (2006). *Joint statement on the role of community colleges in international education*. Retrieved at http://www.aacc.nche.edu/About/Positions/Pages/ps10012006.aspx

California Colleges for International Education (CCIE). (2018). *Mission statement*. Retrieved from http://www.ccieworld.org/missionstatement.htm

College Consortium for International Studies (CCIS). (2018a). *About CCIS*. Retrieved from www.ccisabroad.org/about

College Consortium for International Studies (CCIS). (2018b). *Program search*. Retrieved from www.ccisabroad.org/programsearch

Community Colleges for International Development (CCID). (2018). *About Us*. Retrieved from www.ccidinc.org

Dembicki, M. (2015). Growing interest in community colleges spreads internationally. Retrieved from: https://www.studyusa.com/en/a/347/growing-interest-in-community-colleges-spreads-internationally.

Fernandez, M. (2015). A global community's college. *The New York Times*. Retrieved from https://www.nytimes.com/2015/11/01/education/edlife/houston-community-college-international-students.html

Florida Consortium for International Education (FCIE). (2018a). *Mission*. Retrieved from www.fcie.org/about/mission

Florida Consortium for International Education (FCIE). (2018b). *About FCIE*. Retrieved from www.fcie.org/about

Heisel, M., & Kissler, G. (2010). *Financial strategies for expanding study abroad: Models, mission, management, and means for growth*. NAFSA. Retrieved from https://www.nafsa.org/Professional_Resources/Browse_by_Interest/Education_Abroad/Network_Resources/Education_Abroad/Financial_Strategies_for_Expanding_Study_Abroad__Models,_Mission,_Management,_and_Mea ns_for_Growth/

Hess, G. (1982). *Freshmen and sophomores abroad: community colleges and overseas academic programs*. New York, NY: Teachers College-Press.

Institute of International Education. (2016). *Open Doors*. Retrieved from http://www.iie.org/Research-and-Publications/Open-Doors/Data

Korbel, L. (2007). In union there is strength: the role of state global education consortia in expanding community college involvement in global education. In International Reform Efforts and Challenges in Community Colleges (pp. 47-57). San Francisco, CA: Jossey-Bass.

McLean, J. (1990). Consortial approaches to international education. In Developing International Education Programs (pp. 47-56). San Francisco, CA: Jossey-Bass. doi:10.1002/cc.36819907007

Nevadomski Berdan, S. (2014). *Busting the 10 top study abroad myths*. Retrieved from https://www.huffingtonpost.com/stacie-nevadomski-berdan/busting-the-top-10-study-abroad_b_4175861.html

Raby, R. L., & Valeau, E. J. (Eds.). (2016). *International education at community colleges*. New York, NY: Palgrave Macmillan. doi:10.1057/978-1-137-53336-4

Stearns, P. (2009). *Educating global citizens in colleges and universities: Challenges and opportunities*. New York, NY: Routledge, Taylor and Francis Group.

Chapter 19
How to Survive and Thrive as a Community College Consortium:
A Case Study of the Maryland Community College International Education Consortium

Gregory F. Malveaux
Montgomery College, USA

ABSTRACT

Some state and regional study abroad and international education-based consortia of community colleges have been struggling to remain operational. Key outside factors that have created trials include the United States' (US) economic downturn that ensued from 2007-2009, ongoing regulations set by government officials, and internal logistical challenges such as changes in leadership at member institutions, alterations in financial aid requirements, and emphasis placed on degree completion. There has been much analysis on "why" these consortia exist in the field; in contrast, this chapter focuses on "how" they persist. The Maryland Community College International Education Consortium (MCCIEC) is one of the nation's state consortia that continue to be active and flourish, navigating through economic trials, governmental policies that offset international student entry in to American higher education, and common logistical issues; this chapter uses MCCIEC as an illustrative model to show how community college consortia may function to prosper. MCCIEC uses four main approaches—1) gaining higher administrative buy-in, 2) encouraging full institutional support at membership colleges, 3) incorporating strong incentives for member activity, and 4) stimulating growth—to not only survive, but to thrive.

DOI: 10.4018/978-1-5225-6252-8.ch019

INTRODUCTION AND BRIEF HISTORY OF STATE AND LOCAL CONSORTIA

For the sake of clarity, the term "consortium" or "consortia" refers to a formal association of institutions in a region or state desiring to band their financial and human resources to offer collaborative programs for all member institutions (Korbel, 2007). In particular, the type of consortia considered for this chapter are those predominately made of community college members; they focus on study abroad and international education for students, professional development opportunities for college faculty and staff members, and curriculum development in global education.

In order to better understand the rise of current consortia, it is helpful to have some historical context. The 1980s and 1990s brought forth a major influx of community college collaboration and the increase of consortia from state to state. This new growth was due, in no small part, to a decade of cooperation that began in 1993 between the American Council on International Intercultural Education (ACIIE) and the Stanley Foundation (Korbel, 2007). The partnership brought widespread dialogue about the role community colleges play in preparing a globally competent citizenry, and a series of thirty state and regional seminars were held between 1995 and 2000 (Korbel, 2007). As a result of these seminars, hundreds of colleges initiated or enhanced global education initiatives on their own campuses, and ten global education consortia were established, joining the previously created consortia of the past decade and a half (Korbel, 2007). To further assist this growth, another national organization, Community Colleges for International Development (CCID), strongly advocated for consortia development among community colleges.

A pioneer in the field, Linda Korbel, former Executive Director for the American Council on International Intercultural Education (ACIIE), put forth, in 2007, an extensive list of active consortia, which included the Maryland Community College International Education Consortium (MCCIEC) (Korbel, 2007). The following are some major challenges that these consortia continue to encounter.

ADDRESSING THE CHALLENGES OF A COMMUNITY COLLEGE CONSORTIA

Economic Issues

Just a little over a decade has passed and various active consortia listed in 2007 are no longer functioning. This is due in no small part to economic strains incurred during and following the 2007-2009 US economic recession. Even though a small number of its members come from community colleges, telling is the Forum on Education Abroad's 2009 report that a 60% drop in study abroad enrollment at colleges and universities occurred from the following year, and that 60% of its members, who make up a large number of program directors, said that their budgets had been cut in the past year due to the economic downturn (Forum on Education Abroad, 2009). The same time that directors' budgets diminished, so did their activity in community college consortiums; since 2007, 25% of the active community college consortiums listed by Korbel have become inactive. As directors incurred budget cuts, this should not have been the time for them to "cut and run." Just the opposite. It should have been the time to use the state or local consortia as a lifeline to keep global studies active at the home institution. Why not lean on this resource when you truly need it? For the consortia groups that remain, as previously noted, there are ongoing challenges to remain operational. Those surviving consortia show that even in the face of budget cuts at membership institutions, a consortium can implement certain approaches to sustain itself and thrive, while its membership and functionality grow.

US Policy Concerns

A recent concern for many program directors is a decrease in study abroad enrollment due to restrictions placed on international students by the current administration. The current administration has expressed intention to dissolve the Deferred Action for Children Arrivals (DACA) program which protects 800,000 young undocumented immigrants from deportation. Even with attempts by college officials to reassure this student group that they are supported, feelings of anxiety pervade college campuses throughout the country. In a 2017 survey, administrators at 250 US colleges and universities reported a 40 percent decline in international applications (Redden, 2017). The impact is clearly felt at community colleges where international students have a major presence. Over 91,000 international students are enrolled at two-year institutions (Institute of International Education, 2017, making up nearly 7% of total student enrollment. And much of study abroad budgets come from international student fees and tuition (Raby, 2008).

My own institution, Montgomery College (MC), exemplifies a community college where international students have been a hallmark for active participation in study abroad. This student population represents over 165 nations at our college, and on average, annually, 20% of all MC study abroad participants have been international students (Montgomery College, 2018b). However, international student participation in study abroad at MC has dropped by half since the previous year, from 20% to 10% of our total study abroad student participants, leading to lost revenue of over $23,000.

But a far more expansive loss than economics is international students' loss of confidence with being protected while studying abroad. Some media groups have been shortsighted with claims that a Supreme Court-backed travel restriction on certain countries will leave little impact. Yet, international students, including those from my own institution, who are not from restricted countries, with legal visas, hesitate to leave the US due to concerns with airport detainment and/or being blocked from re-entering the US. It is a strange time. Even with the knowledge that I have as a study abroad coordinator and a leader in the field, my understanding of international students' rights during overseas travel has become less clear; and as I advise the aforementioned students, I cannot guarantee their return to the US, should they study abroad. In the face of this challenge, directors can embrace consortium participation as a means to offset lower program enrollment and economic impacts resulting from decreased international student engagement.

A college may not be able to alter current and future government regulations, but a consortium model, with emphasis placed on addressing community college issues, can provide distinct approaches to bolster program development for its members, and bring sustainability to the consortium.

Logistical Issues That May Compromise Sustainability

Common institutional shifts can disrupt consortium collaboration. Here are some concerns that consortia developers and leaders need to consider based on my experiences as the chairperson of a state-wide consortium, MCCIEC.

Institutional Leadership Changes

Consistent changes occur with member institutions' upper administration. A newly appointed college president or vice president may not provide the same institutional support for study abroad and international education initiatives. It is the responsibility of the college's consortium member(s) to inform leadership about the new president, and to assist with creating a meeting between him/her and consortium leadership. During this meeting, consortium leaders need to share with the new senior administration the consortium objectives, membership benefits, and the Memorandum of Understanding (MOU); in addition, they need to understand the concerns and expectations of that senior administrator. Often, these concerns can begin to be addressed by that institution's faculty and staff members. Recently, a new college president from a member institution questioned retaining MCCIEC membership due to anxieties with being held liable student injuries sustained on a consortium program. She was unaware, as noted in the MOU, we "ensure that a reputable travel provider with current liability insurance and a clearly defined cancellation policy" is in place, and the provider institution, not the home institution, accepts liability, along with the travel agency, for what occurs on its programs. These details assuaged the president's fears.

Changes in Financial Aid Requirements

Alterations in financial aid requirements can put a strain on consortium resources. Consortium colleges will often vary in ways that they disseminate student financial aid; such distribution can alter from year to year at the same institution. For example, in just the last two years my institution has tightened its financial aid distribution, limiting it only to courses that fall within a student's declared major. With consideration to the policy of MCCIEC, the home institution is charged with awarding financial aid as appropriate; and doing the necessary research and putting forth the proper paperwork to distribute financial aid directly to the study abroad agency. It is imperative for the home institution's consortium representative to communicate with their financial aid officer, and vice versa, about any potential changes in policy, and then immediately report modifications to the consortium chairperson and members.

Increasing Emphasis on Degree Completion

Another possible stressor on consortium membership comes from growing emphasis placed on degree completion. For instance, our home institution administrators have placed greater weight on students completing a 60 credit hour track in their discipline of study, and dissuade students from taking courses outside of this. Our college's 1 and 2 credit course offerings have been reduced, to aid an uninterrupted path to degree completion. Students may be advised to forgo study abroad courses that do not match a home college course. A college chancellor's approach—"We're making sure our students are having intrusive advising so they're not taking unnecessary courses" (Smith, 2015)—is pervasive at community colleges. It is the policy of MCCIEC, as noted in the MOU, for the home institution to "advise and monitor student progress toward educational goals and determine potential transferability of course credit when appropriate." MCCIEC respects the degree of stringency in which member colleges advise students with course selections.

Supporting Documentation for Global Initiatives

Consortium members have a range of institutional support for global education, depending on disparities with staffing, publicity, or financing. It can range from full institutional support openly related in the college mission statement, to being viewed by senior administration as a second thought, to having no support. The consortium must strive to serve the needs of all of its members with their varying degrees of home institution backing. It is infrequent for a community college to have a mission statement with language promoting global outreach. Consortium members who have such support should often emphasize, to colleagues and community groups, a desire to meet the college's mission by expanding global education. It should serve as an important reminder to administrators and campus groups that broad-based institutional support is crucial. However, even if your college does not foster global outreach through its mission statement, a commitment may come from other publicized, institutional documents. For example, Montgomery College's strong support for global education is clearly defined in its "Academic Affairs Initiatives." One of the initiatives closely mirrors much of my work at the college: "Expand Global Partnerships and International Opportunities" by "foster[ing] new opportunities for students, staff, faculty, and Academic Affairs units to work with international governments, businesses, and institutions of higher education in order to provide a twenty-first century education for our students and much-needed services and expertise to our colleagues abroad." Search out all institutional public decrees and documents, beyond that of the mission statement. Keep the consortium, which is in place to assist with promoting your programs, informed about the level of support that you are receiving from your institution.

THE DEVELOPMENT OF MCCIEC

This section profiles the advancement of the Maryland Community College International Education Consortium which serves as a case study for a successful community college state consortium. Its formulation was unique, and there is no exact formula for creating a state consortium. However, its early development and strategies for success provide instructive background. These strategies include: 1) gaining senior administration buy-in, 2) cultivating broad-based institutional support for consortium members, 3) providing strong incentives for active membership, and 4) stimulating growth.

Historical Development

In 1999, then acting International Education Coordinator at Frederick Community College (FCC), Peg Mauzy, spearheaded the idea to form MCCIEC. Prior to MCCIEC's start, she had been assisting students with study abroad programs in London through the Foundation for International Education (FIE). She not only aided FCC students, but collaborated with a few other in-state community college coordinators to open study abroad to their students. This activity, along with attending an inspirational seminar, "The First-Year Experience: First-Year Seminar Instructor Training Workshop," in which she gained information on the importance of working with diverse and international student populations, provided incentive to take action with creating a state consortium. She desired to start a consortium primarily to expand program opportunities for FCC students, as well as for community college students in the state.

With the support from then acting President, Patricia Stanley, and a few faculty colleagues involved in FCC global initiatives, Mauzy set out to get input and collaboration from every community college in the state. She, along with President Stanley and a member of the Bursar's Office, made calls to the colleges to share the goal of having a consortium, and to invite a representative to come to a large meeting to discuss "how they could be aided by the consortium, what concerns they had, and what they felt should be in a MOU" (Mauzy, interview, July 30, 2018). Mauzy also took the time to meet with interested individuals face-to-face, on or off of their campus—"from the janitor to the president, and everyone in between" (Mauzy, interview, July 30, 2018). "We found that person on every campus who had interest. And they, along with my president and/or I, would advocate to their president" (Mauzy, interview, July 30, 2018).

Mauzy's energy to build a state-wide collaboration, combined with the full support of her president, gave MCCIEC an early advantage to succeed; this level of support from a community college president to cultivate study abroad and international education is uncommon. Not to say they did not encounter early challenges. Mauzy reflects, "A few colleges were very localized. It was harder to convince them that their students could do study abroad. With a personal meeting with my president present, they came around. These small schools were harder [to give buy-in], but they did not want to be left out from the other schools" (Mauzy, interview, July 30, 2018). Next, multiple meetings were held by the 16 Maryland community college representatives, made up of faculty, staff, and administrators, to construct a MOU.

Senior Administration Buy-In

Having the support of college presidents and vice presidents does not guarantee a consortium's security; however, it does add a major safeguard for survival. A consortium will be stronger by having buy-in from senior administrators from the start. With this support, the consortium is more likely to have continuity of membership and participation from each college. Annual MCCIEC dues are sent to the main representative of each membership college, and this director/staff/faculty member passes the invoice on to their supervisor. With the signature of the college president on the consortium's MOU, as is the case with MCCIEC, membership is more likely to be renewed without question. If that signature does not exist, the representative's supervisor may take it upon him/herself to determine whether membership should continue. It is not likely the supervisor will override the president's commitment. Since the inception of MCCIEC, every college that signed on has remained a member.

However, one cannot ignore the fact that new college presidents may not have the same level of commitment to global education and the consortium. Quick and direct address of the upper administrator's concerns is the best approach to retain the partnering college in the consortium. The provider institution, which delivers the particular study abroad experience, should take on the responsibility of ensuring a reputable travel agency is in place with current liability insurance and a clearly defined cancellation policy. Also, it is necessary for consortia leadership to periodically review and update MOU standards to address current trends, and take on procedures that best protect students from risks, and home institutions from liability.

Transition of leadership within the consortium should be non-disruptive. Having periodic elections for governing positions, with new appointees resulting from majority rule by members, has allowed for smooth transitions. Like most consortiums, MCCIEC, has a governance structure with positions that include Chairperson, Treasurer, Secretary, and Web-designer. In addition, there are a few committees, including a Risks Assessment Team, and a Conference Selection Committee. Elections for all governing positions take place every two years. One may be re-elected to the same position until voted out.

- **MCCIEC's Approach to Getting Statewide Senior Administration Buy-In:** Stakeholders involved with drafting a consortium MOU should be college presidents, administrators, faculty and staff who have interest in cultivating global programs, as well individuals Legal Counsel, Financial Aid, Transcripts, and the Bursar. Once a consortium MOU is created through input by as many state community college representatives as possible, it should be presented at a well-attended meeting of college presidents for approval. In the case of MCCIEC, this would need to occur at the Maryland Council of Community College Chief Academic Officers (M4CAO) meeting where senior officers are organized into 40 affinity groups, working to achieve continuous improvement in all aspects of Maryland's community colleges. Most presidents in attendance had already spoken or met with Peg Mauzy and/or President Stanley about the potential MCCIEC consortium membership and its opportunities to expand study abroad and international education programs. All 16 community college presidents were in attendance at the meeting, and a few days later, Mauzy was handed the MOU, by President Stanley, with the signatures of all 16 presidents. MCCIEC was born.
- **A History of Success:** Upper administration buy-in to help safeguard the lifeline of a consortium is not a new concept. Significant consortium growth occurred nationally during the 1980s as groups sought support by college presidents at community colleges, and many groups, including the expansive California Colleges for International Education (CCIE), a nationally recognized nonprofit advocacy organization that advances international education for community college students, also expect college presidents to sign an agreement to adhere to consortium guidelines with membership (Raby, Culton, & Valeau, 2014). Again, MCCIEC adapted this approach. Senior administrators gave their signed pledge to have their college be an active contributor to MCCIEC. To their credit, they took this pledge seriously, and continue to provide their faculty and staff encouragement, if not economic incentives (membership dues, conference fees, and hosting meetings), to remain involved. During and since the period of economic recession from 2007-2009, many senior administrators from membership colleges looked to MCCIEC for economic and innovative opportunities to help offset their college's fiscal challenges. The Institute of International Education correctly asserts that university officials who look to form collaborations during crisis gain partnerships that can bring valuable research, teaching and service opportunities to be shared (4 Things, 2018). Senior administrators of member colleges were shrewd enough to recognize this with MCCIEC, and through participation with the consortium, many sustained important study abroad and international education initiatives.

Senior administrative support can take a consortium only but so far. There needs to be additional measures taken by each affiliate college to create a college-wide culture that aims to support the consortium.

Broad-Based Institutional Support With Each Consortium Member

In addition to having support from the college president, broad-based institutional support—having buy-in from offices of the Bursar, Financial Aid, Academic Advising, Registrar, Finance, and Risk Management and/or Legal Counsel—further safeguards the viability of international education programs. These broad stakeholders' involvement helps to protect the program in case of leadership changes. They should have knowledge of the students who want to study abroad through the consortium, and be willing to support them. Here are some ways that these stakeholders can assist their institution with consortium functions:

Bursar

With regard to student payments, these officials understand how the set-up the college's data system might play a role in which payment structure works best – whether the travel is considered a "course fee" with the bursar's office, a "program fee," or is paid via another office or mechanism. Also, they will work in conjunction with financial aid on preferences for how and where the funds are applied to student bills, in case a certain structure will ease students' use of aid at their school. As noted in its MOU, with MCCIEC "the institutions agree to revenue sharing. Each home institution pays the provider institution $100.00 per credit hour per student. This revenue is only collected if the student takes the course(s) for credit or audit. This payment is to support the instructional costs incurred by the provider institution and will be collected by the end of each fiscal year." The bursar aids the revenue model related in the MOU of MCCIEC by "developing a mechanism to transfer $100 per credit tuition revenue to the Provider Institution by the end of each fiscal year" as well as "develop a mechanism to have the student pay any study abroad/trip fees in a time frame set up by the provider institution. The home Institution will send these collected funds to the provider institution in a timely manner."

Financial Aid

It is beneficial to have officers facilitating student payments, who will give financial aid recommendations on payment structure and timing for study abroad students. First, ask the Financial Aid Office for their recommendations on how to structure and time student payments for a program. If needed, contact area institutions that facilitate strong financial aid for study abroad, and contact them for details to present to your college's office as a model. In establishing your study abroad payment due dates, if possible, have them coincide with key financial aid events, such as when refund checks become available to students. I recommend, as it is the case with MCCIEC, that it be the duty of the home institution to award financial aid as appropriate; the home institution's representative should have close communications with the Financial Aid Office. For example, an essential regulation that impacts how our financial aid officer and I advise students is "Federal Regulations require schools to only pay for the cost of courses in a declared program of study. Federal Financial Aid affected by this regulation includes Pell, SEOG and Teach grants, Federal Direct Stafford and Plus loans & Work-Study program. Currently this regulation does not apply to state or privately funded scholarships . . ." (Montgomery College, 2018a). Students are clearly warned that "if you are receiving financial aid, your aid will be awarded only for courses that are identified in your major. To avoid losing financial aid it is critical that you are taking required classes for your major" (Montgomery College, 2018c). Again, member institutions must closely work with their financial aid official on best approaches for dispensing financial aid for consortium programs.

Academic Advisor

The home institution should be in charge with assisting students with selections for overseas courses that merge with their major of study and degree completion. In the case of our college, students are strongly advised to retain a degree seeking track and are specifically informed that "your major will determine course selection, transfer planning, and recommendations regarding internships and related experiential learning activities that will enhance your educational experience" (Montgomery College, 2018c). Study abroad is considered a part of this "experiential" learning. The student's academic advisor, along with their study abroad advisor and the registrar, all emphasize that the student needs to select study abroad classes within their major, including consortium offerings. However, there should be some flexibility—for instance, the advisor can consider if a student could take an overseas course as an elective.

Registrar

This branch aids transferability of credits from a consortium program to the home institution. The registrar should consider the courses advised by an academic advisor, and determine transferability of course credits to the home institution, as well as to outside universities. The registrar should assist with recording completed consortium course credits into the student's official transcript. All participants in a state-run consortium should abide by their state's Code of Regulations, particularly with regards to the Academic Regulations. This helps for the consortium to hold consistent policies for admission, graduation, and awarding of academic credits. Developers of a state consortium need to include this policy and language in the established MOU. For example, the MCCIEC MOU states that we "agree that institutional policies for admission, graduation, and the awarding of academic credit shall be consistent with the State's minimum requirements for colleges as outlined in the Code of Maryland Regulations, Subtitle 02, Academic Regulations." Also, with credits awarded, and noted in the MCCIEC MOU, "a course offered by a Provider Institution and adopted by a Home Institution may carry the Home Institution's course title and number if the course is equivalent to a course currently offered by the Home Institution. Each college will also abide by its own institutional calendar but will make every effort to accommodate graduating students who are enrolled in MCCIEC courses." More specifically, with the MCCIEC model, there are "three potential ways to handle course work from the provider institution: 1) take the course(s) for credit, 2) take the course(s) for audit; or, if allowed by the provider institution, 3) take the trip without any course work or credit earned." If the home institution does not have an equivalent course to the provider institution's course, the former should provide alternative ways to issue course credit to the student, such as an "umbrella," "special topic," and/or "global perspective" course. For a well-organized, collaborative process, there needs to be active involvement by the Registrar's Office for advising and providing transferability of credits (in a statewide collaboration).

Finance

The finance office is often the larger division that the bursar is under. This distinction is being noted because the bursar not only assists with student accounts, but disperses Educational Assistance Program (EAP) funds, which can be used for travel expenses for approved professional conferences, including MCCIEC's annual conference. Therefore, the finance office for MCCIEC affiliates should be aware of coming MCCIEC conferences/forums in order to assist in distributing funds for faculty and staff participation. Further, the finance office should aid the consortium Treasurer by assisting with setting up a consortium account within the institution. Each college pays $200 for its annual membership fee, used to maintain MCCIEC administrative costs. It is better to have this account with the Treasurer's college, as opposed to a bank, in order to avoid fraudulent activity, and to sustain ongoing accountability.

Risk Management

Mainly it is the role of the International Education Director, or one of a similar role, at the provider institution, to take on risk management. As related in the MCCIEC MOU, they "1) ensure students have been oriented to travel and liability issues and potential transferability of credit course(s); 2) determine if any ADA accommodation issues exist, and if needed, inform the student's home institution transferability of credit course(s); 3) executes travel experience, monitors student behavior, and maintains standards as indicated in provider institution's policies and procedures; 4) assists students with disabilities in determining their needs, investigating possible options, and, if appropriate, making necessary arrangements. Due to the nature of study abroad experiences, the community colleges may not be able to provide accommodations for students with disabilities." It is important to coordinate with Legal Counsel to manage risks. In addition, as it should be the case for any state consortium, each study abroad and/or international education office should have representation on a designated consortium committee to assess and manage program risks. I feel compelled to note that nationwide interviews with global program leaders revealed

there is a bit of reticence . . . to disclose information about their programs, or to openly share risk-management documents . . . Unnecessary concerns about judgment could limit the effectiveness of program delivery, and put people at unnecessary risk. (Malveaux, 2016, p. 172)

It has been my goal to use MCCIEC as a "safe zone" for information sharing among program leaders; I recommend other consortia leaders to take on the same mindset.

Use College Mission Statements to Aid Institutional Buy-In

In order to also acquire broad-based institutional support for global programs and consortium membership, point out language in the college's mission statement. Look for words such as "global" and "diversity," as these are a natural fit for study abroad and international education. Notice the verbiage taken from various consortium members' mission statements:

- **Community College of Baltimore County:** "We value the diversity of people, cultures, ideas and viewpoints and we honor the dignity of all persons . . . We are committed to preparing students to be active citizens, ready to meet the challenges of an increasingly diverse world and a changing global marketplace (Community College of Baltimore County, 2018).
- **Frederick Community College:** "In traditional and alternative learning environments, we anticipate and respond to the needs of our local, regional, and global communities" (Frederick Community College, 2018).
- **Harford Community College:** "We embrace differences, respect intellectual and academic freedom, promote critical discourse, and encourage socio-cultural and global awareness (Harford Community College, 2018).

It is an advantage for community colleges that have mission statements which include language that embraces diversity and/or global awareness. Even if the college mission statement lacks such language, point to such language in the mission statements of competitive institutions to make a case.

MAJOR INCENTIVES FOR MEMBER ACTIVITY

There must be strong inducements for individual institutions to remain active members and to loyally pay an annual membership fee. As retirees depart and new hires arrive at their institutions, consider the motivations in place to acquire new membership. MCCIEC incentives are the type that are also commonly incorporated with other consortia—assist with increasing student participation and add additional study abroad program offerings; provide professional development activities for faculty and staff; and improve student access to courses. The MCCIEC "Statement of Purpose" (2015), details some of these incentives as a means to "bridge the gaps through (1) improving the accessibility, quality, and diversity of study abroad opportunities for Maryland community college students and (2) serving as a resource for Maryland community colleges to share strategies for success in study abroad and to collaborate on initiatives for mutual benefit" (MCCIEC, Statement of purpose, 2015, para. 3). Specifically, MCCIEC,

1. Enables students from all MCCIEC member institutions to participate in study abroad programs sponsored by other member institutions:
   a. Allows institutions with few or no study abroad programs of their own to offer their students study abroad opportunities;
   b. Allows institutions that sponsor abroad programs a greater chance of reaching target enrollment and running their programs;
2. Enables students to pay in-county tuition rates and use some types of financial aid for study abroad courses;
3. Enables the home institution to collect tuition, fees, and FTE [full time equivalents] for its students who enroll in study abroad at other institutions; and
4. Serves as a resource for all Maryland community colleges to develop and improve their study abroad programs under the guidance of experienced colleagues with established programs (consulting on such topics as liability and risk, insurance, vendor relationships, and others) (MCCIEC, Statement of purpose, 2015, para. 4).

Increased Access and Offerings

Statewide, MCCIEC members feel fortified by the access and range of program offerings for students. Rather than be limited to their home college's offerings, students can seamlessly enroll in classes and study abroad program offerings throughout the state; all while paying in-county tuition rates and having access to financial aid. Leaders of MCCIEC share, with leaders in the field, the belief that "community colleges serve a greater proportion of lower income and minority students than any other postsecondary institution, and this open access philosophy is precisely the means that make international knowledge and experience accessible to students who would not otherwise be able to participate" (Raby, Culton, & Valeau, 2014, p. 79). This is the philosophy that all consortia leaders should have as part of their mission or statement of purpose.

A consortium should fuel member program offerings, particularly "institutions with few or no study abroad programs of their own to offer their students study abroad opportunities," as noted in the MCCIEC MOU. All members have a say in the planning cycle for consortium program offerings—this endeavor is put into a group meeting agenda; attending members discuss, decide, and share (through the chairperson) the plan with all members; and non-attendees of the meeting can give additional, online feedback. Once the program calendar is confirmed by the chairperson, it is posted in the "Current & Upcoming Programs" page of the MCCIEC website. Occasionally, there are competing program offerings; two colleges hope to offer short term programs at a similar location and time. This is why it is essential for college representatives to share their college program offerings as soon as they are aware, even years in advance, to avoid consortium program overlap. When the overlap occurs, one college may either move their program to a different time period, or the institutions merge their two programs into one collaborative program.

Resources to Bank

In addition to improved program access for students, consortium members feel incentive to remain active members due to vast shared resources. There is no need for study abroad coordinators and international education directors to "go at it alone" with creating and implementing programs. To maintain consortium organization, and to have the ability to share important information with members, there needs to be a bank of documents that members can access. This may include lists of reputable travel agencies to assist with study abroad program design; a pool of waivers of liability (legal counsel from each college should be consulted); instructive literature on best practices for study abroad; listings of consortium committees with descriptions of their functions and tasks; and other documents that simply make life easier for directors of study abroad and international education. All members can use the banked documents for their college's benefit.

Human Resources

Then there is the natural benefit of human resources. "[MCCIEC] serves as a resource for all Maryland community colleges to develop and improve their study abroad programs under the guidance of experienced colleagues with established programs (consulting on such topics as liability and risk, insurance, vendor relationships, and others)" (MCCIEC, Statement of purpose, 2015, para. 4). The consulting, or "information-sharing" sessions often begin with a general question such as, "so why did you choose to approach this in that way?" At MCCIEC meetings we encourage open dialogue meant to aid one another's program development, and time is etched out in the agenda for this purpose. However, I recommend that information-sharing takes place at the end of the agenda in order to accomplish other set goals. Careful, if not well-regulated, information-sharing can use up the entire meeting time; this just speaks to the eagerness of members to bolster their knowledge in the field. Such discussions have moved in many directions at MCCIEC meetings—sharing new and current strategies in the field that were acquired at a professional conference; post-program communication on effective and less-than-effective techniques used in a study abroad program; impacts and best practices to consider with new and upcoming state and federal policies that could affect program approaches; and analysis of risk reduction and gained cultural competence for students in particular countries, to name a few examples. Use your valuable human resources, and make meetings a safe-haven for members to learn from and teach one another. Each member should have an equal, active voice, which makes them feel professionally valued. This culture makes most eager to return to future meetings. Their return, coupled with increasing membership, equals consortium longevity.

Student Scholarships

In addition to financial aid, many students need another resource in scholarship funds to make study abroad a financial reality. With consent from members, a small percentage of annual membership dues can be set aside for student scholarships. The awards should be available to students from all membership colleges, and all of the consortium college representatives should have the opportunity to periodically serve on the selection committee.

Also, outside scholarship sources should be offered to students, and consortium representatives should communicate with one another about ongoing opportunities. Some national organizations that provide student study abroad scholarship opportunities are Benjamin A. Gilman, Fulbright, Generation Study Abroad, Fund for Education Abroad, Harry S. Truman Foundation, and Rotary Ambassadorial Scholarship. Study abroad providers also give scholarships for students taking their programs. Again, consortium representatives need to continue to discuss scholarship opportunities, new and old, with students at their home institutions.

STIMULATING GROWTH WITH FORUMS: MCCIEC CASE STUDY

Consortium expansion comes from both statewide memberships, as well as through new partnerships with national and international groups that share your mission. There may be no better way to attract all of these groups than to have an annual forum or conference.

A "forum" can be described as a discussion group in which ideas related to a subject, under examination, can be raised and evaluated on an equal and informal basis. The MCCIEC forum is nearly identical to hosting a conference—a large group meets for about a week in which various workshops and discussions, relative to an overarching theme, occur each day. MCCIEC leadership prefers to use the term "forum," as opposed to "conference," to emphasize that discussion and debate can occur on an equal and informal basis. Yet, like a conference, it is well-organized, and at least one moderator is present to keep participants on task. Statewide members, along with outside experts, are able to showcase innovative research and knowledge in the field through workshops and seminars.

Forum Attendees

Forums, or conferences, if you prefer, serve to galvanize members and expand consortium membership. Faculty, staff and administrators from any affiliated college are eligible to register for the forum. These are typically individuals with strong interest in global education: faculty and staff who desire to create and/or lead international programs; instructors who want to internationalize their curriculum; directors of study abroad and international education who desire program expansion; and administrators who want to better understand impacts and potential liabilities related to global education programs at their institution. While these groups tend to make up the bulk of attendees, community members may also participate in the forum—travel agents, non-profit group leaders, and global education enthusiasts, to name a few.

Marketing Involved and Benefits Received From a Forum Approach

Marketing the Consortium

In advance of the forum, a state-wide "call for proposals" to lead workshops for professional development, is issued to employees at membership colleges. This notice is disseminated by consortium representatives to department Vice Presidents, Deans, and Chairpersons to share with employees college-wide. An appointed selection committee picks the favored proposals, and awardees are able to use institutional funds to support this professional development. Marketing for professional development, and the forum itself, is necessary for strong attendance. A consortium cannot aid membership institutions with dwindling budgets unless it has a solid foundation, generates new and existing membership participation, and continually presents current strategies for community college program success in global education. The forum approach nurtures these consortium standards.

Process of the Forum and How It Draws Participant Interest

Again, an automatic gain for statewide college faculty and staff who give workshops at the forum is professional development and all that it allots, including conference funding from the home institution. Even if an institution does not provide its employees professional development funding, in my experience, with enough perks, faculty and staff often choose to "pay out of pocket" to attend the forum. There are three factors to take into account when planning a forum which MCCEIC has used to draw attendees.

Offer at a convenient time period for statewide college employees. The forum should be brief, occurring for no longer than about one week. It should accommodate participants' work schedules, and therefore be held during commonly occurring spring, summer or winter recess periods.

Keep it affordable as participation in the forum should be relatively inexpensive, especially for an overseas conference with everything included (registration, accommodations, flights, conference materials, regional venues, and breakfast meals). MCCIEC has been able to keep forum costs below $2,000. Reputable agencies who desire to be the chosen provider for the forum have strong incentive to provide group discounts and competitive rates due to the large number of participants, and ease of arrangements for a forum.

Offer convenient, attractive, and intriguing meeting locations to encourage participation. Many will be drawn to attend a forum at an exotic location that is relevant to global issues and occurrences. Yet, the location should be relatively close to the US. MCCIEC has been highly successful with drawing forum interest with locations that take an eight-or-less hour flight; this is most practical so not to over-exhaust participants or burn up valuable forum time with travel. A study abroad director will consider a number of factors when constructing a study abroad program. "Coordinators and faculty leaders must consider national trends, research scholarly sites, merge semester course curriculum to the study abroad experience, match appropriate disciplines to combine with the itinerary, and take various other steps to create a valuable program" (Malveaux, 2016, p. 114). Similarly, in their design of a consortium forum, leaders must scrutinize trends that impact study abroad, global locations of interest, developments in higher education academia, new educational and governmental policies of impact, and much more.

Effective Implementation and Inclusivity With a Forum

There should be a rather expansive theme to the forum so that presentation proposers may merge their area of discipline into a viable, globally-oriented workshop. For example, the last MCCIEC forum had the somewhat open-ended theme, "Strategic Partnerships for Global Learning." A consortium selection committee should receive a healthy range of proposal topics. When selecting workshop leaders, you will want to offer a wide variety of workshop topics to fit the inclusive theme of the forum; and try to select presenters from various membership colleges to show convincing inclusivity at the event. This kind of implementation drew presentations in disciplines ranging from Behavioral Science to Economics, Mathematics to Mortuary Science, and everything between. At the conclusion of the forum, all of the 24 faculty and staff presenters were interested in furthering their research—designing faculty-led study abroad programs at their home institutions, becoming members of the consortium, and/or taking part in a forum debriefing session at the next general MCCIEC meeting. With faculty and staff who return to home institutions throughout the state, driven to design and apply new, innovative, international initiatives that expand college curriculum and program offerings, there is natural incentive for administrators to share future forum opportunities. Consequently, MCCIEC gets "a bump" in membership after each forum.

Reputable Agency as a Partner

Though mentioned briefly in the previous chapter section on "Senior Administration Buy-In," it is worth reiterating the importance of partnering with a reputable travel agency to set up forum logistics; MCCIEC stresses this for each and every program. Agency assistance with reserving a conference room, accommodations, flights, and venues allow forum leaders more flexibility and time to manage workshop schedules. In addition, it is important to organize visits to colleges and universities in the region so that forum attendees get a better understanding of the contrasts between US and overseas educational systems. It is a reasonable request to ask foreign administrators and employees to give short presentations and/or orientation sessions about their departments. Plus, a visit to the global education office is essential.

Putting on a Forum to Reinforce Consortia Membership

As it has been the case for MCCIEC, a consortium forum should bring increased awareness and membership to a consortium. Past presenters take on the dual role of being advocates, encouraging their colleagues to participate and/or present at the next forum, and fuel program growth within their institution. However, one may question, "Even if new faculty-led program offerings come as a result of the forum, how is this favorable when you don't have the student numbers or resources to fill them?" This is the point of the consortium—fill the gaps. Through the consortium, students outside of your college bolster low-enrolled and/or new programs as they take advantage of an array of program options (thanks in part to your college offerings), increased access, seamless transferability of credits, and other perks).

Global Partnerships to Expand the Consortium

Further expansion of consortium program offerings can result from merging with global partners; and the forum design can be manipulated to achieve this goal. For example, at the MCCIEC Forum in England and South Wales, conference attendees met with English and Welsh administrators from various departments at prestigious institutions, including the University of Westminster, Queen Mary University of London, Roehampton University, and Swansea University in South Wales. During those meetings, our consortium members took advantage of the opportunity to start forging partnerships with university officials to have student study abroad, student exchange, global classrooms, and foreign faculty guest lecturers.

However, the main goal for these university visits was to find a strong partner to join in a "2+2 program" approach. It exemplifies the type of global initiative that consortium leadership should use to expand their offerings and vitality. The 2+2 program is a growing trend in community colleges and higher education (Chen, 2017). With this type of program, a student begins in a community college with a two-year associate degree, and the coursework taken at the community college then transfers to a four year program, allowing the student to complete a bachelor's degree in the same amount of time it would have taken if they had gone to the four-year institution right out of high school (Chen, 2017). With this partnership, the community college and four-year school work together to ensure all of the courses they offer complement each other for an overall, comprehensive degree program; and the seamless transition process ensures students do not waste any time or money on classes that will not be a good fit for their final goals (Chen, 2017). For MCCIEC, the most suitable institute to create a 2+2 program was Swansea University in South Wales, due to the university's wide array of course and discipline offerings, and a well-established history of successful 2+2 programs already in place with dozens of American institutions, including one from our own state of Maryland. MCCIEC forum organizers already had meaningful communication with administrators from Swansea University at national conferences. Our consortium group was looking for an additional academic opportunity to better serve all consortium member students who wanted a direct route for transferring to an overseas, 4 year institution to earn a Bachelor's degree. One of the most sought after places for consortium member education abroad students is the United Kingdom (UK). Swansea University was also an ideal partner because it is a top 30 research intensive university in the UK (World University Rankings, 2018) with course offerings that paired well with our consortium colleges in the areas of Liberal Arts, Science-Technology-Engineering-Math (STEM), and Business Administration. Swansea University provides a clear pathway for our graduating students to transfer and earn a Bachelor's degree in the UK.

Meetings at Swansea University were well-integrated into the forum agenda to allow maximum use of time to explore a 2+2 agreement. This dovetailed well into the overarching forum theme of "Strategic Partnerships for Global Learning." Since the forum, a number of consortium members went on to coordinate with Swansea University administrators to finalize transferability of credits and degree completion from one institution to the other. It would have been difficult to create such a partnership without their walking the grounds of Swansea University, and making direct contact with administrators and faculty from various departments of interest. Quite simply, a Swansea University visit gave forum attendees the ability to discuss their colleges' needs with Swansea University administrators and staff. This close dialogue gave each the measure of confidence necessary to believe a 2+2 partnership would be a successful endeavor. I highly recommend that consortium groups add global outreach to their objectives when conducting a forum or conference in order to cultivate consortium growth.

CONCLUSION

Local and state community college consortia of study abroad and international education came into prominence in the 1990s, due in no small part to a decade of coordination between the American Council on International Intercultural Education and the Stanley Foundation. However, in the last decade many of these consortia have been struggling to remain active, and some have had to fully disband. The US economic downturn from 2007-2009, US governmental policies for international students, and natural logistical challenges have caused increased strains on community college consortia. This chapter addresses how such consortia persist and thrive under these circumstances. The Maryland Community College International Education Consortium (MCCIEC) serves as a model for sustaining growth among state or local community college consortia with its strategies for acquiring higher administration buy-in, urging full institutional support at membership colleges, applying strong incentives for member activity, and increasing overall growth.

RECOMMENDATIONS

These are recommendations for sustaining state or local consortia while keeping membership active:

- When building your consortium, get buy-in from senior administrators from the start by having them sign a Memorandum of Understanding.
- Expect consortium members to strive for broad-based institutional support.
- To garner home institution support for global programs and consortium activities, point to language in the college's mission statement and other publicized documents or decrees.
- Provide increased student access, seamless class enrollment, and pathways to financial aid for global education and study abroad program opportunities in the consortium.
- Organize a bank of shared resources for consortium members.
- Use your human resources within the consortium.
- Provide an annual forum or conference for consortium members, and the colleagues of members.
- To broaden the impact of the consortium forum, encourage presenters to use their findings to create faculty-led study abroad programs at their home institutions, to become members of the consortium, and to encourage colleagues to present at future forums.
- Develop global partnerships.

REFERENCES

4 Things Your Institution Can Do to Support Education in Crisis. (2018). *Institute of International Education: The Power of International Education* [Blog]. Retrieved from: https://www.iie.org/Learn/Blog/2015-April-4-Things-Your-Institution-Can-Do-To-Support-Education-In-Crisis

Chen, G. (2017, May 17). 2+2 programs going strong at community colleges nationwide. *Community College Review Blog*. Retrieved from: www.communitycollegereview.com/blog/2-2-programs-going-strong-at-community-colleges-nationwide

Community College of Baltimore County. (2018). *Mission and values.* Retrieved from: /www.ccbcmd.edu/about-ccbc/mission-and-values

Fischer, K. (2009, September 15). Overseas study is down, and the economy takes the blame. *Chronicle of Higher Education.* Retrieved from www.chronicle.com/article/Overseas Study Is Down-and/48420

Forum on Education Abroad. (2009, September 15). *Survey on the impact of the global economic crisis on education abroad.* Retrieved from: https://forumea.org/wp-content/uploads/2014/10/ForumEducationAbroadeconsurvey9-09.pdf

Frederick Community College. (2018). *About FCC.* Retrieved from: https://www.frederick.edu/about-fcc.aspx

Harford Community College. (2018). *Mission, vision, values.* Retrieved from: https://www.harford.edu/about/mission.aspx

Insley, A. (2016, December 22). Transferring from a community college - 2 + 2 agreements. *Study Abroad USA Magazine.* Retrieved from: https://studyusa.com/en/a/1004/ https://studyusa.com/en/a/1004/transferring-from-a-community-college-2-+-2-agreements

Institute of International Education. (2017). *Open Doors (Italicized).* New York: Institute of International Education.

Korbel, L. A. (2007, June 19). In union there is strength: The role of state global education consortia in expanding community college involvement in global education. In International Reform Efforts and Challenges in Community Colleges, New Directions for Community Colleges. San Francisco, CA: Jossey-Bass.

Malveaux, G. F. (2016). *Look before leaping: Risks, liabilities, and repair of study abroad in higher education.* Lanham, MD: Rowman & Littlefield.

Maryland Community College International Education Consortium. (2015). *Statement of Purpose.* Unpublished Documents from the MCCIEC.

Maryland Community College International Education Consortium. (2018a). *How to maintain federal financial aid eligibility in a declared major of study.* Retrieved from: file:///C:/Users/Montgomery%20College/Downloads/ CPOS-FAQs.pdf

Maryland Community College International Education Consortium. (2018b). *Admissions and Records: Resources for International Students.* Retrieved from: http://cms.montgomerycollege.edu/edu/department2.aspx?id=10078

Maryland Community College International Education Consortium. (2018c). *Student Advising Tool Kit.* Retrieved from: http://cms.montgomerycollege.edu/generalstudies/student-advising-toolkit/

Raby, R. L. (2008). *Expanding education abroad at U.S. community colleges.* New York: Institute of International Education.

Raby, R. L., Culton, D. R., & Valeau, E. J. (2014, March 22). Collaboration: Use of consortia to promote international education. In Strengthening community colleges through international collaboration. San Francisco, CA: Jossey-Bass.

Redden, E. (2017, March 13). Will international students stay away? *Inside Higher Education.* Retrieved from: https://www.insidehighered.com/news/2017/03/13/nearly-4-10-universities-report-drops-international-student-applications

Smith, A. A. (2015, June 8). 2 + 2 Shouldn't = 5. *Inside Higher Education.* Retrieved from: https://www.insidehighered.com/news/2015/06/08/two-year-transfers-are-finding-not-all-their-credits-go-them

World University Rankings. (2018). Swansea University. Retrieved from: https://www.timeshighereducation.com/world-university-rankings/swansea-university

Compilation of References

100, 000 Strong in the Americas. (2018). *Meet the winners*. Retrieved from http://www.100kstrongamericas.org/category/meet-the-winners/

4 Things Your Institution Can Do to Support Education in Crisis. (2018). Institute of International Education: The Power of International Education [Blog]. Retrieved from: https://www.iie.org/Learn/Blog/2015-April-4-Things-Your-Institution-Can-Do-To-Support-Education-In-Crisis

Aall, P. R., Helsing, J. W., & Tidwell, A. C. (2007). Addressing conflict through education. In I. W. Zartman (Ed.), *Peacemaking in international conflict: methods & techniques* (pp. 327–353). Washington, DC: United States Institute of Peace.

Accrediting Commission for Community and Junior Colleges. (2018). Western Association of Schools and Colleges. Retrieved from: https://accjc.org/

Ahn, Y., & Janke, M. C. (2011). Motivations and benefits of the travel experience of older adults. *Educational Gerontology*, *37*(8), 653–673. doi:10.1080/03601271003716010

Allen, T. O., & Zhang, Y. (2016). Dedicated to their degrees adult transfer students in engineering baccalaureate programs. *Community College Review*, *44*(1), 72–86. doi:10.1177/0091552115617018

Alliance for Peacebuilding. (n.d.). *What is Peacebuilding?* Retrieved from http://www.allianceforpeacebuilding.org/what-is-peacebuilding/

Altbach, P. G., & De Wit, H. (2016). Internationalization and global tensions: Lessons from history. In P. G. Altbach (Ed.), *Global perspectives on higher education*. Baltimore, MD: John Hopkins University Press.

Amani, M. & Kim, M. M. (in press) Study Abroad Participation at Community Colleges: Students' Decision and Influential Factors. *Community College Journal of Research and Practice, 42*, 678-92.

Amani, M. (2011). *Study abroad decision and participation at community colleges: Influential factors and challenges from the voices of students and coordinators* (Dissertation). George Washington University.

Amani, M. (2011). *Study abroad decision and participation at community colleges: Influential factors and challenges from the voices of students and coordinators* (Doctoral dissertation). Available from Proquest Dissertations and Theses database. (UMI No. 3438831)

Amani, M. (2011). *Study abroad decision and participation at community colleges: Influential factors and challenges from the voices of students and coordinators* (Unpublished doctoral dissertation). George Washington University, Washington, DC.

Amani, M., & Kim, M. M. (2017). Study abroad participation at community colleges: Students' decision and influential factors. *Community College Journal of Research and Practice*, *41*(10), 1–15. doi:10.1080/10668926.2017.1352544

Compilation of References

American Association of Colleges and Universities. (2015). *Global learning VALUE rubric.* American Association of Colleges and Universities Value Rubric Development Project. Retrieved from https://www.aacu.org/value/rubrics/global-learning

American Association of Community Colleges (AACC). (2017). *ACC international programs and services.* Retrieved from http://www.aacc.nche.edu/About/PInternational.aspx

American Association of Community Colleges (AACC). (2017). *Fast facts from our fact sheet.* Retrieved from http://www.aacc.nche.edu/AboutCC/Pages/fastfactsfactsheet.aspx

American Association of Community Colleges (AACC). (2018). *Fast facts from our fact sheet.* Retrieved from http://www.aacc.nche.edu/AboutCC/Pages/fastfactsfactsheet.aspx

American Association of Community Colleges and Association of Community College Trustees. (2006). Joint statement on the role of community colleges in international education. Retrieved at http://www.aacc.nche.edu/About/Positions/Pages/ps10012006.aspx

American Association of Community Colleges. (2017). *Fast facts 2017.* Retrieved from https://www.aacc.nche.edu/research-tends/fast-facts/

American Association of Community Colleges. (2018). *Fast facts 2018.* Retrieved from https://www.aacc.nche.edu/research-trends/fast-facts/

American Association of Community Colleges. (2018). *Fast Facts*. Retrieved from: http://www.aacc.nche.edu

American Council on Education (ACE). (2016). *Survey Responses by Institution Type*. Washington, DC: Center for International and Global Engagement. Retrieved from http://www.acenet.edu/news-room/Documents/Mapping-Internationalization-Tables-2017.pdf

American Council on Education. (2012). *Mapping Internationalization on U.S. Campuses: 2012 Edition* (Rep.). Washington, DC: American Council on Education. Retrieved from http://www.acenet.edu/news-room/Documents/Mapping-Internationalizationon-US-Campuses-2012-full.pdf

American Council on Education. (2012). *Mapping internationalization on U.S. campuses: 2012 edition.* Retrieved from http://www.acenet.edu/news-room/Documents/MappingInternationalizationUS Campuses2012-full.pdf

American Council on Education. (2013-2014). *Internationalization in action: Internationalizing the curriculum.* Retrieved from http://www.acenet.edu/news-room/Pages/Internationalization-in-Action.aspx

American Council on Education. (2017). *ACE releases signature mapping internationalization on U.S. campuses report.* Retrieved from http://www.acenet.edu/news-room/Pages/ACE-Releases-Signature-Mapping-Internationalization-on-U-S-Campuses-Report.aspx

American Council on Education. (2017). *Mapping internationalization on U.S. campuses* (2017 edition). Washington, DC: American Council on Education.

Anastasakos, V. (2013). Teaching peace through short-term study abroad. In D. J. Smith (Ed.), *Peacebuilding in community colleges: a teaching resource* (pp. 105–117). Washington, DC: United States Institute of Peace.

Anderson, B. D. (2007). *Students in a global village: The nexus between choice, expectation, and experience in study abroad* (Unpublished doctoral dissertation). The University of Texas, Austin, TX.

Anderson, P. H., Lawton, L., Rexeisen, R. J., & Hubbard, A. C. (2006). Short-term study abroad and intercultural sensitivity: A pilot study. *International Journal of Intercultural Relations*, *30*(4), 457–469. doi:10.1016/j.ijintrel.2005.10.004

Andreotti, V., Stein, S., Pashby, K., & Nicolson, M. (2016). Social cartographies as performative devices in research on higher education. *Higher Education Research & Development, 35*(1), 84–99. doi:10.1080/07294360.2015.1125857

Anne Arundel Community College. (n.d.). *Law enforcement and criminal justice, social justice option*. Retrieved from https://catalog.aacc.edu/preview_program.php?catoid=16&poid=5853&returnto=2431

Arden-Ogle, E. (2009). *Study abroad and global competence: Exemplary community college programs which foster elements of achievement* (Dissertation). Oregon State University, Corvallis, OR.

Arps, K. (2013). *Study abroad for community college students*. Retrieved from Monterey Institute of International Studies website: http://sites.miis.edu/kristenarps/files/2013/12/Study-Abroad-at-Community-Colleges-Presentation.pdf

Association of American Colleges and Universities. (n.d.). *Intercultural knowledge and competence VALUE rubric*. Retrieved from https://www.aacu.org/value/rubrics/intercultural-knowledge

Ayers, D. F. (2005). Neoliberal ideology in community college mission statements: A critical discourse analysis. *The Review of Higher Education, 28*(4), 527–549. doi:10.1353/rhe.2005.0033

Ayers, D. F., & Palmadessa, A. L. (2015). The community college and a rising global imaginary: An analysis of practical reasoning, 1950-2013. *The Journal of Higher Education, 86*(6), 864–892.

BaileyShea. C. (2009). *Factors that affect American college students' participation in study abroad* (Unpublished doctoral dissertation). University of Rochester, Rochester, NY.

Bailey, T. R., Jaggars, S. S., & Jenkins, D. (2015). *Redesigning America's community colleges: A clearer path to student success*. Cambridge, MA: Harvard University Press. doi:10.4159/9780674425934

Bandyopadhyay, S., & Bandyopadhyay, K. (2015). Factors influencing student participation in college study abroad program. *Journal of International Education Research, 11*(2), 87–94.

Bandyopadhyay, S., & Bandyopadhyay, K. (2015). Factors influencing student participation in college study abroad programs. *Journal of International Education Research, 11*(2), 87–94.

Banks-Santilli, L. (2014). First-Generation college students and their pursuit of the American dream. *Journal of Case Studies in Education, 5*(1), 1–32.

Barash, D., & Webel, C. (2002). *Peace and conflict studies*. Thousand Oaks, CA: Sage Publications.

Barclay Hamir, H., & Gozik, N. (2018). *Promoting inclusion in education aboard: A handbook of research and practice*. Herndon, VA: Stylus Publishing, LLC.

Bartzis, O. L., Kirkwood, K. J., & Mulvihill, T. M. (2016). Innovative approaches to study abroad at Harper College and Fox Valley Technical College. In R. L. Raby & E. J. Valeau (Eds.), *International education at community colleges: Themes, practices, and case studies* (pp. 237–246). Palgrave Macmillan. doi:10.1057/978-1-137-53336-4_17

Bauman, G. L., Bustillos, L. T., Bensimon, E. M., Brown, M. C. II, & Bartee, R. D. (2005). *Achieving equitable educational outcomes with all students: The institution's roles and responsibilities*. Washington, DC: Association of American Colleges and Universities.

Bauman, S. S. M., Wang, N., DeLeon, C. W., Kafentzis, J., Zavala Lopez, M., & Lindsey, M. S. (2004). Nontraditional students' service needs and social support resources: A pilot study. *Journal of College Counseling, 7*(1), 13–17. doi:10.1002/j.2161-1882.2004.tb00254.x

Beitz, C. R. (1979). *Political theory and international relations*. Princeton, NJ: Princeton University Press.

Compilation of References

Bennett, M. J. (1986). A developmental approach to training intercultural sensitivity. International Journal of Intercultural Relations, 10(2), 179-186.

Bennett, M. J. (1993). Towards ethnorelativism: A developmental model of intercultural sensitivity (revised). In R. M. Paige (Ed.), *Education for the Intercultural Experience*. Yarmouth, ME: Intercultural Press.

Bennett, M. J. (2012). Paradigmatic assumptions and a developmental approach to intercultural learning. In *Student Learning Abroad: What our students are learning, what they're not and what we can do about it* (pp. 90–114). Sterling, VA: Stylus.

Bird v. Lewis & Clark College, 104 F. Supp. 2d 1271 (D. Or. 2000) aff'd, 303 F.3d 1015 (9th Cir. 2002).

Bird v. Lewis & Clark College, 303 F.3d 1015 (9th Cir. 2002).

Bissonnette, B., & Woodin, S. (2013). Building support for internationalization through institutional assessment and leadership engagement. In Resituating the community college in a global context (p. 11-26). San Francisco: Jossey-Bass Publications. Doi:10.1002/cc20045

Blair, D. P., Phinney, L., & Phillippe, K. A. (2001). *International programs at community colleges*. Washington, DC: American Association of Community Colleges.

Blake-Campbell, B. (2014). More Than Just a Sampling of Study Abroad: Transformative Possibilities at Best. *The Community College Enterprise*, *20*(2), 60–71.

Boggs, G. R., & Irwin, J. (2007). What every community college leader needs to know: Building leadership for international education. In E. J. Valeau & R. L. Raby (Eds.), International reform efforts and challenges in community colleges (pp. 25-30). San Francisco, CA: Jossey-Bass. doi:10.1002/cc.278

Boggs, G. R., & Irwin, J. (2007). What every community college leader needs to know: Building leadership for international education. In International reform efforts and challenges in community colleges (pp. 25-30). San Francisco: Jossey-Bass.

Boggs, G. R. (2010). The evolution of the community college in America: Democracy colleges. *Community College Journal*, *82*(4), 36–39.

Bolen, M. C. (2014). *A guide to outcomes assessment in education abroad*. Carlisle, PA: Publication of the Forum on Education Abroad.

Bonet, G., & Walters, B. (2016). High impact practices: Student engagement and retention. *College Student Journal*, *50*(2), 224–235.

Bourdieu, P. (1986). The forms of capital (R. Nice, Trans.). In J. Richardson (Ed.), Handbook of theory and research for the sociology of education (pp. 241-258). New York: NY: Greenwood Press.

Bourdieu, P. (1977). *Outline of theory and practice* (R. Nice, Trans.). Cambridge, UK: Cambridge University Press. doi:10.1017/CBO9780511812507

Boutros-Ghali, B. (1992). *An agenda for peace: Preventive diplomacy, peacemaking, and peace-keeping: report of the Secretary-General pursuant to the statement adopted by the summit meeting of the Security Council on 31 January 1992*. New York, NY: United Nations.

Brennan, M., Frost, R., Hagadorn, E., Martin, M., & Natali, J. (2005) Education abroad and the career development of community college students: Four case studies. In M. Tillman (Ed.), Impact of Education Abroad on Career Development: Four Community College Case Studies II (pp. 7-16). Stamford, CT: American Institute for Foreign Study Publications.

Brennan, M., & Dellow, D. A. (2013). International students as a resource for achieving comprehensive internationalization. *New Directions for Community Colleges, 2013*(161), 27–37. doi:10.1002/cc.20046

Brenner, A. (2016). Transformative learning through education abroad: A case study of a community college program. In R. L. Raby & E. J. Valeau (Eds.), *International education at community colleges: Themes, practices, research, and case studies (pp. 370-90)*. New York, NY: Palgrave. doi:10.1057/978-1-137-53336-4_21

Brint, S., & Karabel, J. (1989). *The diverted dream: Community colleges and the promise of educational opportunity in America, 1900-1985*. New York, NY: Oxford University Press.

Brubaker, C. (2017). Re-thinking re-entry: New approaches to supporting students after study zbroad. *Die Unterrichtspraxis/Teaching German, 50*(2), 109.

Burdzinski, D. R. (2014). *Attitudes about globalization, internationalization, and the role of student affairs administrators in internationalizing Florida's community and state colleges* (Doctoral dissertation). Retrieved from ProQuest Dissertations and Theses. (UMI No. 3615607)

Butler, D. C. (2016). *Comprehensive internationalization: Examining the what, why, and how at community colleges*. Retrieved from ProQuest Dissertations and Theses. (UMI No. 10111570)

Byun, S., Meece, J. L., Irvin, M. J., & Hutchins, B. (2012). The role of social capital in educational aspirations of rural youth. *Rural Sociology, 77*(3), 355–379. doi:10.1111/j.1549-0831.2012.00086.x PMID:24039302

California Colleges for International Education (CCIE). (2018). *Education Abroad*. Accessed at: www.ccieworld/studyabroad

California Colleges for International Education (CCIE). (2018). *Mission statement*. Retrieved from http://www.ccieworld.org/missionstatement.htm

California Colleges for International Education. (2018). *Mission*. Retrieved from http://www.ccieworld.org/missionstatement.htm

California Colleges for International Education. (2018). *Study abroad*. Retrieved from http://ccieworld.org/saprograms.php

California Community Colleges Chancellor's Office. (2017). *Management information systems data mart*. Retrieved from: http://datamart.cccco.edu/

California Community Colleges Chancellor's Office. (2018). Datamart. *California Community Colleges*. Retrieved from: https://www.cccco.edu/

California Community Colleges Chancellor's Office. (2018). *Management information systems data mart – Statewide enrollment status summary report of Fall 2017 students by ethnicity*. Retrieved from https://datamart.cccco.edu/Students/Enrollment_Status.aspx

Carl Sandburg College. (2015). *July 1, 2015 to June 30, 2016 budget*. Retrieved from http://www.sandburg.edu/About/Budgets-And-Financial-Information/2016-budget- final.pdf

Carl Sandburg College. (2016). *Experiencing the Holocaust*. Retrieved from https://livesandburg-my.sharepoint.com/personal/jhutchings_sandburg_edu/Documents/Sandburg/Abroad/Experiencing%20the%20Holocaust.mp4?slrid=fc73409e-8031-5000-d3fa-b27af9cb4128

Carley, S., & Tudor, R. K. (2010) Assessing the impact of short-term study abroad. *Journal of Global Initiatives: Policy, Pedagogy, Perspective, 1*(2), Article 5. Available at: https://digitalcommons.kennesaw.edu/jgi/vol1/iss2/5

Carlson, J. S., Burn, B., Useem, J., & Yachimowicz. (1990). *Study abroad: The experience of American undergraduates*. New York: Greenwood Press.

Compilation of References

Carroll Community College. (2016). *Carroll community college catalogue: 2016-2017*. Westminster, MD: Carroll Community College.

Carroll Community College. (2017). *Institutional assessment effectiveness report*. Westminster, MD: Carroll Community College.

Castro-Salazar, R., Merriam-Castro, K., & Perez Lopez, Y. A. (2016). Building a world class college: Creating a global community at Pima community college. In R. L. Raby & E. J. Valeau (Eds.), *International Education at Community Colleges: Themes, Practices, Research, and Case Studies*. New York, NY: Palgrave Macmillian Publishers. doi:10.1057/978-1-137-53336-4_12

Catholic Relief Services. (n.d.). *Peacebuilding*. Retrieved from https://www.crs.org/our-work- overseas/program-areas/peacebuilding

Center for Advanced Language Acquisition. (2017). *Maximizing Study Abroad*. Retrieved from http://carla.umn.edu/maxsa/

Center for Community College Student Engagement. (2017). *The community college student report*. Retrieved from http://www.ccsse.org/aboutsurvey/biblio/page1.cfm

Center for Global Education. (2017). *Global Scholars*. Retrieved from http://www.globalscholar.us/

Center for Global Education. (2018a). *Globaled.us*. Retrieved from http://globaled.us/index.asp

Center for Global Education. (2018b). GlobalScholar.us. Retrieved from http://globaled.us/index.asp

Center for Global Education. (2018c). SAFETI. Retrieved from http://globaled.us./index.asp

Chang, J. C. (2005). Faculty-student interaction at the community college: A focus on students of color. *Research in Higher Education*, *46*(7), 769–802. doi:10.100711162-004-6225-7

Chen, G. (2017, May 17). 2+2 programs going strong at community colleges nationwide. *Community College Review Blog*. Retrieved from: www.communitycollegereview.com/blog/2-2-programs-going-strong-at-community-colleges-nationwide

Chen, Y., & Starobin, S. S. (2017). Measuring and examining general self-efficacy among community college students: A structural equation modeling approach. *Community College Journal of Research and Practice*, *42*(2), 1–19. doi:10.1080/10668926.2017.1281178

Chieffo, L. (2000). *Determinants of student participation in study abroad programs at the university of Delaware: A quantitative study* (Dissertation). University of Delaware, Newark, DE.

Chieffo, L. (2000). *Determinants of student participation in study abroad programs at the university of Delaware: A quantitative study* (Unpublished doctoral dissertation). University of Delaware, Newark, DE.

Chieffo, L., & Griffiths, L. (2004). Large-scale assessment of student attitudes after a short-term study abroad program. *Frontiers: The Interdisciplinary Journal of Study Abroad*, *10*, 165–177. Retrieved from https://frontiersjournal.org/wp-content/uploads/2015/09/CHIEFFO-GRIFFITHS-FrontiersX-LargeScaleAssessmentofStudentAttitudeafteraShort-TermStudyAbroadProgram.pdf

Chieffo, L., & Spaeth, C. (2017). *The guide to successful short-term programs abroad* (3rd ed.). Annapolis, MD: NAFSA.

Clark, B. M. (2013). *Faculty perceptions of the importance of internationalizing the general education curriculum in the Florida college system* (Doctoral dissertation). Retrieved from ProQuest Dissertations and Theses. (UMI No. 3558998)

Clark, B. (1960). The cooling-out function in higher education. *American Journal of Sociology*, *65*(6), 569–576. doi:10.1086/222787

Cloughly, C. (1991). Integrating study abroad into the undergraduate liberal arts curriculum: Eight institutional case studies. In *Factors influencing students' decisions to study abroad* (pp. 65–86). Westport, CT: Greenwood Publishing Group, Inc.

Coffey, A., & Atkinson, P. (1996). *Making sense of qualitative data: Complimentary research strategies*. Thousand Oaks, CA: Sage Publications, Inc.

Cohen, A. M., Brawer, F. B., & Kisker, C. B. (2014). *The American community college* (6th ed.). San Francisco, CA: Jossey-Bass.

Coker, J. S., Heiser, E., & Taylor, L. (2018). Student outcomes associated with short-term and semester study abroad programs. *Frontiers: The Interdisciplinary Journal of Study Abroad, 30*(2), 92–105. Retrieved from https://frontiersjournal.org/wp-content/uploads/2018/04/Coker-Heiser-Taylor-XXX-2-Student-Learning-Outcomes.pdf

Coker, J. S., Heiser, E., Taylor, L., & Book, C. (2017). Impacts of experiential learning depth and breadth on student outcomes. *Journal of Experiential Education, 40*(1), 5–23. doi:10.1177/1053825916678265

College Consortium for International Studies (CCIS). (2018a). *About CCIS*. Retrieved from www.ccisabroad.org/about

College Consortium for International Studies (CCIS). (2018b). *Program search*. Retrieved from www.ccisabroad.org/programsearch

CollegeBoard. (2008, January). *Winning the skills race and strengthening America's middle class: An action agenda for community colleges*. Retrieved from http://professionals.collegeboard.com/profdownload/winning_the_skills_race.pdf

Colorado Community College System. (n.d.). *Common course numbering system*. Retrieved from https://www.cccs.edu/educator-resources/common-course-numbering-system/

Commission on the Abraham Lincoln Study Abroad Fellowship Program. (2005). *Global competence & national needs: 640 One million Americans studying aboard*. Retrieved from https://www.aifs.com/pdf/lincoln_final_report.pdf

Commission on the Abraham Lincoln Study Abroad Fellowship Program. (2005). *Global competence and national needs: One million Americans studying abroad*. Washington, DC: US State Department.

Community College of Baltimore County. (2018). *Mission and values*. Retrieved from: /www.ccbcmd.edu/about-ccbc/mission-and-values

Community College Review. (2015). *What is a community college?* Retrieved from http://www.communitycollegereview.com/blog/what-is-a-community-college

Community College Review. (2017). *Tuition Statistics*. Retrieved from: https://www.communitycollegereview.com/avg-tuition-stats/national-data

Community Colleges for International Development (CCID). (2018). *About Us*. Retrieved from www.ccidinc.org

Compton, J., Cox, E., & Laanan, F. (2006). Adult learners in transition. *New Directions for Student Services, 114*(114), 73–80. doi:10.1002s.208

Consortium for Analysis of Student Success through International Education. (2018). Retrieved from https://www.usg.edu/cassie

Cook, J. (1996). Community self-help international development projects. In N. Tarrow & R. L. Raby (Eds.), *Dimensions of the community college: International, intercultural, and multicultural perspectives*. New York, NY: Routledge.

Compilation of References

Copeland, J. M., McCrink, C. L., & Starratt, G. K. (2017). Development of the community college internationalization index. *Journal of Studies in International Education*, *21*(4), 349–374. doi:10.1177/1028315317697541

Corps, P. (1996). *At home in the world: The Peace Corps story*. Washington, DC: Peace Corps.

Council for the Advancement of Standards in Higher Education. (2015). *CAS professional standards for higher education* (9th ed.). Washington, DC: Wells.

Council for the Advancement of Standards in Higher Education. (2018). CAS Standards. In *CAS Professional Standards for Higher Education* (9th ed.). Cabot, AZ: Author. Retrieved from: http://www.nafsa.org/_/File/_/eaps_ statement.pdf

Council on International Intercultural Exchange. (1988). *Educating for global competence: Report of the Advisory Council for International Educational Exchange*. New York, NY: Council on International Intercultural Exchange.

Covarrubias, R. (2012). Unseen disadvantage: How American universities' focus on independence undermines the academic performance of first-generation college students. *Journal of Personality and Social Psychology*, *102*(6), 178–197. PMID:22390227

Cragg, J. G. (1971). Some statistical models for limited dependent variables with application to the demand for durable goods. *Econometrica*, *39*(5), 829–844. doi:10.2307/1909582

Craig, S. (1999). Study abroad 101: The basic facts. *The Black Collegian*, 138-143.

Creswell, J. W., & Poth, C. N. (2018). *Qualitative inquiry & research design: Choosing among five approaches*. Los Angeles, CA: Sage.

Crotty, M. (1998). *The foundations of social research: Meaning and perspective in the research process*. London, UK: Sage.

Crozier, G. (2006). 'There's a war against our children': Black educational underachievement revisited. *British Journal of Sociology of Education*, *26*(5), 585–598. doi:10.1080/01425690500293520

Cultural Services French Embassy in the United States. (2017). *Community college abroad in France - A new and affordable opportunities to study in France*. Retrieved from http://frenchculture.org/about-us/press-room/4887-community-college-abroad-france-new-and-affordable-opportunities-study

Curran, S. J. (2007, November-December). The career value of education abroad. *International Educator*, 48-52.

Cuyahoga Community College. (2018). *Course survey*. Cleveland, OH: Cuyahoga Community College.

Cuyahoga Community College. (2018). *Study Abroad*. Retrieved from http://www.tri-c.edu/ programs/studyabroad/index.html

Daoust, I., & Epperson, C. (2013). Teaching human rights and international humanitarian law. In D. J. Smith (Ed.), *Peacebuilding in community colleges: a teaching resource* (pp. 149–163). Washington, DC: United States Institute of Peace Press.

Davidjsmithconsulting.com. (2013a). *Madison College Receives Peacebuilding Support Award*. Retrieved from https://davidjsmithconsulting.com/2013/07/10/madison-college-receives-peacebuilding-support-award/

Davidjsmithconsulting.com. (2013b). *ICRC Expert Speaks at Anne Arundel Community College as part of USIP/IIE Public Education for Peacebuilding Support Program*. Retrieved from https://davidjsmithconsulting.com/2013/03/10/icrc-expert-speaks-at- anne-arundel-community-college-as-part-of-usipiie-public-education-for-peacebuilding- support-program/

Davidjsmithconsulting.com. (2017). *U.S. and Canadian Community College Peacebuilding Programs and Initiatives (including peace studies, conflict resolution, social justice, justice studies, human rights, and mediation)*. Retrieved from https://davidjsmithconsulting.com/north-american-community-college- peacebuilding-programs-and-initiatives-including-peace-studies-conflict-resolution- social-justice-justice-studies-human-rights-and-mediation/

Davis, K. (2013). Community building through a peace and social justice institute. In D. J. Smith (Ed.), *Peacebuilding in community colleges: a teaching resource* (pp. 93–104). Washington, DC: United States Institute of Peace Press.

Dawn.Com. (2011, April 19). *Four girls killed in Paris inferno*. Retrieved from: https://www.dawn.com/news/622237

de Wit, H. (2011). Globalisation and internationalisation of higher education (Introduction to online monograph). *Revista de Universidad y Sociedad del Conocimiento (RUSC)*, *8*(2), 241-248. Retrieved from http://rusc.uoc.edu/ojs/index.php/rusc/article/view/v8n2-dewit/v8n2-dewit-eng

Deardorff, D. K. (2011). Assessing intercultural competence. *New Directions for Institutional Research*, *149*(149), 65–79. doi:10.1002/ir.381

Deardorff, D. K. (2014). Outcomes assessment in international education. *Industry and Higher Education*, *75*, 8–10.

Deardorff, D. K. (2015). *Demystifying outcomes assessment for international educators: A practical approach*. Sterling, VA: Stylus Publishing.

Delaware Technical Community College. (2015). *Mission, Vision, Strategic Directions and Values Statement*. Retrieved from https://www.dtcc.edu/about/mission-vision-and-strategic-directions

Delaware Technical Community College. (2017). *Curriculum Guidelines*. Retrieved from https://efiles.dtcc.edu/CURR_GUIDE/Archive/Curriculum%20 Guidelines%20201851.pdf

Delaware Technical Community College. (2018). *Exit surveys: 2010-2018*. Dover, DE: Delaware Technical Community College Study Abroad Program.

Delaware Technical Community College. (2018). *FY2019-2021 College Plan Goals and Objectives: International Education*. Dover, DE: Delaware Technical Community College.

Dembicki, M. (2015). Growing interest in community colleges spreads internationally. Retrieved from: https://www.studyusa.com/en/a/347/growing-interest-in-community-colleges-spreads-internationally.

Dennis, J. M., Phinney, J. S., & Chuateco, L. I. (2005). The role of motivation, parental support, and peer support in the academic success of ethnic minority first-generation college students. *Journal of College Student Development*, *46*(3), 223–236. doi:10.1353/csd.2005.0023

Dishman, L. (2016). These are the biggest skills that new graduates lack. *Fast Company*. Retrieved from https://www.fastcompany.com/3059940/these-are-the-biggest-skills-that-new-graduates-lack

Donohue, D., & Altaf, S. (2012, May). *Learn by doing: expanding international internships/work abroad opportunities for U.S. STEM students—A briefing paper from IIE's Center for Academic Mobility Research*. Retrieved from www.file://C:/ Users/Montgomery%20College/Downloads/Learn%20by%20Doing%20Final.pdf

Draper, K. (2015). CTE and global education: The perfect marriage. *Education Week*.

Duncan-Andrade, J. M. R., & Morrell, E. (2008). *The art of critical pedagogy: Possibilities for moving from theory to practice in urban schools*. New York, NY: Peter Lang. doi:10.3726/b12771

Dutschke, D. (2009). Campus internationalization initiatives and study abroad. *College and University*, *84*(3), 67–73.

Compilation of References

Dwyer, M. M. (2004). Charting the impact of studying abroad. *International Educator, 13*(1), 14–20.

Dwyer, M. M. (2004). More is better: The impact of study abroad program duration. *Frontiers: The Interdisciplinary Journal of Study Abroad, 10*, 151–164. Retrieved from https://frontiersjournal.org/wp-content/uploads/2015/09/DWYER-FrontiersX-MoreIsBetter.pdf

Education Advisory Board. (2017). *Survey: 70% of community college students work—and for many, it's too much.* Retrieved from EAB website: https://www.eab.com/daily-briefing/2015/10/29/seventy-percent-of-community-college-students-work

Emert, H. A., & Pearson, D. L. (2007). Expanding the vision of international education: Collaboration, assessment, and intercultural development. *New Directions for Community Colleges, 2007*(138), 67–75. doi:10.1002/cc.283

Engberg, M. E., & Fox, K. (2011). Exploring the relationship between undergraduate service- learning experiences and global perspective-taking. *Journal of Student Affairs Research and Practice, 48*(1), 85–105. doi:10.2202/1949-6605.6192

Engle, L. (2012). The rewards of qualitative assessment appropriate to study abroad. *Frontiers: The Interdisciplinary Journal of Study Abroad, 22*, 111–126.

Engle, L., & Engle, J. (2003). Study Abroad Levels: Toward a Classification of Program Types 1. *Frontiers: The Interdisciplinary Journal of Study Abroad, 9*(1), 1–20.

Engle, L., & Engle, J. (2003). Study abroad levels: Toward a classification of program types. *Frontiers: The Interdisciplinary Journal of Study Abroad, 9*, 1–20.

Farnsworth, K. A. (2013). Peace, conflict resolution, and the essential need for international education. In D. J. Smith (Ed.), *Peacebuilding in community colleges: a teaching resource* (pp. 29–39). Washington, DC: United States Institute of Peace Press.

Farrugia, C., & Bhandari, R. (2016). *Open Doors*. New York, NY: Institute of International Education.

Farrugia, C., Bhandari, R., Baer, J., Robles, C., & Andrejko, N. (2017). *Open Doors 2017 Report on International Educational Exchange*. New York: Institute of International Education.

Farrugia, C., & Sanger, J. (2017). *Gaining an employment edge: The impact of study abroad on 21st century skills and career prospects in the United States, 2013-2016*. New York, NY: Institute for International Education.

Farrugia, C., & Sanger, J. (2017). *Gaining an employment edge: The impact of study abroad on 21st century skills and career prospects in the United States*. New York, NY: Institute of International Education. Retrieved from https://www.iie.org/Research-and-Insights/Publications/Gaining-an-Employment-Edge---The-Impact-of-Study-Abroad

Farrugia, C., & Sanger, J. (2017). *Gaining an employment edge: The impact of study abroad on the 21st-century skills and career prospects in the United States, 2013-2016*. New York, NY: Institute of International Education.

Fay v. Thiel College, 55 Pa. D. & C.4th 353 (Com. Pl. 2001).

Fernandez, M. (2015). A global community's college. *The New York Times*. Retrieved from https://www.nytimes.com/2015/11/01/education/edlife/houston- community-college-international-students.html

Fink, J., Davis, J., & Takeshi, Y. (2017). *What happens to students who take community college "Dual Enrollment" courses in high school?* Community College Research Center (CCRC). Retrieved from: https://ccrc.tc.columbia.edu/publications/what-happens-community-college-dual- enrollment-students.html

Fischer, K. (2009, September 15). Overseas study is down, and the economy takes the blame. *Chronicle of Higher Education*. Retrieved from www.chronicle.com/article/Overseas-Study-Is-Down-and/48420

Fischer, K. (2012). In study abroad, men are hard to find. *The Chronicle of Higher Education.* Retrieved from http://chronicle.com/article/In-Study-Abroad-Men-Are-Hard/130853

Fitzduff, M., & Jean, I. (2011). *Peace education: State of the field and lessons learned from USIP grantmaking (Publication No. 74).* Washington, DC: United States Institute of Peace.

Florida Consortium for International Education (FCIE). (2018a). *Mission.* Retrieved from www.fcie.org/about/mission

Florida Consortium for International Education (FCIE). (2018b). *About FCIE.* Retrieved from www.fcie.org/about

Flyvbjerg, B. (2006). Five misunderstandings about case-study research. *Qualitative Inquiry, 12*(2), 219–245. doi:10.1177/1077800405284363

Flyvbjerg, B. (2011). Case Study. In N. K. Denzin & Y. S. Lincoln (Eds.), *The Sage Handbook of Qualitative Research* (4th ed.; pp. 301–316). Thousand Oaks, CA: Sage.

Forage, P. C. (2013). Field training for humanitarians and peacebuilders. In D. J. Smith (Ed.), *Peacebuilding in community colleges: a teaching resource* (pp. 189–198). Washington, DC: United States Institute of Peace Press.

Forum on Education Abroad. (2009, September 15). *Survey on the impact of the global economic crisis on education abroad.* Retrieved from: https://forumea.org/wp-content/uploads/2014/10/ForumEducationAbroadeconsurvey9-09.pdf

Forum on Education Abroad. (2017). *State of the field 2017.* Retrieved from https://forumea.org/wp-content/uploads/2018/03/ForumEA-State-of-the-Field-18-web- version.pdf

Forum on Education Abroad. (2018). *Forum's standards focus on health and safety Standards of Practice.* Retrieved from: https://forumea.org/resources/standards-of-good- practice/standard-8/

Forum on Education Abroad. (2018). *Glossary.* Retrieved from https://forumea.org/resources/glossary

Forum on Education Abroad. (2018). *Membership Listing.* Retrieved from: https://forumea.org/about-us/who-we-are/member-listing/

Foucault, M. (1984). What is Enlightenment? In P. Rabinow (Ed.), *The Foucault Reader* (pp. 31–50). New York, NY: Pantheon.

Frederick Community College. (2018). *About FCC.* Retrieved from: https://www.frederick.edu/about-fcc.aspx

Frost, R. A., & Raby, R. L. (2009). Democratizing study abroad: Challenges of open access, local commitments, and global competence in community colleges. In R. Lewin (Ed.), *Handbook of practice and research in study abroad* (pp. 170–190). New York: Routledge.

Furrh v. Arizona Board of Regents, 676 P.2d 1141 (Ariz. Ct. App. 1983).

Furst, M., & Ebersole, T. (2012). *Global Distinction: A Student Pathway to Global Competence, Presentation to The League for Innovation.* Retrieved from https://www.league.org/innovation-showcase/going-global-students-distinction

Gaia, A. C. (2015). Short-term faculty-led study abroad programs enhance cultural exchange and self-awareness. *International Education Journal: Comparative Perspectives, 14*(1), 21-31. Retrieved from https://openjournals.library.sydney.edu.au/index.php/IEJ/article/viewFile/7627/8839

Gaia, A. C. (2015). Short-term faculty-led study abroad programs enhance cultural exchange and self-awareness. *International Education Journal: Comparative Perspectives, 14*(1), 21–31.

Gillborn, D. (2005). Education policy as an act of white supremacy: Whiteness, critical race theory and education reform. *Journal of Education Policy, 20*(4), 485–505. doi:10.1080/02680930500132346

Compilation of References

Gipson, J., Mitchell, D., & McLean, C. (2017). An investigation of high-achieving African- American students attending community colleges: A mixed methods research study. *Community College Journal of Research and Practice*, *41*(3), 1–13. doi:10.1080/10668926.2017.1299652

Gleazer, E. J., Jr. (1975, March 24). *Memorandum to Community College Presidents*. American Association of Community and Junior Colleges.

Glesne, C. (2010). *Becoming qualitative researchers: An introduction*. Pearson.

Golden West College. (n.d.). *Peace conference 2018 – Golden West College*. Retrieved from http://www.goldenwestcollege.edu/peace-conference/

Golden West College. (n.d.). *Peace studies program - Golden West College*. Retrieved from http://www.goldenwestcollege.edu/peace/

Golden West College. (n.d.). *Previous peace conferences*. Retrieved from http://www.goldenwestcollege.edu/peace/past-events/

González Canché, M. S. (2018). Geographical network analysis and spatial econometrics as tools to enhance our understanding of student migration patterns and benefits in the U.S. higher education network. *The Review of Higher Education*, *41*(2), 169–216. doi:10.1353/rhe.2018.0001

Gonzalez, L. M., Stein, G. L., & Huq, N. (2013). The influence of cultural identity and perceived barriers on college-going beliefs and aspirations of Latino youth in emerging immigrant communities. *Hispanic Journal of Behavioral Sciences*, *35*(1), 103–120. doi:10.1177/0739986312463002

Gorlewski, Ey. (2014). Partnerships and advocacy. In Education Abroad for Advisers and Administrators. Washington, DC: NAFSA.

Green, M. F. (2007). Internationalizing community colleges: Barriers and strategies. In International reform efforts and challenges in community colleges (pp. 15-24). San Francisco: Jossey-Bass.

Green, M. F. (2007). Internationalizing community colleges: Barriers and strategies. New Directions for Community Colleges, 138, 15-24. Doi:10.1002/cc.277

Green, M. F., & Siaya, L. (2005). *Measuring internationalization at community colleges.* Report from the American Council on Education Center for Institutional and International Initiatives. Retrieved from http://www.acenet.edu/newsroom/Documents/Measuring-CommunityCollege.pdf

Green, M., & Olsen, C. (2003). *Internationalizing the campus: A user's guide*. Washington, DC: American Council on Education.

Groennings, S., & Wiley, D. S. (Eds.). (1990). *Group portrait: Internationalizing the disciplines*. New York, NY: The American Forum.

Hamir, H. B., & Gozik, N. (2018). *Promoting Inclusion in Education Abroad: A handbook of Research and Practice*. Stylus.

Hammer, M. R., Bennett, M. J., & Wiseman, R. (2003). Measuring intercultural sensitivitiy: The intercultural development inventory. *International Journal of Intercultural Relations*, *27*(4), 421–443. doi:10.1016/S0147-1767(03)00032-4

Hanover Research. (2014). *Trends in higher education marketing, recruitment, and technology*. Washington, DC: Hanover Research.

Harder, A., Andenoro, A., Roberts, T., Stedman, N., Newberry, M. I., Parker, S., & Rodriguez, M. (2015). Does study abroad increase employability? *NACTA Journal*, *59*(1).

Harder, N. J. (2011). Internationalization efforts in United States community colleges: A comparative analysis of urban, suburban, and rural institutions. *Community College Journal of Research and Practice*, *35*(1-2), 152–164. doi:10.1080/10668926.2011.525186

Hardin, C. J. (2008). Adult students in higher education: A portrait of transitions. *New Directions for Higher Education*, *144*(1), 49–57. doi:10.1002/he.325

Harford Community College. (2018). *Mission, vision, values*. Retrieved from: https://www.harford.edu/about/mission.aspx

Harper, S. R., & Quaye, S. J. (2009). Beyond sameness, with engagement and outcomes for all: An introduction. In S. R. Harper & S. J. Quaye (Eds.), *Student engagement in higher education: Theoretical perspectives and practical approaches for diverse populations* (pp. 1–15). New York, NY: Routledge.

Harrell, A., Sterner, G., Alter, T., & Lonie, J. (2017). Student perceptions of the impact of their diverse study abroad experiences. *NACTA Journal*, *61*(1).

Harris, I. M., & Morrison, M. L. (2013). *Peace education*. Jefferson, NC: McFarland & Company.

Harvey, D. (2007). *A brief history of neoliberalism*. Oxford, UK: Oxford University Press.

Heisel, M., & Kissler, G. (2010). *Financial strategies for expanding study abroad: Models, mission, management, and means for growth*. NAFSA. Retrieved from https://www.nafsa.org/Professional_Resources/Browse_by_Interest/Education_Abroad/Network_Resources/Education_Abroad/Financial_Strategies_for_Expanding_Study_Abroad__Models,_Mission,_Management,_and_Means_for_Growth/

Helms, R. M., & Brajkovic, L. (2017). *Mapping internationalization on U.S campuses* (2017 edition). Washington, DC: American Council on Education. Retrieved from http://www.acenet.edu/news-room/Documents/Mapping-Internationalization-2017.pdf

Helms, R. M., Brajkovic, L., & Struthers, B. (2017). *Mapping Internationalization on U.S. Campuses* (2017 edition). Washington, DC: American Council or Education.

Hemming, L. K., & Bosley, W. G. (2012). Facilitating intercultural learning abroad. In M. Vande Berg, R. M. Paige, & K. Hemming Lou (Eds.), *Student Learning Abroad: what our students are learning, what they're not and what we can do about it* (pp. 335–359). Sterling, VA: Stylus.

Henry, R. (1985). California's Community Colleges and International Education: Legal Issues. Santa Rosa, CA: School and College Legal Services of California. (Unpublished Document)

Hernandez, M., Wiedenhoeft, M., & Wick, D. (Eds.). (2014). *NAFSA's guide to education abroad for advisors and administrators* (4th ed.). Annapolis, MD: NAFSA.

Hess, G. (1982). *Freshmen and sophomores abroad: community colleges and overseas academic programs*. New York, NY: Teachers College-Press.

Hess, G. (1982). *Freshmen and sophomores abroad: Community colleges and overseas academic programs*. New York: Teachers College Press.

Hett, J. (1993). *Development of an instrument to measure global-mindedness* (Unpublished doctoral dissertation). University of San Diego, San Diego, CA.

Hicks, C., & Jones, S.J. (2011, Fall). At issue: survival tactics for small, rural-serving community colleges. *The Community College Enterprise*, 28-45.

Compilation of References

Higher Education Marketing. (2016). *7 signs your website is sabotaging student recruitment.* Retrieved from http://www.higher-education-marketing.com/blog/website-student-recruitment

Hodara, M., & Jaggars, S. S. (2014). An examination of the impact of accelerating community college students' progression through developmental education. *The Journal of Higher Education, 85*(2), 246–276. doi:10.1353/jhe.2014.0006

Hossler, D., & Gallagher, K. S. (1987). Studying student college choice: A three-phase model and the implications for policymakers. *College and University, 62*(3), 207–221.

Hovland, K. (2014). *Global learning: defining, designing and demonstrating.* Joint publication of NAFSA and AAC&U. Washington, DC: NAFSA Publications. Institute of International Education (IIE).

Hovland, K. (2017). *Open Doors Report.* New York, NY: Academic Press.

Hovland, K. (2018). *Study Abroad Matters: Linking Higher Education to the Contemporary Workplace through International Experience.* Washington, DC: IIE Publications.

Hovland, K. (2010). *Global learning: aligning student learning outcomes with study abroad. The Center for Capacity Building in Study Abroad. NAFSA and APLU.* Washington, DC: NAFSA Publications.

Howard Community College (HCC). (2017a). College catalog: PSYC 101 General Psychology. *Howard Community College SmartCatalog, 2017-2018.* Retrieved from http://howardcc.smartcatalogiq.com/en/2017-2018/Catalog/Courses/PSYC-Psychology/100/PSYC-101

Howard Community College (HCC). (2017b). College catalog: BMGT 100 Introduction to Business. *Howard Community College SmartCatalog, 2017-2018.* Retrieved from http://howardcc.smartcatalogiq.com/2017-2018/Catalog/Courses/BMGT-Business/100/BMGT-100

Howley, C., Chavis, B., & Kester, J. (2013). 'Like human beings': Responsive relationships and institutional flexibility at a rural community college. *Journal of Research in Rural Education, 28*(8), 1–14.

Hubbard, A., Rexeisen, R., & Watson, P. (2018). *AIFS study abroad alumni outcomes: A longitudinal study of personal, intercultural and career development based on a survey of our alumni from 1990 to 2017.* American Institute of Foreign Study (AIFS). Retrieved from https://www.aifsabroad.com/outcomes2018.pdf

Hudzik & McCarthy. (2012). *Leading Comprehensive Internationalization: Strategies and Tactics for Action.* Washington, DC: NAFSA.

Hudzik, J. K. (2011). Comprehensive internationalization: From concept to action. Washington, DC: NAFSA.

Hudzik, J. K. (2011). Comprehensive internationalization: From concept to action. Washington, DC: NAFSA: Association of International Educators.

Hudzik, J. K., & McCarthy, A. (2012). Leading comprehensive internationalization: Strategies and tactics for action. Washington, DC: NAFSA.

Hudzik, J. K., & McCarthy, J. S. (2012). Leading comprehensive internationalization: Strategies and tactics for action. Washington, DC: NAFSA: Association of International Educators.

Hudzik, J. K. (2011). *Comprehensive Internationalization: From Concept to Action.* Washington, DC: Association of International Educators.

Hulstrand, J. (2011, September). Developing Education Abroad at Community Colleges. *International Educator,* 46-49.

Hulstrand, J. (2013). Should they go? Academic and disciplinary considerations for education abroad. *International Educator, 22*(4).

Hulstrand, J. (2016). Advancing faculty-led programs at community colleges. *International Educator.* Retrieved from: www.nafsa.org/_File/_/ie_ novdec16_education_abroad.pdf

Hulstrand, J. (2016, November-December). Advancing faculty-led programs at community colleges. *International Educator*, 44-47.

Hunter, B., White, G. P., & Godbey, G. C. (2006). What does it mean to be globally competent? *Journal of Studies in International Education, 10*(3), 267–285. doi:10.1177/1028315306286930

Insley, A. (2016, December 22). Transferring from a community college - 2 + 2 agreements. *Study Abroad USA Magazine*. Retrieved from: https://studyusa.com/en/a/1004/ https://studyusa.com/en/a/1004/transferring-from-a-community-college-2-+-2-agreements

Institute for Intercultural Communication. (2018). *Summer Institute for Intercultural Education*. Retrieved from http://intercultural.org/siic.html

Institute for International Education (IIE). (2017a). *Community college education abroad data tables (2002-2017)*. Retrieved from www.iie.org/en/Research-and-Insights/Open-Doors/Data/Community-College-Data-Resource/Community-College---Study-Abroad/Leading-Institutions/

Institute for International Education (IIE). (2017b). *Education abroad data tables*. Retrieved from www.iie.org/en/Research-and-Insights/Open-Doors/Data/Study-Abroad/Leading-Institutions/2016-17

Institute for International Education. (2017). *Open doors Community college education abroad data tables*. Retrieved from: https://www.iie.org/en/Research-and-Insights/Open-Doors/Data/Community-College-Data-Resource/Community-College---Study-Abroad/Leading-Institutions/2015-16

Institute of International Education. (2008). *Expanding education abroad at U.S. community colleges*. Retrieved from https://www.iie.org/Research-and-Insights/Publications/Expanding-Education-Abroad-at-US-Community-Colleges

Institute of International Education. (2014). *Generation study abroad*. Retrieved from: https://www.iie.org/Programs/Generation-Study-Abroad

Institute of International Education. (2014). *Press release Open Doors 2014: International students in the United States and study abroad by American students are at all-time high*. Retrieved from http://www.iie.org/Who-We-Are/News-and-Events/Press-Center/Press-Releases/2014/2014-11-17-Open-Doors-Data

Institute of International Education. (2016). *Open Doors*. Retrieved from http://www.iie.org/Research-and-Publications/Open-Doors/Data

Institute of International Education. (2017). *Open Doors (Italicized)*. New York: Institute of International Education.

Institute of International Education. (2017). *Open doors 2017*. Retrieved from https://www.iie.org/Research-and-Insights/Open-Doors

Institute of International Education. (2017). *Open Doors 2017: Report on international educational exchange*. Retrieved from http://www.iie.org/Research-and-Publications/Open-Doors

Institute of International Education. (2017). *Open doors report on international educational exchange*. New York, NY: Institute for International Education.

Institute of International Education. (2017). *Open doors*. Retrieved from: https://www.iie.org/opendoors

Compilation of References

Institute of International Education. (2017). *Profile of U.S. study abroad students, 2004/05-2015/16*. Open Doors Report on International Educational Exchange. Retrieved from https://www.iie.org/Research-and-Insights/Open-Doors/Data/US-Study-Abroad/Student-Profile

Institute of International Education. (2017a). *Open doors 2017 executive summary*. Retrieved from https://www.iie.org/Why-IIE/Announcements/2017-11-13-Open-Doors-2017-ExecutiveSummary

Institute of International Education. (2017a). *U.S. Study Abroad at Associate's Institutions, 2005/06 - 2015/16*. Open Doors Report on International Educational Exchange.

Institute of International Education. (2017b). *Host Regions of U.S. Study Abroad at Associate's Institutions, 2001/02 - 2015/16*. Open Doors Report on International Educational Exchange.

Institute of International Education. (2017b). *Profile of U.S. study abroad students, 2004/05-2015/16*. Retrieved from https://www.iie.org/Research-and-Insights/Open- Doors/Data/US-Study-Abroad/Student-Profile

Institute of International Education. (2017c). *Duration of U.S. Study Abroad at Associate's Institutions, 2000/01 - 2015/16*. Open Doors Report on International Educational Exchange.

Institute of International Education. (2017d). *Race and Ethnicity Student Characteristics for U.S. Study Abroad, 2015/16*. Open Doors Report on International Educational Exchange.

Institute of International Education. (2017e). *Field of Study Student Characteristics for U.S. Study Abroad, 2015/16*. Open Doors Report on International Educational Exchange.

Institute of International Education. (2018a). *IIE generation study abroad initiative*. Retrieved from https://www.iie.org/en/Programs/Generation-Study-Abroad

Institute of International Education. (2018b). *Heiskell award*. Retrieved from https://www.iie.org/Research-and-Insights/Best-Practices-Resource

Institute of International Education. (n.d.). *About USIP support*. Retrieved from https://www.iie.org/Programs/USIP-Support/About

Institute of International Education. (n.d.). *Support recipients*. Retrieved from https://www.iie.org/Programs/USIP-Support/Support-Recipients

Institute on International Education (IIE). (2017). *Open Doors Report*. New York, NY: IIE.

Interassociational Advisory Committee on Safety and Responsibility in Education Abroad. (2001). *Responsible education abroad: Good practices for health & safety*. Retrieved from https://www.nafsa.org/Professional_Resources/Browse_by_Interest/ Education_Abroad/Network_Resources/Education_Abroad/Responsible_ Study_Abroad__Good_Practices_for_Health___Safety/

Ivey, T. (2009). *Curriculum internationalization and the community college* (Doctoral dissertation). Retrieved from http://thescholarship.ecu.edu/handle/10342/2212

Jackson, M. J. (2005, Fall). Breaking the barriers to overseas study for students of color and minorities. *IIE Networker*, 16-18.

Jacob, J. (2017). Adults and community college degrees. *Chronicle of Higher Education*. Retrieved from https://www.insidehighered.com/views/2017/10/09/community-colleges-should-focus-more-educating-adults-essay

Jaquette, O., & Parra, E. E. (2014). Using IPEDS for panel analyses: Core concepts, data challenges, and empirical applications. In M.B. Paulsen (Ed.), Higher education: Handbook of theory and research (vol. 29, pp. 467-533). New York: Springer Science+Business Media.

Jasmine Jahanshahi Fire Safety Foundation. (2018). *Homepage.* Retrieved From: http://www.firesafetyfoundation.org

Jenkins, D., Lahr, H., Fink, J. & Ganga, E. (2018). *What we are learning about guided pathways.* Community College Research Center.

Jenkins, S. K. (2013, January 1). *Faculty perceptions of, and experiences with, African American male students at a community college* (Dissertation). The University of North Carolina at Charlotte. ERIC NU. (ED558944)

Jenkins, D., & Weiss, M. (2011). *Charting pathways to completion for low-income community college students.* New York, NY: Teachers College, Columbia University.

Johnson County Community College. (n.d.). *Peacebuilding and nonviolence: Beyond the Cliches November 2-4, 2017.* Retrieved from http://www.jccc.edu/conferences/peacebuilding/

Jones, S. R.-K., Rowan-Kenyon, H. T., Ireland, S. M.-Y., Niehaus, E., & Skendall, K. C. (2012). The meaning students make as participants in short-term immersion programs. *Journal of College Student Development, 53*(2), 201–220. doi:10.1353/csd.2012.0026

Kasper, H. T. (2002). The changing role of community college. *Occupational Outlook Quarterly, 46*(4), 14–21.

Kasworm, C. (2007). *Adult Undergraduate Student Identity: A Proposed Model.* Paper presented at the American Educational Research Association, Chicago, IL.

Kasworm, C. (1990). Adult undergraduates in higher education: A review of past research perspectives. *Review of Educational Research, 60*(3), 345–372. doi:10.3102/00346543060003345

Keese, J., & O'Brien, J. (2011). Learn by going: Critical issues for faculty-led study-abroad programs. *The California Geographer, 51,* 2–24.

Kehl, K., & Morris, J. (2008). Differences in global-mindedness between short-term and semester-long study abroad participants at selected private universities. *Frontiers: The Interdisciplinary Journal of Study Abroad, 15,* 67–79. Retrieved from https://frontiersjournal.org/wp-content/uploads/2015/09/KEHL-MORRIS-FrontiersXV- DifferencesinGlobalMindednessbetweenShortTermandSemesterLongStudyAbroadPartici pants.pdf

Kenny, G. (2014). Five questions to identify key stakeholders. *Harvard Business Review.* Retrieved from: https://hbr.org/2014/03/five-questions-to-identify-key-stakeholders

King v. Board of Control of Eastern Michigan University, 221 F. Supp. 2d 783 (E.D. Mich. 2002).

Knight, J. (2003). Updating the definition of internationalization. *Industry and Higher Education, 33,* 2–3.

Knight, J. (2004). Internationalization remodeled: Definition, approaches, and rationales. *Journal of Studies in International Education, 8*(1), 5–31. doi:10.1177/1028315303260832

Kolodner, M. (2016). *Fewer than one in seven community college students transfer and gets a bachelor's degree---but there is new hope.* The Hechinger Report.

Korbel, L. (2007). In union there is strength: the role of state global education consortia in expanding community college involvement in global education. In International Reform Efforts and Challenges in Community Colleges (pp. 47-57). San Francisco, CA: Jossey-Bass.

Compilation of References

Korbel, L. A. (2007, June 19). In union there is strength: The role of state global education consortia in expanding community college involvement in global education. In International Reform Efforts and Challenges in Community Colleges, New Directions for Community Colleges. San Francisco, CA: Jossey-Bass.

Korbelak, S. (2014, April). *The internationalization of community college education: Moving beyond food, flags, and festivals.* Panel presentation at a meeting entitled Internationalization of U.S. Education in the 21st Century: The Future of International and Foreign Language Studies at the College of William & Mary, Williamsburg, VA. Retrieved from www.wm.edu/offices/revescenter/globalengagement/internationalization/ papers%20and%20presentations/StacyKorbelakpresentation2014.pptx

Kowarski, L. (2010). Colleges help students to translate the benefits of study abroad. *Chronicle of Higher Education*. Retrieved from the Chronicle of Higher Education website: https://www.chronicle.com/article/Colleges-Help-Students-to/123653

Kuh, G. D. (2008). *High-Impact educational practices: A brief overview.* Washington, DC: American Association of Colleges and Universities. Retrieved from http://www.aacu.org/leap/hip.cfm

Kuh, G. D. (2008). *High impact educational practices: What they are, who has access to them, and why they matter.* Washington, DC: Association of American Colleges and Universities.

Kuh, G. D. (2008). *High-Impact educational practices: What they are, who has access to them, and why they matter.* Washington, DC: Association of American Colleges and Universities. Retrieved from www.aacu.org/publications/

Kumari, S. (2017). *Leadership in higher education: Role of persons-in-charge of internationalization efforts in community colleges* (Dissertation). University of South Florida.

Ladson-Billings, G., & Tate, W. F. (1995). Toward a critical race theory of education. *Teachers College Record*, *97*(1), 47.

Lambert, R. A. (1989). *International studies and the undergraduate.* Washington, DC: American Council on Education.

Lederach, J. P. (1997). *Building peace: sustainable reconciliation in divided societies.* Washington, DC: U.S. Institute of Peace Press.

Levin, J. S. (2001). *Globalizing the community college: Strategies for change in the twenty-first century.* New York, NY: Palgrave MacMillan. doi:10.1057/9780312292836

Levin, J. S. (2002). Global culture and the community college. *Community College Journal of Research and Practice*, *26*(2), 121–145. doi:10.1080/106689202753385474

Levin, J. S. (2007). *Nontraditional students and community colleges: The conflict of justice and neoliberalism.* New York, NY: Palgrave MacMillan. doi:10.1057/9780230607286

Levin, J. S. (2017). *Community colleges and new universities under neoliberal pressures: Institutional change, institutional stability.* New York, NY: Palgrave MacMillan. doi:10.1057/978-1-137-48020-0

Levin, J. S., Viggiano, T., López Damián, A. I., Morales Vazquez, E., & Wolf, J. P. (2017). Polymorphic students: New descriptions and conceptions of community college students from the perspectives of administrators and faculty. *Community College Review*, *45*(2), 119–143. doi:10.1177/0091552116679731

Lewin, R. (2009). The Handbook of practice and research in study abroad: higher education and the quest for global citizenship. Association of American colleges and universities.

Lilley, K., Barker, M., & Harris, N. (2017). The global citizen conceptualized: Accommodating ambiguity. *Journal of Studies in International Education*, *21*(1), 6–21. doi:10.1177/1028315316637354

Liu, W., & Opotow, S. (2014). Aggression and violence. In P. T. Coleman, M. Deutsch, & E. C. Marcus (Eds.), *The handbook of conflict resolution theory and practice* (pp. 681–707). San Francisco, CA: Jossey-Bass.

Loberg, L. (2012). *Exploring factors that lead to participation in study abroad* (Dissertation). University of California at Los Angeles.

Lobosco, K. (2017, June 29). *Illinois is starving state colleges and universities*. Retrieved from http://money.cnn.com/2017/06/29/pf/college/illinois-budget-higher-education/index.html

Long, J., & Sullivan, B. (2011). *Historical dictionary of Hinduism*. Lanham, MD: Scarecrow Press.

Lu, C., Reddick, R., Dean, D., & Pecero, V. (2015). Coloring up study abroad: Exploring black students' decision to study in China. *Journal of Student Affairs Research and Practice*, *52*(4), 440–451. doi:10.1080/19496591.2015.1050032

Lucas, J. M. (2009). *Where are all the males?: A mixed methods inquiry into male study abroad participation* (Doctoral dissertation). Retrieved from Dissertations and Theses database. (UMI No. 3381358)

Luo, J., & Jamieson-Drake, D. (2015). Predictors of study abroad intent, participation, and college outcomes. *Research in Higher Education*, *56*(1), 29–56. doi:10.100711162-014-9338-7

Ma, J., & Baum, S. (2016). *Trends in community colleges: Enrollment, prices, student debt and completion*. College Board Research Brief: April 2016. Retrieved from: https://trends.collegeboard.org/sites/default/files/trends-in-community-colleges-research- brief.pdf

Maill, H., Ramsbotham, O., & Woodhouse, T. (2011). *Contemporary conflict resolution*. Cambridge, UK: Polity.

Malkay, R., & Pisani, M. J. (2011). Internationalizing the community college experience. *Community College Journal of Research and Practice*, *35*(11), 825–841. doi:10.1080/10668920802201377

Malveaux, G. (2016). *Look before leaping: Risks, liability, and repair of study abroad in higher education*. Lanham, MD: Rowman & Littlefield.

Malveaux, G. F. (2016). *Look Before Leaping: Risks, Liabilities and Repair of Study Abroad in Higher Education*. Lanham, MD: Rowman & Littlefield.

Malveaux, G. F. (2016). *Look before leaping: Risks, liabilities, and repair of study abroad in higher education*. Lanham, MD: Rowman & Littlefield.

Manns, D. (2014). Redefining the role, scope, and mission of community colleges in an international context. *Community College Journal of Research and Practice*, *38*(8), 705–709. doi:10.1080/10668926.2014.897079

Martínez-Alemán, A. M., Pusser, B., & Bensimon, E. M. (Eds.). (2015). *Critical approaches to the study of higher education: A practical introduction*. Baltimore, MD: John Hopkins University Press.

Maryland Community College International Education Consortium. (2015). *Statement of Purpose*. Unpublished Documents from the MCCIEC.

Maryland Community College International Education Consortium. (2018a). *How to maintain federal financial aid eligibility in a declared major of study*. Retrieved from: file:///C:/Users/Montgomery%20College/Downloads/ CPOS-FAQs.pdf

Maryland Community College International Education Consortium. (2018b). *Admissions and Records: Resources for International Students*. Retrieved from: http://cms.montgomerycollege.edu/edu/department2.aspx?id=10078

Maryland Community College International Education Consortium. (2018c). *Student Advising Tool Kit*. Retrieved from: http://cms.montgomerycollege.edu/generalstudies/student-advising-toolkit/

Mazzarol, T., & Soutar, G. N. (2002). "Push-Pull" factors influencing international student destination choice. *International Journal of Educational Management, 16*(82).

McClenney, K., Marti, C. N., & Adkins, C. (2012). *Student engagement and student outcomes: Key findings from CCSSE validation research*. Austin, TX: Community College Survey of Student Engagement. Retrieved from www.ccssc.org/aboutsurvey/docs/CCSSE%20Validation%20Summary.pdf

McDonough, P. (1994). Buying and selling higher education: The social construction of the college applicant. *The Journal of Higher Education, 65*, 427–446.

McDonough, P. (1997). *Choosing colleges: How social class and schools structure opportunity*. Albany, NY: SUNY University Press.

McLean, J. (1990). Consortial approaches to international education. In Developing International Education Programs (pp. 47-56). San Francisco, CA: Jossey-Bass. doi:10.1002/cc.36819907007

McRaven, N., & Somers, P. (2017). Internationalizing a community college: A view from the top. *Community College Journal of Research and Practice, 41*(7), 436–446. doi:10.1080/10668926.2016.1195306

Merriam, S. B. (2002). *Qualitative research in practice: Examples for discussion and analysis*. San Francisco, CA: Jossey-Bass.

Merriam, S. B. (2007). *Qualitative research and case study applications in education*. San Francisco, CA: Jossey-Bass.

Mezirow, J. (2000). *Learning as transformation: Critical perspectives on a theory in progress*. San Francisco, CA: Jossey-Bass.

Mignolo, W. D., & Tlostanova, M. V. (2006). Theorizing from the borders: Shifting to geo-and body-politics of knowledge. *European Journal of Social Theory, 9*(2), 205–221. doi:10.1177/1368431006063333

Miller, C. A., & King, M. E. (2005). *A glossary of terms and concepts in peace and conflict studies*. Geneva: University for Peace.

Miller, M., & Kissinger, D. (2007). Connecting rural community colleges to their communities. In P. Eddy and J. Murray, eds. Rural community colleges: Teaching, learning, and leading in the heartland. *New Directions for Community Colleges, 137*(Spring), 27–34. doi:10.1002/cc.267

Miller-Perrin, C., & Thompson, D. (2014). Outcomes of global education: External and internal change associated with study abroad. *New Directions for Student Services, 146*(146), 77–89. doi:10.1002s.20093

Milofsky, A., & Berdan, K. (Eds.). (2011). *Peacebuilding toolkit for educators: high school lessons*. Washington, DC: United States Institute of Peace.

Modood, T. (2004). Capitals, ethnic identity and educational qualifications. *Cultural Trends, 13*(50), 87–105. doi:10.1080/0954896042000267170

Moschetti, R. V., & Hudley, C. (2015). Social capital and academic motivation among first-generation community college students. *Community College Journal of Research and Practice, 39*(2), 235–251. doi:10.1080/10668926.2013.819304

Murray Brux, J., & Fry, B. (2010). Multicultural students in study abroad: Their interests, their issues, and their constraints. *Journal of Studies in International Education, 14*(5), 508–527. doi:10.1177/1028315309342486

Musil, C. M. (2006). *Assessing Global Learning: Matching Good Intentions with Good Practice*. Washington, DC: American Association of Colleges and Universities Publications.

NAFSA Task Force. (2010). *Assessment and evaluation for international educators.* Accessed from http://www.nafsa.org/uploadedFiles/NAFSA_Home/Resource_Library_Assets/ Networks/RS/Assess%20and%20Eval%20in%20IE.pdf

NAFSA. (2015). *2015 Global learning colloquia presentations and handouts.* Retrieved from https://www.nafsa.org/Programs_and_Events/Global_Learning_Colloquia/2015_Global_Learning_Colloquia_Presentations_and_Handouts

NAFSA. (2015). *Education abroad advising e-learning courses.* Retrieved from: http://www.nafsa.org/Professional_Resources/Learning_and_Training/e-Learning_ Courses/Courses/Education_Abroad_Advising/

NAFSA. (2016). *2016 Global learning colloquia presentations and handouts.* Retrieved from https://www.nafsa.org/Programs_and_Events/Global_Learning_Colloquia/2016_Global_Learning_Colloquia_Presentations_and_Handouts

NAFSA. (2016). *Trends in US study abroad.* Retrieved from http://www.nafsa.org/Policy_and_Advocacy/Policy_Resources/Policy_Trends_and_Data/ Trends_in_U_S__Study_Abroad/

NAFSA. (2017). *2017 Global learning colloquia presentations and handouts.* Retrieved from https://www.nafsa.org/Programs_and_Events/Global_Learning_Colloquia/2017_Global_Learning_Colloquia_Presentations_and_Handouts

NAFSA. (2017). *NAFSA International Education Professional Competencies.* Accessed from www.nafsa.org/competencies

NAFSA. (2017). *Region XII Calendar.* Retrieved from: http://www.nafsa.org/Connect_and_Network/NAFSA_Regions/Region_XII/Resources/

NAFSA. (2018). *2018 global learning signature programs: Presentations and handouts.* Retrieved from http://www.nafsa.org/Programs_and_Events/Global_Learning_Colloquia/2018_Global_Learning_Signature_Programs__Presentations_and_Handouts

NAFSA. (2018). *Education Abroad Knowledge Community.* Retrieved from www.nafsa.org

NAFSA. (2018). *Responsible education abroad: Good practices for health and safety.* Retrieved from: https://www.nafsa.org/uploadedFiles/responsible_ education_abroad.pdf

NAFSA. (2018). *Statement of ethical principles.* Retrieved from: http://www.nafsa.org/About_Us/About_NAFSA/Leadership_and_ Governance/NAFSA_s_Statement_of_Ethical_Principles/

Nair, I., & Henning, M. (2017). *Models of global learning.* Washington, DC: Association of American Colleges and Universities.

National Center for Education Statistics. (2016). *Digest of Education Statistics.* Retrieved from https://nces.ed.gov/programs/digest/

National Center on Education Statistics. (2009). *Integrated Postsecondary Education Data System (IPEDS).* Retrieved from: http://nces.ed.gov/ipeds/

National Survey of Student Engagement. (2018). *High-Impact practices.* Retrieved from http://nsse.indiana.edu/html/high_impact_practices.cfm

Navarro-Castro, L., & Nario-Galace, J. (2008). *Peace education: a pathway to a culture of peace.* Quezon City, Philippines: Center for Peace Education.

Nevadomski Berdan, S. (2014). *Busting the 10 top study abroad myths.* Retrieved from https://www.huffingtonpost.com/stacie-nevadomski-berdan/busting-the-top-10-study- abroad_b_4175861.html

Noddings, N. (2005). Global citizenship: promises and problems. In N. Noddings (Ed.), *Educating citizens for global awareness* (pp. 1–21). New York, NY: Teachers College Press.

Compilation of References

Nunley, C., Bers, T., & Manning, T. (2011). *Learning outcomes assessment in community colleges*. National Institute for Learning Outcome's Assessment. Retrieved from www.learningoutcomesassessment.org

Nussbaum, M. (2006). *Frontiers of justice: Disability, nationality, species membership*. Cambridge, MA: Harvard University Press.

Nyaupane, G., Paris, C. M., & Teye, V. (2010). Study abroad motivations, destination selection and pre-trip attitude formation. *International Journal of Tourism Research*, *13*(3), 205–217. doi:10.1002/jtr.811

O'Connor, G., Farnsworth, K. A., & Utley, M. E. (2013). Internationalization of general education curricula in community colleges: A faculty perspective. *Community College Journal of Research and Practice*, *37*(12), 966–978. doi:10.1080/10668926.2010.515512

Oberstein-Delvalle, E. (1999). *Study abroad programs in three California community colleges* (Dissertation). Pepperdine University, Malibu, CA.

Oberstein-Delvalle, E. (1999). *Study abroad programs in three California community colleges* (Unpublished doctoral dissertation). Pepperdine University, Malibu, CA.

OECD. (2016). *Getting skills right: Assessing and anticipating changing skill needs*. Paris: OECD Publishing; doi:10.1787/9789264252073-

OECD/Asia Society. (2018). *Teaching for global competence in a rapidly changing world*. Retrieved from: https://asiasociety.org/sites/default/files/inline-files/teaching-for-global- competence-in-a-rapidly-changing-world-edu.pdf

Ogden, A., & Barnes, B. E. (2018, July 5). Expanding education abroad through faculty engagement [blog post]. Retrieved from: https://isatoday.wordpress.com/2018/07 /05/expanding-education-abroad-through-faculty-engagement/

Olsen, T., & Lipinsky, B. (2017). *Peace studies and conflict resolution – Study abroad syllabus*. Cleveland, OH: Cuyahoga Community College.

Olssen, M., & Peters, M. A. (2005). Neoliberalism, higher education and the knowledge economy: From the free market to knowledge capitalism. *Journal of Education Policy*, *20*(3), 313–345. doi:10.1080/02680930500108718

Opp, D., & Gosetti, P. P. (2014). The role of key administrators in internationalizing the c ommunity college. In Strengthening Community Colleges Through Institutional Collaborations (pp. 67-75). San Francisco, CA: Jossey-Bass.

Opp, R. D., & Gosetti, P. P. (2014). The role of key administrators in internationalizing the community college student experience. *New Directions for Community Colleges*, *165*(165), 67–75. doi:10.1002/cc.20092

Oredein, A. E. (2016). *Faculty perceptions of factors affecting the internationalization of general education curriculum in Mississippi community colleges* (Doctoral dissertation). Retrieved from ProQuest Dissertations and Theses. (UMI No. 10100418)

Paige, R. M., Fry, G. W., Stallman, E. M., Josić, J., & Jon, J. (2009). Study abroad for global engagement: The long-term impact of mobility experiences. *Intercultural Education*, *20*(Supplement 1), S29–S44. doi:10.1080/14675980903370847

Paige, R. M., & Vande Berg, M. (2012). Why students are and are not learning abroad. In M. Vande Berg, R. M. Paige, & K. H. Lou (Eds.), *Student learning abroad: what our students are learning, what they're not* (pp. 29–58). Sterling, VA: Stylus.

Paneno v. Centres for Academic Programmes Abroad Ltd., 13 Cal. Rptr. 3d 759 (Cal. Ct. App. 2004).

Parsons, R. L. (2010). The effects of an internationalized university experience on domestic students in the United States and Australia. *Journal of Studies in International Education*, *14*(4), 313–334. doi:10.1177/1028315309331390

Partlo, M., & Ampaw, F. (2018). Using income effects to market undergraduate education abroad participation in higher education. *Journal of Marketing for Higher Education, 28*(1), 66–89. doi:10.1080/08841241.2018.1425230

Pashby, K., & Andreotti, V. D. O. (2016). Ethical internationalisation in higher education: Interfaces with international development and sustainability. *Environmental Education Research, 22*(6), 771–787. doi:10.1080/13504622.2016.1201789

Patriquin, W. M. (2016). *Developing intercultural competence in community college career and technical programs* (Doctoral dissertation). Retrieved from ProQuest Dissertations and Theses. (UMI No. 10193559)

Peace Alliance. (n.d.). *Domestic peacekeeping*. Retrieved from https://peacealliance.org/issues-advocacy/domestic-peacekeeping/

Peace and Justice Initiative Newsletter. (2015). Going global, sister school with Kenya institute. *Peace and Justice Initiative Newsletter, 6*, 13.

Peace and Justice Studies Association. (n.d.). *Directory of peace studies and conflict resolution programs*. Retrieved from https://pjsa.lib.miamioh.edu/

Peifer, J., & Meyer-Lee, E. (2017). Program Design for Intercultural Development. In The Guide to Successful Short-Term Programs Abroad (3rd ed.; pp. 157–170). Washington, DC: NAFSA.

Pelton, W. (2017). Administrative Processes. In The Guide to Successful Short-Term Programs Abroad (3rd ed.; pp. 45-63). Washington, DC: NAFSA.

Pennington, K., Williams, M., & Karvonen, M. (2006). Challenges facing rural community colleges: Issues and problems today and over the past 30 years. *Community College Journal of Research and Practice, 30*(8), 641–655. doi:10.1080/10668920600746086

Peralta Community College District. (2015). *Board policies & district administrative procedures home*. Retrieved from: http://web.peralta.edu/trustees/files/2013/12/AP-4026-Philosphy-and-Criteria-for-Study-Abroad-Education-DRAFT-revised-8-6-15.pdf

Peralta Community College District. (2015). *Strategic plan home, our mission*. Retrieved from: http://web.peralta.edu/strategicplan/

Peralta Community College District. (2015). *Study abroad booklet*. Retrieved from: http://web.peralta.edu/international/wp-content/uploads/2008/09/PCCD-Study-Abroad-Booklet.pdf

Peralta Community College District. (2015-2016). *2015-2016 Strategic goals and institutional objectives*. Retrieved from: http://web.peralta.edu/strategicplan/files/2009/02/PCCD-2015-2016-Strategic-Goals-and-Institutional-Objectives1.docx

Peralta Community College District. (2016). *Board policies & district administrative procedures home*. Retrieved from: http://web.peralta.edu/trustees/files/2013/12/AP-5500-Standards-of-Student-Conduct-Discipline-Procedures-and-Due-Process5.pdf

Peralta Community College District. (2018). *Career and technical education home*. Retrieved from: http://web.peralta.edu/cte/

Peralta Community College District. (2018). *Pre-Travel study abroad information form*. Retrieved from: https://www.surveymonkey.com/r/peraltapretravel

Perna, L. W. (2006). Studying college access and choice: A proposed conceptual model. In J. C. Smart (Ed.), *Higher education: Handbook of theory and research* (Vol. 21, pp. 99–157). New York: Springer Press.

Compilation of References

Person, A., Rosenbaum, J. E., & Deil-Amen, R. (2006). Student planning and information problems in different college structures. *Teachers College Record*, *108*(3), 374–396. doi:10.1111/j.1467-9620.2006.00655.x

Petzoid, K., & Peter, T. (2015). The social norm to study abroad: Determinants and effects. *Higher Education*, *69*(8), 885–900. doi:10.100710734-014-9811-4

Pitman, T., Broomhall, S., McEwan, J., & Majocha, E. (2010). Adult learning in educational tourism. *Australian Journal of Adult Learning*, *50*(2), 219–238.

Pogge, T. W. M. (1989). *Realizing Rawls*. Ithaca, NY: Cornell University Press.

Povich, E. (2018). *More community colleges are offering bachelor's degrees — and four-year universities aren't happy about it*. Retrieved from http://www.pewtrusts.org/en/research-and-analysis/blogs/stateline/2018/04/26/more-community-colleges-are-offering-bachelors-degrees

Próspero, M., & Vohra-Gupta, S. (2007). First generation college students: Motivation, integration, and academic achievement. *Community College Journal of Research and Practice*, *31*(12), 963–975. doi:10.1080/10668920600902051

Pussar, B., & Levin, J. (2009). *Re-imagining community colleges in the 21st century*. Retrieved From https://cdn.americanprogress.org/wp-content/uploads/issues/2009/12/pdf/ community_colleges_reimagined.pdf

Quezada, R. L., & Cordeiro, P. A. (2016). Creating and enhancing a global consciousness among students of color in our community colleges. In International education at community colleges: Themes, practices, research, and case studies (pp. 335-355). New York, NY: Palgrave.

Quijano, A. (2007). Coloniality and modernity/rationaleity. *Cultural Studies*, *21*(2-3), 168–178. doi:10.1080/09502380601164353

Raby, R. L. (1995). *Internationalizing the curriculum: Ideals vs. reality*. Paper presented at the Annual Conference of the Association of California Community College Administrators, San Jose, CA.

Raby, R. L. (1996). International, Intercultural, and Multicultural Dimensions of Community Colleges in the United States. In Dimensions of the Community College: International and Inter/Multicultural Perspectives. Garland Pub., Inc.

Raby, R. L. (1997). *Community college models: Myths and realities of access and equality*. ERIC ED402973.

Raby, R. L. (2006, Fall). *Community college study abroad: Making study abroad accessible to all students*. Retrieved from: http://www.iienetwork.org

Raby, R. L. (2007). Internationalizing the Curriculum: On- and Off-Campus Strategies. In International Reform Efforts and Challenges in Community Colleges. Jossey-Bass.

Raby, R. L. (2008). *Expanding Education Abroad at U.S. Community Colleges*. IIE Study Abroad White Paper Series 3 (September 2008). New York: NY: Institute for International Education Press.

Raby, R. L. (2008). *Expanding education abroad at U.S. community colleges*. IIE Study Abroad White Paper Series 3. New York: NY: Institute for International Education Press.

Raby, R. L. (2008). *Expanding education abroad at U.S. community colleges*. New York: Institute of International Education.

Raby, R. L. (2008). *IIE study abroad white paper series number 3: Expanding education abroad at U.S. community colleges*. New York: Institute for International Education.

Raby, R. L. (2008). *Meeting America's global education challenge: Expanding education abroad at U.S. community colleges*. New York: Institute for International Education.

Raby, R. L. (2008, September). *Expanding education abroad at U.S. community colleges.* New York, NY: Institute of International Education Study Abroad.

Raby, R. L. (2008, September). *Meeting America's global education challenge: Expanding education abroad at U.S. Community colleges* (Institute of International Education Study Abroad White Paper Series 3). New York: Institute for International Education Press.

Raby, R. L. (2012). Re-Imagining international education at community colleges. *Audem: International Journal of Higher Education and Democracy, 3,* 81-99. Retrieved from https://muse.jhu.edu/issue/27073

Raby, R. L. (2016, July 18). *Community college education abroad foundation and future concerns.* Retrieved from: https://www.diversitynetwork.org/news/298875/Community-College-Education-Abroad-Foundation-and-Future-Concerns.htm

Raby, R. L., & Rhodes, G. M. (2018). Promoting education abroad among community college students: Overcoming obstacles and developing inclusive practices. In H. Barclay Hamir & N. Gozik (Eds.), Promoting Inclusion in Education Abroad: A Handbook of Research and Practice (pp. 114-133). Sterling, VA: Stylus.

Raby, R. L., & Sawadogo, G. (2005). Community colleges and study abroad. In NAFSA's Guide to Education Abroad for Advisers and Administrators (3rd ed.). New York: NAFSA Publications.

Raby, R. L., & Valeau, E. J. (2007). Community college international education: Looking back to forecast the future. In International Reform Efforts and Challenges in Community Colleges (pp. 5-14). San Francisco, CA: Jossey-Bass.

Raby, R. L., Culton, D. R., & Valeau, E. J. (2014). Collaboration: Use of consortium to promote international education. In Strengthening Community Colleges Through Institutional Collaborations (pp. 77-87). San Francisco, CA: Jossey-Bass.

Raby, R. L., Culton, D. R., & Valeau, E. J. (2014, March 22). Collaboration: Use of consortia to promote international education. In Strengthening community colleges through international collaboration. San Francisco, CA: Jossey-Bass.

Raby, R. L. (2007). Internationalizing the curriculum: On- and off-campus strategies. *New Directions for Community Colleges, 138*(138), 57–66. doi:10.1002/cc.282

Raby, R. L. (2008). *Expanding education abroad at U.S. community colleges (IIE Study Abroad White Paper Series, Issue No. 3).* New York, NY: Institute of International Education. Retrieved from https://www.iie.org/Research-and-Insights/Publications/Expanding-Education-Abroad-at-US-Community-Colleges

Raby, R. L. (2008). *Expanding Education Abroad at U.S. Community Colleges.* New York: Institute for International Education Press.

Raby, R. L. (2012). Re-Imagining International Community Colleges *Audem. International Journal of Higher Education and Democracy, 3,* 81–99.

Raby, R. L. (2012). Re-imagining international education at community colleges. *Audem: International Journal of Higher Education and Democracy, 3,* 81–98.

Raby, R. L. (2012). Re-Imagining international education at community colleges. *Audem: International Journal of Higher Education and Democracy, 3,* 81–99.

Raby, R. L. (2012). Reimagining international education at community colleges. *AUDEM: The International Journal of Higher Education and Democracy, 3*(1), 81–98.

Raby, R. L. (2018). Adult students studying abroad through community colleges. In E. Brewer & A. C. Ogden (Eds.), *Critical Perspectives on Education Abroad: Leveraging the Educational Continuum.* New York, NY: Stylus.

Compilation of References

Raby, R. L., & Rhodes, G. M. (2005). *Barriers for Under-Represented Students Participation in California Community College Study Abroad Programs*. Sacramento, CA: Chancellor's Office of California Community Colleges, Fund for Instructional Improvement Publications.

Raby, R. L., & Rhodes, G. M. (2018). Promoting education abroad among community college students: Overcoming obstacles and developing inclusive practices. In *Promoting Inclusion in Education Abroad*. London: Stylus.

Raby, R. L., Rhodes, G. M., & Biscarra, A. (2014). Community college study abroad: Implications for student success. *Community College Journal of Research and Practice*, *38*(2-3), 174–183. doi:10.1080/10668926.2014.851961

Raby, R. L., & Tarrow, N. (Eds.). (1996). *Dimensions of the community college: International and inter/multicultural perspectives*. New York, NY: Garland.

Raby, R. L., & Valeau, E. J. (2007). Community college international education: Looking back to forecast the future. *New Directions for Community Colleges*, *2007*(138), 5–14. doi:10.1002/cc.276

Raby, R. L., & Valeau, E. J. (2007). International reform efforts and challenges in community colleges. In *New Directions*. San Francisco, CA: Jossey-Bass.

Raby, R. L., & Valeau, E. J. (2016). *International education at community colleges: Themes, practices, research, and case studies*. New York, NY: Palgrave Macmillian Publishers. doi:10.1057/978-1-137-53336-4

Rapoza, K. (2015). What will become of China's ghost cities? *Forbes*. Retrieved from https://www.forbes.com/sites/kenrapoza/2015/07/20/what-will-become-of-chinas-ghost-cities/4/#683ed15927b2

Rawls, J. (1971). *A theory of justice*. Cambridge, MA: Harvard University.

Redden, E. (2017, March 13). Will international students stay away? *Inside Higher Education*. Retrieved from: https://www.insidehighered.com/news/2017/03/13/nearly-4-10-universities-report-drops-international-student-applications

Rhodes, G., DeRomana, I., & Pedone, X. (2018). *Education Abroad & Other International Travel. Center for Disease Control (CDC) Yellow Book*. Retrieved from: https://wwwnc.cdc.gov/travel/yellowbook/2018/advising-travelers-with-specific- needs/education-abroad-other-international-student-travel

Rhodes, T. (2009). *Assessing outcomes and improving achievement: Tips and tools for using the rubrics*. Washington, DC: Association of American Colleges and Universities.

Richardson, J., Kemp, S., Malinen, S., & Haultain, S. A. (2013). The academic achievement of students in a New Zealand university: Does it pay to work? *Journal of Further and Higher Education*, *37*(6), 864–882. doi:10.1080/0309877X.2012.699517

Richland College. (n.d.). *Richland college path for peace*. Retrieved from https://alt.richlandcollege.edu/peace-poles/

Rivera, L. A. (2015). *Pedigree: How elite students get elite jobs*. Oxford, UK: Princeton University Press. doi:10.1515/9781400865895

Robertson, J. (2016). *The community college student's social construction of global learning in the Florida college system* (Doctoral dissertation). Orlando, FL: University of Central Florida.

Robertson, J. (2014). Student interest in international education at the community college. *Community College Journal of Research and Practice*, *39*(5), 473–484. doi:10.1080/10668926.2013.879377

Robertson, J. J., & Blasi, L. (2017). Community college student perceptions of their experiences related to global learning: Understanding the impact of family, faculty, and the curriculum. *Community College Journal of Research and Practice*, *41*(11), 697–718. doi:10.1080/10668926.2016.1222974

Rosenbaum, J. E., Deil-Amen, R., & Person, A. E. (2007). *After admission: From college access to college success*. New York, NY: Russell Sage Foundation.

Rural Community College Alliance. (2017). *Opening doors they alone open*. Retrieved from http://ruralccalliance.org/opening-doors

Sáenz, V. B., García-Louis, C., & Drake, A. P. (2017). Leveraging their family capital: How Latino males successfully navigate the community college. *Community College Review*, *45*(5), 1–17.

Salisbury, M. H., Paulsen, M. B., & Pascarella, E. T. (2010). To see the world or stay at home: Applying an integrated student choice model to explore the gender gap in the intent to study abroad. *Research in Higher Education*, *51*(7), 615–640. doi:10.100711162-010-9171-6

Salisbury, M. H., Paulsen, M. B., & Pascarella, E. T. (2011). Why do all the study abroad students look alike? Applying an integrated student choice model to explore differences in the factors that influence white and minority students' intent to study abroad. *Research in Higher Education*, *52*(2), 123–150. doi:10.100711162-010-9191-2

Salisbury, M. H., Umbach, P. D., Paulsen, M. B., & Pascarella, E. T. (2009). Going global: Understanding the choice process of the intent to study abroad. *Research in Higher Education*, *50*(2), 119–143. doi:10.100711162-008-9111-x

Sanchez, C. M., Fornerino, M., & Zhang, M. (2006). Motivations and the intent to study abroad among U.S., French, and Chinese Students. *Journal of Teaching in International Business*, *18*(1), 27–52. doi:10.1300/J066v18n01_03

Sandoval-Lucero, E., Maes, J. B., & Klingsmith, L. (2014). African American and Latina(o) community college students' social capital and student success. *College Student Journal*, *48*(3), 522–533.

Savicki, V., & Brewer, E. (2015). *Assessing Study Abroad: Theory, Tools and Practice*. Sterling, VA: Stylus Publishing.

SECUSSA List-Serve. (2018, April 9). *Discussion Thread on Credit Options for Study Abroad*. Author.

Seltzer, R. (2017, July 10). Picking up the pieces in Illinois. *Inside Higher Education*. Retrieved from https://www.insidehighered.com/news/2017/07/10/illinois-leaders-re-evaluate-higher-education-after-first-state-budget-two-years

Shahjahan, R. A. (2013). Coloniality and a global testing regime in higher education: Unpacking the OECD's AHELO initiative. *Journal of Education Policy*, *28*(5), 676–694. doi:10.1080/02680939.2012.758831

Shahjahan, R. A., & Kezar, A. J. (2013). Beyond the "national container" addressing methodological nationalism in higher education research. *Educational Researcher*, *42*(1), 20–29. doi:10.3102/0013189X12463050

Sheehy, K. (2014, November 4). *5 politicians who started at community colleges*. Retrieved from https://www.usnews.com/education/community-colleges/articles/2014/11/04/5-politicians-who-started-at-community-colleges

Shiri, S. (2013). Learners' Attitudes toward regional dialects and destinations preferences in study abroad. *Foreign Language Annals*, *46*(4), 565–587. doi:10.1111/flan.12058

Shirley, S. (2006). *The gender gap in post-secondary study abroad: Understanding and marketing to males* (Unpublished doctoral dissertation). University of North Dakota, Grand Forks, ND.

Shooshtari, N. H., & Manuel, T. A. (2009). Curriculum internationalization at AACSB schools: Immersive experiences, student placement, and assessment. *Journal of Teaching in International Business*, *25*(2), 134–156. doi:10.1080/08975930.2014.888965

Sideli, K. (2001, Spring). Outcomes assessment and study abroad programs: Commentary on the results of a SECUSSA/IIE electronic sampling. *International Educator*, 30.

Compilation of References

Silverman, S. C., Sarvenaz, A., & Stiles, M. R. (2009). Meeting the needs of commuter, part-time, transfer, and returning students. In Student engagement in higher education: Theoretical perspectives and practical approaches for diverse populations (pp. 223-242). New York, NY: Routledge.

Simon, J., & Ainsworth, J.W. (2012). Race and socioeconomic status differences in study abroad participation. The role of habitus, social networks, and cultural capital. *ISRN Education*.

Simon, P. (1980). *The tongue-tied American: Confronting the foreign language crisis*. New York, NY: Crossroad.

Smith, A. A. (2015, June 8). 2 + 2 Shouldn't = 5. *Inside Higher Education*. Retrieved from: https://www.insidehighered.com/news/2015/06/08/two-year-transfers-are-finding-not-all-their-credits-go-them

Smith, D. J. (2002, March 21). Let's give peace sign a chance. *Baltimore Sun*. Retrieved from http://articles.baltimoresun.com/2002-03-21/news/0203210153_1_peace-sign-nuclear-disarmament-popular-culture

Snodderly, D. R. (2011). *Peace terms glossary of terms for conflict management and peacebuilding*. Washington, DC: United States Institute of Peace Press.

Snow College. (2017). *EDUC 2851. Global perspectives on education, Latin America syllabus. Instructor: Richard Squire*. Ephraim, UT: Snow College.

Snow College. (n.d.). *Core themes, goals, and objectives*. Retrieved from https://www.snow.edu/academics/office/themes.html

Snyder, T. D., de Brey, C., & Dillow, S. A. (2018). *Digest of Education Statistics 2016 (NCES 2017-094)*. Washington, DC: National Center for Education Statistics, Institute of Education Sciences, U.S. Department of Education. Retrieved from https://nces.ed.gov/pubs2017/2017094.pdf

Soares, L., Gagliardi, J. S., & Nellum, C. J. (2017). *The post-traditional learners manifesto revisited: Aligning post-secondary education with real life for adult student success*. Retrieved from: http://www.acenet.edu/news-room/Pages/The-Post-Traditional-Learners-Manifesto-Revisited.aspx

Soares, L. (2013). *Post-traditional learners and the transformation of postsecondary education: A manifesto for college leaders*. Washington, DC: American Council on Education.

Solorzano, D. G., & Yosso, T. J. (2001). Critical race and LatCrit theory and method: Counter- storytelling. *International Journal of Qualitative Studies in Education: QSE*, *14*(4), 471–495. doi:10.1080/09518390110063365

Solorzano, D., & Delgado Bernal, D. (2001). Critical race theory, transformational resistance, and social justice: Chicana and Chicano students in an urban context. *Urban Education*, *36*, 308–342. doi:10.1177/0042085901363002

Soria, K. M., & Stebleton, M. J. (2012). First-Generation students' academic engagement and retention. *Teaching in Higher Education*, *17*(6), 673–685. doi:10.1080/13562517.2012.666735

Sparks, P. J., & Nuñez, A. (2014). The role of postsecondary institutional urbanicity in college persistence. *Journal of Research in Rural Education*, *29*(6), 1–19.

Spellings, M. (2006). *A test of leadership: Charting the future of U.S. higher education*. Washington, DC: United States Department of Education.

Spencer, S. E., & Tuma, K. (2002). The guide to successful short-term programs abroad. Washington, DC: NAFSA.

Starman, A. B. (2013). The case study as a type of qualitative research. *Journal of Contemporary European Studies*, *1*, 28–43.

Stearns, P. (2009). *Educating global citizens in colleges and universities: Challenges and opportunities.* New York, NY: Routledge, Taylor and Francis Group.

Steger, M. B. (2008). *Globalisms: The great ideological struggle of the twenty-first century.* Lanham, MD: Rowman & Littlefield Publishers.

Stein, S. (2017). Internationalization for an uncertain future: Tensions, paradoxes, and possibilities. *The Review of Higher Education, 41*(1), 3–32. doi:10.1353/rhe.2017.0031

Stein, S., Andreotti, V. D. O., & Suša, R. (2016). 'Beyond 2015', within the modern/colonial global imaginary? Global development and higher education. *Critical Studies in Education,* 1–21. doi:10.1080/17508487.2016.1247737

Sterns, P. (2010). Global Education & Liberal Education. *Liberal Education, 96*(3). Retrieved from https://www.aacu.org/publications-research/periodicals/global-education-liberal-education

Stovall, M. (2001). Using success courses for promoting persistence and completion. In Beyond access: Methods and models for increasing retention and learning among minority students (pp. 45–54). San Francisco, CA: Jossey Bass.

Strange, H., & Gibson, H. J. (2017). An investigation of experiential and transformative learning in study abroad programs. *Frontiers: The Interdisciplinary Journal of Study Abroad, 29,* 85–100.

Strayhorn, T. L., & Johnson, R. M. (2014). Black female community college students' satisfaction: A national regression analysis. *Community College Journal of Research and Practice, 38*(6), 534–550. doi:10.1080/10668926.2013.866060

Stroud, A. H. (2010). Who plans (not) to study abroad? An examination of U. S. student intent. *Journal of Studies in International Education, 14*(5), 491–507. doi:10.1177/1028315309357942

Stutton, S. B., & Obst, D. (Eds.). (2011). *Developing strategic international partnerships: Models for initiating and sustaining innovative institutional linkages. Global Education Research Reports.* New York: Institute of International Education and the AIFS Foundation.

Sutin, S., Derrico, D., Raby, R. L., & Valeau, E. (2011). *Increasing effectiveness of the community college financial model: A global perspective for the global economy.* New York: Palgrave MacMillan. doi:10.1057/9780230120006

Sutton, R. C., & Rubin, D. L. (2010). *Documenting the academic impact of study abroad: Final report of the GlOSSARI project* [PowerPoint slides]. Retrieved from http://glossari.uga.edu/datasets/pdfs/FINAL.pdf

Sutton, R. C., & Rubin, D. L. (2010). *Documenting the academic impact of study abroad: Final report of the GLOSSARI project.* Paper presented at NAFSA National Conference, Kansas City, MO.

Sutton, R. C., & Rubin, D. L. (2004). The GLOSSARI project: Initial findings from a system-wide research initiative on study abroad learning outcomes. *Frontiers: The Interdisciplinary Journal of Study Abroad, 10*(Fall), 65–82.

Swart, W. J., & Spaeth, C. (2017). Designing the Academic Course: Principles and Practicalities. In The Guide to Successful Short-Term Programs Abroad (3rd ed.; pp. 103-155). Washington, DC: NAFSA.

Sweeney, K. (2013). Inclusive excellence and underrepresentation of students of color in study abroad. *Frontiers: The Interdisciplinary Journal of Study Abroad, 23.* Retrieved from https://frontiersjournal.org/wp-content/uploads/2015/09/SWEENEY-FrontiersXXIII- InclusiveExcellenceandUnderrepresentationofStudentsofColorinStudyAbroad.pdf

Thackurdeen v. Duke University, 2014 WL 3886037 (S.D.N.Y. Aug. 8, 2014).

The Forum on Education Abroad. (2011). *Code of Ethics for Education Abroad* (2nd ed.). Carlisle, PA: The Forum on Education Abroad. Retrieved from: https://forumea.org/resources/standards-of-good-practice/code-of-ethics

Compilation of References

The Forum on Education Abroad. (2015). *Standards of Good Practice for Education Abroad* (5th ed.). Carlisle, PA: The Forum on Education Abroad.

The Forum on Education Abroad. (2017a). *Forum History*. Retrieved from https://forumea.org/about-us/mission/history/

The Forum on Education Abroad. (2017b). *Guidelines*. Retrieved from https://forumea.org/resources/standards-of-good-practice/standards-guidelines

Thomas, T. (2016). Community college education abroad and business internship programs cultivation of competency in communicating, collaborating, and critical thinking. In R. L. Raby & E. J. Valeau (Eds.), *International education at community colleges: Themes, practices, research, and case studies*. New York, NY: Palgrave Macmillian Publishers. doi:10.1057/978-1-137-53336-4_23

Tillman, M. (2010). *Diversity in international education hands-on workshop: Summary Report*. Washington, DC: American Institute for Foreign Study.

Tillman, M. (2014). *On the linkage of international experience and student employability, in career integration: Reviewing impact of experience abroad on employment*. CAPA & Learning Abroad Center, University of Minnesota. Retrieved from https://www.capa.org/sites/default/files/Career_Integration_Booklet_lowres.pdf

Tillman, M. (Ed.). (2005). *Impact of education abroad on career development: Four community college case studies*. Stamford, CT: American Institute for Foreign Study.

TNeCampus. (n.d.). *Earn an associate degree online in Tennessee*. Retrieved from https://tnecampus.org/associates

Treat, T., & Hagedorn, L. S. (2013). Resituating the community college in a global context. *New Directions for Community Colleges*, *2013*(161), 5–9. doi:10.1002/cc.20044

Twombly, S. B., Salisbury, M. H., Tumanut, S. D., & Klute, P. (2012). Special Issue: Study Abroad in a New Global Century--Renewing the Promise, Refining the Purpose. *ASHE Higher Education Report*, *38*(4), 1–152.

Twombly, S. B., Salisbury, M. H., Tumanut, S. D., & Klute, P. (2012). Study abroad in a new global century—Renewing the promise, refining the purpose. *ASHE Higher Education Report*, *38*(4), 1–152. Retrieved from http://eds.a.ebscohost.com/

U. S. Department of Agriculture, Economic Research Service. (2017). *Rural education at a glance: 2017 edition*. Retrieved from https://www.ers.usda.gov/webdocs/publications/83078/eib-171.pdf?v=42830

U.S. Department of Education, Institute of Education Sciences, National Center for Education Statistics. (2018). *Detailed fields of study by U.S citizenship at associate's institutions*. Washington, DC: National Postsecondary Student Aid Study (NPSAS).

U.S. Department of Education. (2017-2018). *2017-2018 federal student aid handbook*. Retrieved from https://ifap.ed.gov/fsahandbook/attachments/1415FSAHdbkAppendices FSAGlossaryAppendixA.pdf

U.S. Department of Education. (2017-2018). *International education: Study abroad*. Retrieved from http://www2.ed.gov/students/internatl/abroad/edpicks.jhtml

U.S. Institute of Peace. (2017). *Study abroad*. Retrieved from https://www.usip.org/public-education/students/study-abroad

UNESCO. (2018). *What is global citizenship education?* Retrieved from https://en.unesco.org/themese/gced/definition

University of California Education Abroad Programs. (2018). *Health and Safety*. Retrieved at: http://eap.ucop.edu/ForParents/Pages/health_safety.aspx

University of the Pacific. (2017). *What's Up with Culture?* Retrieved from: http://www2.pacific.edu/sis/culture/

US Department of State. (2018). *US passports & international travel.* US Department of State - Bureau of Consular Affairs. Retrieved from http://travel.state.gov/content/passports/english/country/guatemala.html

USA Study Abroad. (2017). *Study abroad data.* Retrieved from: https://studyabroad.state.gov/

Valeau, E. J., & Raby, R. L. (2016). Building the pipeline for community college international education leadership. In R. L. Raby & E. J. Valeau (Eds.), *International Education at Community Colleges: Themes, Practices, Research, and Case Studies* (pp. 163–173). New York, NY: Palgrave Macmillian. doi:10.1057/978-1-137-53336-4_11

Valencia College. (n.d.a). *Peace and justice institute, Advisory Council.* Retrieved March 1, 2018, from https://valenciacollege.edu/PJI/advisory-council.cfm

Valencia College. (n.d.b). *Peace and justice institute, about.* Retrieved from http://valenciacollege.edu/pji/about.cfm

Valencia College. (n.d.c). *Peace and justice institute, past speakers.* Retrieved from http://valenciacollege.edu/PJI/programs/past-speakers.cfm

Valencia College. (n.d.d). *Peace and justice institute, programs.* Retrieved from http://valenciacollege.edu/PJI/programs/global-peace-week.cfm

Van Der Meid, J. S. (2003). Asian Americans: Factors influencing the decision to study abroad. *Frontiers: The Interdisciplinary Journal of Study Abroad, 9*(4), 71–110.

Van Noy, M., & Heidkamp, M. (2017). *Working for adults: State policies and community college practices to better serve adult learners at community colleges during the great recession and beyond.* Retrieved from: https://www.dol.gov/odep/pdf/WorkingForAdults.pdf

Viggiano, T., López Damián, A. I., Morales Vázquez, E., & Levin, J. S. (2018). The others: Equitable access, international students, and the community college. *Journal of Studies in International Education, 22*(1), 71–85. doi:10.1177/1028315317725883

Wake Forest University. (2017). *WISE Conference.* Retrieved December 30, 2017, from http://global.wfu.edu/global-campus/wise-conference/

West, C. (2012). *Engaging stakeholders in internationalization: Strategies for collaboration.* NAFSA. Retrieved from: https://www.nafsa.org/uploadedFiles/Chez_NAFSA/Find_Resources/Internationalizing_ Higher_Education/engaging_stakeholders.pdf

West, C. (2015, October). Assessing learning outcomes for study abroad. *International Educator,* 36-41.

White, D. (2007). It takes a campus to run a study abroad program. In The Guide to Successful Short-Term Programs Abroad (pp. 29–37). Washington, DC: NAFSA.

Wick, D. J. (2011). *Study abroad for students of color: A third space for negotiating agency and identity* (Unpublished doctoral dissertation). San Francisco State University.

Willett, T., Pellegrin, N., & Cooper, D. (2013). *Study abroad impact technical report.* Retrieved from http://globaled.us/cccsoar/docs/CCC-SOAR-StudyAbroadTechReportFinal.pdf

Williams, F. (2007). *Study abroad and Carnegie doctoral/research extensive universities: Preparing students from underrepresented racial groups to live in a global environment* (Unpublished doctoral dissertation). Virginia Commonwealth University, Richmond, VA.

Williams, M. R., Pennington, K. L., Couch, G., & Dougherty, M. A. (2007). Preparing rural community college professionals. *Community College Enterprise, 13*(1), 23–35.

Willis, T. Y. (2016). Microaggressions and intersectionality in the experiences of Black women studying abroad through community colleges: Implications for practice. In International education at community colleges: Themes, practices, research, and case studies (pp. 167-186). New York: Palgrave Macmillian Publishers.

Wood, J. L., & Harris, F., III. (2015). The effect of academic engagement on sense of belonging: A hierarchical, multilevel analysis of Black men in the community colleges. *Spectrum: A Journal on Black Men, 4*(1), 21–47. doi:10.2979pectrum.4.1.0

Woolf, M. (2007). Impossible things before breakfast: Myths in education abroad. *Journal of Studies in International Education, 11*(3-4), 496–509. doi:10.1177/1028315307304186

World University Rankings. (2018). Swansea University. Retrieved from: https://www.timeshighereducation.com/world-university-rankings/swansea-university

Yankey, J. B. (2014). *Dude, where's my passport?: An exploration of masculine identity of college men who study abroad.* Graduate Theses and Dissertations. 13666. Iowa State University. Retrieved from https://lib.dr.iastate.edu/cgi/viewcontent.cgi?article=4673&context=etd

Yin, R. (1989). *Case study research: Design and method.* Newbury Park, CA: Sage.

Yosso, T. J. (2005). Whose culture has capital? A critical race theory discussion of community cultural wealth. *Race, Ethnicity and Education, 8*(1), 69–91. doi:10.1080/1361332052000341006

Zaki, H. (2016). *CCBC's center for global education: External review report, August 2016* (Unpublished manuscript). National Endowment for the Humanities, Washington, DC.

Zamani-Gallaher, E. M., Leon, R. A., & Lang, J. (2016). Self-authorship beyond borders: Reconceptualizing college and career readiness. In R. L. Raby & E. J. Valeau (Eds.), *International education at community colleges: Themes, practices, research, and case studies (pp. 146-66).* New York, NY: Palgrave. doi:10.1057/978-1-137-53336-4_8

Zhang, Y. (2011). Education abroad in the U.S. Community Colleges. *Community College Review, 39*(2), 181–200. doi:10.1177/0091552111404552

Zhang, Y. L., Lui, J., & Hagedorn, L. S. (2013). Post transfer experiences: Adult undergraduate students at a research university. *Journal of Applied Research in the Community College, 21*, 31–40.

About the Contributors

Gregory F. Malveaux, Ph.D., is a Professor of English and Literature, and Coordinator of Study Abroad at Montgomery College. He has been a study abroad coordinator and international education director in higher education for nearly two decades. Dr. Malveaux is the co-Chairperson of the Maryland Community College International Education Consortium and serves on the board for the College Consortium for International Studies. In addition, he is an accomplished writer and editor; his most recent work being *Look Before Leaping: Risks, Liabilities, and Repair of Study Abroad in Higher Education* (Rowman & Littlefield). He has traversed more than sixty countries and has led student, faculty and community-based study abroad programs to Africa, Asia, Central America, South America, and Europe. His passion to be a global citizen led him to pursue overseas studies in Africa, teach ESOL throughout Southeast Asia, Chair the English and U.S. Business Department at Nation University in Thailand, and serve as a study abroad specialist in American higher education.

Rosalind Latiner Raby, Ph.D., is a Senior Lecturer at California State University, Northridge in the Educational Leadership and Policy Studies Department of the College of Education and is an affiliate faculty for the ELPS Ed.D. Community College program. She also serves as the Director of California Colleges for International Education, a non-profit consortium whose membership includes ninety-one California community colleges. Dr. Raby is the past-NAFSA Education Abroad Knowledge Community College chair for NAFSA, and the past-NAFSA Region XII Community College Coordinator. Dr. Raby received her Ph.D. in the field of Comparative and International Education from UCLA and since 1984, has worked with community college faculty and administrators to help them internationalize their campuses. Dr. Raby has been publishing in the field of community college internationalization since 1985. Her latest books on community college internationalization are *International Education at Community Colleges: Themes, Practices, and Case Studies (Palgrave)* and *Handbook on Comparative Issues of Community Colleges and Global Counterparts.* (Springer).

* * *

Monija Amani, Ed.D., Senior Assistant Dean, Director of Global Programs and Partnerships, Georgetown University. With over two decades of experience in academic and student affairs, Monija Amani has been involved in the development and implementation of curricular and co-curricular programs at the undergraduate and graduate levels. She holds a master's degree in rehabilitation counseling and a doctoral degree in higher education administration from The George Washington University. Prior to joining the McDonough team, she worked at George Washington University where she coordinated the

About the Contributors

overall delivery of masters and education specialist degree programs, as well as graduate certificates in traumatic brain injury. She has taught courses in administration of higher education and qualitative research design and methodology. She also serves as a committee member on doctoral dissertations and engages in applied research related to global education and student development.

Julie Baer, Ed.M., is a Research Specialist in the IIE Center for Academic Mobility Research and Impact at the Institute of International Education (IIE) where she conducts research on the *Open Doors®* project, a large-scale annual survey of international educational exchange in the United States. Her experience includes analyzing trends in international academic mobility in U.S. higher education across sectors and using geospatial analysis to highlight trends in educational access. She holds an Ed.M. in International Education Policy from the Harvard Graduate School of Education and a Bachelor's degree from Centre College.

Tanith Fowler Corsi, M.A., has been professionally active in the field of international higher education for over 20 years in the Washington, DC area at universities, non-profit organizations and private companies. Tanith oversaw global education offices at George Mason University and the Catholic University of America and acted as a Senior Director at NAFSA. Most recently Tanith worked as Director of Membership & Outreach at the College Consortium of International Studies before joining VIU's Academic Affairs team. Tanith was born and raised Monaco in Europe where she completed a French Baccalaureate in Literature & Philosophy. She earned a bachelor's degree in International Relations at the University of California, Riverside, and completed her master's degree in International Communication at America University in Washington, DC. In addition to English, Tanith is fluent in French and conversational in Italian and Spanish. Her travel experiences include countries in Europe, as well as Latin America, Africa, Australia and Asia.

Rebekah de Wit, Ph.D., is the director of global education and an associate professor at the Community College of Baltimore County. She has worked in international education since 1999 and has served as director at both two- and four-year institutions, overseeing study abroad, international student services, intensive and academic English programs, and co-curricular initiatives. She has also served as a faculty member and coordinator of languages. She co-chairs the Maryland state consortium for community college international educators and also serves on the board of the Maryland International Education Consortium.

William David Fell, Ph.D., is an Associate Professor of English at Carroll Community College in Westminster, Maryland. In 2000, he received his Ph.D. in British Literature from the University of Illinois at Urbana-Champaign. Since then, he has taught at Carroll, teaching courses in composition, writing about literature, British literature, and world literature. He also teaches for the college's Hill Scholars honors cohort. Since 2009, he has co-led Carroll's travel program to Europe, which has included England, Scotland, Ireland, France, Italy, and Greece. His personal travels have also included Austria, the Czech Republic, and Spain. He currently resides in Westminster, Maryland.

Mary Beth Furst, Ed.D., is a Lecturer in Marketing at the Robert H. Smith School of Business at the University of Maryland. She teaches foundational marketing classes at the undergraduate and MBA level. Prior to joining the Smith School, Mary Beth was a professor of business at Howard Community

College where she developed curriculum and faculty. She also taught courses in marketing and business at the Whiting School of Engineering at Johns Hopkins University. Mary Beth earned her doctorate in education from Johns Hopkins University School of Education and focused her dissertation work on improving student retention and degree completion. Her teaching goal is to expand students' understanding of the interconnected global business environment. She facilitates student learning and the development of skills needed to be successful in the marketing profession through real-world experiences both in class and through study abroad.

Drew Gephart, M.S., is the International Services Manager for the Peralta Community College District located in Oakland, California. He currently develops and manages enrollment for special programs related to international education, as well as oversees all study abroad programs. Drew organized the district's first annual study abroad fair in 2014 and was awarded a scholarship of $15,000 to provide six Peralta students $2,500 each to study abroad. He also presented at the Institute of International Education's conference on "Models and Best Practices in Internationalization at the Community College" and NAFSA's Region XII conference on "Designing Effective Familiarization Tours for International Recruitment Partners". Drew has written two successful proposals for the California Colleges for International Education (CCIE) grants to support the internationalization of the Peralta Colleges and strengthening of the international programs. Drew earned his Master's Degree in Educational Leadership from California State University, East Bay.

Allan Goodman, Ph.D., is the sixth President of the Institute of International Education. He is also the CEO of the Institute of International Education. He is the author of books on international affairs published by Harvard, Princeton and Yale University presses. Previously, he was Executive Dean of the School of Foreign Service and Professor at Georgetown University. He was the first American professor to lecture at the Foreign Affairs College of Beijing, helped create the first U.S. academic exchange program with the Moscow Diplomatic Academy for the Association of Professional Schools of International Affairs, and developed the diplomatic training program of the Foreign Ministry of Vietnam. He has a Ph.D. in Government from Harvard, an M.P.A. from the John F. Kennedy School of Government and a B.S. from Northwestern University. Dr. Goodman has received awards from Georgetown, Johns Hopkins, South Florida, and Tufts universities, the Légion d'honneur from France, and the Royal Norwegian Order of Merit. He was awarded the inaugural Gilbert Medal for Internationalization by Universitas 21.

Ann Hubbard, Doctoral Candidate, is a vice president with AIFS Study Abroad where she is responsible for university relations for customized programs and academic assessment initiatives. Ann is conducting a longitudinal study of AIFS alumni on the intercultural, personal and professional outcomes of study abroad. Having previously worked in a campus-based education abroad office for 20 years, she has conducted intercultural training, developed faculty-led programs, and taught an honors seminar. She is a doctoral candidate in Higher Education Internationalisation at Università Cattolica del Sacro Cuore in Milan, and a QUIP reviewer for The Forum on Education Abroad.

Mikyong Minsun Kim, Ph.D., is an Associate professor in the Department of Educational Leadership, the Graduate School of Education and Human Development at the George Washington University. She was a visiting professor at Kassel University, Germany in 2017-2018. She has served as a consultant and grant reviewer at NSF and provided expert testimony before the US Commission on Civil Rights.

About the Contributors

She also served as president and board member of the Korean American Researchers Association for several years. Her teaching and research interests are relatively broad, including equity and opportunity issues, college impact, special colleges for special student populations (e.g., historically black institutions, women only colleges), marginalized groups in educational settings, state and inter-state tuition policies, comparative and international higher education, bridging K-12, higher education, and work, organizational analysis, and research design.

Jayme Kreitinger, M.S., is the Executive Director for the College Consortium for International Studies (CCIS), a consortium of U.S. and international member institutions and a 501(3)(c) education non-profit dedicated to increasing access and opportunity in study abroad. Jayme has broad experience leading international education, global strategies, and education abroad. Jayme joins CCIS from Georgetown University where she led graduate school education abroad and international degree initiatives. Prior to her tenure at Georgetown, she launched two new Department of State exchange programs with Tunisia through the NGO IREX. Jayme formerly led Education Abroad at Montana State University. Jayme was awarded a Fulbright Research Grant to Jordan where she studied sports as a tool for development and intercultural understanding. She specializes regionally in the Middle East and North Africa and speaks Spanish and Arabic.

Anne-Marie McKee, Ed.D., is an accomplished higher education professional with more than 25 years in the field. Currently, she creates and implements international programming and teaches business communications at Volunteer State Community College in Gallatin, Tennessee. Dr. McKee is seasoned in creating and building international programs from the ground up through proven competencies in grant writing and administration, project and program management, and staff development. In addition to her love for student success, Dr. McKee enjoys traveling with her college-aged daughters and has even spent the weekend in a tree house! Dr. McKee holds a B.S. in Communications/Journalism from the University of Tennessee, a Masters in Administrative Science from the University of Montana, and a Ed. D. from Union University in Jackson, Tennessee.

Gary Rhodes, Ph.D., is a Professor in the College of Education and Director of the Center for Global Education at California State University at Dominguez Hills (CSUDH). As a Professor, he is responsible for teaching, research and community service. He is also Director of the Center for Global Education, a national research and resource center supporting the internationalization of higher education. Dr. Rhodes areas of expertise include: Internationalization of Higher Education; Study Abroad Program Development and Administration; Impact of Study Abroad on Student Academic and Professional Success, Integrated International Learning; Diversity and Study Abroad; and, Health, Safety, Crisis and Risk Management for Study Abroad. He publishes articles and presents widely at US and international conferences.

Jennifer Robertson, Ed.D., currently serves as Valencia College's executive dean of the Poinciana Campus. Prior to this position, she served as the director of the Study Abroad and Global Experiences office at Valencia and executive director of the Florida Consortium for International Education since 2011. Dr. Robertson has a master's degree in business administration and completed a doctoral program at the University of Central Florida in educational leadership. She has lived and worked throughout Latin America and owned a language school in Puerto Rico prior to coming to Florida. Dr. Robertson is fluent in Spanish and learning Portuguese to better serve our Central Florida communities.

Carola Smith, M.A., serves as Acting Dean of Educational Programs at Santa Barbara City College where she also co-chairs the college's International Education Committee. In her current role, she provides oversight for SBCC's International Programs and the Business Division. Ms. Smith frequently presents both at regional and national international education conferences and is an active member of NAFSA, CCIE, and the Forum on Education Abroad. She came to the US as an international student and earned her Bachelors and Masters Degree as well as her Teaching Certificate in English as a Second Language from the University of California, Santa Barbara. She has lived and traveled abroad extensively and considers herself as a product of international education. For the past 5 years, Ms. Smith has served in a variety of leadership roles within the NAFSA Academy for International Education, and she is currently finishing her second term as Academy Chair.

David J. Smith, J.D., M.S., is an educational consultant supporting higher education in advancing peacebuilding awareness. He directs the National Community College Peacebuilding Seminar. Formerly, a senior manager and senior program officer at the U.S. Institute of Peace, he is president of Forage Center for Peacebuilding and Humanitarian Education. He served on the faculty of Harford Community College in Maryland as an associate (tenured) professor and was a U.S. Fulbright Scholar teaching at the University of Tartu (Estonia). David currently teaches part-time at the School for Conflict Analysis and Resolution at George Mason University and the School of Education at Drexel University. He is the editor of *Peacebuilding in Community Colleges: A Teaching Resource* (U.S. Institute of Peace Press, 2013) and the author of *Peace Jobs: A Student's Guide to Starting a Career Working for Peace* (Information Age Publishing, 2016).

Taryn Tangpricha, M.A., has served as International Education Director for Delaware Technical Community College since 2010. In this role, she oversees study abroad programming, a multi-campus Global Understanding Series, the faculty and staff professional development abroad, and serves as Principal Designated School Official (PDSO). Taryn previously served as Deputy Director for the International Scholar Laureate Program and Global Young Leaders Conference, as well as an English teacher with the Japan Exchange and Teaching Program. She earned a M.A. in International Education from The George Washington University in 2007 and a B.A. from Sewanee: The University of the South, in 2001.

Marc Thomas, Ed.D., taught political science for 15 years at community colleges in Michigan, launching his work in international education as faculty leader for a community college student internship in Japan in 2005. He was selected twice as Visiting Scholar for the Japan Center for Michigan Universities in Hikone, Japan. This work inspired completion of a Master of Education in Global Studies from the University of Illinois, along with dedication to research and writing for NAFSA and other organizations. He coordinated international programs at Lansing Community College in Michigan for five years and now serves as Assistant Dean at the Colorado Mountain College in Leadville.

Tiffany Viggiano, M.Ed is a Doctoral Candidate. At the time that this chapter was written she was a visiting researcher working with the Higher Education Studies Team (HIEST) at the University of Jyväskylä on a Fulbright Finland grant. Her research interests include critical internationalization studies, community colleges, and global responsibility. Her work has been published in the Community College Review, the Journal of Higher Education, and the Journal of Studies in International Education. Previous projects have explained the multiple identities of community college students and the International

About the Contributors

Access Paradox. Upcoming projects will explore the multiple definitions of global responsibility and the ways in which Californian institutions of higher education have institutionalized the inequitable treatment of international students.

Melissa Whatley, Doctoral Candidate in the University of Georgia's Institute of Higher Education. Her research focuses on the social stratification of U.S. education abroad opportunity with emphasis on institutional policy and practice and the two-year postsecondary sector. Her work has appeared in journals such as the *Journal of Studies in International Education* and the *NAFSA Research Symposium Series*. She presents research regularly at conferences such as the annual meetings of the Association for the Study of Higher Education and the American Educational Research Association. She is co-recipient of the 2018 Harold Josephson Award for Professional Promise in International Education awarded by the Association of International Education Administrators.

Dawn Wood, M.S., currently serves as Dean of International Programs for Kirkwood Community College. With over 20 years of experience in international education, Ms. Wood is currently responsible for forwarding the international vision and global commitment of Kirkwood Community College. Ms. Wood graduated with a Bachelor's degree in International Business and Psychology from the University of Northern Iowa. She also holds a Master's Degree in International Management with an emphasis in International Education and Training from the School for International Training. Ms. Wood has experience living and working abroad and has travelled extensively throughout the world. She has served as a leader and presented at many international conferences including involvement in several international education organizations including NAFSA: Association of International Educators for several years, Phi Beta Delta, Professional International Educators Roundtable, StudyIowa, Community Colleges for International Development and Global Education Network.

K. Siobhan Wright, MFA, is the Communication Arts Chair and Co-Travel Study Coordinator at Carroll Community College in Westminster, Maryland. She earned an MFA in 1989 from Penn State University and a BA from SUNY-Fredonia in 1985. Her interest in crossing borders began in childhood when she learned that Grand Island, New York, where she was born and raised, nearly touches the International Boundary between the United States and Canada.

Index

A

academic year 26, 73, 90-91, 95-99, 121, 132, 178, 185, 193-194, 215
access 1-4, 6-7, 12-13, 15, 31, 42-43, 47, 49, 54, 57, 59, 63, 69, 75, 77, 90-92, 94, 99, 101, 103, 108, 121-123, 126-127, 131-132, 138-139, 143, 160, 179, 185, 189, 203, 242, 249, 255-261, 263, 275-276, 279
administrative buy-in 265
advocacy 172-174, 178, 259
anecdotal evidence 72
assessment 38, 41-42, 50, 54, 64-65, 69, 72-73, 75-82, 84-86, 123, 177, 217-218, 237, 239, 260, 270

B

budget 2, 4, 46-47, 50, 134, 158, 160-166, 168-170, 175, 177, 180, 230-231, 234-235, 255-257, 267
budget cuts 175, 177, 180, 255-256, 267

C

Career and Technical students 242
choice to study abroad 1, 4
Code of Ethics 49
collaboration 37, 42, 44-45, 47, 55, 63, 68, 113, 127-128, 144, 172, 177-181, 232, 257-261, 263, 266-267, 270, 273
community college 1-10, 12-15, 22-25, 27-31, 33, 37-38, 41-42, 46, 49-50, 53, 55-60, 63-67, 69, 72-78, 86, 90-94, 99-103, 107-111, 113-116, 120-123, 125-126, 131-135, 137, 140, 142-144, 147-154, 156, 158-159, 161, 168, 172-174, 178-181, 184-195, 201, 203-205, 207-208, 213-215, 217, 228-233, 235-236, 242-245, 252, 255-257, 260-262, 265-267, 269-270, 275, 278, 280-281
conflict 59, 189-190, 200, 202-203, 205-207, 209, 212
consortia 3-4, 6, 9, 38, 181, 258, 265-267, 270, 274-275, 279, 281
Core Competencies 73
court cases 53-54, 60, 64
critical humanism 184, 186, 195

D

diversity 9, 11-12, 39, 41, 158, 166, 169, 173-174, 189-190, 194, 215, 231, 274-275

E

education abroad 1-7, 9-15, 22, 24, 29-31, 33, 37-50, 53-61, 66-69, 75, 90-95, 98, 101, 110, 115, 124, 126, 132, 134, 139-140, 148, 156, 159, 162, 169, 172-173, 175-177, 180-181, 194, 200-201, 231, 242, 244, 255, 257-263, 266, 277, 280
education environment 72
engagement 14, 22, 39, 46, 101, 120-121, 131-132, 134-137, 141, 143-144, 153, 176, 181, 189, 200-202, 208, 212, 214, 216, 219, 229, 231, 235, 252, 261, 267

F

Faculty Development 223
faculty encouragement 91, 93-94, 101, 134, 141
Faculty-Led Programs 28, 40, 159, 179, 234, 236, 260
Faculty-Led Study Abroad Programs 60, 279
federal funding, 94, 98
Forum on Education Abroad 37-38, 43, 49, 56, 110, 115, 266
Fundraising 31, 115-116, 177-178

G

general education requirements 213
generate revenue 255-256

Index

Generation Study Abroad 22, 25, 31, 158, 163, 165, 170, 277
global competence 75-76, 80, 91, 191, 193, 228, 235
Global Distinction 213 214, 216
global education 40, 56, 66, 132, 188, 201, 204, 217, 228, 230, 233, 235, 239, 257, 266, 269-270, 277-279
Global Engagement 200-201, 212, 235
global justice 184-186
Global Knowledge 133, 200-201, 212, 243
global learning 25, 72-78, 86, 108-109, 111, 116-117, 204, 218, 257, 261, 279-280
global mission 255-257
growth 1-2, 5, 9, 24, 26, 29-30, 33, 37, 39, 78-82, 84-86, 120, 127, 136, 140, 143-144, 169, 214, 235, 256-257, 265-266, 269, 277, 279-281

H

Health and safety 43, 48, 53-61, 64-66, 69, 123, 260
Heiskell Award 22, 31, 217
higher education 1, 11, 24, 26, 31, 38-39, 55-56, 62, 72-74, 86, 90, 92-94, 101, 103, 107-108, 110, 120, 132, 159, 175, 187, 191-192, 202, 204, 207, 228, 230, 233, 237, 255-256, 259, 265, 269, 278, 280
humanism 184-188, 190, 195
hybrid model 147-156

I

IIE Open Doors 77, 163
institutional choices 1, 13
institutional profile characteristics 90, 92, 94, 103
institutional profiles 90-92, 94, 99, 103
institutional stakeholders 73, 140
institutional support 10, 13-14, 47, 59, 67, 107, 173, 181, 215, 230, 265, 268-269, 271, 274, 281
Integrated Postsecondary Education Data System (IPEDS) 90, 92, 94
Interassociational Advisory Committee on Safety and Responsibility in Education Abroad 55
Internationalization 4, 24-25, 31, 38-39, 67, 73, 91, 99-100, 110, 117, 121, 124, 132, 142, 169, 173, 175-176, 184-188, 190, 213-220, 223, 230, 235, 255-256, 258, 261-263
internationalization activities 184-185, 187

L

language 26, 40, 58, 63, 72-73, 79-80, 84, 86, 132-134, 139-140, 142-143, 153, 160-161, 166, 168, 174-176, 179, 201, 206, 216, 218, 236-237, 244, 247-248, 251-252, 269, 273-274
leadership 4, 13, 50, 59, 62-63, 67-69, 74, 85, 117, 120-128, 140, 160, 165, 174-177, 180-181, 204-205, 215, 250, 252, 259, 265, 268, 270-271, 277, 280
Learning outcomes 14, 25, 38, 40, 42, 54, 69, 72-73, 75-82, 84-86, 176, 233-234, 237
life-changing experiences 72
lifelong learners 147-150, 153-154, 156

M

Marketing 3-4, 8-9, 24, 30, 49, 107, 111, 113, 117, 123, 125, 153, 156, 162-163, 165, 169, 278
Maryland Community College International Education Consortium (MCCIEC) 265-266, 281
Minority Students 28-29, 94, 107-108, 116, 194, 275
mission 2, 4, 22, 39-41, 50, 57, 64, 75, 91, 108, 110-111, 117, 120-121, 124, 126, 128, 132, 147-148, 150, 152, 156, 160-161, 163, 175-176, 180, 184-186, 189-190, 192, 195, 216, 229, 233, 235-236, 239, 255-259, 261-262, 269, 274-275, 277

O

organizational culture 73, 75

P

paradigms of discourse 184, 186, 188
Peace Education 202, 212
Peace Studies 202-203, 205-208, 212
Peacebuilding 200-209, 212
Pell Grant 96
professional development 47, 66-67, 101, 124, 127, 158, 162, 176, 178, 181, 213, 219, 234, 258-259, 261-263, 266, 275, 278

Q

quantitative information 73

323

R

resource limitations 46, 213
resources 24, 31, 37-38, 40, 42-43, 46, 50, 56, 61, 64, 69, 76-77, 92, 99, 103, 115, 120 121, 123, 125, 127, 140-141, 143, 158, 160, 162, 165, 169-170, 173, 215, 218, 235, 255-263, 266, 268, 276, 279
restricted resources 255-256
rural community college 147-148, 228-230

S

SAFETI Clearinghouse 56
service-learning 242-243
small community college 147, 150-151, 156, 235
socioeconomic status 96, 101-103, 134, 154
staffing 59-60, 62, 107, 158, 175, 180, 263, 269
stakeholders 31, 45, 47, 73, 107, 111, 113, 120, 128, 140, 175, 185-186, 189, 192-193, 195, 271
Standards of Good Practice 37-38, 56
strategic directions 120-121, 124
strategic planning 116, 172, 235
student body 39, 57, 94, 96, 99, 101, 108, 128, 175, 213

Student Enrollment 10, 96, 107, 120-121, 255-256, 267
student participation 33, 94, 111, 115, 141, 154, 161, 164, 231, 267, 275
student population 11, 13, 39, 41, 50, 58, 90-92, 94-96, 99-101, 158, 174, 176, 216, 229, 267
students 1, 3-6, 8-10, 12-15, 22-33, 37, 39-50, 53-54, 56-69, 73-80, 82, 85-86, 90-103, 107-111, 113-117, 120-127, 131-132, 134-144, 147-156, 159-160, 162-170, 172-181, 185, 187, 189-190, 192-194, 201, 203-209, 213-219, 221, 223, 228-229, 231-237, 239, 242-252, 255-262, 266-277, 279-281
study abroad 1-12, 14-15, 22-33, 37-38, 40-41, 43-45, 47, 53-69, 72-74, 76-82, 84-86, 90-101, 103, 107-111, 113-117, 120-128, 131-144, 147-156, 158-170, 172-181, 184-195, 201, 204-209, 213-216, 231-232, 234-235, 242-248, 250-252, 255, 257-259, 261-263, 265-281
study abroad coordinators 64, 131, 135, 141, 143, 276

T

The Forum on Education Abroad 37-38, 43, 49, 56, 110, 115, 266

Purchase Print, E-Book, or Print + E-Book

IGI Global books are available in three unique pricing formats:
Print Only, E-Book Only, or Print + E-Book. Shipping fees apply.

www.igi-global.com

Recommended Reference Books

Cultural Awareness and Competency Development in Higher Education
ISBN: 978-1-5225-2145-7
© 2017; 408 pp.
List Price: $210

Cases on STEAM Education in Practice
ISBN: 978-1-5225-2334-5
© 2017; 375 pp.
List Price: $195

Writing and Composing in the Age of MOOCs
ISBN: 978-1-5225-1718-4
© 2017; 457 pp.
List Price: $270

Administration, Policy, and Leadership in Higher Education
ISBN: 978-1-5225-0672-0
© 2017; 678 pp.
List Price: $295

Formative Assessment Practices for Pre-Service Teacher Practicum Feedback
ISBN: 978-1-5225-2630-8
© 2018; 209 pp.
List Price: $145

Technological Pedagogical Content Knowledge (TPACK) Framework for K-12 Teacher Preparation
ISBN: 978-1-5225-1621-7
© 2017; 173 pp.
List Price: $135

Do you want to stay current on the latest research trends, product announcements, news and special offers?
Join IGI Global's mailing list today and start enjoying exclusive perks sent only to IGI Global members.
Add your name to the list at **www.igi-global.com/newsletters.**

Publisher of Peer-Reviewed, Timely, and Innovative Academic Research

IGI Global
DISSEMINATOR OF KNOWLEDGE

www.igi-global.com | Sign up at www.igi-global.com/newsletters | facebook.com/igiglobal | twitter.com/igiglobal | linkedin.com/igiglobal

Ensure Quality Research is Introduced to the Academic Community

Become an IGI Global Reviewer for Authored Book Projects

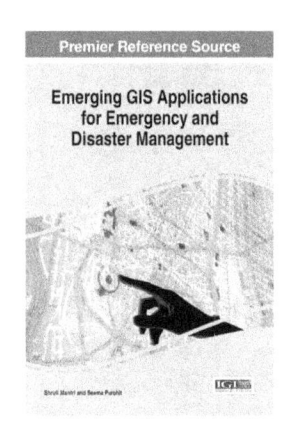

The overall success of an authored book project is dependent on quality and timely reviews.

In this competitive age of scholarly publishing, constructive and timely feedback significantly expedites the turnaround time of manuscripts from submission to acceptance, allowing the publication and discovery of forward-thinking research at a much more expeditious rate. Several IGI Global authored book projects are currently seeking highly qualified experts in the field to fill vacancies on their respective editorial review boards:

Applications may be sent to:
development@igi-global.com

Applicants must have a doctorate (or an equivalent degree) as well as publishing and reviewing experience. Reviewers are asked to write reviews in a timely, collegial, and constructive manner. All reviewers will begin their role on an ad-hoc basis for a period of one year, and upon successful completion of this term can be considered for full editorial review board status, with the potential for a subsequent promotion to Associate Editor.

If you have a colleague that may be interested in this opportunity, we encourage you to share this information with them.

IGI Global
DISSEMINATOR OF KNOWLEDGE
www.igi-global.com

Celebrating 30 Years of Scholarly Knowledge Creation & Dissemination

InfoSci®-Books

A Collection of 4,000+ Reference Books Containing Over 87,000 Full-Text Chapters Focusing on Emerging Research

This database is a collection of over 4,000+ IGI Global single and multi-volume reference books, handbooks of research, and encyclopedias, encompassing groundbreaking research from prominent experts worldwide. These books are highly cited and currently recognized in prestigious indices such as: Web of Science™ and Scopus®.

Librarian Features:
- No Set-Up or Maintenance Fees
- Guarantee of No More Than A 5% Annual Price Increase
- COUNTER 4 Usage Reports
- Complimentary Archival Access
- Free MARC Records

Researcher Features:
- Unlimited Simultaneous Users
- No Embargo of Content
- Full Book Download
- Full-Text Search Engine
- No DRM

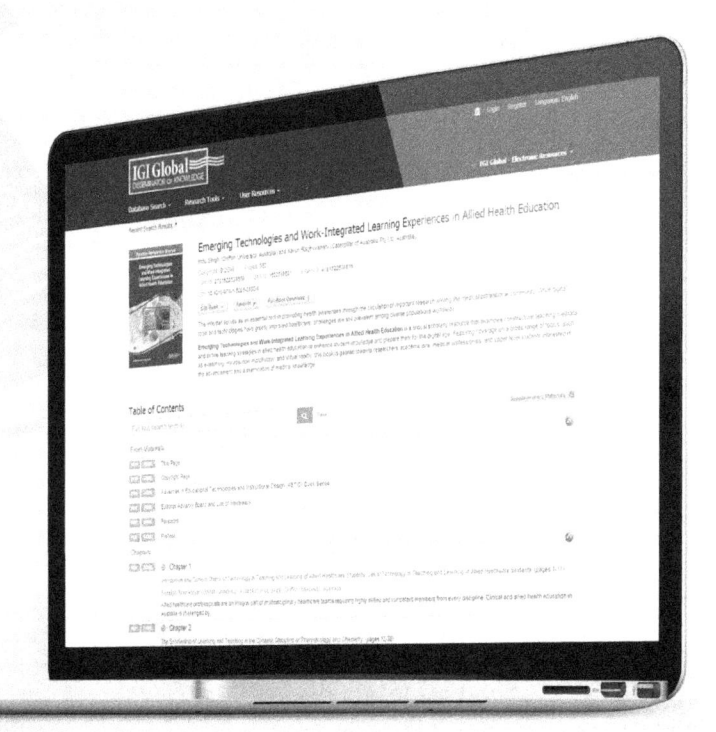

To Find Out More or To Purchase This Database:
www.igi-global.com/infosci-books
eresources@igi-global.com • Toll Free: 1-866-342-6657 ext. 100 • Phone: 717-533-8845 x100

IGI Global
DISSEMINATOR OF KNOWLEDGE
www.igi-global.com

IGI Global Proudly Partners with

eContent Pro International

Enhance Your Manuscript with eContent Pro International's Professional Copy Editing Service

Expert Copy Editing

eContent Pro International copy editors, with over 70 years of combined experience, will provide complete and comprehensive care for your document by resolving all issues with spelling, punctuation, grammar, terminology, jargon, semantics, syntax, consistency, flow, and more. In addition, they will format your document to the style you specify (APA, Chicago, etc.). All edits will be performed using Microsoft Word's Track Changes feature, which allows for fast and simple review and management of edits.

Additional Services

eContent Pro International also offers fast and affordable proofreading to enhance the readability of your document, professional translation in over 100 languages, and market localization services to help businesses and organizations localize their content and grow into new markets around the globe.

IGI Global Authors Save 25% on eContent Pro International's Services!

Scan the QR Code to Receive Your 25% Discount

The 25% discount is applied directly to your eContent Pro International shopping cart when placing an order through IGI Global's referral link. Use the QR code to access this referral link. eContent Pro International has the right to end or modify any promotion at any time.

Email: customerservice@econtentpro.com

econtentpro.com

Are You Ready to Publish Your Research?

IGI Global
DISSEMINATOR OF KNOWLEDGE

IGI Global offers book authorship and editorship opportunities across 11 subject areas, including business, healthcare, computer science, engineering, and more!

Benefits of Publishing with IGI Global:

- Free one-to-one editorial and promotional support.
- Expedited publishing timelines that can take your book from start to finish in less than one (1) year.
- Choose from a variety of formats including: Edited and Authored References, Handbooks of Research, Encyclopedias, and Research Insights.
- Utilize IGI Global's eEditorial Discovery® submission system in support of conducting the submission and blind-review process.
- IGI Global maintains a strict adherence to ethical practices due in part to our full membership to the Committee on Publication Ethics (COPE).
- Indexing potential in prestigious indices such as Scopus®, Web of Science™, PsycINFO®, and ERIC – Education Resources Information Center.
- Ability to connect your ORCID iD to your IGI Global publications.
- Earn royalties on your publication as well as receive complimentary copies and exclusive discounts.

Get Started Today by Contacting the Acquisitions Department at:
acquisition@igi-global.com

Available to Order Now

Order through www.igi-global.com with **Free Standard Shipping**.

The Premier Reference for Information Science & Information Technology

100% Original Content
Contains 705 new, peer-reviewed articles with color figures covering over 80 categories in 11 subject areas

Diverse Contributions
More than 1,100 experts from 74 unique countries contributed their specialized knowledge

Easy Navigation
Includes two tables of content and a comprehensive index in each volume for the user's convenience

Highly-Cited
Embraces a complete list of references and additional reading sections to allow for further research

Included in:
InfoSci-Books

Encyclopedia of Information Science and Technology Fourth Edition
A Comprehensive 10-Volume Set

Mehdi Khosrow-Pour, D.B.A. (Information Resources Management Association, USA)
ISBN: 978-1-5225-2255-3; © 2018; Pg: 8,104; Release Date: July 2017

For a limited time, receive the complimentary e-books for the First, Second, and Third editions with the purchase of the *Encyclopedia of Information Science and Technology, Fourth Edition* e-book.*

The **Encyclopedia of Information Science and Technology, Fourth Edition** is a 10-volume set which includes 705 original and previously unpublished research articles covering a full range of perspectives, applications, and techniques contributed by thousands of experts and researchers from around the globe. This authoritative encyclopedia is an all-encompassing, well-established reference source that is ideally designed to disseminate the most forward-thinking and diverse research findings. With critical perspectives on the impact of information science management and new technologies in modern settings, including but not limited to computer science, education, healthcare, government, engineering, business, and natural and physical sciences, it is a pivotal and relevant source of knowledge that will benefit every professional within the field of information science and technology and is an invaluable addition to every academic and corporate library.

Pricing Information

Hardcover: **$5,695**   E-Book: **$5,695**   Hardcover + E-Book: **$6,895**

Scan for Online Bookstore

Both E-Book Prices Include:
- *Encyclopedia of Information Science and Technology, First Edition E-Book*
- *Encyclopedia of Information Science and Technology, Second Edition E-Book*
- *Encyclopedia of Information Science and Technology, Third Edition E-Book*

*Purchase the Encyclopedia of Information Science and Technology, Fourth Edition e-book and receive the first, second, and third e-book editions for free. Offer is only valid with purchase of the fourth edition's e-book through the IGI Global Online Bookstore.

Recommend this Title to Your Institution's Library: www.igi-global.com/books

www.igi-global.com/infosci-ondemand

InfoSci-OnDemand

Continuously updated with new material on a weekly basis, InfoSci®-OnDemand offers the ability to search through thousands of quality full-text research papers. Users can narrow each search by identifying key topic areas of interest, then display a complete listing of relevant papers, and purchase materials specific to their research needs.

Comprehensive Service
- Over 110,800+ journal articles, book chapters, and case studies.
- All content is downloadable in PDF format and can be stored locally for future use.

No Subscription Fees
- One time fee of $37.50 per PDF download.

Instant Access
- Receive a download link immediately after order completion!

"It really provides an excellent entry into the research literature of the field. It presents a manageable number of highly relevant sources on topics of interest to a wide range of researchers. The sources are scholarly, but also accessible to 'practitioners'."

- Lisa Stimatz, MLS, University of North Carolina at Chapel Hill, USA

"It is an excellent and well designed database which will facilitate research, publication and teaching. It is a very very useful tool to have."

- George Ditsa, PhD, University of Wollongong, Australia

"I have accessed the database and find it to be a valuable tool to the IT/IS community. I found valuable articles meeting my search criteria 95% of the time."

- Lynda Louis, Xavier University of Louisiana, USA

Recommended for use by researchers who wish to immediately download PDFs of individual chapters or articles.
www.igi-global.com/e-resources/infosci-ondemand

IGI Global
DISSEMINATOR of KNOWLEDGE
www.igi-global.com

CPSIA information can be obtained
at www.ICGtesting.com
Printed in the USA
LVHW061453090719
623566LV00013B/290/P